# International Human Rights Law

# International Human Rights Law

**Douglas Lee Donoho**

PROFESSOR OF LAW
NOVA SOUTHEASTERN UNIVERSITY
SHEPARD BROAD COLLEGE OF LAW

WITH CONTRIBUTIONS BY JAMES WILETS
PROFESSOR, NOVA SOUTHEASTERN UNIVERSITY, SHEPARD BROAD COLLEGE OF LAW
CHAIR, INTER-AMERICAN CENTER FOR HUMAN RIGHTS

CAROLINA ACADEMIC PRESS
Durham, North Carolina

eISBN  978-1-61163-824-0

Library of Congress Cataloging-in-Publication Data

Names: Donoho, Douglas Lee, author. | Wilets, James D., author.
Title: International human rights law / Douglas Lee Donoho ; with
   contributions by James Wilets.
Description: Durham, North Carolina : Carolina Academic Press, LLC, 2017. |
   "Electronic course book." | Includes bibliographical references and index.
Identifiers: LCCN 2016051955| ISBN 9781531003890 (alk. paper) | ISBN
   9781611638240 (ebook)
Subjects: LCSH: International law and human rights. | International law and
   human rights--United States.
Classification: LCC KZ1266 .D66 2017 | DDC 341.4/8--dc23
LC record available at https://lccn.loc.gov/2016051955

Carolina Academic Press, LLC
700 Kent Street
Durham, North Carolina 27701
Telephone (919) 489-7486
Fax (919) 493-5668
www.cap-press.com

Printed in the United States of America
2020 Printing

# Contents

# Introduction and Preface

This electronic course book provides a student-oriented examination of the law of international human rights. Although human rights are hardly a recent invention, the advent of their international protection is one of the most profound developments of the modern era. For centuries, governments acted with impunity regarding the treatment of their own people. The horrors of World War II, however, germinated a new conception of international law that dramatically altered this legal landscape. How governments treat their own citizens and others is no longer strictly an internal domestic matter but rather the concern of all humankind. This concern now manifests itself not simply through moral approbation but also through legal constraints created through international law and, sometimes, incorporated into domestic legal systems. International law is now a central feature of the effort to progressively achieve human freedom and dignity for all.

Although great progress has been made, clearly all is not good. You will learn that millions still suffer the torment of torture, imprisonment for their ideas, religious persecution, overt discrimination, and even execution at the hands of their own government. Even recently, civil war, genocide, systematic rape, and ethnic cleansing have ruined the lives of millions and created more than 40 million refugees and displaced persons worldwide.[1]

The United States itself, although a post-World War II leader in the promotion of human rights,[2] now faces serious and credible charges of egregious human rights

---

1. The United Nations currently estimates that there are more than 43 million refugees and displaced persons worldwide. The precise number of refugees and displaced persons is difficult to pin down. The CIA "Fact Book" provides a country specific listing.

2. The longer term human rights history of the United States unquestionably also reflects deep flaws, particularly regarding the rights of African-Americans, Native Americans, and women. See, for example, the Report of the Brown University Trustees on their own university's connections with the slave trade. In the Report, the Trustees note that the United States experience with slavery was unique to world history. As noted by the report of the Brown University Steering Committee on Slavery and Justice (the "Brown Report"). The Brown Report states:

> If American slavery has any claims to being historically "peculiar," its peculiarity lay in its rigorous racialism, the systematic way in which racial ideas were used to demean and deny the humanity of people of even partial African descent. This historical legacy would

People stand on a street lined with damaged buildings in the besieged area of Homs January 27, 2014. Photo Yazan Homsy, Reuters.

abuses relating to the torture and inhumane treatment of prisoners of war and terrorism suspects. Homelessness, poverty, police brutality, deplorable prison conditions, and many forms of discrimination continue unabated in the United States despite our enormous resources. The advent of DNA evidence has exposed glaring flaws in the American criminal justice system with the exoneration of hundreds of convicted defendants, including those who previously faced execution on death row. Perhaps most startling, all of these injustices exist in a nation whose people profoundly believe in human rights.

The materials which follow explore how international law and institutions work to progressively prevent violations of human rights and improve how national governments treat their own citizens. You will soon find that studying human rights can be both distressing and uplifting. We will examine situations that are disturbing, ugly and depressing. The existing international system for protecting rights un-

---

make the process of incorporating the formerly enslaved as citizens far more problematic in the United States than in other New World slave societies.

. . .

Few if any societies in history carried this logic further than the United States, where people of African descent came to be regarded as a distinct "race" of persons, fashioned by nature for hard labor. Id. at 8, 84.

doubtedly has deep flaws. Nevertheless, you will also see that international law has helped achieve substantial progress in human rights and offers the promise of a better way moving forward. You should think critically as you learn about how the current system works. One need not believe in the system (you may or may not) in order to believe in and work for the attainment of its ultimate goal: The enjoyment of fundamental rights and freedoms for all people everywhere.

## Format and Organization

The readings that follow often include web-based materials. When a link to a video clip is provided, use your discretion to skip through parts that you don't find useful, especially if the clip is long (over 10 minutes). When a website link is to textual materials, review the linked page as carefully as seems appropriate to the task at hand. Some links, as noted in their accompanying text, provide explanations or definitions central to our topic — you should study such material carefully. For added explanations and elaboration, you can follow any related links that the webpage itself provides if you think it will be helpful to you. Other links provided in the course materials provide general background, often describing factual situations or points of potential interest — these you should read, if at all, as carefully as your own interest dictates.

Every chapter provides either a set of questions to answer or a problem (or both). *The questions and problems are designed to provide basic guidance to students regarding what they ought to focus on and understand from the materials — the questions are meant to be answered and are not (I hope) esoteric abstractions posed merely for contemplation.*

Since this course book is designed primarily for law students, most chapters focus on legal concepts and institutions with an emphasis on the practice of law. I anticipate that many students will have had little or no exposure to international law which is, of course, the core legal foundation for the international human rights system. Consequently, early chapters examine international law basics relevant to the human rights system. While some particular human rights topics are addressed in distinct, separate chapters (such as the rights of women and sexual minorities), many current human rights issues or topic areas are instead presented as illustrations within the chapters, which focus on various legal aspects of the current international system. The chapter headings, with internal hyperlinks provided in the Table of Contents, should provide adequate guidance for finding such specific topic and factually based material.

# Chapter 1

# What Are International Human Rights?

## A. Introduction

The primary objective of this first chapter is to understand the basic premises of the international human rights system and examine its historical antecedents. We will also begin to examine the legal foundation for the international system by considering the concept of "rights." After finishing this chapter you should be able to provide answers to some basic questions that are more complex than you may initially believe. *Review the following material, including linked video clips, which provides important history and context that should help you think through the answers to the following important questions.*

- What is a "right"?
- Who has rights and against whom do they apply?
- What is the significance of the modifiers "international" and "human" when attached to a right?
- In what ways are human rights different from other rights such as Constitutional or civil rights?
- What does international law have to do with the realization of human rights?
- Why is there an international system for the protection of such rights?

## B. Historical Antecedents: World War II & the Holocaust

### 1. The Limited Scope of International Law Prior to World War II

The general concept of rights—that is, legal protection of certain individual interests against encroachment by society and government—has a long history found in many diverse cultures.[3] Clear textual expressions of rights, such as the English Magna Carta of 1215, the American Declaration of Independence, the French Declaration of the Rights of Man, and the Bill of Rights emerged from the Western enlightenment and 18th Century political thought. Such historical examples of individual rights protection, however, are distinct from modern international human rights in a number of important ways that will become increasingly clear as you study the subject. The most important of these distinctions involve the unique source of legal authority behind international human rights, their rationale, and their universal character.

Prior to World War II, virtually all governments generally accepted the premise that international law was properly concerned exclusively with the relationship between nation states. While some practices, such as the slave trade, were occasionally the subject of international agreement and condemnation, individual rights were simply not generally considered part of international relations.[4]

The consequence of this narrow view of international relations was that human rights were primarily considered an "internal matter" outside the competency of international law. Indeed, rights were primarily just part of the inevitable domestic legal battles over property, personal liberty, and the entitlements of citizenship. Thus, how any particular government treated its own citizens was not a legitimate subject matter for international law but rather solely within the domestic affairs of each nation state. A government's treatment of its own citizens was not simply outside the scope of international law — as a purely domestic matter it was also considered beyond the legitimate concerns of other countries and inappropriate for international scrutiny. In essence, international law provided almost no legal protections for individuals against the actions of their own governments.

Secondly, even though many domestic legal systems recognized certain individual rights prior to World War II, such rights were generally limited in scope, not generally linked to basic human dignity and not remotely universal. The American Bill of Rights, for example, only protects a limited set of political, property, and liberty interests that did not originally apply to African slaves, indigenous people,

---

3. Relatively brief but informative descriptions of the history of rights can be found at the University of Minnesota Human Rights Resource Center, Wikipedia, and Human Rights Web. A longer academically oriented debate on this history, including the role of the anti-slave movement, can be found on the Harvard Law Review On-Line Forum.

4. At least one scholar assigns great significance to the international anti-slavery movement in development of modern international human rights. *See* Jenny S. Martinez, *The Slave Trade and the Origins of International Human Rights Law* (Oxford Press, 2012). *But see* Philip Alston, *Does the Past Matter? On the Origins of Human Rights*, 126 Harv. L. Rev. 2043 (2013) (disputing Professor Martinez' ultimate position and providing an exposition on competing viewpoints about the origins and development of universal rights). Professor James Wilets adds this important distinction: "during this period of slavery individual rights were simply not generally considered part of international relations. In part, this was because slavery, like piracy, was deemed an 'international crime,' not capable of being regulated by only one country. Thus, piracy and slavery fell into a narrow category of crimes that were regulated internationally, but the concept did not extend to countries' treatment of their own citizens."

women, or children. Profoundly important human needs such as food, shelter, work, and education were not considered part of the individual rights calculus. Such rights were not intended for all humans as essential to their humanity but rather as protection for certain interests of just certain people (originally for the primary benefit of white, working or landed European males).

## 2. The Catalyst for Change: World War II Atrocities

The atrocities of World Wars and the horror of World War II and the Holocaust, in particular, were catalysts for fundamental change in these premises. Review the following accounts of the Holocaust and consider how these terrible events relate to the purposes of an international system for protection of individual rights.

a. Adolf Hitler to His Army Commanders, August 22, 1939:

I HAVE ISSUED THE COMMAND - AND I'LL HAVE ANYBODY WHO UTTERS BUT ONE WORD OF CRITICISM EXECUTED BY A FIRING SQUAD - THAT OUR WAR AIM DOES NOT CONSIST IN REACHING CERTAIN LINES, BUT IN THE PHYSICAL DESTRUCTION OF THE ENEMY. ACCORDINGLY, I HAVE PLACED MY DEATH-HEAD FORMATIONS IN READINESS - FOR THE PRESENT ONLY IN THE EAST - WITH ORDERS TO THEM TO SEND TO DEATH MERCILESSLY AND WITHOUT COMPASSION, MEN, WOMEN, AND CHILDREN OF POLISH DERIVATION AND LANGUAGE. ONLY THUS SHALL WE GAIN THE LIVING SPACE (LEBENSRAUM) WHICH WE NEED. WHO, AFTER ALL, SPEAKS TODAY OF THE ANNIHILATION OF THE ARMENIANS?

ADOLF HITLER, AUGUST 22, 1939, ACCORDING TO REPORTS RECEIVED BY THE ASSOCIATED PRESS BUREAU CHIEF IN BERLIN, LOUIS LOCHNER

Inscription from the United States Holocaust Memorial Museum in Washington D.C.

Photo by Fedayee, Wikimedia Commons.

b. Testimony of Hermann Graebe at Nuremberg (German engineer with the Jung, A.G., Construction Company)

On the 5 October 1942, when I visited the building office at Dubno, my foreman told me that in the vicinity of the site Jews from Dubno, had been shot in three large pits, each about thirty metres long and three metres deep. About fifteen hundred persons had been killed daily. All were to be liquidated. As the shootings had taken place in his presence he was still very upset.

Moennikes and I went straight to the pits. Nobody prevented us. I heard a quick succession of shots from behind one of the mounds of earth. The people who had got off the lorries — men, women and children of all ages — had to undress upon the order of an SS man, who carried a riding or a dog whip. They had to put their clothes on separate piles of shoes, top clothing, and underclothing.

I saw a heap of shoes that must have contained eight hundred to one thousand pairs, great piles of clothes and undergarments. Without screaming or weeping these people undressed, stood in family groups, kissed each other, said their farewells, and waited for a sign from another SS man, who stood near the pit, also with a whip in his hand.

During the fifteen minutes that I stood near the pit, I did not hear anyone complain or beg for mercy. I watched a family of about eight, a man and a woman, both about fifty, with their children, aged about one, eight and ten, and two grown up daughters of about twenty to twenty–four.

An old woman with snow-white hair was holding the one-year-old child in her arms, singing something to it and tickling it. The child was crowing with delight. The man and wife were looking on with tears in their eyes.

The father was holding the hand of a boy about ten, speaking to him softly. The boy was fighting back his tears. The father pointed to the sky, stroked the boy's head and seemed to explain something to him.

At that moment the SS man at the pit shouted something to his comrade, who separated off about twenty persons and ordered them to go behind the mound of earth. Among them was the family I have mentioned.

I still clearly remember a dark-haired, slim girl who pointed to herself as she passed close to me and said, "Twenty-Three." I walked to the other side of the mound and found myself standing before an enormous grave. The people lay so closely packed, one on top of the other, that only their heads were visible.

Nearly all had blood running over their shoulders from their heads. Some of them were still moving. Some lifted an arm and turned a head to show that they were still alive.

The pit was already two-thirds full. I estimated that it already contained about one thousand people. I looked round for the man who had shot them. He was an SS man who was sitting on the edge of the narrow end of the pit, his legs dangling into it. He had a sub-machine gun across his knees and was smoking a cigarette.

The people, completely naked, went down some steps which had been cut in the clay wall of the pit and climbed over the heads of those already lying there, to the place indicated by the SS man. They laid down in front of the dead or injured people. Some of them caressed those who were still alive and spoke to them softly.

Then I heard a series of shots. I looked into the pit and saw that the bodies were twitching or that the heads lay motionless on top of the bodies which lay before them. Blood was pouring from their necks.

International Military Tribunal, Nuremberg, November 10, 1945, Nur. Doc. PS 2992.

The famous quote below illustrates how human rights are interrelated, and how, as Martin Luther King Jr. perceptively stated: "No one is free until we are all free."

Rev. Martin Niemoller, 1945:

> **First they came for the Communists, and I didn't speak up, because I wasn't a Communist.**
>
> **Then they came for the Jews, and I didn't speak up, because I wasn't a Jew.**
>
> **Then they came for the Catholics, and I didn't speak up, because I was a Protestant.**
>
> **Then they came for me, and by that time there was no one left to speak up for me.**

c. Visual Reminders of the Holocaust

There are many documentaries, both long and short, available on the internet that provide visual evidence relating to the Holocaust. Many of these clips are graphic and very difficult to watch. These two clips, <u>one</u> and <u>two</u>, provide reasonable accounts of the Holocaust and are not as graphic as many others.

You may, of course, easily find alternative video documentation such as the Steven <u>Spielberg video archive</u> at the United States Holocaust Memorial Museum or the website "<u>Syncrocloud</u>." In the alternative, you might prefer to review the very informative <u>Wikipedia Holocaust pages</u> instead. Although not the first genocidal atrocity in the world, the Holocaust was particularly appalling not only because of the number of lives lost but also because it was organized and systematically perpetrated by government. As described below, a fundamental aspect of rights as a legal construct involves the relationship between individuals and government.

## 3. The Complex Nature of "Rights" As a Legal Concept

The Holocaust and other atrocities committed during World War II, including those committed by <u>Japanese forces</u> in the Asian theatre, were instrumental to the creation of the modern international human rights system. The concept of individual rights had, of course, existed long before the war and had played a fundamental role in many religions and cultures. Examples cited above, including the French <u>Dec-</u> <u>laration of the Rights of Man</u> and the <u>Bill of Rights</u>, are clear illustrations of how rights developed through history as a legal construct to protect the interests of certain individuals in society.

Under the traditional Western view, the exclusive purpose of rights as a legal institution is to protect the individual from certain kinds of governmental action. In essence, rights are legal institutions that prevent governments, and democratic majorities, from abusing certain interests of the individual. Historically, such rights were designed almost exclusively to preserve economic, political, and personal liberties from governmental interference. This <u>classic liberal</u> perspective that rights act solely as a check on government abuse may be contrasted with a broader view of rights that would include affirmative obligations on governments to ensure basic human needs.

a. Western Liberal Premises

Consider the following excerpt from the website of a free market and libertarian oriented <u>organization</u> that articulates the traditional, generally Western, and conservative viewpoint on the nature of rights:

<u>What Is Classical Liberalism?</u>

**By John C. Goodman**

**Characteristics of Individual Rights.**

The Bill of Rights proclaims that individuals have "rights." But what does it mean to have a right? Are some rights fundamentally different from others? In the classical liberal tradition, rights have several characteristics, including the following:

**Rights Are Relational.**

. . . They limit the morally permissible actions government may take to interfere with the lives of individuals who are governed.

. . . .

**Fundamental Rights Imply Negative Obligations.**

For example, the right to free speech implies a (negative) obligation on the part of others not to interfere with your speaking. It does not create the (positive) obligation to provide you with a platform, a microphone, and an audience. . . .

. . . .

**Fundamental Rights Do Not Come from Government.**

Not only do rights not get their legitimacy from government, but — as the Declaration of Independence so eloquently states — it is the other way around. Government gets its legitimacy from the existence of rights. In the view of Locke, Jefferson, and others, rational, moral people form governments for the express purpose of protecting rights. . . .

**Substantive Rights versus Police Powers of the State.**

. . . .

In the classical liberal world, people are free to pursue their own interests so long as they do not violate the rights of others. They are free to trade with others or not to trade. They are free to associate with others or not to associate. . . .

A potential problem arises when government exercises its police powers in defense of rights. A classical liberal citizen clearly has the right not to be seized or searched at random. But suppose a government official suspects the citizen is a thief and that he harbors contraband. Suppose also that after a search, seizure, and trial, the citizen is proved to be guilty. How can we describe these government acts using the language of rights?

Under certain circumstances, rights are *defeasable*. That is, they are justifiably set aside. . . .

**Rights versus Needs**

To appreciate the classical liberal concept of individual rights, it is as important to understand what is being rejected as it is to understand what is being asserted. To say that individuals have the right to pursue their own happiness implies that they are not obliged to pursue the happiness of others. Put differently, the right to life, liberty, and the pursuit of happiness implies that people are not obligated to serve the needs, concerns, wishes, and wants of others. This does not mean that everyone has to be selfish. It does imply that everyone has a right to be selfish.

. . . .

**The Collectivist Notion of Rights**

It is worth noting that all forms of collectivism in the 20th century rejected this classical notion of rights and all asserted in their own way that need is a claim. For the communists, the needs of the class (proletariat) were a claim against every individual. . . .

Despite the fact that 20th century collectivists opposed the classical liberal concept of rights, very rarely did they attack the notion of *rights* as such. Instead, they often tried to redefine the concept of *right* in a way that virtually eviscerated any meaningful notion of liberty. For example, in his 1944 State of the Union Address, President Franklin D. Roosevelt called for a "second Bill of Rights" which included the following:

- The right to a useful and remunerative job in the industries or shops or farms or mines of the nation.

- The right to earn enough to provide adequate food and clothing and recreation.

- The right of every farmer to raise and sell his products at a return which will give him and his family a decent living.
- The right of every businessman, large and small, to trade in an atmosphere of freedom from unfair competition and domination by monopolies at home or abroad.
- The right of every family to a decent home.
- The right to adequate medical care and the opportunity to achieve and enjoy good health.
- The right to adequate protection from the economic fears of old age, sickness, accident, and unemployment.
- The right to a good education.

Note that these rights are very different from the rights Locke, Jefferson, and the Founding Fathers had in mind. Among the characteristics of Roosevelt's rights are the following:

1) *They imply positive obligations on the part of others.* . . .

. . . .

3) *As a practical matter, only government action could insure such rights.*

b. A Broader International Perspective on the Nature of Rights

In substantial ways, international human rights are undoubtedly grounded in, and have evolved from, the Western perspective on individual rights — similar in ways to the version of rights described above. International rights are legal claims or entitlements made against society and government. With some important and evolving exceptions, most international rights are also designed to protect and promote the interests of individuals from government intrusion. Although much broader, the substantive content of international human rights also strongly parallels this Western heritage. A great number of international human rights have identical counterparts within domestic legal systems and focus on prohibiting certain governmental action rather than requiring affirmative government intervention to aid those in need.

However, you will discover that international human rights are not simply a legal extension of Western civil liberties brought to the international stage. Among other things, international human rights is a much broader concept taking into account a wide range of human needs and interests. The international concept of rights is not limited to preventing government abuse of individuals but rather also recognizes that governments and societies may have affirmative obligations to promote full human dignity. Thus, the international view of rights would reject the suggestion, in the excerpt above, that rights to food, water, and shelter "eviscerated any meaningful notion of liberty," recognizing instead that human dignity requires more than the freedom to speak your mind, exercise your religious beliefs, and pursue material wealth.

A good place to start unraveling how international human rights are different from their Western liberal counterparts is with the label. What is the significance of the modifiers "international" and "human" when attached to the word "rights"?

**INTERNATIONAL**: Identifying a right as "international" has several important legal implications. Most importantly, it identifies the source of legal authority upon which a claimed right exists. Just as "constitutional rights" are established as law by virtue of their adoption in the domestic constitution, international rights are established as legally recognizable claims through the international legal system.

There are a number of important legal consequences of this simple fact. Individual interests are not *international human rights* because they are important or moral or treasured by many but, rather, *because they have been recognized as an international legal obligation through established international legal processes.* This also implies that the legal status of such rights is similarly based on and limited by international legal principles. This means, we will learn, that even if a right is established as part of international law, the right is not automatically part of any domestic legal system but rather constitutes an obligation between nations. By agreeing to an international right of free speech, the United States has essentially promised other nations that it will provide that right to its own citizens. This legal obligation, however, is an international one between nations that does not necessarily or automatically have consequences within the U.S. domestic legal system. The obvious corollary is that international rights also may often depend on international forms of enforcement and protection where corresponding domestic adoption of the rights is lacking.

In subsequent lessons we will examine more precisely the important relationship between international human rights law and domestic law. For now, it is enough to recognize that international human rights are created by, subject to, and enforceable through international law. This characteristic distinguishes international human rights from rights, such as constitutional or civil rights, owing their origin and legal authority to domestic processes.

**HUMAN**: The qualifying word "human" also serves to distinguish international human rights from other kinds of individual rights. First, it defines who is entitled to their protection in the broadest of terms. All human beings are entitled to "human rights" because, after all, they are humans. There are no other qualifications needed. In contrast, constitutional or "civil" rights are typically created by governments and are applicable to only defined circumstances, such as citizenship or lawful residency. For example, U.S. Constitutional rights often only protect individuals within the territorial jurisdiction of the United States. A Mexican citizen is not entitled to the Fourth Amendment's protection against unreasonable search and seizures in Mexico, even if carried out by United States federal agents.[5] An unlawful alien might not be entitled to the same degree of protection against discrimination under the Equal Protection Clause as are citizens or lawful residents.[6] In contrast to "constitutional"

---

5. *See, e.g.*, <u>U.S. v. Verdugo-Urquidez</u>, 494 U.S. 259 (1990).
6. *See, e.g.*, <u>Plyer v. Doe</u>, 457 U.S. 202 (1982).

or "civil" rights, the modifier "human" implies a right that requires only one prerequisite — that the holder be a human being.[7]

Secondly, the word human suggests a broader class of interests subject to protection. Rights which are human rights refer to those interests that all humans share. These are interests sufficiently important to basic human dignity that all humans are entitled to. These may include not only civil, political, and physical freedoms, but also, perhaps, shelter, clean water, and education. If an interest is sufficiently universal and sufficiently important to "humanness" to be deemed worthy of international protection, it may be defined as an international human right. Thus, in contrast to the classic Western liberal view, international human rights may imply affirmative obligations on the part of governments to provide a wide range of basic human needs and interests.

**RIGHTS**: As suggested by the excerpts above, there may sometimes be disputes over precisely what it means to describe something as a "right." At their core, however, rights are a legal concept that provide protection to individuals against certain kinds of governmental action. In this sense, international human rights trump (no pun intended) other kinds of laws and restrict how governments may treat individuals within their jurisdiction, much like US Constitutional rights often trump state or federal law. A right is a claim or entitlement that serves as legal protection for the individual against certain government action, or entitles individuals to the government's protection or provision of essential human needs.

**LAW**: International human rights may become law, binding both internationally and, under certain conditions, within domestic legal systems. Attaining this status means that a right is not merely aspirational but rather constitutes a binding legal obligation with consequences for governments and the rights holder. We will see that the process by which international human rights become binding law is distinct from familiar domestic law processes. Similarly, critical distinctions exist between international versus domestic legal obligations over their legal status, effect, and enforceability. Nevertheless, international human rights may exhibit all the essential attributes of binding law, enforceable against governments for protection of individuals.

## 4. Putting It Together: The Founding Premises of International Human Rights

Although the concept of rights has a long history, the idea that rights are an appropriate subject within international law is of recent vintage and owes its genesis primarily to the horrors of World War II as described above. Prior to World War II,

---

7. For many international rights there is also the requirement that the government has consented to be bound to recognition of the right as a matter of international law. However, a number of important rights forming Customary International Law have achieved universal acceptance and no longer depend upon affirmative state consent.

the existence of any particular individual right was strictly a matter of domestic, national law. In other words, whether an individual could freely speak his mind, follow his religious beliefs, or be represented by a lawyer when accused of a crime was solely determined by the law of the national jurisdiction in which he was located. The international community did not generally consider a government's treatment of its own citizens to be a subject matter within the jurisdiction or competence of international law.

After the war, however, this paradigm radically changed. The initial step occurred when the victorious allied countries created "war crimes" tribunals in Nuremberg, Germany and Tokyo, Japan. Government officials were convicted at these tribunals and punished for "war crimes," "crimes against peace," and "crimes against humanity." The charges included not only wrongs committed against citizens of other countries but also for atrocities committed by the German government against its own citizens. In this sense, these tribunals differed from war crime trials that had taken place previously in which only violations of the rules of warfare, or "war crimes," were prosecuted.

Soon after the war, the international community endorsed the idea that rights form part of international law by endorsing the protection of human rights as a fundamental purpose of the newly founded United Nations. The U.N. Charter proclaims as one of its essential purposes: "[T]o reaffirm faith in fundamental human rights, in the dignity and worth of the human person, in the equal rights of men and women and of nations large and small . . . ." Thus began the emergence of human rights as a central subject of international law and the relationship between nations. In a departure from traditional international law, several new premises of the international system emerged. First, how governments treat their own citizens is an appropriate, if not vital, subject for international law and relations. Second, international protections for individuals should exist to safeguard against the potential abuses of their own governments. Third, internationalizing rights means that there are in fact universal interests and needs that all humans share regardless of nationality, gender, culture, or ethnicity. As we will see, however, "the devil is in the details."

Appropriate to the war atrocities that gave rise to international rights, one of the first rights to become part of international law was the prohibition against genocide. *Never again* remains a central purpose of *internationalizing* rights.

The term *genocide* is usually attributed to author Raphael Lemkin, who in 1944 combined the Greek word *genos* — race — with the Latin word *cide* — killing. The United Nations 1948 Convention on the Prevention and Punishment of the Crime of Genocide defines genocide this way:

> In the present Convention, genocide means any of the following acts committed with intent to destroy, in whole or in part, a national, ethnical, racial, or religious group, as such:
>
> (a) Killing members of the group;
>
> (b) Causing serious bodily or mental harm to members of the group;

(c) Deliberately inflicting on the group conditions of life calculated to bring about its physical destruction in whole or in part;

(d) Imposing measures intended to prevent births within the group;

(e) Forcibly transferring children of the group to another group.

Consider the right against genocide in light of the introductory material presented above and the events described below. *What does it mean to say there is an **international right** against genocide?*

## 5. The Grim Reality: "Never Again" Or "Again and Again"?

Each link below provides a short textual description of major modern genocidal atrocities. They include at least three major genocides since the widespread adoption of the Genocide Convention.

### Recent to Past Occurrences

Bosnia-Herzegovina: 1992–1995 — 200,000 Deaths

Rwanda

Pol Pot in Cambodia: 1975–1979 — 2,000,000 Deaths

Nazi Holocaust: 1938–1945 — 6,000,000 Deaths

Rape of Nanking: 1937–1938 — 300,000 Deaths

Stalin's Forced Famine: 1932–1933 — 7,000,000 Deaths

Armenians in Turkey: 1915–1918 — 1,500,000 Deaths

Links from History.com

The most recent genocides referenced in this list, Bosnia, Rwanda, and Cambodia, are examined in later chapters in greater detail. For now, think critically about the potential role of international law and human rights in addressing the vexing question:

**Who Is Next?**

Who's At Risk, http://endgenocide.org/conflict-areas/

Sudan & the Darfur: http://www.24hoursfordarfur.org/

DR Congo: http://endgenocide.org/conflict-areas/dr-congo/

            http://worldwithoutgenocide.org/genocides-and-conflicts/congo

Syria: http://www.genocidewatch.org/syria.html ;

Don't Be Surprised If the Next Genocide Happens In Syria

**Does the international right against genocide mean anything, or is it simply pious rhetoric?**

# Chapter 2

# Basic Principles of International Law Relevant to Human Rights

## A. Introduction

In the previous chapter we learned that international human rights are distinct from other forms and sources of rights by virtue of their grounding in international law. To fully understand such rights from a legal perspective you must also understand the nature of the international legal system and important basic principles about international legal obligations. This chapter essentially presents a primer on international law focusing on those aspects of international law that are most important to human rights. An important, if simple, starting point involves a clarification in terminology. International law generally speaks in terms of "states" and "state parties" rather than nations, countries or governments. The notion of "state" here closely resembles nationhood and largely reflects membership in the United Nations. Governments that represent the state may come and go but the state itself, as an international entity, is bound by international law.

Your primary objective for this chapter should be to gain a clear understanding of the international legal process through which international human rights obligations are created and implemented as well as the essential legal requirements and limitations of such obligations. After completing this chapter you should understand:

(1) The general functions of international law and how it is distinct from domestic law;

(2) What a treaty is, what it requires to be binding, and the effect of reservations;

(3) What customary international law is and how it is established;

(4) What jus cogens is and its relationship to treaties and customary law; and

(5) How international legal obligations are implemented or enforced.

As you study the materials you should consider whether international law is or can be enforced in a meaningful fashion. The chapter ends with a set of questions that probe what you have learned and what you should know. It would be prudent to review those questions now in order to improve your focus as you read the materials.

# B.  General Characteristics of the International Legal System

Virtually all educated adults, even law students, come to the study of international law with certain assumptions about the general characteristics of a legal system grounded in their understanding of the domestic legal order. Rules follow set hierarchical patterns, are the product of well-defined legislative and administrative processes, are interpreted and applied by judicial or administrative bodies, and are enforced through the coercive power of state imposed sanction. In essence, there are well delineated processes involving legislative, judicial and executive authority that create and apply a hierarchy of binding legal obligations on those governed.

Although the international legal system does exhibit many of the characteristics associated with "law" as traditionally understood by most US law students, there are significant differences that must be considered to fully appreciate its complex nature.

It is still accurate to say that the international legal system is characterized by a loose, decentralized political process under which the existence of binding legal obligations depends upon the specific consent of the state being bound. Processes for authoritative interpretation and application of rules are relatively weak and effective enforcement through sanctions frequently non-existent. The reasons for this situation ultimately rest in the continuing prominence of state sovereignty.

The Restatement of the Law, Third, Foreign Relations Law of the United States notes that:

> The absence of central legislative and executive institutions had led to skepticism about the legal quality of international law. Many observers consider international law to be only a series of precepts of morality or etiquette, of cautions and admonitions lacking in both specificity and binding quality. Governments, it is sometimes assumed, commonly disregard international law and observe it only when they deem it to be in their interest to do so.

> These impressions are mistaken. International law is law like other law, promoting order, guiding, restraining, regulating behavior. States, the principal addressees of international law, treat it as law, consider themselves bound by it, attend to it with a sense of legal obligation and with concern for the consequences of violation. . . . It is part of the law of the United States, respected by Presidents and Congresses, and by the States, and given effect by the courts.

Do you agree with the Restatement's position that international law is "law like other law"? The Restatement's assertion that international law *matters* and does have concrete effects on state behavior is undoubtedly true. Indeed, there is at least some empirical research[8] confirming Professor Louis Henkin's iconic statement that: "almost all nations observe almost all principles of international law and almost all of their international obligations almost all of the time."[9] Professor Anthony D'Amato, presenting the more dubious argument that international law is generally just as effective as domestic law, astutely points out that states have an important incentive to comply with international legal obligations based on reciprocal benefits.[10] I stop at stop signs mostly because I hope and expect that you will do the same for our mutual safety. Similarly, states comply with their legal obligations in order to reinforce a system of mutual compliance.

Other scholars have attempted to explain "why international law matters" in terms of "reputational costs" of non-compliance,[11] "legitimacy" and "fairness" of process,[12] and the "internalization" of international obligations within domestic processes.[13] It is noteworthy that the prevailing theoretical viewpoints on compliance rarely rely on, and often reject, coercion or sanction to explain state behavior.

Recognition of the limited role that sanction and authoritative enforcement plays in international law illustrates that analogies to models of domestic law and a preoccupation with state "compliance" may be misleading. A significant function of international law, and human rights in particular, may be the promotion of certain goals (such as peace and recognition of rights) and long term influence on thinking as well as behavior (such as the internalization or incorporation of respect for rights into domestic societies).[14] Even when states fail to obey international human rights norms in a strict sense, the existence of such norms may influence their conduct, provide legal grounds for other states to demand change and weaken the offending government's domestic legitimacy. International human rights are an excellent example of how international law's functions are diverse and evolutionary.

Overemphasis on international enforcement and the weaknesses of international legal processes also begs an important underlying question — is effective and mandatory international governance with authoritative enforcement of human rights "from above" a good idea? Should human rights advocates seek the creation of international institutions with binding interpretive, dispute resolution and enforcement

---

8. Professor Harold Koh's article examining various theories about state compliance with international law lists some of this research which he says "have confirmed [Henkin's] optimistic but hedged" assertion. *See* Harold Hongiu Koh, *Review Essay: Why Do Nations Obey International Law*, Faculty Scholarship Series. Paper 2101.

9. Louis Henkin, How NATIONS BEHAVE 47 (2nd Ed 1979).

10. Anthony D'Amato, *Is International Law Really "Law"?*, Northwestern University Law Review, Vol. 79, 1984 also available at SSRN.

11. Beth A. Simmons, *International Law and State Behavior: Commitment and Compliance in International Monetary Affairs*, 94 American Political Science Review 819 (2000).

12. Thomas M. Franck, *Legitimacy in the International System*, 82 AM. J. INT'L L. 705, 705 (1988); Thomas M. Franck, FAIRNESS IN INTERNATIONAL LAW AND INSTITUTIONS (1995).

13. Harold H. Koh, *Transnational Legal Process*, 75 Neb. L. Rev. 181, 183–84, 204 (1994); Harold Hongiu Koh, *Review Essay: Why Do Nations Obey International Law*, Part III.

14. *See, e.g.*, Robert Howse & Ruti Teitel, *Beyond Compliance: Rethinking Why International Law Really Matters*, Global Policy, Vol.1, Issue 2, May 2010.

authority analogous to domestic systems? How would such authoritative international processes coexist with domestic democratic ideals of self-governance, particularly for contestable rights involving moral and social issues such as abortion, capital punishment, sexual freedoms or free speech (blasphemy, pornography, hate and incitement)? Are international decision makers sufficiently accountable, sufficiently familiar with local cultural and social norms and sufficiently respectful of domestic processes to be entrusted with such authority?

Strong international enforcement has great appeal in an era still marked by widespread and egregious violations of human rights throughout the world — but perhaps one should be careful about what she wishes for. Subsequent lessons will further explore such questions but for now it is important to begin thinking critically about the nature of international law and how it relates to the goal of achieving respect for basic human rights.

From Cartoon Movement

## C. Sources of International Law: Treaties, Customary International Law and General Principles of Law

### 1. Overview

Legal obligations within international law come from sources and in forms quite distinct from those common in domestic legal systems. The absence of legislative, judicial or executive processes means that nearly all international obligations are created through negotiated agreement or based on state practices. In essence, the dominance of state sovereignty has resulted in a system of legal obligations almost entirely dependent upon state consent. In general, any particular state is bound by any particular international legal obligation only when it agrees to be bound. Even then, the precise contours and scope of such obligations are dictated largely within the discretion of each state (for example, through treaty reservations). Because there rarely are authoritative processes for interpretation or binding applications of international rules, the applied meaning and intent of international obligations is frequently unresolved, fragmented or left to each bound state to determine by its own terms.

The <u>Statute of the International Court</u> of Justice identifies the three commonly accepted sources of international legal obligations:

Article 38

1. The Court, whose function is to decide in accordance with international law such disputes as are submitted to it, shall apply:

   a. international conventions, whether general or particular, establishing rules expressly recognized by the contesting states;

   b. international custom, as evidence of a general practice accepted as law;

   c. the general principles of law recognized by civilized nations; . . .

The third "source" of international law set out in this definition, General Principles, represents the idea that legal principles which are ubiquitous to domestic legal systems are also, therefore, part of international law. It has largely been used to fill in gaps in international legal practice and litigation supplying universally accepted principles such as res judicata. Thus far, general principles have had no significant role in international human rights law.

The following material describes the other two essential forms or "sources" of international law in greater detail and reviews the critical features of each. Although perhaps a bit boring, these technical legal characteristics of international law are critically important to human rights. Pay attention.

## 2. Treaties ("Conventional Law")

a. General Characteristics

Let's defy academic orthodoxy and consider the following well stated definition of an international treaty found at Wikipedia:

> A **treaty** is an express agreement under <u>international law</u> entered into by actors in international law, namely <u>sovereign states</u> and <u>international organizations</u>. A treaty may also be known as an **(international) agreement**, **protocol**, **covenant**, contract, **convention**, **pact**, or **exchange of letters**, among other terms. Regardless of terminology, all of these forms of agreements are, under international law, equally considered treaties and the rules are the same.

Treaties can be loosely compared to contracts: both are means of willing parties assuming obligations among themselves, and a party to either that fails to live up to their obligations can be held liable under international law.

A treaty is an official, express written agreement that states use to legally bind themselves.

As noted in this definition, treaties are essentially international agreements between nations (either bilateral or multilateral) creating legal obligations between them. Although it is common to compare treaties to contracts, the analogy is indeed "loose." The primary similarity is limited to the existence of a binding negotiated consensual agreement. Treaties do not require consideration, the promises may be unilateral, their breaches rarely lead to well-defined consequences involving compensation or specific performance and the rules governing their formation, interpretation and termination bear little resemblance to the law of contracts.

In general, the obligations created in a treaty consist of promises by each of the state parties to each other to act, or refrain from acting, in defined ways. In this sense, the promises made create legal rules but, unlike other forms of law, the rules created apply only between the parties to the treaty. In this sense, all treaties create reciprocal obligations focused on the relationship between states as states.

*Importantly, however, human rights treaties do more than this.* The promises made in a human rights treaty are specifically intended to create benefits for a third, non-state party — the individual human beings within the state's jurisdiction. By joining human rights treaties, the United States is not simply promising other countries that it will respect rights, it is also promising all human beings within its jurisdiction that it will do so. Similarly, while many treaties are not intended to have direct domestic legal consequences, human rights treaties demand such consequences and have little meaning unless incorporated into domestic law and practice. Subsequent chapters will closely examine this critical relationship between various forms of international law and domestic systems.

The essential international rules regarding treaties are reviewed below with an emphasis on human rights conventions. These rules, ironically enough, are elaborated in great detail in a treaty called the Vienna Convention on the Law of Treaties [alternative source here]. The Convention, often called the "treaty on treaties," came into force in 1980 and had been adopted by 114 state parties as of 2016. This diagram from Wikipedia's description of the Convention shows its acceptance around the world (ratifications in dark green, signatories in yellow, non-parties in red):

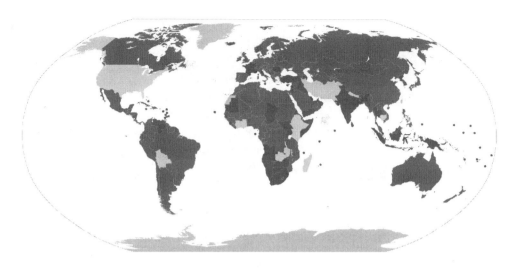

### b. Rules on Formation — Consent, Signature & Ratification

Virtually all significant international human rights treaties are multilateral conventions sponsored and promoted by an inter-governmental organization such as the United Nations. As a body of rules, treaties are often referred to as "conventional" law. The treaty text is typically developed through auspices of the organization by representatives of interested states, adopted by the organization (through resolution) and then opened for signature and ratification by states. Since *state consent to be bound is a necessary prerequisite* to a binding legal obligation, many treaties specify by their terms how such consent may be manifested.

Under the Vienna Convention Article 11 consent to be bound may be manifested in a variety of ways but in human rights this uniformly involves a two or three step process. The first step is typically "signature" by the state representative, which signifies agreement over the negotiated text, preliminary endorsement of the treaty and an *intention to consider its adoption* as a binding legal obligation, commonly referred to as "ratification." Under Article 18 of the Vienna Convention signatories to a treaty are "obligated to refrain from acts which would defeat the objects and purposes of the treaty" pending ratification. In essence, the signing state must not violate the central purposes of the treaty pending ratification unless and until it expresses clear intent to not become a party. Signed but unratified human rights treaties have been common for the United States given the rigorous Constitutional prerequisite of a 2/3 supermajority Senatorial consent.

The second step in forming a binding treaty obligation is manifesting official consent, almost always through either ratification or "accession." What ratification entails depends on the relevant domestic processes of each state. In some states ratification requires participation of the domestic legislature and in others it is exclusively an executive function. The process applicable in the United States is described in Chapter 4. Accession is similar but typically involves approval of the treaty through other domestic processes with formal adoption signified by depositing at the designated authority a notification with the signature of the authorized representative of the state. It is most typically used to join treaties already signed and ratified by a group of other states.

Finally, under most treaties, the instrument of ratification (or accession) must be "deposited" at a designated authority such as the United Nations' Secretary General. The deposit of ratifications not only allows for centralization of information about the treaty and its parties but also determines when multilateral treaties "enter into force." A standard practice with human rights treaties is to require a certain number of state adoptions as prerequisite to creating binding legal effect.

c. Reservations

Article 2 of the Vienna Convention defines a reservation as "a unilateral statement, however phrased or named, made by a State, when signing, ratifying, accepting, approving or acceding to a treaty, whereby it purports to exclude or to modify the legal effect of certain provisions of the treaty in their application to that State." A reservation, in essence, purports to exempt the state party from application of a particular part of the treaty. It seems odd, of course, that participants in a legal system can choose which parts of the law they will adhere to and which they will ignore. However, the practice of allowing reservations is a reflection of the continuing dominance of state sovereignty — states may not be bound to legal obligations without their consent.

In human rights, reservations are routine, extensive and problematic. Reservation practices by the United States provide a good illustration. Every human rights treaty that the United States has ratified includes numerous reservations virtually eliminating any U.S. obligations regarding any provision that might cause a change in previously existing U.S. law or practice. Take, for example, ratification of the CCPR, for which the Senate imposed five "reservations," five "understandings," and three "declarations." The reservations include, "the right, subject to its Constitutional constrains, to impose capital punishment on any person (other than a pregnant woman) duly convicted under existing or future laws permitting the imposition of capital punishment, including such punishment for crimes committed by persons below eighteen years of age." They also assert that the U.S. is bound by Article 7's prohibition against "cruel, inhuman or degrading treatment or punishment" only to the extent "prohibited by the Fifth, Eighth and/or Fourteenth Amendments to the Constitution of the United States."

The Senate also expressly declared that "provisions of Articles 1 through 27 of the Covenant are not self-executing" (essentially not part of U.S. domestic law) and attached a "proviso" declaring that: "Nothing in this Covenant requires or authorizes legislation, or other action, by the United States of America prohibited by the Constitution of the

United States as interpreted by the United States."[15] In effect, the reservations, understandings and declarations were designed to eviscerate all potential legal consequences associated with joining the treaty. A list of U.S. reservations to various human rights treaties is available at the University of Minnesota Human Rights Library.

The U.S. practice of imposing numerous reservations limiting its obligations under human rights treaties is hardly unique, however. The U.N. website provides the text of more than 100 reservations and international responses ("objections') to them regarding the same treaty.

Obviously imposing reservations that eliminate all possible changes in domestic law would appear inconsistent with the very concept of international human rights standards. What is the point of ratifying a treaty only upon the condition that those international standards will not change anything?

# AMERICAN EXCEPTIONALISM

By Kip Lyall

Similarly troubling is the vexing problem of "incompatible reservations" that are manifestly inconsistent with a treaty's central purposes. Many Islamic states, for example, have joined the Convention on the Elimination of Discrimination Against Women only after imposing reservations concerning Sharia religious law and family codes that clearly allow or require the precise types of discrimination

---

15. *See* U.S. Reservations, Declarations, and Understandings, International Covenant on Civil and Political Rights, 138 Cong. Rec. S4781-01 (daily ed., April 2, 1992).

that the Convention was designed to eliminate.[16] At least from a Western perspective, such reservations essentially assert: "we agree to an obligation to not discriminate against women, except for the part about treating men and women the same."

## "Does my bum look big in this?"

By Royston Robertson

---

16. Syria, for example, imposed the following reservation: "subject to reservations to article 2; article 9, paragraph 2, concerning the grant of a woman's nationality to her children; article 15, paragraph 4, concerning freedom of movement and of residence and domicile; article 16, paragraph 1 (c), (d), (f) and (g), concerning equal rights and responsibilities during marriage and at its dissolution with regard to guardianship, the right to choose a family name, maintenance and adoption; article 16, paragraph 2, concerning the legal effect of the betrothal and the marriage of a child, inasmuch as this provision is incompatible with the provisions of the Islamic Shariah; and article 29, paragraph 1, concerning arbitration between States in the event of a dispute." In a similar vein Algeria invoked exceptions preserving its religious based family code: "Article 16: The Government of the People's Democratic Republic of Algeria declares that the provisions of article 16 concerning equal rights for men and women in all matters relating to marriage, both during marriage and at its dissolution, should not contradict the provisions of the Algerian Family Code." There are many other examples of such reservations available at the UN CEDAW website.

By Dan Piraro, <u>Bizarro Cartoons</u>

While reservations are generally permissible under international rules unless the treaty prohibits them,[17] there are some important limitations on a state's right to impose reservations. Under Article 19 of the Vienna Convention, states may not impose reservations which are "incompatible with the object and purpose of the treaty." Under Articles 20 and 21, other state parties may also object to any reservation with various complicated legal consequences depending upon the nature of the treaty.

---

17. A few important multilateral treaties, such as the Convention on the Law of the Sea and Rome Treaty creating the International Criminal Court, prohibit reservations.

Traditionally, these range from eliminating the particular obligation between the reserving state and objecting state, to rendering the reserving state no longer party to the treaty at all (either vis-à-vis objecting states or entirely).

The proper legal remedy or consequence of an incompatible reservation creates a conundrum that has been hotly contested in academic literature.[18] One potential consequence would be to excise, ignore or "sever" the invalid reservation from the state's ratification. This would leave the state bound as if no reservation had been imposed. This approach, however, would seem clearly inconsistent with state sovereignty and the prerequisite of consent to be bound. On the other hand, if the invalid reservation cannot be severed (because of consent) allowing the state to remain party to the treaty would have the practical effect of allowing it the benefit of its incompatible reservation. The state would be party to the treaty except for those provisions for which it's invalid, but non-severable, reservation was imposed. This result would appear inconsistent with the very purposes of the human rights treaty and allow the anomalous result that states could enjoy the benefits of treaty membership (reputation, et cetera) despite maintaining invalid reservations incompatible with the treaty's fundamental purposes. A third possibility would follow the more traditional international law approach finding that the invalid reservations render the state no longer party to the treaty at all. This alternative might slavishly respect state sovereignty and preserve the treaty's integrity, but it would seem counterproductive to the goals of the international human rights system.

Ultimately, the dilemma for the human rights system is that the somewhat complicated and ambiguous international rules regarding the effect of invalid or rejected reservations fits poorly with the purposes of an international human rights system. Allowing incompatible reservations would seem to undermine the goal of creating universal minimum standards for basic human dignity. Yet, disallowing them and attempting to impose upon states obligations that they have objected to (through the reservation) will lead to withdrawal or reluctance to join treaties in the first place.

In practice, invalid reservations have not led to severance — that is, the imposition of obligations despite the reservation. State consent still appears to be a steadfast prerequisite and states are simply not bound by rules to which they object even if those objections appear incompatible with the treaty. Efforts to the contrary have met with stiff state resistance. Recognizing the problem of unbridled reservations, the "Human Rights Committee," an international body which monitors compliance with the CCPR, asserted its own authority as the final arbiter regarding the validity of reservations. It also expressed the view that invalid reservations

---

18. A relatively easy to read and thoughtful response to the problem of incompatible reservations to human rights treaties is presented in Ryan Goodman, *Human Rights Treaties, Invalid Reservations and State Consent*, 96 Am J. Int'l L 531 (2002). Professor Goodman reviews the debate and suggests an approach which presumes invalid reservations are severable unless clear state intent to the contrary is shown.

were essentially inoperable rendering the party bound as if no reservation had been imposed.[19]

A number of states, including the United States and France, immediately rejected both views and disputed the authority of the Committee.[20] This reaction demonstrates not only that states will likely strongly resist any approach to reservations that binds them despite the imposition of a reservation but also the underlying problem of process. Currently there are no human rights institutions with the authority to definitively judge the compatibility of reservations and bind the state parties to such judgments. Moreover, reservations are not only standard international law practice but also essential to promoting state adoption of international treaty obligations and progressive realization of rights. One might reasonably believe that it is much better to have states become members of human rights treaties with problematic reservations than for them not to join at all. Nevertheless, adoption of human rights treaties without reservations remains an obvious priority for the international human rights system.

### d. Interpretation

As with any other form of law, treaty language must often be interpreted when intended meaning is ambiguous or unclear. This is particularly true of human rights treaties which, perhaps by design, typically describe state obligations in very general

---

19. Human Rights Committee's <u>General Comment No. 24</u>, *see* UN Doc. CCPR/C/21/Rev.1/Add. 6 (1994). *See* Report of the Human Rights Committee, GAOR, 50<sup>th</sup> Sess., Supp. No. 40, vol. 1, at 119 (1996). The heart of the Committee's rationale appears in the following excerpt:

"The function of the first Optional Protocol is to allow claims in respect of [the Covenant's] rights to be tested before the Committee. Accordingly, a reservation to an obligation of a State to respect and ensure a right contained in the Covenant, made under the first Optional Protocol when it has not previously been made in respect of the same rights under the Covenant, does not affect the State's duty to comply with its substantive obligation. A reservation cannot be made to the Covenant through the vehicle of the Optional Protocol but such a reservation would operate to ensure that the State's compliance with that obligation may not be tested by the Committee under the first Optional Protocol. And because the object and purpose of the first Optional Protocol is to allow the rights obligatory for a State under the Covenant to be tested before the Committee, a reservation that seeks to preclude this would be contrary to object and purpose of the first Optional Protocol, even if not of the Covenant."

20. The United States, United Kingdom, and France strongly objected to the HRC's position and have indicated that they do not consider the HRC position binding. *See* Observations by the United States on General Comment 24, 3 INT HUM RTS REP. 265 (1996); Observations on General Comment No. 24 (52), U.N. GAOR, 50th Sess., Supp. No. 40, Vol. I, Annex V, at 126–27, U.N. Doc. A/50/40 (1995)(observations on General Comment No. 24 (52) by United Kingdom and Northern Ireland); Report of the Human Rights Committee, U.N. GAOR, 51st Sess., Annex VI, U.N. Doc. A/51/40 (1996) (observations of France to Article 40). The International Law Commission has suggested that this approach is contrary to prevailing international law. ILC legal counsel issued a similar opinion regarding reservations under CEDAW. In a similar vein, the HRC announced in 1997 that North Korea's attempt to withdraw from the CCPR was impermissible. Human Rights Comm., General Comment No. 26, 1997, U.N. Doc. CCPR/C/21/Rev.1/Add.9 (1997) (on continuity of obligations under the Covenant).

terms. The <u>Vienna Convention</u> states that treaties are to be interpreted "in good faith" according to the "ordinary meaning given to the terms of the treaty in their context and in the light of its object and purpose." For human rights treaties this implies recognition that such treaties are designed to protect the interests of individuals and not those of the state parties.[21] Since human rights treaties are multilateral, it also suggests that the "mutual intent" of the state parties may control over the specific intentions of any particular state party.

These general rules, both familiar and reasonable, hardly reveal the complex problem of interpretation in a legal system lacking authoritative institutional processes. Later chapters examine institutional authority and the processes of interpretation in greater detail. For now, consider the following brief excerpt from an article by Professor Donoho describing some of these complexities:

**Donoho, *Autonomy, Self-Governance, and the Margin of Appreciation: Developing a Jurisprudence of Diversity within Universal Human Rights*, 15 Emory Int'l L. Rev. 391 (2001)**

\*\*\*

Giving Meaning to Rights: Mediating Claims of Diversity through Case-by-Case Decision Making and Interpretation

Even a casual observer of the international human rights system will discover a plethora of generally stated, abstract norms covering most aspects of human behavior. For some governments and human rights advocates, the existence of this catalogue of generally stated, abstract norms is frequently the end of the inquiry rather than the beginning. This simplified view, much like vague assertions about "universality," fails to account for a more complex legal reality. Standing alone, generally stated abstract norms such as equal protection, privacy, free speech, or family life are even more indeterminate internationally than they are within domestic legal orders. The specific meaning and potential application of such elastic concepts is simply not self-evident within the enormously diverse settings of the international community. Indeed, vagueness and abstraction are the foundations that support widespread adoption of human rights treaties by widely divergent states in the first instance, often concealing an underlying lack of consensus over specific meaning.

---

21. The Inter-American Court has expressed this viewpoint as follows: "Modern human rights treaties in general, and the American Convention in particular, are not multilateral treaties of the traditional type concluded to accomplish the reciprocal exchange of rights for the mutual benefit of the contracting States. Their object and purpose is the protection of the basic rights of individual human beings irrespective of their nationality, both against the State of their nationality and all other contracting states. In concluding these human rights treaties, the States can be deemed to submit themselves to a legal order within which they, for the common good, assume various obligations, not in relation to other states, but towards all individuals within their jurisdiction [2nd advisory opinion, 1982 . . . ]."

Thus, widespread state agreement to a treaty regime protecting "privacy" or respect for "the best interests of the child" does not by itself imply consensus over whether such rights protect certain specific behavior. As in domestic legal systems, the specific meaning of such abstractions must be developed over time through a process of interpretation and application. Internationally, such questions of interpretation involve a complex matrix of legal and practical considerations including state intent, institutional mandate, context, and the nuanced interplay between national implementation and international supervision. In this regard, choices regarding institutional authority and the appropriate methods and goals of interpretation are critical to the development of the specific parameters of human rights obligations. ***

International Mechanisms for Interpreting the Meaning of Rights

The process of interpretation and application of international human rights norms may take place in a variety of forums and on different levels. Within the existing international human rights system most of these opportunities for interpretation are somewhat underdeveloped. Given the primacy of national implementation, the first layer of interpretation will theoretically be made by national authorities. Like the proverbial fox in the human rights henhouse, state parties themselves get the first crack at giving rights specific meaning. In practice, however, most states treat their human rights obligations as mere paper promises, often relying on the hollow pretext that their existing domestic legal system already fully satisfies their international obligations. The unfortunate reality is that most states simply ignore their international obligations altogether until pressed to respond through international scrutiny. ***

A second and more obvious source of interpretation occurs in the work of international human rights institutions. A poorly rationalized mixture of ill-defined mandates, circumscribed powers, cumbersome mechanisms, and often overlapping substantive norms generally clouds the potential role of these institutions in developing the meaning of rights. Unfortunately, the international human rights system is generally characterized by a multiplicity of non-authoritative interpretative sources.

***

Institutions such as the Human Rights Committee (HRC) necessarily engage in a significant amount of interpretive activity while pursuing their mandate to monitor the implementation of rights by state parties. Typically called "committees" and composed of experts selected by the state parties, these institutions are limited in their powers and mandate. In general, a committee's monitoring work is conducted by reviewing state parties' own self-serving reports regarding implementation and releasing "General Comments." [A number of] the committees, most notably the HRC, also engage in quasi-judicial activities that are described further below.

\*\*\*

At best, the state reporting process and the general comments allow the expression of various interpretations of rights that may slowly inch the international community toward some common understandings. In this sense, they serve an important promotional function that arguably should be less concerned with accommodations of diversity than the quasi-judicial processes described below. These mechanisms have, however, primarily been designed by the state parties to provide essentially toothless monitoring and supervision of national implementation of the treaties that created them. Overall, the potential that such mechanisms will generate significant interpretive work designed to accommodate concerns for diversity and autonomy appears limited.

The most significant opportunity to mediate the competing claims of universality and diversity in the meaning of rights occurs in those forums that have been authorized to serve quasi-judicial, adjudicatory functions. The individual complaint procedures available under the Inter-American and European regional human rights systems provide the most important examples. There are also [several] treaty-based committees, including most prominently the HRC, that have been authorized to hear individual petitions brought against those states that consent to the process.

The work of regional human rights organizations on individual complaints perhaps represents the international community's most significant opportunity to address [interpretation] issues within the international human rights system. Although distinct from domestic judicial processes in many significant respects, these international petitioning procedures often involve many of the same jurisprudential issues that face domestic courts. In each process, for example, an individual claims that some specific action or omission by government violates a right that is set out in an authoritative — albeit usually in general, abstract — text. The decision maker is called upon to give the abstract right a specific meaning that will resolve the concrete dispute between the government and claimant, while inevitably balancing a mixture of competing interests. Domestic judicial experience teaches us that such concrete cases have great potential for giving shape and specific content to the meaning of rights and for developing standards by which to evaluate critical competing interests.

The practical meaning of free speech only begins to take form when, for example, a tribunal is required to evaluate specific challenges to sedition laws, prohibitions on commercial speech, criminalization of pornography, or aggressive defamation laws. Every such challenge raises subtle and complex questions regarding the meaning of free speech that may only be adequately addressed when actual circumstances (i.e., context, countervailing public interests, and actual consequences to the individual) are taken into account by the decision maker. In essence, the concreteness of the dispute allows interpretive opportunities that are far more significant to the development of rights than those available through the other, more general, supervisory and monitoring functions of international organizations.

Thus, the tension between universal rights, self-governance, autonomy, and diversity may perhaps best be played out in the context of concrete dispute resolution. The critical question is how international institutions cast in this role may effectively accommodate diversity and yet preserve, promote, and develop universal human rights values. It is imperative in this regard that international human rights institutions develop a coherent jurisprudence regarding the decision making and interpretation processes that account for the tension between the international community's competing universalist and relativist impulses.

e. Dispute Resolution and Remedies for Breach

What happens when a state breaches its international legal obligations? Violations of both treaties and customary international law (see below) constitute an international wrong to the non-breaching parties. As might be expected, demands for cessation, restitution, compensation and suspension of reciprocal performance are commonly invoked. The Restatement of Foreign Relations purports to summarize the general rules of remedies with specific reference to international human rights obligations:

Restatement § 703

(1)  A state party to an international human rights agreement has, as against any other state party violating the agreement, the remedies generally available for violation of an international agreement, as well as any special remedies provided by the agreement.

(2)  Any state may pursue international remedies against any other state for a violation of the customary international law of human rights (§ 702).

(3)  An individual victim of a violation of a human rights agreement may pursue any remedy provided by that agreement or by other applicable international agreements.

**Comment:**

*a. Remedies for violation of international human rights obligations.* Under international law, a breach of an international obligation, whether deriving from customary law or from international agreement, gives rise to international remedies against the violating state. These remedies include the right to make an international claim; to resort to the International Court of Justice or other international tribunal to whose jurisdiction the complaining and responding states have submitted; and in some circumstances to some measures of self-help. See §§ 901–905. For this purpose, human rights agreements are no different from other international agreements. Unless the human rights agreement provides or clearly implies otherwise, the ordinary remedies are available to any state party against a state party violating the agreement, even if the violation did not affect nationals of the claimant state or any other particular interest of that state. ***

Some international human rights agreements provide for special "implementing machinery," for example complaint before an international human rights committee. See Reporters' Note 2. Unless the agreement provides or clearly implies the contrary, such special remedies generally supplement rather than replace the traditional remedies between states.

In the sense described by the Restatement potential remedies for treaty violations would appear similar to those available for wrongs committed under domestic law. In practice, however, remedies under international law are quite distinct for three related reasons. First, treaty violations typically (but not always[22]) involve state defendants who, as independent sovereign actors, are rarely subject to higher authority. Second, there is a paucity of effective and authoritative dispute resolution processes in the international system from which appropriate remedies can issue.[23] Third, effective enforcement mechanisms binding on the breaching state are often nonexistent or very limited. This lack of readily available and effective institutional remedies for violations of international law has traditionally caused states to rely often upon self-help measures, such as unilateral sanctions and negotiated settlement.

In some areas, however, the international legal system has evolved more effective dispute settlement processes within particular treaty regimes. The World Trade Organization, for example, has developed a system of dispute resolution that is binding, mostly respected, and generally authoritative. More importantly for present purposes, there is a variety of developing international dispute resolution mechanisms available for violations of human rights treaties. In every instance, with one possible exception,[24] the institution has jurisdiction exclusively for the particular treaty that created it. All of these mechanisms, which most prominently include the European Court of Human Rights, the Inter-American Court of Human Rights and international criminal tribunals, are explored in detail in subsequent chapters.

---

22. Some treaty obligations, such as those relating to crimes against humanity, extend to private actors who may be found liable for their violation. *See, e.g.*, Kadic v. Karadžić, 70 F. 3d. 232 (1995).

23. While some treaty disputes are, by mutual agreement, resolved by the International Court of Justice, few alleged treaty violations fall within the Court's jurisdiction.

24. The Inter-American Court of Human Rights has asserted, under Article 64 of the American Convention, to have authority to issue advisory opinions interpreting and applying *any* human rights treaty obligation (that is, obligations under other treaties) of those states subject to its jurisdiction by virtue of the Convention. *See* Advisory Opinion OC-1/82 (Peru).

In almost all cases these international dispute resolution processes and the remedies provided are distinct in important ways from those commonly found in domestic legal systems. Perhaps the most important of these distinctions is that there generally are no enforcement mechanisms with *effective coercive power* over breaching states. Even at the WTO, enforcement is a misnomer — the favored remedy is cessation of wrongful conduct, there are no fines or other forms of sanction, compensation consists primarily of the withdrawal of reciprocal trade benefits, and then only when the breaching party fails ultimately to conform to the rules. As detailed in subsequent chapters, weak enforcement of remedies is particularly true for international human rights although some international institutions, such as the European Court of Human Rights, have reason to boast about voluntary state compliance.

Treaty breaches in the context of human rights raise a number of distinct considerations to keep in mind. First, while a violation of human rights does implicate the interests of other states, it is primarily an individual person who has suffered the wrong. States may and sometimes do complain about breaches of human rights treaties but it is the potential protection of an individual that makes remedies a critical issue. Remedies in this context, particularly compensation and injunctive relief, take on special significance as harms to the individual are typically both tangible and measurable. Second, human rights violations involve harms that are usually done to the individual by his or her own government. This fact directly implicates a domestic legal system as well as international. Most major human rights treaties expressly obligate state parties to provide "effective" domestic remedies for violations. Article 2 (3) of the CCPR is typical:

3.  Each State Party to the present Covenant undertakes:

(a)  To ensure that any person whose rights or freedoms as herein recognized are violated shall have an effective remedy, notwithstanding that the violation has been committed by persons acting in an official capacity;

(b)  To ensure that any person claiming such a remedy shall have his right thereto determined by competent judicial, administrative or legislative authorities, or by any other competent authority provided for by the legal system of the State, and to develop the possibilities of judicial remedy;

(c)  To ensure that the competent authorities shall enforce such remedies when granted.

Because almost all international procedures require exhaustion of such domestic remedies, it is presumed that remedies will in the first instance be shaped by domestic legal processes. Third, an admittedly tepid but evolving institutional structure for remedying human rights violations exists on the international level. If domestic law were adequate to the task there would be no need for an international system for the protection of human rights — but sadly it is not. These international processes for seeking individual remedies are all created and controlled by particular treaties and vary considerably in method, process and effectiveness. Several subsequent chapters are devoted to their study.

### f. Withdrawal, Termination or Denunciation

What happens when a state wishes to terminate its legal obligations created by ratifying a treaty?[25] In light of continuing dominance of state sovereignty one might think this question has an easy answer — the state, being legally bound only by virtue of its own consent, simply takes its ball and goes home. The Vienna Convention rules and actual state practice, however, appear more complicated. After all, a state's withdrawal from a treaty, also called "denunciation," affects other state parties and the mutuality of the original obligations. Similarly, unilateral state withdrawal from a treaty obligation may be inconsistent with the treaty's underlying purposes. This would seem particularly true with regard to multilateral human rights treaties involving adoption of universal minimum standards based on recognized essentials for basic human dignity. Such treaties are designed to progressively achieve implementation of rights inherently possessed by everyone simply by virtue of being human. They are created to benefit and are "owned" by the people living within the state and not the state itself as a legal entity.

Obviously, states may always withdraw from a treaty that so provides, typically after notice and some reasonable time period.[26] Under Article 44 of the Vienna Convention withdrawal from a treaty must, with some limited exceptions, be as to the whole treaty. Generally states may not, unless the treaty so provides, withdraw from only parts of a treaty. In the human rights context there have been several prominent illustrations of these basic rules involving denunciations of treaty obligations by several Caribbean and Latin American countries.[27]

Starting around 1997, Jamaica, Trinidad & Tobago and Guyana all announced withdrawal from the Optional Protocol to the Covenant on Civil and Political Rights, which allowed the Human Rights Committee to hear complaints from individuals involving alleged violations of rights. Each country had become disgruntled with decisions of the Committee involving capital punishment. The countries quickly "reacceded" to the Optional Protocol with a reservation excluding capital punishment from the Committee's jurisdiction. At the same time, Trinidad & Tobago and Guy-

---

25. An informative review and analysis of treaty withdrawal is presented in: Lawrence Helfer, Chapter 25, Terminating Treaties.

26. An example of this includes the American Convention on Human Rights, Article 78, which allows withdrawal after five years membership upon one year notice. Trinidad and Tobago opted to withdraw from the Convention in 1998 asserting that the system's delay in reviewing claims involving capital punishment frustrated the expeditious administration of justice and would cause violations of its Constitution, based on case law from the Privy Council (Pratt (A.C. P.C. 1993) and Morgan cases). *See* Trinidad Denunciation. The "Bolivarian Republic of Venezuela" similarly denounced the Convention on September 10, 2012.

27. *See* Amnesty International, Document — Caribbean: Unacceptably limiting human rights protection.

ana also withdrew from the American Convention on Human Rights in order to preclude review of death penalties sentences by the Inter-American Court of Human Rights.

The Human Rights Committee later declared, over 4 dissenting views, that Trinidad & Tobago's reservation excluding capital cases (in its "re-accession") was incompatible with the Optional Protocol of the Covenant on Civil and Political Rights. Extending the controversy created earlier in its General Comment No. 24, the Human Rights Committee then ignored the reservation and considered a communication involving the death penalty to be admissible.[28] The country subsequently refused to participate in further proceedings. In recent news some UK politicians have even proposed withdrawal from the European Convention on Human Rights in light of adverse rulings concerning deportation of terrorism suspects.

An even more controversial question involves withdrawal from treaties that are silent on the issue. Here the Vienna Convention provides in Article 56 that states may only withdraw from such treaties if it is shown that the parties intended this possibility or it is implied by the nature of the treaty itself. These rules were put to practical effect in 1996 when North Korea announced its intent to withdraw from the Covenant on Civil and Political Rights. The Human Rights Committee, entrusted with monitoring state compliance with the treaty, declared in General Comment 26 (61) that the treaty was not susceptible of denunciation.[29] The U.N. Secretary General, whose authority over the issue is unclear, also rejected North Korea's attempt to withdraw from this major human rights treaty. The country eventually resumed participation in the treaty processes.

g. Derogation of Obligations

Withdrawal from a treaty must be distinguished from the right, authorized in many human rights treaties, to temporarily suspend or "derogate" from certain rights in times of national emergency. Article 15 of the European Convention on Human Rights provides an example:

Article 15 — Derogation in time of emergency

1. In time of war or other public emergency threatening the life of the nation any High Contracting Party may take measures derogating from its obligations under this Convention to the extent strictly required by the exigencies of the situation, provided that such measures are not inconsistent with its other obligations under international law.

---

28. Rawle Kennedy v. Trinidad & Tobago, Communication No. 845/1999, available at: http://www.ohchr.org/Documents/Publications/SDecisionsVol7en.pdf

29. Human Rights Committee, General Comment 26 (61), General Comments under article 40, paragraph 4, of the International Covenant on Civil and Political Rights, Adopted by the Committee at its 1631st meeting.

2. No derogation from Article 2, except in respect of deaths resulting from lawful acts of war, or from Articles 3, 4 (paragraph 1) and 7 shall be made under this provision.

3. Any High Contracting Party availing itself of this right of derogation shall keep the Secretary General of the Council of Europe fully informed of the measures which it has taken and the reasons therefor. It shall also inform the Secretary General of the Council of Europe when such measures have ceased to operate and the provisions of the Convention are again being fully executed.

Similar derogation provisions appear in <u>Article 4 of the CCPR</u> , Article 27 of the <u>Economic, Social and Cultural Rights Covenant</u>,[30] and Article 27 of the <u>American Convention on Human Rights</u>. Typically derogations are subject to specific exclusions (rights not allowing for derogation) and conditions or prerequisites such as necessity, proportionality and non-discrimination. The European Court of Human Rights has developed considerable jurisprudence regarding derogations under the European Convention that is likely to be persuasive under other treaty regimes as well.[31] The website of the <u>Geneva Academy</u>'s Rule of Law in Armed Conflict Project provides a <u>concise summary</u> of this jurisprudence and the somewhat more restrictive views of the CCPR's Human Rights Committee.

---

30. Article 27 is both more specific and restrictive than its counterpart CCRP:

*Article 27. Suspension of Guarantees*

1. In time of war, public danger, or other emergency that threatens the independence or security of a State Party, it may take measures derogating from its obligations under the present Convention to the extent and for the period of time strictly required by the exigencies of the situation, provided that such measures are not inconsistent with its other obligations under international law and do not involve discrimination on the ground of race, color, sex, language, religion, or social origin.

2. The foregoing provision does not authorize any suspension of the following articles: Article 3 (Right to Juridical Personality), Article 4 (Right to Life), Article 5 (Right to Humane Treatment), Article 6 (Freedom from Slavery), Article 9 (Freedom from Ex Post Facto Laws), Article 12 (Freedom of Conscience and Religion), Article 17 (Rights of the Family), Article 18 (Right to a Name), Article 19 (Rights of the Child), Article 20 (Right to Nationality), and Article 23 (Right to Participate in Government), or of the judicial guarantees essential for the protection of such rights.

3. Any State Party availing itself of the right of suspension shall immediately inform the other States Parties, through the Secretary General of the Organization of American States, of the provisions the application of which it has suspended, the reasons that gave rise to the suspension, and the date set for the termination of such suspension.

31. *See, e.g., Lawless v Ireland* (No 3) (1961) 1 EHRR 15; *Ireland v United Kingdom* (1978) Series A No 35; A and Others v. United Kingdom, Application no. 3455/05, Council of Europe: European Court of Human Rights, 19 February 2009. The Human Rights Committee *Landinelli Silva v Uruguay* (1981) HRC Comm. No 34/1978 at paras 8.3. *See also* Siracusa Principles on the Limitation and Derogation Provisions in the International Covenant on Civil and Political Rights (1985), 7(1) Human Rights Quarterly 3.

## 3. Customary International Law

### a. General Characteristics

As a form of binding positive legal obligation, customary international law (CIL) is an odd duck. Born perhaps from necessity in an era lacking the infrastructure to readily create binding multilateral treaties, customary international law rules are generated not by overt agreement but rather by what states do and say over time. The Restatement on Foreign Relations § 102, provides a commonly accepted general definition:

> "(2) Customary international law results from a general and consistent practice of states followed by them from a sense of legal obligation."

Two key ingredients appear in the Restatement definition of CIL: (1) a general and consistent practice of states, and (2) conformity to the practice as a legal obligation, commonly referred to as the "psychological factor" of "opinio juris." In essence, CIL consists of state practices that have "crystalized" into law as the international community comes to expect that those practices are legally required of them. As states interact, makes demands, respond and acquiesce to the actions of other states, their patterns of behavior and rhetoric create legal expectations with the same legal consequences as rules created through treaties. Once formed, these rules are theoretically binding on all states that have not expressly and persistently objected to them. Express consent to CIL is not required.

Rules regarding national territorial seas provide a good example of how CIL develops, works in practice and relates to the modern reliance on treaties. As early as the 17th century, coastal states began to assert sovereign authority over the waters adjacent to their shores. Precisely how far from shore this authority could lawfully reach was, of course, a matter of dispute and concern for all seafaring nations. As states asserted their authority by boarding vessels, distributing permits to fish and allowing passage, the "cannon shot" rule developed—allowing absolute authority over seas extending 3 miles from the shore, approximately the distance of a cannon shot. Because states eventually began to enforce and follow this 3 mile limitation, *treating it as a legal obligation*, CIL was formed. Eventually, led by the United States, the 3 mile rule was abandoned through contrary practices and declarations of authority which resulted in a 12 mile territorial sea, a 24 mile "contiguous zone," and 200 mile "exclusive economic zone." By 1982, these practices were adopted, or "codified," into conventional law through the United Nations Convention on the Law of the Sea.[32]

### b. Customary International Law & Human Rights: The Contested "Modern" View

Needless to say, CIL is often amorphous and contested. Disputes over the existence of a claimed rule and its contours are inevitable given the soft variables that

---

32. The Coastal Survey division of NOAA provides a more detailed description of the historical development of the law of the sea.

define it — sufficient state practice and opinio juris. Inevitably, there is a difference between what states say, what they do and what they believe is legally obligated. When states routinely endorse the Universal Declaration of Human Rights in non-binding resolutions at the U.N. General Assembly does this imply recognition of a binding customary law obligation to adhere to its provisions? If 150 countries ratify a multilateral human rights treaty such as the CCPR does this provide evidence of "widespread, uniform practice" rendering the treaty rights part of CIL binding even on non-participants?

In this sense it is easy to understand the modern prominence and functional superiority of treaties as a source of international law. In sharp contrast to CIL, treaties create legal obligations through textually memorialized, express and negotiated agreement over the rules. Legitimate disputes over the existence of a legal obligation are rare, state consent to the obligation typically includes ratification endorsed through domestic political processes and there is a text which defines obligations with at least some minimal clarity. Treaty obligations ultimately enjoy the legitimacy of a deliberative process that the states themselves have consented to and may reject.

One might expect then, in a modern world with efficient means for negotiating consensual sets of rules in written form, custom as a source of law would fade from view. It has not, however. The continuing saliency of CIL is largely due to one of its unique, perhaps unintended, characteristics and its utility for promoting international human rights. Under CIL there is no requirement of express consent to be bound. It also fairly easy, if controversial, to find evidence of "state practice" in the multitude of non-binding resolutions and declarations endorsing human rights standards by inter-governmental organizations like the U.N.[33] Similarly, widespread adoption of multilateral human rights treaties is often cited, even by the Restatement of Foreign Relations,[34] as evidence of state practice and CIL.

Take note of the position espoused by the Restatement on what constitutes evidence of customary international law, particularly its view of state "pronouncements" articulated in (2)(d):

---

33. The Restatement of Foreign Relation Law asserts this position in the "comments" to §102:

"The practice of states that builds customary law takes many forms and includes what states do in or through international organizations. Comment b. The United Nations General Assembly in particular has adopted resolutions, declarations, and other statements of principles that in some circumstances contribute to the process of making customary law, insofar as statements and votes of governments are kinds of state practice, Comment b, and may be expressions of *opinio juris*, Comment c. The contributions of such resolutions and of the statements and votes supporting them to the lawmaking process will differ widely, depending on factors such as the subject of the resolution, whether it purports to reflect legal principles, how large a majority it commands and how numerous and important are the dissenting states, whether it is widely supported (including in particular the states principally affected), and whether it is later confirmed by other practice."

34. The Restatement clearly articulates this position: "(3) International agreements create law for the states parties thereto and may lead to the creation of customary international law when such agreements are intended for adherence by states generally and are in fact widely accepted."

### § 103 Evidence of International Law

(1)  Whether a rule has become international law is determined by evidence appropriate to the particular source from which that rule is alleged to derive (§ 102).

(2)  In determining whether a rule has become international law, substantial weight is accorded to

(a)  judgments and opinions of international judicial and arbitral tribunals;

(b)  judgments and opinions of national judicial tribunals;

(c)  the writings of scholars;

(d)  pronouncements by states that undertake to state a rule of international law, when such pronouncements are not seriously challenged by other states.

The Restatement comments to sections 102 and 103 add this more controversial perspective regarding resolutions of international organizations and multilateral treaties:

> ... agreements open to all states, however, are increasingly used for general legislation, whether to make new law, as in human rights (Introduction to Part VII), or for codifying and developing customary law, as in the Vienna Convention on the Law of Treaties. ... International agreements may contribute to customary law. See Comment i.
>
> *c. Declaratory resolutions of international organizations.* States often pronounce their views on points of international law, sometimes jointly through resolutions of international organizations that undertake to declare what the law is on a particular question, usually as a matter of general customary law. International organizations generally have no authority to make law, and their determinations of law ordinarily have no special weight, but their declaratory pronouncements provide some evidence of what the states voting for it regard the law to be. The evidentiary value of such resolutions is variable. Resolutions of universal international organizations, if not controversial and if adopted by consensus or virtual unanimity, are given substantial weight. ...

In *Principles of Public International Law*, Professor Ian Brownlie lists a similar set of sources as evidence of custom:

> "The material sources of custom are very numerous and include the following: diplomatic correspondence, policy statements, press releases, the opinions of official legal advisers, official manuals on legal questions, e.g. manuals of military law, executive decisions and practices, orders to naval forces etc., comments by governments on drafts produced by the International Law Commission, state legislation, international and national judicial decisions, recitals in treaties and other international instruments, a pattern of treaties in the same form, the practice of international organs, and resolutions relating to legal questions in the United Nations General Assembly."

In this respect, consider whether reference to the U.S. Uniform Commercial Code provides a strained but useful analogy to Customary International Law. Reflect on how the concept of "Customary International Law" compares to the legal concept of "Course of Dealing and Usage of Trade" found in the Uniform Commercial Code, imposed on parties to a dispute when there is no contract provision or applicable statutory law directly on point. In other words, could the concepts of "course of dealing" and particularly "usage of trade" be invoked to bind parties that have not specifically consented to the imposition of those rules?[35]

It is easy to understand why human rights advocates, but not so much states, love the "modern" CIL. The effect of these factors put together is the inevitable claim that all states are bound by most human rights norms regardless of their overt consent, even when they have not chosen to ratify human rights treaties. Endorsing this approach, it is common for human rights advocates, non-governmental organizations and U.N. agencies to assert that, at minimum, the entire Universal Declaration of Human Rights is now part of binding CIL. This position is sometimes bolstered by the argument that the Universal Declaration is essentially a state endorsed interpretation of the treaty based obligation to respect universal rights found in Article 55 and 56 of the United Nations Charter. Under this expansive view of customary law, obligations are essentially implicitly created thus avoiding the inherent limitations of an international system still dominated by sovereignty, consent and lack of hierarchical legal order. Professor Sullivan expressed it this way:

> "In many ways, CIL holds a privileged position in the international legal system. Customary law is universal. While treaties require explicit and affirmative approval, rules of customary law bind all states. Customary law is cheap. Customary law flows directly from the act of governance, thus resulting in minimal transaction costs. In contrast, treaties, if consummated at all, incur heavy transaction costs at the international level to achieve state accession and at the domestic level to accomplish ratification and incorporation. Customary law is organically produced. Customary practices become law while no one is watching. In contrast, the process of treaty ratification is fraught with political peril and thus subject to political assassination. Most

---

35. 1.Uniform Commercial Code

Uniform Commercial Code § 1-205. Course of Dealing and Usage of Trade.

(1) A course of dealing is a sequence of previous conduct between the parties to a particular transaction which is fairly to be regarded as establishing a common basis of understanding for interpreting their expressions and other conduct.

(2) A usage of trade is any practice or method of dealing having such regularity of observance in a place, vocation or trade as to justify an expectation that it will be observed with respect to the transaction in question. The existence and scope of such a usage are to be proved as facts. If it is established that such a usage is embodied in a written trade code or similar writing the interpretation of the writing is for the court.

. . .

importantly, customary law is dynamic. Once ratified, the subject matter governed by treaties is subjugated to the preeminence of text, thus impeding innovation and institutionalizing status quo biases."[36]

Extensive reliance on CIL by human rights advocates, despite soft empirical support based on state practice, has stirred considerable academic controversy and challenges to the legitimacy of CIL as a source of binding authority within the U.S. legal system.[37] Consider the following critique of the modern CIL and think about its implications for international human rights. Is Professor Kelly's critical assessment of CIL correct or overblown?

J. Patrick Kelly, The Twilight of Customary International Law, 40 Va. J. Int'l L. 449 (2000)

\*\*\*

International legal theory is in disarray. Despite the rapid internationalization of commerce and finance, there is neither a common understanding of how customary international legal norms are formed, nor agreement on the content of those norms. Scholars and nations declare with equal conviction that torture is or is not a violation of the customary international law ("CIL") of human rights, that states are or are not responsible for their failure to prevent significant injury to the environment of another states, and that states have or do not have an international obligation to pay full compensation for the expropriation of foreign-owned property. Under the indeterminate and manipulable theory of CIL, all of these positions are tenable. CIL is then a matter of taste. As such, it cannot function as a legitimate source of substantive legal norms in a decentralized world of nations without a broad base of shared values.

\*\*\*

In this article, I argue that CIL should be eliminated as a source of international legal norms and replaced by consensual processes. My goal is not to undermine international law, but to encourage the use of more democratic, deliberative processes in formulating this law. My argument has three components. First, the substantive CIL norms of the literature lack the authority of customary law and therefore are not binding on states. CIL lacks authority

---

36. Scott Sullivan, *Networking Customary International Law*, 61 Kan.L.Rev. 659 (2013).

37. A representative sample of such critiques might include: John O. McGinnis & Ilya Somin, *Should International Law Be Part of Our Law?*, 59 Stan. L. Rev. 1175, 1179 (2007) ("democracy deficit"); Curtis A. Bradley & Mitu Gulati, *Customary International Law and Withdrawal Rights in an Age of Treaties*, 21 Duke J. Comp. & Int'l L. 1, 4-7 (2010)(describing CIL as "riddled with uncertainty" and summarizing issues). *See also* Andrew T. Guzman, *Saving Customary International Law*, 27 Mich. J. Int'l L. 115, 116, 117 (2005) ("virtually everyone agrees that the theory and doctrine of CIL is a mess"); George Norman & Joel P. Trachtman, *The Customary International Law Game*, 99 Am. J. Int'l L. 541, 541 (2005) ("[CIL] is under attack as . . . doctrinally incoherent."); Curtis A. Bradley & Jack L. Goldsmith, *Customary International Law as Federal Common Law: A Critique of the Modern Position*, 110 Harv. L. Rev. 815, 838–42 (1997).

as law, because such norms are not, in fact, based on the implied consent or general acceptance of the international community that a norm is obligatory. Both implied consent and general acceptance are fictions used at different historical periods to justify the universalization of preferred norms. In a world of many cultures and values, general acceptance is neither ascertainable nor verifiable.

Second, CIL has evolved into a meaningless concept that furnishes neither a coherent nor objective means of determining the norms of international law, how and when they come into existence, and which nations are bound. As an undefined and indeterminate source, it is unable to perform its assigned function as a relatively objective source of international norms based on social fact. Third, the CIL process lacks procedural legitimacy. The process of norm formation, as actually practiced, violates the basic notion of democratic governance among states and is a particularly ineffective way to generate substantive norms that will command compliance. Few nations participate in the formation of norms said to be customary. The less powerful nations and voices are ignored. There is little consideration of alternatives and trade-offs in reconciling diverse values and interests. Consequently, CIL should be discarded as a source of law and replaced by consent based processes that permit wide participation, the discussion of alternatives, and the commitment of nations to their norms.

\*\*\*

The current debate in CIL theory is between those who espouse a traditional notion of customary law based on general and consistent acts of state practice over an extended period of time and advocates of "new CIL," who would expand CIL to include norms articulated in non-binding resolutions by the majority of states at international fora and to norms in multilateral treaties even though not agreed to by all. With the rise of "new CIL" CIL appears to be of growing importance. \*\*\*

This article raises a more fundamental critique of CIL. I challenge the basic assumption of international legal theory that CIL is a legitimate form of lawmaking in the international community. I argue that the substantive norms of both traditional CIL and "new CIL" are non-empirical forms of CIL deduced from subjective principles. Such "non-empirical" custom lacks the authority of the international community and hence is inappropriate for resolving disputes in both domestic and international fora. \*\*\*

Moreover, I believe that the CIL process lacks procedural legitimacy — i.e., concern with how rules are formed. I argue that the CIL process is inconsistent with democratic values and lacks the procedural safeguards necessary to produce norms that will be perceived as legitimate by the nations of the world. Few nations participate in the formation of CIL, and the process is not deliberative. Thus, the customary international legal process is an unacceptable means of developing legal norms in a diverse world society when other more efficacious and legitimate means are available.

Objections to the more expansive approach to customary law are typically grounded in the fact that states make statements and vote in favor of non-binding resolutions *precisely because they are non-binding.* Some have argued, therefore, that finding customary obligations on the basis of state rhetoric, multilateral treaties and non-binding resolutions is both a non-sequitur and directly contrary to actual state intent, mistakenly focusing more on what states proclaim rather than on what they actually practice. The distinction between rhetoric and practice is a murky one. Many governments continue to violate the international prohibition against torture. Does this indicate an absence of "practice" sufficient to establish a customary international law rule against torture? Or does the fact that states universally deny allegations of torture even while practicing it (except perhaps for the United States, which chose to redefine torture rather than deny it), instead confirm the existence of the rule?

However one views the expansive "modern" approach to customary international law of human rights, it undoubtedly creates a number of conundrums still waiting for resolution. How can one explain how the assertion of a legally non-binding rhetorical position or endorsement of non-binding resolution creates a binding legal obligation in a system grounded on state consent? How can the widespread adoption of human rights treaties by some states lead to the conclusion that other states which have refused to join them are nevertheless bound to the same legal rules through custom? Doesn't the decision not to join a treaty demonstrate intent not to be bound by the principles it declares? Ultimately, proponents of the modern view of custom are challenging vestiges of the traditional international legal system itself — the premise that states, as equal and independent sovereigns, may not be bound absent their consent. In the absence of an international legislature, this may be the only option in challenging an unjust, inhumane world order.

Not surprisingly, there is little evidence that states themselves have endorsed the expansive approach to the creation of customary law. What about the courts? In several cases, the International Court of Justice appears to have adopted a more modern approach to finding custom.[38] In addition, the expansive view of custom, which has the potential for significantly expanding the protection that human rights can offer, has sometimes found a positive reception in litigation before United States and other domestic courts. As described in Chapters 4 and 5, lower United States courts have tended to follow a mixed approach with references to actual state "practice" appearing to be little more than a formality with regard to some well recognized rights such as torture. These chapters examine such litigation and the role of both customary and conventional law within domestic systems in greater detail.

---

38. *See, e.g.,* Military and Paramilitary Activities in and Against Nicaragua (Nicar. v. U.S.), Merits, 1986 ICJ REP. 14

### c. Remedies for Violations of Customary Human Rights Obligations

The next chapter explores the substantive content of current international human rights, including customary international law, in greater detail. It is important to recognize at this point that customary international human rights law, despite ongoing academic disputes over its content and legitimacy, is nevertheless binding on all states and its violations subject to appropriate remedies. However, significant institutional and jurisdictional limitations on international enforcement of customary human rights law exists.

Other than the International Court of Justice, which itself has very limited jurisdiction over states and disputes, there are no international institutions under whose jurisdiction customary law violations generally fall. A temporary and limited exception to this observation would be the ad hoc International Criminal Tribunals for the former Yugoslavia and Rwanda. Both of these institutions relied heavily on principles of customary international law involving crimes against humanity and war crimes, but had limited temporal and geographic jurisdiction, which is at an end.[39] As described in subsequent chapters, most international human rights institutions are designed exclusively to implement the terms of a specific treaty regime that created them rather than customary law.

This means that domestic enforcement of customary human rights law is critical to rendering such norms meaningful. Note the following position taken by the Restatement of Foreign Relations on the subject of remedies for customary international human rights obligations:

> ***Comments to §703***
>
> ***b. Remedies for violation of customary law of human rights.*** Since the obligations of the customary law of human rights are ***erga omnes*** (obligations to all states), § 702, Comment o, any state may pursue remedies for their violation, even if the individual victims were not nationals of the complaining state and the violation did not affect any other particular interest of that state. . . .
>
> ***c. Remedies of individual victims.*** In general, individuals do not have direct international remedies against a state violating their human rights except where such remedies are provided by international agreement. See § 906. Whether they have a remedy under the law of a state depends on that state's law. See Reporters' Note 7. International human rights agreements generally require a state party to provide such remedies. See, e.g., International Covenant on Civil and Political Rights, Article 2(3). Failure to provide such remedies would constitute an additional violation of the agreement. . . .

---

39. *See* Chapter 11, *infra.*

## 4. Jus Cogens

The term jus cogens refers to an uncertain set of overriding principles of international law for which no state consent is required and no derogation permitted. Jus cogens norms are also known as "peremptory" norms since they sit at the apex of international law hierarchy and theoretically allow for no dissent or deviation. Like international human rights, the concept of jus cogens is of comparatively recent origin and its endorsement by states, as opposed to academics and international organizations,[40] is uncertain at best.[41] In part because jus cogens norms are inconsistent with the basic precept of state sovereignty and consent, their existence and legitimacy is sometimes also disputed by scholars.[42] Nevertheless, the Vienna Convention on Treaties, the Restatement of Foreign Relations, many international law scholars and a number of international judicial bodies, all endorse the concept.[43]

Acceptance or rejection of jus cogens by governments is uncertain. The Vienna Convention, however, suggests that jus cogens is, much like customary law, the product of widespread acceptance by state of the norm as peremptory:

> "A treaty is void if, at the time of its conclusion, it conflicts with a peremptory norm of general international law. For the purposes of the present Convention, a peremptory norm of general international law is a norm accepted and recognized by the international community of states as a whole as a norm from which no derogation is permitted and which can be modified only by a subsequent norm of general international law having the same character."

---

40. Professor Andrea Bianchi described the development of jus cogens this way: "If it may be temerity of sorts to say that the contours of *jus cogens* have been moulded by international lawyers, to hold that the latter have created the humus on which the notion could thrive is certainly an accurate representation of its development. In this respect, international lawyers have acted as 'magicians,' administering the rites of *jus cogens* and invoking its magical power. Acting under the different guise of scholars, counsel, international judges, and legal advisers, international lawyers have succeeded in making *jus cogens* part and parcel of the fabric of the international law discourse." Andrea Bianchi, *Human Rights and the Magic of Jus Cogens*, 19 EJIL 493 (2008).

41. For a review of the history and disputes over jus cogens, *See* Paul Stephan, *The Political Economy of Jus Cogens,* 44 Vand. J. Trans. L. 1073 (2011). Professor Stephan reports that a number of major states, including the United States, have not ratified the Vienna Convention on Treaties at least in part because of its endorsement of jus cogens in Article 53. Id. at 1088–90. The former Soviet Union joined the treaty but imposed a reservation rejecting application of jus cogens to any international dispute. *Id.*

42. E.g., Anthony D'Amato, *It's a Bird, It's a Plane, It's Jus Cogens!,* 6 Conn. J. of Int'l L. 1-6 (1990); George Schwarzenberger, International Jus Cogens? 43 Tx L. Rev. 455/ 467 (1965); Gordon A. Christenson, Jus Cogens: *Guarding Interests Fundamental to International Society,* 28 VA. J. INT'L L. 585 (1988); Gennady M. Danilenko, *International Jus Cogens: Issues of Law-Making,* 2 Eur. J. Int'l L. 42 (1991); A. Mark Weisburd, *The Emptiness of the Concept of* Jus Cogens, *as Illustrated by the War in Bosnia-Herzegovina,* 17 Mich. J. Int'l L. 1 (1995).

43. Prosecutor v. Furundžija, International Criminal Tribunal for the Former Yugoslavia, 2002, 121 *International Law Reports* 213 (2002); Al-Adsani v. United Kingdom, App. No. 35763/97, paras. 9–13 (Nov. 21, 2001), *available at* ‹ http://www.echr.coe.int/eng/judgments.htm; Vienna Convention on Treaties, Article 53.

Given this approach and debates over legitimacy, identification of precisely which norms of international law might be jus cogens is also far from clear. It is frequently assumed that the basic obligation of states to comply with their treaty obligations, known by the Latin phrase "pacta sunt servanda," must be jus cogens. Without such a rule the system itself could not function. Many other candidates have been suggested including the U.N. Charter's prohibition on the use of force (raising the somewhat perverse implication that peremptory status apparently does not depend upon actual state compliance).[44]

With almost no state response or involvement, human rights advocates, scholars and international human rights bodies have frequently urged that particular human rights norms constitute jus cogens. Since jus cogens norms are binding without specific state consent and superior to other forms of legal obligation, their appeal for human advocates is understandable. Not only is state consent to the obligation irrelevant, violations of jus cogens arguably eliminate any official immunity from liability for the public officials that perpetrate them.[45]

By circumventing overt state consent, jus cogens of human rights also implicitly empowers international organizations and human rights bodies to challenge governments that abuse rights, without regard to state consent or membership in a treaty. Plausible candidates likely to be endorsed by the international community as jus cogens would include torture, genocide, crimes against humanity, slavery, summary executions and apartheid. The Restatement of Foreign Relations endorses this view in the Reporter Notes to §702, which suggests "Not all human rights norms are jus cogens, but those in clauses (a) to (f) have that quality."

Some scholars have pointed out that the "rhetorical charm" of jus cogens may conceal a certain underlying incoherence in the concept and the regrettable reality that scholars and advocates, not states, are its biggest fans. Consider the following tongue in cheek indictment by Professor D'Amato.

### Anthony D'Amato, *It's a Bird, It's a Plane, It's Jus Cogens!*, Connecticut Journal of International Law, Vol. 6, No. 1, pp. 1–6, 1990

If an International Oscar were awarded for the category of Best Norm, the winner by acclamation would surely be *jus cogens*. Who has not succumbed to its rhetorical power? Who can resist the attraction of a supernorm against which all ordinary norms of international law are mere 97-pound weaklings?

---

44. *See* Restatement Comments 702. *See e.g.*, International Law Commission, Commentaries to 2001 Draft Articles on Responsibility of States for Internationally Wrongful Acts, Art. 40, ¶¶ 4–6, *in Report of the International Law Commission on the Work of Its Fifty-third Session*, U.N. GAOR, 56th Sess., Supp. No. 10, U.N. Doc. A/56/10 (2001) (suggesting that *jus cogens* norms include the prohibition of aggression, slavery and slave trade, genocide, racial discrimination and apartheid, torture, international humanitarian law in armed conflict and self-determination). *See also* Prosecutor v. Furundžija, No. IT-95-17/1-T, (Dec. 10, 1998), ¶ 155, *reprinted in* 38 ILM 317 (1999), ¶ 155 (discussing torture as a peremptory norm).

45. Various forms of immunity (sovereign, official, diplomatic) are examined in Chapter 8 *infra*.

To be sure, a critic may object that *jus cogens* has no substantive content; it is merely an insubstantial image of a norm, lacking flesh and blood. Yet lack of content is far from disabling for a protean supernorm. Indeed, the sheer ephemerality of *jus cogens* is an asset, enabling any writer to christen any ordinary norm of his or her choice as a new *jus cogens* norm, thereby in one stroke investing it with magical power. Nor does there appear to be any limit to the number of norms that a writer may promote to the status of supernorm. Consider the gaggle of substantive norms, sharing in common their newly anointed *jus cogens* status, that have been collected by Karen Parker and Lyn Beth Neylon in a recent article. These authors claim that the right to life is a norm of *jus cogens*, as are the prohibitions against torture and apartheid. Indeed, having attained this measure of momentum — faster than a speeding bullet — the authors end by claiming that the entire body of human rights norms are norms of *jus cogens*.

However, Ms. Parker and Ms. Neylon, perhaps in a moment of weakness, admit that "not all commentators agree that the whole of human rights law presently constitutes imperative rules of *jus cogens*." They cite Rosalyn Higgins' observation that while treaties "undoubtedly contain elements" that are peremptory, that fact alone does not lead to the view that all human rights are *jus cogens*. I confess to breathing a sigh of relief when Professor Higgins' down-to-earth comment was mentioned, for I had feared that the next step Ms. Parker and Ms. Neylon might take would be the investiture of every single norm of international law — not just human rights norms — with the heady status of *jus cogens*. If that had happened, we would have wound up with something like the popular caricature of German Law: "that which is not expressly prohibited is compulsory."

The long bull market in *jus cogens* stock began when Professor Grigory Tunkin proclaimed in 1974 that the Brezhnev doctrine, which he called "proletarian internationalism," is a norm of *jus cogens*. Shares skyrocketed on all international exchanges when the World Court found in the Nicaragua case that the international prohibition on the use of force was "a conspicuous example of a rule of international law having the character of *jus cogens*." This pronouncement should be taken in context — that of a kitchen-sink approach to the sources of international law. In an expansive decision, the World Court found it just as easy to promote an ordinary norm into an imperative norm as to create out of thin air an ordinary norm. The only requirement for either of these transformative processes of legal legerdemain to be effected was the garnering of a majority vote of the judges present at The Hague.

Demonstrating slightly greater restraint than the judges were the rapporteurs of the Third Restatement of the Foreign Relations Law of the United States, who conceded that "not all human rights norms are peremptory norms (*jus cogens*), but those in clauses (a) to (f) of this section are, and an international agreement that violates them is void." As usual, neither the rapporteurs of the

Restatement nor the judges of the Nicaragua case give the reader the slightest clue as to how they came to know that their favorite norms have become *jus cogens* norms. \*\*\*

What shall we do with the Pandora's Box approach to supernorms taken by Professor Janis [that they cannot be changed]? Can't we find a little weakness in it? Isn't there some kryptonite that will sap the powers of these invincible supernorms? The Vienna Convention on the Law of Treaties made an attempt along these lines. It provides that a norm of *jus cogens* "can be modified only by a subsequent norm of general international law having the same character." At least this introduces a second, competing Pac-Man — one supernorm can be swallowed by a subsequent one. But the drafters of the Convention failed to tell us how such a subsequent norm can itself arise. Perhaps that is no serious omission; after all, they did not tell us how the initial peremptory norm arose, so they should not be faulted for failure to reveal the origins of subsequent norms. But conceding that much to the drafters of the Vienna Convention, would it not be the case that as soon as one of their subsequent peremptory norms starts to arise and attempts to "modify" a previous supernorm, the existing supernorm will do a reverse flip and stomp out the subsequent norm? After all, it is only normal to expect that any established supernorm will be on the lookout for incipient competitive supernorms, turn sharply upon them as soon as they get close, and rub them out. \*\*\*

# D.  Review Questions

You should be able, based on the readings provided above, to answer each of the following questions.

1. The United States and 191 other nations are parties to the United Nations Charter. Read the text of the <u>Charter</u>, a multilateral treaty that creates the United Nations and sets out some basic rules of international conduct. Many authors describe such multilateral treaties as analogous to a contract.

- Please paraphrase the "contract like" promise made between the United States and other members of the United Nations in Articles 55 and 56 of the Charter.

- Who or what owes these "contract-like" obligations and to whom?

- Where, if at all, do the citizens of the United States fit into this contract analogy?

2. There were only about 50 original member states in the United Nations in 1948 when the General Assembly voted its approval for the <u>Universal Declaration of Human Rights</u>. However, the member states that subsequently joined the U.N. have many times voted for General Assembly resolutions endorsing the Universal Declaration as the "universal standard for international human rights."

- Are these member states bound by the provisions of the Universal Declaration?
- What is the best legal theory supporting the view that all nations are bound by the Universal Declaration?
- Why might that view be problematic in light of the non-binding status of General Assembly Resolutions?

3. The United States is a party to the <u>Covenant on Civil and Political Rights</u> (CCPR). Examine Article 2.

- What are the United States' legal obligations under Article 2?
- To whom do these obligations run?

4. The United States has invoked a number of reservations to articles of the CCPR, found at <u>http://www1.umn.edu/humanrts/usdocs/civilres.html</u>.

- What legal effect do such reservations have on our obligations under that treaty?
- What happens if such reservations are believed incompatible with the treaty by other parties or international organizations responsible for supervising their implementation?

5. The international legal order is premised on state consent.

- What is the legal significance of declaring a right to be "jus cogens" with regard to this premise?
- If jus cogens does not depend upon state consent, how can the existence of any particular jus cogens human right be authoritatively determined?

# Chapter 3

# What Rights Are Humans Entitled to Under International Law?

## A. Introduction & Overview

The goal of this chapter is simple but important. What rights are humans entitled to under international law? The premise of this chapter is that knowledge about the substantive content of the current catalogue of international human rights and the history of their evolution is fundamental to understanding the international system. For now, our goal is the big picture — reviewing major multilateral human rights treaties and the subjects those treaties involve, as well as identifying rights clearly established as part of customary international law. This overview includes consideration of possible distinctions among different kinds of rights and the historical development of the existing catalogue of norms. In subsequent chapters, a more detailed picture of what these various rights may entail will emerge as the materials address specific human rights issues.

**Your assignment** is to review the material below (the treaty texts are hyperlinked) and then read any major newspaper published within this month (or internet news feeds) and spot possible violations of international rights. Focus first on the so-called "International Bill of Rights" described below. Do not analyze the text of these treaties from a detailed legal perspective but rather read them over carefully to get a solid understanding about what rights are protected and how they are described. Also review more generally other treaties linked below under the heading "Other Important Global Human Rights Treaties" in order to understand the range of subjects and interests covered within the international system.

- What international human rights norms defined within these treaties seem to apply to the news events you have found?

- Do those rights clearly prohibit or condemn what happened?

- Are there plausible interpretations of those rights that make violations seem less or more certain?

- Are the states involved legally bound to those treaties without reservations?

- If not, are there customary international law rights or jus cogens norms that might apply?

Make a list of what you find, correlating events to various international rights and their legal sources.

# B.  Treaty Based Human Rights

## 1. U.N. Charter

In many ways, international human rights start with the United Nations Charter. The Charter preamble provides:

WE THE PEOPLES OF THE UNITED NATIONS DETERMINED

- to save succeeding generations from the scourge of war, which twice in our lifetime has brought untold sorrow to mankind, and

- to reaffirm faith in fundamental human rights, in the dignity and worth of the human person, in the equal rights of men and women and of nations large and small, and

- to establish conditions under which justice and respect for the obligations arising from treaties and other sources of international law can be maintained, and

- to promote social progress and better standards of life in larger freedom . . . [establish the United Nations].

This affirmation of a human rights oriented purpose is followed later by Articles 55 & 56, which provide:

Article 55

With a view to the creation of conditions of stability and well-being which are necessary for peaceful and friendly relations among nations based on respect for the principle of equal rights and self-determination of peoples, the United Nations shall promote:

1. higher standards of living, full employment, and conditions of economic and social progress and development;

2. solutions of international economic, social, health, and related problems; and international cultural and educational cooperation; and

3. universal respect for, and observance of, human rights and fundamental freedoms for all without distinction as to race, sex, language, or religion.

Article 56

All Members pledge themselves to take joint and separate action in co-operation with the Organization for the achievement of the purposes set forth in Article 55.

These are lofty and inspiring aspirations but exactly what are the human rights and freedoms that each U.N. member state promises to "respect" and "observe"? The Charter doesn't say. It seems obvious that the Charter's inchoate human rights provisions are, by themselves, far too vague to establish affirmative, meaningful legal obligations. Thankfully, the U.N. has made great progress since its founding in providing specific, substantive content to these promises. The most important source of this normative development has been through the creation and adoption of multilateral human rights treaties. It is helpful to review the sometimes bumpy historical path that led from the U.N. Charter's open-ended promises to the development of the current extensive catalogue of convention based human rights.

## 2. The "International Bill of Rights"

a. Universal Declaration of Human Rights: The Blueprint

Soon after its creation, the United Nations General Assembly adopted the 1948 Universal Declaration of Human Rights by non-binding resolution.

Eleanor Roosevelt [who chaired the drafting committee] with Spanish Version of the Universal Declaration (picture from Wikipedia commons). Audio of Mrs. Roosevelt is available at the UN website.

The Declaration was meant to serve both as a statement of principles and a precursor to development of a universal binding international treaty defining essential human rights. The Declaration's preamble clearly suggests that its original purposes were exclusively hortatory:

Now, Therefore, THE GENERAL ASSEMBLY proclaims

THIS UNIVERSAL DECLARATION OF HUMAN RIGHTS as a common standard of achievement for all peoples and all nations, to the end that every individual and every organ of society, keeping this Declaration constantly in mind, shall strive by teaching and education to promote respect for these rights and freedoms and by progressive measures, national and international, to secure their universal and effective recognition and observance, both among the peoples of Member States themselves and among the peoples of territories under their jurisdiction.

The Declaration has, however, outgrown this role. The U.N. has described the Declaration this way:

Today, the Universal Declaration, translated into [467] national and local languages, is the best known and most cited human rights document in the world. The foundation of international human rights law, the Universal Declaration serves as a model for numerous international treaties and declarations and is incorporated in the constitutions and laws of many countries.

Although technically non-binding,[46] the Declaration has been endorsed countless times by various inter-governmental organizations and states as the universal standard for human rights.[47] This universal endorsement has led to suggestions that the Declaration, in whole or part, has morphed over time into binding customary international law. In a similar vein, some scholars see the Declaration as an authoritative interpretation of the Charter's obligation to respect universal rights.[48]

These theoretical positions are, of course, both plausible and contestable. State endorsement of the Declaration as a statement of hortatory goals, is distinct from recognition that it creates legally binding and enforceable international obligations. Perhaps more significantly, almost all of the rights found in the Declaration are ar-

---

46. Eleanor Roosevelt described the non-binding nature of the Declaration in her statement presenting it to the General Assembly for consideration: "In giving our approval to the declaration today, it is of primary importance that we keep clearly in mind the basic character of the document. It is not a treaty; it is not an international agreement. It is not and does not purport to be a statement of law or of legal obligation. It is a declaration of basic principles of human rights and freedoms, to be stamped with the approval of the General Assembly by formal vote of its members, and to serve as a common standard of achievement for all peoples of all nations." Statement of Eleanor Roosevelt to the U.N. General Assembly, December 9, 1948.

47. For example, see Vienna Declaration and Programme of Action, World Conference on Human Rights, 22d plen. mtg. (June 25, 1993), pmbl., T1 3, 8, U.N. Doc. A/CONF.157/24 (Part 1) at 20–46 (1993).

48. See Thomas Buergenthal, *The Evolving International Human Rights System*, 100 Am. J. Int'l L. 783, 787 (2006); Barry E. Carter & Philip R. Trimble, INTERNATIONAL LAW, 898–900 (1995) (arguing that the Universal Declaration has become binding customary international law). *See generally* H. Hannum, *The Status and Future of the Customary International Law of Human Rights: The Status of the Universal Declaration of Human Rights in National and International Law*, 25 Ga. J. Int'l & Comp. L. 287 (1996). *See also* Restatement (third) of Foreign Relations Law 701, comment d (1987) ("[I]t is increasingly accepted that states parties to the [United Nations] Charter are legally obligated to respect some of the rights recognized in the Universal Declaration.")

ticulated in very general abstract terms. This is consistent with the premise that the Declaration was designed to set general standards of achievement that would differ in their particular manifestations within the world's many diverse societies. In essence, to say that the rights declared are now legally binding as part of customary law begs the more important questions about their specific meaning and application, and whether such decisions are to be made by national or international authorities.

Many of the rights contained in the Declaration (Articles 3–21) are primarily grounded in Western liberal traditions. These include familiar rights to equal protection, due process, marriage, property, expression, association, religion and suffrage. A number of other provisions, however, reference broader human needs suggesting affirmative obligations for governments. Article 25, for example, provides that:

> "Everyone has the right to a standard of living adequate for the health and well-being of himself and of his family, including food, clothing, housing and medical care and necessary social services, and the right to security in the event of unemployment, sickness, disability, widowhood, old age or other lack of livelihood in circumstances beyond his control."

Sometimes subject to derision, Article 24 adds the "right to rest and leisure, including reasonable limitation of working hours and periodic holidays with pay."

Although the Declaration's selection of fundamental rights might show a fairly distinct Western orientation (perhaps not surprising given the make-up of the United Nation's 50 original member states), the inclusion of some basic economic and social rights demonstrates international recognition that human dignity requires more than liberty alone. The U.N.'s own description of the Declaration (no longer available on its website) reveals this perspective:

> The Universal Declaration covers the range of human rights in 30 clear and concise articles. The first two articles lay the universal foundation of human rights: human beings are equal because of their shared essence of human dignity; human rights are universal, not because of any State or international organization, but because they belong to all of humanity. The two articles assure that human rights are the birthright of everyone, not privileges of a select few, nor privileges to be granted or denied. ***

> The first cluster of articles, 3 to 21, sets forth civil and political rights to which everyone is entitled. . . .

> The second cluster of articles, 22 to 27, sets forth the economic, social and cultural rights to which all human beings are entitled. The cornerstone of these rights is Article 22, acknowledging that, as a member of society, everyone has the right to social security and is therefore entitled to the realization of the economic, social and cultural rights "indispensable" for his or her dignity and free and full personal development. Five articles elaborate the rights necessary for the enjoyment of the fundamental right to social security, including economic rights related to work, fair remuneration and leisure, social rights concerning an adequate standard of living for health,

well-being and education, and the right to participate in the cultural life of the community. . . .

You should start by reviewing the <u>text of the Declaration</u>. This <u>link</u> from the University of Minnesota presents a helpful abbreviation of the rights found in the Declaration, article by article. If you prefer an artful and visually pleasing review of the Declaration you can watch this <u>video</u> or its <u>alternative</u> featuring well-known media stars reciting key provisions.

### b. The 1966 Covenants

The 1948 Universal Declaration's promise as blueprint for a binding universal human rights treaty was quickly stymied by cold war politics and philosophical disagreements regarding the proper role of government and international law. The Universal Declaration itself reflected brewing international political disputes[49] and the seeds of a major, and sometimes controversial, distinction among rights — the arguably false dichotomy between forbearance and affirmative assistance. This distinction, often described in terms of "negative" versus "positive" rights,[50] has played a significant role in the historical development of the current catalogue of international human rights. Our own constitutional rights and civil liberties, such as free speech, suffrage and the prohibition against unreasonable search and seizure, generally fall in the former category, reflecting our Western, liberal orientation concerning the relationship between individuals and government. Under this viewpoint the function of rights is to forbid the government from unreasonably interfering with defined liberties, to prevent governmental abuse of the individual.

The alternative, "less-Western," view of rights defines their function more broadly. Under this view, rights include affirmative government obligations to provide certain essential needs. If shelter, water, food, physical security and education are needs essential to human dignity and universally so, then it is not unreasonable to believe that governments are obligated to ensure that all humans have them. While it is possible to view human needs for health, food or education in "negative rights" terms — that is, just don't interfere — such interests generally require affirmative action by government and allocation of resources in order to be meaningfully realized.

Such distinctions are somewhat simplistic and often overstated. Some rights can be seen both ways: the right to work might be seen as a prohibition against government interference with your pursuit of livelihood or it could suggest that governments must devote resources towards providing everyone with meaningful employment. Similarly, even "negative rights" require some affirmative government

---

49. *See* Tai-Heng Cheng, *The Universal Declaration of Human Rights at Sixty: Is It Still Right For the United States?* 41 Corn. Int'l L. J. 251 (2008) (reviewing the political influences on the drafting and formation of the Universal Declaration).

50. For reasonably accurate additional background and description of philosophical debate <u>Wikipedia summary</u>.

action and allocation of resources for their effective protection. Indeed, virtually every modern government and society, whether socialist or liberal in orientation, endorses protection of both negative and affirmative rights on some level. Nevertheless, such distinctions have played a prominent role in the development of the current catalogue of international human rights and continue to influence their interpretation and enforcement prospects.

In the years following adoption of the Universal Declaration, the U.N. and its membership were heavily constrained by the competing influences of the United States and Soviet Union. The distinctions described above conformed to the dogma underlying the conflict of western capitalism and international communism, among other tensions played out in the "cold war." As a result, the U.N. membership simply could not or would not agree on what kinds of rights should be contained in a universal human rights treaty. Put in simplistic terms, Western states resisted the creation of affirmative obligations while socialist states insisted that such rights were all that really mattered. In a world full of autocratic and repressive governments it is also undoubtedly true that many states were perfectly happy with such a stalemate.

After two decades of debate, the U.N. finally reached a compromise by agreeing to create two distinct comprehensive human rights treaties. Reflecting the conceptual division described above, these two proposed treaties, which were opened for ratification in 1966, focused on distinct kinds of rights. The International Covenant on Civil and Political Rights (CCPR) concerns liberties and freedoms familiar to most Americans.[51] The International Covenant on Economic, Social and Cultural Rights (CESCR) involves very different interests, which many Americans would consider vital to human dignity but not necessarily the obligation of governments. These include things like the right to education, cultural life, health, shelter, work and an "adequate standard of living." These two treaties, together with the Universal Declaration, are now often informally referred to as "the International Bill of Rights." This term is one of convenience and advocacy only — there is no particular legal significance to its use under international law. In any case, the two covenants now form the foundation of a universal system of international rights. Both Covenants are widely adopted. A compilation of membership in all major U.N. sponsored human rights treaties, along with reservations, can be found at the U.N. Treaty Collection.

As shown in dark green on the map below, membership in the CCPR is now very substantial. There were 168 state parties to the CCPR as of 2016, including the United States (which has not, however, adopted either of the CCPR's optional protocols).

---

51. Note that the Covenant also has two optional protocols that will be reviewed in later chapters. These protocols authorize submission of individual petitions about government violations to the "Human Rights Committee" and promote abolition of the death penalty.

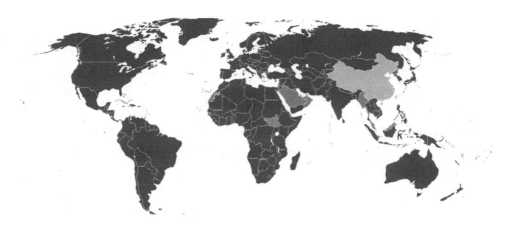

■ State party

■ Signatory that has not ratified

■ State party that attempted to withdraw

■ Non-state party, non-signatory

Image used courtesy of Dudeman5685, <u>Creative Commons, Wikipedia</u>.

Membership in the CESCR is equally widespread but of slightly different composition. There were, as of 2016, 164 state parties to the CESCR (whose 2008 optional protocol came into effect upon its 10th ratification in 2013). The United States is a signatory but not a party as shown in the <u>membership map</u> below in light green.

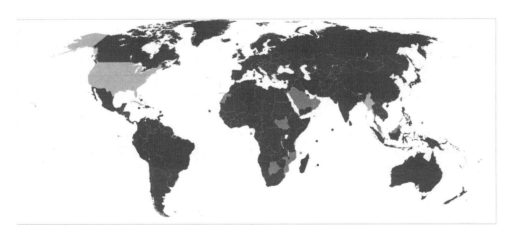

■ signed and ratified    ■ signed but not ratified    ■ neither signed nor ratified

Image used courtesy of Louperivois, Creative Commons, Wikipedia.

## 3. Post-Covenant Developments: The Evolving Network of Global Human Rights Treaties

The U.N. Treaty Collection webpage provides a link to essentially every U.N. sponsored treaty relating to human rights. Use it for an overview of the current catalogue of international human rights. You will see that treaty based human rights developed under U.N. auspices are very extensive, covering many aspects of social and political life. Some of these treaties, such as the Children's Convention, focus on the specific vulnerable groups. Others, such as the Conventions against torture and genocide, focus on specific human rights issues. These treaties are distinct in this respect from the two 1966 Covenants which cover a broad range of rights applicable to everyone.

The U.N. categorizes nine of its sponsored treaties as "core," a designation seemingly earned by virtue of membership and the existence of treaty based enforcement mechanisms. As can be seen from the following chart, some of these treaties have been widely, almost universally, adopted.

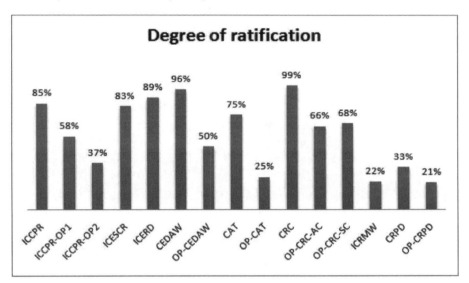

The treaties described by the U.N. as "core" are listed below with links to U.N. pages. The list includes several Optional Protocols to the treaties which mostly focus on implementation and supervisory mechanisms.

The UN also provides a helpful summary of rights found in the various major treaties. Wikipedia presents well-organized and clear summaries of the Civil and Political Rights Covenant and Economic and Social Rights Covenant. A summary of CEDAW (Women's Rights Convention) can be found at CEDAW2015.org. The UN HCHR also provides a summary of the Children's Convention. Review these various summaries to get a better idea about the current substantive scope of the current catalogue of conventional human rights. It goes without saying, of course, that such summaries don't purport to be precise for purposes of legal analysis—look at them only to get an idea about what rights and interests are protected.

| | | Date | Monitoring Body |
|---|---|---|---|
| ICERD | International Convention on the Elimination of All Forms of Racial Discrimination | 21 Dec 1965 | CERD |
| ICCPR | International Covenant on Civil and Political Rights | 16 Dec 1966 | CCPR |
| ICESCR | International Covenant on Economic, Social and Cultural Rights | 16 Dec 1966 | CESCR |
| CEDAW | Convention on the Elimination of All Forms of Discrimination against Women | 18 Dec 1979 | CEDAW |
| CAT | Convention against Torture and Other Cruel, Inhuman or Degrading Treatment or Punishment | 10 Dec 1984 | CAT |
| CRC | Convention on the Rights of the Child | 20 Nov 1989 | CRC |
| ICMW | International Convention on the Protection of the Rights of All Migrant Workers and Members of Their Families | 18 Dec 1990 | CMW |
| CPED | International Convention for the Protection of All Persons from Enforced Disappearance | 20 Dec 2006 | CED |
| CRPD | Convention on the Rights of Persons with Disabilities | 13 Dec 2006 | CRPD |
| ICESCR-OP | Optional Protocol to the Covenant on Economic, Social and Cultural Rights | 10 Dec 2008 | CESCR |
| ICCPR-OP1 | Optional Protocol to the International Covenant on Civil and Political Rights | 16 Dec 1966 | CCPR |
| ICCPR-OP2 | Second Optional Protocol to the International Covenant on Civil and Political Rights, aiming at the abolition of the death penalty | 15 Dec 1989 | CCPR |
| OP-CEDAW | Optional Protocol to the Convention on the Elimination of Discrimination against Women | 10 Dec 1999 | CEDAW |
| OP-CRC-AC | Optional protocol to the Convention on the Rights of the Child on the involvement of children in armed conflict | 25 May 2000 | CRC |

|  |  | *Date* | *Monitoring Body* |
|---|---|---|---|
| OP-CRC-SC | Optional protocol to the Convention on the Rights of the Child on the sale of children, child prostitution and child pornography | 25 May 2000 | CRC |
| OP-CRC-IC | Optional Protocol to the Convention on the Rights of the Child on a communications procedure | 14 Apr 2014 | CRC |
| OP-CAT | Optional Protocol to the Convention against Torture and Other Cruel, Inhuman or Degrading Treatment or Punishment | 18 Dec 2002 | SPT |
| OP-CRPD | Optional Protocol to the Convention on the Rights of Persons with Disabilities | 12 Dec 2006 | CRPD |

It is important to note two distinct sources of human rights treaty obligations which are not directly part of the list of U.N. sponsored treaties and other instruments, (although most can be accessed from the U.N. Treaty Database.) First, there are currently three important regional human rights treaties — the American Convention on Human Rights, the European Convention on Human Rights and African Convention on Human and Peoples' Rights. We will review each of these in subsequent chapters. Second, there are also a series of global treaties, commonly called the Geneva Conventions, which create important international obligations during armed conflicts. These obligations, involving war crimes, humanitarian law and crimes against humanity, are distinct from but closely related to international human rights. These conventions form part of the evolving international law on criminal liability under the jurisdiction of the newly established Permanent International Criminal Court. These obligations are also examined in later chapters.

**Which of the above treaties has the United States ratified?** Recall that the United States is only subject, under international law, to those treaty obligations to which it expressly consents. In the context of international human rights, virtually all treaties are subject to the advice and consent of the Senate.

To date, the United States has ratified only a few major human rights treaties, most prominently the CCPR, the Genocide Convention, the Torture Convention and the Convention on the Elimination of Racial Discrimination. Correspondingly, the U.S. has failed to ratify a number of other important and widely adopted treaties. For example, only the United States and Somalia have failed to ratify the Convention on the Rights of the Child. The United States is only one of seven countries, including Iran, Somalia and Sudan, that has failed to ratify the Convention on the Elimination of All Forms of Discrimination Against Women (CEDAW or Woman's Convention).

It has also refused to agree to virtually all optional enforcement mechanisms created through the treaty process (for example, the optional protocol to the CCPR).

A chart summarizing U.S. ratifications and a list of human rights treaty ratifications by country can be found at the University of Minnesota website. The Office of the U.N. High Commissioner for Human Rights provides a "Chart disclosing the status of ratifications of human rights treaties" in addition to ratification and reservations information available from the U.N. Treaty Collection, Chapter IV, Human Rights.

## C.  Customary International Human Rights

We learned from the prior chapter that customary international law consists of those widespread, uniform practices of states that are followed from a sense of legal obligation. Traditionally such practices "crystalized" into law over time as states developed expectations that failures to adhere to the practice would lead to legal consequences (such as they are) within the international system. Improved communication, widely adopted multilateral treaties and the advent of global forums such as the United Nations has sped this process, even leading to claims that "instant" customary law is possible. At least in the context of human rights, there has also been a shift in focus from empirical practices (what states actually do) to rhetorical practices (what states say). A greater emphasis is placed under this view, one might say, on "opinio juris" rather than on actual conduct. As noted in Chapter Two, this shift in focus to a "modern" approach to customary international law is controversial and has not been overtly endorsed by states themselves (as opposed to scholars and jurists).[52]

Thus, it might reasonably be said that the consistent denial and rhetorical rejection of torture is more critical to the formation of custom than the inconvenient fact that a great number of countries routinely engage in it. The act of denial itself is strong evidence that states believe a legal obligation exists. Similarly, repeated endorsement of a right through resolutions adopted at the U.N. and other intergovernmental forums might reasonably be seen as evidence of custom. Since there is no authoritative process for determining the content of customary law, this has led inevitably to a proliferation of claims about human rights. The appeal which custom-

---

52. There are many excellent expositions of the debate over the formation of customary human rights law. *See, e.g.,* Anthea Elizabeth Roberts, *Traditional and Modern Approaches to Customary International Law: A Reconciliation,* 95 Am. J. Int'l L. 757 (2001); Neils Petersen, *Customary Law Without Custom? Rules, Principles, and the Role of State Practice in International Norm Creation,* 23 Am. U. Int'l L. Rev. 275 (2008). This debate should be distinguished from a related debate over the status of customary international law within the domestic law of the United States. *Compare* Curtis A. Bradley & Jack L. Goldsmith, *Customary International Law as Federal Common Law: A Critique of the Modern Position,* 110 Harv. L. Rev. 815 (1997) *with* William Dodge, *Customary International Law and the Question of Legitimacy,* 120 Harv. L. Rev. Forum 19 (2007).

ary law holds for advocates is obvious — states are bound by customary law regardless whether or not they have overtly consented to the obligation. This more expansive approach to customary international law undoubtedly holds significant promise for enhancing human rights protection.

The Restatement's position on customary human rights, which relies heavily on U.N. declarations and treaties, has been influential on this issue:

**Foreign Relations Law of the United States 3d**

**§ 702. Customary International Law of Human Rights**

A state violates **international law** if, as a matter of state policy, it practices, encourages, or condones

(a) genocide,

(b) slavery or slave trade,

(c) the murder or causing the disappearance of individuals,

(d) torture or other cruel, inhuman, or degrading treatment or punishment,

(e) prolonged arbitrary detention,

(f) systematic racial discrimination, or

(g) a consistent pattern of gross violations of internationally recognized human rights.

## *Reporters' Notes*

1. **Customary law of human rights.** This section adopts the view that customary international law prohibits the particular human rights violations indicated, if the violations are state policy. This view is accepted by virtually all states; *** no state claims the right to commit the practices set forth in this section as state policy, and few, if any, would deny that they are violations of international law. Other rights may already have become customary law and international law may develop to include additional rights. It has been argued that customary international law is already more comprehensive than here indicated and forbids violation of any of the rights set forth in the Universal Declaration. See s 701, Reporters' Note 4; McDougal, Lasswell, and Chen, Human Rights and World Public Order 273–74, 325–27 (1980); Waldock, "Human Rights in Contemporary International Law and the Significance of the European Convention," in The European Convention on Human Rights 15 (1963) (British Inst. Int'l & Comp. L., Int'l L. Ser. No. 11).

\*\*\*

11. **Human rights law and jus cogens**. Not all human rights norms are jus cogens, but those in clauses (a) to (f) have that quality. \*\*\*

The Restatement's following position on gender discrimination illustrates some of the central issues surrounding the definition of customary human rights norms. While universally endorsed by Western societies, a great number of states do not honor the prohibition against gender discrimination in any recognizable fashion. The Restatement nevertheless suggests that the prohibition against gender discrimination "may already be a principle of customary international law." Is this legally justifiable or just wishful thinking?

**Restatement (Third) of Foreign Relations Law, 702**

**Comment:**

n. **Gender discrimination**. The United Nations Charter (Article 1(3)) and the Universal Declaration of Human Rights (Article 2) prohibit discrimination in respect of human rights on various grounds, including sex. Discrimination on the basis of sex in respect of recognized rights is prohibited by a number of international agreements, including the Covenant on Civil and Political Rights, the Covenant on Economic, Social and Cultural Rights, and more generally by the Convention on the Elimination of All Forms of Discrimination Against Women, which, as of 1987, had been ratified by 91 states and signed by a number of others. The United States had signed the Convention but had not yet ratified it. See Introductory Note to this Part. The domestic laws of a number of states, including those of the United States, mandate equality for, or prohibit discrimination against, women generally or in various respects. Gender-based discrimination is still practiced in many states in varying degrees, but freedom from gender discrimination as state policy, in many matters, may already be a principle of customary international law. Discrimination by a state that does not constitute a violation of customary law may violate a particular international agreement if practiced by a state party.

**What is the proper role for customary international law of human rights and how should its content be determined?**

# Chapter 4

# International Rights as Domestic Obligations

## A. Introduction and Overview

What is the relationship between international legal obligations and domestic law? If a country enters into a treaty promising to respect human rights does it thereby create obligations that are binding and enforceable within its domestic legal system? The answer to this question is of critical importance to human rights but regrettably complex and sometimes uncertain. As a starting premise recognize that international law does not generally require that states make their international obligations directly binding within, or legally part of, their domestic systems, although a treaty could explicitly require this obligation. Historically, many if not most states have considered the international legal system and international obligations as distinct from their various domestic legal systems.[53] In effect, states themselves decided whether and how any particular international obligation would be treated vis-a-vis their domestic law. This traditional approach reflected the fact that almost all international obligations involved the relationship between various countries *as nations* and did not directly relate to domestic conditions within those states.

Modern international human rights obligations, however, are distinct from these more traditional types of international obligations. The obligations created, while still in the form of promises that run between states, are expressly designed to benefit individuals through changes in the domestic legal order. Reflecting this characteristic, it is common for international human rights treaties to declare or "recognize" certain rights and demand that state parties "respect," "give effect" or "ensure" their realization within their domestic jurisdiction. Thus, a primary obligation imposed by international human rights treaties is to "give effect" to the rights declared in the treaty **under domestic law**. Indeed, the premise of most human rights treaties is that

---

53. Curtis Bradley, *Breard, Our Dualist Constitution, and the Internationalist Conception*, 51 Stan.L.Rev. 529, 531 (1999) (providing supporting citations in footnote 8).

the fundamental mechanism for ensuring international rights is their implementation and protection as part of each domestic legal system.

Two critical factors support the rationale of this domestic focus for implementation of rights. First, current international enforcement mechanisms are embryonic and lack the tools for effective enforcement. You can make your own judgements in that regard after studying Chapters 7, 8 & 9. Second, and perhaps more importantly, domestic implementation portends greater legitimacy for rights as they are initially interpreted and enforced through democratically accountable processes.

## 1. Incorporation: Traditional Distinctions between Monism and Dualism

There are at least three major pathways through which this "domestication" of international human rights obligations might happen. First, states might choose to directly adopt or otherwise give automatic domestic recognition to the treaty or customary rule — that is, routinely treat its international obligations as part of the domestic legal system on par with other sources of domestic law. This approach to international obligations is commonly referred to as "monism," in contrast to the more prevalent "dualist" approach described below. In such states, human rights treaty obligations form part of enforceable domestic law as soon as the obligation is created. Since international law and domestic law are considered parts of a unitary system, the international obligation is binding before domestic courts without further action or special requirements. There are some notable examples. Certain states, such as Costa Rica, the Netherlands, France, the Czech Republic and perhaps Germany, often treat international treaty obligations, particularly those involving individual rights, as part of domestic law, ipso facto.[54]

The second and third pathways for domestic legal status reflect the so-called "dualist" orientation toward international law which prevails in the majority of states. Under a dualist approach, an international human rights obligation is not automatically part of domestic law but rather represents strictly an international legal obligation. The obligation only becomes binding or legally effective within the domestic system if overtly adopted, or "incorporated," through some domestic process, typically via appropriate domestic implementing legislation. Reflecting this dualist approach, the second pathway to domestic legal status is through an act of direct incorporation in which the treaty itself is adopted through legislation as part of domestic law. It is possible, of course, that a treaty might itself require direct domestic incorporation as a part of its obligations but currently most human rights treaties do not expressly do so. This is sometimes referred to as giving the treaty "direct effect" since it typically authorizes domestic courts to directly enforce the treaty's provisions. This approach, which is further explored in later chapters, is common among European states under the European Convention on Human Rights.

---

54. *See generally* THE ROLE OF DOMESTIC COURTS IN TREATY ENFORCEMENT: A COMPARATIVE STUDY at 9–15, 209–211 (David Sloss, Editor, Cambridge University Press 2009).

The third pathway to domestic legal status is similar to the second except that the state does not give the treaty direct effect but rather indirectly "puts into effect" the obligations through legislation that effectuates or implements such obligations. Under this approach, the state controls the manner and extent to which the international obligation becomes an effective part of domestic law — rights and remedies being based not on the treaty itself directly but rather on domestic implementing legislation. The United States has taken this approach as reflected in statutes which selectively implement provisions of the Conventions against Torture and Genocide, allowing only criminal liability against certain perpetrators under limited circumstances.

It is important to note that, even when incorporated, the precise status that such international norms may have within the domestic legal hierarchy — superior, on par, or inferior to regular domestic legislation and Constitutional provisions — is a distinct question that also varies among states.[55]

## B.  The Critical Role of Incorporation: Domestication of International Norms

In considering potential domestic applications for human rights it is important to recognize initially that nearly all *human rights treaties are premised on the primacy of domestic implementation and enforcement.* While international processes and institutions have been created to monitor and scrutinize such enforcement their role is generally subsidiary to national processes and, to date, these institutions typically lack enforcement capacity. Thus, domestic implementation and enforcement of human rights is both contemplated by the treaties and essential to the international system's ultimate goal of modifying every government's treatment of its own citizens.

The <u>International Covenant on Civil and Political Rights</u> (CCPR) emphatically illustrates this point. Under Article 2 the state party's essential legal obligations are outlined in a fashion that makes clear the primacy of domestic enforcement. Each state must "respect and ensure" rights "recognized" in the treaty by taking "necessary steps . . . to adopt such law or measures as may be necessary to give effect to the rights," and provide "effective remedy" before "competent judicial, administrative or

---

55. Even among states taking a monist, direct incorporation approach to international obligations, there may be variations in the precise legal status such obligations have within the hierarchy of domestic law. A critical consideration would be if the treaty provisions were considered superior to ordinary domestic legislation. Although the question is complicated, some states such as the Netherlands apparently treat international human rights obligations as superior to its own constitutional principles. Alec Stone Smith, *On The Constitutionalisation of the Convention: The European Court of Human Rights as a Constitutional Court*, at 9 (2009) (citing Article 93 of the Dutch Constitution). Yale *Faculty Scholarship Series*. Paper 71.

legislative authorities . . . ."[56] The significance of this domestic focus becomes even more apparent when one considers the ambiguous and anemic authority of the Human Rights Committee, the international institution that has supervisory jurisdiction over this particular treaty. The HRC, which is examined along with other similar institutions in later chapters, has virtually no enforcement powers and only limited legal authority vis-à-vis state parties.

Identical or similar language to that of the CCPR is found in many of the major multilateral human rights treaties sponsored by the United Nations. This nearly universal focus on domestic implementation and enforcement might be best explained by the fact that nearly all states jealously guard their sovereign prerogatives and prefer, for both good and nefarious reasons, to retain control over the implementation of rights. It is, however, equally true that primary reliance on domestic enforcement enjoys the benefits of enhanced legitimacy as domestic institutions, accountable and organic, implement and enforce rights in light of prevailing political, social, and cultural conditions. It also takes advantage of the relatively greater resources and effectiveness of domestic legal systems over alternative, typically toothless and underfunded, international processes that inevitably lack coercive power.

Direct application of international law by domestic institutions to challenge domestic governmental actors is undoubtedly central to an effective human rights system. In essence, this form of enforcement involves petitions or suits asking the domestic institutions (courts or alternative administrative processes) to redress domestic government action on international law grounds. An illustration of this type of domestic enforcement would include a suit challenging a state practice of jailing juvenile offenders with adult prisoners on grounds that such a practice is forbidden by Article 10 of the CCPR. More controversially, it might also include civil suits seek-

---

56. Article 2

1. Each State Party to the present Covenant undertakes to respect and to ensure to all individuals within its territory and subject to its jurisdiction the rights recognized in the present Covenant, without distinction of any kind, such as race, colour, sex, language, religion, political or other opinion, national or social origin, property, birth or other status.

2. Where not already provided for by existing legislative or other measures, each State Party to the present Covenant undertakes to take the necessary steps, in accordance with its constitutional processes and with the provisions of the present Covenant, to adopt such laws or other measures as may be necessary to give effect to the rights recognized in the present Covenant.

3. Each State Party to the present Covenant undertakes:

(a) To ensure that any person whose rights or freedoms as herein recognized are violated shall have an effective remedy, notwithstanding that the violation has been committed by persons acting in an official capacity;

(b) To ensure that any person claiming such a remedy shall have his right thereto determined by competent judicial, administrative or legislative authorities, or by any other competent authority provided for by the legal system of the State, and to develop the possibilities of judicial remedy;

(c) To ensure that the competent authorities shall enforce such remedies when granted.

ing compensation for violations of international human rights law by <u>U.S. public offi-cials who tortured</u>, or approved the torture, of a terrorism suspect within the United States or abroad. <u>Extraordinary rendition</u>,[57] <u>secret overseas prisons</u> ("black sites") and the long term detention of suspects at <u>Guantanamo</u> Bay Cuba without charges or trials, are other obvious and troubling examples of how domestic implementation of international rights is of profound importance. <u>Racial bias</u> in capital punishment, prosecution of <u>juvenile defendants as adults</u>, unaddressed <u>homelessness</u>, obstacles to <u>voting</u> and bans on <u>same sex marriage</u> all provide further illustrations of domestic practices that might be challenged under international human rights norms.

The sobering reality regarding domestic implementation, however, is that most countries outside of Europe, including the United States, have generally refused to fully incorporate international standards of human rights protection into domestic law or otherwise genuinely and effectively implement such obligations. Indeed, many states instead adopt the patently false stance that all of their international human rights obli-gations are already fully effectuated and protected within their domestic legal order. There is an obvious gap between the promises and actual performance of states regard-ing the implementation of human rights within their domestic legal systems.[58] With disheartening frequency, ratification of human rights treaties serves as "window dress-ing" rather than a force for meaningful change. In the case of the United States, its failure to "domesticate" international human rights can be contrasted with the extent to which it has incorporated numerous international economic legal obligations into domestic law, such as those created under the World Trade Organization and NAFTA.

The remainder of this chapter focuses on the process of domestic implementation and the relationship between international human rights law and domestic legal sys-tems, with a focus on the United States and Europe.

## C. Incorporating Human Rights Obligations into Domestic Legal Orders: The Contrasting European and U.S. Examples

### 1. The Shining European Example

There is only limited empirical evidence available regarding the degree to which states effectively "domesticate" and enforce their international human rights

---

57. Extraordinary rendition is the term used to describe the practice of transferring a suspect from one country to another, often to secret facilities for "enhanced" interrogation, without judicial processes.

58. *See, e.g.,* Hafner-Burton & Tsutsui, *Human Rights in a Globalizing World: The Paradox of Empty Promises*, 110 American Journal of Sociology, 1373 (2005) (providing some empirical evi-dence); Hathaway, *Do Human Rights Treaties Make A Difference?*, 111 Yale L.J.1935 (2002) (finding inverse correlation between ratification and human rights performance) also available at Yale <u>Fac-ulty Scholarship Series</u>.

obligations. Sadly, domestic implementation would appear to be the apparent exception not the norm for most of the world. The best illustrations of active domestic enforcement of international human rights against domestic officials have undoubtedly come from within Europe under the <u>European Convention on Human Rights</u>. In a 2008 study, Professors Stone Sweet and Keller concluded that the Convention has had enormous impact on the domestic legal systems of its member states. These researchers identified "domestication" of the treaty through "incorporation into national legal orders" as the most critical causal factor.[59] More specifically, "Other things being equal, the ECHR is most effective where Convention rights, *de jure* and *de facto*: (1) bind all national officials in the exercise of public authority; (2) possess at least supra-legislative status (they occupy a rank superior to that of statutory law in the hierarchy of legal norms), and (3) can be pleaded directly by individuals before judges who may directly enforce, while disapplying conflicting norms."[60]

Although the extent and methods of implementation vary,[61] the 47 members of the Convention provide "direct effect" and often "supra-legislative force" to the treaty,

---

59. A EUROPE OF RIGHTS, Ch.11, 682–84 (Oxford Press, Alec Stone Sweet and Helen Keller, Editors, 2008).

60. Id. at 683.

61. *See, e.g.,* Guesseppi Martinico, *Is the European Convention Going to Be 'Supreme'? A Comparative-Constitutional Overview of ECHR and EU Law before National Courts,* <u>23 European J. Int'l L. 401</u> ( 2012). Professor Martinico provides this now common summarization of approaches: "In a recent book, Keller and Stone Sweet underscored the variety of national constitutional provisions regarding the ECHR. Indeed, looking at these provisions (and those applicable to EU law) one easily appreciates the diversity of national approaches with respect to the domestic authority of European laws:

1. First, some constitutions reserve a particular status to EU law, distinguishing it from 'normal' public international law. An example is Italy, where Article 117 of the Constitution states: '[l]egislative power belongs to the state and the regions in accordance with the constitution and within the limits set by European Union law and international obligations'. Accordingly, many commentators have stressed the distinction between the effects of EU obligations and international ones.

2. Secondly, some constitutions acknowledge the special status of international human rights treaties (or some of them). In Spain and Portugal (see, respectively, Article 10 of the Spanish Constitution6 and Article 16 of the Portuguese Constitution) such declarations provide an interpretative support for constitutional human rights provisions.

3. Thirdly, some constitutions seem not to distinguish between international and EU law.

According to another classification, the ECHR's status in the domestic order may be summarized as follows:

a) Some constitutions attribute constitutional rank to the ECHR, as in Austria and the Netherlands ('the world's most monist state').

b) In some states, instead, the ECHR has a super-legislative ranking (e.g., in France, Belgium, Spain, and Portugal).

c) In other states (the UK), finally, the ECHR has a legislative ranking. Countries like Italy and Germany seemingly belong in the third group (if one reads their constitutions) but local Constitutional Courts clarified that the ECHR has a special force that exceeds the normal constitutional discipline of international norms."

thereby promoting effective domestic enforcement of its provisions.[62] The system reinforces the primacy of domestic enforcement by denying international redress before the European Court of Human Rights for individuals who do not first exhaust their claims before national institutions.[63]

The United Kingdom provides a useful example of the European model of domestic enforcement that also reflects earlier lessons concerning domestic incorporation of international obligations. The United Kingdom ratified the European Convention on Human Rights as an original member of the Council of Europe in 1951. As a common law "dualist" oriented country, however, the Convention was not actionable before British courts until incorporated into domestic law and made enforceable in the 1998 Human Right Act. This act, which came into force in 2000, allows citizens of the U.K. to bring actions before domestic institutions claiming violations of the Convention by domestic public officials.[64] By way of illustration, in 2012, the British courts held in *Burnip, Trengove, Gorry v SSWP* [2012] EWCA Civ 629, that U.K. housing benefit laws violated the Convention's provisions against discrimination by failing to accommodate certain disabilities. In Cadder v Her Majesty's Advocate, (Scotland) [2010] UKSC 43, the U.K. Supreme Court declared that the Scottish practice of interviewing criminal suspects without the assistance of counsel was incompatible with the Convention's right to a fair trial (Article 6).[65]

National court decisions enforcing (or denying) Convention rights are subject to review by the European Court of Human Rights, an intentional body created by the Convention. Controversial rulings by the European Court of Human Rights rejecting interpretations of the treaty relating to terrorism suspects caused threats by British leaders in 2013 to jettison the Act and the Convention. Threats of withdrawal or refusals to abide by international decisions reflect the inherent tension between domestic sovereignty and international supervision of rights, a subject that is addressed in subsequent chapters. Compliance with decisions by international institutions could be described, of course, as a form of domestic enforcement but is distinct from direct implementation by domestic institutions. Enforcement within the European

---

62. *See, e.g.,* Alec Stone Smith, *On The Constitutionalisation of the Convention: The European Court of Human Rights as a Constitutional Court,* at 9 (2009) (citing Article 93 of the Dutch Constitution). Yale *Faculty Scholarship Series.* Paper 71, available at Yale Digital Commons; Martinico, *Is The European Convention Going to Be 'Supreme'? A Comparative-Constitutional Overview of ECHR and EU Law Before National Courts,* 23 European J. Int'l L. 401 (2012), also available at: http://ejil.oxfordjournals.org/ .

63. An important characteristic of the European system of human rights is that the primacy of national implementation and enforcement leads to variations in the practical interpretation of some rights. As described in later chapters, the European Convention does not contemplate complete unanimity over the meaning of its various abstract human rights provisions among its 47 member states. *See* Chapter Nine *infra.*

64. Ireland provides a similar example. The Government of Ireland, however, was even slower to fulfill the obligation to incorporate the Convention and only partially did so in the European Convention on Human Rights Act of 2003.

65. Note that such decisions do not automatically void the offending domestic legislation in the United Kingdom under the domestic doctrine of parliamentary supremacy.

system, including compliance with the edicts of the European Court of Human Rights, is examined in much greater detail in later chapters.

The European example shows that incorporation or "domestication" of international rights is a necessary precursor, in most instances, to meaningful domestic implementation and enforcement. Put another way, effective enforcement of international rights largely depends upon whether those rights have been made part of domestic law with appropriate remedies provided. There is, however, no reliable empirical basis to know how widespread direct incorporation or "domestication" of human rights norms is outside of Europe. In an excerpt provided below, Professor Buergenthal suggests anecdotal evidence that there is a growing trend toward giving human rights treaties domestic legal effect. The actual significance of any such domestication of rights would depend on their status within the domestic legal hierarchy, the authority of courts to invalidate domestic law or conduct based on such international norms, the recognition of individual causes of action and enforcement mechanisms. Unfortunately, given the continuing dominance of dualist approaches to international law and the terrible human rights performance of most countries, it is reasonable to suspect that direct incorporation remains somewhat uncommon globally. The European example, however, surely suggests that promotion of direct incorporation and domestication of rights should be a priority of the international human rights system.

## 2. The Not So Shiny Example: The United States' Failure to Domesticate International Obligations

### a. Constitutional Framework

It would seem clear from the Constitutional text quoted below that treaty obligations of the United States constitute binding and supreme federal law. After all, that is what Article VI actually says.

Article VI (Supremacy Clause)

> This Constitution, and the Laws of the United States which shall be made in Pursuance thereof; and all Treaties made, or which shall be made, under the Authority of the United States, shall be the supreme Law of the Land; and the Judges in every State shall be bound thereby, anything in the Constitution or Laws of any State to the Contrary notwithstanding.

Early in our history, however, the Supreme Court announced that the domestic legal status of treaties was not that simple. The United States is clearly not a monist state. According to Justice John Marshall:

> Our constitution declares a treaty to be the law of the land. It is, consequently, to be regarded in courts of justice as equivalent to an act of the legislature, wherever it operates of itself, without the aid of any legislative provision. But when the terms of the stipulation import a contract, when either of the parties engages to perform a particular act, the treaty addresses

itself to the political, not the judicial department; and the legislature must execute the contract, before it can become a rule for the court.

Thus was born the U.S. doctrine distinguishing between "self-executing" and "non-self-executing" treaties.

### b. Doctrine of Self-Executing Treaties

### i. Overview

Despite the language of Article VI, Chief Justice Marshall's ruling established that not all ratified treaties are automatically the supreme law of the land, operative in American courts. Instead, the domestic legal status of a treaty depends upon the intent of the President and Senate in ratifying the treaty.

Some treaties are ratified with the intent that they become operative domestic law binding in the courts without further action by Congress. These treaties are referred to as "self-executing" treaties. Such treaties have the same legal status as a federal statute and, in cases of conflict between the two, the last in time prevails. Like other forms of federal law, a self-executing treaty is subject to the Constitution but is supreme over all state law. A self-executing treaty must, like other federal law, be considered and applied by both federal and state courts in resolving disputes. An example of this somewhat rare bird is the Convention on the International Sale of Goods or CISG. This treaty spells out a series of rules similar to those found in the Uniform Commercial Code that are to apply to most international sales transactions involving U.S. participants. Although not expressly stated, the treaty envisions by design (purposes, textual language and legislative history) direct application of its provisions in U.S. domestic courts without the need for implementing legislation.[66]

It is important to recognize that having the status as a self-executing treaty does not necessarily imply a private cause of action to sue for enforcement of its provisions. Just as with federal statutes, some treaties do not give rise for claims of compensation or enforcement. This question is further addressed in the next chapter. Nevertheless, such treaties are, in effect, domestic federal law.

Other ratified treaties, however, are not intended for immediate domestic legal consequences such as application by the courts. Such "non-self-executing" treaties cannot be used in the courts unless and until Congress enacts legislation implementing their provisions. Such "non-self-executing treaties" are international obligations of the United States but are not domestic law until Congress chooses to incorporate

---

66. Delchi Carrier, 71 F.3d at 1027 (2d Cir. 1995) ("[t]he CISG . . . [is] a self-executing agreement . . ."); Chicago Prim Packers, Inc. v. Northam Food Trading Co., 408 F.3d 894, 897 (7th Cir. 2000); Filanto, 789 F. Supp. At 1237 (S.D.N.Y. 1992). For the Supreme Court's latest pronouncements regarding the doctrine of self-execution *see Medellin v. Texas*, 128 S. Ct. 1346, 1357 (2008) ("Because a treaty ratified by the United States is 'an agreement among sovereign powers,' we have also considered as 'aids to its interpretation' the negotiation and drafting history of the treaty as well as 'the post-ratification understanding' of signatory nations."). Id. at 1364–66 (". . . we have held treaties to be self-executing when the textual provisions indicate that the President and Senate intended for the agreement to have domestic effect.").

them into the domestic legal system. They essentially have no domestic legal effect (save perhaps for limited interpretive purposes as described below) even though the United States has an international obligation to obey them. If implemented or "incorporated" by legislation, a non-self-executing treaty becomes enforceable before the courts but only in accordance with the terms of the implementing statute. As described below, Congress has on several occasions implemented some portions of ratified human rights treaties but only for limited purposes.

ii. When Is a Treaty Self-Executing?

The intent of the President and the Senate is the traditional touchstone for determining whether a treaty is self-executing. How to determine this intent, when it is not explicitly expressed, is more uncertain. Most courts have focused on the treaty's language, purposes, context and legislative history. Compare the following section of the Restatement of Foreign Relations Law with excerpts from the Supreme Court's most recent pronouncement on the issue also appearing below. Is subsection (4) of the Restatement, suggesting a somewhat mild presumption of self-executing status, an accurate portrayal of the prevailing rules?

Restatement § 111. International Law and Agreements as Law of the United States

\*\*\*

(4) An international agreement of the United States is "non-self-executing"

(a) if the agreement manifests an intention that it shall not become effective as domestic law without the enactment of implementing legislation,

(b) if the Senate in giving consent to a treaty, or Congress by resolution, requires implementing legislation, or

(c) if implementing legislation is constitutionally required.

**Comment:**

311(3).

\*\*\*

*h. Self-executing and non-self-executing international agreements.* In the absence of special agreement, it is ordinarily for the United States to decide how it will carry out its international obligations. Accordingly, the intention of the United States determines whether an agreement is to be self-executing in the United States or should await implementation by legislation or appropriate executive or administrative action.\*\*\*

Whether a treaty is self-executing is a question distinct from whether the treaty creates private rights or remedies. See Comment g.

c. Legal Status of Treaties within the U.S. Hierarchy of Laws

What is the precise legal status of self-executing versus non-self-executing treaties under U.S. law? Where do self-executing treaties fit within the hierarchy of U.S. law? Consider the following excerpt from an article by Professor Kirgis describing the legal status of treaties in U.S. domestic law. Also note his discussion of the status of customary international law and international agreements that the President enters into without the advice and consent of the Senate (so-called "executive agreements").

### Frederic Kirgis, <u>ASIL Insights, May 1997, International Agreements and U.S. Law</u>

There is confusion in the media and elsewhere about United States law as it relates to international agreements, including treaties. The confusion exists with respect to such matters as whether "treaty" has the same meaning in international law and in the domestic law of the United States, how treaties are ratified, how the power to enter into international agreements is allocated among the Executive Branch, the Senate and the whole Congress, whether Congress may override an existing treaty, and the extent to which international agreements are enforceable in United States courts.

Under international law a "treaty" is any international agreement concluded between states or other entities with international personality (such as public international organizations***

"Treaty" has a much more restricted meaning under the constitutional law of the United States. It is an international agreement that has received the "advice and consent" (in practice, just the consent) of two-thirds of the Senate and that has been ratified by the President. ***

As a matter of domestic law within the United States, Congress may override a pre-existing treaty or Congressional-Executive agreement of the United States. To do so, however, would place the United States in breach of the obligation owed under international law to its treaty partner(s) to honor the treaty or agreement in good faith. Consequently, courts in the United States are disinclined to find that Congress has actually intended to override a treaty or other internationally binding obligation. Instead, they struggle to interpret the Congressional act and/or the international instrument in such a way as to reconcile the two.

***

All treaties are the law of the land, but only a self-executing treaty would prevail in a domestic court over a prior, inconsistent act of Congress. A non-self-executing treaty could not supersede a prior inconsistent act of Congress in a U. S. court. ***

Even if a treaty or other international agreement is non-self-executing, it may have an indirect effect in U. S. courts. The courts' practice, mentioned above, of interpreting acts of Congress as consistent with earlier international agreements applies to earlier non-self-executing agreements as well as to self-executing ones, since in either case the agreement is binding internationally and courts are slow to place the United States in breach of its international obligations***

### d. Self-Execution and Human Rights Treaties Ratified by the United States

Thus far, no international human rights treaty has been found by the United States Courts to be self-executing. The following brief excerpt from an opinion by the California Supreme Court regarding the human rights provisions of the U.N. Charter illustrates a common rationale:[67]

> It is clear that the provisions of the preamble and of article 1 of the Charter which are claimed to be in conflict with the alien land law are not self-executing. They state general purposes and objectives of the United Nations Organization and do not purport to impose legal obligations on the individual member nations or to create rights in private persons. It is equally clear that none of the other provisions relied on by plaintiff is self-executing. Article 55 declares that the United Nations "shall promote . . . universal respect for, and observance of, human rights and fundamental freedoms for all without distinction as to race, sex, language, or religion," and in article 56, the member nations "pledge themselves to take joint and separate action in cooperation with the Organization for the achievement of the purposes set forth in Article 55." Although the member nations have obligated themselves to cooperate with the international organization in promoting respect for, and observance of, human rights, it is plain that it was contemplated that future legislative action by the several nations would be required to accomplish the declared objectives, and there is nothing to indicate that these provisions were intended to become rules of law for the courts of this country upon the ratification of the charter.
>
> The language used in articles 55 and 56 is not the type customarily employed in treaties which have been held to be self-executing and to create rights and duties in individuals.

This logic would seem to apply with equal force to treaties like the <u>Covenant on Civil and Political Rights</u>, in which Article 2 explicitly obligates member states to take domestic action implementing the rights recognized:

> Article 2
>
> 1. Each State Party to the present Covenant undertakes to respect and to ensure to all individuals within its territory and subject to its jurisdiction the rights recognized in the present Covenant, without distinction of any kind, such as race, colour, sex, language, religion, political or other opinion, national or social origin, property, birth or other status.
>
> 2. Where not already provided for by existing legislative or other measures, each State Party to the present Covenant undertakes to take the necessary steps, in accordance with its constitutional processes and with the provisions of the present Covenant, to adopt such laws or other measures as

---

67. <u>Sei Fujii v. State of California</u>, 38 Cal. 2d 718 (1952).

may be necessary to give effect to the rights recognized in the present Covenant.

3. Each State Party to the present Covenant undertakes:

(a) To ensure that any person whose rights or freedoms as herein recognized are violated shall have an effective remedy, notwithstanding that the violation has been committed by persons acting in an official capacity;

(b) To ensure that any person claiming such a remedy shall have his right thereto determined by competent judicial, administrative or legislative authorities, or by any other competent authority provided for by the legal system of the State, and to develop the possibilities of judicial remedy;

(c) To ensure that the competent authorities shall enforce such remedies when granted.

Even more daunting to human rights advocates than this rationale is the fact that the U.S. Senate is apparently well aware of the self-execution doctrine. As a result, nearly every human rights treaty ratified by the United States to date has been approved by the Senate with an express declaration that the treaty is non-self-executing. Generally speaking, the United States has adopted the position that it retains complete discretion regarding how it may choose to fulfill its human rights treaty obligations. The importance of this is that almost none of the human rights treaty obligations of the United States are part of our domestic law, except for the few instances in which Congress has passed implementing legislation.

In this regard, Congress has passed legislation implementing some aspects of just a few treaties, including the Convention Against Torture (CAT) (18 U.S.C. § 2340) and Genocide Convention (18 U.S.C. §§ 1091–93). These two implementation statutes create federal crimes for torture and genocide when committed by certain individuals but otherwise exclude "any substantive or procedural right enforceable by law by any party in any proceeding." In 1998, Article 3 of CAT, which forbids deportation of any person who faces a substantial risk of torture in the receiving country, was also implemented. Now, under current regulations, an alien is entitled to protection from "removal" from the United States if the alien can prove "that it is more likely than not that he or she would be tortured if removed to the proposed country of removal." 8 C.F.R. § 1208.16(c)(2)-(3). The Torture Victim Protection Act, which is examined in the next chapter, is a further example of implementation on limited terms. While the statute creates a cause of action for victims of torture as required by CAT, it does so only in relation to acts committed by foreign public officials.

### e. Growing Movement Toward Domestic Implementation by Other Nations?

To what degree do other governments "domesticate" their international human rights obligations? As detailed in the next chapter, European countries commonly incorporate their international human rights treaty obligations into domestic law. Outside of Europe, and perhaps Latin America, the empirical evidence is sketchy at best. At least some scholars, however, believe that there is a significant trend in that direction. Consider Judge Buergenthal's viewpoint in the excerpt below.

> Buergenthal, *The Evolving International Human rights System*, 100 A.J.I.L. 683 (2006) (available on JSTOR)

> ... The proliferation of human rights treaties and the emergence of international and regional human rights tribunals with jurisdiction to interpret and apply these treaties have prompted an increasing number of states to accord human rights treaties a special status in their national constitutions.

> ... One of the most interesting constitutional provisions in this regard is Article 10(2) of the Spanish Constitution of 1978, which reads as follows: "The norms relative to basic rights and liberties which are recognized by the Constitution shall be interpreted in conformity with the Universal Declaration of Human Rights and the international treaties and agreements on those matters ratified by Spain." ...

> Other countries, among them Argentina, have conferred constitutional rank on human rights treaties. Argentina did so when it amended its Constitution in 1994 and adopted a new Article 75(22). That provision confers constitutional rank on various international human rights instruments, including the American Convention on Human Rights and the two International Covenants on Human Rights. . . .

> In this regard, it is also noteworthy that the Austrian law ratifying the European Convention on Human Rights declared the treaty to have the normative rank of a constitutional law.

> A large number of countries, particularly in Europe and Latin America, consider many provisions of various human rights treaties, especially those guaranteeing civil and political rights such as the European and American Conventions and the International Covenant on Civil and Political Rights to be self-executing in character. As such, they become directly applicable domestic law. . . .

> The foregoing national constitutional developments hold great importance for the protection of human rights. They make it possible for international human rights treaties and the decisions of international tribunals applying these instruments to have a direct impact on the domestic administration of justice. That, in the long run, is the best way to ensure the effective implementation of internationally guaranteed human rights.

f. The Domestic Legal Status of Customary International Law

In **The Paquete Habana**, 175 U.S. 677, 700, 20 S.Ct. 290, 299, 44 L.Ed. 320 (1900) the Supreme Court declared that:

> "International law is part of our law, and must be ascertained and administered by the courts of justice of appropriate jurisdiction, as often as questions of right depending upon it are duly presented for their determination . . .

where there is no treaty and no controlling executive or legislative act or judicial decision. . . ."

We will see in the next chapter that this phrase has frequently been invoked by U.S. federal courts in human rights cases justifying reliance upon customary international law in the absence of a binding and self-executing treaty obligation. Generally the courts have assumed that CIL is part of federal law and therefore superior to inconsistent state law. A recent spate of xenophobic, undoubtedly unconstitutional, state laws purporting to prohibit the consideration of international or "foreign" law by state courts might test out this assumption.[68] Assuming no inconsistent controlling federal law, CIL would also seem to control the conduct of federal officials. Thus, given the dearth of self-executing international human rights obligations within the U.S. domestic system, customary human rights law is of vital importance.

There are, however, some lingering ambiguities and challenges regarding its status and effect. If treaties must be self-executing in order to become operative domestic law, is customary law subject to the same restriction? Decisions of the lower U.S. courts, examined in the next chapter, don't address this issue directly but rather seem to assume that CIL is always applicable regardless whether domestic political institutions have weighed in. Does this mean that a customary international law norm can be applied by a U.S. court even when the same rule appears in a treaty that the Senate has declared to be non-self-executing? While current case law amply supports the proposition that customary law is part of our domestic law does it create a cause of action for its enforcement by individuals? These and other concerns have caused some scholars to challenge the "legitimacy" of customary international law as a rule for decision in domestic courts.[69] When we examine human rights litigation in United States courts in the next chapter, we will address such questions in greater detail.

g. The Interpretation Angle: The Charming Betsy Doctrine

Chief Justice Marshall stated in *Murray v. Schooner Charming Betsy*, 6 U.S. (2 Cranch) 64, 118, 2 L.Ed. 208 (1804) that "an Act of Congress ought never to be construed to violate the law of nations if any other possible construction remains . . . . . . ."

---

68. The website <u>Gavel to Gavel</u> reports 44 bills in 21 states that, to varying degrees, attempt to the limit the use of "Sharia," "foreign" and sometimes "international" law. Most of these attempts have failed although as many as <u>seven states have banned</u> "foreign law." Oklahoma, however, passed a state constitutional amendment in 2010 providing that "courts shall not look to the legal precepts of other nations or cultures. Specifically, the courts shall not consider international law or Sharia Law." The amendment was later <u>struck down</u> by a federal court on Establishment Clause grounds.

69. A critique of customary law offered by Professors Bradley and Goldsmith in *Customary International Law as Federal Common Law: A Critique of the Modern Position*, 110 Harv. L. Rev. 815, 821, 838–42 (1997) (arguing the modern application of CIL in federal court cases is inconsistent with "representative democracy, federal common law, separation of powers, and federalism,") has generated an on-going debate. For a recent article summarizing various points of view and adding another refutation of the critique *see* Carlos Vasquez, *Customary International Law as U.S. Law: A Critique of the Revisionist and Intermediate Positions and a Defense of the Modern Position*, 86 Notre Dame Law Review 1495 (2011).

The Restatement of Foreign Relations, Third, § 114, expresses the doctrine in this way: "Where fairly possible, a United States statute is to be construed so as not to conflict with international law or with an international agreement of the United States." This general rule of interpretation has relevance in human rights, particularly for non-self-executing treaties, and has been adopted in a number of other countries.[70]

In essence, the Charming Betsy canon of interpretation suggests that existing domestic law (at least federal law) must be interpreted in light of the United States' international human rights treaty obligations even if those treaties are not directly binding in the courts because of their non-self-executing status. Essentially, there is a presumption that our government would not take actions in violation of U.S. international obligations. This presumption makes treaties that have not yet been incorporated into domestic law relevant even if not directly applicable as controlling law. Note that a similar presumption applies under the Vienna Convention on Treaties when the United States has signed, but not yet ratified, a treaty. A similar but legally distinct issue is whether U.S. court may legitimately rely upon international and foreign country practices, or foreign domestic law, when interpreting both treaties and Constitutional rights.

The practical implications of "interpretive incorporation" under the Charming Betsy canon are varied, nuanced and limited. At its most powerful ebb the doctrine might conceivably cause a court to prohibit governmental actions which were clearly inconsistent with our international treaty obligations — condemning, for example, executive branch use of "enhanced" interrogation not otherwise authorized by Congress. In its least influential form, the U.S. Supreme Court has occasionally used both unincorporated treaty obligations and foreign country practices to confirm or bolster a particular interpretation of domestic law, or what one author has described as "gilding the lily."[71] At minimum, courts should interpret ambiguous domestic statutes and regulations in ways consistent with our ratified but unincorporated treaties. The most obvious limitation on the doctrine is that Congress is free to violate our unincorporated treaty obligations if it so chooses. If domestic law is clear, American courts will apply such law even if it violates a prior treaty obligation.

Reliance on treaties and other international legal standards has been contentious, however, particularly with regard to the death penalty. The following section explores the implications of the Charming Betsy canon and related reliance on foreign country practices by examining the United States Supreme Court's approach to the death penalty. The cases also are instructive regarding the relationship between international law and domestic law generally.

---

70. *See* Melissa Waters, *Creeping Monism: The Judicial Trend Toward Interpretive Incorporation of Human Rights Treaties*, 107 Col. L. Rev. 628 (2007). *See, e.g.,* Minister for Immigration & Ethnic Affairs v. Teoh (1995) 128 A.L.R. 353, 365 (Austl.)( "[R]atification . . . of an international convention is not to be dismissed as a merely platitudinous or ineffectual act,. . . . [it] is a positive statement by the Executive Government of this country to the world and to the Australian people that the Executive Government will act in accordance with the Convention).

71. Waters, *supra* note 70 at 655. *See, e.g.* Atkins v. Virginia, 536 U.S. 304, 316 (2002); Lawrence v. Texas, 539 U.S. 558 (2003); Roper v. Simmons, 543 U.S. 551 (2005).

# D.  Treaties within U.S. Domestic Law: Case Study of Capital Punishment & the Vienna Convention on Consular Relations

## 1. Interpretation of the 8th Amendment and the Execution of Juveniles

While many human rights treaties prohibit the death penalty for juvenile offenders (those under 18 at the time of their crime), the United States has either not ratified such treaties or imposed an explicit reservation relating to capital punishment. Should American courts nevertheless consider international human rights standards and the practices of other nations in interpreting the meaning of "cruel and unusual punishment" under the 8th Amendment? In *Thompson v. Oklahoma*, 487 U.S. 815 (1988) the Supreme Court faced the issue in judging whether capital punishment violated the Constitution when imposed on a defendant who was under the age of 16 at the time of his crime. In ruling that it did, Justice Stevens relied significantly on such sources:

\*\*\*

The authors of the Eighth Amendment drafted a categorical prohibition against the infliction of cruel and unusual punishments, but they made no attempt to define the contours of that category. They delegated that task to future generations of judges, who have been guided by the "evolving standards of decency that mark the progress of a maturing society."

\*\*\*

The conclusion that it would offend civilized standards of decency to execute a person who was less than 16 years old at the time of his or her offense is consistent with the views that have been expressed by respected professional organizations, by other nations that share our Anglo-American heritage, and by the leading members of the Western European community. Thus, the American Bar Association and the American Law Institute have formally expressed their opposition to the death penalty for juveniles. Although the death penalty has not been entirely abolished in the United Kingdom or New Zealand (it has been abolished in Australia, except in the State of New South Wales, where it is available for treason and piracy), in neither of those countries may a juvenile be executed. The death penalty has been abolished in West Germany, France, Portugal, The Netherlands, and all of the Scandinavian countries, and is available only for exceptional crimes such as treason in Canada, Italy, Spain, and Switzerland. Juvenile executions are also prohibited in the Soviet Union.

\*\*\*

FN34\*\*\* In addition, three major human rights treaties explicitly prohibit juvenile death penalties. Article 6(5) of the International Covenant on Civil and Political Rights, Annex to G. A. Res. 2200, 21 U.N.GAOR Res. Supp.

(No. 16) 53, U.N.Doc. A/6316 (1966) (signed but not ratified by the United States), reprinted in 6 International Legal Material 368, 370 (1967); Article 4(5) of the American Convention on Human Rights, O.A.S. Official Records, OEA/Ser.K/XVI/1.1, Doc. 65, Rev. 1, Corr. 2 (1970) (signed but not ratified by the United States), reprinted in 9 International Legal Material 673, 676 (1970); Article 68 of the Geneva Convention Relative to the Protection of Civilian Persons in Time of War, August 12, 1949, 6 U.S.T. 3516, 3560, T.I.A.S. No. 3365 (ratified by the United States).

As any court observer might expect, Justice Scalia dissented from this approach in the following terms expressed in a footnote:

\*\*\*

The plurality's reliance upon Amnesty International's account of what it pronounces to be civilized standards of decency in other countries, *ante* at 487 U.S. 830–31 and n. 34, is totally inappropriate as a means of establishing the fundamental beliefs of this Nation. \*\*\* In the present case, therefore, the fact that a majority of foreign nations would not impose capital punishment upon persons under 16 at the time of the crime is of no more relevance than the fact that a majority of them would not impose capital punishment at all, or have standards of due process quite different from our own.

Subsequently, in *Roper v. Simmons*, 543 U.S. 551 (2005), the Supreme Court declared that capital punishment may not be imposed on defendants who were under 18 at the time of their crime. In reaching this result Justice Kennedy once again relied, in part, on international legal sources.

This case requires us to address, for the second time in a decade and a half, whether it is permissible under the Eighth and Fourteenth Amendments to the Constitution of the United States to execute a juvenile offender who was older than 15 but younger than 18 when he committed a capital crime. In *Stanford* v. *Kentucky*, 492 U. S. 361 (1989), a divided Court rejected the proposition that the Constitution bars capital punishment for juvenile offenders in this age group. We reconsider the question.

\*\*\*

Our determination that the death penalty is disproportionate punishment for offenders under 18 finds confirmation in the stark reality that the United States is the only country in the world that continues to give official sanction to the juvenile death penalty. This reality does not become controlling, for the task of interpreting the Eighth Amendment remains our responsibility. Yet at least from the time of the Court's decision in *Trop*, the Court has referred to the laws of other countries and to international authorities as instructive for its interpretation of the Eighth Amendment's prohibition of "cruel and unusual punishments." 356 U.S., at 102–103 (plurality opinion).

\*\*\*

As respondent and a number of *amici* emphasize, Article 37 of the United Nations Convention on the Rights of the Child, which every country in the world has ratified save for the United States and Somalia, contains an express prohibition on capital punishment for crimes committed by juveniles under 18. *** No ratifying country has entered a reservation to the provision prohibiting the execution of juvenile offenders. Parallel prohibitions are contained in other significant international covenants. See CCPR, Art. 6(5), 999 U. N. T. S., at 175 (prohibiting capital punishment for anyone under 18 at the time of offense) (signed and ratified by the United States subject to a reservation regarding Article 6(5), as noted, *supra*, at 13); American Convention on Human Rights: Pact of San José, Costa Rica, Art. 4(5), Nov. 22, 1969, 1144 U. N. T. S. 146 (entered into force July 19, 1978) (same); African Charter on the Rights and Welfare of the Child, Art. 5(3), OAU. CAB/LEG/24.9/49 (1990) (entered into force Nov. 29, 1999) (same).

. . . fair to say that the United States now stands alone in a world that has turned its face against the juvenile death penalty.

***

The opinion of the world community, while not controlling our outcome, does provide respected and significant confirmation for our own conclusions.

## 2. Violations of the Vienna Convention on Consular Relations

As of 2012, there were approximately 125 foreign nationals on death row in the United States. These persons have been duly convicted of capital crimes and received the full panoply of Constitutional rights required for all criminal convictions. Many of them, however, did not receive one form of protection required in the <u>Vienna Convention on Consular Relations</u>, an international treaty to which the United States is a party. Article 36 of the Convention essentially requires that states notify each other when their nationals are charged with crimes in the foreign jurisdiction. This allows the foreign defendant's home state to consult with and provide a defense for its citizen — if it chooses. It similarly requires that the defendant be informed of his right to consult with his home nation's local consular offices. Since many countries may choose to assist in their national's legal representation, such rights are not insignificant and may induce diplomatic interventions as well. Recent interpretation and application of this treaty in a series of capital cases reveals much about the tentative relationship between American treaty obligations and domestic law. A full understanding requires that one trace the progression of several cases.

In 1992, Angel Francisco Breard, a citizen of Paraguay, was tried by a jury and sentenced to death in Virginia for attempted rape and capital murder. Breard filed a motion for habeas corpus in federal court on grounds that Virginia had failed to inform him of his rights under the Vienna Convention. The federal courts held that the claim had been waived because Breard had failed to raise it in the state courts. In *Breard v. Greene*, 523 U.S. 371 (1998), the Supreme Court agreed that the claim was procedurally barred and also concluded that Breard could not, in any case, show prejudice in his original trial and conviction (essentially harmless error). The Breard decision is referenced extensively in the Court's subsequent decisions in this area. In 1997, Jose Ernesto Medellin was convicted of the brutal rape and murder of two adolescent girls. Unlike Breard, Medellin raised the Vienna Convention issue on direct appeal, alleging that he was never notified of his right to seek assistance from the Mexican government. After Texas state courts rejected his claims, he brought a 2003 habeas petition in the federal courts, which found the claim procedurally barred and the violation non-prejudicial.

In the meantime, also in 2003, Mexico sued the United States before the International Court of Justice alleging some 50 violations of the Convention's notification requirement, including the Medellin case. The World Court had jurisdiction because the U.S. had adopted an optional protocol to the Convention that gave the Court jurisdiction to hear disputes under the Convention. In 2004, the ICJ ruled against the United States in *Case Concerning Avena and Other Mexican Nationals (Mex. v. U. S.)*, 2004 I.C.J. 12 (2004), holding that the Mexican defendants were entitled to reconsideration of their convictions.

On March 7, 2005, apparently displeased with the Avena judgment, the U.S. withdrew from the Optional Protocol that provided the ICJ's jurisdiction. Medellin's case was then accepted for review by the U.S. Supreme Court. However, before the case was heard, President Bush issued a memorandum order requiring state courts to review the convictions of foreign nationals who were never advised of their Convention rights. The Supreme Court promptly dismissed Medellin's case in light of President Bush's order, returning the case to the state courts (for a second habeas corpus petition).

While Medellin's second habeas petition was under consideration in Texas, the U.S. Supreme Court decided the case of *Sanchez-Llamas v. Oregon*, 548 U.S. 331 (2006). In *Sanchez-Llamas* the Court held that violations of the Convention did not require the suppression of evidence at trial (evidence obtained before the defendant was informed of his right to consult with the foreign Consulate) and that state imposed procedural requirements must be respected and followed even if they result in waiver of Convention based claims. Most controversially, however, the Court also suggested that rulings of the ICJ regarding interpretation of U.S. treaty obligations were not binding on U.S. courts.

The oral argument, briefs and full written opinion in Sanchez-Llamas can be found at Oyez.

i. MOISES SANCHEZ-LLAMAS v. OREGON, 548 U.S. 331 (2006)

Chief Justice Roberts delivered the opinion of the Court.

Article 36 of the Vienna Convention on Consular Relations (Vienna Convention or Convention), Apr. 24, 1963, [1970] 21 U. S. T. 77, 100–101, T. I. A. S.

No. 6820, addresses communication between an individual and his consular officers when the individual is detained by authorities in a foreign country. These consolidated cases concern the availability of judicial relief for violations of Article 36. We are confronted with three questions. *First*, does Article 36 create rights that defendants may invoke against the detaining authorities in a criminal trial or in a post-conviction proceeding? *Second*, does a violation of Article 36 require suppression of a defendant's statements to police? *Third*, may a State, in a post-conviction proceeding, treat a defendant's Article 36 claim as defaulted because he failed to raise the claim at trial? We conclude, even assuming the Convention creates judicially enforceable rights, that suppression is not an appropriate remedy for a violation of Article 36, and that a State may apply its regular rules of procedural default to Article 36 claims. We therefore affirm the decisions below.

\*\*\*

Article 36 of the Convention concerns consular officers' access to their nationals detained by authorities in a foreign country. The article provides that "if he so requests, the competent authorities of the receiving State shall, without delay, inform the consular post of the sending State if, within its consular district, a national of that State is arrested or committed to prison or to custody pending trial or is detained in any other manner." Art. 36(1) (b), *id.*, at 101.

\*\*\*

Along with the Vienna Convention, the United States ratified the Optional Protocol Concerning the Compulsory Settlement of Disputes (Optional Protocol or Protocol), Apr. 24, 1963, [1970] 21 U. S. T. 325, T. I. A. S. No. 6820. The Optional Protocol provides that "[d]isputes arising out of the interpretation or application of the Convention shall lie within the compulsory jurisdiction of the International Court of Justice [(ICJ)]," and allows parties to the Protocol to bring such disputes before the ICJ. *Id.*, at 326. The United States gave notice of its withdrawal from the Optional Protocol on March 7, 2005. Letter from Condoleezza Rice, Secretary of State, to Kofi A. Annan, Secretary-General of the United Nations.

B

Petitioner Moises Sanchez-Llamas is a Mexican national. In December 1999, he was involved in an exchange of gunfire with police in which one officer suffered a gunshot wound in the leg. Police arrested Sanchez-Llamas and gave him warnings under *Miranda* v. *Arizona*, 384 U.S. 436 (1966), in both English and Spanish. At no time, however, did they inform him that he could ask to have the Mexican Consulate notified of his detention.

\*\*\*

Before trial, Sanchez-Llamas moved to suppress the statements he made to police. He argued that suppression was warranted because the statements were made involuntarily and because the authorities had failed to comply with Article 36 of the Vienna Convention. The trial court denied the motion. The case proceeded to trial, and Sanchez-Llamas was convicted and sentenced to 2012 years in prison.

\*\*\*

Because we conclude that Sanchez-Llamas and Bustillo are not in any event entitled to relief on their claims, we find it unnecessary to resolve the question whether the Vienna Convention grants individuals enforceable rights. Therefore, for purposes of addressing petitioners' claims, we assume, without deciding, that Article 36 does grant Bustillo and Sanchez-Llamas such rights.

A

Sanchez-Llamas argues that the trial court was required to suppress his statements to police because authorities never told him of his rights under Article 36.

\*\*\*

It would be startling if the Convention were read to require suppression. The exclusionary rule as we know it is an entirely American legal creation. . . . More than 40 years after the drafting of the Convention, the automatic exclusionary rule applied in our courts is still "universally rejected" by other countries. . . . It is implausible that other signatories to the Convention thought it to require a remedy that nearly all refuse to recognize as a matter of domestic law. There is no reason to suppose that Sanchez-Llamas would be afforded the relief he seeks here in any of the other 169 countries party to the Vienna Convention.

\*\*\*

Of course, it is well established that a self-executing treaty binds the States pursuant to the Supremacy Clause, and that the States therefore must recognize the force of the treaty in the course of adjudicating the rights of litigants. *See, e.g., Hauenstein* v. *Lynham,* 100 U.S. 483(1880). And where a treaty provides for a particular judicial remedy, there is no issue of intruding on the constitutional prerogatives of the States or the other federal branches. Courts must apply the remedy as a requirement of federal law. \*\*\* But where a treaty does not provide a particular remedy, either expressly or implicitly, it is not for the federal courts to impose one on the States through lawmaking of their own.

\*\*\*

B

The Virginia courts denied petitioner Bustillo's Article 36 claim on the ground that he failed to raise it at trial or on direct appeal. The general rule in federal habeas cases is that a defendant who fails to raise a claim on direct appeal is barred from raising the claim on collateral review.

***

This is not the first time we have been asked to set aside procedural default rules for a Vienna Convention claim. . . . In *Breard*, the petitioner failed to raise an Article 36 claim in state court — at trial or on collateral review — and then sought to have the claim heard in a subsequent federal habeas proceeding. *Id.*, at 375. He argued that "the Convention is the 'supreme law of the land' and thus trumps the procedural default doctrine." *Ibid*. We rejected this argument as "plainly incorrect," . . . In light of *Breard*'s holding, Bustillo faces an uphill task in arguing that the Convention requires States to set aside their procedural default rules for Article 36 claims.

***

Bustillo's second reason is less easily dismissed. He argues that since *Breard*, the ICJ has interpreted the Vienna Convention to preclude the application of procedural default rules to Article 36 claims. The *LaGrand Case (F. R. G.* v. *U. S.)*, 2001 I. C. J. 466 (Judgment of June 27) *(LaGrand)*, and the *Case Concerning Avena and other Mexican Nationals (Mex.* v. *U. S.)*, 2004 I. C. J. No. 128 (Judgment of Mar. 31) *(Avena)* . . .

Bustillo argues that *LaGrand* and *Avena* warrant revisiting the procedural default holding of *Breard*. In a similar vein, several *amici* contend that "the United States is *obligated* to comply with the Convention, *as interpreted by the ICJ*." Brief for ICJ Experts 11 (emphases added). We disagree. Although the ICJ's interpretation deserves "respectful consideration," *Breard, supra*, at 375, we conclude that it does not compel us to reconsider our understanding of the Convention in *Breard*.

***

Nothing in the structure or purpose of the ICJ suggests that its interpretations were intended to be conclusive on our courts. The ICJ's decisions have "*no binding force* except between the parties and in respect of that particular case," Statute of the International Court of Justice, Art. 59, 59 Stat.1062, T. S. No. 993 (1945) . . . .. The ICJ's principal purpose is to arbitrate particular disputes between national governments. *Id.*, at 1055 (ICJ is "the principal judicial organ of the United Nations"); see also Art. 34, *id.*, at 1059 ("Only states [*i.e.*, countries] may be parties in cases before the Court"). While each member of the United Nations has agreed to comply with decisions of the ICJ "in any case to which it is a party," United Nations Charter, Art. 94(1), 59 Stat.1051, T. S. No. 933 (1945), the Charter's procedure for noncompliance — referral to the Security Council by the aggrieved state — contemplates quintessentially *international* remedies, Art. 94(2), *ibid*** Moreover, shortly after *Avena*, the United States withdrew from the Optional Protocol concerning

Vienna Convention disputes. Whatever the effect of *Avena* and *LaGrand* before this withdrawal, it is doubtful that our courts should give decisive weight to the interpretation of a tribunal whose jurisdiction in this area is no longer recognized by the United States.

***

We therefore conclude, as we did in *Breard*, that claims under Article 36 of the Vienna Convention may be subjected to the same procedural default rules that apply generally to other federal-law claims.

The judgments of the Supreme Court of Oregon and the Supreme Court of Virginia are affirmed.

It is so ordered.

**MEDELLIN REDUX:**

After rendering its decision in Sanchez-Llamas, the Supreme Court once again accepted certiorari in the case of Medellin whose second habeas corpus petition (grounded in President Bush's memorandum order and the Avena decision) was rejected by the Texas state courts. An excerpt of the Court's discussion regarding the non-binding status of ICJ decisions and non- self-executing treaties, appears below.

ii. Jose Ernesto Medellin v. Texas, 552 U.S.

**491 (2008)**

Chief Justice Roberts delivered the opinion of the Court.

The International Court of Justice (ICJ), located in The Hague, is a tribunal established pursuant to the United Nations Charter to adjudicate disputes between member states. In the *Case Concerning Avena and Other Mexican Nationals* (*Mex. v. U. S.*), 2004 I. C. J. 12 (Judgment of Mar. 31) (*Avena*), that tribunal considered a claim brought by Mexico against the United States. The ICJ held that, based on violations of the Vienna Convention, 51 named Mexican nationals were entitled to review and reconsideration of their state-court convictions and sentences in the United States. This was so regardless of any forfeiture of the right to raise Vienna Convention claims because of a failure to comply with generally applicable state rules governing challenges to criminal convictions.

In *Sanchez-Llamas* v. *Oregon*, 548 U. S. 331 (2006) — issued after *Avena* but involving individuals who were not named in the *Avena* judgment — we held that, contrary to the ICJ's determination, the Vienna Convention did not preclude the application of state default rules. After the *Avena* decision, President George W. Bush determined, through a Memorandum to the Attorney General (Feb. 28, 2005), App. to Pet. for Cert. 187a (Memorandum or President's Memorandum), that the United States would "discharge its international obligations" under *Avena* "by having State courts give effect to the decision."

\*\*\*

We granted certiorari to decide two questions. *First*, is the ICJ's judgment in *Avena* directly enforceable as domestic law in a state court in the United States? *Second*, does the President's Memorandum independently require the States to provide review and reconsideration of the claims of the 51 Mexican nationals named in *Avena* without regard to state procedural default rules? We conclude that neither *Avena* nor the President's Memorandum constitutes directly enforceable federal law that pre-empts state limitations on the filing of successive habeas petitions. We therefore affirm the decision below.

I A   \*\*\*

Petitioner José Ernesto Medellin, a Mexican national, has lived in the United States since preschool. A member of the "Black and Whites" gang, Medellin was convicted of capital murder and sentenced to death in Texas for the gang rape and brutal murders of two Houston teenagers. \*\*\* Local law enforcement officers did not, however, inform Medellin of his Vienna Convention right to notify the Mexican consulate of his detention. . . .

Medellin first raised his Vienna Convention claim in his first application for state post-conviction relief. The state trial court held that the claim was procedurally defaulted because Medellin had failed to raise it at trial or on direct review. The trial court also rejected the Vienna Convention claim on the merits, finding that Medellin had "fail[ed] to show that any non-notification of the Mexican authorities impacted on the validity of his conviction or punishment." *Id.*, at 62. The Texas Court of Criminal Appeals affirmed. *Id.*, at 64–65.

\*\*\*

While Medellin's application for a certificate of appealability was pending in the Fifth Circuit, the ICJ issued its decision in *Avena*. The ICJ held that the United States had violated Article 36(1) (b) of the Vienna Convention by failing to inform the 51 named Mexican nationals, including Medellin, of their Vienna Convention rights. 2004 I. C. J., at 53–55. In the ICJ's determination, the United States was obligated "to provide, by means of its own choosing, review and reconsideration of the convictions and sentences of the [affected] Mexican nationals." *Id.*, at 72. The ICJ indicated that such review was required without regard to state procedural default rules. *Id.*, at 56–57.

\*\*\*

This Court granted certiorari. *Medellin* v. *Dretke*, 544 U.S. 660, 661 (2005) (*per curiam*) (*Medellin I*). Before we heard oral argument, however, President George W. Bush issued his Memorandum to the United States Attorney General, providing:

I have determined, pursuant to the authority vested in me as President by the Constitution and the laws of the United States of America, that the

United States will discharge its international obligations under the decision of the International Court of Justice in [*Avena*], by having State courts give effect to the decision in accordance with general principles of comity in cases filed by the 51 Mexican nationals addressed in that decision. App. to Pet. for Cert. 187a.

Medellin, relying on the President's Memorandum and the ICJ's decision in *Avena*, filed a second application for habeas relief in state court. *Ex parte Medellin*, 223 S. W. 3d 315, 322–323 (Tex. Crim. App. 2006). \*\*\*

The Texas Court of Criminal Appeals subsequently dismissed Medellin's second state habeas application as an abuse of the writ. \*\*\* We again granted certiorari.

II

Medellin first contends that the ICJ's judgment in *Avena* constitutes a "binding" obligation on the state and federal courts of the United States. He argues that "by virtue of the Supremacy Clause, the treaties requiring compliance with the *Avena* judgment are *already* the 'Law of the Land' by which all state and federal courts in this country are 'bound.'" Reply Brief for Petitioner 1. Accordingly, Medellin argues, *Avena* is a binding federal rule of decision that pre-empts contrary state limitations on successive habeas petitions.

No one disputes that the *Avena* decision — a decision that flows from the treaties through which the United States submitted to ICJ jurisdiction with respect to Vienna Convention disputes — constitutes an *international* law obligation on the part of the United States. But not all international law obligations automatically constitute binding federal law enforceable in United States courts. The question we confront here is whether the *Avena* judgment has automatic *domestic* legal effect such that the judgment of its own force applies in state and federal courts.

This Court has long recognized the distinction between treaties that automatically have effect as domestic law, and those that — while they constitute international law commitments — do not by themselves function as binding federal law. \*\*\*

\*\*\*

Medellin and his *amici* nonetheless contend that the Optional Protocol, United Nations Charter, and ICJ Statute supply the "relevant obligation" to give the *Avena* judgment binding effect in the domestic courts of the United States. Reply Brief for Petitioner 5–6. Because none of these treaty sources creates binding federal law in the absence of implementing legislation, and because it is uncontested that no such legislation exists, we conclude that the *Avena* judgment is not automatically binding domestic law.

A

The interpretation of a treaty, like the interpretation of a statute, begins with its text. *Air France* v. *Saks*, 470 U.S. 392, 396–397 (1985). ***

The most natural reading of the Optional Protocol is as a bare grant of jurisdiction. *** The Protocol says nothing about the effect of an ICJ decision and does not itself commit signatories to comply with an ICJ judgment. The Protocol is similarly silent as to any enforcement mechanism.

The obligation on the part of signatory nations to comply with ICJ judgments derives not from the Optional Protocol, but rather from Article 94 of the United Nations Charter — the provision that specifically addresses the effect of ICJ decisions. Article 94(1) provides that "[e]ach Member of the United Nations *undertakes to comply* with the decision of the [ICJ] in any case to which it is a party." 59 Stat. 1051 (emphasis added). The Executive Branch contends that the phrase "undertakes to comply" is not "an acknowledgement that an ICJ decision will have immediate legal effect in the courts of U. N. members," but rather "a *commitment* on the part of U. N. Members to take *future* action through their political branches to comply with an ICJ decision." Brief for United States as *Amicus Curiae* in *Medellin I*, O. T. 2004, No. 04–5928, p. 34.

We agree with this construction of Article 94. The Article is not a directive to domestic courts. It does not provide that the United States "shall" or "must" comply with an ICJ decision, nor indicate that the Senate that ratified the U. N. Charter intended to vest ICJ decisions with immediate legal effect in domestic courts. Instead, "[t]he words of Article 94 . . . call upon governments to take certain action." ***

The remainder of Article 94 confirms that the U. N. Charter does not contemplate the automatic enforceability of ICJ decisions in domestic courts. Article 94(2) — the enforcement provision — provides the sole remedy for noncompliance: referral to the United Nations Security Council by an aggrieved state.

The U. N. Charter's provision of an express diplomatic — that is, nonjudicial — remedy is itself evidence that ICJ judgments were not meant to be enforceable in domestic courts. ***, as the President and Senate were undoubtedly aware in subscribing to the U. N. Charter and Optional Protocol, the United States retained the unqualified right to exercise its veto of any Security Council resolution.

***

Moreover, the consequences of Medellin's argument give pause. An ICJ judgment, the argument goes, is not only binding domestic law but is also unassailable. As a result, neither Texas nor this Court may look behind a judgment and quarrel with its reasoning or result. (We already know, from

*Sanchez-Llamas*, that this Court disagrees with both the reasoning and re-sult in *Avena*.) Medellin's interpretation would allow ICJ judgments to over-ride otherwise binding state law; there is nothing in his logic that would exempt contrary federal law from the same fate. See, *e.g.*, *Cook* v. *United States*, 288 U.S. 102, 119 (1933) (later-in-time self-executing treaty supersedes a federal statue if there is a conflict). And there is nothing to prevent the ICJ from ordering state courts to annul criminal convictions and sentences, for any reason deemed sufficient by the ICJ. Indeed, that is precisely the relief Mexico requested. *Avena*, 2004 I. C. J., at 58–59.

***

In short, and as we observed in *Sanchez-Llamas*, "[n]othing in the structure or purpose of the ICJ suggests that its interpretations were intended to be conclusive on our courts." *** We do not suggest that treaties can never af-ford binding domestic effect to international tribunal judgments — only that the U. N. Charter, the Optional Protocol, and the ICJ Statute do not do so. And whether the treaties underlying a judgment are self-executing so that the judgment is directly enforceable as domestic law in our courts is, of course, a matter for this Court to decide. See *Sanchez-Llamas, supra*, at 353–354.

***

## III

Medellin next argues that the ICJ's judgment in *Avena* is binding on state courts by virtue of the President's February 28, 2005 Memorandum. *** Ac-cordingly, we must decide whether the President's declaration alters our conclusion that the *Avena* judgment is not a rule of domestic law binding in state and federal courts.

## A

*** In this case, the President seeks to vindicate United States interests in ensuring the reciprocal observance of the Vienna Convention, protecting re-lations with foreign governments, and demonstrating commitment to the role of international law. These interests are plainly compelling.

***

The President has an array of political and diplomatic means available to enforce international obligations, but unilaterally converting a non-self-executing treaty into a self-executing one is not among them. The responsi-bility for transforming an international obligation arising from a non-self-executing treaty into domestic law falls to Congress. *Foster*, 2 Pet., at 315; *Whitney*, 124 U. S., at 194; *Igarta-De La Rosa*, 417 F. 3d, at 150. As this Court has explained, when treaty stipulations are "not self-executing they can only be enforced pursuant to legislation to carry them into effect." *Whit-

*ney, supra*, at 194. Moreover, "[u]ntil such act shall be passed, the Court is not at liberty to disregard the existing laws on the subject." *Foster, supra*, at 315.

The requirement that Congress, rather than the President, implement a non-self-executing treaty derives from the text of the Constitution, which divides the treaty-making power between the President and the Senate. *\*\*\**

A non-self-executing treaty, by definition, is one that was ratified with the understanding that it is not to have domestic effect of its own force. That understanding precludes the assertion that Congress has implicitly authorized the President — acting on his own — to achieve precisely the same result.

***

The President may comply with the treaty's obligations by some other means, so long as they are consistent with the Constitution. But he may not rely upon a non-self-executing treaty to "establish binding rules of decision that preempt contrary state law." Brief for United States as *Amicus Curiae* 5.

2

The judgment of the Texas Court of Criminal Appeals is affirmed.

Oral argument, briefs and the opinion in Medellin v. Texas can be found at Oyez. Medellín was executed at 9:57 pm on August 5, 2008, after his last-minute appeals were rejected by the Supreme Court. The Houston Chronical reported that Governor Rick Perry's spokesman responded to the ICJ's demand for a stay by saying, "The world court has no standing in Texas and Texas is not bound by a ruling or edict from a foreign court. It is easy to get caught up in discussions of international law and justice and treaties. It's very important to remember that these individuals are on death row for killing our citizens."

# Chapter 5

# Civil Liability as a Method of Domestic Enforcement of International Human Rights

## A. Introduction & Overview

In previous chapters we reviewed the relationship between international human rights and domestic law. We learned that many countries continue to treat international law as distinct from enforceable domestic law, only sometimes implementing or directly incorporating human rights obligations into the domestic legal system. This creates the anomalous circumstance that the state may be obligated internationally to "observe" or "respect" human rights that are not legally applicable or actionable before its domestic institutions. This chapter focuses on the practical implications of incorporation by examining how international human rights have been enforced within domestic legal systems, particularly before United States courts.

This chapter reviews specific examples and methods of enforcement within the U.S. legal system involving civil compensation. Chapter Six examines use of the criminal law processes to vindicate human rights. You will discover that, despite many obstacles, there are a number of important ways in which international law is being used in U.S. courts to remedy violations of international human rights. Before addressing these options you should consider the following important observations about the U.S. approach to its international obligations.

## 1. The "Domestication Gap": U.S. Failure to Incorporate International Human Rights Treaties

As detailed in the subsections that follow, domestic enforcement of international human rights has had a mixed record in the United States. Actions challenging domestic practices by American public officials based upon international human rights law have been limited and rarely successful before U.S. courts. On the other hand, actions seeking redress for violations committed overseas by foreign public officials against aliens have had considerably more historical success. The continuing viability of such "foreign violations" litigation, however, has been cast into considerable doubt by recent Supreme Court decisions. It is safe to say that, at present, there are significant obstacles to effective enforcement of international human rights before U.S. courts. Why is this true?

One reason for the somewhat limited success of human rights enforcement in American courts should be clear from earlier lessons. Multilateral treaties, an essential and primary source of international rights, are almost never incorporated in U.S. domestic law. To date, the Senate has uniformly declared that every international human rights treaty ratified by the United States is non-self-executing. Following such declarations, the courts have thus far refused to find any U.S. human rights treaty obligations directly applicable within our domestic system. A second significant obstacle has involved the question of remedies. Some courts, including the U.S. Supreme Court, have also resisted the idea that treaty provisions, even if seemingly applicable, create individual rights actionable within the courts — that is, treaty obligations don't necessarily create causes of action for individual victims.

The upshot of these two limitations is that international treaty obligations may only become legally enforceable before American courts if Congress chooses to implement their provisions through legislation, including the provisions of a cause of action. However, only a relatively small number of U.S. international human rights treaty obligations have been domesticated through implementing legislation in this way. These implementing statutes selectively create civil or criminal liability for certain violations but are limited in their scope of application. For example, as detailed below, the Torture Victim Protection Act creates civil liability for torture or extrajudicial executions but only when committed by a foreign official and the victim has exhausted local remedies in the foreign jurisdiction. In essence, even when international rights have been domestically implemented by the United States through legislation it has been done in a piecemeal, narrow fashion. The TVPA and other relevant statutes are further examined in detail in subsequent sections of this chapter.

## 2. Invoking Customary International Human Rights in the United States Courts

In contrast to treaty obligations, U.S domestic courts have been far more amenable to human rights claims based on customary international law. One simple reason for this is that customary law is not subject to the doctrine of self-execution and has historically been treated as part of domestic federal law. Thus, even though customary international human rights law is far narrower in substance than treaty law, it has a very distinct advantage since it is incorporated into domestic law without the need for Congressional approval.

As you will see, however, American courts' receptiveness to customary human rights law has almost exclusively been reserved for claims brought by aliens against foreign public officials for actions outside of the United States. The legal vehicle for such claims has been a jurisdictional statute first passed in 1789, commonly referred to as the "Alien Torts Statute" or "Alien Torts Claims Act," 42 U.S.C. § 1350 (ATCA or ATS). The ATS provides that "the district courts shall have original jurisdiction of any civil action by an alien for a tort only, committed in violation of the law of nations or a treaty of the United States." As described below, alien human rights victims have successfully used the statute to bring customary international law claims before federal courts against government officials from many countries including Uruguay, Ethiopia, Guatemala, Haiti, Bosnia and the Philippines, among others. In recent years, a spate of cases has also been brought against large, multinational corporations under the ATS alleging complicity in government human rights violations overseas.

The continuing viability of these lines of ATS "foreign directed" litigation has recently been challenged by two Supreme Court cases, *Sosa* and *Kiobel*, each of which is set forth later in this chapter. In *Sosa*, the Supreme Court significantly limited the availability of ATS claims by narrowly defining which international rights may be brought before federal courts. Subsequently, in 2013, *Kiobel* further and dramatically narrowed when claims regarding overseas human rights violations may be brought by applying a presumption against extraterritorial application of the ATS. The materials which follow describe the various methods of enforcement at play in the United States before turning to the implications of these two cases.

## B. Methods of Domestic Enforcement of International Human Rights in the United States Generally

### 1. Overview

The history of human rights litigation in the United States suggests several important variations in how such rights have been enforced before American courts. For a variety of reasons, these variations are characterized by subtle but important distinctions relating to the types of relief sought, the locus of challenged conduct and alienage of the parties. Most obviously, civil claims seeking monetary or injunctive relief are subject to different legal conditions than criminal prosecutions. Similarly, claims brought against U.S. public officials may differ from those brought against foreign defendants in terms of jurisdiction and defenses. Similarly, suing foreign governments or corporate defendants raises distinct legal issues from those applicable to individual defendants. Even among individual defendants, high public officials such former heads of state, may enjoy special defenses attributable to their status. While perhaps not always inherently coherent, such distinctions are clearly reflected in existing case law and therefore explored in the materials that follow. Because the ATS, followed by the TVPA, have been the most prominent vehicles for the application of international human rights law within the United States we will begin with those statutes and civil remedies against individual foreign defendants.

## 2. Civil Suits in American Courts for Foreign Human Rights Violations: ATS & TVPA Litigation Against Individual Foreign Defendants

Civil suits asking for money damages against foreign public officials for abuses occurring abroad have been a common and often successful form of human rights litigation in the United States. As noted above, the two primary vehicles for such litigation have been the ATS, beginning with the Filartiga case in 1980, and the 1991 TVPA. We will study the evolution and current status of such litigation in U.S. courts using a problem based on actual events. Your assignment is to evaluate potential liabilities regarding the following case based on the materials which follow it, including recent decisions by the Supreme Court. (You should ignore any statute of limitations issues.)

Photo by author, Santiago, Chile

### a. Facts: CASO QUEMADOS

The following is an account of actual events that took place in Chile in 1986.

In September, 1973, a violent military coup lead by General Augusto Pinochet overthrew the democratically elected government of Chile. In the years following the coup, the military government instituted a series of brutal repressive measures designed to eliminate what it perceived to be leftist threats to the "traditional Chilean way of life." These included the arrest of anyone suspected of socialist or leftist political thinking, rampant torture and murder of political opposition, and a brutal, repressive military presence in all of the poor neighborhoods surrounding the capital city, Santiago. On a regular basis, heavily armed military vehicles and police conducted raids into the lower class neighborhoods of Santiago in an effort to both round up suspected opponents of the government and terrorize and silence the local population.

In 1986, a naturalized U.S. citizen named Rodrigo Rojas DeNegri decided to return to Chile, the land of his birth. His mother had been exiled from Chile by the Pinochet regime in 1976. Upon his arrival in Chile, Rojas, who was 17 years old, soon became interested in documenting the civil unrest and turmoil that had engulfed his former native land. He began to collect a photographic record of events in Chile often attending street rallies and other public demonstrations against the military dictatorship.

On July 2, 1986, Rojas went to a street intersection that had been designated for a public demonstration against the military regime. Groups of teenagers and others had piled discarded tires and other debris into the streets surrounding the intersection in an effort to keep the police and military vehicles from easily disrupting the demonstration. As Rojas stood around the intersection with a group of other teenagers, a military van with dozens of soldiers pulled up near them. As the soldiers leaped from the vehicle, Rojas and the other teenagers quickly ran away from the scene. However, one of Rojas' young friends, 15-year-old Carmen Gloria Quintana tripped and fell. Rojas stopped to help her up and was quickly captured, along with Quintana, by the pursuing soldiers.

Lieutenant Pedro Fernández Dittus was in command. At first the soldiers merely mimicked the two teenagers and pushed them around as they asked for the names of anti-government activists. The interrogation then became more brutal. A soldier hit Rojas in the mouth with the butt of his rifle, breaking Rojas' teeth. As Rojas fell to the ground another soldier cracked his ribs and kicked him in the head. As the teenager lay helplessly on the ground, one of the soldiers doused him and the nearby Quintana with kerosene. A soldier then lit a match and set the two teenagers on fire. Each time the teenagers attempted to put out the flames the soldiers knocked them back to the ground.

After the teenagers lost consciousness, the soldiers wrapped their smoldering bodies in dirty blankets and drove them to the outskirts of town where they were dumped into an irrigation ditch and left for dead. Some hours later, Rojas miraculously managed to regain consciousness and helped Quintana out of the ditch. The two teenagers were horribly burned with third degree burns over 70% of their bodies. Although some workers soon found them and brought them to a hospital, within four days Rojas was dead. Carmen Gloria Quintana (a Chilean citizen) survived, but was horribly and permanently disfigured.[72]

---

72. After the military regime of Pinochet was forced from power in 1990, at least a small measure of justice for the victims was achieved in the Chilean courts. In 1993, Fernández Dittus was sentenced to 600 days in prison for his responsibility in the burnings. In 2000, a court ordered the

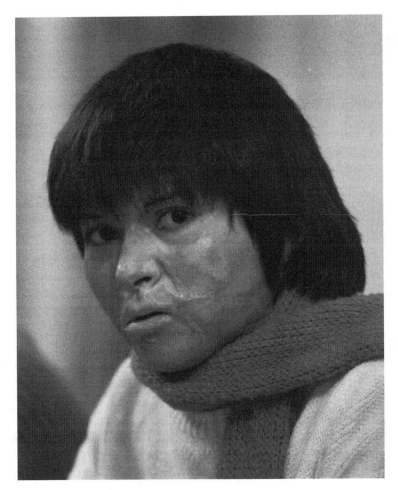

Wikipedia Commons, Photographs by Rob Croes

Please view these very brief video clips:
http://www.youtube.com/watch?v=VAL-J4fm76o
http://www.youtube.com/watch?v=r2ZcXVytZYo&NR=1

**1. Could Quintana and the Estate of Rojas successfully sue Lieutenant Fernandez Dittus, assuming he now resides in Miami Beach, Florida, in the United States Courts utilizing a claim that their international human rights were violated?**

**2. Could Rojas and Quintana sue the Republic of Chile or the estate of former head of state, Augusto Pinochet, for involvement in these violations of international human rights?**

---

government to pay Quintana 251.7 million pesos (about U$500,000) in compensatory damages. *See* Handbook of Reparations.

b. Statutory Resources

i. Alien Torts Claim Statute, 28 U.S.C. § 1350 (judiciary act of 1789)

The district courts shall have original jurisdiction of any civil action by an alien for a tort only, committed in violation of the law of nations or a treaty of the United States.

ii. Torture Victim Protection Act of 1991, 28 U.S.C. § 1350

**Section 1. Short Title.**

This Act may be cited as the 'Torture Victim Protection Act of 1991.'

**Sec. 2. Establishment of civil action.**

**(a) Liability.** — An individual who, under actual or apparent authority, or color of law, of any foreign nation —

**(1)** subjects an individual to torture shall, in a civil action, be liable for damages to that individual; or

**(2)** subjects an individual to extrajudicial killing shall, in a civil action, be liable for damages to the individual's legal representative, or to any person who may be a claimant in an action for wrongful death.

**(b) Exhaustion of remedies.** — A court shall decline to hear a claim under this section if the claimant has not exhausted adequate and available remedies in the place in which the conduct giving rise to the claim occurred.

**(c) Statute of limitations.** — No action shall be maintained under this section unless it is commenced within 10 years after the cause of action arose.

**Sec. 3. Definitions.**

**(a) Extrajudicial killing.** — For the purposes of this Act, the term 'extrajudicial killing' means a deliberated killing not authorized by a previous judgment pronounced by a regularly constituted court affording all the judicial guarantees which are recognized as indispensable by civilized peoples. Such term, however, does not include any such killing that, under international law, is lawfully carried out under the authority of a foreign nation.

**(b) Torture.** — For the purposes of this Act —

**(1)** the term 'torture' means any act, directed against an individual in the offender's custody or physical control, by which severe pain or suffering (other than pain or suffering arising only from or inherent in, or incidental to, lawful sanctions), whether physical or mental, is intentionally inflicted on that individual for such purposes as obtaining from that individual or a third person information or a confession, punishing that individual for an act that individual or a third person has committed or is suspected of having committed, intimidating or coercing that individual or a third person, or for any reason based on discrimination of any kind; and

**(2)** mental pain or suffering refers to prolonged mental harm caused by or resulting from —

**(A)** the intentional infliction or threatened infliction of severe physical pain or suffering;

**(B)** the administration or application, or threatened administration or application, of mind altering substances or other procedures calculated to disrupt profoundly the senses or the personality;

**(C)** the threat of imminent death; or

**(D)** the threat that another individual will imminently be subjected to death, severe physical pain or suffering, or the administration or application of mind altering substances or other procedures calculated to disrupt profoundly the senses or personality.

iii. Foreign Sovereign Immunity Act, 28 U.S.C.A. 1601, et seq

### § 1604. Immunity of a foreign state from jurisdiction

Subject to existing international agreements to which the United States is a party at the time of enactment of this Act a foreign state shall be immune from the jurisdiction of the courts of the United States and of the States except as provided in sections 1605 to 1607 of this chapter.

### § 1605. General exceptions to the jurisdictional immunity of a foreign state

(a) A foreign state shall not be immune from the jurisdiction of courts of the United States or of the States in any case —

(1) in which the foreign state has waived its immunity either explicitly or by implication, notwithstanding any withdrawal of the waiver which the foreign state may purport to effect except in accordance with the terms of the waiver;

(2) in which the action is based upon a commercial activity carried on in the United States by the foreign state; or upon an act performed in the United States in connection with a commercial activity of the foreign state elsewhere; or upon an act outside the territory of the United States in connection with a commercial activity of the foreign state elsewhere and that act causes a direct effect in the United States;

(3) ***;

(4) ***;

(5) not otherwise encompassed in paragraph (2) above, in which money damages are sought against a foreign state for personal injury or death, or damage to or loss of property, occurring in the United States and caused by the tortious act or omission of that foreign state or of any official or employee of that foreign state while acting within the scope of his office or employment; ***

(6) \*\*\*;

(7)  not otherwise covered by paragraph (2), in which money damages are sought against a foreign state for personal injury or death that was caused by an act of torture, extrajudicial killing, aircraft sabotage, hostage taking, or the provision of material support or resources (as defined in section 2339A of title 18) for such an act if such act or provision of material support is engaged in by an official, employee, or agent of such foreign state while acting within the scope of his or her office, employment, or agency, except that the court shall decline to hear a claim under this paragraph —

(A)  if the foreign state was not designated as a state sponsor of terrorism under section 6(j) of the Export Administration Act of 1979 (50 U.S.C. App. 2405(j)) or section 620A of the Foreign Assistance Act of 1961 (22 U.S.C. 2371) at the time the act occurred, unless later so designated as a result of such act . . .; and

(B)  even if the foreign state is or was so designated, if —

(i)  the act occurred in the foreign state against which the claim has been brought and the claimant has not afforded the foreign state a reasonable opportunity to arbitrate the claim in accordance with accepted international rules of arbitration; or

(ii)  neither the claimant nor the victim was a national of the United States (as that term is defined in section 101(a)(22) of the Immigration and Nationality Act) when the act upon which the claim is based occurred.

### c. Case Law: Suits against Foreign Government Actors for Violations of Human Rights

In 1980, the Second Circuit Court of Appeals ushered in a new era of human rights enforcement. At the urging of lawyers from the Center for Constitutional Rights, the court endorsed a then novel claim that an alien victim of human rights violations that occurred overseas could sue their tormentor for civil damages in federal court pursuant to a little known jurisdictional statute, 28 U.S.C.§ 1350 — now known as the Alien Tort Statute or ATS. Based on this precedent, and on the later enacted TVPA, literally hundreds of victims have since sought redress for overseas human rights violations before the U.S. federal courts. Recent Supreme Court decisions have, however, cast some doubt on the continuing viability of such "foreign violation" litigation. The cases presented below trace its evolution, critical developments and current status.

### i. Filartiga v. Pena-Irala, 630 F.2d 876 (2nd Cir. 1980)

IRVING R. KAUFMAN, Circuit Judge:

Upon ratification of the Constitution, the thirteen former colonies were fused into a single nation, one which, in its relations with foreign states, is bound both to observe and construe the accepted norms of international law, formerly known as the law of nations. \*\*\*

Implementing the constitutional mandate for national control over foreign relations, the First Congress established original district court jurisdiction over "all causes where an alien sues for a tort only (committed) in violation of the law of nations." Judiciary Act of 1789, ch. 20, s 9(b), 1 Stat. 73, 77 (1789), codified at 28 U.S.C. s 1350. Construing this rarely-invoked provision, we hold that deliberate torture perpetrated under color of official authority violates universally accepted norms of the international law of human rights, regardless of the nationality of the parties. Thus, whenever an alleged torturer is found and served with process by an alien within our borders, s 1350 provides federal jurisdiction. Accordingly, we reverse the judgment of the district court dismissing the complaint for want of federal jurisdiction.

I

The appellants, plaintiffs below, are citizens of the Republic of Paraguay. Dr. Joel Filartiga, a physician, describes himself as a longstanding opponent of the government of President Alfredo Stroessner, which has held power in Paraguay since 1954. His daughter, Dolly Filartiga, arrived in the United States in 1978 under a visitor's visa, and has since applied for permanent political asylum. The Filartigas brought this action in the Eastern District of New York against Americo Norberto Pena-Irala (Pena), also a citizen of Paraguay, for wrongfully causing the death of Dr. Filartiga's seventeen-year old son, Joelito. Because the district court dismissed the action for want of subject matter jurisdiction, we must accept as true the allegations contained in the Filartigas' complaint and affidavits for purposes of this appeal.

The appellants contend that on March 29, 1976, Joelito Filartiga was kidnapped and tortured to death by Pena, who was then Inspector General of Police in Asuncion, Paraguay. Later that day, the police brought Dolly Filartiga to Pena's home where she was confronted with the body of her brother, which evidenced marks of severe torture. As she fled, horrified, from the house, Pena followed after her shouting, "Here you have what you have been looking for so long and what you deserve. Now shut up." The Filartigas claim that Joelito was tortured and killed in retaliation for his father's political activities and beliefs.

Shortly thereafter, Dr. Filartiga commenced a criminal action in the Paraguayan courts against Pena and the police for the murder of his son. As a result, Dr. Filartiga's attorney was arrested and brought to police headquarters where, shackled to a wall, Pena threatened him with death. This attorney, it is alleged, has since been disbarred without just cause.

During the course of the Paraguayan criminal proceeding, which is apparently still pending after four years, another man, Hugo Duarte, confessed to the murder. Duarte, who was a member of the Pena household, FN1 claimed that he had discovered his wife and Joelito in flagrante delicto, and that the crime was one of passion. The Filartigas have submitted a photograph of

Joelito's corpse showing injuries they believe refute this claim. Dolly Filartiga, moreover, has stated that she will offer evidence of three independent autopsies demonstrating that her brother's death "was the result of professional methods of torture." Despite his confession, Duarte, we are told, has never been convicted or sentenced in connection with the crime.

> FN1. Duarte is the son of Pena's companion, Juana Bautista Fernandez Villalba, who later accompanied Pena to the United States.

In July of 1978, Pena sold his house in Paraguay and entered the United States under a visitor's visa. He was accompanied by Juana Bautista Fernandez Villalba, who had lived with him in Paraguay. The couple remained in the United States beyond the term of their visas, and were living in Brooklyn, New York, when Dolly Filartiga, who was then living in Washington, D. C., learned of their presence. Acting on information provided by Dolly the Immigration and Naturalization Service arrested Pena and his companion, both of whom were subsequently ordered deported on April 5, 1979 following a hearing. They had then resided in the United States for more than nine months.

Almost immediately, Dolly caused Pena to be served with a summons and civil complaint at the Brooklyn Navy Yard, where he was being held pending deportation. The complaint alleged that Pena had wrongfully caused Joelito's death by torture and sought compensatory and punitive damages of $10,000,000. The Filartigas also sought to enjoin Pena's deportation to ensure his availability for testimony at trial. The cause of action is stated as arising under "wrongful death statutes; the U. N. Charter; the Universal Declaration on Human Rights; the U. N. Declaration Against Torture; the American Declaration of the Rights and Duties of Man; and other pertinent declarations, documents and practices constituting the customary international law of human rights and the law of nations," as well as 28 U.S.C. s 1350, Article II, sec. 2 and the Supremacy Clause of the U. S. Constitution. Jurisdiction is claimed under the general federal question provision, 28 U.S.C. s 1331 and, principally on this appeal, under the Alien Tort Statute, 28 U.S.C. s 1350.

***

Judge Nickerson stayed the order of deportation, and Pena immediately moved to dismiss the complaint on the grounds that subject matter jurisdiction was absent and for forum non conveniens. On the jurisdictional issue, there has been no suggestion that Pena claims diplomatic immunity from suit. The Filartigas submitted the affidavits of a number of distinguished international legal scholars, who stated unanimously that the law of nations prohibits absolutely the use of torture as alleged in the complaint. Pena, in support of his motion to dismiss on the ground of forum non conveniens, submitted the affidavit of his Paraguayan counsel, Jose Emilio

Gorostiaga, who averred that Paraguayan law provides a full and adequate civil remedy for the wrong alleged. Dr. Filartiga has not commenced such an action, however, believing that further resort to the courts of his own country would be futile.

***

Judge Nickerson heard argument on the motion to dismiss on May 14, 1979, and on May 15 dismissed the complaint on jurisdictional grounds.

***

The district court continued the stay of deportation for forty-eight hours while appellants applied for further stays. These applications were denied by a panel of this Court on May 22, 1979, and by the Supreme Court two days later. Shortly thereafter, Pena and his companion returned to Paraguay.

II

Appellants rest their principal argument in support of federal jurisdiction upon the Alien Tort Statute, 28 U.S.C. s 1350, which provides: "The district courts shall have original jurisdiction of any civil action by an alien for a tort only, committed in violation of the law of nations or a treaty of the United States." Since appellants do not contend that their action arises directly under a treaty of the United States, a threshold question on the jurisdictional issue is whether the conduct alleged violates the law of nations. In light of the universal condemnation of torture in numerous international agreements, and the renunciation of torture as an instrument of official policy by virtually all of the nations of the world (in principle if not in practice), we find that an act of torture committed by a state official against one held in detention violates established norms of the international law of human rights, and hence the law of nations.

The Supreme Court has enumerated the appropriate sources of international law. The law of nations "may be ascertained by consulting the works of jurists, writing professedly on public law; or by the general usage and practice of nations; or by judicial decisions recognizing and enforcing that law." . . . . The Paquete Habana, 175 U.S. 677, 20 S.Ct. 290, 44 L.Ed. 320 (1900), ***

Habana is particularly instructive for present purposes, for it held that the traditional prohibition against seizure of an enemy's coastal fishing vessels during wartime, a standard that began as one of comity only, had ripened over the preceding century into "a settled rule of international law" by "the general assent of civilized nations." Id. at 694, 20 S.Ct. at 297; accord, id. at 686, 20 S.Ct. at 297. Thus it is clear that courts must interpret international law not as it was in 1789, but as it has evolved and exists among the nations of the world today. See Ware v. Hylton, 3 U.S. (3 Dall.) 198, 1 L.Ed. 568 (1796) (distinguishing between "ancient" and "modern" law of nations).

***

... to paraphrase that Court's statement, id. at 428, 84 S.Ct. at 940, there are few, if any, issues in international law today on which opinion seems to be so united as the limitations on a state's power to torture persons held in its custody.

\*\*\*

Turning to the act of torture, we have little difficulty discerning its universal renunciation in the modern usage and practice of nations. Smith, supra, 18 U.S. (5 Wheat.) at 160–61, 5 L.Ed. 57. The international consensus surrounding torture has found expression in numerous international treaties and accords.

\*\*\*

There now exists an international consensus that recognizes basic human rights and obligations owed by all governments to their citizens . . . . There is no doubt that these rights are often violated; but virtually all governments acknowledge their validity. . . . We have been directed to no assertion by any contemporary state of a right to torture its own or another nation's citizens.

\*\*\*

Having examined the sources from which customary international law is derived the usage of nations, judicial opinions and the works of jurists we conclude that official torture is now prohibited by the law of nations. The prohibition is clear and unambiguous, and admits of no distinction between treatment of aliens and citizens. . . . We therefore turn to the question whether the other requirements for jurisdiction are met.

\*\*\*

Appellee submits that even if the tort alleged is a violation of modern international law, federal jurisdiction may not be exercised consistent with the dictates of Article III of the Constitution. The claim is without merit. Common law courts of general jurisdiction regularly adjudicate transitory tort claims between individuals over whom they exercise personal jurisdiction, wherever the tort occurred. \*\*\*

It is not extraordinary for a court to adjudicate a tort claim arising outside of its territorial jurisdiction. A state or nation has a legitimate interest in the orderly resolution of disputes among those within its borders, and where the lex loci delicti commissi is applied, it is an expression of comity to give effect to the laws of the state where the wrong occurred. . . . . . Here, where in personam jurisdiction has been obtained over the defendant, the parties agree that the acts alleged would violate Paraguayan law, and the policies of the forum are consistent with the foreign law, FN 18 state court jurisdiction would be proper. Indeed, appellees conceded as much at oral argument.

FN18. Conduct of the type alleged here would be actionable under 42 U.S.C. s 1983 or, undoubtedly, the Constitution, if performed by a government official.

*\*\**

The Filartigas urge that 28 U.S.C. s 1350 be treated as an exercise of Congress's power to define offenses against the law of nations. While such a reading is possible, see Lincoln Mills v. Textile Workers, 353 U.S. 488, 77 S.Ct. 912, 1 L.Ed.2d 972 (1957) (jurisdictional statute authorizes judicial explication of federal common law), we believe it is sufficient here to construe the Alien Tort Statute, not as granting new rights to aliens, but simply as opening the federal courts for adjudication of the rights already recognized by international law. \*\*\*

> . . . FN22. We recognize that our reasoning might also sustain jurisdiction under the general federal question provision, 28 U.S.C. s 1331. We prefer, however, to rest our decision upon the Alien Tort Statute, in light of that provision's close coincidence with the jurisdictional facts presented in this case.

*\*\**

Pena also argues that "(i)f the conduct complained of is alleged to be the act of the Paraguayan government, the suit is barred by the Act of State doctrine." This argument was not advanced below, and is therefore not before us on this appeal. We note in passing, however, that we doubt whether action by a state official in violation of the Constitution and laws of the Republic of Paraguay, and wholly unratified by that nation's government, could properly be characterized as an act of state. . . . . Paraguay's renunciation of torture as a legitimate instrument of state policy, however, does not strip the tort of its character as an international law violation, if it in fact occurred under color of government authority. . . . .

Finally, we have already stated that we do not reach the critical question of forum non conveniens, since it was not considered below.

*\*\**

In the twentieth century the international community has come to recognize the common danger posed by the flagrant disregard of basic human rights and particularly the right to be free of torture. . . . Indeed, for purposes of civil liability, the torturer has become like the pirate and slave trader before him hostis humani generis, an enemy of all mankind. Our holding today, giving effect to a jurisdictional provision enacted by our First Congress, is a small but important step in the fulfillment of the ageless dream to free all people from brutal violence.

Filartiga opened the federal court house door for aliens seeking redress for egregious human rights violations committed by foreign perpetrators so long as personal jurisdiction could be established. Perhaps not surprisingly, a great number of these villains have fled their home countries after regime change, seeking a comfortable safe haven in the United States. Human rights advocates, such as the Center for Justice and Accountability, actively sought out and sued them. By one author's count, there have been "about 173 judicial opinions regarding the ATS" since Filartiga was decided.[73] Although many of the decisions favorable to plaintiffs have come in the form of default judgments and actual collection of damages has been rare, such litigation has both vindicated the victim's rights and made the United States a hostile retirement destination for brutal dictators and their henchmen.

### ii. Enter the TVPA

Although most federal courts across the United States eventually endorsed Filartiga, the D.C. Circuit decided a case in 1984 that raised doubts about the existence of a cause of action for human rights violations based on customary international law.[74] Not long thereafter, Congress responded and reinforced the premises of Filartiga, at least in part, by passing the 1991 TVPA. This statute, the text of which appears above, creates a federal cause of action for victims (American or foreign) of foreign based torture or extrajudicial execution. Because Congress enacted the TVPA with the Filartiga case and the ATS well in mind, courts have consistently allowed plaintiffs to pursue TVPA claims, and customary law claims under the ATS, simultaneously. Observe that TVPA claims are limited, as specified in the statute, to torture and extrajudicial executions while ATS claims may involve any recognized customary law right that meets the criteria recently established by the Supreme Court in *Sosa* (set forth below). Consider the following case which analyzes the important concept of command responsibility under the TVPA.

### iii. TVPA Litigation & Command Responsibility

**Ford v. Garcia, 289 F.3d 1283 (11th Cir. 2002)**

Kravitch, Circuit Judge:

The main issue presented in this appeal, one of first impression in the federal courts, is the allocation of the burden of proof in a civil action involving the command responsibility doctrine brought under the Torture Victim Protection Act. ***

*I. Background*

Three nuns and one layperson (the "churchwomen"), all Americans engaged in missionary and relief work in El Salvador, were abducted, tortured, and murdered in December 1980 by five members of the Salvadoran

---

73. Donald Earl Childress, III, *The Alien Tort Statute, Federalism, and the Next Wave of Transnational Litigation*, 100 Georgetown L.J. 709 (2012) *citing*, Julian G. Ku, *The Curious Case of Corporate Liability Under the Alien Tort Statute: A Flawed System of Judicial Lawmaking*, 51 Va. J. Int'l L. 353, 357 (2011).

74. Tel Oren v. Libyan Arab Republic, 726 F.2d 774 (1984).

National Guard (the "Guardsmen"). Approximately three years later, in response to American pressure to punish the responsible parties, the Guardsmen were convicted of the crimes and sentenced to prison terms. In the period before and after this tragic incident, thousands of civilians in El Salvador were victimized by violence during a civil war in which both communist and colonialist forces competed with the government for control of the country. At the time of the murders and directly before, Defendant General Carlos Eugenio Vides Casanova was Director of the Salvadoran National Guard and Defendant General Jose Guillermo Garcia was El Salvador's Minister of Defense. Both defendants currently reside in Florida.

Subsequent to the murders of the churchwomen, Congress passed the Torture Victim Protection Act of 1991 ("TVPA") . . . The TVPA allows victims of violations of international law, or those victims' representatives, to bring a civil cause of action in federal district court against commanders under the international law doctrine of command responsibility. FN2 This doctrine makes a commander liable for acts of his subordinates, even where the commander did not order those acts, when certain elements are met. Relying on the TVPA, Plaintiffs-Appellants, for and on behalf of the estates of the churchwomen, filed suit against Defendants- Appellees in 1999 seeking to recover damages for the torture and murders. Appellants invoked the doctrine of command responsibility and alleged that the executions at issue were part of a pattern and practice of extrajudicial killings committed by the Salvadoran National Guard under Appellees' command.

***

FN 2. "However, a higher official need not have personally performed or ordered the abuses in order to be held liable. Under international law, responsibility for torture, summary execution, or disappearances extends beyond the person or persons who actually committed those acts anyone with higher authority who authorized, tolerated or knowingly ignored those acts is liable for them." S. Rep. No. 102-249, at 9 (1991).

At trial, Appellants offered evidence of the great number of atrocities committed against civilians at the hands of the Salvadoran military in the months preceding the churchwomen's deaths. The Generals conceded that they were aware of a pattern of human rights abuses in El Salvador during their tenures as Minister of Defense and Director of the National Guard, but argued that they did not have the ability to control their troops during this period. As part of their defense, Appellees called Edwin Corr, U.S. Ambassador to El Salvador from 1985 to 1988, to testify as both a fact and expert witness. After deliberations, the jury returned a verdict for Appellees. Appellants argue on appeal that the jury instructions given at trial contained material misstatements of law ***.

## II. Discussion

### A. The Jury Instructions

Appellants contend that the jury instructions in this case contained errors of law which placed on them the burden of establishing elements that they are not required to prove under either the TVPA or the international law which the TVPA has adopted. The instructions required Appellants to prove by a preponderance of the evidence first that the Guardsmen were under Appellees' "effective command," defined as the legal authority and the practical ability of the Generals to control the guilty troops, and second, that the Generals failed to take all reasonable steps to prevent or repress the murders of the churchwomen. Appellants argue that both of these showings are properly affirmative defenses that the Appellees had the burden of proving at trial. Finally, Appellants contend that the district court's instructions erroneously included proximate cause as a required element before liability could be established under the TVPA and command responsibility doctrine.

### 1. The Command Responsibility Instruction

\*\*\*

The essential elements of liability under the command responsibility doctrine are: (1) the existence of a superior-subordinate relationship between the commander and the perpetrator of the crime; (2) that the commander knew or should have known, owing to the circumstances at the time, that his subordinates had committed, were committing, or planned to commit acts violative of the law of war; and (3) that the commander failed to prevent the commission of the crimes, or failed to punish the subordinates after the commission of the crimes. Although the TVPA does 1289 not explicitly provide for liability of commanders for human rights violations of their troops, legislative history makes clear that Congress intended to adopt the doctrine of command responsibility from international law as part of the Act. Specifically identified in the Senate report is *In re Yamashita*, 327 U.S. 1 (1946), a World War II era case involving the command responsibility doctrine in habeas review of the conviction of a Japanese commander in the Philippines by an American military tribunal.

\*\*\*

Despite Appellants' assertions that the district court's definition of "effective command" misplaced the burden of persuasion, we find no plain error. *In re Yamashita* did not explicitly address the allocation of the burdens on the elements of command responsibility.

\*\*\*

The recently constituted international tribunals of Rwanda and the former Yugoslavia have applied the doctrine of command responsibility since *In re Yamashita*, and therefore their cases provide insight into how the doctrine should be applied in TVPA cases. Recent international cases consistently have found that effective control of a commander over his troops is required before liability will be imposed under the command responsibility doctrine. The consensus is that "[t]he concept of effective *control* over a subordinate in the sense of a material ability to prevent or punish criminal conduct, however that control is exercised is the threshold to be reached in establishing a superior- subordinate relationship. . . . " *Prosecutor v. Delalic* (Appeals Chamber ICTY, Feb. 20, 2001) ¶ 256; *accord id.* at ¶ 266; *Prosecutor v. Aleksovski,* Judgment (Appeals Chamber ICTY, March 24, 2000) ¶ 76; *Prosecutor v. Blaskic,* Judgment (Trial Chamber ICTY, March 3, 2000) ¶¶ 295, 302 ("Proof is required that the superior has effective control over the persons committing the violations of international humanitarian law in question, that is, has the material ability to prevent the crimes and to punish the perpetrators thereof.");

***

In the end, then, there is ample authority contrary to Appellants' argument that Defendants bore the burden of persuasion on effective control. Decisions by the Yugoslav and Rwanda tribunals seem to allocate the burden of persuasion to plaintiffs on the issue of defendants' effective control.

***

AFFIRMED.

Although vindication in most foreign violation claims has been largely symbolic rather than leading to monetary compensation, there have been some exceptions. Consider the following news report regarding a successful "foreign violation" litigation relying on the TVPA.

SAN FRANCISCO CHRONICLE

*Florida jury convicts 2 Salvadoran generals of atrocities $54.6 million awarded to three torture victims*

**By Robert Collier**

Chronicle Staff Writer

**Wednesday, July 24, 2002; Page A — 12**

Reopening a bloody wound from two decades ago, a U.S. federal court in Florida on Tuesday found two retired Salvadoran generals responsible for torture, rape and other atrocities committed during El Salvador's civil war.

The jury in West Palm Beach ordered Carlos Eugenio Vides Casanova and Jose Guillermo Garcia to pay $54.6 million to three torture victims. . . .

Both generals were trained at the U.S. Army's School of the Americas, and both received U.S. Legion of Merit awards from the State Department. They retired to the Miami area in 1989.

... The jury found that the generals had known their troops were torturing and murdering civilians but failed to try to stop it or punish those responsible. ...

"If you're a former torturer from another country, you might want to leave the United States before somebody serves you with a lawsuit." Sandra Coliver, executive director of the Center for Justice and Accountability. ...

E-mail Robert Collier at rcollier@sfchronicle.com.

©2002 San Francisco Chronicle.

Are there other human rights abusers, perhaps lurking around in your neighborhood?

South Florida Haven for the Craven, <u>Latin American dictators love South Florida</u>, Miami New Times, September 16, 2010, by Tim Elfrink

**Forget Epcot. Screw the Wizarding World of Harry Potter.** Put down that glossy guidebook to Orlando hotel bargains before we sic our guerrillas on your pastel-pants-wearing ass.

This is South Florida, *muchacho*, the retirement home of army strongmen, torturers, and every other unsavory character from the Southern Hemisphere. We make Casablanca look like a Daffy Duck cartoon.

Why, then, shouldn't we celebrate our heritage as a second home to the worst leaders of Western civilization? (Hey, they're building a freaking library for George W. Bush in Texas.) So here it is: a guidebook to the bastards who have tried to flee international tribunals and angry drug lords by settling in South Florida. Want to see where these guys lived while hiding out in our hood? Yeah, we did too. So we plumbed property records, consulted historians, and dived into overflowing boxes of lawsuits ....

Follow the link above if interested in the *New Times* listing of the misdeeds, names and South Florida addresses of some unsavory guests now living among us.

iv. Limitations on ATS Claims: Identifying Causes of Action

**SOSA V. ALVAREZ-MACHAIN, 542 U.S. 692 (2004)**

***

Justice Souter delivered the opinion of the Court.

The two issues are whether respondent Alvarez-Machain's allegation that the Drug Enforcement Administration instigated his abduction from Mexico for criminal trial in the United States supports a claim against the Government under the Federal Tort Claims Act (FTCA or Act), 28 U.S.C.§1346 (b)(1), §§2671-2680, and whether he may recover under the Alien Tort Statute (ATS), 28 U.S.C. §1350. We hold that he is not entitled to a remedy under either statute.

## I

We have considered the underlying facts before, United States v. Alvarez-Machain, 504 U.S. 655, 112 S. Ct. 2188 (1992). In 1985, an agent of the Drug Enforcement Administration (DEA), Enrique Camarena-Salazar, was captured on assignment in Mexico and taken to a house in Guadalajara, where he was tortured over the course of a 2-day interrogation, then murdered. Based in part on eyewitness testimony, DEA officials in the United States came to believe that respondent Humberto Alvarez-Machain (Alvarez), a Mexican physician, was present at the house and acted to prolong the agent's life in order to extend the interrogation and torture. Id. at 657, 112 S. Ct 2188.

In 1990, a federal grand jury indicted Alvarez for the torture and murder of Camarena-Salazar, and the United States District Court for the Central District of California issued a warrant for his arrest . . . . The DEA asked the Mexican Government for help in getting Alvarez into the United States, but when the requests and negotiations proved fruitless, the DEA approved a plan to hire Mexican nationals to seize Alvarez and bring him to the United States for trial. As so planned, a group of Mexicans, including petitioner Jose Francisco Sosa, abducted Alvarez from his house, held him overnight in a motel, and brought him by private plane to El Paso, Texas, where he was arrested by federal officers.

Once in American custody, Alvarez moved to dismiss the indictment on the ground that his seizure was "outrageous governmental conduct," . . . .and violated the extradition treaty between the United States and Mexico. The District Court agreed, the Ninth Circuit affirmed, and we reversed, id., at 670, 112 S. Ct. 2188, holding that the fact of Alvarez's forcible seizure did not affect the jurisdiction of a federal court. The case was tried in 1992, and ended at the close of the Government's case, when the District Court granted Alvarez's motion for a judgment of acquittal.

In 1993, after returning to Mexico, Alvarez began the civil action before us here. He sued Sosa, Mexican citizen and DEA operative Antonio Garate-Bustamante, five unnamed Mexican civilians, the United States, and four DEA agents. . . . So far as it matters here, Alvarez sought damages from the United States under the FTCA, alleging false arrest, and from Sosa under the ATS, for a violation of the law of nations. The former statute authorizes suit "for . . . personal injury . . . caused by the negligent or wrongful act or omission of any employee of the Government while acting within the scope of his office or employment." 28 U.S.C. § 1346 (b)(1). The latter provides in its entirety that "[t]he district courts shall have original jurisdiction of any civil action by an alien for a tort only, committed in violation of the law of nations or a treaty of the United States." §1350.

The District Court granted the Government's motion to dismiss the FTCA claim, but awarded summary judgment and $25,000 in damages to Alvarez on the ATS claim. A three-judge panel of the Ninth Circuit then affirmed the ATS judgment, but reversed the dismissal of the FTCA claim. 266 F. 3d 1045 (2001).

A divided en banc court came to the same conclusion. 331 F. 3d at 641. As for the ATS claim, the court called on its own precedent, "that [the ATS] not only provides federal courts with subject matter jurisdiction, but also creates a cause of action for an alleged violation of the law of nations." ***

We granted certiorari in these companion cases to clarify the scope of both the FTCA and the ATS. . . . We now reverse in each.

## II

[Editor's Note: The FTCA claim was dismissed based on an explicit statutory exception to waiver of sovereign immunity for claims "arising in a foreign country," 28 U.S.C.§ 2680(k).]

***

## III

Alvarez has also brought an action under the ATS against petitioner, Sosa, who argues (as does the United States supporting him) that there is no relief under the ATS because the statute does no more than vest federal courts with jurisdiction, neither creating nor authorizing the courts to recognize any particular right of action without further congressional action. Although we agree the statute is in terms only jurisdictional, we think that at the time of enactment the jurisdiction enabled federal courts to hear claims in a very limited category defined by the law of nations and recognized at common law. We do not believe, however, that the limited, implicit sanction to entertain the handful of international law *cum* common law claims understood in 1789 should be taken as authority to recognize the right of action asserted by Alvarez here.

## A

***

The parties and *amici* here advance radically different historical interpretations of this terse provision. Alvarez says that the ATS was intended not simply as a jurisdictional grant, but as authority for the creation of a new cause of action for torts in violation of international law. We think that reading is implausible. As enacted in 1789, the ATS gave the district courts "cognizance" of certain causes of action, and the term bespoke a grant of jurisdiction, not power to mold substantive law. *** In sum, we think the statute was intended as jurisdictional in the sense of addressing the power of the courts to entertain cases concerned with a certain subject.

But holding the ATS jurisdictional raises a new question, this one about the interaction between the ATS at the time of its enactment and the ambient law of the era. Sosa would have it that the ATS was stillborn because there could be no claim for relief without a further statute expressly authorizing adoption of causes of action. *Amici* professors of federal jurisdiction and legal history take a different tack, that federal courts could entertain claims once the jurisdictional grant was on the books, because torts in violation of the law of nations would have been recognized within the common law of the time. Brief for Vikram Amar et al. as *Amici Curiae*. We think history and practice give the edge to this latter position.

1

\*\*\*

There was, finally, a sphere in which these rules binding individuals for the benefit of other individuals overlapped with the norms of state relationships. Blackstone referred to it when he mentioned three specific offenses against the law of nations addressed by the criminal law of England: violation of safe conducts, infringement of the rights of ambassadors, and piracy. 4 Commentaries 68. An assault against an ambassador, for example, impinged upon the sovereignty of the foreign nation and if not adequately redressed could rise to an issue of war. See Vattel 463–464. It was this narrow set of violations of the law of nations, admitting of a judicial remedy and at the same time threatening serious consequences in international affairs, that was probably on minds of the men who drafted the ATS with its reference to tort.

\*\*\*

The second inference to be drawn from the history is that Congress intended the ATS to furnish jurisdiction for a relatively modest set of actions alleging violations of the law of nations.

\*\*\*

The sparse contemporaneous cases and legal materials referring to the ATS tend to confirm both inferences, that some, but few, torts in violation of the law of nations were understood to be within the common law.

\*\*\*

In sum, although the ATS is a jurisdictional statute creating no new causes of action, the reasonable inference from the historical materials is that the statute was intended to have practical effect the moment it became law. The jurisdictional grant is best read as having been enacted on the understanding that the common law would provide a cause of action for the modest number of international law violations with a potential for personal liability at the time.

IV

\*\*\*

We assume, too, that no development in the two centuries from the enactment of §1350 to the birth of the modern line of cases beginning with Filartiga v. Pena-Irala, 630 F.2d 876 (2D Cir. 1980), has categorically precluded federal courts from recognizing a claim under the law of nations as an element of common law; Congress has not in any relevant way amended §1350 or limited civil common law power by another statute. Still, there are good reasons for a restrained conception of the discretion a federal court should exercise in considering a new cause of action of this kind. Accordingly, we think courts should require any claim based on the present-day law of nations to rest on a norm of international character accepted by the civilized world and defined with a specificity comparable to the features of the 18th-century paradigms we have recognized. This requirement is fatal to Alvarez's claim.

***

Second, along with, and in part driven by, that conceptual development in understanding common law has come an equally significant rethinking of the role of the federal courts in making it. Erie R. Co. v. Tompkins, 304 U.S. 64 (1938), was the watershed in which we denied the existence of any federal "general" common law ... And although we have even assumed competence to make judicial rules of decision of particular importance to foreign relations, such as the act of state doctrine, see Banco Nacional de Cuba v. Sabbatino, 376 U.S. 398 (1964), the general practice has been to look for legislative guidance before exercising innovative authority over substantive law. It would be remarkable to take a more aggressive role in exercising a jurisdiction that remained largely in shadow for much of the prior two centuries.

Third, this Court has recently and repeatedly said that a decision to create a private right of action is one better left to legislative judgment in the great majority of cases.

***

Fourth, the subject of those collateral consequences is itself a reason for a high bar to new private causes of action for violating international law, for the potential implications for the foreign relations of the United States of recognizing such causes should make courts particularly wary of impinging on the discretion of the Legislative and Executive Branches in managing foreign affairs. . . . Since many attempts by federal courts to craft remedies for the violation of new norms of international law would raise risks of adverse foreign policy consequences, they should be undertaken, if at all, with great caution.

***

Congress as a body has done nothing to promote such suits. Several times, indeed, the Senate has expressly declined to give the federal courts the task of interpreting and applying international human rights law, as when its ratification of the International Covenant on Civil and Political Rights declared that the substantive provisions of the document were not self-executing. 138 Cong. Rec. 8071 (1992).

These reasons argue for great caution in adapting the law of nations to private rights.

***

We must still, however, derive a standard or set of standards for assessing the particular claim Alvarez raises, and for this case it suffices to look to the historical antecedents. Whatever the ultimate criteria for accepting a cause of action subject to jurisdiction under §1350, we are persuaded that federal courts should not recognize private claims under federal common law for violations of any international law norm with less definite content and acceptance among civilized nations than the historical paradigms familiar when §1350 was enacted. See, *e.g., United States v. Smith, 5 Wheat. 153, 163–180, n.a, 5 L. Ed. 57 (1820)* (illustrating the specificity with which the law of nations defined piracy). This limit upon judicial recognition is generally consistent with the reasoning of many of the courts and judges who faced the issue before it reached this Court. See Filartiga, supra, at 890 ("[F]or purposes of civil liability, the torturer has become—like the pirate and slave trader before him—*hostis humani generis,* an enemy of all mankind"); Tel-Oren, supra, at 781 (Edwards, J., concurring) (suggesting that the "limits of section 1350' reach" be defined by "a handful of heinous actions—each of which violates definable, universal and obligatory norms"); see also In re Estate of Marcos Human Rights Litigation, 25 F.3d 1467 (9th Cir. 1994)("Actionable violations of international law must be of a norm that is specific, universal, and obligatory"). And the determination whether a norm is sufficiently definite to support a cause of action should (and, indeed, inevitably must) involve an element of judgment about the practical consequences of making that cause available to litigants in the federal courts. FN 21

> FN 21
>
> This requirement of clear definition is not meant to be the only principle limiting the availability of relief in the federal courts for violations of customary international law, though it disposes of this case. For example, the European Commission argues as *amicus curiae* that basic principles of international law require that before asserting a claim in a foreign forum, the claimant must have exhausted any remedies available in the domestic legal system, and perhaps in other fora such as international claims tribunals. . . .

Another possible limitation that we need not apply here is a policy of case-specific deference to the political branches. For example, there are now pending in federal district court several class actions seeking damages from various corporations alleged to have participated in, or abetted, the regime of apartheid that formerly controlled South Africa. See In re South

African Apartheid Litigation, 238 F. Supp. 2d 1379 (JPML 2002) (granting a motion to transfer the cases to the Southern District of New York). The Government of South Africa has said that these cases interfere with the policy embodied by its Truth and Reconciliation Commission, which "deliberately avoided a 'victors' justice' approach to the crimes of apartheid and chose instead one based on confession and absolution, informed by the principles of reconciliation, reconstruction, reparation and goodwill." . . . In such cases, there is a strong argument that federal courts should give serious weight to the Executive Branch's view of the case's impact on foreign policy. . . .

Thus, Alvarez's detention claim must be gauged against the current state of international law, looking to those sources we have long, albeit cautiously, recognized.

***

To begin with, Alvarez cites two well-known international agreements that, despite their moral authority, have little utility under the standard set out in this opinion. He says that his abduction by Sosa was an "arbitrary arrest" within the meaning of the Universal Declaration of Human Rights (Declaration), G.A. Res. 217A (III), U.N. Doc. A/810 (1948). And he traces the rule against arbitrary arrest not only to the Declaration, but also to article nine of the International Covenant on Civil and Political Rights (Covenant), Dec. 19, 1996, 999 U.N.T.S. 171, to which the United States is a party, and to various other conventions to which it is not. But the Declaration does not of its own force impose obligations as a matter of international law. *** And, although the Covenant does bind the United States as a matter of international law, the United States ratified the Covenant on the express understanding that it was not self-executing and so did not itself create obligations enforceable in the federal courts. See *supra,* at 2763. Accordingly, Alvarez cannot say that the Declaration and Covenant themselves establish the relevant and applicable rule of international law. He instead attempts to show that prohibition of arbitrary arrest has attained the status of binding customary international law.

***

Any credible invocation of a principle against arbitrary detention that the civilized world accepts as binding customary international law requires a factual basis beyond relatively brief detention in excess of positive authority.

***

Whatever may be said for the broad principle Alvarez advances, in the present, imperfect world, it expresses an aspiration that exceeds any binding customary rule having the specificity we require. Creating a private cause of action to further that aspiration would go beyond any residual common law discretion we think it appropriate to exercise. It is enough to hold that a single illegal detention of less than a day, followed by the transfer of custody to lawful authorities and a prompt arraignment, violates no norm of customary international law so well defined as to support the creation of a federal remedy.

\*\*\*

The judgment of the Court of Appeals is *Reversed.*

Justice Scalia, with whom THE CHIEF JUSTICE and Justice THOMAS join, concurring in part and concurring in the judgment.

There is not much that I would add to the Court's detailed opinion, and only one thing that I would subtract: its reservation of a discretionary power in the Federal Judiciary to create causes of action for the enforcement of international-law-based norms. Accordingly, I join Parts I, II, and III of the Court's opinion in these consolidated cases. Although I agree with much in Part IV, I cannot join it because the judicial lawmaking role it invites would commit the Federal Judiciary to a task it is neither authorized nor suited to perform.

\*\*\*

We Americans have a method for making the laws that are over us. We elect representatives to two Houses of Congress, each of which must enact the new law and present it for the approval of a President, whom we also elect. For over two decades now, unelected federal judges have been usurping this lawmaking power by converting what they regard as norms of international law into American law. Today's opinion approves that process in principle, though urging the lower courts to be more restrained.

This Court seems incapable of admitting that some matters — *any* matters — are none of its business. . . . In today's latest victory for its Never Say Never Jurisprudence, the Court ignores its own conclusion that the ATS provides only jurisdiction, wags a finger at the lower courts for going too far, and then — repeating the same formula the ambitious lower courts *themselves* have used — invites them to try again.

\*\*\*

## 3. The Corporate Alien Tort: ATS Litigation against Multinational Corporations

### a. Background & Overview

One of the most controversial applications of the ATS involves the potential liability of multinational corporations for their alleged complicity in human rights violations. One of the earliest cases was *Doe v. Unocal Corporation*. In *Unocal*, plaintiffs alleged that Unocal knew of, encouraged and provided material support for the Burmese military's enslavement, torture, rape and extra-judicial execution of villagers in connection with construction of a jointly owned natural gas pipeline in Burma. In 2002, the Ninth Circuit held that plaintiffs had sufficiently alleged violations of the law of nations under ATS and that issues of fact existed as to whether Unocal aided and abetted Myanmar military's perpetration of forced labor, murder, and rape (but not torture). While scheduled for en banc review, the case was settled for $500 million dollars just after the Supreme Court issued its opinion in *Sosa*. The Ninth Circuit then vacated the prior lower court and appellate opinions.

A significant number of ATS lawsuits against multinational corporations have been filed since *Unocal*. One law firm reported to its clients that:

> "That wave continues to crest in cases against corporations. Plaintiffs have invoked ATCA in more than 100 cases against corporate defendants. Since 2000, more than 60 such cases have been filed under ATCA, and plaintiffs firms and nongovernmental organizations even specialize in these actions. Plaintiffs now are relying on traditional causes of action — securities fraud, breach of fiduciary duty, assault and false advertising — in bringing their human rights claims. Targeted businesses span a spectrum of industries, from transportation to manufacturing to industrial chemicals, although extractive and financial companies face suits most frequently. And the potential liability in these emotionally charged cases, often involving graphic allegations of murder, torture, environmental devastation, and Dickensian working conditions, is substantial."

From: Five Tips to <u>Avoid the Human Rights Litigation Trap</u>

As these cases have progressed through the courts they have raised a variety of important legal issues, including application of *Sosa* to determine the contours of actionable violations. For example, in <u>*Bowoto v. Chevron Corporation*</u> (9th Circuit, Sept. 10, 2010) the Ninth Circuit approved a jury verdict in favor of Chevron relating to incidents resulting in the death of protesters in the Nigerian oil fields. Among other things, the Court held that corporations are potentially liable for torture under ATS but that they are not "individuals" subject to suit under the TVPA (a view later endorsed by the Supreme Court). In <u>*Aldana v Del Monte*</u>, 416 F.3d 1242 (11th Cir. 2005), in which plaintiffs alleged human rights violations by a Del Monte subsidiary during labor dispute in Guatemala, the 11th Circuit upheld claims of torture but dismissed causes of action for cruel & degrading treatment and arbitrary detention as not cognizable under the ATS.

The Second Circuit took a relatively expansive approach to the cause of action question in <u>*Abdullahi v. Pfizer*</u>, 562 F.3d 163 (2d Cir. 2009) holding that claims against Pfizer alleging non-consensual medical experimentation on children in Nigeria could go forward under the ATS. Finally, in <u>*Romero v. Drummond*</u>, the plaintiffs alleged that Drummond collaborated with paramilitaries who carried out the murder of three union leaders. The judge allowed the case to go to the jury on a theory that the defendants aided and abetted an actionable "war crime" under the ATS. After a three-week trial, the jury found for the defendants. On appeal, the Eleventh Circuit held that the ATS permits causes of action for extra-judicial killings based on a theory of corporate aiding and abetting.

According to one report, there have been about seventeen plaintiff favorable settlements among the more than 150 cases filed under the ATS and TVPA against corporate defendants.[75] Along with these successes, there have been at least two adverse jury decisions against plaintiffs seeking to hold multinational corporations responsible for human rights violations.[76]

Claims based on the TVPA against corporate defendants, however, have now been foreclosed by the Supreme Court in _Mohamad v. Palestinian Authority_, 102 S.Ct. 1702 (2012). In _Mohamad_, the plaintiffs alleged that the Palestinian Authority and Palestinian Liberation Organization, among others, tortured and killed Azzam Rahim, a naturalized American citizen, during a trip to the West Bank. Resolving a split in the Circuits, the Supreme Court held that "the text of the statute persuades us that the Act authorizes liability solely against natural persons."

Since nearly all human rights claims against corporations allege only indirect involvement in the relevant human rights violations, one of the most critical legal issues in these cases involves liability for complicity. In <u>Khulumani v. Barclay National Bank, Ltd., 504 F. 3d 252 (2d Cir. 2007) (per curiam)</u>, the Second Circuit held that the ATS conferred jurisdiction over numerous multinational corporations that allegedly collaborated with the former government of South Africa in maintaining apartheid in violation of customary international law. _Id._ at 260. This decision, however, lacked a majority position regarding the standards for finding actionable complicity. The decision's rationale was recently confirmed by the Second Circuit. In <u>Presbyterian Church of Sudan v. Talisman Energy</u>, 582 F. 3d 244 (2009), the court sets out a standard for determining actionable complicity that requires more than mere knowledge or acquiescence:

> "Plaintiffs-Appellants are Sudanese who allege that they are victims of human rights abuses committed by the Government of the Sudan in Khartoum ('the Government') and that Talisman Energy, Inc. ('Talisman'), a Canadian corporation, aided and abetted or conspired with the Government to advance those abuses that facilitated the development of Sudanese oil concessions by Talisman affiliates. ***
>
> We hold that under the principles articulated by the United States Supreme Court in Sosa v. Alvarez-Machain, 542 U.S. 692 (2004), the standard for imposing accessorial liability under the ATS must be drawn from international law; and that under international law, a claimant must show that the defendant provided substantial assistance with the purpose of facilitating

---

75. _See also_ Drimmer, Lamoree, _Think Globally, Sue Locally: Trends and Out-of-Court Tactics in Transitional Tort Actions,_ 29 Berk. J. Int'l L. 456 (2011).

76. _See_ Bowoto v. Chevron Corp., 621 F.3d 1116 (9th Cir. 2010); Romero v. Drummond Co., 552 F.3d 1303 (11th Cir. 2008).

the alleged offenses. Applying that standard, we affirm the district court's grant of summary judgment in favor of Talisman, because plaintiffs presented no evidence that the company acted with the purpose of harming civilians living in southern Sudan."

b. *Kiobel*, Extraterritoriality & ATS Claims: What Remains?

Among the many cases brought against multinational corporations in recent years, one eventually made its way to the United States Supreme Court. The Court's decision in *Kiobel*, set forth below, drastically curtails the scope of cases subject to the ATS based on a presumption against its extraterritorial application. Although the decision specifically involved corporate defendants it has obvious potential application to both corporate and individual foreign defendants. Read the case critically, including the dissent and purposefully vague concurrence of Justice Kennedy, to determine precisely what is left of the ATS and Filartiga style litigation. What questions remain unanswered?

### Kiobel v. Royal Dutch Petroleum, 569 U.S. _____, 133 S. Ct. 1569 (2013)

Chief Justice ROBERTS delivered the opinion of the Court.

Petitioners, a group of Nigerian nationals residing in the United States, filed suit in federal court against certain Dutch, British, and Nigerian corporations. Petitioners sued under the Alien Tort Statute, 28 U.S.C. § 1350, alleging that the corporations aided and abetted the Nigerian Government in committing violations of the law of nations in Nigeria. The question presented is whether and under what circumstances courts may recognize a cause of action under the Alien Tort Statute, for violations of the law of nations occurring within the territory of a sovereign other than the United States.

I

Petitioners were residents of Ogoniland, an area of 250 square miles located in the Niger delta area of Nigeria and populated by roughly half a million people. When the complaint was filed, respondents Royal Dutch Petroleum Company and Shell Transport and Trading Company, p.l.c., were holding companies incorporated in the Netherlands and England, respectively. Their joint subsidiary, respondent Shell Petroleum Development Company of Nigeria, Ltd. (SPDC), was incorporated in Nigeria, and engaged in oil exploration and production in Ogoniland. According to the complaint, after concerned residents of Ogoniland began protesting the environmental effects of SPDC's practices, respondents enlisted the Nigerian Government to violently suppress the burgeoning demonstrations. Throughout the early 1990's, the complaint alleges, Nigerian military and police forces attacked Ogoni villages, beating, raping, killing, and arresting residents and destroying or looting property. Petitioners further allege that respondents aided and abetted these atrocities by, among other things, providing the Nigerian forces with food, transportation, and compensation, as well as by allowing the Nigerian military to use respondents' property as a staging ground for attacks.

Following the alleged atrocities, petitioners moved to the United States where they have been granted political asylum and now reside as legal residents. See Supp. Brief for Petitioners 3, and n. 2. They filed suit in the United States District Court for the Southern District of New York, alleging jurisdiction under the Alien Tort Statute and requesting relief under customary international law. The ATS provides, in full, that "[t]he district courts shall have original jurisdiction of any civil action by an alien for a tort only, committed in violation of the law of nations or a treaty of the United States." 28 U.S.C. § 1350. According to petitioners, respondents violated the law of nations by aiding and abetting the Nigerian Government in committing (1) extrajudicial killings; (2) crimes against humanity; (3) torture and cruel treatment; (4) arbitrary arrest and detention; (5) violations of the rights to life, liberty, security, and association; (6) forced exile; and (7) property destruction. The District Court dismissed the first, fifth, sixth, and seventh claims, reasoning that the facts alleged to support those claims did not give rise to a violation of the law of nations. The court denied respondents' motion to dismiss with respect to the remaining claims, but certified its order for interlocutory appeal pursuant to § 1292(b).

The Second Circuit dismissed the entire complaint, reasoning that the law of nations does not recognize corporate liability. 621 F.3d 111 (2010). We granted certiorari to consider that question. 565 U.S. ____, 132 S.Ct. 472, 181 L.Ed.2d 292 (2011). After oral argument, we directed the parties to file supplemental briefs addressing an additional question: "Whether and under what circumstances the [ATS] allows courts to recognize a cause of action for violations of the law of nations occurring within the territory of a sovereign other than the United States." 565 U.S. ____, 132 S.Ct. 1738, 182 L.Ed.2d 270 (2012). We heard oral argument again and now affirm the judgment below, based on our answer to the second question.

## II

Passed as part of the Judiciary Act of 1789, the ATS was invoked twice in the late 18th century, but then only once more over the next 167 years. *** The statute provides district courts with jurisdiction to hear certain claims, but does not expressly provide any causes of action. We held in *Sosa v. Alvarez–Machain*, 542 U.S. 692, 714, 124 S.Ct. 2739, 159 L.Ed.2d 718 (2004), however, that the First Congress did not intend the provision to be "stillborn." The grant of jurisdiction is instead "best read as having been enacted on the understanding that the common law would provide a cause of action for [a] modest number of international law violations." *Id.,* at 724, 124 S.Ct. 2739. We thus held that federal courts may "recognize private claims [for such violations] under federal common law." *Id.*, at 732, 124 S.Ct. 2739. The Court in *Sosa* rejected the plaintiff's claim in that case for "arbitrary arrest and detention," on the ground that it failed to state a violation of the law of nations with the requisite "definite content and acceptance among civilized nations." *Id.*, at 699, 732, 124 S.Ct. 2739.

The question here is not whether petitioners have stated a proper claim under the ATS, but whether a claim may reach conduct occurring in the territory of a foreign sovereign. Respondents contend that claims under the ATS do not, relying primarily on a canon of statutory interpretation known as the presumption against extraterritorial application. That canon provides that "[w]hen a statute gives no clear indication of an extraterritorial application, it has none," *Morrison v. National Australia Bank Ltd.*, 561 U.S. ____, ____, 130 S.Ct. 2869, 2878, 177 L.Ed.2d 535 (2010), and reflects the "presumption that United States law governs domestically but does not rule the world," *Microsoft Corp. v. AT & T Corp.*, 550 U.S. 437, 454, 127 S.Ct. 1746, 167 L.Ed.2d 737 (2007).

This presumption "serves to protect against unintended clashes between our laws and those of other nations which could result in international discord." *EEOC v. Arabian American Oil Co.*, 499 U.S. 244, 248, 111 S.Ct. 1227, 113 L. Ed.2d 274 (1991) (*Aramco*). As this Court has explained:

"For us to run interference in . . . a delicate field of international relations there must be present the affirmative intention of the Congress clearly expressed. It alone has the facilities necessary to make fairly such an important policy decision where the possibilities of international discord are so evident and retaliative action so certain." *Benz v. Compania Naviera Hidalgo, S.A.*, 353 U.S. 138, 147 [77 S.Ct. 699, 1 L.Ed.2d 709] (1957). The presumption against extraterritorial application helps ensure that the Judiciary does not erroneously adopt an interpretation of U.S. law that carries foreign policy consequences not clearly intended by the political branches.

*** 

Indeed, the danger of unwarranted judicial interference in the conduct of foreign policy is magnified in the context of the ATS, because the question is not what Congress has done but instead what courts may do. This Court in *Sosa* repeatedly stressed the need for judicial caution in considering which claims could be brought under the ATS, in light of foreign policy concerns. *** These concerns, which are implicated in any case arising under the ATS, are all the more pressing when the question is whether a cause of action under the ATS reaches conduct within the territory of another sovereign.

These concerns are not diminished by the fact that *Sosa* limited federal courts to recognizing causes of action only for alleged violations of international law norms that are " 'specific, universal, and obligatory.' " *Id.*, at 732, 124 S.Ct. 2739 (quoting *In re Estate of Marcos, Human Rights Litigation,*

25 F.3d 1467, 1475 (C.A.9 1994)). As demonstrated by Congress's enactment of the Torture Victim Protection Act of 1991, 106 Stat. 73, note following 28 U.S.C. § 1350, identifying such a norm is only the beginning of defining a cause of action. See *id.*, § 3 (providing detailed definitions for extrajudicial killing and torture); *id.*, § 2 (specifying who may be liable, creating a rule of exhaustion, and establishing a statute of limitations). Each of these decisions carries with it significant foreign policy implications.

The principles underlying the presumption against extraterritoriality thus constrain courts exercising their power under the ATS.

### III

Petitioners contend that even if the presumption applies, the text, history, and purposes of the ATS rebut it for causes of action brought under that statute. *** But to rebut the presumption, the ATS would need to evince a "clear indication of extraterritoriality." *Morrison,* 561 U.S., at ____, 130 S.Ct., at 2883. It does not.

To begin, nothing in the text of the statute suggests that Congress intended causes of action recognized under it to have extraterritorial reach. The ATS covers actions by aliens for violations of the law of nations, but that does not imply extraterritorial reach — such violations affecting aliens can occur either within or outside the United States. Nor does the fact that the text reaches *"any* civil action" suggest application to torts committed abroad; it is well established that generic terms like "any" or "every" do not rebut the presumption against extraterritoriality. ***

Petitioners make much of the fact that the ATS provides jurisdiction over civil actions for "torts" in violation of the law of nations. They claim that in using that word, the First Congress "necessarily meant to provide for jurisdiction over extraterritorial transitory torts that could arise on foreign soil." Supp. Brief for Petitioners 18. For support, they cite the common-law doctrine that allowed courts to assume jurisdiction over such "transitory torts," including actions for personal injury, arising abroad.

***

Under the transitory torts doctrine, however, "the only justification for allowing a party to recover when the cause of action arose in another civilized jurisdiction is a well founded belief that it was a cause of action in that place." *** In the end, nothing in the text of the ATS evinces the requisite clear indication of extraterritoriality.

Nor does the historical background against which the ATS was enacted overcome the presumption against application to conduct in the territory of another sovereign. See *Morrison, supra,* at ____, 130 S.Ct., at 2883 (noting that "[a]ssuredly context can be consulted" in determining whether a cause of action applies abroad). We explained in *Sosa* that when Congress passed the ATS, "three principal offenses against the law of nations" had been identified by Blackstone: violation of safe conducts, infringement of the rights of ambassadors, and piracy. 542 U.S., at 723, 724, 124 S.Ct. 2739; see 4 W. Blackstone, Commentaries on the Laws of England 68 (1769). The first two offenses have no necessary extraterritorial application.

\*\*\*

The third example of a violation of the law of nations familiar to the Congress that enacted the ATS was piracy. Piracy typically occurs on the high seas, beyond the territorial jurisdiction of the United States or any other country. See 4 Blackstone, *supra,* at 72 ("The offence of piracy, by common law, consists of committing those acts of robbery and depredation upon the high seas, which, if committed upon land, would have amounted to felony there"). This Court has generally treated the high seas the same as foreign soil for purposes of the presumption against extraterritorial application. \*\*\* Petitioners contend that because Congress surely intended the ATS to provide jurisdiction for actions against pirates, it necessarily anticipated the statute would apply to conduct occurring abroad.

Applying U.S. law to pirates, however, does not typically impose the sovereign will of the United States onto conduct occurring within the territorial jurisdiction of another sovereign, and therefore carries less direct foreign policy consequences. Pirates were fair game wherever found, by any nation, because they generally did not operate within any jurisdiction. See 4 Blackstone, *supra,* at 71. We do not think that the existence of a cause of action against them is a sufficient basis for concluding that other causes of action under the ATS reach conduct that does occur within the territory of another sovereign; pirates may well be a category unto themselves.

\*\*\*

Finally, there is no indication that the ATS was passed to make the United States a uniquely hospitable forum for the enforcement of international norms. As Justice Story put it, "No nation has ever yet pretended to be the custos morum of the whole world. . . ." *United States v. The La Jeune Eugenie,* 26 F. Cas. 832, 847 (No. 15,551) (C.C.Mass.1822). It is implausible to suppose that the First Congress wanted their fledgling Republic — struggling to receive international recognition — to be the first. Indeed, the parties offer no evidence that any nation, meek or mighty, presumed to do such a thing.

The United States was, however, embarrassed by its potential inability to provide judicial relief to foreign officials injured in the United States. Bradley, 42 Va. J. Int'l L., at 641. Such offenses against ambassadors violated the law of nations, "and if not adequately redressed could rise to an issue of war." \*\*\* The ATS ensured that the United States could provide a forum for adjudicating such incidents. See *Sosa, supra,* at 715–718, and n. 11, 124 S.Ct. 2739. Nothing about this historical context suggests that Congress also intended federal common law under the ATS to provide a cause of action for conduct occurring in the territory of another sovereign.

Indeed, far from avoiding diplomatic strife, providing such a cause of action could have generated it. Recent experience bears this out. See *Doe v. Exxon Mobil Corp.*, 654 F.3d 11, 77–78 (C.A.D.C.2011) (Kavanaugh, J., dissenting in part) (listing recent objections to extraterritorial applications of the ATS by Canada, Germany, Indonesia, Papua New Guinea, South Africa, Switzerland, and the United Kingdom). Moreover, accepting petitioners' view would imply that other nations, also applying the law of nations, could hale our citizens into their courts for alleged violations of the law of nations occurring in the United States, or anywhere else in the world. The presumption against extraterritoriality guards against our courts triggering such serious foreign policy consequences, and instead defers such decisions, quite appropriately, to the political branches.

We therefore conclude that the presumption against extraterritoriality applies to claims under the ATS, and that nothing in the statute rebuts that presumption. "[T]here is no clear indication of extraterritoriality here," *Morrison*, 561 U.S., at ____, 130 S.Ct., at 2883, and petitioners' case seeking relief for violations of the law of nations occurring outside the United States is barred.

IV

On these facts, all the relevant conduct took place outside the United States. And even where the claims touch and concern the territory of the United States, they must do so with sufficient force to displace the presumption against extraterritorial application. See *Morrison*, 561 U.S. ____, 130 S.Ct., at 2883–2888. Corporations are often present in many countries, and it would reach too far to say that mere corporate presence suffices. If Congress were to determine otherwise, a statute more specific than the ATS would be required.

The judgment of the Court of Appeals is affirmed.

Justice KENNEDY, concurring.

The opinion for the Court is careful to leave open a number of significant questions regarding the reach and interpretation of the Alien Tort Statute. In my view that is a proper disposition. *** Other cases may arise with allegations of serious violations of international law principles protecting persons, cases covered neither by the TVPA nor by the reasoning and holding of today's case; and in those disputes the proper implementation of the presumption against extraterritorial application may require some further elaboration and explanation.

***

Justice BREYER, with whom Justice GINSBURG, Justice SOTOMAYOR and Justice KAGAN join, concurring in the judgment.

I agree with the Court's conclusion but not with its reasoning.

***

Unlike the Court, I would not invoke the presumption against extraterritoriality. Rather, guided in part by principles and practices of foreign relations law, I would find jurisdiction under this statute where (1) the alleged tort occurs on American soil, (2) the defendant is an American national, or (3) the defendant's conduct substantially and adversely affects an important American national interest, and that includes a distinct interest in preventing the United States from becoming a safe harbor (free of civil as well as criminal liability) for a torturer or other common enemy of mankind. See *Sosa v. Alvarez–Machain,* 542 U.S. 692, 732, 124 S.Ct. 2739, 159 L.Ed.2d 718 (2004) ("'[F]or purposes of civil liability, the torturer has become — like the pirate and slave trader before him — *hostis humani generis,* an enemy of all mankind.'" (quoting *Filartiga v. Pena–Irala,* 630 F.2d 876, 890 (C.A.2 1980) (alteration in original))). See also 1 Restatement (Third) of Foreign Relations Law of the United States §§ 402, 403, 404 (1986). In this case, however, the parties and relevant conduct lack sufficient ties to the United States for the ATS to provide jurisdiction.

***

Recognizing that Congress enacted the ATS to permit recovery of damages from pirates and others who violated basic international law norms as understood in 1789, *Sosa* essentially leads today's judges to ask: Who are today's pirates? See 542 U.S., at 724–725, 124 S.Ct. 2739 (majority opinion). We provided a framework for answering that question by setting down principles drawn from international norms and designed to limit ATS claims to those that are similar in character and specificity to piracy. *Id.,* at 725, 124 S.Ct. 2739.

In this case we must decide the extent to which this jurisdictional statute opens a federal court's doors to those harmed by activities belonging to the limited class that *Sosa* set forth *when those activities take place abroad.* To help answer this question here, I would refer both to *Sosa* and, as in *Sosa,* to norms of international law. See Part II, *infra.*

In my view the majority's effort to answer the question by referring to the "presumption against extraterritoriality" does not work well. That presumption "rests on the perception that Congress ordinarily legislates with respect to domestic, not foreign matters." *Morrison v. National Australia Bank Ltd.,* 561 U.S. ____, ____, 130 S.Ct. 2869, 2877–2888, 177 L.Ed.2d 535 (2010). See *ante,* at 1664. The ATS, however, was enacted with "foreign matters" in mind. The statute's text refers explicitly to "alien[s]," "treat [ies]," and "the law of nations." 28 U.S.C. § 1350. The statute's purpose was to address "violations of the law of nations, admitting of a judicial remedy and at the same time threatening serious consequences in international affairs." *Sosa*, 542 U.S., at 715, 124 S.Ct. 2739. And at least one of the three kinds of activities that we found to fall within the statute's scope, namely piracy, *ibid.*, normally takes place abroad. See 4 W. Blackstone, Commentaries on the Law of England 72 (1769).

The majority cannot wish this piracy example away by emphasizing that piracy takes place on the high seas. See *ante,* at 1667. That is because the robbery and murder that make up piracy do not normally take place in the water; they take place on a ship. And a ship is like land, in that it falls within the jurisdiction of the nation whose flag it flies. See *McCulloch v. Sociedad Nacional de Marineros de Honduras,* 372 U.S. 10, 20–21, 83 S.Ct. 671, 9 L. Ed.2d 547 (1963); 2 Restatement § 502, Comment *d*

∗∗∗

The majority also writes, "Pirates were fair game wherever found, by any nation, because they generally did not operate within any jurisdiction." *Ibid.* I very much agree that pirates were fair game "wherever found." Indeed, that is the point. That is why we asked, in *Sosa,* who are today's pirates? Certainly today's pirates include torturers and perpetrators of genocide. And today, like the pirates of old, they are "fair game" where they are found. Like those pirates, they are "common enemies of all mankind and all nations have an equal interest in their apprehension and punishment." 1 Restatement § 404 Reporters' Note 1, p. 256 (quoting *In re Demjanjuk,* 612 F. Supp. 544, 556 (N.D.Ohio 1985) (internal quotation marks omitted)). See *Sosa, supra,* at 732, 124 S.Ct. 2739. And just as a nation that harbored pirates provoked the concern of other nations in past centuries, see *infra,* at 1674, so harboring "common enemies of all mankind" provokes similar concerns today.

II

∗∗∗

The Restatement (Third) of Foreign Relations Law is helpful. Section 402 recognizes that, subject to § 403's "reasonableness" requirement, a nation may apply its law (for example, federal common law, see 542 U.S., at 729–730, 124 S.Ct. 2739) not only (1) to "conduct" that "takes place [or to persons or things] within its territory" but also (2) to the "activities, interests, status, or relations of its nationals outside as well as within its territory," (3) to "conduct outside its territory that has or is intended to have substantial effect within its territory," and (4) to certain foreign "conduct outside its territory . . . that is directed against the security of the state or against a limited class of other state interests." In addition, § 404 of the Restatement explains that a "state has jurisdiction to define and prescribe punishment for certain offenses recognized by the community of nations as of universal concern, such as piracy, slave trade," and analogous behavior.

Considering these jurisdictional norms in light of both the ATS's basic purpose (to provide compensation for those injured by today's pirates) and *Sosa's* basic caution (to avoid international friction), I believe that the statute provides jurisdiction where (1) the alleged tort occurs on American soil, (2) the defendant is an American national, or (3) the defendant's conduct substantially and adversely affects an important American national interest, and that includes a distinct interest in preventing the United States from becoming a safe harbor (free of civil as well as criminal liability) for a torturer or other common enemy of mankind.

I would interpret the statute as providing jurisdiction only where distinct American interests are at issue.

***

As I have indicated, we should treat this Nation's interest in not becoming a safe harbor for violators of the most fundamental international norms as an important jurisdiction-related interest justifying application of the ATS in light of the statute's basic purposes — in particular that of compensating those who have suffered harm at the hands of, *e.g.,* torturers or other modern pirates. Nothing in the statute or its history suggests that our courts should turn a blind eye to the plight of victims in that "handful of heinous actions."

***

International norms have long included a duty not to permit a nation to become a safe harbor for pirates (or their equivalent).

More recently two lower American courts have, in effect, rested jurisdiction primarily upon that kind of concern. In *Filartiga,* 630 F.2d 876, an alien plaintiff brought a lawsuit against an alien defendant for damages suffered through acts of torture that the defendant allegedly inflicted in a foreign nation, Paraguay. Neither plaintiff nor defendant was an American national and the actions underlying the lawsuit took place abroad. The defendant, however, "had . . . resided in the United States for more than ninth months" before being sued, having overstayed his visitor's visa. *Id.,* at 878–879. Jurisdiction was deemed proper because the defendant's alleged conduct violated a well-established international law norm, and the suit vindicated our Nation's interest in not providing a safe harbor, free of damages claims, for those defendants who commit such conduct.

In *Marcos,* the plaintiffs were nationals of the Philippines, the defendant was a Philippine national, and the alleged wrongful act, death by torture, took place abroad. *In re Estate of Marcos, Human Rights Litigation,* 25 F.3d 1467, 1469, 1475 (C.A.9 1994); *In re Estate of Marcos Human Rights Litigation,* 978 F.2d 493, 495–496, 500 (C.A.9 1992). A month before being sued, the defendant, "his family, . . . and others loyal to [him] fled to Hawaii," where the ATS case was heard. *Marcos,* 25 F.3d, at 1469. As in *Filartiga,* the court found ATS jurisdiction.

And in *Sosa* we referred to both cases with approval, suggesting that the ATS allowed a claim for relief in such circumstances. 542 U.S., at 732, 124 S.Ct. 2739.

***

Many countries permit foreign plaintiffs to bring suits against their own nationals based on unlawful conduct that took place abroad. ***

Other countries permit some form of lawsuit brought by a foreign national against a foreign national, based upon conduct taking place abroad and seeking damages. Certain countries, which find "universal" criminal "jurisdiction" to try perpetrators of particularly heinous crimes such as piracy and genocide, see Restatement § 404, also permit private persons injured by that conduct to pursue *"actions civiles,"* seeking civil damages in the criminal proceeding.*** Moreover, the United Kingdom and the Netherlands, while not authorizing such damages actions themselves, tell us that they would have no objection to the exercise of American jurisdiction in cases such as *Filartiga* and *Marcos.* Netherlands Brief 15–16, and n. 23.

At the same time Congress has ratified treaties obliging the United States to find and punish foreign perpetrators of serious crimes committed against foreign persons abroad.

***

Congress, while aware of the award of civil damages under the ATS — including cases such as *Filartiga* with foreign plaintiffs, defendants, and conduct — has not sought to limit the statute's jurisdictional or substantive reach. Rather, Congress has enacted other statutes, and not only criminal statutes, that allow the United States to prosecute (or allow victims to obtain damages from) foreign persons who injure foreign victims by committing abroad torture, genocide, and other heinous acts. See, *e.g.,* 18 U.S.C. § 2340A(b)(2) (authorizing prosecution of torturers if "the alleged offender is present in the United States, irrespective of the nationality of the victim or alleged offender"); § 1091(e)(2)(D) (2006 ed., Supp. V) (genocide prosecution authorized when, "regardless of where the offense is committed, the alleged offender is . . . present in the United States"); note following 28 U.S.C. § 1350, § 2(a) (private right of action on behalf of individuals harmed by an act of torture or extrajudicial killing committed "under actual or apparent authority, or color of law, of any foreign nation"). See also S.Rep. No. 102–249, *supra,* at 1671–1672 (purpose to "mak[e] sure that torturers and death squads will no longer have a safe haven in the United States," by "providing a civil cause of action in U.S. courts for torture committed abroad").

***

## III

Applying these jurisdictional principles to this case, however, I agree with the Court that jurisdiction does not lie. The defendants are two foreign corporations. Their shares, like those of many foreign corporations, are traded on the New York Stock Exchange. Their only presence in the United States consists of an office in New York City (actually owned by a separate but affiliated company) that helps to explain their business to potential investors. See Supp. Brief for Petitioners 4, n. 3 (citing *Wiwa v. Royal Dutch Petroleum Co.,* 226 F.3d 88, 94 (C.A.2 2000)); App. 55. The plaintiffs are not United States nationals but nationals of other nations. The conduct at issue took place abroad. And the plaintiffs allege, not that the defendants directly engaged in acts of torture, genocide, or the equivalent, but that they helped others (who are not American nationals) to do so.

Under these circumstances, even if the New York office were a sufficient basis for asserting general jurisdiction, but see *Goodyear Dunlop Tires Operations, S.A. v. Brown,* 564 U.S. ____, 131 S.Ct. 2846, 180 L.Ed.2d 796 (2011), it would be farfetched to believe, based solely upon the defendants' minimal and indirect American presence, that this legal action helps to vindicate a distinct American interest, such as in not providing a safe harbor for an "enemy of all mankind." Thus I agree with the Court that here it would "reach too far to say" that such "mere corporate presence suffices." *Ante,* at 1669.

I consequently join the Court's judgment but not its opinion.

You can listen to the oral argument in Kiobel before the Supreme Court at: http://www.c-spanvideo.org/program/308614-1

## c. Interpretation and Application of *Kiobel*

## i. Daimler v. Bauman, 571 U.S. 310 (2014)

GINSBURG, J., delivered the opinion of the Court, in which ROBERTS, C.J., and SCALIA, KENNEDY, THOMAS, BREYER, ALITO, and KAGAN, JJ., joined. SOTOMAYOR, J., filed an opinion concurring in the judgment.

This case concerns the authority of a court in the United States to entertain a claim brought by foreign plaintiffs against a foreign defendant based on events occurring entirely outside the United States. The litigation commenced in 2004, when twenty-two Argentinian residents filed a complaint in the United States District Court for the Northern District of California against DaimlerChrysler Aktiengesellschaft (Daimler), a German public stock company, headquartered in Stuttgart, that manufactures Mercedes–Benz vehicles in Germany. The complaint alleged that during Argentina's 1976–1983 "Dirty War," Daimler's Argentinian subsidiary, Mercedes–Benz Argentina (MB Argentina) collaborated with state security forces to kidnap, detain, torture, and kill certain MB Argentina workers, among them, plaintiffs or persons closely related to plaintiffs. Damages for the alleged human-rights violations were sought from Daimler under the laws of the United States, California, and Argentina. Jurisdiction over the lawsuit was predicated on the California contacts of Mercedes–Benz USA, LLC (MBUSA), a subsidiary of Daimler incorporated in Delaware with its principal place of business in New Jersey. MBUSA distributes Daimler-manufactured vehicles to independent dealerships throughout the United States, including California.

Most of the Court's opinion justifies its conclusion that there is no basis for asserting personal jurisdiction over the named corporate defendants. This in itself has caused significant controversy for apparently <u>creating new significant limits on personal</u> jurisdiction over foreign corporations. At the end of the opinion the Court then added:

> Finally, the transnational context of this dispute bears attention. The Court of Appeals emphasized, as supportive of the exercise of general jurisdiction, plaintiffs' assertion of claims under the Alien Tort Statute (ATS), 28 U.S.C. § 1350, and the Torture Victim Protection Act of 1991 (TVPA), 106 Stat. 73, note following 28 U.S. C. § 1350. See 644 F.3d at 927 ("American federal courts, be they in California or any other state, have a strong interest in adjudicating and redressing international human rights abuses."). Recent decisions of this Court, however, have rendered plaintiffs' ATS and TVPA claims infirm. See Kiobel v. Royal Dutch Petroleum Co., 569 U.S. ___, 133 S. Ct. 1659, 1669 (2013) (presumption against extraterritorial application controls claims under the ATS); Mohamad v. Palestinian Authority, 566 U.S. ___, 132 S. Ct. 1702, 1705 (2012) (only natural persons are subject to liability under the TVPA).

ii. Balintulo v. Daimler, 727 F. 3d 174 (2d Cir. 2013)

Before CABRANES, HALL, and LIVINGSTON, Circuit Judges.

JOSÉ A. CABRANES, Circuit Judge:

The question presented is whether to issue a writ of mandamus to resolve in favor of the defendants this long-lived litigation under the Alien Tort Statute ("ATS") — a statute, passed in 1789, that was rediscovered and revitalized by the courts in recent decades to permit aliens to sue for alleged serious violations of human rights occurring abroad.

***

We consider this question in light of the Supreme Court's recent decision that federal courts may not, under the ATS, recognize common-law causes of action for conduct occurring in another country.

In these putative class-action suits brought on behalf of those harmed by the decades-long South African legal regime known as "apartheid," the plaintiffs assert that the South African subsidiary companies of the named corporate defendants — Daimler, Ford, and IBM (the "defendants") — aided and abetted violations of customary international law committed by the

South African government. In short, the plaintiffs claim that these subsidiary companies sold cars and computers to the South African government, thus facilitating the apartheid regime's innumerable race-based depredations and injustices, including rape, torture, and extrajudicial killings.

*＊＊*

Now on appeal for over four years, this case has been overtaken by recent events. Most significantly, the Supreme Court held, as a matter of United States law, that federal courts may not, under the ATS, recognize common-law causes of action for conduct occurring in the territory of another sovereign. *Kiobel v. Royal Dutch Petroleum Co.,* ____U.S. ____, 133 S.Ct. 1659, 1668–69, 185 L.Ed.2d 671 (2013). Additionally, the South African government—which had previously opposed the suits because they "interfere[d] with the policy embodied by its Truth and Reconciliation Commission," *Sosa v. Alvarez–Machain,* 542 U.S. 692, 733 n. 21, 124 S.Ct. 2739, 159 L.Ed.2d 718 (2004)—reversed its position in September 2009 after a change in governmental leadership. After this series of twists and turns, the parties submitted supplemental briefing, and we have now reached a decision.

The opinion of the Supreme Court in *Kiobel* plainly bars common-law suits, like this one, alleging violations of customary international law based solely on conduct occurring abroad. Because of that unambiguous holding, the defendants will be able to obtain their desired relief (dismissal of all claims) in the District Court through a motion for judgment on the pleadings . . .

### ii.

As we have now made clear, *Kiobel* forecloses the plaintiffs' claims because the plaintiffs have failed to allege that any relevant conduct occurred in the United States. The plaintiffs resist this obvious impact of the *Kiobel* holding on their claims. The Supreme Court's decision, they argue, does not preclude suits under the ATS based on foreign conduct when the defendants are American nationals, or where the defendants' conduct affronts significant American interests identified by the plaintiffs. *See* Plaintiffs' Letter Br. at 6–13. Curiously, this interpretation of *Kiobel* arrives at precisely the conclusion reached by Justice Breyer, who, writing for himself and three colleagues, only concurred in the judgment of the Court affirming our decision to dismiss all remaining claims brought under the ATS. *See Kiobel,* 133 S.Ct. at 1671 (Breyer, J., concurring). The plaintiffs' argument, however, seeks to evade the bright-line clarity of the Court's actual holding—clarity that ensures that the defendants can obtain their desired relief without resort to mandamus. We briefly highlight why the plaintiffs' arguments lack merit.

### a.

The Supreme Court's *Kiobel* decision, the plaintiffs assert, "adopted a new presumption that ATS claims must 'touch and concern' the United States with 'sufficient force' to state a cause of action." Plaintiffs Letter Br. 6 (quoting

*Kiobel,* 133 S.Ct. at 1669). The plaintiffs read the opinion of the Court as holding only that "mere corporate presence" in the United States is insufficient for a claim to "touch and concern" the United States, but that corporate citizenship in the United States is enough. *Id.* at 11 ("[I]nternational law violations committed by U.S. citizens on foreign soil 'touch and concern' U.S. territory with 'sufficient force' to displace the *Kiobel* presumption."). Reaching a conclusion similar to that of Justice Breyer and the minority of the Supreme Court in *Kiobel,* the plaintiffs argue that whether the relevant conduct occurred abroad is simply one prong of a multi-factor test, and the ATS still reaches extraterritorial conduct when the defendant is an American national. *Id.* at 8–11.

We disagree. The Supreme Court expressly held that claims under the ATS cannot be brought for violations of the law of nations occurring within the territory of a sovereign other than the United States. *Kiobel,* 133 S.Ct. at 1662, 1668–69. The majority framed the question presented in these terms no fewer than three times; it repeated the same language, focusing solely on the location of the relevant "conduct" or "violation," at least eight more times in other parts of its eight-page opinion; and it affirmed our judgment dismissing the plaintiffs' claims because "all the relevant conduct took place outside the United States," *id.* at 1669. Lower courts are bound by that rule and they are without authority to "reinterpret" the Court's binding precedent in light of irrelevant factual distinctions, such as the citizenship of the defendants. . . . Accordingly, if all the relevant conduct occurred abroad, that is simply the end of the matter under *Kiobel.*

***

As the Court observed in *Morrison,* "the presumption against extraterritorial application would be a craven watchdog indeed if it retreated to its kennel whenever *some* domestic activity is involved in the case." 130 S.Ct. at 2884. But since *all* the relevant conduct in *Kiobel* occurred outside the United States — a dispositive fact in light of the Supreme Court's holding — the Court had no reason to explore, much less explain, how courts should proceed when *some* of the relevant conduct occurs in the United States. FN 26

> FN 26 Although joining in the opinion of the Court, Justice Alito, joined by Justice Thomas, indicated a desire to adopt a broader holding, requiring that the "domestic conduct" be "sufficient" to constitute a violation of an appropriate international law norm. *Kiobel,* 133 S.Ct. at 1670 (Alito, J., concurring). The Court did not adopt Justice Alito's broader reasoning, but it did not reject it either; the majority simply left open any questions regarding the permissible reach of causes of action under the ATS when "*some* domestic activity is involved in the case."

***

The complaint alleges only vicarious liability of the defendant corporations based on the actions taken within South Africa by their South African subsidiaries. . . . *Because the defendants' putative agents did not commit any relevant conduct within the United States giving rise to a violation of customary international law* [emphasis added] — that is, because the asserted "violation[s] of the law of nations occurr[ed] outside the United States," *Kiobel*, 133 S.Ct. at 1669 — the defendants cannot be *vicariously liable* for that conduct under the ATS.

## d. Bucking the *Kiobel* Tide?

### i. Sexual Minorities Uganda v. Scott Lively, 2013 WL 4130756 (August 14, 2013)

MEMORANDUM AND ORDER REGARDING DEFENDANT'S MOTIONS TO DISMISS, PONSOR, U.S.D.J.

## I. INTRODUCTION

Plaintiff Sexual Minorities Uganda is an umbrella organization located in Kampala, Uganda, comprising member organizations that advocate for the fair and equal treatment of lesbian, gay, bisexual, transgender, and intersex (LGBTI) people in that east African country. Defendant Scott Lively is an American citizen residing in Springfield, Massachusetts who, according to the complaint, holds himself out to be an expert on what he terms the "gay movement." Lively is also alleged to be an attorney, author, and evangelical minister.

Plaintiff alleges that in concert with others Defendant — through actions taken both within the United States and in Uganda — has attempted to foment, and to a substantial degree has succeeding in fomenting, an atmosphere of harsh and frightening repression against LGBTI people in Uganda.

The complaint asserts five counts, <u>three invoking the jurisdiction of the federal Alien Tort Statute, 28 U.S.C. § 1350 ("ATS")</u>, and two under state law. Plaintiff seeks compensatory, punitive, and exemplary damages; declaratory relief holding that Defendant's conduct has been in violation of the law of nations; and injunctive relief enjoining Defendant from undertaking further actions, and from plotting and conspiring with others, to persecute Plaintiff and the LGBTI community in Uganda.

Defendant has filed two motions to dismiss, offering in essence five arguments.

First, the court lacks jurisdiction because international norms do not bar persecution based on sexual orientation or gender identity with sufficient clarity and historical lineage to make it one of the narrow set of claims for which the ATS furnishes jurisdiction.

Second, the court cannot recognize a claim under the ATS for actions taken outside the United States, as the Supreme Court has recently held in *Kiobel v. Royal Dutch Petroleum*, 133 S. Ct. 1659 (2013).

Third, Plaintiff lacks standing to bring this case either on behalf of itself as an organization or on behalf of members of the LGBTI community in Uganda.

Fourth, the right of free speech described in the First Amendment to the United States Constitution prohibits any attempt by Plaintiff to restrict expression, however distasteful, through court action.

Finally, the two claims asserted under Massachusetts state law lack any adequate legal foundation.

For the reasons set forth at length below, none of these arguments is persuasive. As to the first argument, many authorities implicitly support the principle that widespread, systematic persecution of individuals based on their sexual orientation and gender identity constitutes a crime against humanity that violates international norms.

It is a somewhat closer question whether this crime constitutes what Justice Souter has termed one of the "relatively modest set of actions alleging violations of the law of nations" for which the ATS furnishes jurisdiction. *Sosa v. Alvarez-Machain*, 542 U.S. 692, 720 (2004). However, aiding and abetting a crime against humanity is a well established offense under customary international law, and actions for redress of this crime have frequently been recognized by American courts as part of the subclass of lawsuits for which the ATS furnishes jurisdiction. Given this, the allegations set forth in the Amended Complaint are more than adequate at this stage to require denial of Defendant's motion to dismiss. Moreover, given the elasticity of the legal standard for ATS jurisdiction, it is fairer and more prudent to address the *Sosa* issue on a fully developed record, following discovery.

Second, the restrictions established in *Kiobel* on extraterritorial application of the ATS do not apply to the facts as alleged in this case, where Defendant is a citizen of the United States and where his offensive conduct is alleged to have occurred, in substantial part, within this country. Indeed, Defendant, according to the Amended Complaint, is alleged to have maintained what amounts to a kind of "Homophobia Central" in Springfield, Massachusetts. He has allegedly supported and actively participated in worldwide initiatives, with a substantial focus on Uganda, aimed at repressing free expression by LGBTI groups, destroying the organizations that support them, intimidating LGBTI individuals, and even criminalizing the very status of being lesbian or gay. *Kiobel* makes clear that its restrictions on extraterritorial application of American law do not apply where a defendant and his or her conduct are based in this country.

Third, clear authority supports Plaintiff's standing here.

Fourth, the argument that Defendant's actions have constituted mere expression protected under the First Amendment is, again, premature. Accepting the allegations of the complaint, as the court must at this stage, sufficient facts are alleged, with specific names, dates, and actions, to support the claim that Defendant's behavior crossed well over any protective boundary established by the First Amendment.

Fifth, and finally, the arguments attacking the claims under Massachusetts state law have not been convincingly developed. Having denied the motions to dismiss the federal claims, the court will retain the state law claims pending discovery and, if appropriate, reconsider them on a fuller record in connection with a motion for summary judgment.

Compare the District Court's opinion in *Sexual Minorities Uganda* with the following ATS decision by a different lower court after *Kiobel*. Take particular note of the various lower court decisions that the court cites dismissing cases after *Kiobel* and the reasons given. They paint a dismissal picture for the so-called "foreign cubed" cases but at the same time reveal a few glimmers of hope regarding cases with a significant connection to the United States.

ii. Chen Gang, et al, v. Zhao Zhizhen, 2013 W.L. 5313411 (D. Conn. Sept. 20, 2013)

ROBERT N. CHATIGNY, District Judge.

Plaintiffs, on behalf of themselves and others similarly situated, bring this action pursuant to the Alien Tort Statute ("ATS"), 28 U.S.C. § 1350, and the Torture Victims Protection Act ("TVPA"), 106 Stat. 73 (1992) (codified at 28 U.S.C. § 1350 note), alleging that the named defendant Zhao Zhizhen has committed torts in violation of international and domestic law. The defendant is alleged to be liable under theories of aiding and abetting, command responsibility, and conspiracy for torture, arbitrary arrest and detention, crimes against humanity and violation of the rights to life, liberty, security of persons and peaceful assembly and association.***

Plaintiffs are all residents of the Peoples Republic of China, refugees from that country, or aliens who visited that country. SAC (ECF No. 85) ¶¶ 1, 15. In China, primarily in the city of Wuhan, plaintiffs were subjected to persecution and human rights abuses due to their adherence to Falun Gong, a spiritual practice based on the teachings of Li Hongzhi. *Id.* ¶¶ 2, 5. The defendant, a Chinese citizen, "exercised authority over media and related brainwashing and propaganda activities of the People's Republic of China," *id.* ¶ 16, as part of a "nationwide . . . crackdown against Falun Gong practitioners." *Id.* ¶ 5.

***

They were also physically tortured by Chinese security forces: shocked with electric batons, handcuffed to beds while their bodies were stretched in opposite directions and hung from ceilings with handcuffs. *See id.* ¶ 24. The defendant "personally, and in collaboration with others, mobilized, instigated, ordered, [and] aided and abetted" these abuses. *Id.* ¶ 3.

***

III. *Discussion*

After careful review of the SAC and the parties' submissions, it is apparent that the Court lacks jurisdiction over the plaintiffs' ATS claims. . . .

The [Kiobel] Court noted that "even where claims touch and concern the territory of the United States, they must do so with sufficient force to displace the presumption against extraterritorial application" in order to confer jurisdiction. *Id.*

The plaintiffs have seized on the Court's "touch and concern" language, arguing that their claims are distinguishable because they impact the United States to a greater extent than the claims in *Kiobel,* "a paradigmatic 'foreign-cubed' case — foreign defendant, foreign plaintiff, and exclusively foreign conduct — lacking any connection to the United States beyond 'mere corporate presence.'" Pls. Supp. Br. (ECF No. 115) at 2. Plaintiffs argue that this case sufficiently touches and concerns the United States because (1) the defendant "specifically directed" his propaganda campaign toward United States citizens and residents-through CACA's website, for example; (2) a refusal to provide redress for serious violations of international law would deprive the plaintiffs of the only relief available to them; and (3) there is no risk of international discord in this case because the U .S. Department of State has not indicated that the case should be dismissed. *See id.* at 7.

Despite plaintiffs' attempts to distinguish their claims from those in *Kiobel,* this case is also a paradigmatic "foreign cubed" case. The plaintiffs are all "past or present residents of the People's Republic of China, or visitors to that country", SAC ¶ 1, the defendant is a Chinese citizen, *id.* ¶ 10, and the alleged violations of international law that the defendant allegedly aided and abetted-torture, arbitrary arrest and detention, crimes against humanity and violation of the rights to life, liberty, security of persons and peaceful assembly and association — all took place entirely abroad, in "Mainland China." *See id.* ¶ 2. Under *Kiobel,* the ATS does not confer jurisdiction over such exclusively extraterritorial claims.

*See Balintulo v. Daimler AG,* 09–2778–CV L, 2013 WL 4437057, at *7 (2d Cir. Aug. 21, 2013) ("[C]laims under the ATS cannot be brought for violations of the law of nations occurring within the territory of a sovereign other than the United States."); Hua *Chen v. Honghui Shi,* 09 CIV. 8920 RJS, 2013 WL 3963735 (S.D.N.Y. Aug. 1, 2013) (finding no jurisdiction under the ATS over claims of "torture, genocide, violation of the right to life, arbitrary arrest and imprisonment, and violation of freedom of thought, conscience, and religion" brought by "members of the Falun Gong movement who currently reside in the United States" because "all of the abuses took place in China"); *Ahmed–Al–Khalifa v. Minister of Interior, Fed. Republic of Nigeria,* 5:13–CV–172–RSGRJ, 2013 WL 3991961, at *2 (N.D.Fla. Aug. 2, 2013) ("In light of *Kiobel,* the ATS cannot confer subject-matter jurisdiction onto Plaintiff's claims because the violations at issue occurred outside the United States."); *Ahmed–Al–Khalifa v. Trayers,* 313–CV–00869CSH, 2013 WL 3326212, at *2 (D.Conn. July 1, 2013) ("The Alien Tort Statute cannot confer jurisdiction in this Court over conduct committed outside of the United States."); *Al Shimari v. CACI Int'l, Inc.,* 1:08–CV–827 GBL/JFA, 2013 WL 3229720, at *10 (E.D. Va. June 25, 2013) ("Plaintiffs' ATS claims are barred because the ATS does not provide jurisdiction over their claims, which involve tortious conduct occurring exclusively outside the territory of the United States."); *Mohammadi v. Islamic Republic of Iran,* CIV.A. 09–1289 BAH, 2013 WL 2370594, at *15 (D.D.C. May 31, 2013) ("[T]o the extent that the plaintiffs seek to pursue claims under the ATS . . . for conduct that occurred entirely within the sovereign territory of Iran, those claims are also barred under the holding of *Kiobel.*"). *Compare with Sexual Minorities Uganda v. Lively,* 12–CV–30051–MAP, 2013 WL 4130756, at *2 (D.Mass. Aug. 14, 2013) (finding that the *Kiobel* restrictions on extraterritorial application of the ATS did not apply where the defendant was a citizen of the United States and where the alleged conduct occurred in substantial part within the United States).

***

Without subject matter jurisdiction under the ATS, the Court also lacks jurisdiction over plaintiffs' TVPA claim. *See Kadic v. Karadzic,* 70 F.3d 232, 246 (2d Cir.1995) ("Though the Torture Victim Act creates a cause of action for official torture, this statute, unlike the Alien Tort Act, is not itself a jurisdictional statute.").

The court in Chen Gang concludes that it lacks jurisdiction to hear TVPA claims if extraterritoriality problems render the ATS inapplicable. One obvious response to the court might involve 28 U.S.C. § 1331, federal question jurisdiction. Consider this question in light of following interpretations of Kiobel's aftermath by two legal commentators.

### e. Response of Legal Commentators to *Kiobel*

Julian Ku, <u>Opinio Juris</u>, *Goodbye ATS? U.S. Appeals Court Dismisses South African Apartheid ATS Case and Rejects Narrow Reading of Kiobel*

The Second Circuit's <u>decision in Balintulo v. Daimler*</u> (already discussed at length by John Bellinger at <u>Lawfare</u>) is one of the first major U.S. court opinions to apply the Supreme Court's decision in *Kiobel*. It is pretty much a complete smackdown of the ATS plaintiffs, and for any hopes they might have that the *Kiobel* decision's bar on extraterritoriality for ATS suits would be read narrowly. While they were at it, the Court pretty much kills every other kind of ATS lawsuit as well. In particular, it rejects the notion that mere corporate nationality in the U.S. would be enough to overcome the *Kiobel* bar. ***

The Second Circuit also dismissed the plaintiffs' claim that the fact that there was some affirmative steps in support of the agents' conduct in South Africa, this would be enough to displace the presumption. The key holding is that the conduct giving rise to the violation of the law of nations must occur in the U.S.

\*\*\*

I agree with the Court that this approach ("relevant conduct that violates the law of nations") is the most natural reading of *Kiobel*, I am less confident it fits with the historical purpose of the ATS, which did seem to have a particular interest in providing remedies against U.S. nationals. Although it seems clear from the history that the ATS was largely aimed at U.S. nationals in United States territory, there seems some possibility that it would apply to the actions of U.S. nationals abroad.

In any event, this reading of *Kiobel* is pretty much everything corporate ATS defendants could ask for, especially U.S. ones that might have been uncertain about their status. I doubt the Supreme Court will revisit this anytime soon, so expect a spirited en banc petition to get this reversed by the full appeals court. If that doesn't happen, the only remaining question is how much conduct in the U.S. would satisfy Kiobel (knowledge? active participation?). Balintulo doesn't resolve that question.

It also doesn't resolve whether *Filartiga*-like lawsuits involving foreign nationals who committed violations abroad but whom are now living in the U.S. can still be sued. Under *Balintulo*, I think the answer is no, which would mean the end of almost every ATS lawsuit against foreign government officials. If *Balintulo* is followed, the era of ATS lawsuits in the U.S. is coming to an end.

Burt Neuborne, <u>NYU Journal of International Law and Politics</u>, April 2013, *Some Quick Thoughts on Transnational Human Rights Litigation in American Courts After Kiobel*

The hope that the ATS would permit entrepreneurial lawyers to choreograph international human rights cases involving: (1) alien plaintiffs; (2) alien corporate defendants; and (3) acts wholly occurring abroad into an American court in an effort to take advantage of American discovery rules, Rule 23 class actions, and an independent judiciary is now history. All nine Justices in *Kiobel* slammed that door, which was probably a pipe dream in the first place. Chief Justice Roberts, writing for five Justices, including the maddeningly vague Justice Kennedy, ruled that the presumption against extraterritorial legislation blocked use of the ATS as a source of federal jurisdiction when neither the plaintiffs, nor the defendants, nor the operative facts had a significant link with the territorial United States. Mere corporate presence for the purposes of general jurisdiction over the defendant could not, ruled the Chief Justice, constitute the significant link to the territorial

United States needed to rebut the presumption against extraterritorial legislation.

Although the grant by the United States of political asylum to the injured plaintiffs in *Kiobel* might have been deemed a significant link, and while it is a stretch to apply a presumption against extraterritorial effect to a jurisdictional statute designed to permit the efficient enforcement of customary international law claims that are binding throughout the civilized world, the Roberts opinion asks and answers the hard question of why the Delphic ATS should be read to make the United States judiciary the arbiter of worldwide international human rights claims having little or nothing to do with the United States. As I read the Breyer concurrence for the Court's four liberals, they do not disagree that it would have been a form of judicial imperialism for the United States to make itself into a worldwide human rights tribunal in settings having little or nothing to do with the United States — except for general jurisdiction over a corporate defendant.

But the *Kiobel* majority says little or nothing about how to decide ATS cases where a significant link to the territorial United States exists, either because the injured plaintiff is a United States national, the defendant is a United States resident, and/or a significant proportion of the operative facts took place within the United States. The Breyer concurrence indicates that the ATS will apply in many such cases. The Roberts majority is silent on whether one or more of such links will rebut the presumption against extraterritoriality. The swing-vote Kennedy concurrence is purposefully vague on the issue. So, much ATS litigation will continue, albeit in a narrower set of cases involving allegations of significant links to the territorial United States. We can look forward to years of uncertainty, split decisions, and an eventual return trip to a reconstituted Court.

I want to ask a different question. Is it necessary — or wise — to continue to view the ATS as the principal source of judicial authority to hear transnational human rights cases in US courts? Remember that the core provisions of customary international law discussed in *Sosa* are part of both the federal and state common law. As such, they provide a cause of action for damages entirely apart from the ATS which was held in *Sosa* to be solely a jurisdictional statute. Two alternative federal jurisdictional statutes are available. First, a cause of action under core customary international law would arise under the laws of the United States for the purposes of 28 U.S.C. sec. 1331, providing general federal question jurisdiction. While the exchange between Justices Souter and Scalia at nn. 19 and 20 in *Sosa* counsel caution about the use of 1331 as a jurisdictional base for a customary international law claim, both Justice Scalia and Justice Souter were talking about using 1331 to expand the pool of judicially enforceable customary international law claims, not about using it to enforce the core claims that are already enforceable under the ATS. While the *Erie* problem must be confronted, it seems clear to me that *Sosa* recognizes that federal common law, including core customary international law, survived *Erie* and is enforceable in federal court.

The second possible source of federal jurisdiction is diversity or alienage jurisdiction under 28 U.S.C. § 1332. If complete diversity exists and the jurisdictional amount is satisfied, customary international law claims are merely a form of common law fully enforceable in a diversity case. In order to minimize *Erie*, I would characterize the customary international law claim as part of the common law of the state in which the federal court sits. Alternatively, it could be enforceable as federal common law, although 1331 would seem to be the more logical vehicle. In deciding whether 1332 jurisdiction exists, remember, first, that the named-plaintiff in a class action is the sole measure of the class's citizenship; and, second, that as long as one class member satisfies the jurisdictional amount, everyone else can come in under 28 U.S.C. § 1367 supplemental jurisdiction.

Entirely apart from federal jurisdiction, maybe it's time to explore the international human rights enforcement capabilities of state courts. As long as general jurisdiction of the defendant exists in a particular state, a customary international law claim should be enforceable in state court as a matter of state common law. Just as the federal government adopts customary international law as a form of federal common law, states are free to adopt international norms as part of the state common law, and are duty-bound to enforce federal common law if they would enforce a parallel state law claim. If you choose to deploy a state common law claim premised on customary international law, remember that you can bring it in state court, or use 1367 to pendent the state common law claim onto your federal common law claim under 1331, or your common law claim under 1332.

Finally, whatever the availability of American courts, it's long past time to take judicial *fora* in other settings more seriously as enforcement engines for international human rights. We should be working to add clear civil jurisdiction to the Rome court to enforce core claim of customary international law on behalf of victims. The evolution of aggregate litigation options in many foreign courts opens yet another door. The bottom line is that *Filartiga* survives. *Sosa* survives. A visionary, but unrealistic hope about the use of American courts as a worldwide enforcement arm for international human rights has been dashed. But the struggle goes on.

### f. Common Defenses to ATS and TVPA Claims

### i. Overview

After the double barrel legal assault on the ATS mounted by the Supreme Court in *Sosa*, and *Kiobel*, alien plaintiffs face substantial obstacles in vindicating human rights abuses before U.S. courts. Recognized causes of action will be limited to the most egregious violations of international human rights law similar to piracy and must "touch and concern" the United States sufficiently to overcome a presumption against hearing claims involving foreign based conduct. Based on early lower court decisions it seems clear that mere corporate presence or residency will not usually be enough. However, as witnessed by the *Sexual Minorities Uganda* case, a glimmer of hope for such cases remains. In that case the defendant was a U.S. citizen and at least some of the challenged conduct occurred in the United States. What if the only U.S. connection is that the victim or defendant is a U.S. citizen or permanent resident?

At least for torture and extrajudicial executions plaintiffs may still seek redress against foreign conduct under the TVPA. However, the Supreme Court also limited application of the TVPA in the *Mohamed* case, declaring that corporate defendants did not fall within its statutory causes of action for torture or extrajudicial executions. (The Supreme Court refrained in *Kiobel* from resolving a spit among federal circuit courts regarding whether the ATS can be applied to corporate entities at all.[77]) Assuming that a plaintiff survives these hurdles now erected for ATS and TVPA claims, they must also face other defenses, prominent among them sovereign and other immunities. In the following case the Supreme Court ruled that the Foreign Sovereign Immunities Act does not apply to individual defendants, with some exceptions, even though they act under color of government authority.

ii. Sovereign Immunity under the FSIA in Human Rights Cases

**Mohamed Ali Samantar v. Bashe Abdi Yousuf, et al**, Supreme Court of United States. 560 U.S. 305, 130 S. Ct. 2278 (2010)

JUSTICE STEVENS delivered the opinion of the Court.

From 1980 to 1986 petitioner Mohamed Ali Samantar was the First Vice President and Minister of Defense of Somalia, and from 1987 to 1990 he served as its Prime Minister. Respondents are natives of Somalia who allege that they, or members of their families, were the victims of torture and extrajudicial killings during those years. They seek damages from petitioner based on his alleged authorization of those acts. The narrow question we must decide is whether the Foreign Sovereign Immunities Act of 1976 (FSIA or Act), 28 U. S. C. §§1330, 1602 *et seq.*, provides petitioner with immunity from suit based on actions taken in his official capacity. We hold that the FSIA does not govern the determination of petitioner's immunity from suit.

*** 

Although characterizing the statute as silent on its applicability to the officials of a foreign state, the District Court followed appellate decisions

---

77. *Compare* Doe I v. Nestle USA, Inc. ____ F.3d ____, 2013 WL 6670945 (9th Cir. 2013) (corporations are subject to ATS) *with* Kiobel v. Royal Dutch Petroleum Co., 621 F. 3d 111, 149 (2d Cir. 2010) (corporation are not subject to the ATS since not capable of committing violations of human rights under international law).

holding that a foreign state's sovereign immunity under the Act extends to "'an individual acting in his official capacity on behalf of a foreign state,'" but not to "'an official who acts beyond the scope of his authority.'" *Id.,* at 47a . . . The court rejected respondents' argument that petitioner was necessarily acting beyond the scope of his authority because he allegedly violated international law. The Court of Appeals reversed, rejecting the District Court's ruling that the FSIA governs petitioner's immunity from suit. It acknowledged "the majority view" among the Circuits that "the FSIA applies to individual officials of a foreign state." 552 F. 3d 371, 378 (CA4 2009). It disagreed with that view, however, and concluded, "based on the language and structure of the statute, that the FSIA does not apply to individual foreign government agents like [petitioner]." *Id.,* at 381. \*\*\*

What we must now decide is whether the Act also covers the immunity claims of foreign officials. . . .

### III

The FSIA provides that "a foreign state shall be immune from the jurisdiction of the courts of the United States and of the States" except as provided in the Act. §1604. Thus, if a defendant is a "foreign state" within the meaning of the Act, then the defendant is immune from jurisdiction unless one of the exceptions in the Act applies. See §§1605-1607 (enumerating exceptions). The Act, if it applies, is the "sole basis for obtaining jurisdiction over a foreign state in federal court." *Argentine Republic v. Amerada Hess Shipping Corp.* 488 U.S. 428, 439 (1989). The question we face in this case is whether an individual sued for conduct undertaken in his official capacity is a "foreign state" within the meaning of the Act.

The Act defines "foreign state" in §1603 as follows:

"(a) A 'foreign state' . . . includes a political subdivision of a foreign state or an agency or instrumentality of a foreign state as defined in subsection (b).

"(b) An 'agency or instrumentality of a foreign state' means any entity —

"(1) which is a separate legal person, corporate or otherwise, and

"(2) which is an organ of a foreign state or political subdivision thereof, or a majority of whose shares or other ownership interest is owned by a foreign state or political subdivision thereof, and

"(3) which is neither a citizen of a State of the United States as defined in section 1332(c) and (e) of this title, nor created under the laws of any third country."

\*\*\*

It is true that an individual official could be an "agency or instrumentality," if that term is given the meaning of "any thing or person through which action is accomplished," .... Congress has specifically defined "agency or instrumentality" in the FSIA, and all of the textual clues in that definition cut against such a broad construction. . . . the terms Congress chose simply do not evidence the intent to include individual officials within the meaning of "agency or instrumentality."

***

Moreover, elsewhere in the FSIA Congress expressly mentioned officials when it wished to count their acts as equivalent to those of the foreign state, which suggests that officials are not included within the unadorned term "foreign state." . . .

***

In sum . . . Reading the FSIA as a whole, there is nothing to suggest we should read "foreign state" in §1603(a) to include an official acting on behalf of the foreign state, and much to indicate that this meaning was not what Congress enacted.

***

Finally, our reading of the FSIA will not "in effect make the statute optional," . . . Even if a suit is not governed by the Act, it may still be barred by foreign sovereign immunity under the common law. And not every suit can successfully be pleaded against an individual official alone. Even when a plaintiff names only a foreign official, it may be the case that the foreign state itself, its political subdivision, or an agency or instrumentality is a required party, because that party has "an interest relating to the subject of the action" and "disposing of the action in the person's absence may . . . as a practical matter impair or impede the person's ability to protect the interest." Fed. Rule Civ. Proc. 19(a)(1)(B). If this is the case, and the entity is immune from suit under the FSIA, the district court may have to dismiss the suit, regardless of whether the official is immune or not under the common law. . . . Or it may be the case that some actions against an official in his official capacity should be treated as actions against the foreign state itself, as the state is the real party in interest. . . .

And we think this case, in which respondents have sued petitioner in his personal capacity and seek damages from his own pockets, is properly governed by the common law because it is not a claim against a foreign state as the Act defines that term. Although Congress clearly intended to supersede the common-law regime for claims against foreign states, we find nothing in the statute's origin or aims to indicate that Congress similarly wanted to codify the law of foreign official immunity.

***

We emphasize, however, the narrowness of our holding. Whether petitioner may be entitled to immunity under the common law, and whether he may have other valid defenses to the grave charges against him, are matters to be addressed in the first instance by the District Court on remand.

### iii. Other Immunities for Government Officials

In *Samantar,* the Supreme Court unanimously decided that immunity granted under the FSIA would not apply to an individual foreign government official. Thus, while a human rights claim against the government or its agencies would be barred under the FSIA (except for certain "terrorist" states), the individual government official may be sued in his or her individual capacity (unless the government itself is an indispensable party or the real party in interest who would be required to pay damages or provide other relief). The court left open, however, the possibility that other types of immunities and defenses outside of the FSIA might apply, influenced by State Department advice and input.

The defendant in *Samantar,* who had served in various high government positions during the time period relevant to the plaintiffs' claims, asserted two common law immunities on remand to the district court—the status based "head of state" immunity for high level government officials and the conduct based "official act immunity" for action taken in official capacity. The State Department submitted a "Statement of Interest" (SOI) urging rejection of both defenses, emphasizing two points. First, head of state immunity must be asserted by, and can be waived by, the foreign government not the defendant. In this case this was not possible since there was no recognized government in Somalia. Second, the defendant was a resident of the United States at the time of suit and, taking advantage of the protections of American law, generally should not be entitled to foreign derived immunities.

The Fourth Circuit affirmed the district court's denial of the claimed immunities, asserting several important rationales. First, the court held that a SOI from the executive branch regarding status based "head of state" immunity is binding on the courts. This, the court asserted, is true even if the claims involve alleged violations of jus cogens norms of international human rights.[78]

Second, in contrast to "head of state" immunity, the Executive Branch's position on the conduct based "official act" immunity was not binding on the courts but merely influential. More importantly, the court concluded that:

> "Under international and domestic law, officials from other countries are not entitled to foreign official immunity for jus cogens violations, even if the acts

---

78. In Manoharan v. Rajapaksa, 711 F.3d 178 (9th Cir. 2013), a suit involving claims against the then sitting President of Sri Lanka, the court affirmed this approach following a "two step" process. A defendant first requests a "suggestion of immunity" from the State Department (status based immunity such as head of state). If the State Department agrees with the asserted immunity, the court is then bound by that determination. The court in Manoharan also held that the TVPA did not statutorily eliminate such immunities.

were performed in the defendant's official capacity." . . . "Because this case involves acts that violated jus cogens norms, including torture, extrajudicial killings and prolonged arbitrary imprisonment of politically and ethnically disfavored groups, we conclude that Samantar is not entitled to conduct-based official immunity under the common law, which in this area incorporates international law."[79]

We will revisit the question of immunities later when reviewing extraterritorial criminal prosecutions for universal crimes involving human rights, such as the case brought against former Chilean dictator, Augusto Pinochet.

### iv. Other Miscellaneous Defenses Including Exhaustion of Remedies

Apart from immunities, the federal courts have also addressed a variety of other potential defenses including international comity, political questions, act of state, forum non-conveniens, lack of state action and exhaustion of remedies. These defenses will not be reviewed here in favor of supplying some basic references for further study. *See, e.g.*, Sarei v. Rio Tinto, 550 F. 3d 822 (9th Cir. 2008, *en banc*) *reversed and remanded on other grounds*, 133 S.Ct. 1995 (Mem. 2013) (reconsideration in light of Kiobel), (war crimes, crimes against humanity, racial discrimination and environmental torts relating to international mining operations in Papua New Guinea — political questions, acts of state, international comity and exhaustion of local remedies) *See also* Sarei v. Rio Tinto, *PLC*, 722 F.3d 1109 (9th Cir. 2013) (en banc affirmance of D. Ct. dismissal of action in light of Kiobel); Saleh v. Titan Corp., 580 F.3d 1 (D.C. Circuit 2009)(dismissing claims by Iraqi detainees at Abu Ghraib prison against private contractors hired by U.S. military for lack of state action and preemption). *See generally* Regina Waugh, *Exhaustion of Remedies and the Alien Tort Statute* , 28 Berkeley J. Int'l L. 555 (2010); *Defending Actions in the United States Arising From Alleged Foreign-Based Torts*, 57 Rocky Mountain Mineral L. INST 8-1 (2011).

### g. Putting It All Together: The Aftermath of *Sosa* and *Kiobel*, Claims & Defenses

The case of Chilean leftist songwriter Victor Jara (performing here and here; covered by Bruce Springsteen here) provides a glimpse at the potential future of foreign violation cases in the United States. Jara, along with thousands of other intellectuals and perceived opponents of the Junta, was rounded up by the military during the 1973 coup in Chile and taken to the national soccer stadium. After being recognized as a popular folk singer, he was then tortured and eventually shot 44 times. In 2012, some 40 years later, Chilean authorities charged eight retired Army officers in his death. One of his killers, lieutenant Pedro Barrientos, had since taken up permanent residence in Deltona, Florida, and was sued by Jara's widow in 2013 under the TVPA and ATS (complaint).

---

79. Yousuf v. Samantar, 699 F. 3d 763 (4th Circ. 2012).

Image by reddartfrog on deviantart.com

### Chile: 3 More Charged in Victor Jara Murder

SANTIAGO, Chile — Sep 3, 2014, 9:31 PM ET

Chile charged three more people on Wednesday in the murder of folk singer Victor Jara during the country's 1973 military coup.

A judge in Santiago charged former military officers Hernan Chancon Soto and Patricio Vasquez Donoso with taking part in the Sept. 16, 1973 killing. He also charged ex-army prosecutor Ramon Melo Silva as an accomplice. They join a list of eight former army officers who were charged in late 2012 and early 2013 in the killing of the communist singer and songwriter.

"This decision has to be celebrated and we hope this investigation can continue," Jara's widow, Joan Jara, said at a press conference. "We know this marks a milestone."

Jara, whose songs tackled social and political issues, was swept up with thousands of other supporters of socialist President Salvador Allende during a military coup led by Gen. Augusto Pinochet.

Last year, Jara's family filed a civil lawsuit in the United States accusing former Chilean army Lt. Pedro Barrientos Nunez of ordering soldiers to torture the singer. The lawsuit also said Barrientos personally fired the fatal shot while playing a game of "Russian roulette" inside a locker room in Santiago's Estadio Chile, where some 5,000 supporters of Allende were being detained.

. . .

Please review the Jara complaint at the link above. Note in particular the allegations relating to sources of law, jurisdiction and causes of action. **In light of what you now understand about the law in this area how would you rule if you were a judge considering a motion to dismiss this complaint and why? What legal theory and critical contacts with the United States should be emphasized?** (Note the materials below relating to the involvement of U.S. officials like Henry Kissinger in Chile.)

Here is what the jury thought.

Pascale Bonnefoy, NY Times, JUNE 27, 2016, <u>Florida Jury Finds Former Chilean Officer Liable in '73 Killing</u>

SANTIAGO, Chile — Four decades after the bullet-riddled body of the Chilean folk singer Víctor Jara was discovered in the mayhem of the military coup that upended his country, Mr. Jara's family found some measure of justice on Monday in a Florida courtroom.

A federal jury in Orlando concluded that a former Chilean Army officer who had emigrated to the United States and worked as a short-order cook was liable for the torture and extrajudicial killing of Mr. Jara at the Chilean sports stadium where he was held after the 1973 coup that brought Gen. <u>Augusto Pinochet</u> to power.

The court awarded Mr. Jara's family $28 million in damages.

The former officer, Pedro Pablo Barrientos, 67, a naturalized American citizen and resident of Deltona, Fla., near Daytona Beach, was a defendant in a civil suit brought under an American law aimed at helping victims of human rights violations committed overseas.

<u>Video clip of Jara</u> singing

## 4. *Filartiga*-Style Actions Overseas: The Case against Henry Kissinger

**Larry Rohter, <u>Victims of Pinochet Regime Target Kissinger in Courts</u>,** March 29, 2002 (*Copyright © 2002, Chicago Tribune*)

SANTIAGO, Chile — With a trial of Gen. Augusto Pinochet increasingly unlikely here, victims of the Chilean military's 17-year dictatorship are now pressing legal actions in Chilean and U.S. courts against Henry Kissinger and other Nixon administration officials who supported plots to overthrow Salvador Allende, the Socialist president, in the early 1970s.

In perhaps the most prominent of the cases, an investigating judge here has formally asked Kissinger, a former national security adviser and secretary of state, and Nathaniel Davis, the U.S. ambassador to Chile at the time, to respond to questions about the killing of an American citizen, Charles Horman, after the deadly military coup that brought Pinochet to power on Sept. 11, 1973.

. . . . the initiation of legal action in Chile against Pinochet and the declassification of some American documents led her to file a new suit in Chile 15 months ago.

Relatives of Gen. Rene Schneider, commander of the Chilean armed forces when he was assassinated in October 1970 by other military officers, have taken a different approach. Alleging summary execution, assault and civil rights violations, they filed a $3 million lawsuit in Washington last fall [September 11, 2001] against Kissinger, former CIA Director Richard Helms and other Nixon-era officials who, according to declassified U.S. documents, were involved in plotting a military coup to keep Allende from power.

## 5. Domestic Enforcement of Human Rights against U.S. Government Actors

### a. Overview

In contrast to ATS and TVPA claims against foreign defendants (at least historically), human rights litigation against U.S. public officials has had limited success. One of the earliest cases relying on human rights law to challenge U.S. conduct abroad is a good illustration of why. In Sanchez-Espinoza v. Reagan, 770 F.2d 202 (1985), twelve Nicaraguan plaintiffs (among others) sought damages from U.S. public officials for financing, training and directing attacks against innocent Nicaraguan civilians by the "Contras," an anti-government military group. Plaintiffs relied on, among other things, the ATS for jurisdiction and alleged violations of international law such as "summary execution, murder, abduction, torture, rape, wounding, and the destruction of private property and public facilities."[80] The District Court dismissed the claims essentially on grounds that they were non-justiciable political questions. The D.C. Court of Appeals, in an opinion written by Antonin Scalia and joined by Ruth Bader Ginsburg (both then Circuit Court Judges), did not disagree but instead dismissed the claims on alternative grounds. To the extent that the plaintiffs challenged conduct of U.S. officials or their agents taken in their official capacity, their claims would be barred by sovereign immunity. To the extent such claims relied on private, non-official conduct, there would be no violation of international law which generally only applies to state actors. Scalia also reasoned that such claims should not be entertained by courts because of their potential interference with "sensitive" matters of foreign affairs.

In contrast to *Sanchez*, the federal district court in Jama v. INS, 22 F.Supp.2d 353 (1998), was far more amenable to claims that U.S. officials and their agents (private

---

80. 770 F.2d at 205.

contractors) could be sued for violations of international law occurring in the United States. Plaintiffs in *Jama* alleged that Immigration and Naturalization Service officials and their agents had subjected them to a multitude of physical and emotional abuses while in detention awaiting resolution of their political asylum claims. The court's description of the legal basis for the plaintiffs' claims is instructive regarding the role of treaties and customary law:

> Plaintiffs have included among their papers in opposition to the motion to dismiss nineteen treaties, charters on human rights, conventions and other international instruments articulating the rights of refugees and seekers of asylum and condemning or prohibiting in general or specific terms many of the kinds of abuses which are alleged in the complaint.

> In order for a treaty to confer rights enforceable by private parties it must be self-executing, that is, a treaty which requires no legislation to make it operative. *Frolova v. Union of Soviet Socialist Republics*, 761 F.2d 370 (7th Cir.1985). Unless a treaty is self-executing, it must be implemented by legislation before it can give rise to a private right of action enforceable in a court of the United States. *Dreyfus v. Von Finck*, 534 F.2d 24 (2d Cir.1976), *cert. denied*, 429 U.S. 835, 97 S.Ct. 102, 50 L.Ed.2d 101 (1976).

> None of the treaties or other international instruments which plaintiffs have submitted are self-executing. Plaintiffs recognize that these treaties do not per se provide a basis for suit under the ATCA. Rather, they are submitted for another purpose — to support a claim under the "law of nations" or international law, which is also a basis for an ATCA action: "The complaint alleges violations of customary international law and not specific treaties. The complaint alleges that defendants' abuses of plaintiff asylum seekers violated customary international law *as informed by* various international human rights treaties and other international human rights instruments." (Plaintiffs' Brief at p. 21) (Emphasis on original).

***

> For the purposes of the present motions, the allegations of the complaint must be accepted as true and all reasonable inferences favorable to plaintiffs must be drawn from them. When this is done, it is evident that the totality of the treatment to which plaintiffs were subjected violated customary international law as it is now established.

***

> The mental and physical abuses which are alleged to have been inflicted upon plaintiffs violate the international human rights norm of the right to be free from cruel, unhuman and degrading treatment. The ATCA confers federal subject matter jurisdiction when i) an alien sues, ii) for a tort iii) committed in violation of the law of nations (i.e., international law), *Kadic*, 70 F.3d at 238. The complaint sufficiently alleges all three jurisdictional requirements.

Because the ATCA provides jurisdiction over plaintiffs' claims based on international law, it is unnecessary to decide if 28 U.S.C. § 1331 (federal question jurisdiction) provides an independent basis for jurisdiction. See discussion in *Kadic*, 70 F.3d at 246.

Although the court in Jama clearly recognized that the ATS (ATCA) could be potentially used to bring customary international law claims against U.S. public officials, it also recognized several important obstacles to such claims generally. As in *Sanchez*, the court held that the United States itself and its agency (INS) could not be sued by virtue of sovereign immunity. Even individual defendant officials might be entitled to immunity under some circumstances (such as in *Sanchez*) and plaintiffs must factually demonstrate that the defendant was individually responsible for violating the international norm.

In both *Sanchez* and *Jama* the plaintiffs were aliens entitled to rely on the ATS. American citizens, however, would not be entitled to invoke this statute and, in any case, would typically have a number of domestic legal alternatives for seeking remedies against public officials. Consider the following case brought by a U.S. citizen alleging violations of international human rights by a California judge. The case provides a good illustration of the obstacles facing lawsuits in U.S. courts against American public officials based on international rights. Note in particular the plaintiff's reliance on jus cogens as a source of law and the court's discussion of implied causes of action.

b. Civil Suits against U.S. Public Officials for Domestic Violations of Human Rights: A Shocking Lack of International Protections?

**Hawkins v. Comparet-Cassani**, 33 F. Supp. 2d 1244 (C.D. Cal. 1999) (reversed on other grounds, 251 F.3d 1230 (9th Cir. 2001)

PREGERSON, District Judge.

\*\*\*

## BACKGROUND

The plaintiff, Ronnie Hawkins ("Hawkins"), was tried and convicted of one count of felony burglary and one count of felony theft in April 1998 before Los Angeles County Municipal Court Judge Comparet-Cassani, a named defendant in this case. On June 30, 1998, Hawkins appeared before Judge Comparet-Cassani to have a motion heard and for sentencing. Due to alleged threats of violence to the Court, the Los Angeles County Sheriff received a court order to place a "stun belt" on Hawkins. At this hearing, Judge Comparet-Cassani claims that Hawkins made several statements out of order and acted in a generally disruptive manner. As a result, Judge Comparet-Cassani ordered a courtroom deputy to activate the stun belt.

\*\*\*

Hawkins alleges that the stun belt operates by delivering a current of 50,000 volts of electricity. This shock "stuns" the victim into submission.

\*\*\*

The complaint requests the following relief: (1) a declaratory judgment that using the stun belt is unconstitutional; (2) an injunction prohibiting the defendants from using the stun belt; (3) compensatory damages against all defendants, punitive damages against all defendants except Los Angeles County, and punitive damages of $50,000,000 against Judge Comparet-Cassani; and (4) costs of the suit and attorney's fees.

## MOTIONS AT ISSUE

First, the defendants move under Federal Rule 12(b)(6) to dismiss all claims against all defendants. Defendants argue that several defendants are immune from suit and that Hawkins failed to state a claim upon which relief can be granted. Additionally, the defendants move to dismiss counts I, II, IV and X of the plaintiff's amended complaint for failure to state a claim.

\*\*\*

### 4. Claims under international law (Counts I and II)

The plaintiff makes two claims under international law. First, the plaintiff claims that the defendants violated jus cogens norms of international law. Second, the plaintiff argues that the defendants violated jus dispositivum international law — i.e., the violation of various treaties which the United States signed and ratified.

a. Violations of jus cogens international law (Count I)

The plaintiff claims that the defendants' acts amount to torture under international law, and therefore the defendants violated jus cogens norms of international law. Jus cogens norms of international law comprise the body of laws that are considered so fundamental that they are binding on all nations whether the nations have consented to them or not. See Siderman de Blake v. Republic of Argentina, 965 F.2d 699, 714 (9th Cir.1992). To determine the scope of jus cogens international law, courts look to several different sources including treaties, state practice, legal decisions, and works of noted jurists. See id. at 714–15. In this regard, several courts have found that torture is a violation of jus cogens norms of international law. \*\*\* These cases define torture as:

any act by which severe pain or suffering, whether physical or mental, is intentionally inflicted on a person for such purposes as obtaining from him or a third person information or a confession, punishing him for an act he or a third person has committed or is suspected of having committed, or intimidating or coercing him or a third person, or for any reason based on discrimination of any kind, when such pain or suffering is inflicted by or at the instigation of or with the consent or acquiescence of a public official or other person acting in an official capacity.

***

All of the cases, however, that found a cognizable right under jus cogens norms of international law involved either acts committed on a foreign citizen or acts committed by a foreign government or government official. There is no reported case of a court in the United States recognizing a cause of action under jus cogens norms of international law for acts committed by United States government officials against a citizen of the United States. See White v. Paulsen, 997 F.Supp. 1380, 1383 (E.D.Wash.1998) (rejecting this type of action). Therefore, the plaintiff is inviting this Court to define a new cause of action against state officers in the United States when they act against a citizen of this country.

It is clear that jus cogens norms of international law are part of the laws of the United States. See The Paquete Habana, 175 U.S. 677, 700, 20 S.Ct. 290, 44 L.Ed. 320 (1900). However, the law of nations does not in itself create a personal right of action for individual citizens. See White, 997 F.Supp. at 1383. Instead, "[w]hether and how the United States wished to react to such violations are domestic questions." In Re Estate of Marcos Human Rights Lit., 25 F.3d 1467, 1475 (9th Cir.1994), quoting Tel-Oren v. Libyan Arab Republic, 726 F.2d 774, 777–78 (D.C.Cir.1984) (Edwards, J., concurring).

It is also clear, however, that federal courts may imply a personal right of action for violations of jus cogens norms of international law. See, e.g., White, 997 F.Supp. at 1383; see also, Bivens v. Six Unknown Named Agents of the Fed. Bureau of Narcotics, 403 U.S. 388, 91 S.Ct. 1999, 29 L.Ed.2d 619 (1971). In Bivens, the Supreme Court held that where federally protected rights are invaded then the "courts will be alert to adjust their remedies so as to grant the necessary relief." Bivens, 403 U.S. at 392, 91 S.Ct. 1999. However, courts do not automatically recognize a Bivens claim anytime there is a federally protected right that does not have an express remedy. See Schweiker v. Chilicky, 487 U.S. 412, 414, 108 S.Ct. 2460, 101 L.Ed.2d 370 (1988). Instead, "federal courts also must consider whether there exist 'special factors counseling hesitation in the absence of affirmative action by Congress.'" White, 997 F.Supp. at 1384, quoting Bivens, 403 U.S. at 396, 91 S.Ct. 1999.

Here, as in White, there are several factors which counsel against the Court implying a Bivens right of action in this case. First, in the Court's view, there are existing remedies for plaintiff's causes of action. Indeed, the plaintiff has filed several different claims under domestic laws such as the Eighth Amendment's prohibition of cruel and unusual punishment. Moreover, many of the claims barred in this Court due to Eleventh Amendment concerns could have been brought in a California state court.

Additionally, the Court notes, as did the White court, that Congress has acted in the field of torture. Congress enacted the Torture Victim Protection Act of 1991. This Act creates a private right of action for victims of torture taken under color of law in a foreign nation. Pub.L. 102-256, Mar. 12, 1992, 106 Stat. 73, codified at 28 U.S.C. § 1350. Although this statute appears to be limited to acts of foreign officials, it represents congressional attempts to address the issue of a private remedy for acts of torture. Courts normally give great deference to congressional policy determinations regarding whether to afford individuals personal rights of action for particular violations. See Schweiker, 487 U.S. at 423, 108 S.Ct. 2460. Likewise, this Court is hesitant to create a new cause of action in a circumstance where the Legislature has stated that domestic law affords adequate remedies. See White, 997 F.Supp. at 1384–85.

Finally, this Court is also hesitant to interfere in an area that is traditionally entrusted to the legislative and executive branches. It is these two branches which must interpret what international obligations the United States will undertake and how to implement them domestically. See id. at 1385; Handel v. Artukovic, 601 F.Supp. 1421, 1428 (C.D.Cal.1985) (stating, "To imply a cause of action from the law of nations would completely defeat the critical right of the sovereign to determine whether and how international rights should be enforced in that municipality.").

For these reasons, the Court finds that "the special factors counseling hesitation" the Bivens Court discussed are present in the current case. Therefore, the Court GRANTS the defendants' motion to dismiss Count I of the plaintiff's amended complaint with prejudice.

b. Violations of jus dispositivum international law (Count II)

It is well settled that treaties are part of the supreme law of the land. U.S. Const. Art VI, cl. 2. However, it is also well settled that treaties may be modified by subsequent statutes enacted by Congress or other executive agreements. See Moser v. United States, 341 U.S. 41, 45, 71 S.Ct. 553, 95 L.Ed. 729 (1951). Therefore, although treaties are supreme over the laws of the several states, they are basically on par with federal law, and certainly are not superior to the Constitution.

As stated above, the Eleventh Amendment prohibits a federal court from hearing many of the plaintiff's claims. There is nothing to suggest that these international treaties grant district courts subject matter jurisdiction in cases where it would normally not exist under the Eleventh Amendment.

The plaintiff claims that the actions herein violate five "treaties" to which the United States is a signatory: the Universal Declaration of Human Rights; the Declaration on the Protection of All Persons from Being Subjected to Torture; the American Convention on Human Rights; the International Covenant on Civil and Political Rights; and the European Convention for the Protection of Human Rights and Fundamental Freedoms. The plaintiff states that violations of these treaties entitle him to recover damages and to receive declaratory and injunctive relief.

The Supreme Court has stated that treaties are only enforceable in United States courts if either the treaty is self-executing or the Legislature passes legislation implementing the provisions of a treaty. ***

Therefore, the Court must examine each treaty the plaintiff cites to see if it is self-executing under the Iran and Saipan tests.

The first two "treaties" which the plaintiff cites, the Universal Declaration of Human Rights and the Declaration on the Protection of All Persons from Being Subjected to Torture, are not treaties at all. . . . Instead, they are non-binding resolutions of the United Nations General Assembly. See Siderman de Blake, 965 F.2d at 719. As such, they are only intended to "represent[ ] evidence of customary international law." Id. They are not intended to be legally binding or create self-executing rights like other international treaties. Id. Therefore, the plaintiff cannot state a claim under these resolutions.

Although the American Convention on Human Rights is a treaty to which the United States is a signatory, the United States has not yet ratified this treaty. *** Therefore, this treaty is not binding on the United States. *** Consequently, the plaintiff cannot state a claim under this treaty.

Additionally, the United States is not a signatory nor has it ratified the European Convention for the Protection of Human Rights and Fundamental Freedoms. Therefore, this treaty is not binding on the United States and the plaintiff cannot state a claim under it.

The United States, however, has signed and ratified the International Covenant on Civil and Political Rights and the Convention Against Torture and Other Cruel, Inhuman or Degrading Treatment or Punishment. Several courts have looked at these treaties and have concluded that they are not self-executing. *** Furthermore, when the Senate ratified these treaties it did so "with the express proviso that they were not self-executing." Extradition of Cheung, 968 F.Supp. at 803 n. 17. Additionally, Congress has not enacted implementing legislation. Id. Therefore, these treaties do not create a private right of action under which the plaintiff can successfully state a claim.

For these reasons, the defendants' motion to dismiss Count II of plaintiff's amended complaint is GRANTED.

Metropolitan News-Enterprise , Wednesday, December 5, 2001, Page 3

### Board of Supervisors Agrees to $2.5 Million in Settlement Payments

By a MetNews Staff Writer

The county Board of Supervisors yesterday agreed to pay more than $2.5 million in lawsuit settlements, including $275,000 to a Long Beach man whose criminal case made national news when he was jolted in court with a 50,000-volt stun belt.

Ronnie Hawkins, a career criminal, was shocked by sheriff's deputies during his sentencing hearing in 1998 when Los Angeles Municipal Court Judge Joan Comparet-Cassani, now a Superior Court judge, ordered the jolt after Hawkins interrupted her repeatedly and violated her orders not to tell jurors that he was HIV-positive or that he was facing a 25-year-to-life sentence . . . .

Hawkins was awarded a second trial and was convicted by a second jury of stealing $265 worth of aspirin. The conviction was his third strike under California's three strikes law. Hawkins is currently appealing his 25 years to life sentence.

The Ninth U.S. Circuit Court of Appeals ruled in May that the belts may no longer be used to subdue defendants who are just being verbally disruptive, but they can be used on defendants who are flight risks or are a threat to others in the courtroom.

### c. The Case for Domestic Accountability of U.S. Officials for Actions Overseas

The United States has had a long, unfortunate history associated with supporting authoritarian regimes in Latin America. This history has included substantial material assistance to forces responsible for brutal repression, thousands of extra-judicial executions and practices such as torture, arbitrary imprisonment and "<u>disappearances.</u>" Review the brief news excerpts below and consider whether U.S. officials should be held accountable for their role in facilitating human rights abuses overseas.

### i. Editorial, *Reagan and War Crimes*, Consortium News, 1999

Some readers might be offended by the thought of us blaming Ronald Reagan for arming and protecting war criminals who inflicted mass murder and genocide on Guatemalans.

But the point of this special report is that the United States invites the charge of hypocrisy when it accuses "enemy" leaders of war crimes, while it turns a blind eye to equally horrific slaughters committed by allies, sometimes guided and protected by the U.S. government . . . .

In the 1980s, U.S.-backed forces committed widespread massacres, political murders and torture. Tens of thousands of civilians died. Many of the dead were children. Soldiers routinely raped women before executing them.

There can be no doubt, too, that President Reagan was an avid supporter of the implicated military forces, that he supplied them with weapons and that he actively sought to discredit human rights investigators and journalists who exposed the crimes. . . .

Without doubt, it is safer for an American journalist or politician to wag a finger at Milosevic or at the killers in Rwanda or at the Khmer Rouge than it is to confront the guilt that pervaded Ronald Reagan's presidency . . . .

In that sense, this issue's special report addresses more than President Reagan's personal guilt. The larger question is whether the United States still has the political capacity — and the moral integrity — to confront its own complicity in shameful war crimes committed against the people of Latin America . . . .

ii. Editorial, *Overdue Apology Clinton Addresses a Shameful U.S. Role in Guatemala*

Pittsburgh Post-Gazette, Friday, March 12, 1999, available through <u>Google Newspaper Archives</u>

For decades the Guatemalan army and internal security forces fought insurgents and anyone they believed might be a sympathizer. Over time that definition was applied to a larger and larger group of people, until ultimately the entire Indian population was suspect.

Labor leaders, student activists, priests, intellectuals and anyone who questioned economic inequity and the lack of civil liberties were routinely kidnapped and summarily executed, while entire rural villages were razed. Massacre, torture, rape and murder were widely used and accepted tools in the counter-insurgency.

And throughout it all, the United States supplied money, training and support. It all fit into a broader Cold War policy embracing anti-communism in all its manifestations . . . .

This week, President Clinton on a tour of Central America took the welcome and important step of apologizing for American involvement and pledging that such lapses of foreign policy decency and judgment would not happen again. He said the United States would no longer take part in campaigns of repression but would "continue to support the peace and reconciliation process in Guatemala. . . .

iii. Tim Weiner, *C.I.A. May Dismiss Chief Officer Involved in Guatemala*, NY Times, Thursday, September 28, 1995

Breaking with the past, the CIA will dismiss, demote or discipline up to a dozen officers, including the former chief of covert operations in Latin America, for shielding suspect agents and stifling reports of human-rights abuses in Guatemala, government officials said Wednesday.

The director of central intelligence, John M. Deutch, is weighing an internal review board's recommendations to dismiss the former Latin American division chief and a former station chief in Guatemala, and demote or discipline as many as 10 other officers . . . .

The board's recommendations came six months after the exposure of the agency's longstanding ties to senior Guatemalan military officers suspected of human-rights abuses, including murder. Scores of senior officers in the Guatemalan army, which has killed tens of thousands of civilians and tortured thousands more in a long campaign against a small guerrilla force, have served as CIA agents.

The agency declined to comment.***

### d. Domestic Accountability for Human Rights Violations in the War on Terror?

The actions of U.S. officials in the context of the "War on Terror" have raised the issue of domestic accountability under international human rights law to new saliency. Could U.S. officials responsible for "water boarding" and other "enhanced interrogation" techniques during the administration of George W. Bush be held liable, or charged with crimes, for violation of the international norms against torture? Has President Barak Obama violated international human rights law by creating a "kill list" of suspected terrorists who are selected for assassination via drone strikes? Recall that the ATS only covers alien plaintiffs, and that the TVPA only applies to the conduct of foreign officials. U.S. officials are often entitled to immunities for official conduct and courts are reluctant to judge actions by the executive branch involving foreign affairs and national defense. It should be fairly apparent based on the limited case law described above that suits against U.S. public officials based on international human rights law would face substantial obstacles. Should U.S. officials face accountability under international human rights standards?

# Chapter 6

# Using Domestic Criminal Prosecutions to Enforce International Human Rights

## A. Introduction and Overview

It is not uncommon within domestic legal systems that certain wrongful conduct, such as battery, can create both civil and criminal liability. Similarly, while most international rights are clearly not designed or intended to create criminal liability, a relatively small but vital sub-set of those rights involve physical harms to others and lend themselves to potential criminal culpability. Human rights violations commonly subject to criminal prosecution currently include genocide, torture, extra-judicial execution, and "disappearances." Others may potentially include human trafficking, exploitation of children as soldiers, and apartheid. Conduct which violates "humanitarian law" relating to armed conflict, primarily war crimes and crimes against humanity, are also primarily enforced through criminal culpability. It is now common for states to define at least some egregious human rights violations as crimes under their domestic law, although not in strict compliance with international definitions. In a "preliminary survey update" released in 2012, Amnesty International reported that:

> ". . . 166 (approximately 86%) of the 193 UN member states have defined one or more of the four crimes under international law (war crimes, crimes against humanity, genocide and torture) as crimes in their national law. As noted below, however, not only have many states failed to define all of these crimes under international law as crimes under national law, but in many instances the definitions are not consistent with the strictest requirements of international law, creating a serious impunity gap. 24 states apparently have not defined any of them as crimes in their national law."[81]

---

81. Amnesty International, *Universal Jurisdiction: A Preliminary Survey of Legislation Around the World — 2012 Update* at 12. Professor Goodman has cast some doubt about the accuracy of the Amnesty Report on the website "Just Security."

There are, of course, many important distinctions between criminal and civil liability which are relevant to human rights enforcement. Many of these distinctions derive from the contrasting goals involved. For most human rights norms, enforcement goals tend to focus on inducing legal change, modification of government policies or actions and, to a lesser but growing extent, compensating victims of abuse for their losses. In contrast, enforcement through criminal liability is primarily focused on punishing and deterring individual perpetrators, typically government officials, for their wrong-doing. Since criminal prosecution leads to punishment including loss of liberty, the defendant is also entitled to protection of his own human rights relating to jurisdiction, fair trial and procedure.

This chapter focuses on domestic criminal prosecutions for certain human rights violations. In subsequent chapters we examine the development of international criminal processes designed to prosecute violations of human rights associated with humanitarian law that take place during armed conflict. You will discover that, prompted by the unfortunate circumstance of experience and need, international criminal processes focused on war crimes and crimes against humanity have undergone an impressive evolution in the last two decades. Despite some noteworthy success in prosecuting major figures, however, these international institutions have neither the resources nor physical capacity to reach most perpetrators of international human rights crimes. Therefore, national institutions pursuing domestic prosecutions, particularly in the jurisdictions affected, is a critical but underdeveloped alternative.

Within most domestic systems, any particular human rights violation will only be criminally prosecuted if the domestic legal order first chooses to "domesticate" that international right by criminalizing its violation. The prosecution, while derived from an international obligation, would be for crimes defined and forbidden under domestic law. Prosecutors and courts within the United States, for example, could not prosecute a suspected torturer until that international human rights violation was also defined as a crime under federal or state law. This would be true even for a self-executing human rights treaty, if such a thing existed. For a limited number of human rights violations, it is not uncommon for international treaties to require member states to do precisely that—criminalize violations of certain rights as part of the states' international obligations.

Both the Genocide Convention and Convention Against Torture, for example, require state parties to criminalize violations under domestic law. They also adopt the principle of "*aut dedere aut judicare*" (Latin for "either deliver or judge"), which requires member states to either criminally prosecute or extradite violators, preventing jurisdictional safe havens. The Geneva Conventions, the primary source of humanitarian law outlawing war crimes and crimes against humanity, also require states to investigate, prosecute or extradite those who commit "grave breaches" of the Conventions.[82] In at least one important instance, international criminal law even

---

82. First Geneva Convention, Article 49; Second Geneva Convention, Article 50; Third Geneva Convention, Article 129; Fourth Geneva Convention, Article 146.

defers to domestic criminal processes whenever possible. The jurisdiction of the International Criminal Court over the prosecution of international crimes is subsidiary to domestic prosecutorial processes when available and utilized. Note that the potential for extradition of a human right violator to a willing prosecuting state usually also depends on domestic criminalization of that international right. Most extradition treaties require "dual criminality" — that is, the alleged violation must be recognized as a crime in both the sending and receiving states.

Once a human rights violation has been domestically criminalized, prosecution follows normal domestic rules and procedures which, in the context of human rights, may often engender particular jurisdictional issues involving international law. When a defendant is a national of the prosecuting state or has committed the violation within its territory there is little doubt that prosecution would meet both constitutional and international jurisdictional rules. Prosecution in the state of origin, however, is often not a realistic possibility for human rights violations. Historically, the most egregious violations of human rights take place under conditions in which the rule of law has been seriously compromised and genuine enforcement mechanisms are lacking. When conditions for prosecution improve after regime change, such perpetrators frequently flee the place of their crimes and seek sanctuary in distant places.

When is it permissible for other states to take jurisdiction and prosecute an accused non-national for conduct taking place outside its territory? Can the United States lawfully prosecute extra-territorial violations of international human rights law committed by foreign defendants? May Iran, North Korea and all other states do the same? International law provides some increasingly definitive answers to this critical question of jurisdiction and its appropriate limits, although serious issues and controversy remain.

After reviewing the international law backdrop regarding jurisdictional issues, we will examine current U.S. law criminalizing certain human rights violations. This study includes a review of how the United State government has utilized immigration law, both civil and criminal, to either prosecute or return foreign human rights violators to their home countries to face criminal charges. The next section of the chapter then examines efforts to use criminal processes in other countries. This includes the case of Chilean Dictator Augusto Pinochet and the effort to extradite him from the United Kingdom to Spain for crimes committed in Chile. This section also asks you to consider whether U.S. officials could or should be held criminally responsible for human rights violations allegedly committed in the "War on Terror."

After studying this material you should be able to answer the following questions:

1. What do international rules defining the limits on state jurisdiction currently provide regarding domestic criminal prosecution of human rights violations?

2. Which particular international human rights violations have been criminalized within the United States and under what limitations?

3. What is Universal Jurisdiction and what are the primary policy implications regarding its widespread use to vindicate human rights?

4. How are immigration laws used in the United States to indirectly vindicate and enforce human rights?

5. What are the potential benefits and downsides of widespread use of criminal law and universal jurisdiction to prosecute alleged violations of human rights?

To put a practical face on these questions as you study the materials, think about and evaluate two possible criminal prosecutions involving current world events. First, evaluate the actions of the radical self-proclaimed Islamic State in Iraq and Syria ("ISIS," also known as ISIL, which stands for Islamic State in Iraq and the Levant). Consider any sources of news on ISIS you want or this article from <u>SLATE</u>. Second, applying the same criteria, evaluate whether U.S. officials could be criminally prosecuted here or abroad for actions taken in the war of terrorism including the use of "enhanced interrogation" techniques and drone based "targeted killings." You will find materials discussing this particular question in the later part of this chapter.

## B. International Law Limits on Domestic Jurisdiction and the Rise of Universal Jurisdiction

With regard to prosecuting human rights violations that take place overseas, jurisdiction is a particularly sensitive issue. While international law recognizes the plenary power of a state to control conduct occurring within its territory, it has traditionally imposed limits upon the power of any particular state to reach conduct taking place outside of its borders—that is, the extra-territorial application of its laws. The reason for this is obvious—if Iran could lawfully criminalize and seek to punish American citizens who defame the Koran in the United States it would undoubtedly create significant political conflict and inevitable disruptions of peaceful international relations.

As if on cue, an <u>Egyptian court recently tried in absentia</u> and sentenced to death seven Coptic Christians living in the United States and the controversial Florida "pastor" Terry Jones for promoting a low-budget internet anti-Islamic video. (The video, "Innocence of Muslims," sparked riots in the Middle East by portraying the Prophet Muhammad as a fraud, womanizer and buffoon. Jones' sentence was reduced to seven years.) Even if only for show or domestic political consumption, such attempts at extraterritorial application of law and legal processes will obviously rankle the U.S. government and American public, and vice versa if played in reverse.

And yet, it is also inevitably true that conduct and events taking place outside a particular state's territory will raise issues of critical and legitimate concern to that state. If an Iranian were to produce counterfeit U.S. passports or conspire to commit terrorist attacks on Americans overseas, the United States would legitimately seek to proscribe such overseas conduct, and punish its individual perpetrators wherever they might be. Should the same logic apply to perpetrators of torture, genocide and war crimes—the enemies of all humankind?

In response to such jurisdictional quandaries, international law provides a set of generally well-recognized rules defining the scope of state jurisdiction. While the term "jurisdiction" generally refers to the authority or power of an institution over subjects and actors, various applications of jurisdictional authority are distinguishable. International law, for example, distinguishes the power to "prescribe" rules (e.g., defining criminal conduct) from the power to enforce or adjudicate those rules in various circumstances. The Restatement articulates these distinctions in this way:

Restatement of Foreign Relations Law, Third § 401

Under international law, a state is subject to limitations on

(1) jurisdiction to prescribe, i.e., to make its law applicable to the activities, relations, or status of persons, or the interests of persons in things, whether by legislation, by executive act or order, by administrative rule or regulation, or by determination of a court;

(2) jurisdiction to adjudicate, i.e., to subject persons or things to the process of its courts or administrative tribunals, whether in civil or in criminal proceedings, whether or not the state is a party to the proceedings;

(3) jurisdiction to enforce, i.e., to induce or compel compliance or punish noncompliance with its laws or regulations, whether through the courts or by use of executive, administrative, police, or other nonjudicial action.

These distinctions and the corresponding rules on the limits of state power to prescribe, enforce and adjudicate have particular importance to domestic criminal prosecutions of international human rights violators. It is possible, for example, to believe that a particular state may have sufficient interests to prescribe certain conduct but would not be justified in using its law enforcement powers to find and capture violators residing in other countries. Such extra-territorial use of law enforcement would, by definition, invade the territory of other states and violate their sovereignty. Because enforcement in this sense could be extremely disruptive to international relations, most criminal prosecutions of human rights violations depend on the physical presence of the defendant, which can be secured peacefully via regularized extradition or through happenstance. The physical presence of the defendant also enhances justifications for adjudication assuming that due process and genuinely neutral procedures are followed.

Consider the following articulation of the international rules on the power to prescribe as provided by the U.S. Restatement of Foreign Relations Law, Third:

§ 402. BASES OF JURISDICTION TO PRESCRIBE

Subject to § 403, [a general overarching rule of "reasonableness"] a state has jurisdiction to prescribe law with respect to

(1) (a)  conduct that, wholly or in substantial part, takes place within its territory;

  (b)  the status of persons, or interests in things, present within its territory;

(c) conduct outside its territory that has or is intended to have substantial effect within its territory;

(2) the activities, interests, status, or relations of its nationals outside as well as within its territory; and

(3) certain conduct outside its territory by persons not its nationals that is directed against the security of the state or against a limited class of other state interests.

It should be immediately obvious that the first premise of these international rules is that states have plenary jurisdiction to criminalize any conduct that takes place within their territory but only limited jurisdiction over events and people outside of national boundaries. The underlying premise might be described as a general prohibition against extra-territorial applications of domestic law. There are, however, several important variations or exceptions. The first, often called nationality jurisdiction, is that states are generally entitled to control the conduct of their own nationals wherever they might be. The United States has the power, for example, to criminalize torture by a U.S. national even if it takes place in another country. This power is constrained in some fashion by the fact that the foreign state in which the national's conduct takes place would also have jurisdiction to prescribe. Thus, a U.S. national suspected of torture would simultaneously be subject to the foreign state's law on torture if the relevant conduct took place within that foreign state's sovereign territory.

Second, states also can exercise jurisdiction over conduct occurring outside their territory that has an intended, substantial effect within their borders. The example of terrorism demonstrates the justification for this type of jurisdiction. The United States has the authority under international law to criminalize and prosecute those who, while outside U.S. territory, plan and put into motion acts of terrorism designed to cause injuries within the United States. The United States can, for example, lawfully prosecute foreign nationals who place a bomb on a jet overseas that is designed to explode on U.S. soil. Note here how distinct limitations on the power to enforce and adjudicate may impose limits on the practical significance of this jurisdiction to outlaw the conduct.

Third, states can reach overseas conduct that threatens state security or its essential functions as a sovereign. This so-called "protective jurisdiction" is not generally relevant to human rights and has been restricted to subjects such as counterfeiting, nationality and immigration. One can imagine circumstances involving terrorism in which a state might also invoke such a basis for jurisdiction.

Fourth, some states extend their jurisdiction to include wrongs committed *against* their nationals overseas (as distinguished from nationality jurisdiction under which the national is the actor). Sometimes called "passive personality jurisdiction," this form of extra-territorial power is rejected by many states and exercised rarely. The United States currently asserts such jurisdiction only with regard to acts of terrorism (which by definition are directed not just at the victim but also at the United States itself) and war crimes.

Finally, and most significantly for human rights, many states now endorse a concept called "universal jurisdiction." The Restatement articulates the concept in Section 404:

> A state has jurisdiction to define and prescribe punishment for certain offenses recognized by the community of nations as of universal concern, such as piracy, slave trade, attacks on or hijacking of aircraft, genocide, war crimes, and perhaps certain acts of terrorism, even where [no other basis of jurisdiction] is present.

Under universal jurisdiction, all states have the power to prosecute certain universally condemned and egregious crimes. It posits that some conduct is so universally condemned that all states have the power to outlaw and prosecute its perpetrators regardless of nationalities or where it took place. The court referenced this idea in *Filartiga* when it described the torturer and slave trader as "*hostes humani generis*" — enemies of all human kind. Under universal jurisdiction, the prosecution is justified by the need to vindicate the interests of the entire international community. This rationale was clearly expressed by the Israeli Supreme Court regarding the prosecution of Adolf Eichmann for his crimes in Germany committed many years prior to Israel's existence:

> "Not only do all the crimes attributed to the appellant bear an international character, but their harmful and murderous effects were so embracing and widespread as to shake the international community to its very foundations. The State of Israel therefore was entitled, pursuant to the principle of universal jurisdiction and in the capacity of a guardian of international law and an agent for its enforcement, to try the appellant. That being the case, no importance attaches to the fact that the State of Israel did not exist when the offences were committed."[83]

Universal jurisdiction now plays a prominent part in the evolving role of domestic courts in enforcing international human rights through criminal processes. While the historical antecedents of universal jurisdiction are found in "state-less" international crimes such as piracy, most states and international bodies have now extended the concept of universal jurisdiction to at some of the following four types of international human rights crimes — torture, genocide, war crimes and crimes against humanity. In a "preliminary survey update" released in 2012 Amnesty International reported that:

> ". . . it appears that 147 (approximately 76.2%) states have provided universal jurisdiction over one or more crimes under international law and 91 (approximately 47.1%) states have provided universal jurisdiction over ordinary crimes under national law, even when the conduct does not involve conduct amounting to a crime under international law, in most instances permitting

---

83. Attorney General of Israel v. Eichmann, 36 Int'l L. Rep. 277, 304 (Israel Sup. Ct. 1962).

their courts in certain circumstances to exercise universal jurisdiction over some conduct that amounts to a crime under international law."[84]

The Amnesty report notes significant variations in the degree to which states criminalize and recognize universal jurisdiction for the four international human rights crimes included in its study.[85] The report, which does not address other crimes potentially subject to universal jurisdiction, also describes national definitions of human rights crimes as "seriously flawed," primarily for omissions that could lead to impunity. Nevertheless, it is clear that the principle of universal jurisdiction is now widely accepted around the world, at least for war crimes, torture, genocide and crimes against humanity.

Having the authority to criminalize certain human rights violations does not necessarily mean, however, that the state may legally utilize its law enforcement power to investigate, capture and prosecute any particular defendant. The authority to define crimes is distinct from using state power to enforce them internationally. The reason for this distinct limitation is simple. Basic international norms of territorial sovereignty would forbid one state from taking direct law enforcement activities within the territory of another state without permission. Many states have cooperative arrangements with each other regarding law enforcement culminating in extradition treaties. Thus, if a state criminalizes a particular human rights violation, it might also seek extradition of perpetrators of the crimes so defined, including those based on universal jurisdiction. Such extraditions would ultimately require the cooperation of the "sending" state in which the perpetrator was found, subject to specific conditions and limits on extradition, including "dual criminality." (A list of countries with which the United States has an extradition treaty can be found at 18 U.S.C. § 3181 — a statute which also outlines U.S. cooperation with international criminal tribunals for Rwanda and the former Yugoslavia.) In essence, cooperation and consent among states is a necessary prerequisite to actual enforcement and adjudication. This practical requirement may explain why, despite widespread crimi-

---

84. Amnesty International, *Universal Jurisdiction: A Preliminary Survey of Legislation Around the World — 2012 Update* at 12.

85. The Amnesty Report states

"... at least 142 (approximately 73.6%) UN member states have included at least one war crime as a crime under national law and at least 136 (approximately 70.5%) UN member states have provided for universal jurisdiction over such crimes .... at least 92 (approximately 47.7%) UN member states have included at least one crime against humanity as a crime under national law and at least 80 (approximately 41.5%) UN member states have provided for universal jurisdiction over such crimes .... at least 118 (approximately 61.1%) UN member states have included genocide as a crime under national law and at least 94 (approximately 48.7%) UN member states have provided for universal jurisdiction over genocide .... at least 95 (approximately 49.2%) UN member states have included torture as a separate crime under national law (not as a war crime or crime against humanity) and at least 85 (approximately 44%) UN member states have provided for universal jurisdiction over this crime." *Id*. at 12–13.

nalization of some human rights crimes and acceptance of universal jurisdiction, actual prosecutions have not been very common.[86]

As noted above, several international human rights treaties require that member states criminalize violations, prosecute perpetrators or extradite them to willing states. Some of these treaties also appear to give a clear nod in favor of universal jurisdiction, which reinforces the technically distinct "*aut dedere aut judicare*" obligation. The Torture Convention (CAT), for example, expressly requires that member states not only criminalize violations (Art. 4) but also prosecute or extradite any perpetrator found within their territorial control *regardless of where the crime took place* (Art. 5–7). While not as explicit, the Geneva Conventions similarly provide that, with regard to grave breaches during international conflicts, states are: "under the obligation to search for persons alleged to have committed, or to have ordered to be committed, such grave breaches, and shall bring such persons, regardless of their nationality, before its own courts." (For more detailed information on the obligation to penalize violations of humanitarian law see "Information Kit on National Enforcement.") These treaties, at least impliedly, would appear to not only authorize assertions of universal jurisdiction, they would demand it.[87]

---

86. The Amnesty report states, without providing specifics, that "Since the Second World War, prosecutions based on universal jurisdiction have been instituted, although not all have led to a final judgment, in Argentina, Austria, Australia, Belgium, Canada, Denmark, Finland, France, Germany, Israel, Netherlands, Norway, Paraguay, Senegal, Spain, Sweden, Switzerland, the United Kingdom and the United States of America." In 2005, a United Kingdom court convicted an Afghan, Sarwar Zardad, for torture which took place in Afghanistan against Afghan victims. In 2013, the United Kingdom brought charges of torture against a former Nepalese Colonel, Kumar Lama, who was visiting the U.K. The charges related to events taking place during the 2005 Nepalese civil war.

87. In an expert study conducted under the joint auspices of the European Union and African Union it was suggested that the following treaties require or permit universal jurisdiction: "Provisions to this effect are found in Convention for the Suppression of Unlawful Seizure of Aircraft, The Hague, 16 December 1970, 860 UNTS 105, article 4(2); Convention for the Suppression of Unlawful Acts against the Safety of Civilian Aircraft, Montreal, 23 September 1971, 974 UNTS 177, article 5(2); Convention on the Prevention and Punishment of Crimes against Internationally Protected Persons, including Diplomatic Agents, New York, 14 December 1973, 1035 UNTS 167, article 3(2); Convention against the Taking of Hostages, New York, 17 December 1979, 1316 UNTS 205, article 5(2); Convention on the Physical Protection of Nuclear Material, Vienna, 3 March 1980, 1456 UNTS 124, article 8(2); Convention against Torture and Other Cruel, Inhuman or Degrading Treatment or Punishment, New York, 10 December 1984, 1465 UNTS 112, article 5(2); Convention for the Suppression of Unlawful Acts against the Safety of Maritime Navigation, Rome, 10 March 1988, 1678 UNTS 221, article 6(4); Protocol for the Suppression of Unlawful Acts Against the Safety of Fixed Platforms Located on the Continental Shelf, Rome, 10 March 1988, 1678 UNTS 304, article 3(4); Convention against the Recruitment, Use, Financing and Training of Mercenaries, 4 December 1989, New York, UN Treaty Reg. No. 37789, article 9(2); Convention on the Safety of United Nations and Associated Personnel, New York, 9 December 1994, 2051 UNTS 363, article 10(4); Convention for the Suppression of Terrorist Bombings, New York, 15 December 1997, UN Treaty Reg. No. 37517, article 6(4); Second Protocol to the Hague Convention of 14 May 1954 for the Protection of Cultural Property in the Event of Armed Conflict, The Hague, 26 March 1999, UN Treaty Reg. No. 3511, article 16(1)(c); Convention for the Suppression of the Financing of Terrorism, New York, 9 December

Universal jurisdiction is now authorized in the United States for some human rights crimes but certainly not all. The 2007 Genocide Accountability Act, for example, expressly authorized universal jurisdiction by modifying earlier legislation that criminalized Genocide but only for conduct taking place within the United States or committed by a U.S. national. Other examples include statutes criminalizing terrorism, high-jacking, torture and recruitment of child soldiers. At least in some cases the authorization of universal jurisdiction is only partial. For example, the statute criminalizing torture, which appears below, only criminalizes torture occurring "outside of the United States."

Congress is currently considering a bill that would criminalize crimes against humanity, including a fairly extensive list of applicable criminal conduct, but not authorize universal jurisdiction. The 2010 Crimes Against Humanity Act, which was still on the Senate legislative calendar in 2012, *removed* universal jurisdiction from an earlier 2009 version of the bill. For a critique of the proposed bill and universal jurisdiction generally see this linked Heritage Foundation "Web Memo." The United States code also makes "war crimes" involving "grave breaches" of the Geneva Conventions common Article 3 a federal offense wherever they may occur *but only if* the perpetrator or victim is a U.S. national or member of the military.[88]

---

1999, UN Treaty Reg. No. 38349, article 7(4); Convention against Transnational Organized Crime, New York, 15 November 2000, UN Treaty Reg. No. 39574, article 15(4); Convention for the Suppression of Acts of Nuclear Terrorism, New York, 13 April 2005, UN Treaty Reg. No. 44004, article 9(4); Convention for the Protection of All Persons from Enforced Disappearance, New York, 20 December 2006, UN Doc. A/RES/61/177, Annex, article 9(2) (not in force)." Council of the European Union, AU-EU Expert Report on the Principle of Universal Jurisdiction, 8672/09 (2009). This study also surveys the practices of various EU and AU states regarding universal jurisdiction.

88. Compare this approach to that of Canada in implementing the Rome Convention creating the International Criminal Court and criminalizing crimes against humanity and war crimes.

   "S.C. 2000, c. 24 *** 6. (1) Every person who, either before or after the coming into force of this section, commits outside Canada

   (*a*) genocide,

   (*b*) a crime against humanity, or

   (*c*) a war crime, is guilty of an indictable offence and may be prosecuted for that offence in accordance with section 8.***

   8. A person who is alleged to have committed an offence under section 6 or 7 may be prosecuted for that offence if

   (*a*) at the time the offence is alleged to have been committed,

   (i)  the person was a Canadian citizen or was employed by Canada in a civilian or military capacity,

   (ii)  the person was a citizen of a state that was engaged in an armed conflict against Canada, or was employed in a civilian or military capacity by such a state,

   (iii)  the victim of the alleged offence was a Canadian citizen, or

   (iv)  the victim of the alleged offence was a citizen of a state that was allied with Canada in an armed conflict; or

   (*b*) after the time the offence is alleged to have been committed, the person is present in Canada."

# C.  Prosecuting Human Rights Crimes in the United States

## 1. Current U.S. Statutes Criminalizing International Human Rights Violations

a. Genocide

### TITLE 18. CRIMES AND CRIMINAL PROCEDURE, PART I — CRIMES, CHAPTER 50A — GENOCIDE

§ 1091.  Genocide

(a)  Basic offense. — Whoever, whether in time of peace or in time of war, in a circumstance described in subsection (d) and with the specific intent to destroy, in whole or in substantial part, a national, ethnic, racial, or religious group as such —

(1)  kills members of that group;

(2)  causes serious bodily injury to members of that group;

(3)  causes the permanent impairment of the mental faculties of members of the group through drugs, torture, or similar techniques;

(4)  subjects the group to conditions of life that are intended to cause the physical destruction of the group in whole or in part;

(5)  imposes measures intended to prevent births within the group; or

(6)  transfers by force children of the group to another group; or attempts to do so, shall be punished as provided in subsection (b).

(b)  Punishment for basic offense. — The punishment for an offense under subsection (a) is —

(1)  in the case of an offense under subsection (a)(1), [FN1] where death results, by death or imprisonment for life and a fine of not more than $1,000,000, or both; and

(2)  a fine of not more than $1,000,000 or imprisonment for not more than twenty years, or both, in any other case.

(c)  Incitement offense. — Whoever in a circumstance described in subsection (d) directly and publicly incites another to violate subsection (a) shall be fined not more than $500,000 or imprisoned not more than five years, or both.

(d)  Required circumstance for offenses. — The circumstance referred to in subsections (a) and (c) is that —

(1)  the offense is committed within the United States; or

(2)  the alleged offender is a national of the United States (as defined in section 101 of the Immigration and Nationality Act (8 U.S.C. 1101)). [EDITOR'S NOTE: AMENDED BELOW]

(e) Nonapplicability of certain limitations. — Notwithstanding section 3282 of this title, in the case of an offense under subsection (a)(1), an indictment may be found, or information instituted, at any time without limitation.

'Genocide Accountability Act of 2007'.

SEC. 2. GENOCIDE.

Section 1091 of title 18, United States Code, is amended by striking subsection (d) and inserting the following:

(d) Required Circumstance for Offenses- The circumstance referred to in subsections (a) and (c) is that —

> (1) the offense is committed in whole or in part within the United States;

> (2) the alleged offender is a national of the United States (as that term is defined in section 101 of the Immigration and Nationality Act (8 U.S.C. 1101));

> (3) the alleged offender is an alien lawfully admitted for permanent residence in the United States (as that term is defined in section 101 of the Immigration and Nationality Act (8 U.S.C. 1101));

> (4) the alleged offender is a stateless person whose habitual residence is in the United States; or

> (5) after the conduct required for the offense occurs, the alleged offender is brought into, or found in, the United States, even if that conduct occurred outside the United States.

b. Torture

### USCA, TITLE 18. CRIMES AND CRIMINAL PROCEDURE
### PART I — CRIMES, CHAPTER 113C — TORTURE

As used in this chapter —

(1) "torture" means an act committed by a person acting under the color of law specifically intended to inflict severe physical or mental pain or suffering (other than pain or suffering incidental to lawful sanctions) upon another person within his custody or physical control;

(2) "severe mental pain or suffering" means the prolonged mental harm caused by or resulting from —

(A) the intentional infliction or threatened infliction of severe physical pain or suffering;

(B) the administration or application, or threatened administration or application, of mind-altering substances or other procedures calculated to disrupt profoundly the senses or the personality;

(C) the threat of imminent death; or

(D)  the threat that another person will imminently be subjected to death, severe physical pain or suffering, or the administration or application of mind-altering substances or other procedures calculated to disrupt profoundly the senses or personality; and

(3)  "United States" means the several States of the United States, the District of Columbia, and the commonwealths, territories, and possessions of the United States.

### § 2340A. Torture

(a)  Offense. — Whoever outside the United States commits or attempts to commit torture shall be fined under this title or imprisoned not more than 20 years, or both, and if death results to any person from conduct prohibited by this subsection, shall be punished by death or imprisoned for any term of years or for life.

(b)  Jurisdiction. — There is jurisdiction over the activity prohibited in subsection (a) if —

(1)  the alleged offender is a national of the United States; or

(2)  the alleged offender is present in the United States, irrespective of the nationality of the victim or alleged offender.

(c)  Conspiracy. — A person who conspires to commit an offense under this section shall be subject to the same penalties (other than the penalty of death) as the penalties prescribed for the offense, the commission of which was the object of the conspiracy.

### c. Recruitment and Use of Child Soldiers

This Act may be cited as the "Child Soldiers Accountability Act of 2008".

SEC. 2. ACCOUNTABILITY FOR THE RECRUITMENT AND USE OF CHILD SOLDIERS.

(a)  CRIME FOR RECRUITING OR USING CHILD SOLDIERS. — (1) IN GENERAL. — Chapter 118 of title 18, United States Code, is amended by adding at the end the following:

### § 2442. Recruitment or use of child soldiers

(a)  OFFENSE. — Whoever knowingly —

(1)  recruits, enlists, or conscripts a person to serve while such person is under 15 years of age in an armed force or group; or

(2)  uses a person under 15 years of age to participate actively in hostilities; knowing such person is under 15 years of age, shall be punished as provided in subsection (b).

(b)  PENALTY. — Whoever violates, or attempts or conspires to violate, subsection (a) shall be fined under this title or imprisoned not more than 20 years, or both and, if death of any person results, shall be fined under this title and imprisoned for any term of years or for life.

(c) JURISDICTION. — There is jurisdiction over an offense described in subsection (a), and any attempt or conspiracy to commit such offense, if —

(1) the alleged offender is a national of the United States (as defined in section 101(a)(22) of the Immigration and Nationality Act (8 U.S.C. 1101(a)(22)) or an alien lawfully admitted for permanent residence in the United States (as defined in section 101(a)(20) of such Act (8 U.S.C. 1101(a)(20));

(2) the alleged offender is a stateless person whose habitual residence is in the United States;

(3) the alleged offender is present in the United States, irrespective of the nationality of the alleged offender; or

(4) the offense occurs in whole or in part within the United States.

d. War Crimes

18 U.S.C § 2441 — War crimes

(a) Offense. — Whoever, whether inside or outside the United States, commits a war crime, in any of the circumstances described in subsection (b), shall be fined under this title or imprisoned for life or any term of years, or both, and if death results to the victim, shall also be subject to the penalty of death.

(b) Circumstances. — The circumstances referred to in subsection (a) are that the person committing such war crime or the victim of such war crime is a member of the Armed Forces of the United States or a national of the United States (as defined in section 101 of the Immigration and Nationality Act).

(c) Definition. — As used in this section the term "war crime" means any conduct —

(1) defined as a grave breach in any of the international conventions signed at Geneva 12 August 1949, or any protocol to such convention to which the United States is a party;

(2) prohibited by Article 23, 25, 27, or 28 of the Annex to the Hague Convention IV, Respecting the Laws and Customs of War on Land, signed 18 October 1907;

(3) which constitutes a grave breach of common Article 3 (as defined in subsection (d)) when committed in the context of and in association with an armed conflict not of an international character; or

(4) of a person who, in relation to an armed conflict and contrary to the provisions of the Protocol on Prohibitions or Restrictions on the Use of Mines, Booby-Traps and Other Devices as amended at Geneva on 3 May 1996 (Protocol II as amended on 3 May 1996), when the United States is a party to such Protocol, willfully kills or causes serious injury to civilians.

(d)  Common Article 3 Violations. —

(1)  Prohibited conduct. — In subsection (c)(3), the term "grave breach of common Article 3" means any conduct (such conduct constituting a grave breach of common Article 3 of the international conventions done at Geneva August 12, 1949), as follows:

(A)  Torture. — The act of a person who commits, or conspires or attempts to commit, an act specifically intended to inflict severe physical or mental pain or suffering (other than pain or suffering incidental to lawful sanctions) upon another person within his custody or physical control for the purpose of obtaining information or a confession, punishment, intimidation, coercion, or any reason based on discrimination of any kind.

(B)  Cruel or inhuman treatment. — The act of a person who commits, or conspires or attempts to commit, an act intended to inflict severe or serious physical or mental pain or suffering (other than pain or suffering incidental to lawful sanctions), including serious physical abuse, upon another within his custody or control.

(C)  Performing biological experiments. — The act of a person who subjects, or conspires or attempts to subject, one or more persons within his custody or physical control to biological experiments without a legitimate medical or dental purpose and in so doing endangers the body or health of such person or persons.

(D)  Murder. — The act of a person who intentionally kills, or conspires or attempts to kill, or kills whether intentionally or unintentionally in the course of committing any other offense under this subsection, one or more persons taking no active part in the hostilities, including those placed out of combat by sickness, wounds, detention, or any other cause.

(E)  Mutilation or maiming. — The act of a person who intentionally injures, or conspires or attempts to injure, or injures whether intentionally or unintentionally in the course of committing any other offense under this subsection, one or more persons taking no active part in the hostilities, including those placed out of combat by sickness, wounds, detention, or any other cause, by disfiguring the person or persons by any mutilation thereof or by permanently disabling any member, limb, or organ of his body, without any legitimate medical or dental purpose.

(F)  Intentionally causing serious bodily injury. — The act of a person who intentionally causes, or conspires or attempts to cause, serious bodily injury to one or more persons, including lawful combatants, in violation of the law of war.

(G)  Rape. — The act of a person who forcibly or with coercion or threat of force wrongfully invades, or conspires or attempts to invade, the body of a person by penetrating, however slightly, the anal or genital opening of the victim with any part of the body of the accused, or with any foreign object.

(H) Sexual assault or abuse. — The act of a person who forcibly or with coercion or threat of force engages, or conspires or attempts to engage, in sexual contact with one or more persons, or causes, or conspires or attempts to cause, one or more persons to engage in sexual contact.

(I) Taking hostages. — The act of a person who, having knowingly seized or detained one or more persons, threatens to kill, injure, or continue to detain such person or persons with the intent of compelling any nation, person other than the hostage, or group of persons to act or refrain from acting as an explicit or implicit condition for the safety or release of such person or persons.

\*\*\*

(3) Inapplicability of certain provisions with respect to collateral damage or incident of lawful attack. — The intent specified for the conduct stated in subparagraphs (D), (E), and (F) or paragraph (1) precludes the applicability of those subparagraphs to an offense under subsection (a) by reasons of subsection (c)(3) with respect to —

(A) collateral damage; or

(B) death, damage, or injury incident to a lawful attack.

e. Human Trafficking

Title 18 — CRIMES AND CRIMINAL PROCEDURE

PART I — CRIMES

CHAPTER 77 — PEONAGE, SLAVERY, AND TRAFFICKING IN PERSONS

§1596. Additional jurisdiction in certain trafficking offenses

(a) In General. — In addition to any domestic or extra-territorial jurisdiction otherwise provided by law, the courts of the United States have extra-territorial jurisdiction over any offense (or any attempt or conspiracy to commit an offense) under section 1581, 1583, 1584, 1589, 1590, or 1591 if —

[EDITOR'S NOTE: These sections prohibit, respectively, "Peonage"; "Enticement to Slavery"; "Sale into Involuntary Servitude"; "Forced Labor"; "Trafficking with respect to peonage, slavery, involuntary servitude, or forced labor"; and "Sex trafficking of children or by force, fraud, or coercion"]

(1) an alleged offender is a national of the United States or an alien lawfully admitted for permanent residence (as those terms are defined in section 101 of the Immigration and Nationality Act (8 U.S.C. 1101)); or

(2) an alleged offender is present in the United States, irrespective of the nationality of the alleged offender.

(b) Limitation on Prosecutions of Offenses Prosecuted in Other Countries. — No prosecution may be commenced against a person under this section if a foreign government, in accordance with jurisdiction recognized by the United States, has prosecuted or is prosecuting such person for the conduct constituting such offense, except upon the approval of the Attorney General or the Deputy Attorney

General (or a person acting in either such capacity), which function of approval may not be delegated.

## 2. Institutional Framework

Under the statutes provided above, U.S. Attorneys across the country could conceivably bring charges against international human rights criminals much like with any other federal crime. Prosecution of an international crime, however, may carry with it a variety of complications including potential implications for U.S. foreign relations. This is particularly true for foreign defendants and cases involving the exercise of universal jurisdiction. Such prosecutions also may require specialized knowledge. Perhaps in recognition of this, Congress authorized the creation of a specialized "human rights enforcement" section within the Criminal Division of the Department of Justice in the "2009 Human Rights Enforcement Act."

The Human Rights and Special Prosecutions (HRSP) section is authorized to both criminally prosecute human rights crimes and seek civil immigration exclusion orders. Consistent with relevant treaties, the authorizing statute implicitly recognizes a policy of "*aut dedere aut judicare*" — prosecute or extradite to another state willing to do so.

> "(d) In determining the appropriate legal action to take against individuals who are suspected of committing serious human rights offenses under Federal law, the section shall take into consideration the availability of criminal prosecution under the laws of the United States for such offenses or in a foreign jurisdiction that is prepared to undertake a prosecution for the conduct that forms the basis for such offenses.
>
> (e) The term 'serious human rights offenses' includes violations of Federal criminal laws relating to genocide, torture, war crimes, and the use or recruitment of child soldiers under sections 1091, 2340, 2340A, 2441, and 2442 of title 18, United States Code."

The HRSP describes itself in this way:

### Ensuring Accountability for Human Rights Violations and Extraterritorial Violent Crime

> Where U.S. federal jurisdiction exists, HRSP seeks to prosecute human rights violators under the federal criminal statutes proscribing torture, war crimes, genocide, and recruitment or use of child soldiers. The Section also prosecutes human rights violators under U.S. civil immigration and naturalization laws in order to revoke U.S. citizenship or other legal status. Defendants in these cases include both participants in World War II-era Nazi-sponsored acts of persecution and persons who perpetrated more recent human rights violators. HRSP works closely with the Department of Homeland Security and with the FBI to identify, investigate, and prosecute alleged human rights violators.

Undoubtedly out of recognition for foreign policy concerns, DOJ's policy manual (USAM 9-2.139 — Notification, Consultation, and Approval Requirements for Torture, War Crimes, and Genocide Matters) imposes notification and coordination requirements on U.S. prosecutors relying on the federal statutes set out above:

### National Coordination

Matters involving torture (18 U.S.C. §§ 2340 — 2340B), war crimes (18 U.S.C. § 2441), and genocide (18 U.S.C. §§ 1091–1093), and recruitment or use of child soldiers (18 U.S.C. § 2442) raise issues of national and international concern. Successful prosecution of these matters requires both careful coordination within the Department of Justice and careful coordination between the Department and senior officials in the foreign affairs and military communities. The responsibility for this coordination is assigned to the Criminal Division and, in particular, its Human Rights and Special Prosecutions Section (HRSP). If a matter involving torture, war crimes, genocide, or recruitment or use of child soldiers also involves international terrorism, responsibility for coordination will be assigned to the Counterterrorism Section of the National Security Division as provided in this section and USAM 9-2.136.

### Notification Requirements

**Initiation.** When the USAO opens any torture, war crimes, genocide, or child soldiers matter, the USAO shall promptly notify the Human Rights and Special Prosecutions Section (HRSP) of the Criminal Division. The notification should include the names and identifiers, if known, of the subjects of the investigation and a general overview of the investigation. Whenever feasible, notification should be made in advance of any action by the USAO . . .

To date, there has only been a single, but noteworthy prosecution.

## 3. Case Study: U.S. v. Charles Taylor, Jr.

**Taylor's son gets 97 years in prison for torture**, Curt Anderson, January 9, 2009, AP News Service

MIAMI — Charles McArthur Emmanuel, the son of former Liberian President Charles Taylor and head of a savage paramilitary unit known as the "Demon Forces," was sentenced Friday to 97 years in prison for torture overseas in the first U.S. case of its kind.

U.S. District Judge Cecilia M. Altonaga imposed the sentence after describing Emmanuel's actions against people viewed as rebels or opponents of his father as "sadistic, cruel and atrocious."

"It is hard to conceive of any more serious offenses against the dignity and the lives of human beings," Altonaga said. "The international community condemns torture." . . . .

"Our message to human rights violators, no matter where they are, remains the same: We will use the full reach of U.S. law ... to hold you accountable for your crimes," said Matthew Friedrich, acting chief of the U.S. Justice Department's criminal division, in a statement ....

Emmanuel's father, a notorious warlord who left power in 2003 under U.S. pressure, is on trial before a United Nations tribunal in The Hague, Netherlands, for crimes allegedly committed during the Sierra Leone civil war. Emmanuel was born to a girlfriend of Taylor's while he was a college student in Boston in the 1970s.

Victims testified that Emmanuel, as chief of Taylor's Antiterrorist Unit from 1997 to 2003, either personally tortured them or directed others to do so. People were shocked by electric devices, stabbed with bayonets, burned with cigarettes, scalding water and molten plastic, bitten by shovelfuls of ants and imprisoned in water-filled holes topped by iron bars and barbed wire.

Emmanuel personally shot several men to death at a bridge checkpoint and ordered one man beheaded with a large knife, witnesses said ....

Also Friday, the group Human Rights USA filed a lawsuit in Miami federal court on behalf of potentially thousands of Liberian torture victims seeking unspecified damages from Emmanuel or accounts controlled by Taylor that have been frozen by the U.N. ....

## 4. Potential Prosecution of American Actors for Human Rights Violations in the War on Terror

a. The Case against Bush Administration Officials for Torture

Scott Shane, New York Times, January 16, 2009

<u>Remarks on Torture May Force New Administration's Hand</u>

WASHINGTON — Just 14 months ago, at his confirmation hearing, Attorney General <u>Michael B. Mukasey</u> frustrated and angered some senators by refusing to state that <u>waterboarding</u>, the near-drowning technique used on three prisoners by the <u>Central Intelligence Agency</u>, is in fact torture.

This week, at his confirmation hearing, <u>Eric H. Holder Jr.</u>, the attorney general-designate, did not hesitate to express a clear view. He noted that waterboarding had been used to torment prisoners during the Inquisition, by the Japanese in World War II and in Cambodia under the <u>Khmer Rouge</u>.

"We prosecuted our own soldiers for using it in Vietnam," Mr. Holder said. "<u>Waterboarding</u> is torture." ....

Mr. Holder's statement came just two days after the Defense Department official in charge of military commissions at Guantánamo Bay, Cuba, said in an interview with The Washington Post that she had refused to permit a trial for one detainee there, <u>Mohammed al-Qahtani</u>, because she believed he had been tortured . . . .

In recent weeks, Mr. Bush, Vice President Cheney and other officials have strongly defended their counterterrorism methods and credited them with preventing attacks on the United States since 2001. Their implicit argument—that the Obama administration should not question policies that protected Americans—was made more explicit and personal by <u>Michael V. Hayden</u>, the departing C.I.A. director, in a session with reporters on Thursday.

"If I'm going to go to an officer and say, 'I've got a truth commission, or I want to post all your e-mails, or, well, we've got this guy from the bureau who wants to talk to you,'" Mr. Hayden said, it would discourage such a C.I.A. officer from taking risks on behalf of the new president's policies. . . . .

b. The War Crimes Case against the Obama Administration: Use of Targeted Drone Assassinations

i. Overview

Both the Bush and Obama administrations have made extensive use of remotely piloted aircraft, commonly called "drones," to kill suspected terrorists in areas outside of the reach of the U.S. military and intelligence forces. The New America Foundation, whose website provides <u>detailed statistics</u>, reports 370 drone strikes in Pakistan and 99 strikes in Yemen since 2002. Although many "high level" terrorist leaders have been killed in the attacks (58 in Pakistan and 35 in Yemen, including the Yemeni-American cleric Anwar al-Awlaki), a far greater numbers of the deaths have involved civilians and lower level "militants" of more ambiguous status and threat.

(As of 25 December 2013)

| Year | Number of Attacks | Casualties | | | Total |
| | | Militants | Civilians | Unknown | |
| --- | --- | --- | --- | --- | --- |
| 2004 | 1 | 3 | 2 | 2 | 7 |
| 2005 | 3 | 5 | 6 | 4 | 15 |
| 2006 | 2 | 1 | 93 | 0 | 94 |
| 2007 | 4 | 51 | 0 | 12 | 63 |
| 2008 | 36 | 223 | 28 | 47 | 298 |
| 2009 | 54 | 387 | 70 | 92 | 549 |
| 2010 | 122 | 788 | 16 | 45 | 849 |
| 2011 | 73 | 420 | 62 | 35 | 517 |
| 2012 | 48 | 268 | 5 | 33 | 306 |
| 2013 | 26 | 145 | 4 | 4 | 153 |
| Total | 369 | 2,291 | 286 | 274 | 2,851 |

Critics of U.S. drone strikes argue that they result in indiscriminate killings of innocent victims that violate human rights and may constitute war crimes. Good examples of these arguments appear in reports by Amnesty International and Human Rights Watch. In 2013, President Obama defended the program while at the same time announcing constraints. Consider the following commentaries and Obama's retort in weighing the various human rights implications of drones. Some of the legal issues involve the application of international humanitarian law, or laws of war, which we will further consider is subsequent chapters. (If interested in finding out more now, you can find an overview of the legal issues in the Stanford/NYU report "Living Under Drones." You might also consider the legal defense of the use of drones under international law presented by the Heritage Foundation, which includes arguments made by Harold Koh, legal advisor to the State Department.)

Additional background in multimedia formats is available at:

Public Radio International Report (9 minute report including interviews with Amnesty International Representative as well as Pakistani counterviews); and

http://rt.com/news/us-drones-war-crimes-535/ (includes video report condemning U.S. practices); and this Bill Moyer television news report.

ii. The Guardian (Editorial): Is President Obama a suspected war criminal?

> If you have read the recent reports on drone strikes by Ben Emmerson, UN special rapporteur on the promotion and protection of human rights and fundamental freedoms while countering terrorism, Christof Heyns, UN special rapporteur on extrajudicial, summary or arbitrary executions, Amnesty International and Human Rights Watch, there is only one answer to this question . . . and it is not the answer most would want to hear. . . .

> This brings us to the question of whether President Obama's targeted killing program, implemented through the use of drone strikes, complies with both international human rights law and international humanitarian law. *Outside of a defined conflict zone*, international human rights law is the applicable law. This is important because human rights law demands significantly more stringent rules for the use of lethal force than does humanitarian law . . . .

> Amnesty International concluded that it is highly likely that drone strikes in Pakistan fail to "satisfy the law enforcement standards that govern intentional use of lethal force outside armed conflict", and therefore:

> [T]heir deliberate killings by drones . . . very likely violate the prohibition of arbitrary deprivation of life and may constitute extrajudicial executions.

> . . . , there is mounting evidence that the Obama administration's use of drones constitute violations of international law in the form of war crimes . . . .

iii. The Week: Are U.S. drone strikes really war crimes?

**Two new reports say the U.S. has indiscriminately killed civilians in Pakistan and Yemen**, By Peter Weber | October 22, 2013

On Tuesday, human rights groups Amnesty International and Human Rights Watch released separate reports on the use of armed U.S. drones to target al Qaeda and other terrorist groups. . . .

However, the most explosive allegation is that some U.S. drone strikes amount to probable war crimes. Here's Amnesty:

. . . the cases in this report raise serious concerns that the U.S.A. has unlawfully killed people in drone strikes, and that such killings may amount in some cases to extrajudicial executions or war crimes and other violations of international humanitarian law. [Amnesty International]. . . .

Meanwhile, Human Rights Watch looked into six unacknowledged attacks in Yemen between 2009 and 2013, interviewing some 90 people. The group says that the attacks, mostly by drones but also warships and cruise missiles, killed 82 people, at least 57 of them civilians. "Two these attacks were in clear violation of international humanitarian law — the laws of war — because they struck only civilians or used indiscriminate weapons," the report says. The other four "may have violated the laws of war" but "require further investigation."

**So, is the U.S. committing war crimes?** Broadly speaking, war crimes are grave violations of the Geneva Conventions and a few other binding international treaties. The number of civilian deaths in Pakistan and Yemen "suggests they are not 'one-offs' but part of a systematic policy that appears inherently illegal," says Simon Tisdall at *The Guardian*. . . .

Even if the U.S. is guilty of war crimes — as it almost certainly was in torturing prisoners after the al Qaeda attacks of September 2001 — who's going to do anything about it?

iv. Response of President Obama: Speech before the National Defense University, 2013

(White House Press Office. Also available from NY Times including video of President's speech):

But despite our strong preference for the detention and prosecution of terrorists, sometimes this approach is foreclosed. Al Qaeda and its affiliates try to gain foothold in some of the most distant and unforgiving places on Earth. They take refuge in remote tribal regions. They hide in caves and walled compounds. They train in empty deserts and rugged mountains.

In some of these places — such as parts of Somalia and Yemen — the state only has the most tenuous reach into the territory. In other cases, the state lacks the capacity or will to take action. And it's also not possible for America to simply deploy a team of Special Forces to capture every terrorist. Even when such an approach may be possible, there are places where it would pose profound risks to our troops and local civilians — where a terrorist compound cannot be breached without triggering a firefight with surrounding tribal communities, for example, that pose no threat to us; times when putting U.S. boots on the ground may trigger a major international crisis.

\*\*\*

So it is in this context that the United States has taken lethal, targeted action against al Qaeda and its associated forces, including with remotely piloted aircraft commonly referred to as drones.

As was true in previous armed conflicts, this new technology raises profound questions — about who is targeted, and why; about civilian casualties, and the risk of creating new enemies; about the legality of such strikes under U.S. and international law; about accountability and morality. So let me address these questions.

To begin with, our actions are effective. Don't take my word for it. In the intelligence gathered at bin Laden's compound, we found that he wrote, "We could lose the reserves to enemy's air strikes. We cannot fight air strikes with explosives." Other communications from al Qaeda operatives confirm this as well. Dozens of highly skilled al Qaeda commanders, trainers, bomb makers and operatives have been taken off the battlefield. Plots have been disrupted that would have targeted international aviation, U.S. transit systems, European cities and our troops in Afghanistan. Simply put, these strikes have saved lives.

Moreover, America's actions are legal. We were attacked on 9/11. Within a week, Congress overwhelmingly authorized the use of force. Under domestic law, and international law, the United States is at war with al Qaeda, the Taliban, and their associated forces. We are at war with an organization that right now would kill as many Americans as they could if we did not stop them first. So this is a just war — a war waged proportionally, in last resort, and in self-defense.

And yet, as our fight enters a new phase, America's legitimate claim of self-defense cannot be the end of the discussion. To say a military tactic is legal, or even effective, is not to say it is wise or moral in every instance. For the same human progress that gives us the technology to strike half a world away also demands the discipline to constrain that power — or risk abusing it. And that's why, over the last four years, my administration has worked vigorously to establish a framework that governs our use of force against terrorists — insisting upon clear guidelines, oversight and accountability that is now codified in Presidential Policy Guidance that I signed yesterday.

\*\*\*

Beyond the Afghan theater, we only target al Qaeda and its associated forces. And even then, the use of drones is heavily constrained. America does not take strikes when we have the ability to capture individual terrorists; our preference is always to detain, interrogate, and prosecute. America cannot take strikes wherever we choose; our actions are bound by consultations with partners, and respect for state sovereignty.

America does not take strikes to punish individuals; we act against terrorists who pose a continuing and imminent threat to the American people, and when there are no other governments capable of effectively addressing the threat. And before any strike is taken, there must be near-certainty that no civilians will be killed or injured — the highest standard we can set.

Now, this last point is critical, because much of the criticism about drone strikes — both here at home and abroad — understandably centers on reports of civilian casualties. There's a wide gap between U.S. assessments of such casualties and nongovernmental reports. Nevertheless, it is a hard fact that U.S. strikes have resulted in civilian casualties, a risk that exists in every war. And for the families of those civilians, no words or legal construct can justify their loss. For me, and those in my chain of command, those deaths will haunt us as long as we live, just as we are haunted by the civilian casualties that have occurred throughout conventional fighting in Afghanistan and Iraq.

But as Commander-in-Chief, I must weigh these heartbreaking tragedies against the alternatives. To do nothing in the face of terrorist networks would invite far more civilian casualties — not just in our cities at home and our facilities abroad, but also in the very places like Sana'a and Kabul and Mogadishu where terrorists seek a foothold. Remember that the terrorists we are after target civilians, and the death toll from their acts of terrorism against Muslims dwarfs any estimate of civilian casualties from drone strikes. So doing nothing is not an option.

***

Our efforts must be measured against the history of putting American troops in distant lands among hostile populations. In Vietnam, hundreds of thousands of civilians died in a war where the boundaries of battle were blurred. ***

Moreover, our laws constrain the power of the President even during wartime, and I have taken an oath to defend the Constitution of the United States. The very precision of drone strikes and the necessary secrecy often involved in such actions can end up shielding our government from the public scrutiny that a troop deployment invites. It can also lead a President and his team to view drone strikes as a cure-all for terrorism.

And for this reason, I've insisted on strong oversight of all lethal action. *** For the record, I do not believe it would be constitutional for the government to target and kill any U.S. citizen — with a drone, or with a shotgun — without due process, nor should any President deploy armed drones over U.S. soil.

*** But the high threshold that we've set for taking lethal action applies to all potential terrorist targets, regardless of whether or not they are American citizens. ***

Going forward, I've asked my administration to review proposals to extend oversight of lethal actions outside of warzones that go beyond our reporting to Congress. ***

# D. U.S. Immigration Based Civil and Criminal Actions Against Human Rights Violators

The United States has long maintained a policy, not always aggressively implemented, of refusing admission, excluding, or deporting (now called "removal") foreign nationals and naturalized citizens based on their undisclosed involvement in human rights atrocities overseas. This policy may be reinforced, or in some cases inhibited, by the potential extradition of the perpetrator to his country of origin for prosecution. Removing such a person from the United States and returning him to his native land may, of course, have the same consequence as formal extradition. Apart from removal, human rights criminals illegally seeking refuge in the United States have more recently been criminally prosecuted for committing fraud in the immigration process.

## 1. Civil Removal Proceedings

Immigration oriented pursuit of international human rights criminals in the United States began in earnest around 1979 with the establishment of a special section in the criminal division of the Department of Justice. The "Office of Special Investigations" was created with the mandate to find, and seek the denaturalization and expulsion of, former Nazi war criminals. Thousands of suspected war criminals surreptitiously entered the United States after World War II hidden within a multitude of other refugees. It is perhaps noteworthy and sobering to learn that during the Cold War the United States government, prior to the OSI, had knowingly recruited and utilized the services of some Nazi war criminals. (See NY Times, Nazis Were Given 'Safe Haven' in U.S., Report Says.) Believing that the Constitution prevented direct prosecution for such war crimes occurring outside of the United States, the OSI has brought more than 100 successful civil denaturalization and deportation cases against former Nazis since 1979.[89] In The OSI was merged with the Justice Department's newly created HRSP (described above) in 2010.

---

89. Prosecution for the crimes such individuals had committed during the war outside of the United States was believed to be precluded under the U.S. Constitution, presumably under the prohibition against Ex Post Facto prosecutions. Prior to the establishment of OSI the Immigration and Naturalization Service was responsible for seeking deportation of World War II war criminals but was completely ineffectual. See U.S. Attorney's Bulletin, Vol. 54, January, 2006. Most proceeding brought by OSI are in fact civil not criminal in nature.

Paralleling the efforts of the Justice Department, U.S. Immigration & Customs Enforcement (ICE) also attempts to enforce human rights norms by denying entry, prosecuting or removing aliens involved in foreign based human rights violations. This work is the primary responsibility of a section within ICE called the Human Rights Violators & War Crimes Unit which describes it work this way:

> U.S. Immigration and Customs Enforcement's (ICE) Homeland Security Investigations (HSI) operates the Human Rights Violators and War Crimes Unit (HRVWCU) within the National Security Investigations Division (NSID). Preceded by the U.S. Immigration and Naturalization Service, HSI has more than 30 years of experience in successfully investigating human rights violators. The unit conducts investigations focused on human rights violations in an effort to prevent the United States from becoming a safe haven to those individuals who engage in the commission of war crimes, genocide, torture and other forms of serious human rights abuses from conflicts around the globe. When foreign war crimes suspects, persecutors and human rights abusers are identified within U.S. borders, the unit utilizes its powers and authorities to the fullest extent of the law to investigate, prosecute and, whenever possible, remove any such offenders from the United States.

> Since fiscal year 2004, ICE has arrested more than 250 individuals for human rights-related violations under various criminal and/or immigration statutes. During that same period, ICE has denied more than 117 individuals from obtaining entry visas to the United States and created more than 20,000 subject records, which prevented identified human-rights violators from attempting to enter the United States. In addition, ICE successfully obtained deportation orders to physically remove more than 590 known or suspected human rights violators from the United States.

> Currently, ICE is pursuing more than 1,900 leads and removal cases that involve suspected human rights violators from nearly 96 different countries.

### a. Man Linked to Guatemala Massacre Deported

From <u>Immigration and Customs Enforcement Press Release</u>

LOS ANGELES — A former member of the Guatemalan army whom witnesses say participated in a massacre there three decades ago that claimed at least 162 lives was deported to his native country Tuesday, capping an effort by U.S. Immigration and Customs Enforcement (ICE) to investigate the case and win the ex-commando's removal from the United States.

Pedro Pimentel Rios, 54, arrived in Guatemala on board an ICE Air Operations charter removal flight and was immediately turned over to Guatemalan law enforcement officials. The Santa Ana, Calif., maintenance worker is wanted in his native country on criminal charges for his role in the Dos Erres massacre.

(Picture Courtesy of Immigration and Customs Enforcement)

Guatemalan authorities allege Pimentel Rios was among some 20 members of an elite Guatemalan army unit called the Kaibiles who murdered dozens of men, women and children in the village of Las Dos Erres in December 1982. The Kaibiles had gone to the remote Guatemalan settlement seeking to locate left-wing insurgents allegedly responsible for the ambush of an army convoy nearby that resulted in the theft of more than 20 military rifles. After arriving in the village, the Kaibiles began searching for the missing weapons, forcing the residents from their homes and interrogating them about the stolen guns. No rifles were recovered. The soldiers then proceeded to systematically murder the villagers, beginning with the children.

The victims were bludgeoned with sledgehammers and their bodies thrown into the village's well. Other victims were shot or strangled and many of the local women were raped during the two-day ordeal.

In July 2010, ICE charged Pimentel Rios in immigration court with being deportable for having assisted or otherwise participated in extrajudicial killings during the Dos Erres massacre. In May, an immigration judge in Los Angeles cleared the way for Pimentel Rios' repatriation to Guatemala, ruling he was deportable based upon his participation in the extrajudicial killings at Las Dos Erres. The judge's ruling capped an intensive legal effort by ICE to gain Pimentel Rios' removal from the United States following his arrest by ICE Homeland Security Investigations (HSI) agents in Orange County a year ago.

. . . .

Pimentel Rios is the fourth former Kaibil living in the United States linked to the massacre to be targeted by ICE for enforcement action. Two of the others, Gilberto Jordan and Jorge Vincio Sosa Orantes, previously became naturalized U.S. citizens. In Sept. 2010, Gilberto Jordan was sentenced in Florida to 10 years in federal prison for failing to disclose his prior military service and involvement in the killings on his citizenship application. Criminal charges for naturalization fraud are pending in Los Angeles against Sosa, who is awaiting extradition following his arrest by Canadian authorities in January. A fourth Kaibil, Santos Lopez Alonzo, was arrested by ICE HSI agents in Houston and criminally charged in February 2010 with re-entry after deportation.

. . .

Members of the public who have information about foreign nationals suspected of engaging in human rights abuses or war crimes are urged to call the ICE tip line at 1-866-DHS-2423 (1-866-347-2423). Callers may remain anonymous. To learn more about the assistance available to victims in these cases, the public should contact ICE's confidential victim-witness toll-free number at 1-866-872-4973.

Since fiscal year 2004, ICE has arrested more than 200 individuals for human rights-related violations of the law under various criminal and/or immigration statutes. During that same period, ICE obtained deportation orders for and physically removed more than 400 known or suspected human rights violators from the United States.

Pimentel Rios was later convicted in Guatemala, along with five other military officers, and sentenced to 6060 years in prison for his crimes. You can find out about the Las Dos Erres massacre on the website of the Center for Justice and Accountability. Deportation of a human rights criminal is, however, often not as easy as it sounds.

b. Six Nazis Who Will Probably Live Out Their Lives Free in America

May 13, 2011, ABC News, By JASON RYAN

ABCNEWS.com

The conviction of former Nazi and one-time Cleveland autoworker John Demjanjuk for hiding his Nazi war crimes has focused attention on the remaining aging Nazis discovered in America, but legal appeals and international refusal to accept these men suggest they may live out the rest of their lives in the U.S.

There are currently only six remaining Nazi cases left on the books for U.S. investigators to wrap up. One man, Peter Egner, died in February just before an Appeals Court was slated to hear his case.

Demjanjuk, 91, was convicted Thursday by a German court of taking part in the murder of over 28,000 Jews while serving as a prison guard at the Sobibor concentration camp. He was sentenced to five years in prison, but has been let out while he appeals the sentence. [Since died.]

Demjanjuk's legal battles have been underway since 1986 when he was first accused of hiding his Nazi past while living in Cleveland. Repeated trials and appeals have spanned the U.S., Israel and Germany.

. . .

No Country Will Accept Aging Nazis Ordered Deported

But once convicted and stripped of their citizenship, it is proving to be very difficult to deport them. Of the six remaining Nazis who have been discovered in the U.S., all have been ordered to be deported but all are still here and have been appealing the deportation order for as long as seven years.

U.S. officials have told ABC News that the fact is that U.S. cannot find a country that will accept the aging Nazis.

. . .

## 2. Immigration Related Criminal Prosecutions

Apart from removal, foreign human rights violators may also be extradited or prosecuted criminally for lying on their immigration or citizenship applications. The ICE website "fact sheet" describes some of its recent successes including prosecution or removal of participants in human rights violations in Rwanda, Bosnia, Guatemala, Honduras, Argentina, Peru and Liberia. The following news report describes one of several cases involving participants in a massacre in Guatemala.

a. Ex-Guatemalan Soldier Will Be Sentenced for Lying

From ABC News:

RIVERSIDE, Calif. February 10, 2014 (AP)

Former Guatemalan soldier Jorge Sosa was a member of a special force suspected of killing at least 160 people in a remote village more than three decades ago in a massacre that still haunts its few survivors.

In an American court on Monday, the 55-year-old will be sentenced to up to a decade in prison for lying on his U.S. citizenship papers about his alleged role in the slayings.

Federal prosecutors are seeking the maximum prison sentence for the former second lieutenant for failing to disclose his alleged participation in the murders in the Guatemalan hamlet of Dos Erres when he applied to naturalize and are asking a judge strip him of his American citizenship. Sosa's lawyer says his client's lies did not harm anyone, so he should serve no more than a year in prison. . . .

Another member of Sosa's group, Gilberto Jordan, admitted his participation in the same massacre and received a 10-year prison sentence in the United States federal prison for fraudulently obtaining his U.S. citizenship. He was also stripped of his citizenship. In 2011, he was extradited back to Guatemala and thereupon convicted for his participation in the massacre. The next section examines this and other more difficult prosecutions of the political leadership which direct such atrocities.

# E.  The Pinochet Paradigm: Use and Limits of Universal Jurisdiction to Prosecute Foreign Based Human Rights Crimes Unrelated to the Forum

## 1. Overview

Review of the various attempts to bring human rights violators to justice before their own national courts reveals that significant obstacles are perhaps inevitable. Violations of human rights that lead to potential criminal prosecution typically occur under conditions of political repression and national crisis. Repressive regimes are obviously unlikely to allow such prosecutions while still in power and significant political compromises, amnesties, reconciliation processes and immunities inevitably accompany regime change. National institutions critical to domestic, home grown prosecutions often lack the necessary independence, resources and competencies. Political and social conditions also typically complicate the quest for justice — powerful elites, vested interests and even ambivalent public sentiment about past events make prosecution of higher level officials both difficult and controversial.

What then is the appropriate role for other countries in seeking vindication for universal wrongs? If Guatemala or the Sudan is unable or unwilling to prosecute public officials who have committed egregious violations of human rights should other nations pursue such prosecutions in their own courts pursuant to universal jurisdiction? Even if other nations lack any overt direct relationship to the victims, defendants or events, violators of certain human rights are "hostes humani generis" — enemies of all human kind. When and how should universal jurisdiction be used? Can it be used to prosecute a former head of state or other high ranking public officials who would normally be entitled to immunity for conduct in office? Is it a legitimate tool for achieving global justice, or a problematic invitation to meddle in the affairs of other societies and nations? The following case, involving the attempted extradition of the notorious Chilean Dictator Augusto Pinochet from the United Kingdom to Spain,[90] represents the first clear test of the potential use of universal jurisdiction to pursue human rights violators wherever they might be found.

## 2. The Decision: Regina v. Pinochet Ugarte

House of Lords

Lord Browne Wilkinson, Lord Goff of Chieveley, Lord Hope of Craighead, Lord Hutton, Lord Saville of Newdigate, Lord Millett and Lord Phillips of Worth Matravers

---

90. The investigation prompting the request for extradition was directed by Spanish investigating magistrate Baltasar Garzon, a crusading and often controversial figure.

**[2000] 1 A.C. 147)**

*\*\*\**

On 11 September 1973 a right-wing coup evicted the left-wing regime of President Allende. The coup was led by a military junta, of whom Senator (then General) Pinochet was the leader. At some stage he became head of state. The Pinochet regime remained in power until 11 March 1990 when Senator Pinochet resigned.

There is no real dispute that during the period of the Senator Pinochet regime appalling acts of barbarism were committed in Chile and elsewhere in the world: torture, murder and the unexplained disappearance of individuals, all on a large scale. Although it is not alleged that Senator Pinochet himself committed any of those acts, it is alleged that they were done in pursuance of a conspiracy to which he was a party, at his instigation and with his knowledge. He denies these allegations. None of the conduct alleged was committed by or against citizens of the United Kingdom or in the United Kingdom.

In 1998 Senator Pinochet came to the United Kingdom for medical treatment. The judicial authorities in Spain sought to extradite him in order to stand trial in Spain on a large number of charges. Some of those charges had links with Spain. But most of the charges had no connection with Spain. *\*\*\**
Our job is to decide two questions of law: are there any extradition crimes and, if so, is Senator Pinochet immune from trial for committing those crimes.*\*\*\**

Senator Pinochet started proceedings for habeas corpus and for leave to move for judicial review of both the first and the second provisional warrants.

*\*\*\**

The issue is whether the acts amount to an offence under English law.*\*\*\**

**Held:**

(1) that the requirement in section 2 of the Act of 1989 that the alleged conduct which was the subject of the extradition request be a crime under United Kingdom law as well as the law of the requesting state was a requirement that the conduct be a crime in the United Kingdom at the time when the alleged offence was committed; that (Lord Millett dissenting) extraterritorial torture did not become a crime in the United Kingdom until section 134 of the Criminal Justice Act 1988 came into effect on 29 September 1988; and that, accordingly, all the alleged offences of torture and conspiracy to torture before that date and all the alleged offences of murder and conspiracy to murder which did not occur in Spain were crimes for which the applicant could not be extradited *\*\*\**

(2) Allowing the appeal in part (Lord Goff dissenting), that, a former head of state had immunity from the criminal jurisdiction of the United Kingdom for acts done in his official capacity as head of state pursuant to section 20

of the State Immunity Act 1978 when read with article 39(2) of Schedule 1 to the Diplomatic Privileges Act 1964; but that torture was an international crime against humanity and jus cogens and after the coming into effect of the International Convention against Torture and other Cruel, Inhuman or Degrading Treatment or Punishment 1984 there had been a universal jurisdiction in all the Convention state parties to either extradite or punish a public official who committed torture; that in the light of that universal jurisdiction the state parties could not have intended that an immunity for ex-heads of state for official acts of torture *** would survive their ratification of the Convention; that *** since Chile, Spain and the United Kingdom had all ratified the Convention by 8 December 1988 the applicant could have no immunity for crimes of torture or conspiracy to torture after that date; that *** the relevant date when the immunity was lost was 29 September 1988 when section 134 of the Act of 1988 came into effect; that *** and that, accordingly, the applicant had no immunity from extradition for offences of torture or conspiracy to torture which were said to have occurred after 8 December 1988 and the extradition could proceed on those charges . . .

***

**Opinion of the Court**

**Lord Browne-Wilkinson.**

**Outline of the law**

In general, a state only exercises criminal jurisdiction over offences which occur within its geographical boundaries. If a person who is alleged to have committed a crime in Spain is found in the United Kingdom, Spain can apply to the United Kingdom to extradite him to Spain. The power to extradite from the United Kingdom for an "extradition crime" is now contained in the Extradition Act 1989. That Act defines what constitutes an "extradition crime." For the purposes of the present case, the most important requirement is that the conduct complained of must constitute a crime under the law both of Spain and of the United Kingdom. This is known as the double criminality rule.

Since the Nazi atrocities and the Nuremberg trials, international law has recognised a number of offences as being international crimes. Individual states have taken jurisdiction to try some international crimes even in cases where such crimes were not committed within the geographical boundaries of such states. The most important of such international crimes for present purposes is torture which is regulated by the International Convention against Torture and other Cruel, Inhuman or Degrading Treatment or Punishment 1984 (1990) (Cm. 1775). The obligations placed on the United Kingdom by that Convention (and on the other 110 or more signatory states who have adopted the Convention) were incorporated into the law of the United Kingdom by section 134 of the Criminal Justice Act 1988. That Act came into force on 29 September 1988. Section 134 created a new crime under United Kingdom law, the crime of torture. ***

It is quite clear *** that under the Act of 1870 the double criminality rule required the conduct to be criminal under English law at the conduct date not at the request date. ***

*The charges which allege extradition crimes*

I must therefore consider whether, in relation to these two surviving categories of charge, Senator Pinochet enjoys sovereign immunity. But first it is necessary to consider the modern law of torture.

**Torture**

Apart from the law of piracy, the concept of personal liability under international law for international crimes is of comparatively modern growth. The traditional subjects of international law are states not human beings. But consequent upon the war crime trials after the 1939–45 World War, the international community came to recognise that there could be criminal liability under international law for a class of crimes such as war crimes and crimes against humanity. *** At least from that date onwards the concept of personal liability for a crime in international law must have been part of international law. *** Ever since 1945, torture on a large scale has featured as one of the crimes against humanity:***

"Because of the importance of the values it protects, [the prohibition of torture] has evolved into a peremptory norm or jus cogens, that is, a norm that enjoys a higher rank in the international hierarchy than treaty law and even 'ordinary' customary rules. The most conspicuous consequence of this higher rank is that the principle at issue cannot be derogated from by states through international treaties or local or special customs or even general customary rules not endowed with the same normative force . . . ***

The jus cogens nature of the international crime of torture justifies states in taking universal jurisdiction over torture wherever committed. International law provides that offences jus cogens may be punished by any state because the offenders are "common enemies of all mankind and all nations have an equal interest in their apprehension and prosecution:" Demjanjuk v. Petrovsky (1985) 603 F.Supp. 1468; 776 F.2d 571. ***

**The Torture Convention**

*** Under article 5(2) a state party has to take jurisdiction over any alleged offender who is found within its territory. Article 6 contains provisions for a state in whose territory an alleged torturer is found to detain him, inquire into the position and notify the states referred to in article 5(1) and to indicate whether it intends to exercise jurisdiction. Under article 7 the state in whose territory the alleged torturer is found shall, if he is not extradited to any of the states mentioned in article 5(1), submit him to its authorities for the purpose of prosecution. Under article 8(1) torture is to be treated as an extraditable offence and under article 8(4) torture shall, for the purposes of extradition, be treated as having been committed not only in the place where it occurred but also in the state mentioned in article 5(1). ***

**Universal Jurisdiction**

The purpose of the [Torture] Convention was to introduce the principle aut dedere aut punire — either you extradite or you punish: If there is no prosecution by, or extradition to, an article 5(1) state, the state where the alleged offender is found (which will have already taken him into custody under article 6) must exercise the jurisdiction under article 5(2) by prosecuting him under article 7(1).

I gather the following important points from the Torture Convention: (1) torture within the meaning of the Convention can only be committed by "a public official or other person acting in an official capacity," but these words include a head of state. A single act of official torture is "torture" within the Convention; (2) superior orders provide no defence; (3) if the states with the most obvious jurisdiction (the article 5(1) states) do not seek to extradite, the state where the alleged torturer is found must prosecute or, apparently, extradite to another country, i.e. there is universal jurisdiction; (4) there is no express provision dealing with state immunity of heads of state, ambassadors or other officials; (5) since Chile, Spain and the United Kingdom are all parties to the Convention, they are bound under treaty by its provisions whether or not such provisions would apply in the absence of treaty obligation.

**State Immunity**

This is the point around which most of the argument turned. It is of considerable general importance internationally since, if Senator Pinochet is not entitled to immunity in relation to the acts of torture alleged to have occurred after 29 September 1988, it will be the first time so far as counsel have discovered when a local domestic court has refused to afford immunity to a head of state or former head of state on the grounds that there can be no immunity against prosecution for certain international crimes.

It is a basic principle of international law that one sovereign state (the forum state) does not adjudicate on the conduct of a foreign state. The foreign state is entitled to procedural immunity from the processes of the forum state. This immunity extends to both criminal and civil liability. State immunity probably grew from the historical immunity of the person of the monarch. In any event, such personal immunity of the head of state persists to the present day: the head of state is entitled to the same immunity as the state itself. The diplomatic representative of the foreign state in the forum state is also afforded the same immunity in recognition of the dignity of the state which he represents. This immunity enjoyed by a head of state in power and an ambassador in post is a complete immunity attaching to the person of the head of state or ambassador and rendering him immune from all actions or prosecutions whether or not they relate to matters done for the benefit of the state. Such immunity is said to be granted ratione personae.

What then when the ambassador leaves his post or the head of state is deposed? The position of the ambassador is covered by the Vienna Convention on Diplomatic Relations (1961). After providing for immunity from arrest (article 29) and from criminal and civil jurisdiction (article 31), article 39(1) provides that the ambassador's privileges shall be enjoyed from the moment he takes up post; and paragraph (2) provides:

"When the functions of a person enjoying privileges and immunities have come to an end, such privileges and immunities shall normally cease at the moment when he leaves the country, or on expiry of a reasonable period in which to do so, but shall subsist until that time, even in case of armed conflict. However, with respect to acts performed by such a person in the exercise of his functions as a member of the mission, immunity shall continue to subsist."

***

Can it be said that the commission of a crime which is an international crime against humanity and jus cogens is an act done in an official capacity on behalf of the state? I believe there to be strong ground for saying that the implementation of torture as defined by the Torture Convention cannot be a state function. ***

*** The idea that individuals who commit international crimes are *internationally* accountable for them has now become an accepted part of international law. ***

How can it be for international law purposes an official function to do something which international law itself prohibits and criminalises? Thirdly, an essential feature of the international crime of torture is that it must be committed "by or with the acquiescence of a public official or other person acting in an official capacity." As a result all defendants in torture cases will be state officials. Yet, if the former head of state has immunity, the man most responsible will escape liability while his inferiors (the chiefs of police, junior army officers) who carried out his orders will be liable. I find it impossible to accept that this was the intention. ***

As to the charges of murder and conspiracy to murder, no one has advanced any reason why the ordinary rules of immunity should not apply and Senator Pinochet is entitled to such immunity.

For these reasons, I would allow the appeal so as to permit the extradition proceedings to proceed on the allegation that torture in pursuance of a conspiracy to commit torture, including the single act of torture which is alleged in charge 30, was being committed by Senator Pinochet after 8 December 1988 when he lost his immunity. \*\*\*

**Lord Millett. [Essentially a concurring opinion]**

My Lords, I have had the advantage of reading in draft the speech of my noble and learned friend, Lord Browne-Wilkinson. Save in one respect, I agree with his reasoning and conclusions. Since the one respect in which I differ is of profound importance to the outcome of this appeal, I propose to set out my own process of reasoning at rather more length than I might otherwise have done.

State immunity is not a personal right. It is an attribute of the sovereignty of the state. The immunity which is in question in the present case, therefore, belongs to the Republic of Chile, not to Senator Pinochet. It may be asserted or waived by the state, but where it is waived by treaty or convention the waiver must be express. So much is not in dispute.

\*\*\* The idea that individuals who commit crimes recognised as such by international law may be held internationally accountable for their actions is now an accepted doctrine of international law. \*\*\*

\*\*\*

The landmark decision of the Supreme Court of Israel in **Attorney-General of Israel v. Eichmann**, 36 I.L.R. 5 is also of great significance. Eichmann had been a very senior official of the Third Reich. \*\*\* He was abducted from Argentina and brought to Israel, where he was tried in the District Court for Tel Aviv. His appeal against conviction was dismissed by the Supreme Court. \*\*\*

The court dealt separately with the questions of jurisdiction and act of state. Israel was not a belligerent in the Second World War, which ended three years before the state was founded. Nor were the offences committed within its territory. \*\*\* [T]he court also held that the scale and international character of the atrocities of which the accused had been convicted fully justified the application of the doctrine of universal jurisdiction.

The case is authority for three propositions. (1) There is no rule of international law which prohibits a state from exercising extraterritorial criminal jurisdiction in respect of crimes committed by foreign nationals abroad. (2) War crimes and atrocities of the scale and international character of the Holocaust are crimes of universal jurisdiction under customary international law. (3) The fact that the accused committed the crimes in question in the course of his official duties as a responsible officer of the state and in the exercise of his authority as an organ of the state is no bar to the exercise of the jurisdiction of a national court.

\*\*\*

In my opinion, crimes prohibited by international law attract universal jurisdiction under customary international law if two criteria are satisfied. First, they must be contrary to a peremptory norm of international law so as to infringe a jus cogens. Secondly, they must be so serious and on such a scale that they can justly be regarded as an attack on the international legal order. Isolated offences, even if committed by public officials, would not satisfy these criteria. ***

For my own part, I would allow the appeal in respect of the charges relating to the offences in Spain and to torture and conspiracy to torture wherever and whenever carried out. But the majority of your Lordships think otherwise, and consider that Senator Pinochet can be extradited only in respect of a very limited number of charges. ***

## 3. The Aftermath: Exportation of the Pinochet Paradigm Outside of Spain[91]

After the decision above was rendered, the British House of Lords ultimately approved the Spanish extradition request as to a limited number of crimes alleged to have occurred after British accession to the Torture Convention. U.K. foreign minister, Jack Straw, however, eventually denied the extradition request on discretionary grounds related to Pinochet's allegedly failing mental health. Pinochet promptly returned to Chile and had a good laugh at British expense.

The Court's decision, although more limited than many advocates hoped, directly supported the proposition that universal jurisdiction may justify domestic criminal prosecution of certain violations of international human rights in states other than the one in which the offending acts were committed. More controversially, the decision also recognized important limitations on public official immunities. The British and Spanish courts, in essence, recognized that Pinochet, and others like him, could be prosecuted for certain universal crimes through the domestic criminal processes of any state that obtains personal jurisdiction over him.[92] Citing criminal

---

91. Portions of the following text was taken from: Donoho, *Human Rights Enforcement in the Twenty-First Century*, 35 Ga. J. Int'l & Comp. L. 1 (2006).

92. *See, e.g.*, Al-Adsani v. United Kingdom, App. No. 35763/97, paras. 9–13, 54–61 (Nov. 21, 2001) (rejecting claim that torture eliminates state sovereign immunity under international law), *available at* ‹http://www.echr.coe.int/eng/judgments.htm›; Pinochet (No. 3) R., *ex parte* Pinochet Ugarte (Amnesty International Intervening) (No. 3) [2000] AC 147.]. The ICJ has found no state practice of denying head of state/official immunity based on violations of human rights involving war crimes or crimes against humanity. *See* Arrest Warrant of 11 April 2000 (Democratic Republic of the Congo v. Belgium), 2002 I.C.J. 3, ¶¶51–58. *See also* Certain Questions of Mutual Assistance in Criminal Matters (Djib. v. Fr.), 2008 I.C.J. 177, 236, 237. In contrast, the International Criminal Court for the Former Yugoslavia has rejected such immunity. *See* Prosecutor v. Blaškić (Case No. IT-95-14), Appeals Chamber, Judgment on the Request of the Republic of Croatia for the Review of the Decision of Trial Chamber II of 18 July 1997, ¶ 41 (Oct. 29, 1997). *See generally*, Sevrine Knuchel, *State Immunity And The Promise Of Jus Cogens*, 9 Nw. J. Int'l Hum. Rts. 149 (2011); Lee M. Caplan, *State*

investigations or complaints brought in Belgium, Senegal, Austria, Canada, Denmark, France, Germany, the Netherlands, Spain, Switzerland, and the United Kingdom, Professor Diane Orentlicher reports that a "raft of countries have walked through the door the Pinochet case opened." A 2013 Amnesty International Report surveying domestic practices (referenced at the beginning of this chapter) indicates that authorization of universal jurisdiction is now commonplace, at least for genocide, war crimes, torture and crimes against humanity.

The widespread adoption and potential use of universal jurisdiction is not, however, without controversy and significant opposition. Opposition to domestic deployment of universal jurisdiction largely centers on the foreign policy and political implications of the potential prosecution of high level public officials — in essence, the Pinochet paradigm. The experiences of Belgium and Spain, whose laws and practices were among the most expansive regarding the use universal jurisdiction, illustrate this point. The Belgian law, for example, authorized Belgian courts to hear criminal claims, <u>in absentia</u>, alleging war crimes, crimes against humanity and genocide brought not just by state prosecutors but also by private parties, without any circumstantial connection to Belgium whatsoever, and explicitly prohibited official immunity defenses.[93]

Conditions being favorable, a significant number of criminal complaints involving alleged international crimes followed including an arrest warrant issued in 2000 against the Minister of Foreign Affairs for the Democratic Republic of the Congo <u>Abdoulaye Yerodia Ndombasi</u>. The Congolese government objected to the Belgian action and brought a case challenging the legality of the warrant under international law before the International Court of Justice. The ICJ agreed, ruling that the Minister was entitled to immunity under customary international law even for human rights crimes, at least while in office.[94] Professor Dalila Hoover, in an article urging replacement of domestic use of universal jurisdiction with reliance on the International Criminal Court, describes these events and the ensuing "chaos" this way:

> In June 2001, four Rwandan Hutus were convicted in a Belgium court of committing genocide in Rwanda in violation of a Belgian universal jurisdiction statute. The success of the case which marked Belgium's first application of its universal jurisdiction laws resulted in a profusion of complaints. A group of twenty-three Palestinian refugees and survivors, for instance, initiated an action in Belgium seeking to have Prime Minister Ariel Sharon tried for his alleged involvement in the massacre of Palestinians in Sabra and Shatila refugee camps in 1982 while the camps were under Israeli control. A

---

*Immunity, Human Rights, and Jus Cogens: A Critique of the Normative Hierarchy Theory*, 97 Am. J. Int'l L. 741 (2003).

93. *See* R. Baker, *Universal Jurisdiction and the Case of Belgium: A Critical Assessment*, 16 ILSA J. Int'l & Comp. L. 141, 149–155 (2009).

94. *Case Concerning the Arrest Warrant of 11 April 2000 (Democratic Republic of the Congo v. Belgium)* [2002] <u>ICJ 1</u> [2002].

group of Israelis returned the favor by seeking to have Palestinian leader Yasser Arafat tried in Belgium for his alleged role in terrorist attacks in Israel. Instead of rendering justice, Belgium's courts sole retribution created an unprecedented judicial chaos which materially impacted on the international community.

The explosion of lawsuits against official leaders spread throughout Europe. In 2006, Spain launched a criminal case against former Chinese President Jiang Zemin and his Prime Minister LiPeng for participating in genocide in Tibet. In 2009, various Iraqi victims took former U.S. Presidents, George H. W. Bush, William J. Clinton, George W. Bush and his senior officials, Vice-President Dick Cheney, Secretary of State Colin Powell, U.S. President Barack H. Obama, along with four U.K. Prime Ministers to a Spanish court for war crimes, crimes against humanity and genocide committed during the bombing of Baghdad in 1991 and 2003. In that same year, a British court issued an arrest warrant at the behest of pro-Palestinian activists against Israeli opposition leader Tzipi Livni for alleged war crimes committed during Operation Cast Lead, during which she acted as Israeli's Foreign Minister. The warrant was later cancelled after British officials learned that Livni was not in Britain. The Israeli foreign Ministry called the move "an absurdity."

This list which is far from being exhaustive clearly signals new changes in international norms and highlights some of the dangers associated with the exercise of universal jurisdiction. Britain, Belgium, and Spain have since reformed their laws to narrow the scope of universal jurisdiction. Nevertheless, the damage caused remains considerable.[95]

Belgian's 1993 universal jurisdiction law was repealed in 2003 and replaced by rules designed to "filter" politically sensitive cases. Apparently significant pressure from the United States, questioning Belgium's status as the headquarters for NATO, helped induce the change after cases were brought against former President George H. Bush and Dick Cheney alleging war crimes in connection with the Persian Gulf War of 1991.[96] Currently, Belgian courts only exercise jurisdiction over international crimes if the accused is a citizen or resident, or the victim is a citizen or three year resident, or an international treaty requires prosecution. Spain, formerly on the vanguard of universal jurisdiction, has also recently adopted significant changes to its laws, once again to deflect foreign policy and political fallout relating to prosecuting high public officials from other countries.

Spain Seeks to Curb Law Allowing Judges to Pursue Cases Globally, NY Times, By JIM YARDLEY FEB. 10, 2014

---

95. Hoover, Dalila V., *"Universal Jurisdiction not so Universal: A Time to Delegate to the International Criminal Court"* (2011). Cornell Law School Inter-University Graduate Student Conference Papers. Paper 52. http://scholarship.law.cornell.edu/lps_clacp/52 .

96. *See* Richard Bernstein, ***Belgium Rethinks*** *Its Prosecutorial Zeal*, NY Times, April 1, 2003.

MADRID — For nearly two decades, Spanish judges have been the provocateurs of international criminal law, pursuing human rights cases against Argentine military officers, Israeli defense officials or American soldiers in Iraq. Most famously, a Spanish judge opened the case that led to the arrest of the former dictator of Chile, <u>Augusto Pinochet</u> . . . .

They have also complicated diplomacy in unpredictable ways.

Which brings up China. On Monday afternoon, <u>Spain's National Court ordered international warrants</u> for China's former President Jiang Zemin and former Prime Minister Li Peng as part of a case about alleged human rights abuses in Tibet. Infuriated, Chinese diplomats are pressuring the Spanish government to stop the prosecution.

On Tuesday, Spain's Parliament is expected to debate and eventually approve a bill that would do exactly that. . . .

Under that pressure, Spain's government, then controlled by the Socialist Party, <u>weakened the law in 2009</u>, leading to the dismissal of several cases. Human rights advocates argue that a double standard has emerged — where it is acceptable to prosecute abuses in weak countries but not in global powers.

"They are trying to eliminate universal jurisdiction," said Judge Garzón, whose aggressive use of the doctrine later led to his <u>suspension from the Spanish bench in 2010</u>. "That is their goal. They have never believed in it." [97]

Following the lead of Belgium and Spain, the United Kingdom now requires that all prosecutions under universal jurisdiction be approved by the central Director of Public Prosecutions rather than through normal criminal law processes. Were the governments of Belgium, Spain and the United Kingdom correct to limit the potential reach of universal jurisdiction in their courts? Should universal jurisdiction be restricted so as to avoid foreign policy tensions or politically motivated actions? If

---

97. According to one source: "The new law means an end to a dozen investigations including:• The investigation of CIA rendition flights that landed in Spain after 9/11• The murder of Spanish cameraman José Couso in Iraq by US troops in 2003• The 2012 Israeli attack on the Freedom Flotilla delivering humanitarian aid to Gaza• The kidnap, torture and murder of Spanish United Nations official Carmelo Soria in 1976 by the National Intelligence Directorate of Chilean dictator General Augusto Pinochet• The prosecution of China for genocide, torture and crimes against humanity in Tibet• The complaint against four former SS soldiers by a survivor and the families of five Spanish victims of the Nazi concentration camps• The lawsuit involving the alleged killing by the military in 1989 of five Spanish Jesuits in the Central American University in El Salvador• The investigation of several former top Guatemalan officials charged with genocide and torture committed against the Mayan population• The investigation of former officials of the Rwandan government for the genocide of four million people and the murder of nine Spaniards in the 1990s• The investigation into the attack by Iraqi special forces in 2011 against the Ashraf refugee camp, in which 35 people are said to have died and 337 injured• The lawsuit into the alleged crimes of genocide, murder, torture and illegal detention of Sahwaris by the Moroccan authorities• The alleged crimes of genocide and torture against followers of the Falun Gong in China . . ."

so, can it ever be effectively used to pursue claims against high ranking government officials? Consider the circumstances and arguments of former U.S. Secretary of State, Henry Kissinger.

## 4. The Case of Henry Kissinger

Henry Kissinger is, to say the least, a controversial figure in modern American history. He served under President Richard Nixon as National Security Advisor during bombing campaigns in <u>Viet Nam</u>, <u>Cambodia</u> and <u>Laos</u> (1969–73) that killed, by most <u>historical estimates</u>, far more than 100,000 civilians and were, at times, kept secret from Congress. Dr. Kissinger is also widely believed to be the "<u>principle policy architect</u>" of U.S. assistance to the 1973 coup in Chile that replaced the democratically elected Salvador Allende with the now infamous General Pinochet. As U.S. Secretary of State, Kissinger actively supported repressive South and Central American regimes knowing full well that those governments were engaging in widespread and persistent human rights atrocities. After a 1976 coup, <u>Kissinger told</u> Argentine Foreign Minister César Guzzetti, despite knowledge of the notorious "<u>Operation Condor</u>" assassination squads, "we have followed events in Argentina closely" and "wish the new government well. We wish it will succeed . . . If there are things that have to be done, you should do them quickly."

Wikipedia Commons, Archivo General Histórico del <u>Ministerio de Relaciones Exteriores</u> (Chile)

## a. Henry and the Case for Universal Jurisdiction

Dear Henry, <u>Writs and Demos over Chile Coup Hound Kissinger</u>, The Independent, By Hugh O'Shaughnessy and Robert Mendick, 14 April 2002

> The Chilean judge prosecuting Augusto Pinochet for crimes committed during his 17-year dictatorship, is seeking to extradite Henry Kissinger, the former US Secretary of State, to Chile.

> The threat will overshadow a visit to London next week by Mr. Kissinger, who will find himself hounded by an alliance of human rights campaigners and anti-capitalist demonstrators over his alleged connivance at General Pinochet's 1973 coup in Chile, as well as his part in the Vietnam war and America's secret bombing of Cambodia . . . .

> Any application for his extradition, however, would increase the embarrassment and pressure on Mr. Kissinger, who last year quit France in a hurry rather than submit to a summons to appear before Judge Roger Le Loire, who was looking into the disappearance of five French citizens in Chile during the Pinochet years.

***

> Mr. Kissinger is still threatened by a $4.9m civil action from Joyce Horman for the death of her husband, Charles Horman, during Pinochet's 1973 coup, which formed the basis of the film Missing. He is also being sued in Washington by members of the family of the former Chilean army commander, General René Schneider. Schneider was assassinated in Chile in 1970 in what was seen as a plot, aided by the CIA, to prevent the election of the Socialist President Salvador Allende.

## b. Henry's Response: <u>The Pitfalls of Universal Jurisdiction, By Henry Kissinger, Foreign Affairs</u>, July / August, 2001

> In less than a decade, an unprecedented movement has emerged to submit international politics to judicial procedures. It has spread with extraordinary speed and has not been subjected to systematic debate, partly because of the intimidating passion of its advocates. To be sure, human rights violations, war crimes, genocide, and torture have so disgraced the modern age and in such a variety of places that the effort to interpose legal norms to prevent or punish such outrages does credit to its advocates. The danger lies in pushing the effort to extremes that risk substituting the tyranny of judges for that of governments; historically, the dictatorship of the virtuous has often led to inquisitions and even witch-hunts.

> The doctrine of universal jurisdiction asserts that some crimes are so heinous that their perpetrators should not escape justice by invoking doctrines of sovereign immunity or the sacrosanct nature of national frontiers. Two specific approaches to achieve this goal have emerged recently. The first seeks

to apply the procedures of domestic criminal justice to violations of universal standards, some of which are embodied in United Nations conventions, by authorizing national prosecutors to bring offenders into their jurisdictions through extradition from third countries. The second approach is the International Criminal Court (ICC), the founding treaty for which was created by a conference in Rome in July 1998 and signed by 95 states, including most European countries. ***

The notion that heads of state and senior public officials should have the same standing as outlaws before the bar of justice is quite new.

***

Even with respect to binding undertakings such as the genocide convention, it was never thought that they would subject past and future leaders of one nation to prosecution by the national magistrates of another state where the violations had not occurred. Nor, until recently, was it argued that the various U.N. declarations subjected past and future leaders to the possibility of prosecution by national magistrates of third countries without either due process safeguards or institutional restraints.

Yet this is in essence the precedent that was set by the 1998 British detention of former Chilean President Augusto Pinochet as the result of an extradition request by a Spanish judge seeking to try Pinochet for crimes committed against Spaniards on Chilean soil. For advocates of universal jurisdiction, that detention — lasting more than 16 months — was a landmark establishing a just principle. But any universal system should contain procedures not only to punish the wicked but also to constrain the righteous. It must not allow legal principles to be used as weapons to settle political scores. Questions such as these must therefore be answered: What legal norms are being applied? What are the rules of evidence? What safeguards exist for the defendant? And how will prosecutions affect other fundamental foreign policy objectives and interests?

A DANGEROUS PRECEDENT

It is decidedly unfashionable to express any degree of skepticism about the way the Pinochet case was handled. For almost all the parties of the European left, Augusto Pinochet is the incarnation of a right-wing assault on democracy because he led a coup d'état against an elected leader. . . . . .

Disapproval of the Allende regime does not exonerate those who perpetrated systematic human rights abuses after it was overthrown. But neither should the applicability of universal jurisdiction as a policy be determined by one's view of the political history of Chile. The appropriate solution was arrived at in August 2000 when the Chilean Supreme Court withdrew Pinochet's senatorial immunity, making it possible to deal with the charges against him in the courts of the country most competent to judge this history and to relate its decisions to the stability and vitality of its democratic institutions.

On November 25, 1998, the judiciary committee of the British House of Lords [the United Kingdom's highest court] concluded that "international law has made it plain that certain types of conduct . . . are not acceptable conduct on the part of anyone." But that principle did not oblige the lords to endow a Spanish magistrate — and presumably other magistrates elsewhere in the world — with the authority to enforce it in a country where the accused had committed no crime, and then to cause the restraint of the accused for 16 months in yet another country in which he was equally a stranger. It could have held that Chile, or an international tribunal specifically established for crimes committed in Chile on the model of the courts set up for heinous crimes in the former Yugoslavia and Rwanda, was the appropriate forum.

The unprecedented and sweeping interpretation of international law in Ex parte Pinochet would arm any magistrate anywhere in the world with the power to demand extradition, substituting the magistrate's own judgment for the reconciliation procedures of even incontestably democratic societies where alleged violations of human rights may have occurred. It would also subject the accused to the criminal procedures of the magistrate's country, with a legal system that many be unfamiliar to the defendant and that would force the defendant to bring evidence and witnesses from long distances. Such a system goes far beyond the explicit and limited mandates established by the U.N. Security Council for the tribunals covering war crimes in the former Yugoslavia and Rwanda as well as the one being negotiated for Cambodia.

Perhaps the most important issue is the relationship of universal jurisdiction to national reconciliation procedures set up by new democratic governments to deal with their countries' questionable pasts. One would have thought that a Spanish magistrate would have been sensitive to the incongruity of a request by Spain, itself haunted by transgressions committed during the Spanish Civil War and the regime of General Francisco Franco, to try in Spanish courts alleged crimes against humanity committed elsewhere. . . . .

It is an important principle that those who commit war crimes or systematically violate human rights should be held accountable. But the consolidation of law, domestic peace, and representative government in a nation struggling to come to terms with a brutal past has a claim as well. The instinct to punish must be related, as in every constitutional democratic political structure, to a system of checks and balances that includes other elements critical to the survival and expansion of democracy.

Another grave issue is the use in such cases of extradition procedures designed for ordinary criminals. If the Pinochet case becomes a precedent, magistrates anywhere will be in a position to put forward an extradition request without warning to the accused and regardless of the policies the accused's country might already have in place for dealing with the charges. The country from which extradition is requested then faces a seemingly technical legal decision that, in fact, amounts to the exercise of political discretion — whether to entertain the claim or not.

*\*\**

The Pinochet precedent, if literally applied, would permit the two sides in the Arab-Israeli conflict, or those in any other passionate international controversy, to project their battles into the various national courts by pursuing adversaries with extradition requests. When discretion on what crimes are subject to universal jurisdiction and whom to prosecute is left to national prosecutors, the scope for arbitrariness is wide indeed. So far, universal jurisdiction has involved the prosecution of one fashionably reviled man of the right while scores of East European communist leaders — not to speak of Caribbean, Middle Eastern, or African leaders who inflicted their own full measures of torture and suffering — have not had to face similar prosecutions.

*\*\**

## AN INDISCRIMINATE COURT

The ideological supporters of universal jurisdiction also provide much of the intellectual compass for the emerging International Criminal Court. Their goal is to criminalize certain types of military and political actions and thereby bring about a more humane conduct of international relations. To the extent that the ICC replaces the claim of national judges to universal jurisdiction, it greatly improves the state of international law. And, in time, it may be possible to negotiate modifications of the present statute to make the ICC more compatible with U.S. constitutional practice. But in its present form of assigning the ultimate dilemmas of international politics to unelected jurists — and to an international judiciary at that — it represents such a fundamental change in U.S. constitutional practice that a full national debate and the full participation of Congress are imperative. Such a momentous revolution should not come about by tacit acquiescence in the decision of the House of Lords or by dealing with the ICC issue through a strategy of improving specific clauses rather than as a fundamental issue of principle.

*\*\**

For example, can any leader of the United States or of another country be hauled before international tribunals established for other purposes? This is precisely what Amnesty International implied when, in the summer of 1999, it supported a "complaint" by a group of European and Canadian law professors to Louise Arbour, then the prosecutor of the International Criminal Tribunal for the Former Yugoslavia (ICTY). The complaint alleged that crimes against humanity had been committed during the NATO air campaign in Kosovo. Arbour ordered an internal staff review, thereby implying that she did have jurisdiction if such violations could, in fact, be demonstrated. Her successor, Carla Del Ponte, in the end declined to indict any NATO official because of a general inability "to pinpoint individual responsibilities," thereby implying anew that the court had jurisdiction over NATO and American leaders in the Balkans and would have issued an indictment had it been able to identify the particular leaders allegedly involved.

*＊*

Distrusting national governments, many of the advocates of universal jurisdiction seek to place politicians under the supervision of magistrates and the judicial system. . . . .

The advocates of universal jurisdiction argue that the state is the basic cause of war and cannot be trusted to deliver justice. If law replaced politics, peace and justice would prevail. But even a cursory examination of history shows that there is no evidence to support such a theory. The role of the statesman is to choose the best option when seeking to advance peace and justice, realizing that there is frequently a tension between the two and that any reconciliation is likely to be partial. The choice, however, is not simply between universal and national jurisdictions.

MODEST PROPOSALS

The precedents set by international tribunals established to deal with situations where the enormity of the crime is evident and the local judicial system is clearly incapable of administering justice, as in the former Yugoslavia and Rwanda, have shown that it is possible to punish without removing from the process all political judgment and experience. In time, it may be possible to renegotiate the ICC statute to avoid its shortcomings and dangers. Until then, the United States should go no further toward a more formal system than one containing the following three provisions. First, the U.N. Security Council would create a Human Rights Commission or a special subcommittee to report whenever systematic human rights violations seem to warrant judicial action. Second, when the government under which the alleged crime occurred is not authentically representative, or where the domestic judicial system is incapable of sitting in judgment on the crime, the Security Council would set up an ad hoc international tribunal on the model of those of the former Yugoslavia or Rwanda. And third, the procedures for these international tribunals as well as the scope of the prosecution should be precisely defined by the Security Council, and the accused should be entitled to the due process safeguards accorded in common jurisdictions.

In this manner, internationally agreed procedures to deal with war crimes, genocide, or other crimes against humanity could become institutionalized. Furthermore, the one-sidedness of the current pursuit of universal jurisdiction would be avoided. This pursuit could threaten the very purpose for which the concept has been developed. In the end, an excessive reliance on universal jurisdiction may undermine the political will to sustain the humane norms of international behavior so necessary to temper the violent times in which we live.

### c. Henry Could Be Wrong

Kenneth Roth, *The Case for Universal Jurisdiction*, Foreign Affairs, September/ October, 2001

Behind much of the savagery of modern history lies impunity. Tyrants commit atrocities, including genocide, when they calculate they can get away with them. Too often, dictators use violence and intimidation to shut down any prospect of domestic prosecution. Over the past decade, however, a slowly emerging system of international justice has begun to break this pattern of impunity in national courts.

*** 

With growing frequency, national courts operating under the doctrine of universal jurisdiction are prosecuting despots in their custody for atrocities committed abroad. Impunity may still be the norm in many domestic courts, but international justice is an increasingly viable option, promising a measure of solace to victims and their families and raising the possibility that would-be tyrants will begin to think twice before embarking on a barbarous path.

In "The Pitfalls of Universal Jurisdiction" (July/August 2001), former Secretary of State Henry Kissinger catalogues a list of grievances against the juridical concept that people who commit the most severe human rights crimes can be tried wherever they are found. But his objections are misplaced, and the alternative he proposes is little better than a return to impunity.

*** 

What is new is not the concept of extraterritorial jurisdiction but the willingness of some governments to fulfill this duty against those in high places.

### ORDER AND THE COURT

Kissinger's critique of universal jurisdiction has two principal targets: the soon-to-be-formed International Criminal Court and the exercise of universal jurisdiction by national courts. (Strictly speaking, the ICC will use not universal jurisdiction but, rather, a delegation of states' traditional power to try crimes committed on their own territory.) Kissinger claims that the crimes detailed in the ICC treaty are "vague and highly susceptible to politicized application." But the treaty's definition of war crimes closely resembles that found in the Pentagon's own military manuals and is derived from the widely ratified Geneva Conventions and their Additional Protocols adopted in 1977. ***

Kissinger further asserts that the ICC prosecutor will have "discretion without accountability," going so far as to raise the specter of Independent

Counsel Kenneth Starr and to decry "the tyranny of judges." In fact, the prosecutor can be removed for misconduct by a simple majority of the governments that ratify the ICC treaty, and a two-thirds vote can remove a judge. Because joining the court means giving it jurisdiction over crimes committed on the signatory's territory, the vast majority of member states will be democracies, not the abusive governments that self-protectively flock to U.N. human rights bodies, where membership bears no cost.

NO PLACE TO HIDE

National courts come under Kissinger's fire for selectively applying universal jurisdiction. He characterizes the extradition request by a Spanish judge seeking to try former Chilean President Augusto Pinochet for crimes against Spanish citizens on Chilean soil as singling out a "fashionably reviled man of the right." But Pinochet was sought not, as Kissinger writes, "because he led a coup d'état against an elected leader" who was a favorite of the left. Rather, Pinochet was targeted because security forces under his command murdered and forcibly "disappeared" some 3,000 people and tortured thousands more.

Furthermore, in recent years national courts have exercised universal jurisdiction against a wide range of suspects: Bosnian war criminals, Rwandan genocidaires, Argentine torturers, and Chad's former dictator. It has come to the point where the main limit on national courts empowered to exercise universal jurisdiction is the availability of the defendant, not questions of ideology.

Kissinger also cites the Pinochet case to argue that international justice interferes with the choice by democratic governments to forgive rather than prosecute past offenders. In fact, Pinochet's imposition of a self-amnesty at the height of his dictatorship limited Chile's democratic options. Only after 16 months of detention in the United Kingdom diminished his power was Chilean democracy able to begin prosecution. Such imposed impunity is far more common than democratically chosen impunity.

\*\*\*

Kissinger legitimately worries that the nations exercising universal jurisdiction could include governments with less-entrenched traditions of due process than the United Kingdom's. But his fear of governments robotically extraditing suspects for sham or counterproductive trials is overblown. Governments regularly deny extradition to courts that are unable to ensure high standards of due process. And foreign ministries, including the U.S. State Department, routinely deny extradition requests for reasons of public policy.

If an American faced prosecution by an untrustworthy foreign court, the United States undoubtedly would apply pressure for his or her release. If that failed, however, it might prove useful to offer the prosecuting government the face-saving alternative of transferring the suspect to the ICC, with its extensive procedural protections, including deference to good-faith investigations and prosecutions by a suspect's own government. Unfortunately, the legislation being pushed by ICC opponents in Washington would preclude that option.

As a nation committed to human rights and the rule of law, the United States should be embracing an international system of justice, even if it means that Americans, like everyone else, might sometimes be scrutinized.

# F.  Domestic Prosecutions Outside of the United States

## 1. Overview

Domestic criminal prosecution for egregious human rights violations has also been pursued outside of the United States, particularly in nations emerging from authoritarian rule. Inevitably these prosecutions open old wounds and cause internal political conflict while at the same time vindicating critical principles of basic justice. Chile, for example, has lurched through a decades-long process, emerging from the darkness of the Pinochet era (1973–90) with competing claims of amnesties, immunities and reconciliation counter-posed against egregious violations of human rights by military personnel and high public officials. Entrenched political elites and the lurking threat of a still powerful military were clear impediments to aggressive pursuits of justice. This difficult transition from autocracy to democracy in Chile, much like in other <u>Latin American nations</u>, resulted in a decades-long emphasis on "<u>truth and reconciliation</u>" rather than accountability. In very recent years, however, Chilean courts and prosecutors have become increasingly receptive to claims and charges brought against Pinochet era abusers. The <u>2013 World Report</u> from <u>Human Rights Watch</u> describes both significant progress and impediments in this process:

> More than three-quarters of the 3,186 documented killings and "disappearances" during the Augusto Pinochet dictatorship (1973–1990) have been heard by courts or are now under court jurisdiction, according to Diego Portales University's Human Rights Observatory, a nongovernmental organization that monitors progress in human rights trials.

> Between 2000 and September 2011, more than 800 former state security agents had been indicted or convicted, and as of August 2012, 64 agents were serving prison sentences. In many cases, the Supreme Court has used its discretionary powers to reduce sentences against human rights violators in recognition of the time elapsed since the criminal act. Others had their sentences commuted. These practices raise concerns about Chile's fulfillment of its obligation to hold accountable perpetrators of crimes against humanity by imposing appropriate punishments or sanctions.

> A similar pattern has emerged in Argentina where seven years of military rule and its "<u>dirty war</u>" against perceived subversives from 1976–83 resulted

in more than <u>9000 documented cases</u> (and as many as 30,000 suspected) of "disappearances" — individuals, desaparecidos, arrested by the government and never seen again. (Photo <u>gallery here</u>.)

After Argentine courts declared existing amnesty laws void in 2005, a wave of claims and prosecutions followed as described in this account from Human Rights Watch's 2013 <u>World Report section on Argentina</u>:

> As of August 2012, the number of persons accused of crimes against humanity had increased to 1,926, from 922 in 2007, according to CELS. There were 799 people facing charges for these crimes, and 262 who had been convicted and sentenced.

***

> In July 2012, a federal court sentenced Jorge Videla, de facto president from 1976 to 1981, to 50 years in prison for implementing a plan to steal babies from women who gave birth while they were being held in torture centers before they were killed, and to hand them over to military families for adoption. More than 400 babies are estimated to have been affected. Other officers, including the head of the last military junta, Reynaldo Bignone (1982–1983), also received prison sentences. The court concluded that the theft of babies was a "systematic and generalized practice." Videla had been convicted in 1985 for crimes against humanity and was already serving a life sentence.

> The "mega-trial" of state agents responsible for crimes committed at the Navy Mechanics School (ESMA) continued in 2012. In October 2011, a federal court sentenced 12 of the perpetrators to life imprisonment for the illegal arrest, torture, and murder of detainees held at the center. A second trial commenced in November 2012, in which 67 state agents faced similar charges. Seven of them were being tried for their alleged participation in "flights of death," in which prisoners held at ESMA were drugged and dropped from planes into the Atlantic.

Another striking example of the emerging use of criminal processes to vindicate human rights involves the struggle to bring abusers to justice in Guatemala. The UN-backed <u>Historical Clarification Commission</u> found that Guatemalan security forces and paramilitary "death squads" committed genocide by murdering or disappearing some 200,000 people, primarily indigenous Mayans, during <u>Guatemala's prolonged internal conflict</u>. Murder is a polite word that fails to capture the brutality of the campaign against indigenous Guatemalans. Consider this description in the Commission's <u>Report</u>:

> "In the majority of massacres there is evidence of multiple acts of savagery. Acts such as the killing of defenceless children, often by beating them against walls or throwing them alive into pits where the corpses of adults were later thrown; the amputation of limbs; the impaling of victims; the killing of persons by covering them in petrol and burning them alive; the

extraction, in the presence of others, of the viscera (internal organs) of victims who were still alive; the confinement of people who had been mortally tortured, in agony for days; the opening of the wombs of pregnant women, and other similarly atrocious acts, were not only actions of extreme cruelty against the victims, but also morally degraded the perpetrators and those who inspired, ordered or tolerated these actions."

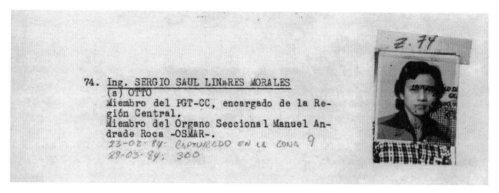

Page from Death Squad Dossier, <u>National Security Archive</u>, George Washington University, (Guatemalan military intelligence dossier on 183 "disappeared" persons between 1983 and 1985).

Exhumation of a mass grave in Comalapa. *Electronic Briefing Book No. 363*, Photograph courtesy of USAID, National Security Archive, George Washington University. An alternative, detailed account of the conflict in Guatemala is available on <u>Wikipedia</u>.

Guatemalan courts, controlled by the military and ruling elites, nevertheless refused to act or found human rights violators immune from prosecution. More recently, however, the prosecution of some military officers has moved forward. In 2011, four retired officers were convicted of participating in the "Dos Erres massacre" and sentenced to over 6000 years in prison (note related immigration actions by the United States described above). In August 2013, the former chief of detectives of the Guatemalan police, Pedro García Arredondo, was sentenced to 70 years in prison for his involvement in the 1981 disappearance of a university student.

Perhaps most significantly, criminal charges were recently brought against the former Guatemalan military dictator, Efrain Rios Montt, for his participation in the brutal "scored earth" campaign against Guatemala's indigenous population in the 1980s. In May, 2013, a Guatemalan court found Montt guilty of genocide and crimes against humanity and sentenced him to 80 years in prison. As described below, this verdict was soon overturned and the prosecutor removed from office.

## 2. Former Leader of Guatemala Is Guilty of Genocide against Mayan Group, <u>NY Times</u>

By ELISABETH MALKIN, Published: May 10, 2013

Photo by Elena Hermosa / Trocaire, Wikipedia Commons

GUATEMALA CITY — A Guatemalan court on Friday found Gen. Efraín Ríos Montt, the former dictator who ruled <u>Guatemala</u> during one of the bloodiest periods of its long civil war, guilty of genocide and crimes against humanity.

The verdict marked the first time a former head of state had been found guilty of genocide in his or her own country.

Judge Yasmín Barrios sentenced General Ríos Montt, 86, to 80 years in prison. His co-defendant, José Mauricio Rodríguez Sánchez, who served as the director of intelligence under the general, was acquitted of the same two charges.

"We are completely convinced of the intent to destroy the Ixil ethnic group," Judge Barrios said as she read the hour long summary of the ruling by the three-judge panel. Over five weeks, the tribunal heard more than 100 witnesses, including psychologists, military experts and Maya Ixil Indian survivors who told how General Ríos Montt's soldiers had killed their families and wiped out their villages. . . . .

The American military had a close relationship with the Guatemalan military well into the 1970s before President Jimmy Carter's administration cut off aid. When General Ríos Montt seized power in March 1982, President Ronald Reagan's administration cultivated him as a reliable Central American ally in its battle against Nicaragua's Sandinista government and Salvadoran guerrillas . . . .

By the end of 1982, however, the State Department had gathered evidence that the army was behind the massacres.

But even then, the administration insisted that General Ríos Montt was working to reduce the violence. After a regional meeting, President Reagan described him as "a man of great personal integrity and commitment." . . . .

After Montt spent a few nights in jail and a few more in the hospital, the Guatemalan Constitutional Court sent the case back to the trial court based on perceived procedural errors.

Consider this excerpt of a NY Times Editorial:

Even if the case goes forward, there are obstacles. Some witnesses have been threatened and will need to be protected so they can testify again . . . .

For 30 years, victims sought to bring General Ríos Montt to justice. His trial has been seen as a turning point both for Guatemala and for the international quest to deal with human rights abuses. The United States, which supported the general and his regime during the war and apologized for that in 1999, provides aid for the justice system. It should urge that the case be pursued through an independent process. It would be a travesty if a mishandled legal proceeding were to deny victims justice now.

Soon after ordering a new trial for Montt, the Court also decreed that the prosecutor, Attorney General Claudia Paz y Paz, must step down from her office before her official term expired.

# Chapter 7

# International Promotion and Enforcement Under the United Nations Charter Based System

## A.  Introduction & Overview

The last few chapters focused on the legal status of international rights within domestic legal systems and the ways in which domestic institutions are developing the capacity to enforce such rights as a part of the domestic legal order. The next several chapters will examine supervision and enforcement of international human rights by global and regional inter-governmental organizations. In essence, we will turn our attention from domestic enforcement of human rights to the activities and processes of international organizations. It is useful to keep in mind some basic distinctions between the various types of international institutions involved in human rights, particularly regarding the role of governments. Some international human rights organizations are properly described as "inter-governmental organizations" (IGOs) because they are created by governments, often have exclusively government membership and, at least on some level, serve purposes defined by those member governments. The United Nation's Human Rights Council, whose work is central to this chapter, is an example of an IGO.

The role of governments in such organizations distinguishes them from international organizations or "bodies" whose members or representatives are to some degree independent of the governments that created the institution. Treaty based "committees of experts" such as the CPRC's Human Rights Committee, and international judicial institutions such as the European Court of Human Rights are good examples of such international organizations. Both of these types of international organizations should be further distinguished from "non-governmental" human rights organizations, commonly called NGOs. The activities, positions and policies of NGOs are not directed by governments, allowing them to serve important independent "watchdog" functions. Human Rights Watch and Amnesty International are NGOs.

For pedagogical convenience it is also helpful to identify at least five major groups of international human rights organizations with reference to their source of authority and focus. These include: (1) institutions created by an international political organization like the United Nations under its Charter ("Charter based" — e.g., the Human Rights Council (successor to the now defunct Commission for Human Rights or CHR)); (2) institutions created by U.N. sponsored multilateral human rights treaties ("treaty based" — e.g., the Human Rights Committee referenced above); (3) institutions created by regional political organizations ("regionals" — e.g., the Inter-American Commission for Human Rights created by the Organization of American States and the European Court of Human Rights created by the European Convention on Human Rights); (4) international institutions created for a particular situation or crisis ("ad hoc" — e.g., the International Criminal Tribunal for the Former Yugoslavia created by the U.N. Security Council); and (5) the permanent International Criminal Court created by the "Rome Convention."

All of these institutions have been created through governmental agreement, all depend upon voluntary government involvement and all derive their powers, jurisdiction and mandates from the treaties, and ultimately the governments, that created them. The specific authority and function of each institution varies depending upon the terms of the international agreement that created them. This chapter will focus on the U.N. Charter based institutions, while subsequent chapters will examine the other institutional frameworks identified above. A starting point for research regarding situations in specific countries involving the work of various U.N. institutions, both Charter and treaty based, is the <u>Universal Human Rights Index</u>.

To facilitate your study of the U.N. Charter based system, focus on answering the following two sets of questions. The first set of questions asks for basic information about U.N. institutions that you need to know in order to understand how the U.N. functions in the field of human rights. You will find that these inquiries are also useful in understanding the institutions that are the focus of our subsequent chapters on treaty based, regional and international criminal institutions. The second set of questions ask you to apply what you have learned to a human rights situation involving government repression of Tibetan and Uyghur (often spelled "Uighur"; pronounced "wee-gur") people in China. Links to reports issued by news organizations and human rights NGOs regarding these ongoing situations immediately follow the questions.

1. Please identify the primary role and functions of the General Assembly, Security Counsel, International Court of Justice, High Commissioner for Human Rights and the HR Council in the UN's efforts to protect human rights. Start by answering the following specific questions which are organized by theme:

a. **Mandate:** Do these institutions enforce, supervise, advise, implement, or simply promote human rights (or none of the above)? What differences are there between these various possible descriptions of institutional mandate?

b. **Organization & Lines of Authority:** What relationship do these institutions have with each other and the rest of the UN? Is there a hierarchy of authority? What is the legal relationship between individual member states and the institutions?

c. **Membership, Status & Constituency:** Who serves on these institutions and in what capacity? Whose interests do they serve?

d. **Powers & Mechanisms:** How are these institutions empowered to act, if at all, to address alleged violations of human rights (i.e., what can they do) and what criteria exist, jurisdictional or otherwise, for the exercise of those powers?

e. **Standards:** What human rights standards do they use? (i.e., what sources of legal obligations do various U.N. institutions rely upon?)

f. **Authority:** Are the actions or decisions of these institutions binding, and if so, on whom?

g. **Enforceability:** How are the actions or decisions of these institutions enforced, if at all?

2. Please explain what the HR Council could do to address the violations of international human rights described in the following reports regarding China. In particular, focus your attention on the situations in the autonomous regions of Tibet and Xinjiang ("sin-jian") — sometimes called the "other Tibet," and "East Turkestan."

a. What human rights would Tibetans, and Uyghurs in Xinjiang, allege that China has violated?

b. What would you argue as the U.S. representative on the Council if seeking to urge Council action?

c. What legal standards or prerequisites are relevant?

d. What would you argue as the Chinese representative on the Council in response to allegations brought by Western countries?

3. Could individual victims of these alleged violations seek redress before any U.N. based institutions, particularly before the Council or its "advisory committee" (formerly "Sub-Commission")?

# B.  Human Rights in China: The Suppression of Uyghur & Tibetan Minorities

## 1. Generally

Please review Amnesty International's <u>2013 Annual Report: China</u> or Human Rights Watch's <u>2013 China Report</u>. These reports will provide you with an overview of China's dismal human rights record generally, as well as an overview of the situations in Tibet and Xinjiang. Next, consult the myriad of other web-based sources that provide information regarding the Chinese government's treatment of the Tibetan and Uyghur ethnic minorities. A few such sources are included below for your convenience but you can rely on other information if you so choose. Finally, consider the specific cases of the Uyghur author, Nurmuhemmet Yasin, and Professor Ilham Tohti, as described below.

**Videos:**

<u>A Uighur/Uyghur was interviewed by Laura Ling in Xinjiang in western China (Current TV) part 1</u>

(Eight-minute Frontline video about young reporter emotionally recounting trip to Xinjiang in which Uyghur man is arrested after an interview and taken away by police)

What's China doing in Tibet? 21st Century Repression, 60+ Years of Brutal Occupation (Six-minute video concerning the more than 100 Tibetans who have self-immolated in protest against Chinese oppression of their religion and culture)

France 24: Seven days in Tibet - EXCLUSIVE REPORT — 05/20/2013 REPORTS (one of many journalistic reports on Chinese repression in Tibet)

Tibet Situation : Critical (Full Length Documentary, by Jason Lansdel)

**Print News Reports on Web**:

Ending the Silence on China's Uighur Repression, (Washington Post, 2013)

China's Uighur Oppression Continues, Beijing hands down a 15-year sentence for speaking to foreign journalists, Wall Street Journal, 2010 (summary of circumstances by Uighur separatist leader, Rebiya Kadeer)

What data reveals about big brother in the Far East — PRC censorship

What does China say in its defense?

## 2. Author Nurmuhemmet Yasin

Biographical information from English Pen (about Pen here)

**D.o.b:** 6 March 1974

**Profession:** Freelance Uighur writer of the Uighur-language *Kashgar Literary Journal*

**Date of arrest:** 29 November 2004

**Sentence:** 10 years in prison

**Expires:** 30 November 2014

**Details of arrest:** Nurmuhemmet Yasin was arrested in Kashgar on 19 November 2004 for the publication of his short story 'Wild Pigeon' ('Yawa Kepter'), first published in the bi-monthly Uighur-language *Kashgar Literature Journal* (issue No. 5). After publication, the story was widely circulated and was recommended for an award by one of the biggest Uighur literary web sites. It also attracted the attention of the Chinese authorities, who apparently consider the fable to be a tacit criticism of their government in the Xinjiang Uighur Autonomous Region. The Chinese authorities confiscated his personal computer, which contained close to 1,600 poems, commentaries, stories and one unfinished novel.

**Trial details:** After a closed trial, during which he was denied access to legal representation, Yasin was sentenced to 10 years in prison. He was convicted for 'inciting Uighur separatism' in his book *Yawa Kepter*. The Kashgar Intermediate Court upheld his sentence on appeal, and he was transferred to Urumchi No. 1 Jail. Yasin has not been allowed any visitors since his arrest. Korash Huseyin, the editor of the *Kashgar Literary Journal*, was sentenced to three years in prison for publishing 'Wild Pigeon'.

**Professional details:** Nurmuhemmet Yasin is an award-winning freelance Uighur writer. He is known for his numerous short stories, essays, and three volumes of poetry: *First Love*, *Crying From the Heart* and *Come on Children*. Some of his work has already been selected for inclusion in Uighur-language middle-school literature textbooks. His short story 'Wild Pigeon' ('Yawa Kepter') was broadcast through Radio Free Asia's Uighur Service and has been translated into English.

**Place of detention:** Urumchi No. 1 Jail.

**Treatment in prison:** Yasin has been permitted no visitors since his arrest.

**Other Details:** Yasin is married with two sons.

**Honorary Member:** American PEN, English PEN and Independent Chinese PEN.

In 2008, Nurmuhemmet Yasin was shortlisted for the inaugural Art Venture Freedom to Create Prize, a unique prize designed to celebrate the role of the arts in promoting human rights and highlighting the forgotten frontline of artists defending their freedom of expression at great personal sacrifice. The nominated piece of work, "Wild Pigeon (Yawa Kepter)" has been translated from Uighur into English and Chinese by Dolkun Kamberi, director of Radio Free Asia's Uighur service. The English translation is available online in two parts: Part One & Part Two.

Please read at least some portion of the Wild Pigeon. This is all it takes to find yourself in prison in the PRC.

## 3. Professor Ilham Tohti

From Pen America:

Status: Convicted

Ilham Tohti, 44, is an ethnically Uyghur economist, writer, and public intellectual, and is a professor at Minzu University of China in Beijing (formerly Central Nationalities University). He is one of the best-known scholars on Uyghur issues, and is a co-founder of the website Uyghur Online, which was designed to promote understanding between Uyghurs and Han Chinese. It is now blocked inside China. Tohti is a member of the Uyghur PEN Center.

Tohti, who was born in Artush, Xinjiang Uyghur Autonomous Region (XUAR), is married with two young sons. His daughter, Jewher Ilham, is studying at Indiana University. He lives in Beijing.

Ilham Tohti is the winner of the 2014 PEN/Barbara Goldsmith Freedom to Write Award.

On September 23, 2014, Tohti was convicted on charges of separatism and sentenced to life in prison—a sentence much more harsh than predicted.

## 4. China's Uighurs — Islamic Extremists or Oppressed Minority?

Andrew Jacobs, <u>Uighur Scholar's Life Sentence Is Seen as Reining in Debate on Minorities in China</u>, New York Times, September 24, 2014

> BEIJING — The news that a Uighur academic, Ilham Tohti, had been sentenced in China to life in prison on charges of separatism drew a torrent of international outrage this week. . . . [R]ights advocates said they could not recall a similarly harsh penalty for a prominent intellectual whose main offense, it appeared, was criticizing government policies . . . .
>
> A slow-boil Uighur insurgency in Xinjiang, the resource-rich expanse of northwest China, has claimed hundreds of lives in a wave of violence over the past year . . . .
>
> By broaching those issues in his classroom, talking to foreign journalists and running an online forum for Uighur issues, prosecutors said, Mr. Tohti had "bewitched" his students, "maliciously hyped Xinjiang-related issues" and "exploited foreign forces to create pressure to make Xinjiang an international matter," according to court documents posted online by his lawyer, Li Fangping . . . .
>
> Although violence has been mounting there since 2009, when ethnic rioting in the regional capital, Urumqi, claimed about 200 lives, the latest policy shift was driven largely by two attacks in the past year. . . .
>
> Earlier this month, a county in southern Xinjiang said it would encourage Han-Uighur intermarriage by showering ethnically mixed couples with cash payments and generous government benefits. . . .
>
> "Forcing Uighurs to assimilate with the Han while flooding the streets with armed troops is not the way to ease the mounting anger and estrangement," said Professor Bovingdon, who, like a number of Western experts on Xinjiang, has been unable to obtain a Chinese visa in recent years.

# C. Principal U.N. Institutions and Their Role in the Protection of Human Rights

In order to understand and evaluate the U.N. Charter based human rights system, you must have a general working knowledge about the legal framework and central institutions of the United Nations. To that end, a primer on the U.N. and its institutions is included below with a focus on their role in protecting human rights. While all of the UN's principal institutions have functions implicating human rights in some fashion, you will find that the Security Council, General Assembly and International Court of Justice have, in practice, somewhat indirect and limited roles. More specialized organs, such as the U.N. "High Commissioner for Human Rights" (UNHCHR) and the Human Rights Council (HR Council) have a mandate dedicated to human rights and central to the U.N. Charter based system. Vital roles are also played by the various sub-entities created under the High Commissioner's or Council's authority such as "advisory committees," "thematic procedures," "working groups" and "rapporteurs" — so-called, "special procedures." After providing necessary background about the U.N. generally, the remainder of this chapter focuses on the High Commissioner, the Council and these various specialized entities and procedures. A useful general resource concerning the human rights functions of the U.N. is Office of the High Commissioner for Human Rights, "<u>Human Rights — A Basic Handbook for U.N. Staff.</u>"

## 1. The United Nations Generally

From: <u>http://www.un.org/en/aboutun/</u>

> The United Nations is an international organization founded in 1945. It is currently made up of 193 Member States. The mission and work of the United Nations are guided by the purposes and principles contained in its founding Charter.
>
> Due to the powers vested in its Charter and its unique international character, the United Nations can take action on the issues confronting humanity in the 21st century, such as peace and security, climate change, sustainable development, human rights, disarmament, terrorism, humanitarian and health emergencies, gender equality, governance, food production, and more.
>
> The U.N. also provides a forum for its members to express their views in the General Assembly, the Security Council, the Economic and Social Council, and other bodies and committees. By enabling dialogue between its members, and by hosting negotiations, the Organization has become a mechanism for governments to find areas of agreement and solve problems together.

In the above passage, the U.N. website describes promotion of human rights as one of its central functions along with the related topics of peace keeping and development. The Charter itself justifies this focus in its preamble and Articles 55–56 by including respect for fundamental rights and freedoms among the organization's primary purposes. The Charter is, however, long on promise and short on details. Both the identification of specific rights and freedoms — the normative question; and the methods of protection — the implementation and process question; were left to future development. As described in earlier chapters, the U.N. has made significant progress regarding the normative questions by playing a critical role in the development of a comprehensive catalogue of internationally recognized human rights standards. U.N. development of successful institutional frameworks for protecting human rights is, unfortunately, still a work in progress subject to significant flaws.

## 2. Principal U.N. Institutions

The UN has five principal institutions, each with defined functions that touch upon human rights in some fashion. Each of these principal organs, the <u>General Assembly,</u> the <u>Security Council</u>, the <u>Economic and Social Council</u>, the <u>International Court of</u>

Published by the United Nations Department of Public Information   DPI/2470 rev.4 — 15-00040 — July 2015

# The United Nations System

Strong UN. Better World. 70

## UN Principal Organs

**General Assembly**

**Security Council**

**Economic and Social Council**

**Secretariat**

**International Court of Justice**

**Trusteeship Council**[9]

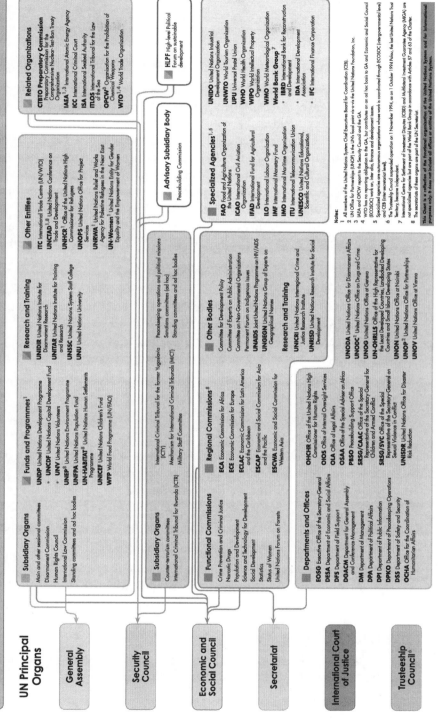

### ■ Subsidiary Organs

Main and other sessional committees
Disarmament Commission
Human Rights Council
International Law Commission
Standing committees and ad hoc bodies

### ■ Funds and Programmes[1]

**UNDP** United Nations Development Programme
 • **UNCDF** United Nations Capital Development Fund
 • **UNV** United Nations Volunteers
**UNEP**[2] United Nations Environment Programme
**UNFPA** United Nations Population Fund
**UN-HABITAT**[2] United Nations Human Settlements Programme
**UNICEF** United Nations Children's Fund
**WFP** World Food Programme (UN/FAO)

### ■ Research and Training

**UNIDIR** United Nations Institute for Disarmament Research
**UNITAR** United Nations Institute for Training and Research
**UNSSC** United Nations System Staff College
**UNU** United Nations University

### ■ Other Entities

**ITC** International Trade Centre (UN/WTO)
**UNCTAD**[1,4] United Nations Conference on Trade and Development
**UNHCR**[1] Office of the United Nations High Commissioner for Refugees
**UNOPS** United Nations Office for Project Services
**UNRWA**[1] United Nations Relief and Works Agency for Palestine Refugees in the Near East
**UN-Women**[1] United Nations Entity for Gender Equality and the Empowerment of Women

### ■ Related Organizations

**CTBTO Preparatory Commission** Preparatory Commission for the Comprehensive Nuclear-Test-Ban Treaty Organization
**IAEA**[1,3] International Atomic Energy Agency
**ICC** International Criminal Court
**ISA** International Seabed Authority
**ITLOS** International Tribunal for the Law of the Sea
**OPCW**[3] Organization for the Prohibition of Chemical Weapons
**WTO**[1,4] World Trade Organization

### ■ Subsidiary Organs

Counter-terrorism committees
International Criminal Tribunal for Rwanda (ICTR)
International Criminal Tribunal for the former Yugoslavia (ICTY)
Mechanism for International Criminal Tribunals (MICT)
Military Staff Committee
Peacekeeping operations and political missions
Sanctions committees (ad hoc)
Standing committees and ad hoc bodies

### ■ Advisory Subsidiary Body

Peacebuilding Commission

### ■ Functional Commissions[8]

Crime Prevention and Criminal Justice
Narcotic Drugs
Population and Development
Science and Technology for Development
Social Development
Statistics
Status of Women
United Nations Forum on Forests

### ■ Regional Commissions[8]

**ECA** Economic Commission for Africa
**ECE** Economic Commission for Europe
**ECLAC** Economic Commission for Latin America and the Caribbean
**ESCAP** Economic and Social Commission for Asia and the Pacific
**ESCWA** Economic and Social Commission for Western Asia

### ■ Other Bodies

Committee for Development Policy
Committee of Experts on Public Administration
Committee on Non-Governmental Organizations
Permanent Forum on Indigenous Issues
**UNAIDS** Joint United Nations Programme on HIV/AIDS
**UNGEGN** United Nations Group of Experts on Geographical Names

### Research and Training

**UNICRI** United Nations Interregional Crime and Justice Research Institute
**UNRISD** United Nations Research Institute for Social Development

### ■ Departments and Offices

**EOSG** Executive Office of the Secretary-General
**DESA** Department of Economic and Social Affairs
**DFS** Department of Field Support
**DGACM** Department for General Assembly and Conference Management
**DM** Department of Management
**DPA** Department of Political Affairs
**DPI** Department of Public Information
**DPKO** Department of Peacekeeping Operations
**DSS** Department of Safety and Security
**OCHA** Office for the Coordination of Humanitarian Affairs
**OHCHR** Office of the United Nations High Commissioner for Human Rights
**OIOS** Office of Internal Oversight Services
**OLA** Office of Legal Affairs
**OSAA** Office of the Special Adviser on Africa
**PBSO** Peacebuilding Support Office
**SRSG/CAAC** Office of the Special Representative of the Secretary-General for Children and Armed Conflict
**SRSG/SVC** Office of the Special Representative of the Secretary-General on Sexual Violence in Conflict
**UNISDR** United Nations Office for Disaster Risk Reduction
**UNODA** United Nations Office for Disarmament Affairs
**UNODC** United Nations Office on Drugs and Crime
**UNOG** United Nations Office at Geneva
**UN-OHRLLS** Office of the High Representative for the Least Developed Countries, Landlocked Developing Countries and Small Island Developing States
**UNON** United Nations Office at Nairobi
**UNOP**[2] United Nations Office for Partnerships
**UNOV** United Nations Office at Vienna

### ■ Specialized Agencies[1,5]

**FAO** Food and Agriculture Organization of the United Nations
**ICAO** International Civil Aviation Organization
**IFAD** International Fund for Agricultural Development
**ILO** International Labour Organization
**IMF** International Monetary Fund
**IMO** International Maritime Organization
**ITU** International Telecommunication Union
**UNESCO** United Nations Educational, Scientific and Cultural Organization
**UNIDO** United Nations Industrial Development Organization
**UNWTO** World Tourism Organization
**UPU** Universal Postal Union
**WHO** World Health Organization
**WIPO** World Intellectual Property Organization
**WMO** World Meteorological Organization
**World Bank Group**[7]
 • **IBRD** International Bank for Reconstruction and Development
 • **IDA** International Development Association
 • **IFC** International Finance Corporation

### ■ HLPF High-level Political Forum on sustainable development

### Notes:

1 All members of the United Nations System Chief Executives Board for Coordination (CEB).

2 UN Office for Partnerships (UNOP) is the UN's focal point vis-à-vis the United Nations Foundation, Inc.

3 IAEA and OPCW report to the Security Council and the GA.

4 WTO has no reporting obligation to the GA, but contributes on an ad hoc basis to GA and Economic and Social Council (ECOSOC) work on, inter alia, finance and development issues.

5 Specialized agencies are autonomous organizations whose work is coordinated through ECOSOC (intergovernmental level) and CEB (inter-secretariat level).

6 The Trusteeship Council suspended operation on 1 November 1994, as on 1 October 1994 Palau, the last United Nations Trust Territory, became independent.

7 International Centre for Settlement of Investment Disputes (ICSID) and Multilateral Investment Guarantee Agency (MIGA) are not specialized agencies but are part of the World Bank Group in accordance with Articles 57 and 63 of the Charter.

8 The secretariats of these organs are part of the UN Secretariat.

This Chart is a reflection of the functional organization of the United Nations System and for informational purposes only. It does not include all offices or entities of the United Nations System.

Justice, and the Secretariat, are described briefly below.[98] The UN's own comprehensive organizational chart (linked here and set out below) identifies the U.N.'s principle institutions and many important subsidiary bodies.

a. General Assembly

### Functions and Powers of the General Assembly

The General Assembly is the main deliberative, policymaking and representative organ of the UN. All 193 Member States of the U.N. are represented in the General Assembly, making it the only U.N. body with universal representation. Each year, in September, the full U.N. membership meets in the General Assembly Hall in New York for the annual General Assembly session, and general debate, which many heads of state attend and address. Decisions on important questions, such as those on peace and security, admission of new members and budgetary matters, require a two-thirds majority of the General Assembly. Decisions on other questions are by simple majority. The General Assembly, each year, elects a GA President to serve a one-year term of office.

Functions and powers of the General Assembly

According to the Charter of the United Nations, the General Assembly may:

- Consider and approve the United Nations budget and establish the financial assessments of Member States;
- Elect the non-permanent members of the Security Council and the members of other United Nations councils and organs and, on the recommendation of the Security Council, appoint the Secretary-General;
- Consider and make recommendations on the general principles of co-operation for maintaining international peace and security, including disarmament;
- Discuss any question relating to international peace and security and, except where a dispute or situation is currently being discussed by the Security Council, make recommendations on it;
- Discuss, with the same exception, and make recommendations on any questions within the scope of the Charter or affecting the powers and functions of any organ of the United Nations;
- Initiate studies and make recommendations to promote international political cooperation, the development and codification of international law, the realization of human rights and fundamental freedoms, and international collaboration in the economic, social, humanitarian, cultural, educational and health fields;
- Make recommendations for the peaceful settlement of any situation that might impair friendly relations among nations;

---

98. The Trusteeship Council was originally designated as a principal institution of the U.N. but ceased active operations in 1994 when the last remaining trust territory, Palau, gained its independence.

- Consider reports from the Security Council and other United Nations organs.

The Assembly may also take action in cases of a threat to the peace, breach of peace or act of aggression, when the Security Council has failed to act owing to the negative vote of a permanent member. In such instances, according to its "Uniting for Peace" resolution of November 1950 (resolution 377 (V)), the Assembly may consider the matter immediately and recommend to its Members collective measures to maintain or restore international peace and security (See "Special sessions and emergency special sessions").

As noted in the UN's own description above, a primary function of the U.N. General Assembly is to provide a forum for nations to "deliberate" and seek consensus on matters of global concern. Since promoting respect for human rights and fundamental freedoms is a primary function of the U.N. generally, appearing in both the preamble and Articles 55 and 56 of the Charter, the General Assembly has historically played a significant role in developing the current catalogue of international human rights norms and, more indirectly, in creating an institutional framework for their protection. Many major international human rights treaties, ranging from the two 1966 Covenants on political and economic rights to the Rome Convention creating the International Criminal Court, owe their genesis to the General Assembly process. As you will discover in the next chapter, many of these independent human rights treaties create their own institutional frameworks. Correspondingly, most of these treaty based institutions for protecting human rights reside within the U.N. umbrella, eventually linked back to the General Assembly.

The General Assembly also has a supervisory role regarding the work of other U.N. sub-entities specifically focused on human rights. Thus, the recently revamped Human Rights Council, examined below, reports directly to the General Assembly (it previously reported to the Economic and Social Council (ECOSOC)). The General Assembly also now elects the Council's membership. Within the General Assembly, human rights issues are generally considered by the Social, Humanitarian and Cultural Affairs Committee — commonly known as the Third Committee. The following excerpt about this General Assembly Committee, taken from the U.N. Third Committee website, illustrates the "deliberative" or "discursive" nature of the General Assembly's human right function — *they do a lot of talking.*

> As in previous sessions, an important part of the Committee's work this year will focus on the examination of human rights questions, including reports of the special procedures of the recently established Human Rights Council. In October 2010, the Committee will hear and interact with 36 such special rapporteurs, independent experts, and chairpersons of working groups of the Human Rights Council.

> The Committee also discusses the advancement of women, the protection of children, indigenous issues, the treatment of refugees, the promotion of fundamental freedoms through the elimination of racism and racial

discrimination, and the promotion of the right to self- determination. The Committee also addresses important social development questions such as issues related to youth, family, ageing, persons with disabilities, crime prevention, criminal justice, and drug control.

At the sixty-fourth session of the General Assembly, the Third Committee considered 64 draft resolutions, more than half of which were submitted under the human rights agenda item alone. These included a number of so-called country-specific resolutions on human rights situations.

Although important, the General Assembly's role with regard to both normative and institutional development of human rights has been a very general one. As an institution, the General Assembly is limited by its extremely cumbersome and bureaucratic processes, overtly political nature, and lack of binding authority. General Assembly resolutions are non-binding, typically deeply tainted by international politics and often simply ignored. Consideration and debate of human rights issues in the General Assembly is prone to empty polemical exercises in political rhetoric as countries applaud their friends and castigate their rivals with little regard for reality. Voting practices also create significant issues of legitimacy. Every member state, no matter how large or small, has one vote in the General Assembly. Thus, the Republic of Nauru with a population of about 13,000 people (just a bit more than Sarah Palin's Wasilla, Alaska) has equal voting power to the Republic of China and the United States.

Aerial view of the Republic of Nauru
Courtesy: U.S. Department of Energy's Atmospheric Radiation Measurement Program

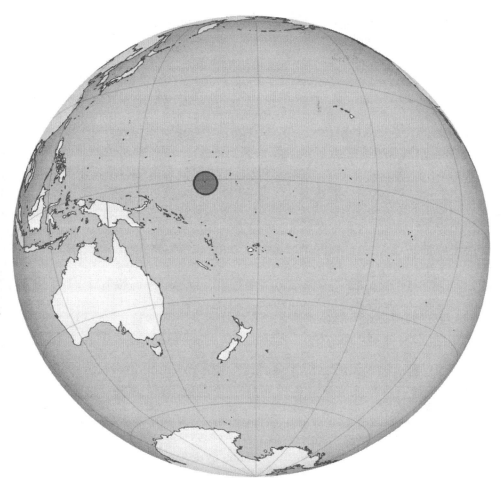

Nauru on the globe. Image created by TUBS, Wikimedia Commons.

Despite these limitations and problems, the General Assembly has nevertheless played an important historical role in promoting respect for human rights.

b. U.N. Security Council

The following excerpt from the U.N. website provides an overview of the Security Council and its functions.

15 members: Five permanent members with veto power and ten non-permanent members, elected by the General Assembly for a two-year term.

Meetings are called at any given time when the need arises.

Rotating presidency: Members take turn at holding the presidency of the Security Council for one month.

Under the Charter, the Security Council has primary responsibility for the maintenance of international peace and security. It has 15 Members, and each Member has one vote. Under the Charter, all Member States are obligated to comply with Council decisions.

The Security Council takes the lead in determining the existence of a threat to the peace or act of aggression. It calls upon the parties to a dispute to settle it by peaceful means and recommends methods of adjustment or terms of settlement. In some cases, the Security Council can resort to imposing sanctions or even authorize the use of force to maintain or restore international peace and security.

The Security Council also recommends to the General Assembly the appointment of the Secretary-General and the admission of new Members to the United Nations. And, together with the General Assembly, it elects the judges of the International Court of Justice.

The Security Council is the only U.N. institution with binding authority over member states. It may order sanctions against recalcitrant states and even authorize the use of military force to enforce its dictates. Pursuant to Charter Articles 25, 48 and 49, U.N. members have agreed to undertake such measures as the Council may order within its defined authority. The scope of this authority, however, is limited to issues of international peace and security. The international community has never recognized a general Security Council power to enforce international law or to police its violation. Thus, neither the Security Council, nor any other UN institution, has any express power to address human rights violations through binding decisions, economic sanctions or other compulsory measures. Absent either an express invitation of the government involved or a threat to international peace, such U.N. actions would appear to be ultra vires. This raises an essential question: Are violations of human rights ever sufficiently a "threat to peace" to justify mandatory orders or authorization of force by the Security Council? The following excerpt considers this potential role.

### Donoho, Evolution or Expediency: The United Nations Response to the Disruption of Democracy, 29 *Cornell Journal of International Law* 329 (1996)

On September 30, 1991, only nine months after the U.N. helped organize and monitor the first free and fair democratic election in Haiti's history, a bloody military coup posed a dramatic challenge to the U.N.'s new-found commitment to democracy. For nearly two years the U.N.'s response to this challenge followed a familiar pattern: the General Assembly passed powerless, non-binding resolutions endorsing the efforts of the Organization of American States (OAS) to return President Jean-Bertrand Aristide to power while the Security Council remained inactive and nearly silent. On June 16, 1993, however, the United Nations arguably entered a brave new world in support of democracy [and human rights]. Citing Chapter VII of the U.N. Charter, the Security Council issued a potentially revolutionary order creating mandatory economic sanctions aimed at restoring Aristide to power. Following another year of continued intransigence by the military, the Council authorized member states to utilize "all necessary means" to restore democracy in Haiti. \*\*\* On July 31, thirty-four months after the coup, the Security Council passed Resolution 940 which, for the first time in U.N. history, authorized member states to utilize force to restore democracy in an independent member state. Accepting the invitation obviously intended for it, the United States eventually announced plans for an "international" invasion force, primarily consisting of U.S. military units, to restore Aristide to power. With the invasion apparently only minutes away, former President Jimmy Carter reached an eleventh-hour agreement with the Haitian military to restore Aristide to power.

\*\*\*

[T]he disruption of democracy in Haiti presented the new world order with an old dilemma: reconciling the demands of rapidly evolving principles of substantive international law, such as self-determination, democratic governance and the promotion of human rights, with states' almost instinctual and atavistic impulses to preserve their sovereign prerogatives. On the surface, the U.N.'s response to the coup in Haiti appears to have been a strong endorsement of democracy [and other human rights] and a potentially powerful means for its protection.

\*\*\*

[The Security Council's] response to the coup in Haiti raises many important questions about the organization's future role in promoting, preserving and restoring democracy and that role's relationship to international peace and security. \*\*\* If the Security Council's authorization of force against Haiti establishes that disruptions of democracy constitute threats to international peace justifying Chapter VII action, even absent an overt military threat, what of similar recent disruptions of democracy such as those occurring in Sudan (1989), Myanmar (1990), Suriname (1990), Peru (1992), Algeria (1992), Sierra Leone (1992), Guatemala (1993), Nigeria (1993), and Gambia (1994)? If the disruption of democracy in Haiti posed a threat to peace, why doesn't the continuing denial of democratic [or other human] rights in China, Saudi Arabia, Cuba, Zaire, Kenya and numerous other U.N. member states similarly pose threats to peace which justify collective action? In other words, if the Security Council is authorized to use mandatory sanctions to restore democracy because its disruption threatens peace, isn't it equally authorized to use sanctions to promote democracy where none exists, or to preserve it where it is threatened? That the fair and logically consistent answers to these questions are politically untenable demonstrates the problematic nature of a Haitian precedent.

\*\*\*

Most importantly, these examples seem to demonstrate that the Security Council will find a threat to peace justifying mandatory collective action only where the permanent five members' interests are affected.

\*\*\*

This lack of consistency arguably reflects decision-making based upon the political interests of powerful states rather than upon principled fact-finding and adherence to standards. Although otherwise laudable, the Council's justifications for acting in Haiti are difficult to distinguish from other even more egregious denials of democracy and human rights violations. Cynics suspect that the only actual distinction is the desire of the United States and France to resolve a crisis which implicated their own national interests.

The author above is hardly sanguine about the potential for utilizing the Security Council's mandatory authority over threats to international peace as a means for addressing human rights violations. Nevertheless, the Council has arguably used its authority on several subsequent occasions to address international crises that appeared primarily to involve egregious violations of human rights rather than overt threats to international peace defined in more traditional ways. Examples of this apparent, but inconsistent, and often ambiguous trend might include the genocide in Bosnia (Res. 819, civilian safe haven, 1993),[99] Rwanda (Res. 918, arms embargo, 1994), Kosovo (Res. 1160, arms embargo, 1998) and the resolution authorizing force to protect Libyans during the so-called Arab Spring (Res. 1973, no-fly zone, 2011). Perhaps most significantly, the Security Council utilized its Article VII mandatory powers to create ad hoc international criminal tribunals to prosecute crimes against humanity occurring in the former Yugoslavia and Rwanda (Res. 955, 1994). In essence, these actions seem to recognize that egregious widespread violations of human rights, at least those occurring during armed conflict, might sometimes constitute a threat to international peace justifying Security Council action.

Even more recent events, however, have once again presented the inescapable reality that the Security Council's capacity to effectively respond to human rights crises is still severely constrained by unfavorable geo-political circumstances. China may do as it pleases in suppressing Tibetans, Russia may annex Crimea, and the United States may hold suspected terrorists indefinitely for years without charges. Perhaps most telling is the Council's inability to respond to well documented horrors committed in the ongoing Syrian civil war, including the government's use of chemical weapons and "barrel bombs" on civilian populations. The crisis in Syria is obviously a breach of international peace and yet the Security Council has remained on the sidelines, regularly stymied by Russian and Chinese vetoes. Apparently over 100,000 deaths, 2 million refugees and indiscriminate murder of children are easily ignored in some quarters. Consider this excerpt from the U.S. State Department's 2013 Country Reports on Human Rights Practices:

---

99. Despite Resolution 819, the United Nations Protection Force failed to protect more than 8,000 innocent refugees who were systematically killed by the forces of Bosnian Serb General Ratko Mladic. Mladic was subsequently indicted by the International Criminal Tribunal for the Former Yugoslavia for war crimes and genocide relating to the Srebrenica massacre and is currently (2014) facing trial.

The Assad regime continued to use indiscriminate and deadly force to quell protests and conducted air and ground-based military assaults on cities, residential areas, and civilian infrastructures, including schools and hospitals throughout the country. For example, on August 21, the regime used sarin gas and artillery to target East Ghouta and Moadamiya al-Sham, suburbs of Damascus, and killed over 1,000 persons. In July the United Nations announced that more than 100,000 persons had been killed since the beginning of the crisis in March 2011. In December the Syrian Observatory for Human Rights (SOHR) estimated that more than 125,835 persons had been killed. As the civil war intensified, the humanitarian situation reached crisis proportions. As of September 1, more than 2.2 million refugees had registered with the Office of the U.N. High Commissioner for Refugees (UNHCR) in neighboring states and North Africa, and more than 6.5 million persons were displaced internally. The figures for internally displaced persons were estimates; actual figures may have been higher. The regime blocked access for humanitarian assistance to reach civilian areas, particularly areas held by opposition groups.

The most egregious human rights problems during the year were the regime's widespread and systematic attacks against civilians; systematic and widespread use of torture; and the perpetuation of massacres, forced displacement, and starvation. The government denied citizens the right to change their government peacefully. The government denied citizens the right to practice freedom of speech, mobility, association, access to legal representation, and medical assistance. The government detained tens of thousands of individuals associated with nongovernmental organizations (NGOs), human rights activists, journalists, humanitarian aid providers, and doctors without access to fair trial.

Other serious problems included kidnappings and disappearances; targeted killing of protesters, bystanders, journalists, and medical professionals; torture and abuse, including of women and children; the use of rape and assault as punishment and a war tactic; poor prison and detention center conditions; arbitrary arrest and detention; denial of fair public trial; arbitrary interference with privacy; and lack of press, internet, and academic freedom.

See more at Secretary of State's Preface.

A new human rights mandate was created for the Security Council in 2002 by the Rome Statute of the permanent International Criminal Court. Under Articles 13 of the Statute, the Court has jurisdiction to investigate and prosecute situations referred to it by the Security Council involving potential genocide, crimes against humanity or war crimes. The Security Council may only refer a situation to the Court if it finds a threat to international peace under Chapter VII of the Charter. The Council has now done this twice, in reference to events in Darfur, Sudan, (Res. 1593, 2005) and Libya (Res. 1970, 2011). In 2014, after a commission created by the U.N. Human Rights

Council issued a <u>damning report</u> describing North Korea's vast system of slave-like prison camps, and other forms of egregious human rights violations. The Security Council <u>met in special session</u> to consider similar action against North Korean leaders. Ultimately such a referral must gain the approval of China, putting its adoption in serious doubt. Similarly, China and Russia have continually rejected proposed Council resolutions referring to <u>Syrian war crimes</u> to the Court, despite <u>photographic proof</u> and <u>U.N. sponsored investigative reports</u> detailing such crimes.[100] Why Libya and Sudan but not Korea and Syria, despite overwhelming evidence of war crimes in those states? The <u>N.Y. Times reported</u> the French UN Ambassador's response to the Chinese and Russian veto of the Syrian war crimes referral: "There is a moment when you realize you are powerless in front of barbarians and their supporters." Such inconsistencies also give credence to the adage "it depends on <u>who your friends are</u>."

### c. Economic and Social Council

The <u>Economic and Social Council</u> (ECOSOC) is the principal U.N. organ charged with coordination of economic development, social and humanitarian issues. It consists of 54 representatives of Member States elected by the General Assembly based on geographic restrictions (with 14 African, 11 Asian, 6 Eastern European, 10 Latin and 13 Western European states represented). It coordinates the work of 14 "specialized" U.N. agencies (such as the World Health Organization, UNICEF, IMF and UNESCO), a host of subsidiary institutional bodies and about 70% of the U.N. budget. Because it serves as a central policy forum regarding a broad range of humanitarian and economic development issues, its functions often overlap with international human rights, particularly those involving social, cultural and economic interests.

In two areas ECOSOC has supervisory functions that directly implicate international human rights. The first involves promotion of the rights of women through the U.N. <u>Commission on the Status of Women</u>. According to ECOSOC's website:

> The Commission on the Status of Women (hereafter referred to as "CSW" or "the Commission") is the principal global policy-making body dedicated exclusively to gender equality and advancement of women. Every year, representatives of Member States gather at United Nations Headquarters in New York to evaluate progress on gender equality, identify challenges, set global standards and formulate concrete policies to promote gender equality and women's empowerment worldwide.

---

100. "Government forces and pro-government militia continue to conduct widespread attacks on civilians, systematically committing murder, torture, rape and enforced disappearance as crimes against humanity. Government forces have committed gross violations of human rights and the war crimes of murder, hostage-taking, torture, rape and sexual violence, recruiting and using children in hostilities and targeting civilians in sniper attacks." *See* Report of the Independent International Commission of Inquiry on the Syrian Arab Republic, A/HRC/25/65, 12 February 2014.

The Commission was established by ECOSOC resolution 11(II) of 21 June 1946 with the aim to prepare recommendations and reports to the Council on promoting women's rights in political, economic, civil, social and educational fields. The Commission also makes recommendations to the Council on urgent problems requiring immediate attention in the field of women's rights.

As part of its work, the Commission on the Status of Women itself is empowered to consider "communications" alleging violations of the human rights of women.

> Any individual, non-governmental organization, group or network may submit communications (complaints/appeals/petitions) to the Commission on the Status of Women containing information relating to alleged violations of human rights that affect the status of women in any country in the world. The Commission on the Status of Women considers such communications as part of its annual programme of work in order to identify emerging trends and patterns of injustice and discriminatory practices against women for purposes of policy formulation and development of strategies for the promotion of gender equality.

***

The Commission is not empowered, however, to render decisions regarding the merits of communications submitted to it, or offer compensation to victims. Therefore, as noted on its website: "the communications procedure does not provide an avenue for the redress of individual grievances."

The second area of active involvement in human rights for ECOSOC involves supervising the work of the Committee on Economic, Social and Cultural Rights. ECOSOC describes the Committee as a:

> body of 18 independent experts that monitors implementation of the International Covenant on Economic, Social and Cultural Rights by its States parties. The Committee was established under ECOSOC Resolution 1985/17 of 28 May 1985 to carry out the monitoring functions assigned to the United Nations Economic and Social Council (ECOSOC) in Part IV of the Covenant.

This important human rights body, which is examined in greater detail in the next chapter, essentially reports to ECOSOC on its work.

d. International Court of Justice (a.k.a. "World Court")

The International Court of Justice, often referred to as the World Court, is the judicial organ of the UN. The Court has 15 judges elected by the General Assembly and Security Council. It does not possess authority to interpret or apply international law generally but rather decides international legal disputes between countries, based on the voluntary participation of the States concerned. States may give the requisite consent to jurisdiction generally for all international disputes ("compulsory jurisdiction"), limited to particular treaties ("treaty based jurisdiction"), or on a case by case basis ("special agreement jurisdiction"). The Court also has "advisory" jurisdiction in which it may render non-binding opinions on international legal issues to U.N. principal institutions and specialized agencies. Except as to this advisory jurisdiction, only nation states may bring cases and appear before the Court. The Court has no specific human rights mandate or particular expertise in the field and its processes have been charitably described as "slow, cumbersome and expensive."[101]

These significant limitations on the Court's jurisdiction, mandate and process explain, in part, why it has played only a modest role in the protection of international human rights. Currently, only about 70 countries accept the Court's general compulsory jurisdiction and often with significant limitations. The United States withdrew its acceptance of compulsory jurisdiction in 1986, disgruntled over the Court's negative view of the Regan administration's facilitation of human rights violations by the Nicaraguan Contras. It could happen, of course, that two states under the Court's compulsory jurisdiction might become embroiled in an inter-state human rights dispute. But such a happenstance will inevitably be rare since states typically lack incentives to challenge each other's human rights records in such a way, at least in the absence of armed conflict or other geo-political dispute. A recent example of a compulsory jurisdiction human rights case linked to armed conflict involved claims by the Democratic Republic of the Congo against Uganda. The Court found that Ugandan armed forces committed violations of human rights and humanitarian law between 1998 and 2003 within the Democratic Republic of the Congo.

More commonly, the Court might gain jurisdiction over a human rights issue by virtue of a treaty that so provides. One recent example is the LaGrand case, reviewed in Chapter 4, which involved claims that the United States had violated the Convention on Consular Relations in death penalty cases involving foreign nationals (at least indirectly a human rights issue). In response to the Court's decision against it in this case, the United States withdrew its consent to jurisdiction for disputes under the treaty. In 1993, Bosnia brought claims of genocide against Serbia under a provision of the Genocide Convention that provided for ICJ jurisdiction. After 13 years of litigation, the Court ruled that Serbia had neither committed nor conspired to commit genocide. Serbia had, however, breached its international obligations under the Genocide Convention by failing to "prevent" genocide and refusing to transfer indicted war criminal Ratko Mladić to the International Criminal Tribunal for the Former Yugoslavia. More recently, the Republic of Georgia brought a petition to the Court under Article 22 of the Convention on the Elimination of Racial Discrimination alleging that the Russian

---

101. *See* John R. Crook, *The International Court of Justice and Human Rights*, 1 NW J. Int'l Human Rights 1 (2004), available at Northwestern Scholarly Commons.

Federation had systematically orchestrated the "mass expulsion" of ethnic Georgians from the separatist regions of South Ossetia and Abkhazia. Such sporadic recourse to the ICJ, while perhaps meaningful to some participants, demonstrates its current limited role in human rights enforcement.

# D. Charter-Based Institutions and Mechanisms with Dedicated Human Rights Mandates

## 1. Overview & Historical Evolution

As described above, the five principle U.N. institutions have important but somewhat indirect and limited human rights functions. A number of other U.N. institutions and "specialized agencies" also play important indirect roles in human rights by virtue of their focus on humanitarian, social and human development issues. These institutions would include the Office of the U.N. High Commissioner for Refugees, U.N. Children's Fund, the World Food Program, the World Health Organization, U.N. Population Fund, U.N. Food and Agriculture Organization, International Labor Organization and the U.N. Development Program.

Most of the heavy lifting in human rights at the UN, however, is left to subsidiary institutional bodies with a dedicated human rights mandate. It is the work of these institutions, with a direct human rights focus, that is most commonly meant when referring to the "UN human rights system." The following excerpt describes the evolution of the U.N. human rights system and provides useful background information about how that system functions. A central distinction drawn by the author is between U.N. Charter based processes and those associated with U.N. sponsored multilateral human rights treaties. Our current focus is on the Charter based processes.

a. Thomas Buergenthal, The Evolving International Human Rights System, 100 A.J.I.L. 683 (2006)

\*\*\*

### II. THE UNITED NATIONS CHARTER

International human rights law, as we know it today, begins with the Charter of the United Nations. According to its Article 1 (3), one of the purposes of the United Nations is the achievement of "international co-operation in . . . promoting and encouraging respect for human rights and for fundamental freedoms for all without distinction as to race, sex, language, or religion." That the U.N. Charter should have listed this subject among the Organization's purposes is not surprising, considering that it was drafted in the aftermath of World War II, the Holocaust, and the murder of millions of innocent human beings. But contrary to what might have been expected given this background, the Charter did not impose any concrete human rights obligations on the U.N. member states. \*\*\*

UN human rights law has evolved over the past sixty years along two parallel paths, one based on the U.N. Charter, the other on the human rights treaties adopted by the Organization. The Charter-based system comprises the human rights principles and institutional mechanisms that different U.N. organs have developed in the exercise of their Charter powers. The treaty-based system consists of a large number of human rights treaties drafted under U.N. auspices that codify much of the international human rights law in existence today. Some of these treaties also establish institutional mechanisms to monitor compliance by the states parties with the obligations imposed by these instruments.

\*\*\*

### *The Charter-Based System*

The U.N. Human Rights Council, the successor to the Human Rights Commission, lies at the center of the Charter-based system, followed by the Commission on the Status of Women and various subsidiary bodies of the Council, such as the Sub-Commission on the Promotion and Protection of Human Rights, formerly the Sub-Commission on the Prevention of Discrimination and Protection of Minorities. Although the Human Rights Commission took the position into the mid-1960s that it lacked the power to act on violations of human rights brought to its attention, that attitude began to change as more and more newly independent states joined the United Nations and campaigned for U.N. antiapartheid measures. They argued that the United Nations had the requisite authority to take such action because a state that practiced apartheid could not be said to be "promoting" human rights without discrimination, as required by Articles 55 and 56 of the Charter. This argument gradually prevailed, prompting the General Assembly to call on South Africa to end apartheid and on Southern Rhodesia to do away with its racial discrimination policies.

The Economic and Social Council followed up with a series of resolutions on the subject. In one of the earliest, ECOSOC authorized the Human Rights Commission "to make a thorough study of situations which reveal a consistent pattern of violations of human rights, as exemplified by the policy of apartheid as practised in the Republic of South Africa . . . , and racial discrimination as practised notably in Southern Rhodesia." This narrow mandate was expanded a few years later when ECOSOC empowered the Commission and its subcommission to act on complaints from groups and individuals that revealed "a consistent pattern of gross and reliably attested violations of human rights." This resolution opened the way for the Commission and subcommission to deal with gross violations of human rights in general, that is, whether or not they involved apartheid or racial discrimination.

These and related ECOSOC resolutions enabled the Human Rights Commission gradually to develop a growing number of U.N. Charter-based mechanisms for dealing with large-scale human rights violations. Today the system consists of mushrooming rapporteur and special-mission components, as well as the Office of the United Nations High Commissioner for Human Rights with its own bureaucracy. (It is too early to say what changes in this practice, if any, the newly established Human Rights Council will adopt.) These institutions derive their normative legitimacy from the Charter itself and from the Universal Declaration of Human Rights.

***

After a restructuring process described further below, the U.N. Charter based system now centers around two primary institutions and a series of subsidiary bodies and processes. The UN High Commissioner for Human Rights was established in 1993 within the U.N. Secretariat to more effectively manage, assist and carry out the various human rights activities of the organization. The Human Rights Council, consisting of national representatives from 47 U.N. member states, was established in 2006 to replace a discredited predecessor, the Commission on Human Rights. It is assisted not only by the High Commissioner but also by an "Advisory Committee" of 18 independent experts.

Like its predecessor, the Human Rights Council engages in a range of activities, directly or through subsidiaries, designed to promote human rights compliance. These include three primary mechanisms which are reviewed below: (1) "Universal Periodic Reports" which involve examination of states' periodic reports on their human rights records; (2) "Complaint Procedures" which consider whether confidential communications regarding alleged violations of human rights demonstrate a "consistent pattern of gross and reliably attested violations" justifying further Council action; and (3) "Special Procedures" which involve consideration of various human rights crises situations on either a country specific, or issue themed, basis through working groups or appointed experts (rapporteurs). Some of the special procedures allow their mandate holder (the experts assigned) to consider individual complaints by victims of alleged human rights violations.

b. Organizational Structure of U.N. Human Rights Institutions

Here is a diagram that sketches out the basic organization of the U.N. human rights system.

### Structure of the UN Human Rights Bodies and Mechanisms

Note: This diagram is not exhaustive. It highlights the major human rights bodies and mechanisms which are covered in this training.

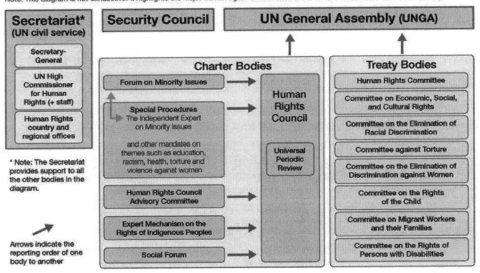

The Chart above, possibly from the UN.org, appears on various websites including the <u>Auschwitz Institute</u>.

## 2. Office of the High Commissioner for Human Rights

During the early years of the U.N. the Secretary General's office maintained a small human rights "division" that eventually became the "UN Human Rights Centre" based in Geneva. In 1992, the General Assembly organized a <u>World Conference on Human Rights</u>, which was subsequently held in Vienna, Austria.[102] The Conference agenda, adopted by the General Assembly, included an evaluation of the effectiveness of U.N. mechanisms and approaches to the promotion of human rights. Following recommendations from the resulting "<u>Vienna Declaration and Programme of Action</u>," the General Assembly passed <u>Resolution 48/141</u> establishing the Under-Secretary General position of High Commissioner for Human Rights. The Resolution defined the High Commissioner's mandate in this way:

> High Commissioner for Human Rights shall be the United Nations official with principal responsibility for United Nations human rights activities

---

102. In a fashion typical of the U.N. but also reflecting deep divides between countries over human rights, the Conference agenda excluded any discussion of ongoing human rights violations or situations. The Conference featured a pitched battle between Western and non-Western countries over whether the meaning of human rights may vary within diverse cultural, social or religious contexts or instead is the same and universal world-wide. *See* Alan Riding, NY Times, *A Rights Meeting, but Don't Mention the Wronged*, June 14, 1993. *See also* D. Donoho, *Autonomy, Self-Governance, and the Margin of Appreciation: Developing A Jurisprudence of Diversity Within Universal Human Rights*, 15 Emory Int'l L. Rev. 391 (2001).

under the direction and authority of the Secretary-General; within the framework of the overall competence, authority and decisions of the General Assembly, the Economic and Social Council and the Commission on Human Rights, the High Commissioner's responsibilities shall be:

(a)  To promote and protect the effective enjoyment by all of all civil, cultural, economic, political and social rights;

(b)  To carry out the tasks assigned to him/her by the competent bodies of the United Nations system in the field of human rights and to make recommendations to them with a view to improving the promotion and protection of all human rights;

***

(d)  To provide, through the Centre for Human Rights of the Secretariat and other appropriate institutions, advisory services and technical and financial assistance, ***;

(f)  To play an active role in removing the current obstacles and in meeting the challenges to the full realization of all human rights and in preventing the continuation of human rights violations throughout the world,*** ;

(i)  To coordinate the human rights promotion and protection activities throughout the United Nations system;

(j)  To rationalize, adapt, strengthen and streamline the United Nations machinery in the field of human rights with a view to improving its efficiency and effectiveness;

(k)  To carry out overall supervision of the Centre for Human Rights;

The High Commissioner, who is nominated by the Secretary General and elected by the General Assembly, now heads the "Office of the High Commissioner for Human Rights" (OHRHR) which replaced the Centre for Human Rights. In 2014, Jordanian Prince Zeid Ra'ad Al Hussein replaced South African lawyer, Navi Pillay as High Commissioner (you can read his opening speech to the Human Rights Council here). The OHRHR has its headquarters in Geneva and maintains offices in 13 country field offices (in human rights trouble spots such as Bolivia, Cambodia, Colombia, Guatemala, Guinea, Mauritania, Mexico, Nepal, the Occupied Palestinian Territories, Kosovo, Togo, and Uganda) and 13 regional centers. OHCHR has two major divisions and four branches that reflect its mandate and functions. These include: the Human Rights Treaties Division (responsible for supporting the work of 10 treaty based institutions that monitor national implementation of major human rights treaties), the Field Operations and Technical Cooperation Division (supports the work of human rights "field" officers and leads "dialogue" with countries about human rights issues), the Human Rights Council and Special Procedures Division (provides substantive and organizational support to the Human Rights Council and its mechanisms), and the Research and Right to Development Division (carries out thematic research and develops training tools). The OHCHR employs more than

1,000 staff members and over 600 international "human rights officers" serving in U.N. peace keeping missions.

It should be obvious from the above description that the OHCHR promotes human rights through programs, provides support for the human rights work of U.N. bodies and U.N. related institutions and responds to human rights situations or crises. This includes deployment of "human rights advisors" to countries such as Chad, Ecuador, Honduras, Kenya, Moldova, Niger, Papua New Guinea, Paraguay, Russia, Rwanda and Tajikistan. It also includes deployment by the OHCHR "Rapid Response Unit" to immediate crisis situations. Since its creation in 2006, the unit has participated in fact finding in Timor-Leste, Western Sahara, Sudan, Liberia, Lebanon, Palestine, Kenya, Togo, Guinea, and Somalia. A recent example of this function occurred in 2014 when the OHCHR announced that it was deploying a team of human rights monitors throughout the Ukraine (by invitation of the government) "to help establish the facts surrounding human rights violations, including in Crimea, and serve to de-escalate tensions in the country."

## 3. Human Rights Council

The General Assembly created the inter-governmental U.N. Human Rights Commission in 1946 with a relatively modest mandate. The Commission's powers and functions were significantly constrained by the state parties, often placing misguided reliance on the Charter-based doctrine of non-intervention in domestic affairs. Consisting of 54 representatives from U.N. member states, the Commission gradually expanded its role eventually undertaking consideration of human rights crises and occasional condemnation of government abuse. In 2006, the U.N. Commission on Human Rights was replaced by the 47 member Human Rights Council. The Commission was replaced essentially because it had lost virtually all its already limited credibility through increased hypocrisy and the politicization of human rights. In the words of former U.N. Secretary General Kofi Annan: "We have reached a point at which the commission's declining credibility has cast a shadow on the reputation of the United Nations system as a whole, and where piecemeal reforms will not be enough." Unfortunately, its replacement, the Human Rights Council, looks remarkably like its predecessor — 47 rather than 54 member states representatives with similar procedures. The member states are elected to the Council on a geographic basis with 13 from the African Group, 13 from the Asian Group, 6 from the Eastern European Group, 8 from the Latin American and Caribbean Group and 7 from the Western Group.

The new Council has adopted at least one new procedure ("Universal Periodic Review") and revamped existing mechanisms in order to revitalize its work. The Council has also organized its work into three basic categories: (1) "universal periodic review" of state self-reporting on human rights compliance; (2) "complaint procedures" for identifying "situations" involving patterns of gross and widespread violations; and (3) "special procedures" consisting of work by appointed experts regarding country or theme specific issues. The Council also works with an "advisory committee" of 18 independent human rights experts who are described by the U.N. as the Council's "think tank."

After reviewing these central Council's mechanisms for promoting human rights, we will evaluate whether the U.N. has now developed Charter based human rights institutions that engender credibility and respect. This link to the "Thematic & Country Chart" prepared for the HRC's 2014, 26th session provides insight regarding the wide range of topics and situations currently falling within the HRC's agenda.

a. Specific Mechanisms & Procedures of the HRC

i. Universal Periodic Reporting

The following informative excerpt was taken from the U.N. OHCHR website:

Basic facts about the UPR

### What is the Universal Periodic Review?

The Universal Periodic Review (UPR) is a unique process which involves a review of the human rights records of all 192 U.N. Member States once every four years. The UPR is a significant innovation of the Human Rights Council which is based on equal treatment for all countries. It provides an opportunity for all States to declare what actions they have taken to improve the human rights situations in their countries and to overcome challenges to the enjoyment of human rights. The UPR also includes a sharing of best human rights practices around the globe. Currently, no other mechanism of this kind exists.

\*\*\*

### When will States have their human rights records reviewed by the UPR?

All U.N. Member States will be reviewed every four years — with 48 States reviewed each year. All the 47 members of the Council will be reviewed during their term of membership. On 21 September 2007, the Human Rights Council adopted a calendar detailing the order in which the 192 U.N. Member States will be considered during the first four-year cycle of the UPR (2008–2011). The reviews will take place during the sessions of the UPR Working Group (see below) which will meet three times a year.

### Who conducts the review?

The reviews are conducted by the UPR Working Group which consists of the 47 members of the Council; however any U.N. Member State can take part in the discussion/dialogue with the reviewed States. Each State review is assisted by groups of three States, known as "troikas", who serve as rapporteurs. The selection of the troikas for each State review is done through a drawing of lots prior for each Working Group session.

### What are the reviews based on?

The documents on which the reviews are based are: 1) information provided by the State under review, which can take the form of a "national report"; 2) information contained in the reports of independent human rights experts and groups, known as the Special Procedures, human rights treaty bodies, and other U.N. entities; 3) information from other stakeholders including non-governmental organizations and national human rights institutions.

### How are the reviews conducted?

Reviews take place through an interactive discussion between the State under review and other U.N. Member States. This takes place during a meeting of the UPR Working Group. During this discussion any U.N. Member State can pose questions, comments and/or make recommendations to the States under review. The troikas may group issues or questions to be shared with the State under review to ensure that the interactive dialogue takes place in a smooth and orderly manner. The duration of the review will be three hours for each country in the Working Group.

### Can non-governmental organizations (NGOs) participate in the UPR process?

Yes. NGOs can submit information which can be added to the "other stakeholders" report which is considered during the review. Information they provide can be referred to by any of the States taking part in the interactive discussion during the review at the Working Group meeting. NGOs can attend the UPR Working Group sessions and can make statements at the regular session of the Human Rights Council when the outcome of the State reviews are considered. OHCHR has released "Technical guidelines for the submission of stakeholders".

### What human rights obligations are addressed?

The UPR will assess the extent to which States respect their human rights obligations set out in: (1) the U.N. Charter; (2) the Universal Declaration of Human Rights; (3) human rights instruments to which the State is party (human rights treaties ratified by the State concerned); (4) voluntary pledges and commitments made by the State (e.g. national human rights policies and/or programmes implemented); and (5) applicable international humanitarian law.

### What is the outcome of the review?

Following the State review by the Working Group a report is prepared by the troika with the involvement of the State under review and assistance from the OHCHR. This report, referred to as the "outcome report", provides a summary of the actual discussion. It therefore consists of the questions, comments and recommendations made by States to the country under review, as well as the responses by the reviewed State.

### How is the review adopted?

During the Working Group session half an hour is allocated to adopt each of the "outcome reports" for the States reviewed that session. These take place no sooner than 48 hours after the country review. The reviewed State has the opportunity to make preliminary comments on the recommendations choosing to either accept or reject them. Both accepted and refused recommendations are included in the report. After the report has been adopted, editorial modifications can be made to the report by States on their own statements, within the following two weeks. The report then has to be adopted at a plenary session of the Human Rights Council. During the plenary session, the State under review can reply to questions and issues that were not sufficiently addressed during the Working Group and respond to recommendations that were raised by States during the review. Time is also allotted to member and observer States who may wish to express their opinion on the outcome of the review and for NGOs and other stakeholders to make general comments.

### What steps are taken as follow up to the review?

The State has the primary responsibility to implement the recommendations contained in the final outcome. The UPR ensures that all countries are accountable for progress or failure in implementing these recommendations. When it comes time for the second review of a State they must provide information on what they have been doing to implement the recommendations made during the 1st review four years earlier. The international community will assist in implementing the recommendations and conclusions regarding capacity-building and technical assistance, in consultation with the country concerned. If necessary, the Council will address cases where States are not cooperating.

### What happens if a State is not cooperating with the UPR?

The Human Rights Council will decide on the measures it would need to take in case of persistent non-cooperation by a State with the UPR.

The United States, a strong supporter of the universal periodic review process, submitted its first report and participated in the Council's review process in 2010. In a follow up response, the State Department (humanrights.gov) announced that it planned to take the process seriously:

"After careful review, the United States accepted in whole or in part 173 of the 228 recommendations it received. In keeping with the United States' enduring commitment to universal human rights and fundamental freedoms at home and abroad, we have adopted a process for carrying out and reviewing our implementation of the recommendations we accepted. Working groups have been formed to oversee implementation efforts in ten thematic categories: Civil Rights and Racial and Ethnic Discrimination, Criminal Justice Issues, Indigenous Issues, National Security, Immigration, Labor and Trafficking, Economic, Social, and Cultural Rights and Measures, The Environment, Domestic Implementation of Human Rights, Treaties and International Human Rights Mechanisms.

These working groups are each led by the government department or agency with the greatest subject matter expertise in that area and are composed of members from other relevant departments and agencies. During the coming months and years, we will reach out to civil society through this working group process, both on the individual working group level and collectively, thus continuing the dialogue that was begun in preparation for our initial review.

Lead agencies for each thematic area, along with information regarding how interested individuals and organizations can engage with each working group."

Available from Humanrights.gov

For an alternative and critical, if somewhat defensive, perspective on the significance of the United States' participation see the Fox News Article, "U.N. Human Rights Council Takes Aim at New Target: United States." In a similar vein, the following link provides a highly edited video of the HRC debate over the U.S. report aimed at criticizing U.S. participation in the process. The video appears to represent the view that the process is hypocritical and merely a political game by highlighting critiques of the U.S. by such human rights stalwarts as Cuba, Iran, and North Korea. Finally, if you are still in a critical mood, consider the conservative Heritage Foundation's viewpoint on U.S. participation in the HRC's periodic report process, captured in the following quote: "By legitimizing the HRC through U.S. membership, the Obama Administration will give credibility to a farcical UPR process that has become little more than a 'mutual praise society' for repressive regimes and created the opportunity for human rights abusers to take unjustified shots at America's human rights record."

ii. Complaint Procedures for Identifying Human Rights Crises: (revised Res. 1503/1235)

Early on in the evolution of the Charter based system the Economic and Social Council authorized the Human Rights Commission and its Sub-Commission on minorities, both now defunct, to respond to complaints from groups and individuals that revealed "a consistent pattern of gross and reliably attested violations of human rights." Originally designed solely for apartheid in South Africa, these so-called "Resolutions 1235 and 1503" procedures eventually were applied to a wide variety of large scale human rights violations leading to both confidential (Res. 1503) and public dialogue, negotiation and condemnation (Res. 1235) of the offending states. Blatant hypocrisy, double standards and politicization in these procedures was one of the reasons that the Commission eventually lost any credibility and good will that it might have ever had.

The Human Rights Council eventually revised and renewed the complaint procedures retaining its traditional focus on large scale violations and confidential responses. The purpose of the procedure is not to provide redress for individual victims but rather identify situations involving widespread abuses. The process relies upon two "working groups" to manage the process, one consisting of independent experts (communication admissibility and significance) and the other state representatives (deciding if a "situation" deserves consideration by the Council and recommended action).

The following excerpt about the complaint procedure was taken from the U.N. OHCHR Website:

### Fifteenth session of the Human Rights Council Working Group on Situations 26 to 30 January 2015

The fifteenth session of the Human Rights Council Working Group on Situations is scheduled to take place from 26 to 30 January 2015, at the Palais des Nations in Geneva.

As a result of the review of the complaint procedure established in accordance with Economic and Social Council resolution 1503, the Human Rights Council, by resolution 5/1 of 18 June 2007, set up a new confidential complaint procedure as an integral part of its institutional architecture. Two distinct working groups, the Working Group on Communications and the Working Group on Situations, have been established with the mandate to examine the communications received under the complaint procedure and to bring to the attention of the Human Rights Council consistent patterns of gross and reliably attested violations of human rights and fundamental freedoms occurring in any part of the world and under any circumstances.

The Working Group on Situations examines communications on the basis of the information and recommendations provided by the Working Group on Communications, and presents to the Council a report on consistent patterns of gross and reliably attested violations of human rights and fundamental freedoms as well as makes recommendations to the Council on the course of action to take. Alternatively, the Working Group on Situations may also decide to keep any situation under review or to dismiss it. So as to ensure that the complaint procedure is victims-oriented, efficient and conducted in a timely manner, the author of a communication and the State concerned are continuously informed of the proceedings at each stage. With this complaint procedure, communications received from individuals, groups or organizations can reach the highest level of the United Nations human rights machinery, the Human Rights Council. The Human Rights Council shall consider consistent patterns of gross and reliably attested violations of human rights and fundamental freedoms brought to its attention by the Working Group on Situations as frequently as needed, but at least once a year.

The Working Group is composed of five representatives of Member States of the Human Rights Council appointed by each regional group to serve in their personal capacity. Members may be re-elected once if nominated. Members of the Working Group meet twice a year for five working days during each session. The proceedings of the Working Group are confidential and are held as private meetings.

At the link below you will find a useful summary of complaint procedures leading to country specific reviews since 2006: <u>History of situations considered since the establishment of the complaint procedure.</u>

iii. Special Procedures (Thematic and Country Specific Activities)

The former Human Rights Commission and its sub-commission had regularly employed the practice of appointing special experts to investigate and report on human rights issues. Typically these appointments would come in the form of individual "Rapporteurs," "Special Representatives," "Independent Experts," or as multi-person "Working Groups" whose mandate focused either on a particular country or thematic issue such as torture. The Human Rights Council has continued this practice in a reorganized form now referred to as "Special Procedures." These typically may include country visits and even consideration of individual communications alleging violations of rights. The mandate holder often is empowered to communicate such allegations to the government involved and seek "clarification" of the situation. The following excerpt describing HRC Special Procedures was taken from the <u>U.N. website,</u> complete with useful links to additional information and topics:

> The special procedures of the Human Rights Council are independent human rights experts with mandates to report and advise on human rights from a thematic or country-specific perspective. *** As of 27 March 2015 there are 41 <u>thematic</u> and 14 <u>country</u> mandates.
>
> With the support of the Office of the United Nations High Commissioner for Human Rights (OHCHR), special procedures undertake <u>country visits;</u> act on individual cases and concerns of a broader, structural nature by sending <u>communications</u> to States and others in which they bring alleged violations or abuses to their attention; conduct thematic studies and convene <u>expert consultations</u>, contribute to the development of international human rights standards, engage in advocacy, raise public awareness, and provide advice for technical cooperation. Special procedures <u>report annually</u> to the Human Rights Council; the majority of the mandates also <u>reports to the General Assembly</u>. Their tasks are defined in the resolutions creating or extending their mandates.
>
> Special procedures are either an individual (called "Special Rapporteur" or "Independent Expert") or a working group composed of five members, one from each of the five United Nations regional groupings: Africa, Asia, Latin America and the Caribbean, Eastern Europe and the Western group. The Special Rapporteurs, Independent Experts and members of the Working Groups are <u>appointed</u> by the Human Rights Council and serve in their personal capacities. They undertake to uphold independence, efficiency, com-

petence and integrity through probity, impartiality, honesty and good faith. They are not United Nations staff members and do not receive financial remuneration. The independent status of the mandate holders is crucial in order to be able to fulfil their functions in all impartiality. A mandate-holder's tenure in a given function, whether it is a thematic or country mandate, is limited to a maximum of six years.

### Country visits

Mandate holders carry out <u>country visits</u> to analyse the human rights situation at the national level. They typically send a letter to the State requesting to visit the country, and, if the State agrees, an invitation to visit is extended. Some countries have issued "<u>standing invitations</u>", which means that they are, in principle, prepared to receive a visit from any thematic special procedures mandate holder. As of 1 January 2015, 109 States had extended standing invitations to the special procedures. After their visits, special procedures' mandate-holders issue a mission report containing their findings and recommendations.

### Communications

Most special procedures receive information on specific allegations of human rights violations and send <u>urgent appeals or letters of allegation</u> to States asking for clarification. Mandate holders may also send letters to States seeking information about new developments, submitting observations, or following-up on recommendations. These letters do not necessarily allege that a violation has taken place or is about to occur. In 2013, a total of 528 communications were sent to 116 countries. 84% of these were joint communications of two or more mandate holders. Communications sent and the responses received are <u>reported</u> at each regular session to the Human Rights Council.

### Nomination, selection and appointment of mandate holders

In its resolution 5/1 the Human Rights Council clarified the parameters related to the <u>selection and appointment</u> of special procedures mandate holders: Candidates can be nominated by Governments, the Regional Groups operating within the United Nations system, international organisations or their offices, non-governmental organizations, other human rights bodies and individuals. A Consultative Group appointed by the Council reviews all applications for Special Procedures' positions and proposes a list of candidates to the President of the Council. Resolution <u>16/21</u> has further strengthened and enhanced transparency in the selection and appointment process of mandate holders. <u>National Human Rights Institutions</u> that comply with the Paris Principles may also nominate candidates. ***

According to <u>resolution 5/1,</u> the following general criteria will be of paramount importance while nominating, selecting and appointing mandate-holders: (*a*) expertise; (*b*) experience in the field of the mandate; (*c*) independence; (*d*) impartiality; (*e*) personal integrity; and (*f*) objectivity. Due consideration should be given to gender balance and equitable geographic representation, as well as to an appropriate representation of different legal systems. *** Technical and objective requirements have been further clarified in HRC decision 6/102.

**Recent Developments**

In 2006–2007 the Human Rights Council engaged in an institution building process, which included a review of the special procedures system. *** The Human Rights Council also adopted resolution 5/2, containing a Code of Conduct for special procedures mandate holders.

In 2011, the Human Rights Council undertook a review of its work and functioning. ***The Council further recognized the importance of ensuring transparent, adequate and equitable funding to support all special procedures according to their specific needs (see HRC resolution 16/21).

Since 2006 several new **thematic mandates** were established:

1. Special Rapporteur on **contemporary forms of slavery** (2007)

2. Special Rapporteur on the human right to safe drinking **water and sanitation** (2008)

3. Special Rapporteur in the field of **cultural rights** (2009)

4. Special Rapporteur on the rights to **freedom of peaceful assembly and of association** (2010)

5. Working Group on the issue of **discrimination against women in law and in practice** (2010)

6. Independent expert on the promotion of a democratic and equitable **international order** (2011)

7. Special Rapporteur on the **promotion of truth, justice, reparation & guarantees of non-recurrence** (2011)

8. Working Group on **transnational corporations and other business enterprises** (2011)

9. Independent Expert on the issue of human rights obligations relating to the enjoyment of a safe, clean, healthy and sustainable **environment** (2012)

10. Independent Expert on **the enjoyment of all human rights by older persons** (2013)

The Human Rights Council also established the following new **country mandates** since 2006:

1. Independent Expert on the situation of human rights in the **Sudan** (2009)

2. Special Rapporteur on the situation of human rights in **the Islamic Republic of Iran** (2011)

3. Independent Expert on the situation of human rights in **Côte d'Ivoire** (2011)

4. Special Rapporteur on the situation of human rights in the **Syrian Arab Republic** (2011)

5. Special Rapporteur on the situation of human rights in **Belarus** (2012)

6. Special Rapporteur on the situation of human rights in **Eritrea** (2012)

7. Independent Expert on the situation of human rights in **Mali** (2013)

8. Independent Expert on the situation of human rights in **Central African Republic** (2013)

To gain a better understanding about the specific work product of the Special Procedures' Thematic Working Groups, Rapporteurs, Experts and Country Visits consider the following excerpt from the Special Rapporteur's Country Visit Report on the United States. You can also find a summary of this work by country in Recommendations of Special Procedures by Country 2007.

iv. Report of the Special Rapporteur on Terrorism, Country Visit to USA, A/HRC/6/17/Add.3

### United States of America

### Introduction

During the period under review, the Special Rapporteur on human rights while countering terrorism visited the United States from 16 to 25 May 2007 (please refer to document A/HRC/6/17/Add.3).

### Conclusions (A/HRC/6/17/Add.3, para. 53)

53. The Special Rapporteur has identified elements of best practice in the United States' fight against terrorism and the compliance of this with human rights and fundamental freedoms, including compensation for victims of terrorism, community outreach, and non-interference with the freedom of the press. He has, in contrast, also identified serious situations of incompatibility between international human rights obligations and the counter-terrorism law and practice of the United States. Such situations include the prohibition against torture, or cruel, inhuman or degrading treatment; the right to life; and the right to a fair trial. He has also identified deficiencies in United States law and practice pertaining to the principle of non-refoulement; the rendition of persons to places of secret detention; the definition of terrorism; non-discrimination; checks in the application of immigration laws; and the obtaining of private records of persons and the unlawful surveillance of persons, including a lack of sufficient balances in that context.

### Recommendations (A/HRC/6/17/Add.3, paras. 54–68)

54. The Special Rapporteur has described his visit to the United States as a step in the process of restoring the role of the United States as a positive ex-

ample for respecting human rights, including in the context of the fight against terrorism, and he hopes that these steps continue to progress. He likewise recommends that the United States take a strong role in the implementation of the United Nations Global Counter-Terrorism Strategy.

55. The Special Rapporteur recommends that the categorization of persons as "unlawful enemy combatants" be abandoned. He calls upon the United States to release or to put on trial those persons detained under that categorization. In the case of those suspected of war crimes, the international community has recognized the need to ensure that there is no impunity for such offending, but the Special Rapporteur is gravely concerned about the increasing risks of an unfair trial as time continues to pass, and he therefore urges a determined effort to proceed with and conclude such prosecutions.

56. The Special Rapporteur further recommends that legislative amendments be made to remove the denial of habeas corpus rights under the Military Commissions Act 2006 and the restrictions upon the ability of Guantánamo Bay detainees to seek full judicial review of their combatant status, with the authority of the reviewing court to order release.

***

59. Due to the various concerns identified in this report pertaining to the composition and operation of military tribunals under the Military Commissions Act of 2006, involving multiple incompatibilities with the CCPR, the Special Rapporteur recommends that these commissions be disestablished. Wherever possible, ordinary civilian courts should be used to try terrorist suspects.

60. In the case of persons charged with war crimes, being those crimes identified in the Rome Statute of the International Criminal Court, such persons may be tried by military courts martial provided that safeguards are in place to check against the exercise of bias or executive interference, including rights of appeal to civilian courts. In any such proceedings, the security classification of information should not interfere with the presumption of innocence or the equality of arms, nor should evidence obtained by any form of torture or cruel, inhuman or degrading treatment be admitted in proceedings. ***

61. Gravely concerned at the enhanced interrogation techniques reportedly used by the CIA, the Special Rapporteur urges the United States to ensure that all its officials and agencies comply with international standards, including article 7 of CCPR, the Convention against Torture and, in the context of an armed conflict, common article 3 of the Geneva Conventions. Noting the United States understanding of cruel, inhuman or degrading punishment, he reminds the Government that there are no circumstances in which cruel, inhuman or degrading treatment may be justified, and recommends that steps be taken to reflect this in its domestic law.

\*\*\*

67. Due to the fact that the United States Attorney General's guidelines on the availability of surveillance warrants under FISA, and the minimization procedures applicable to the surveillance of US persons are classified, the Special Rapporteur recommends that the Government introduce independent mechanisms, preferably involving the judiciary, to ensure that these guidelines and procedures are compliant with both the Constitution and the international obligations of the United States. The Special Rapporteur further urges the Government to extend these, and existing safeguards, to all persons within the jurisdiction and control of the United States, not simply those falling within the definition of "US persons".

68. The Special Rapporteur urges the Government to take steps to introduce independent checks and balances upon the authority of the FBI and other intelligence agencies to use National Security Letters.

The HRC annually hears and debates the findings and recommendations of Special Procedure mandate holders. These events also provide human rights NGOs the opportunity to bring violations to light as they are allowed to respond to the various reports. The links below provide a few, sometimes frustrating, examples of the process with a particular focus on Chinese treatment of Tibetans and Uyghurs.

v. HRC 15th Session: Video, NGO Statements Regarding Treatment of Uyghurs

HRC 23rd Session: NGO Statement Regarding Treatment of Tibetans (start at minute 55 or read transcript) (Item 3: Interactive Dialogue-Report of Special Rapporteur on Extrajudicial, Summary or Arbitrary Executions)

Reply of China:

Reply to the Helsinki Human Rights Foundation groundless accusation against China

Helsinki Human Rights Foundation has always been holding an anti china position. And making attacks on China on a groundless basis. Their statement is full of false statements and lies. We all know that Tibet in China after the democratic transformation in China has undergone great changes in the social economic spheres. Today the freedom and rights enjoyed by people in Tibet is unprecedented today in Tibet. China is a country under the Rule of Law. The Chinese constitution guarantees the right to assembly and other rights. The Human Rights Council is a forum for genuine dialogues and cooperation for all parties. It should not become a venue for the so called Human Rights organizations to usurp this forum to make false accusations and making lies.

Thank you.

**Uh-huh.**

vi. Individual Complaints to Special Procedure Experts

As part of the Special Procedure process some mandate holders are enabled to consider and respond to individual complaints by requesting information concerning the allegations from the relevant government.

The following excerpt from the U.N. website describes this process:

### Communications

Some special procedures mechanisms intervene directly with Governments on specific allegations of violations of human rights that come within their mandates. The intervention can relate to a human rights violation that has already occurred, is ongoing, or which has a high risk of occurring. The process, in general, involves sending a letter to the concerned Government requesting information and comments on the allegation and, where necessary, asking that preventive or investigatory action be taken.

The decision to intervene is at the discretion of the special procedure mandate holder and will depend on the various criteria established by him or her, as well as the criteria laid out in the Code of Conduct. The criteria will generally relate to: the reliability of the source and the credibility of information received; the details provided; and the scope of the mandate. However, it must be emphasized that the criteria and the procedure involved in responding to an individual complaint vary, so it is necessary to submit a communication in accordance with the specific requirements established by each special procedure.

\*\*\*

For specific information concerning the individual communication procedures of each special procedure mandate please consult the individual webpages of thematic mandates or country mandates.

vii. Advisory Committee

As part of the 2006 reforms of the Charter based system an "advisory committee" comprised on "independent experts" was created to assist the HRC.

The following excerpt from the U.N. website describes this advisory committee and its work:

Pursuant to Human Rights Council resolution 5/1, the Human Rights Council Advisory Committee (hereinafter "the Advisory Committee"), composed of 18 experts, has been established to function as a think-tank for the Council and work at its direction. The Advisory Committee replaces the former Sub-Commission on the Promotion and Protection of Human Rights.

\*\*\*

The function of the Advisory Committee is to provide expertise in the manner and form requested by the Council, focusing mainly on studies and research-based advice. Such expertise shall be rendered only upon the latter's request, in compliance with its resolutions and under its guidance.

The Advisory Committee should be implementation-oriented. The scope of its advice should be limited to thematic issues pertaining to the mandate of the Council; namely promotion and protection of all human rights. The Committee shall not adopt resolutions or decisions, but may propose to the Council, within the scope of its work as set out by the Council, suggestions for further enhancing its procedural efficiency, as well as further research proposals within the scope of the work set out by the Council.

# E. Critiquing the Revamped UN Charter Based Human Rights System: Evolution, Expediency or Just More of the Same?

## 1. Some Well-Deserved Criticisms: Continuing Hypocrisy & Double Standards

Muammar al-Gaddafi at the AU summit. U.S. Navy photo by Mass Communication Specialist 2nd Class Jesse B. Awalt.

a. Tom Kuntz, Libya's Late, Great Rights Record, NY Times, March 5, 2011

Until Col. Muammar el-Qaddafi's violent suppression of unrest in recent weeks, the United Nations Human Rights Council was kind in its judgment of Libya. In January, it produced a draft report on the country that reads like an international roll call of fulsome praise, when not delicately suggesting improvements. Evidently, within the 47-nation council, some pots are loath to call kettles black, at least until events force their hand. Last week Libya was suspended from the body, and the report was shelved. Here are excerpts.

- Algeria noted the efforts of the Libyan Arab Jamahiriya [People's Republic] to promote human rights, which reflected the country's commitment to complying with Human Rights Council resolutions and cooperating with the international community.

- Qatar praised the legal framework for the protection of human rights and freedoms, including, inter alia, its criminal code and criminal procedure law, which provided legal guarantees for the implementation of those rights.

- The Syrian Arab Republic praised the Libyan Arab Jamahiriya for its serious commitment to and interaction with the Human Rights Council and its mechanisms.

- [North Korea] praised the Libyan Arab Jamahiriya for its achievements in the protection of human rights, especially in the field of economic and social rights, including income augmentation, social care, a free education system, increased delivery of health care services, care for people with disabilities, and efforts to empower women.

b. Daily News, Editorial, UNseen Abuses: The Clownish United Nations Human Rights Council Hits New Heights of Absurdity

**Sunday, February 22nd 2009**

What do these have in common: genocide in Darfur; child soldiers in Chad and Congo; compulsory sterilization of women in China; suppression of dissent in Cuba, Iran, Syria and Russia; rape as a political weapon in Zimbabwe; sex trafficking in Asia; denial of human rights to minorities and women in Saudi Arabia and other Arab countries?

Answer: None of those gross abuses has drawn the notice of the United Nations Human Rights Council.

No, the council has had other matters to attend to, the vast majority of which focused on Israel. . . .

But now the council has broadened its portfolio. It has turned to brainstorming over the ills likely to flow from the global economic meltdown — meaning, let's figure out how to heap blame on the U.S. It also has decried the human rights threat posed by global warming, declaring:

"The inundation and disappearance of small island States would have implications for the right to self-determination."

Take that, global warming.

As for female genital mutilation in Africa — who cares?

c. Wonk'd: <u>Why the U.N. Human Rights Council Blows,</u> blog Undiplomatic, March 8, 2008

\*\*\* And then, late last week, we have the latest <u>outrage</u>:

A former spokesman for Cuba's foreign ministry was appointed this week to head the United Nations Human Rights Council's advisory committee. Radio Rebelde says Miguel Alfonso Martinez, is president of the Cuban Society of International Law, was appointed this Monday to head the Advisory Committee of the U.N. Human Rights Council.

Oy vey. Oh wait — saying that might get me investigated by the Council.

This isn't the first bad appointment either. Richard Falk, a Princeton professor who has <u>compared</u> Israeli policy in the Gaza Strip to Nazi Germany, is the Council's Special Rapporteur on . . . wait for it . . . Israel. And Jean Ziegler, who once helped Muammar Qaddafi establish a peace prize named after the dictator and who has praised, among others, Robert Mugabe and Fidel Castro, was <u>elected</u> to the Council's Advisory Committee.\*\*\*

d. Frida Ghitis, The Human Rights Council is a Tragic Joke, Miami Herald, 6/25/2010

We should honor BP for protecting the environment. While we're at it, we can name Jack the Ripper to the Commission for the Protection of Women, and make Philip Morris a special advisor on pulmonary health. This would all make perfect sense if we followed the example of United Nations Human Rights Council, one of the most astonishing organizations the world has devised under the U.N. umbrella.

The Council operates as a parody of itself, as if it had been designed by a team of comedians writing theater of the absurd. The reality, however, is that the UNHRC is a disaster that requires some decisive action by countries that truly value human rights, especially the US.

Today's UNHRC stands as one of the greatest obstacles impeding the protection of human rights by the international community. The organization makes a mockery of the suffering of the victims of human-rights abuses, glorifying their tormentors and depriving victims of a desperately needed protective voice. The obscenely dysfunctional UNHRC has removed from the arsenal of civilization a critically needed tool against regimes that brutalize their people. And now, adding to its dazzling performance in the field of human rights, the Council is working its magic against freedom of the press.

The question now is what does the Obama administration — and the world's democratic nations — plan to do about this suppurating sore on the body of the world's foremost international organization?

Where to begin to explain the outrages? Let's look at the Council's Advisory Committee: The group is chaired by Halima Warzazi of Morocco, whose history-making contribution to human rights came when Saddam Hussein used poison gas against Iraq's Kurds in 1988. Warzazi proudly blocked the U.N.'s move to condemn the massacre. The vice-chair of the Committee is the always impressive Swiss diplomat Jean Ziegler, who helped Libya's despot Moammar Qaddafi create the charmingly named "al-Qaddafi International Prize for Human Rights," and became its first winner.

Ziegler who, like the rest of the Council, is obsessed with Israel's sins to the exclusion of any other problem on Earth, has shared the Qaddafi prize honor with Fidel Castro, Louis Farrakhan, Hugo Chávez and other luminaries of freedom. The latest "expert adviser" is Nicaragua's Miguel D'Escoto Brockman, admirer of Mahmoud Ahmadinejad and defender of Omar al-Bashir, the Sudanese president indicted by the International Criminal Court for crimes against humanity.

The Council succeeded the disgraceful U.N. Commission on Human Rights in 2006. CHR was such an embarrassment that it had to be disbanded and replaced. But the new effort is even more of a disaster.

\*\*\*

### e. Sudan's Election to ECOSOC

<u>U.N. Watch</u>: Mia Farrow Condemns U.N. Election of Genocidal Sudan as Vice-President of Top Human Rights Body

*UN Watch's Hillel Neuer: "It's like naming Jack the Ripper to head a women's shelter"*

Contact: <u>media1@unwatch.org</u>

NEW YORK, Jan. 29, 2013 — Mia Farrow, the film star and human rights activist, today condemned the U.N.'s election of Sudan as vice-president of its 54-member Economic and Social Council (ECOSOC), a top U.N. body that regulates human rights groups, shapes the composition of key U.N. women's rights bodies, and adopts resolutions on subjects ranging from Internet freedom to female genital mutilation.

The UN's election of Sudan took place yesterday: <u>click here for U.N. announcement. . . .</u>

"Sudanese president Al Bashir is wanted by the International Criminal Court for crimes against humanity and genocide in the Darfur region of Sudan," said Farrow. "President Al Bashir and his regime are orchestrating a campaign of ethnic cleansing in Sudan's border regions, the Nuba Mountains and the Blue Nile, where some 700,000 civilians face starvation and are denied access to humanitarian aid because of incessant aerial bombardments."

"It's an outrage," said Hillel Neuer, executive director of U.N. Watch, the Geneva-based non-governmental human rights group.

f. The Anti-Israel Obsession

From Wikipedia:

*** As of 2015, Israel had been condemned in 62 resolutions by the Council since its creation in 2006 — the Council had resolved almost more resolutions condemning Israel than on the rest of the world combined. The 50 resolutions comprised almost half (45.9%) of all country-specific resolutions passed by the Council, not counting those under Agenda Item 10 (countries requiring technical assistance). By April 2007, the Council had passed eleven resolutions condemning Israel, the only country which it had specifically condemned. Toward Sudan, a country with human rights abuses as documented by the Council's working groups, it has expressed "deep concern".

The council voted on 30 June 2006 to make a review of alleged human rights abuses by Israel a permanent feature of every council session. The Council's special rapporteur on the Israeli–Palestinian conflict is its only expert mandate with no year of expiry. The resolution, which was sponsored by <u>Organisation of the Islamic Conference</u>, passed by a vote of 29 to 12 with five abstentions. <u>Human Rights Watch</u> urged it to look at international human rights and humanitarian law violations committed by <u>Palestinian</u> armed groups as well. Human Rights Watch called on the Council to avoid the selectivity that discredited its predecessor and urged it to hold special sessions on other urgent situations, such as that in <u>Darfur</u>.

Video: <u>http://vimeo.com/12583916</u> (statement of Hillel Neuer of U.N. Watch regarding HRC bias against Israel)

## 2. Potential Light on the Horizon: A Glass Half Full?

a. Patrick Stewart, <u>The Human Rights Council: Give Credit Where Credit Is Due</u>, **Counsel** on Foreign Relations, The Internationalist, June 1, 2012

Since the creation of the Human Rights Council (HRC) in 2006, U.S. critics have repeatedly tarred the HRC as a feckless haven for human rights abusers and a platform for egregious attacks of Israel. . . . . But critics overlook transformational improvements. The HRC remains deeply imperfect. But thanks to the Obama administration's dogged diplomacy, it has started to turn the corner, gaining "newfound credibility as a human rights watchdog."

This is the compelling conclusion of a new CFR [Council on Foreign Relations] report, "Advancing Human Rights in the U.N. System," by Suzanne Nossel, the new executive director of Amnesty International USA. . . . [ <u>Report is available here</u>.]

On country-specific resolutions, the United States began gradually, working first to secure resolutions for human rights monitoring in countries experiencing political transition (including Guinea and Kyrgyzstan), before moving on to secure more forceful resolutions against regimes committing egregious human rights abuses . . . .

Beyond placing abusers in the "hot seat", the United States has over the past three years scored some impressive victories on thematic resolutions. . . . The result was an historic achievement: passage of a resolution on freedom of expression and religion that contained none of the problematic language — and yet enjoyed widespread support among Muslim countries. Another signature success — virtually unimaginable only a few years ago — was the U.S. victory in engineering the support of a HRC resolution affirming the rights of lesbian, gay, bisexual, and transgender persons.

See also James Traub, U.N. Human Rights Council Condemns Actual Human Rights Abusers! Or, in praise of small victories, Foreign Policy, June 1, 2012

Human Rights Watch Report, <u>U.N. Human Rights Council: Build on Recent Successes, New Member States Critical to Future Progress</u>, September 22, 2011

# Chapter 8

# International Promotion and Enforcement of Right Through the U.N. Treaty Based System

## A. Introduction & Overview

In the last chapter we examined the U.N. Charter based system for the protection of human rights. These institutions, primary among them the U.N. Human Rights Council and High Commissioner for Human Rights, derive their mandate and authority from the principle bodies of the U.N. and ultimately from the Charter itself. A second and distinct branch of the U.N. system for protecting human rights involves the work of specific human rights treaty based institutions. These institutions, their functions, membership and powers, are derived from and controlled by the specific human rights treaty that created them. They typically report back to the U.N. which provides necessary assistance, facilities and funding.

After studying these materials you should be able to answer basic questions about the functions, composition, powers and authority of these various treaty based institutions and evaluate their role in the realization of human rights. The readings below primarily focus on the functions, powers and actions of the ICPRC's Human Rights Committee (HRC) as an illustration of how the treaty based system operates. The HRC is both typical of other treaty based institutions and the most prominent among them. To gain a more practical perspective, you should evaluate the potential role of the HRC (and other treaty institutions) regarding human rights conditions in Venezuela and the cases of Judge María Lourdes Afiuni and Leopoldo Lopez. Information about events in Venezuela is provided below.

As you study the materials focus on answering the following questions.

1. What actions, if any, may the Human Rights Committee take regarding human rights conditions in Venezuela generally?

2. Can an individual victim of alleged human rights violations by the Venezuelan government, such as Judge Afiuni and legislator Lopez, seek redress before the HRC?

- Are there any prerequisites or limitations on such actions?
- What process would be followed to resolve such disputes and find the relevant facts?
- What remedies may the Human Rights Committee provide to individual petitioners?
- Would the Committee's decisions be legally binding and enforceable?

3. Are there other treaty based institutions that might have jurisdiction to consider human rights conditions in Venezuela generally or the cases of Afiuni or Lopez?

4. Do the treaty based institutions such as the HRC actually "enforce" human rights or simply monitor and encourage their implementation?

5. Are the committees accountable for their decisions and if so, to whom? (Do they, or the processes they employ, have legal and democratic legitimacy?)

6. Should such institutions be given the power to render authoritative interpretations and decisions that are binding and enforceable? Do the answers to such questions depend in any way upon which rights are being enforced?

7. What are the current strengths and weaknesses of the treaty based system? How could the system be improved?

## 1. The Treaties

To date, about 50 distinct human rights treaties and protocols have been created under the auspices of the United Nations. As of 2014, there were 26 treaties or protocols deposited with the U.N. and listed on the U.N. treaty database under the category "human rights." Many other human rights related treaties, such as those on human trafficking and refugees, are found under other categories in the database. The UN High Commissioner for Human Rights describes ten of these treaties as "core" instruments — although a more realistic assessment would recognize that some treaties are far more central and widely adopted than others. The list below, with links to the treaty text and related monitoring body, appears on the U.N. High Commissioner's website (the bracketed information on state adoptions has been added by the book authors). Note that many of these "core" multilateral treaties have optional protocols which, being optional, have different membership from the core treaty. For example, the CCPR has two optional protocols; one allows for the treaties' Human Rights Committee to hear petitions from individuals and the other seeks abolition of the capital punishment.

| | | | |
|---|---|---|---|
| ICERD | International Convention on the Elimination of All Forms of Racial Discrimination<br>*[177 state parties including the U.S.]* | 21 Dec 1965 | CERD |
| CCPR | International Covenant on Civil and Political Rights<br>*[168 state parties including the United States]* | 16 Dec 1966 | CCPR |
| CESCR | International Covenant on Economic, Social and Cultural Rights<br>*[162 state parties, not including the U.S.]* | 16 Dec 1966 | CESCR |
| CEDAW | Convention on the Elimination of All Forms of Discrimination against Women<br>*[188 state parties not including the U.S.]* | 18 Dec 1979 | CEDAW |
| CAT | Convention against Torture and Other Cruel, Inhuman or Degrading Treatment or Punishment<br>*[155 state parties including the U.S.]* | 10 Dec 1984 | CAT |
| CRC | Convention on the Rights of the Child<br>*[194 state parties, not including the U.S.]* | 20 Nov 1989 | CRC |
| ICMW | International Convention on the Protection of the Rights of All Migrant Workers and Members of Their Families<br>*[47 state parties, not including the U.S.]* | 18 Dec 1990 | CMW |
| CPED | International Convention for the Protection of All Persons from Enforced Disappearance<br>*[42 state parties, not including the U.S.]* | 20 Dec 2006 | CED |
| CRPD | Convention on the Rights of Persons with Disabilities<br>*[147 state parties, not including the U.S.]* | 13 Dec 2006 | CRPD |
| CESCR-OP | Optional Protocol to the Covenant on Economic, Social and Cultural Rights<br>*[15 parties to optional protocol allowing individual complaints — U.S. is not a party]* | 10 Dec 2008 | CESCR |
| CCPR-OP1 | Optional Protocol to the International Covenant on Civil and Political Rights<br>*[115 parties to optional protocol allowing individual complaints, not including the U.S.]* | 16 Dec 1966 | CCPR |
| CCPR-OP2 | Second Optional Protocol to the International Covenant on Civil and Political Rights, aiming at the abolition of the death penalty<br>*[81 State parties, not including the U.S.]* | 15 Dec 1989 | CCPR |

| | | | |
|---|---|---|---|
| OP-CEDAW | Optional Protocol to the Convention on the Elimination of Discrimination against Women<br>*[17 state parties, not including the U.S.]* | 10 Dec 1999 | CEDAW |
| OP-CRC-AC | Optional protocol to the Convention on the Rights of the Child on the involvement of children in armed conflict<br>*[157 State parties, including the U.S.]* | 25 May 2000 | CRC |
| OP-CRC-SC | Optional protocol to the Convention on the Rights of the Child on the sale of children, child prostitution and child pornography<br>*[168 State parties, including the U.S.]* | 25 May 2000 | CRC |
| OP-CAT | Optional Protocol to the Convention against Torture and Other Cruel, Inhuman or Degrading Treatment or Punishment<br>*[73 State parties, not including the U.S.]* | 18 Dec 2002 | SPT |
| OP-CRPD | Optional Protocol to the Convention on the Rights of Persons with Disabilities<br>*[85 State parties, not including the U.S.]* | 12 Dec 2006 | CRPD |

Together these multilateral human rights treaties and their accompanying supervisory mechanisms make up what is commonly referred to as the U.N. "treaty based system."

## 2. The Treaty Based Mechanisms: General Characteristics

Each of the ten treaties that the U.N. describes as "core" create a monitoring body and procedural mechanism designed to promote their effective implementation. In most cases, at least some of these mechanisms are optional and apply to a state party only if that party consents. As developed further below, there are significant differences in the prestige, effectiveness and significance among these various bodies. The Office of the High Commissioner for Human Rights provides extensive information and links to each "Human Rights Treaty Body," including the brief summaries with webpage links which appear here. (The information in brackets on state parties was added by the authors.)

The Human Rights Committee (CCPR) monitors implementation of the International Covenant on Civil and Political Rights (1966) and its optional protocols *[115 parties to optional protocol allowing individual complaints, not including the U.S.]*;

The <u>Committee on Economic, Social and Cultural Rights (CESCR)</u> monitors implementation of the International Covenant on Economic, Social and Cultural Rights (1966) *[15 parties to optional protocol allowing individual complaints — U.S. is not a party to this treaty]*;

The <u>Committee on the Elimination of Racial Discrimination (CERD)</u> monitors implementation of the International Convention on the Elimination of All Forms of Racial Discrimination (1965) *[54 states accepting Article 14 individual complaints, not including the U.S.]*;

The <u>Committee on the Elimination of Discrimination Against Women (CEDAW)</u> monitors implementation of the Convention on the Elimination of All Forms of Discrimination against Women (1979) and its optional protocol (1999) *[104 parties to protocol allowing individual complaints — U.S. is not a party to this treaty]*;

The <u>Committee Against Torture (CAT)</u> monitors implementation of the Convention against Torture and Other Cruel, Inhuman or Degrading Treatment (1984) *[65 parties accepting Article 22 individual communications, not including the U.S.]*;

The <u>Committee on the Rights of the Child (CRC)</u> monitors implementation of the Convention on the Rights of the Child (1989) and its optional protocols (2000) *[10 parties to 2011 optional protocol allowing individual complaints, the U.S. is not a party to this treaty or optional protocols]*;

The <u>Committee on Migrant Workers (CMW)</u> (2004) monitors implementation of the International Convention on the Protection of the Rights of All Migrant Workers and Members of Their Families (1990) *[10 states accepting Article 77 individual complaints, the U.S. is not a party to this treaty]*;

The <u>Committee on the Right of Persons with Disabilities (CRPD)</u> monitors implementation of the International Convention on the Rights of Persons with Disabilities (2006) *[83 states accepting optional protocol allowing individual complaints, the U.S. is not a party to this treaty or optional protocol]*;

The <u>Committee on Enforced Disappearances</u> (CED) monitors implementation of the International Convention for the Protection of All Persons from Enforced Disappearance (2006); *[17 accept individual complaint procedures, the U.S. is not a party to this treaty]*;

The <u>Subcommittee on Prevention of Torture and other Cruel, Inhuman or Degrading Treatment or Punishment (SPT)</u> established pursuant to the Optional Protocol of the Convention against Torture (OPCAT) (2002) visits places of detention in order to prevent torture and other cruel, inhuman or degrading treatment or punishment *[73 state parties, not including the U.S.]*.

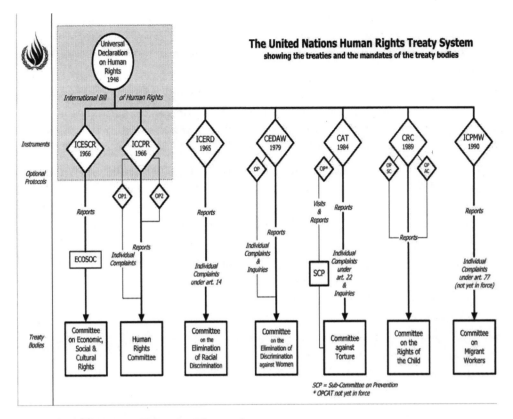

**From OHCHR <u>Fact Sheet On Treaty System</u>**

The monitoring bodies, formally called "committees," are made up of varying numbers of "independent experts" selected by the state parties to the relevant treaty. They are generally not paid and are selected by the member states. They typically meet for one or two sessions every year ranging from one to three weeks. The U.N. offers, for your viewing pleasure, both live and archived <u>webcasts</u> of the various committee sessions. Each treaty, often in combination with an optional protocol to the treaty, creates very similar procedures for conducting the committee's work typically involving three types of activities. First, all of the committees, other than the Sub-Committee on Prevention of Torture (SPT), are authorized to examine mandatory state party periodic reports on implementation.[103] Second, most committees are authorized to provide interpretive guidance on the treaty in the form of "general

---

103. Typically the treaty itself establishes the periodic reporting requirement and the committee's competence to review it. One important committee, CESCR, owes its existence and power to a resolution of ECOSOC. The Committee was established under ECOSOC Resolution 1985/17 (May 28, 1985) to carry out the monitoring functions originally assigned to ECOSOC in Part IV of the Covenant.

comments." Third, all of the committees except for SPT[104] are also empowered to consider "individual communications" alleging violations of the treaty by any state that has specifically consented to that process, often by ratifying an "Optional Protocol."[105] These three common treaty body tools are examined in much greater detail below. A fourth type of implementation mechanism, in the form of "inter-state" complaints, is also available under some of the treaties but has never been utilized. A fairly comprehensive review of the treaty based mechanisms is provided by the OHCHR in "Fact Sheet No. 30."

## 3. Distinctions from Charter Based Mechanisms

These treaty based institutions are distinct from the Charter based institutions in several key respects. First, each committee is created and controlled by the treaty that it monitors. This means that the committee's subject matter jurisdiction and mandate is confined to the terms of that particular treaty. Essentially, the committee is only concerned with the rights recognized in the treaty that created it and with the conduct of those states that have ratified it. Second, the committee members consist of "independent experts" rather than representatives of various states. Although nominated and elected by the state parties, these experts are not meant to represent the interests of the state parties or their home country but rather the cause of human rights. Third, many of the committees are empowered to consider and seek redress for individual cases — claims that a particular state has violated the rights of a particular individual. This function provides an opportunity for both concrete application of rights and individual redress generally lacking in the Charter-based mechanisms. Fourth, the committees are empowered to provide interpretive guidance as to the legal meaning of the rights under their jurisdiction. Although the committees' authoritativeness in this regard is uncertain and sometimes controversial, this process of providing interpretive guidance through "general comments" has potential significance for the development of relevant legal standards.

---

104. The Sub-Committee on the Prevention of Torture is distinct from other U.N. bodies in both approach and mandate. In its own words, SPT "has a preventive mandate focused on an innovative, sustained and proactive approach to the prevention of torture and ill treatment." It tries to accomplish this goal through country visits, confidential dialogue and technical assistance.

105. As of 2014, the optional protocol to the Migrant Worker Convention that authorizes individual complaints was not yet in force.

## B. Case Study: Human Rights, Free Speech & the Judiciary in Venezuela

https://www.cia.gov/library/publications/the-world-factbook/geos/ve.html

## 1. General Human Rights Conditions in Venezuela

Australia Business Insider provides a series of photos depicting recent unrest in Venezuela and government suppression of protest.

U.S. State Department Human Rights Country Report 2015, Venezuela

Simon Romero, NY Times, April 3, 2010, Criticism of Chávez Stifled by Arrests

Human Rights Watch, May 14, 2014, Venezuela: Unarmed Protestors Beaten, Shot

For additional information also see:

Human Rights Watch 2014 World Report, Venezuela

CNN World, 2014, Searching for Truth in Venezuela

## 2. The Case of Judge Afiuni

Juan Forero, Washington Post, April 25, 2010, Venezuelan Judge is Jailed After Ruling Angers President Hugo Chávez

Maria Diaz & William Neuman, NY Times, November 26, 2012, Venezuelan Judge Who Angered Chávez Says She Was Raped While in Prison

International Bar Association Report, April 4, 2014, Executive Summary, Urgent Need for Venezuelan Justice System Reform is Highlighted by Criminal Trial of Judge Afiuni

For additional information also see:

U.N. News Center, 2009, Venezuelan leader violates independence of judiciary — UN rights experts

U.N. News Center, July 30, 2009, Political interference mars justice in Venezuela, says U.N. rights expert

## 3. Treatment of Political Opposition Including Leopoldo Lopez

The Guardian, June 5, 2014, Venezuela opposition leader remaining in jail while awaiting trial

BBC News, June 14, 2014, Venezuela opposition politician Machado questioned over 'plot'

# C. How Treaty Based Processes Function

## 1. Periodic State Reports

a. Generally

**From OHCHR Website:**
**Consideration of State parties' reports**

When a country ratifies one of these treaties, it assumes a legal obligation to implement the rights recognized in that treaty. But signing up is only the first step, because recognition of rights on paper is not sufficient to guarantee that they will be enjoyed in practice. So the country incurs an additional obligation to submit regular reports to the monitoring committee set up under that treaty on how the rights are being implemented.

This system of human rights monitoring is common to most of the U.N. human rights treaties.

To meet their reporting obligation, States must submit an initial report usually one year after joining (two years in the case of the CRC) and then periodically in accordance with the provisions of the treaty (usually every four or five years). In addition to the government report, the treaty bodies may receive information on a country's human rights situation from other sources, including non-governmental organizations, U.N. agencies, other intergovernmental organizations, academic institutions and the press. In the light of all the information available, the Committee examines the report together with government representatives. Based on this dialogue, the Committee publishes its concerns and recommendations, referred to as "concluding observations".

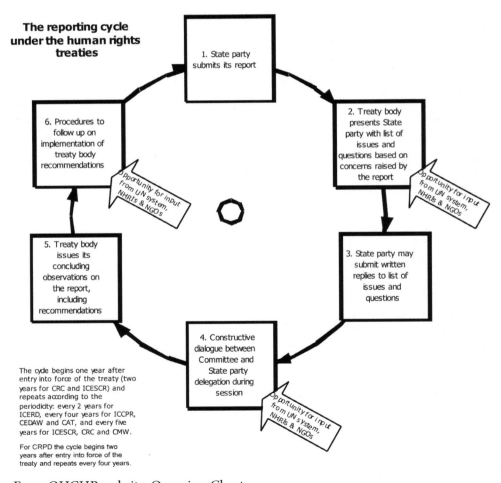

**The reporting cycle under the human rights treaties**

1. State party submits its report

2. Treaty body presents State party with list of issues and questions based on concerns raised by the report

3. State party may submit written replies to list of issues and questions

4. Constructive dialogue between Committee and State party delegation during session

5. Treaty body issues its concluding observations on the report, including recommendations

6. Procedures to follow up on implementation of treaty body recommendations

Opportunity for input from UN system, NHRIs & NGOs

The cycle begins one year after entry into force of the treaty (two years for CRC and ICESCR) and repeats according to the periodicity: every 2 years for ICERD, every four years for ICCPR, CEDAW and CAT, and every five years for ICESCR, CRC and CMW.

For CRPD the cycle begins two years after entry into force of the treaty and repeats every four years.

From OHCHR website, Overview Chart

### b. Report Exhaustion & Overlap: Efforts to Coordinate State Reporting

As the U.N. treaty based system has evolved, state reporting obligations have proliferated. With the recent advent of Universal Periodic Reports required by the Human Rights Council, the U.N. human rights system currently imposes at least 10 distinct reporting obligations on states which have ratified all of the major U.N. sponsored treaties. The reports are reviewed by distinct committees under treaties with distinct obligations and procedures. As noted in a 2012 U.N. Report on Strengthening the Treaty Body System ("Pillay Report"):

> If a State ratifies all nine core treaties and two optional protocols with a reporting procedure, it is bound to submit in the time frame of 10 years approximately 20 reports to treaty bodies, i.e. two annually. The reporting includes a national process followed by a meeting between the State party with the respective treaty body in Geneva (or New York) during a constructive dialogue. A State which is party to all the treaties and submits all its reports on time will participate in an average of two dialogues annually.[106]

Complicating these obligations, there exist significant overlaps in the rights declared in the various treaties. For example, nearly all treaties impose prohibitions on various forms of discrimination. Similarly, the interests of specially protected persons such as women, children, migrant workers and the disabled are inevitably subject to multiple treaties — those covering rights generally and those specifically addressing those vulnerable populations. An OHCHR report on the problem recognized the issue of overlapping or "congruent" obligations among the various treaties:

> *(b) Congruent provisions*
>
> 18. The degree of congruence of obligations across the treaties ranges from absolute congruence where provisions of the treaties have the same scope or objective (and often identical wording) to a broader congruence where provisions are not identical but are related and could therefore be addressed within a thematic framework in the common core document.***
>
> 20. In addition to non-discrimination provisions, there is a high degree of congruence among other provisions of the treaties which would allow information relating to their implementation to be included in the core document. The chart below shows areas of congruence in the substantive provisions of the seven core international human rights treaties.

(See the Chart of Congruence Here.)

---

106. Strengthening the United Nations Human Rights Treaty Body System, Report by the High Commissioner for Human Rights (Pillay) 2012, Submitted to General Assembly as A/66/860, Sixty-sixth session, Agenda item 124, United Nations reform: measures and proposals, 26 June 2012.

The potential for repetition, confusion, conflict, non-compliance and simple exhaustion under these conditions is obvious. The 2012 Pillay Report noted above observes that: "only 16% of States parties report on time; and even with this low compliance rate, four out of nine treaty bodies with a reporting procedure are facing significant and increasing backlogs of reports awaiting consideration. Several regularly make requests to the General Assembly for additional meeting time." The Pillay Report further notes "Under some treaties such as CESCR, CAT and the CCPR, around 20% of States parties have never submitted an initial report; for others like ICRMW, CRPD and the two Optional Protocols to the CRC (with a reporting requirement), the figure is even higher. In other words, a significant proportion of ratifications has never resulted in a report or a review. At the same time, the most widely ratified treaties — the CRC and CEDAW — have succeeded in receiving almost all initial reports due from their 193 and 187 States parties, respectively." Despite this persistent high degree of non-reporting, Committee consideration of submitted reports faced significant backlogs as well. That is to say, even with a plethora of missing reports, the committees have been somewhat overwhelmed by the review process and face backlogs.

The UN has attempted to address these problems and improve the effectiveness of the reporting process by instituting some guidelines and uniform procedures — Compilation of Harmonized Guidelines, HRI/GEN/2/Rev.6 3 June 2009 (there are currently three different versions of the Guidelines on the OHCHR webpage). These guidelines include the use of a "common core" document that a reporting state will submit to all treaty bodies in conjunction with additional treaty specific reporting. The common core document is designed to provide general information about the state, describe its infrastructure for implementing human rights obligations and address certain rights that appear in multiple treaties such as non-discrimination. The U.S. Common Core Document recently submitted to the HRC as part of the U.S. Fourth Periodic Report provides a clear example. Various common core documents submitted to date are accessible at the OHCHR website, including the 2011 Common Core Document of Venezuela.

A second initiative has been adopted by several committees of a new "simplified" optional reporting procedure, which a significant number of states have opted for.[107] The HRC describes it this way:

Simplified Reporting Procedure

New optional reporting procedure adopted by the Human Rights Committee: Focused reports based on replies to lists of issues prior to reporting (LOIPR)/Simplified Reporting Procedure. At its ninety-seventh session, held in October 2009, the Committee started discussing its draft revised reporting guidelines. In this context, it decided to adopt a new reporting procedure whereby it would send States parties a list of issues (a so-called

---

107. The Pillay Report urges adoption of the Simplified Reporting Procedure for all committees and states. Pillay Report, p. 48–50.

"list of issues prior to reporting" (LOIPR)) and consider their written replies in lieu of a periodic report (a so-called "focused report based on replies to a list of issues"). Under the new procedure, the State party's answer would constitute the report for the purposes of Article 40 of the Covenant.

A useful and detailed explanation of these reporting requirements can be found at the <u>International Women's Rights Action Watch</u> (Univ. of Minn.). More detail regarding the various procedures used by the treaty bodies for the treaty specific portion of state reports is available under "<u>working methods</u>" at the High Commissioner's website. You can find all reports and follow up communications submitted by the United States to the various U.N. treaty bodies on the State Department website under <u>U.S. Treaty Reports</u>.

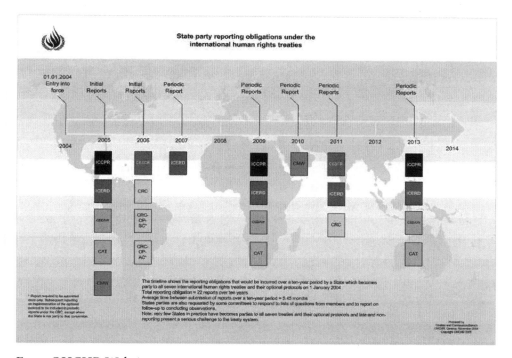

From <u>OHCHR Website</u>.

### c. Committee Evaluation of Reports, Concluding Observations & Reality

State periodic reports to the various treaty based bodies and the Committees' "concluding observations" (as well as other human rights related reports) can be accessed from a <u>searchable database</u> on the OHCHR website. These reports and Committee responses, <u>including those of the HRC</u>, are also available at each Committee's own webpage. You can also access report recommendations (concluding observations) and state responses for all treaty based committees, as well as for the Human Rights Council's Universal Periodic Reports, on a country specific basis through the UN's <u>Universal Human Rights Index</u>.

How forthright and honest is state self-reporting? Consider the following excerpts from the Venezuelan government's 4th Periodic Report to the HRC in 2012 in light of alternative viewpoints presented in the news reports about human rights in Venezuela presented above.

i. Fourth Periodic Report of Venezuela to Human Rights Committee

**Human Rights Committee**

**Consideration of reports submitted by States parties under article 40 of the Covenant**

 **International Covenant on Civil and Political Rights**

Distr.: General
29 April 2013
English
Original: Spanish

**Fourth periodic report of States parties due in 2005**

**Bolivarian Republic of Venezuela**

[18 December 2012]

\*\*\*

3. For Venezuela it is important to highlight the most significant legislative and institutional changes that have occurred in the last 14 years and how these changes have affected economic, political, social and cultural life in the country. Attention will accordingly be drawn to achievements in the building of a new society under the banner of Bolivarian socialism in which the central thrust of political action is to bring lasting dignity to human beings.

4. Our country enjoys true participatory democracy and, since 1998, has held 15 elections in which citizens have been called on both to choose freely their leaders and to decide on issues of importance for the nation. \*\*\* .

5. The policies implemented by the State are designed to give structural responses to historical situations that have infringed on fundamental rights. The law enforcement system has thus been realigned to break with the police culture put in place by previous governments, driven by an imperialistic national security doctrine that repressed and controlled the most excluded groups, criminalized protest and managed poverty but did not eradicate it. The recent establishment of the National Commission for Police Reform (CONAREPOL) and the National University for Security and Police Services underpins efforts to develop a new model for policing, based on the guiding principle of respect for the human rights of every person.

6. Capacity-building in the judiciary — the Public Prosecution Service and other organs of the justice system — together with the strengthening of the Ombudsman's Office as an independent human rights monitoring and advocacy body, has

placed at the service of citizens a robust institutional system for monitoring, investigating and publishing human rights violations.

7. Freedom of expression is fully guaranteed in Venezuela: citizens have the right to obtain truthful, timely, impartial and uncensored information. The translation of this right into reality is seen in the establishment and continued existence of private media outlets and in the encouragement of community media, which co-exist with commercial and public media, ensuring organized communities a means of freely expressing their ideas and viewpoints, which are traditionally barred or excluded from private and commercial media.

∗∗∗

26. A further piece of legislation that guarantees equality and the right not to suffer discrimination is the Social Responsibility in Radio, Television and Electronic Media Act, which expressly states that messages may not be disseminated by radio, television or electronic media that incite or promote hatred and intolerance on grounds of religion, politics, gender difference, racism or xenophobia.

27. The Social Responsibility in Radio, Television and Electronic Media Act lays down penalties for the dissemination of discriminatory messages. ∗∗∗

### Article 19

126. The Constitution of the Bolivarian Republic of Venezuela guarantees freedom of expression with no possibility of censorship; correspondingly, the exercise thereof entails full responsibility for what is expressed. The right to truthful, timely, impartial and uncensored information is also recognized.

127. In order to protect the exercise of these rights, the State has established governing and regulatory bodies and has passed laws on the subject, noteworthy among which is the Social Responsibility in Radio and Television Act, which establishes, in the dissemination and reception of messages, the social responsibility of radio and television service providers, electronic media suppliers, advertisers and independent national producers and users for developing a democratic balance between their duties, rights and interests with a view to promoting social justice and contributing to citizen education, democracy, peace, human rights and the social and economic development of the nation.

∗∗∗

To combat the typical whitewashing often found in self-serving state reports, the HRC accepts and considers information from alternative sources including independent NGOs or "civil society." After a country submits its formal report, the Committee develops a list of issues, assisted by these NGOs, which require a written response by the state prior to the meeting in which the report will be discussed. During its formal sessions the Committee then engages in a form of dialogue with state representatives about the report and these specific flagged issues.

The HRC ultimately publishes "Concluding Observations" describing concerns and recommendations, to which the state also is expected to respond to in subsequent reports (see, for example, U.S. comments to the HRC's "suggestions and recommendations" relating to prior reports in the 2005 US Report). The Committee has also adopted a "follow up" process, including a "Special Rapporteur on Follow Up" to track state responses and compliance with the Committee's "Concluding Observations."[108] (See searchable documentation on follow ups, including that relating to U.S. 2005 report, here.) Other Committees have similarly adopted written follow up processes for state reports.

A video clip of a Committee/ U.S. representative dialogue — involving questions posed by the HRC in 2014 regarding the criminalization of certain everyday activities of homeless people — can be viewed here. After viewing at least some part of this video, consider the following excerpts from the HRC "List of Issues" and "Concluding Observations" regarding the U.S. 3rd (2005) and 4th (2012) Periodic Reports. While it is not necessary for present purposes to study the details of these excerpts, you should both take note of the subjects covered and think about the Committee's role and approach. Also consider whether the Committee's comments demonstrate an understanding of the American legal structure and are well founded based on actual conditions within the United States.

ii. HRC Concluding Observations Regarding 2005 (3rd) Periodic Report of the United States

CCPR/C/USA/CO/3/Rev.1

**Concluding Observations of the HRC regarding 2005 Periodic Report of the United States Under the CPRC:**

***

**Principal subjects of concern and recommendations**

10. The Committee notes with concern the restrictive interpretation made by the State party of its obligations under the Covenant, as a result in particular of (a) its position that the Covenant does not apply with respect to individuals under its jurisdiction but outside its territory, nor in time of war, despite the contrary opinions and established jurisprudence of the Committee and the International Court of Justice; . . .

The State party should in particular . . . consider in good faith the interpretation of the Covenant provided by the Committee pursuant to its mandate.

***

12. The Committee is concerned by credible and uncontested information that the State party has seen fit to engage in the practice of detaining people secretly and in secret places for months and years on end, without keeping the International Committee of the Red Cross informed. ***

---

108. This process is similar to but distinguished from the HRC's Special Rapporteur for Follow Up on Individual Communications. The HRC's positions taken in the reporting process are described as "Concluding Observations" while its decisions taken on individual petitions are called "views."

The State party should immediately cease its practice of secret detention and close all secret detention facilities. ***

13. The Committee is concerned with the fact that the State party has authorized for some time the use of enhanced interrogation techniques, such as prolonged stress positions and isolation, sensory deprivation, hooding, exposure to cold or heat, sleep and dietary adjustments, 20-hour interrogations, removal of clothing and deprivation of all comfort and religious items, forced grooming, and exploitation of detainees' individual phobias. Although the Committee welcomes the assurance that, according to the Detainee Treatment Act of 2005, such interrogation techniques are prohibited by the present Army Field Manual on Intelligence Interrogation, the Committee remains concerned that. . . . (b) no sentence has been pronounced against an officer, employee, member of the Armed Forces, or other agent of the United States Government for using harsh interrogation techniques that had been approved;. . . .

***

14. The Committee notes with concern shortcomings concerning the independence, impartiality and effectiveness of investigations into allegations of torture and cruel, inhuman or degrading treatment or punishment inflicted by United States military and non-military personnel or contract employees, in detention facilities in Guantanamo Bay, Afghanistan, Iraq, and other overseas locations, and to alleged cases of suspicious death in custody in any of these locations. . . .

***

18. The Committee is concerned that, following the Supreme Court ruling in *Rasul v. Bush* (2004), proceedings before Combatant Status Review Tribunals (CSRTs) and Administrative Review Boards (ARBs), mandated respectively to determine and review the status of detainees, may not offer adequate safeguards of due process, . . . .

***

22. The Committee is concerned with reports that some 50% of homeless people are African American although they constitute only 12% of the United States population. (Articles 2 and 26.) The State party should take measures, including adequate and adequately implemented policies, to bring an end to such de facto and historically generated racial discrimination.

23. The Committee notes with concern reports of de facto racial segregation in public schools, reportedly caused by discrepancies between the racial and ethnic composition of large urban districts and their surrounding suburbs, and the manner in which schools districts are created, funded and regulated. The Committee is concerned that the State party, despite measures adopted, has not succeeded in eliminating racial discrimination such as regarding the wide disparities in the quality of education across school districts in metropolitan areas, to the detriment of minority students. It also notes

with concern the State party's position that federal government authorities cannot take legal action if there is no indication of discriminatory intent by state or local authorities. (Articles 2 and 26.)

\*\*\*

25. The Committee notes with concern allegations of widespread incidence of violent crime perpetrated against persons of minority sexual orientation, including by law enforcement officials.

\*\*\*

28. The Committee regrets that many federal laws which address sex-discrimination are limited in scope and restricted in implementation. The Committee is especially concerned about the reported persistence of employment discrimination against women. (Articles 3 and 26.)

\*\*\*

30. The Committee reiterates its concern about reports of police brutality and excessive use of force by law enforcement officials. . . . .

\*\*\*

32. The Committee reiterates its concern that conditions in some maximum security prisons are incompatible with the obligation contained in article 10 (1) of the Covenant to treat detainees with humanity and respect for the inherent dignity of the human person. . . . .

\*\*\*

34. The Committee notes with concern reports that forty-two states and the Federal government have laws allowing persons under the age of eighteen at the time the offence was committed, to receive life sentences, without parole, and that about 2,225 youth offenders are currently serving life sentences in United States prisons. . . . .

\*\*\*

35. The Committee is concerned that about five million citizens cannot vote due to a felony conviction, and that this practice has significant racial implications. . . . . ..

\*\*\*

iii. HRC List of Issues Regarding Fourth Periodic Report of the United States (2013)

Human Rights Committee (CCPR/C/USA/Q/4)

**List of issues in relation to the fourth periodic report of the United States of America (CCPR/C/USA/4 and Corr. 1), adopted by the Committee at its 107th session (11–28 March 2013)**

Constitutional and legal framework within which the Covenant is implemented (art. 2)

1. Please clarify the following issues:

(a) The State party's understanding of the scope of applicability of the Covenant with respect to individuals under its jurisdiction but outside its territory; in times of peace, as well as in times of armed conflict;

(b) Which measures have been taken to ensure that the Covenant is fully implemented by State and local authorities;

***

4. Please provide information on steps taken to address racial disparities in the criminal justice system, including the overrepresentation of individuals belonging to racial and ethnic minorities in prisons and jails. . . .

5. Please clarify which steps have been taken to eliminate and combat all forms of racial profiling against Arabs, Muslims and South Asians, and whether the Guidance Regarding the Use of Race by Federal Law Enforcement Agencies covers profiling based on religion, religious appearance or national origin. Please provide information on the practices and justification of practices involving the surveillance of Muslims in the State party, given that it has not resulted in any prosecution. . . . Please also provide information on steps taken to address discriminatory and unlawful use of "stop and frisk" practices by officers of the New York Police Department.

6. Please provide information on the imposition of criminal penalties on people living on the streets . . . .

7. Please provide information on obstacles to the access of undocumented migrants to health services and higher education institutions, and to federal and state programmes addressing such obstacles.

Right to life (art. 6)

8. Please provide information on:

(a) Death sentences imposed, the number of executions carried out, the grounds for each conviction and sentence, the age of the offenders at the time of committing the crime, and their ethnic origin;

(b) Whether the death penalty has been imposed on people with mental or intellectual disabilities since the 2002 Supreme Court ruling in Atkins v. Virginia exempting people with "mental retardation" from the death penalty; . . . .

(d) Steps taken to ensure that the death penalty is not imposed on the innocent;

***

9. Please provide information on:

(a) The number of victims of gun violence, including in the context of domestic violence, and on steps taken to better protect people against the risks associated with proliferation of firearms. Please also provide information on the applicability of "stand your ground" laws, and whether they provide blanket immunity to persons using force as defined and permitted by such laws; . . . .

*\*\**

10. Regarding the protection of life in armed conflict:

(a) Please clarify how targeted killings conducted through drone attacks on the territory of other States, as well as collateral civilian casualties are in compliance with Covenant obligations. Please clarify how the State party ensures that such use of force fully complies with its obligation to protect life.

*\*\**

11. Please provide information on:

(a) Whether the State party has instigated independent investigations into cases of torture or cruel, inhuman or degrading treatment or punishment of detainees in United States custody outside its territory. Please clarify whether those responsible have been prosecuted and sanctioned, and whether the State party has prosecuted former senior government and military officials who have authorized such torture and abuse;

*\*\**

13. Please provide information on:

(a) Steps taken to address cases of police brutality and excessive use of force, in particular against persons belonging to racial, ethnic or national minorities, as well as undocumented migrants crossing the United States-Mexico border, and to hold responsible officers accountable for such abuses;

*\*\**

14. Please provide information on:

(a) Steps taken to prohibit and prevent corporal punishment of children in schools (including the practice of "paddling"), penal institutions (including as a disciplinary measure in juvenile detention), the home, and all forms of care. Please provide information on measures taken to address the alleged more frequent use of corporal punishment against African-American students and students with disabilities;

(b) The application of criminal law to minors in order to address disciplinary issues arising in schools.

*\*\**

17. Please clarify whether the State party will deal with detainees held in Guantanamo Bay and in military facilities in Afghanistan and Iraq within the criminal justice system, and will end the system of administrative detention without charge or trial. Please clarify whether the State party will grant detainees the right to legal representation. . . .

*\*\**

19. Please clarify:

(a) Whether mandatory detention of immigrants who lack identification documents or are charged with the commission of crimes will be eliminated . . . .

(c) Which steps are taken to ensure that immigrants, in particular those with children, and unaccompanied alien children, are not held in jails or jail-like detention facilities.

20. Please provide information on steps taken to prevent and combat domestic violence, and the impact measured, as well as to ensure that acts of domestic violence are effectively investigated and that perpetrators are prosecuted and sanctioned. . . .

### Elimination of slavery and servitude (art. 8 and 24)

21. Please provide information on steps taken:

(a) To combat human trafficking;

(b) To protect children under 18 years of age living in the State party from being sexually exploited through prostitution, as well as the steps taken to ensure that these children are not dealt with through the criminal justice system.

### Right to privacy (art. 17)

22. Please provide information on steps taken to ensure judicial oversight over National Security Agency surveillance of phone, email and fax communications both within and outside the State party. Please also specify what circumstances, as mentioned in section 206 of the USA Patriot Act, justify "roving" wiretaps.

### Freedom of assembly and association (arts. 21 and 22)

23. Please clarify why agricultural and domestic workers and independent contractors are excluded from the right to organize themselves in trade unions by the National Labor Relations Act and provide information on steps taken to ensure that the right to freedom of association is available to these categories of workers.

\*\*\*

### Right to take part in the conduct of public affairs (art. 25)

26. Please provide information on:

(a) The rationale for prohibiting persons with felony convictions from voting in federal elections once they have completed their sentence. . . .

(b) Measures taken by several states, including restrictions on access to voter registration, more stringent eligibility requirements or purging voters from registration rolls leading to the legal or de facto disenfranchisement of voters;

(c) Steps taken or foreseen to ensure that residents of Washington, D.C., can exercise the right to vote and elect representatives to the Senate and House of Representatives.

\*\*\*

iv. Concluding Observations of the HRC Regarding the Fourth Periodic Report of the United States

Human Rights Committee (CCPR/C/USA/CO/4)

**Concluding observations on the fourth periodic report of the United States of America** \*\*\*

B. Positive aspects . . . .

3. The Committee notes with appreciation the many efforts undertaken by the State party and the progress made in protecting civil and political rights. The Committee welcomes in particular the following legislative and institutional steps taken by the State party:

> (a) Full implementation of article 6, paragraph 5, of the Covenant in the aftermath of the Supreme Court's judgment in *Roper v. Simmons*, 543 U.S. 551 (2005), despite the State party's reservation to the contrary;

> (b) Recognition by the Supreme Court in *Boumediene v. Bush*, 553 U.S. 723 (2008) of the extraterritorial application of constitutional habeas corpus rights to aliens detained at Guantánamo Bay;

> (c) Presidential Executive Orders 13491 — Ensuring Lawful Interrogations, 13492 — Review and Disposition of Individuals Detained at the Guantánamo Bay Naval Base and Closure of Detention Facilities and 13493 — Review of Detention Policy Options, issued on 22 January 2009;

> (d) Support for the United Nations Declaration on the Rights of Indigenous Peoples, announced by President Obama on 16 December 2010;

> (e) Presidential Executive Order 13567 establishing a periodic review of detainees at the Guantánamo Bay detention facility who have not been charged, convicted or designated for transfer, issued on 7 March 2011.

C. Principal matters of concern and recommendations

Applicability of the Covenant at national level

\*\*\*

The State party should:

\*\*\*

> (b) Engage with stakeholders at all levels to identify ways to give greater effect to the Covenant at federal, state and local levels, taking into account that the obligations under the Covenant are binding on the State party as a whole, and that all branches of government and other public or governmental authorities at every level are in a position to engage the responsibility of the State party (general comment. No. 31, para. 4);

> (c) Taking into account its declaration that provisions of the Covenant are non-self-executing, ensure that effective remedies are available for violations of the Covenant, including those that do not, at the same time, constitute vio-

lations of the domestic law of the United States of America, and undertake a review of such areas with a view to proposing to Congress implementing legislation to fill any legislative gaps. The State party should also consider acceding to the Optional Protocol to the Covenant, providing for an individual communication procedure.

***

## Accountability for past human rights violations

5. The Committee is concerned at the limited number of investigations, prosecutions and convictions of members of the Armed Forces and other agents of the United States Government, including private contractors, for unlawful killings during its international operations, and the use of torture or other cruel, inhuman or degrading treatment or punishment of detainees in United States custody, including outside its territory, as part of the so-called "enhanced interrogation techniques". . . .

***

## Racial disparities in the criminal justice system

6. While appreciating the steps taken by the State party to address racial disparities in the criminal justice system, including the enactment in August 2010 of the Fair Sentencing Act and plans to work on reforming mandatory minimum sentencing statutes, the Committee continues to be concerned about racial disparities at different stages in the criminal justice system, as well as sentencing disparities and the overrepresentation of individuals belonging to racial and ethnic minorities in prisons and jails (arts. 2, 9, 14 and 26).

***

## Racial profiling

7. While welcoming plans to reform the "stop and frisk" programme in New York City, the Committee remains concerned about the practice of racial profiling and surveillance by law enforcement officials targeting certain ethnic minorities and the surveillance of Muslims, undertaken by the Federal Bureau of Investigation (FBI) and the New York Police Department (NYPD), in the absence of any suspicion of wrongdoing (arts. 2, 9, 12, 17 and 26).

The State party should continue and step up measures to effectively combat and eliminate racial profiling by federal, state and local law enforcement officials, inter alia, by: . . . .

(c) Abolishing all "stop and frisk" practices.

## Death penalty

8. While welcoming the overall decline in the number of executions and the increasing number of states that have abolished the death penalty, the Committee remains concerned about the continuing use of the death penalty and, in particular,

racial disparities in its imposition that disproportionately affects African Americans, exacerbated by the rule that discrimination has to be proven on a case-by-case basis. . . .

The State party should: . . . .

(e) Consider establishing a moratorium on the death penalty at the federal level and engage with retentionist states with a view to achieving a nationwide moratorium.

\*\*\*

### Targeted killings using unmanned aerial vehicles (drones)

9. The Committee is concerned about the State party's practice of targeted killings in extraterritorial counter-terrorism operations using unmanned aerial vehicles (UAV), also known as "drones," the lack of transparency regarding the criteria for drone strikes, including the legal justification for specific attacks, and the lack of accountability for the loss of life resulting from such attacks. . . . Nevertheless, the Committee remains concerned about the State party's very broad approach to the definition and geographical scope of "armed conflict," including the end of hostilities, the unclear interpretation of what constitutes an "imminent threat," who is a combatant or a civilian taking direct part in hostilities, the unclear position on the nexus that should exist between any particular use of lethal force and any specific theatre of hostilities, as well as the precautionary measures taken to avoid civilian casualties in practice (arts. 2, 6 and 14).

The State party should revisit its position regarding legal justifications for the use of deadly force through drone attacks. It should: . . . .

(c) Provide for independent supervision and oversight of the specific implementation of regulations governing the use of drone strikes; . . . .

(e) Conduct independent, impartial, prompt and effective investigations of allegations of violations of the right to life and bring to justice those responsible;

\*\*\*

### Gun violence

10. While acknowledging the measures taken to reduce gun violence, the Committee remains concerned about the continuing high numbers of gun-related deaths and injuries and the disparate impact of gun violence on minorities, women and children. While commending the investigation by the United States Commission on Civil Rights of the discriminatory effect of the "Stand Your Ground" laws, the Committee is concerned about the proliferation of such laws which are used to circumvent the limits of legitimate self-defence in violation of the State party's duty to protect life (arts. 2, 6 and 26).

The State Party should take all necessary measures to abide by its obligation to effectively protect the right to life. In particular, it should:

(a) Continue its efforts to effectively curb gun violence, including through the continued pursuit of legislation requiring background checks for all private firearm transfers, in order to prevent possession of arms by persons recognized as prohibited individuals under federal law, and ensure strict enforcement of the Domestic Violence Offender Gun Ban of 1996 (the Lautenberg Amendment); and

(b) Review the Stand Your Ground laws to remove far-reaching immunity and ensure strict adherence to the principles of necessity and proportionality when using deadly force in self-defence.

### Excessive use of force by law enforcement officials

11. The Committee is concerned about the still high number of fatal shootings by certain police forces, including, for instance, in Chicago, and reports of excessive use of force by certain law enforcement officers, including the deadly use of tasers, which has a disparate impact on African Americans, and use of lethal force by Customs and Border Protection (CBP) officers at the United States-Mexico border (arts. 2, 6, 7 and 26).

***

### Trafficking and forced labour

14. While acknowledging the measures taken by the State party to address the issue of trafficking in persons and forced labour, the Committee remains concerned about cases of trafficking of persons, including children, for purposes of labour and sexual exploitation, and criminalization of victims on prostitution-related charges. ***

### Immigrants

15. The Committee is concerned that under certain circumstances mandatory detention of immigrants for prolonged periods of time without regard to the individual case may raise issues under Article 9 of the Covenant. It is also concerned about the mandatory nature of the deportation of foreigners, without regard to elements such as the seriousness of crimes and misdemeanors committed, the length of lawful stay in the United States, health status, family ties and the fate of spouses and children staying behind, or the humanitarian situation in the country of destination. Finally, the Committee expresses concern about the exclusion of millions of undocumented immigrants and their children from coverage under the Affordable Care Act and the limited coverage of undocumented immigrants and immigrants residing lawfully in the United States for less than five years by Medicare and Children Health Insurance, all resulting in difficulties for immigrants in accessing adequate health care (arts. 7, 9, 13, 17, 24 and 26).

***

### Corporal punishment

17. The Committee is concerned about corporal punishment of children in schools, penal institutions, the home and all forms of childcare at federal, state and local levels. It is also concerned about the increasing criminalization of students to deal with disciplinary issues in schools (arts. 7, 10 and 24).

\*\*\*

## Non-consensual psychiatric treatment

18. The Committee is concerned about the widespread use of non-consensual psychiatric medication, electroshock and other restrictive and coercive practices in mental health services (arts. 7 and 17).

\*\*\*

## Criminalization of homelessness

19. While appreciating the steps taken by federal and some state and local authorities to address homelessness, the Committee is concerned about reports of criminalization of people living on the street for everyday activities such as eating, sleeping, sitting in particular areas, etc. The Committee notes that such criminalization raises concerns of discrimination and cruel, inhuman or degrading treatment (arts. 2, 7, 9, 17 and 26).

The State party should engage with state and local authorities to:

(a) Abolish the laws and policies criminalizing homelessness at state and local levels; . . . .

## Detainees at Guantánamo Bay

21. While noting the President's commitment to closing the Guantánamo Bay facility and the appointment of Special Envoys at the United States Departments of State and of Defense to continue to pursue the transfer of designated detainees, the Committee regrets that no timeline for closure of the facility has been provided. The Committee is also concerned that detainees held in Guantánamo Bay and in military facilities in Afghanistan are not dealt with through the ordinary criminal justice system after a protracted period of over a decade, in some cases (arts. 7, 9, 10 and 14).

\*\*\*

## National Security Agency surveillance

22. The Committee is concerned about the surveillance of communications in the interest of protecting national security, conducted by the National Security Agency (NSA) both within and outside the United States, through the bulk phone metadata surveillance programme (Section 215 of the USA PATRIOT Act) and, in particular, surveillance under Section 702 of the Foreign Intelligence Surveillance Act (FISA) Amendment Act, conducted through PRISM (collection of communications content from United States-based Internet companies) and UPSTREAM (collection of communications metadata and content by tapping fiber-optic cables carrying Internet traffic) and the adverse impact on individuals' right to privacy. The Committee is concerned that, until recently, judicial interpretations of FISA and rulings of the Foreign Intelligence Surveillance Court (FISC) had largely been kept secret, thus not allowing affected persons to know the law with sufficient precision. \*\*\*

### Juvenile justice and life imprisonment without parole

23. While noting with satisfaction the Supreme Court decisions prohibiting sentences of life imprisonment without parole for children convicted of non-homicide offences (Graham v. Florida), and barring sentences of mandatory life imprisonment without parole for children convicted of homicide offences (Miller v. Alabama) and the State party's commitment to their retroactive application, the Committee is concerned that a court may still, at its discretion, sentence a defendant to life imprisonment without parole for a homicide committed as a juvenile, and that a mandatory or non-homicide-related sentence of life imprisonment without parole may still be applied to adults. The Committee is also concerned that many states exclude 16 and 17 year olds from juvenile court jurisdictions so that juveniles continue to be tried in adult courts and incarcerated in adult institutions (arts. 7, 9, 10, 14, 15 and 24).

The State party should prohibit and abolish the sentence of life imprisonment without parole for juveniles, irrespective of the crime committed, as well as the mandatory and non-homicide-related sentence of life imprisonment without parole. It should also ensure that juveniles are separated from adults during pretrial detention and after sentencing, and that juveniles are not transferred to adult courts. It should encourage states that automatically exclude 16 and 17 year olds from juvenile court jurisdictions to change their laws.

### Voting rights

24. While noting with satisfaction the statement by the Attorney General on 11 February 2014, calling for a reform of state laws on felony disenfranchisement, the Committee reiterates its concern about the persistence of state-level felon disenfranchisement laws, its disproportionate impact on minorities and the lengthy and cumbersome voting restoration procedures in states. The Committee is further concerned that voter identification and other recently introduced eligibility requirements may impose excessive burdens on voters and result in de facto disenfranchisement of large numbers of voters, including members of minority groups. Finally, the Committee reiterates its concern that residents of the District of Columbia (D.C.) are denied the right to vote for and elect voting representatives to the United States Senate and House of Representatives (arts. 2, 10, 25 and 26).

\*\*\*

27. In accordance with rule 71, paragraph 5, of the Committee's rules of procedure, the State party should provide, within one year, relevant information on its implementation of the Committee's recommendations made in paragraphs 5, 10, 21 and 22 above.

### v. Critiquing the Critiques: Does the HRC "Overreach"?

The HRC's "List of Issues" and "Concluding Observations" regarding the United States' periodic reports reveal some serious flaws in the American human rights record. These are particularly evident regarding government conduct in the war against terrorism. The HRC's observations, however, also provide ammunition for critics of the process. Does the HRC demonstrate a working knowledge of U.S. principles of federalism and Constitutional allocations of power between the federal and state governments? Is the committee aware of a U.S. declaration accompanying ratification asserting the limits of federal power over certain subjects? The Committee expresses concerns over alleged widespread police brutality and use of excessive force. There are plenty of reasons, splashed across American media, to believe that excessive force by police occurs far more than it should — after events in Ferguson, Missouri, it seemingly couldn't get worse.

Yet critics of the system will point out that allegations of widespread brutality and a lack of government response may or may not be justified depending upon factual findings and evidence that the Committee has virtually no capacity to gather or evaluate. A similar criticism could be raised about the Committee's "concerns" over allegedly unabated corporal punishment in schools, sexual trafficking and non-consensual mental health treatments — such events do certainly occur but to what degree and under what circumstances? Probably to the surprise of many Americans, somewhere around 19 states still allow some forms of corporal punishment in public schools. The Federal Department of Education estimates that as many as 200,000 children, mostly boys aged between 13–16, were paddled in 2010 — the vast majority in rural areas of Mississippi, Arkansas, Alabama and Texas.[109] You and I might believe that paddling a child for discipline or punishment is a terrible policy but, as practiced and applied, is it a violation of international human rights under the CPRC? More importantly perhaps, the critical question is not whether bad things like domestic violence, homelessness or private discrimination happen but rather how the government responds and takes measures to prevent their occurrence.

On a number of occasions the Committee also appears to involve itself in what critics might reasonably view as policy issues outside the parameters of the express treaty obligations. For example, the Committee expresses its view that disenfranchising felons violates Articles 25 and 26 of the CPRC. Yet, Articles 25 & 26 say nothing whatsoever about when or if a state may disenfranchise a citizen for committing a crime. While one might well agree that the policy is wrong headed and unfair, is it within the authority of the HRC to decide that disallowing the vote of a person because of a felony conviction violates the CCPR? Are such issues properly part of "international policy" reflected in the intended obligations created by the treaty? Similarly, the Committee expresses "concerns" that the United States has failed its treaty obligations by virtue of de facto racial segregation, stand your ground laws, prosecution of illegal aliens, denial of government subsidized health insurance to illegal aliens, and voter eligibility requirements. Yet nothing in the Convention appears to expressly address any of these social issues — all issues deeply imbued with public policy and competing domestic points of view. Absent textual direction, upon

---

109. These statistics appear on the website, corpun.com, which is focused on world-wide corporal punishment research.

what basis does the Committee's expression of concern rest? Is the Committee's interpretation and application of general principles in the treaty binding and authoritative on the various states and the U.S. Congress? Does the Committee have either the legal authority or institutional competency to render such judgments?

On the other hand, if the Committee is overly cautious and narrow in its approach can the treaty serve to promote improved human rights conditions? How could the Committee not call on the U.S. federal government to intervene in matters of police brutality directed at racial minorities? Even if a government has taken many positive steps to respect human rights can it not always do better? All of these questions raise a critical concern for U.N. treaty based bodies: How can the Committees ensure credibility with state parties and yet maintain an effective and critical voice? These observations about the Committee's conclusions demonstrate the difficulties of its task, especially in light of its limited institutional capacities and member state recalcitrance.

d. Shadow Reports & NGO Participation

Given that the state party is self-reporting on its own human rights record it should not be surprising that reports sometimes lack substance and candor. To its credit, the United States has to some degree provided relatively specific and somewhat self-critical reports. This is not, however, the norm. The reporting process is replete with white washing and what might be described as "hollow formalism" — states providing self-serving descriptions of the idyllic human rights conditions within their borders and comprehensive legal protections which are not actually enforced. The committees have combated this problem by allowing the submission and consideration of information collected by NGO's and independent observers. Often prepared as "Shadow Reports," this independent source of information about human rights conditions is undoubtedly essential to the various committees' work. Shadow reports frequently challenge misleading government assertions, add information omitted and provide information on specific alleged violations. They can provide committees with information critical to challenging a state's human rights record and pressing for improvement.

You can find a series of shadow reports prepared for the HRC's review of U.S. periodic reports on the website of the NGO "US Human Rights Network." These reports, which are organized, coordinated and summarized for submission by this NGO from a variety of sources, cover a wide range of topics relating to rights under the Covenant on Civil and Political Rights including critiques of the criminal justice system, voting rights, human trafficking, juveniles in adult prisons, racial profiling, food insecurity, to Guantanamo Bay's indefinite detainees. There is little doubt that this summary, and other shadow reports, legitimately call out both state and federal governments for potential violations of the treaty. It is also apparent, however, that NGOs submitting shadow reports also frequently have their own agendas and political perspectives. Domestic policy debates are often conflated with international human rights aspirations and norms that lack specific definitional content. The reports are, in essence, advocacy.

Peruse the following excerpts from the Human Rights Network's most recent summary of shadow reports that the group submitted to the HRC regarding the U.S. 2014 periodic report. A short excerpt from the group's shadow report to CERD, the Committee that monitors the Convention on the Elimination of Racial Discrimination is also included. The reports make some well-founded allegations and observations that provide the Committees with critical information. You may or may not agree with some of the assertions made in these excerpts as a matter of fact (the Shadow Report alleges, for example, 3000 unpunished "homicides" by law enforcement, and that the U.S. government is using the civil rights legislation to suppress the speech of pro-Palestinian viewpoints) or social policy (pregnant defendants should never be shackled nor illegal immigrants detained). More importantly, however, you should evaluate whether you believe that the assertions of human rights violations represent reasonable interpretations of U.S. treaty obligations. For example, do such obligations prevent states from reducing early voting periods, as alleged in the Report? Keep in mind that the very purpose of a shadow report is advocacy for improved human rights conditions. Given the committees' limited resources, they must necessarily rely heavily on such sources of information that are, at least, independent of the government itself.

i. Illustrative Shadow Reports

a. Shadow Report Submissions Compiled by the U.S. Human Rights Network (on behalf of Member and Partner Organizations) While USHRN recognizes the positive steps the U.S. has made towards the advancement of human rights, it remains concerned about the general trend of the country and the large number of individuals whose rights as provided for under the CCPR remain unprotected, in particular the racial, ethnic, gender, and class disparities that persist in the enjoyment of those rights. The following summary outlines the main points from the 30 shadow reports that comprise this joint submission, and emphasizes shortcomings in the United States' implementation of its fundamental human rights obligations under the CCPR.

A. Constitutional and Legal Framework within which the Covenant is Implemented (art. 2).

Issues 1 and 2: Implementation of the CCPR

A central issue in the United States' failure to fully recognize and implement human rights is the absence of a domestic human rights infrastructure that reaches all levels of government.

\*\*\*

Issue 4: Racial Disparities in the Criminal Justice System

Discrimination and racial disparities persist at every stage of the criminal justice system in the United States. The government continues to create, foster, and perpetuate these inequalities in violation of its obligations Article 2 and Article 26 of the CCPR to ensure all its citizens, regardless of race, are treated equally under the law. Racial minorities, particularly African-American males, are proportionately affected by the U.S. criminal justice system, which is the largest — and maintains the highest incarceration rate — in the world.

As noted in the Joint Submission, Report of the Sentencing Project to the United Nations Human Rights Committee Regarding Racial Disparities in the United States Criminal Justice System, "[r]acial minorities are more likely than white Americans to be arrested; once arrested, they are more likely to be convicted; and once convicted, they are more likely to face stiff sentences."

***

## Issue 5: Racial Profiling

Particularly problematic is the law enforcement practice known as "stop and frisk," which is commonly employed by the New York Police Department (NYPD) — the largest police force in the United States. As noted in the joint submission, Stopped Seized and Under Siege, "[s]tops are both unlawful and discriminatory as they occur overwhelmingly without the reasonable, articulable suspicion of criminal activity as required by the law and at an alarming rate in communities of color. . . ."***

Immigration enforcement policies in the United States frequently result in racial discrimination and profiling of racial and ethnic minority populations in the country. ***

## Issue 6: Criminalization of People Living on the Streets

State policies of criminalization of homelessness routinely penalize individuals for their involuntary status in violation of their right to be free from discrimination under Article 2 and the CCPR.

***

## Issue 7: Access of Undocumented Migrants to Health Services and Higher Education Institutions.

***

## Additional Considerations

Hate Crimes: *** Through systemic failures, such as inadequate data collection and severe underreporting, limited training of law enforcement to investigate and document hate crimes and a failure to devote adequate resources, the U.S. Government has failed to protect minority communities from hate crimes.

Food Insecurity: *** The outcomes of racialized policies in other domains, such as housing, education, transportation, and income, have led to food insecurity among low-income households and people of color. ***

Issue 8: Death Penalty

\*\*\* The death penalty system has wrongfully convicted and sentenced innocent persons to death, executing at least ten individuals despite strong evidence of their innocence. \*\*\*

Racial bias is pervasive in the application of the death penalty in the United States . . . .

Issue 9: Gun Violence

United States "Stand Your Ground" (SYG) laws extend immunity to prosecution or civil suit for the use of deadly force in self-defense beyond the home, without imposing a duty to retreat. SYG laws are overbroad and prone to amplifying existing racial biases. . . . In Florida, data has shown that in cases in which SYG was raised as a defense, a defendant who killed a white person was two times more likely to be convicted of a crime than when a defendant killed an African American person. \*\*\*

Extrajudicial killings and excessive uses of force by U.S. law enforcement officers violates, among others, the inherent right to life (Article 6) and the right to be free from torture or cruel, inhumane or degrading punishment or treatment (Article 7). From the years 2003 to 2009, nearly 3,000 homicides were committed by U.S. law enforcement officers against members of the civilian population, of whom a disproportionate percentage were African American. Police officers have and continue to use excessive force, sexual assault, and other inhuman and degrading treatment, as well as torture, as a means to coerce confessions, including threatening and often dropping detainees in unknown or rival neighborhoods.

\*\*\*

Additional Considerations

**Fukishima Daiichi Disaster Response:** The U.S. Government has failed to address the human rights, particularly the inherent right to life, of communities living in the direct path of a jet stream coming from three Fukushima Daiichi nuclear power plants in Fukushima Prefecture, Japan. . . .

\*\*\*

Reproductive Rights and Abortion:

\*\*\* While bans on abortion harm all women, they have a disproportionate impact on marginalized women, including those who are poor, young, less educated, women of color, and those without access to health insurance or affordable care.

\*\*\*

Issue 16: Treatment of Persons Deprived of Their Liberty

The United States is one of the few countries in the world that continues to shackle pregnant women, a practice that increases substantial medical risks of childbirth and is a painful, demeaning, and needlessly punitive practice that is rarely necessary for safety.***

## Issue 18: Juveniles in Adult Facilities

Youth in the United States continue to be subjected to adult criminal sentences and incarceration in adult facilities despite federal prohibitions against these practices.

***

## Issue 19: Detention of Immigrants

*** The U.S. Government imposes mandatory detention for a wide array of cases, including asylum seekers, others in expedited removal, or persons with criminal convictions, without discretion to release . . . . Mandatory detention for asylum seekers risks re-traumatization of refugees who are already in a psychologically delicate state.

***

## Issue 19 Recommendations

Halt the practice of prosecuting in the criminal justice system, aliens charged with immigration offenses such as unlawful entry.

***

## Additional Considerations

Access to Counsel in Civil Cases: Because a categorical right to counsel in civil cases is not recognized under the federal Constitution, millions of poor and low-income people in the United States are unable to obtain legal representation in facing a crisis such as eviction, domestic violence, workplace discrimination, termination of subsistence income, medical assistance, or loss of child custody . . . .

***

## F. Freedom of Speech and Expression (art. 19)

The U.S. Government continues to use Title VI of the Civil Rights Act to suppress pro-Palestinian viewpoints on college and university campuses by making the unsupported argument that speech critical of Israeli state policies is anti-Semitic.

***

## H. Right to Take Part in the Conduct of Public Affairs (art. 25) Issue 26: Voting Rights (persons with felony convictions, voter disenfranchisement, residents of Washington, D.C.)

***

Several U.S. states retain laws and practices that severely restrict access to voting in contravention of the right to take part in the conduct of public affairs (Article 25) and nondiscrimination principles under Article 2 of the CCPR. These restrictions, which disproportionately affect low-income individuals and racial minorities, include restrictive identification requirements, highly inaccurate lists of individuals to be removed from voter rolls, restrictions on community-based voter registration drives, long waiting lines up to seven hours in some locations, and attempts to cut early in-person voting by several days.

***

The following excerpts from the Summary Shadow Report of the U.S. Human Rights network to the Committee on the Elimination of Racial Discrimination argue that the treaty requires the United States to address non-intentional discriminatory effects[110] and adopt affirmative action programs. It also suggests that law school admission criteria, bar licensing tests, and U.S. agencies' law school accreditation practices have a disparate impact on minorities, thus violating the treaty.

## ii. U.S. Human Rights Network Shadow Report on U.S. Report to CERD

### Art. 1(1) Definition of Discrimination

6. Contrary to the Convention, United States law defines racial discrimination too narrowly. With few exceptions, cognizable racial discrimination requires evidence of *intent* to discriminate. This requirement is contrary to the Convention's framework and does not reflect the real-world operation of discriminatory behavior in contemporary American society. ***

### Art. 1(4) Special measures for "adequate advancement" to ensure equal enjoyment or exercise of human rights and fundamental freedoms

20. Article 1(4) requires a States party to adopt special measures, i.e. affirmative action, as long as circumstances warrant such measures. In 2001, this Committee noted "the persistence of the discriminatory effects of the legacy of slavery, segregation, and destructive policies with regard to Native Americans." This legacy led the Committee to conclude that African Americans and Native Americans are especially vulnerable to contemporary manifestations of past discrimination. These are the types of circumstances for which the Convention deems "special measures" to be warranted to ensure "adequate advancement" for these especially vulnerable populations.

21. Special measures, however, are currently under attack based on notions of rights that are at odds with the Convention's requirements. The use of voter referenda to prohibit states from adopting race-based affirmative action measures is on the rise. While the States party claims its ability to act is

---

110. The Report doesn't appear to distinguish between federal statutory prohibitions on discrimination, which in fact do not always require intent, from Constitutional violations under the equal protection clause.

limited by the principles of federalism and state's rights, it is the duty of all U.S. Government authorities to act in conformity with and to take *affirmative measures* to meet the requirements under the Convention.

***

23. The legal profession provides a particularly sharp picture the continuing need for "special measures." In California, one of the most multi-racial states in the United States, the legal profession is now more that eighty percent white although whites comprise only forty-five percent of the population. The numbers in California are consistent with national trends and data. Persistent barriers to inclusion of racial minorities in the legal profession in the United States constitute race discrimination in education and in employment and lack of equality before the law and in the administration of justice. The serious under-representation of racial minorities in the legal profession is caused in part by continuing overuse of law school admissions and attorney licensing tests with significant disparate impacts on African Americans, Hispanics, and Asian-Americans. Instead of addressing the racial imbalance in the legal profession or the misuse of these discriminatory tests, the United States government, through the Department of Education and, ironically, the Civil Rights Commission, is using its control over accreditation of law schools to undermine efforts to establish greater racial diversity in legal education and in the legal profession.***

e. Other Examples of NGO Shadow Reporting

## i. Center for Reproductive Rights

### Shadow Letter on Nicaragua to the Committee on the Rights of the Child>

**09.27.10** - In September, the Center submitted a shadow letter to the Committee on the Rights of the Child on the situation of sexual and reproductive rights of children and adolescents in Nicaragua. Nicaragua is reporting to the Committee during its 55th session. The shadow letter highlights . . .

### Shadow Letter on Uganda to the CEDAW Committee>

**09.27.10** - In September, the Center submitted a shadow letter to the Committee on the Elimination of Discrimination against Women (CEDAW Committee) on the situation of sexual and reproductive rights in Uganda. Uganda is reporting to the CEDAW Committee during its 47th session in October 2010. . . .

### Shadow Letter: Supplementary Information on Nigeria to the Committee on the Rights of the Child>

**07.08.10** - This letter is intended to supplement the combined third and fourth periodic report submitted by the Federal Republic of Nigeria, which is scheduled to be reviewed by the Committee on the Rights of the Child (the Committee) during its 54th session. . . .

*Report on the United States' Compliance with Its Human Rights Obligations In the Area of Women's Reproductive and Sexual Health>*

**06.01.10** - The United Nations Human Rights Council has introduced a process designed to review countries' compliance with human rights obligations as contained in (1) the Universal Declaration of Human Rights; (2) the United Nations Charter; (3) human rights treaties to which the country is a State Party. . . .

ii. European Network Against Racism

**2012/13 Shadow Reports on racism & discrimination in employment in Europe**

ENAR published a European and twenty-three country-specific Shadow Reports in March 2014, with the support of PROGRESS (2007–2013), the Open Society Foundations and ENAR Foundation.

**Racism and discrimination in employment in Europe — ENAR Shadow Report 2012–13**

iii. International Women's Rights Action Watch: **Shadow Reports on CEDAW**

# 2. Consideration of individual complaints and communications

a. Overview

In addition to the reporting procedure, many of the U.N. Treaty-based Committees can, under certain conditions, receive petitions from individuals who claim that their treaty based rights have been violated. These include — try sorting out this little taste of alphabet soup: HRC, CERD, CAT, CEDAW, CRC, CESCR, CRD, CMW, and CRPD. Critical among these conditions are the requirements that the state party has consented to the process, the petitioner has exhausted domestic remedies, and the complaint is not already pending before other international forums. Two committees, CAT and CEDAW, may also initiate an "inquiry" directed to a state party based on "reliable information" concerning "systematic violations." The following description of the individual petitioning mechanisms is found on the U.N. High Commissioner's website:

Human Rights Bodies — Complaints Procedures

**Complaining about human rights violations**

The ability of individuals to complain about the violation of their rights in an international arena brings real meaning to the rights contained in the human rights treaties.

There are three main procedures for bringing complaints of violations of the provisions of the human rights treaties before the human rights treaty bodies:

- individual communications;
- state-to-state complaints; and
- inquiries.

There are also procedures for complaints which fall outside of the treaty body system — through the Special Procedures of the Human Rights Council and the Human Rights Council Complaint Procedure.

[Author's note: Details about these Charter based complaint procedures can be found in Chapter 7.]

**Individual Communications**

There are nine core international human rights treaties. Each of these treaties has established a "treaty body" (Committee) of experts to monitor implementation of the treaty provisions by its States parties.

Treaty bodies (CCPR, CERD, CAT, CEDAW, CRPD, CED, CMW, CESCR, and CRC) may, under certain conditions, consider individual complaints or communications from individuals.

**Not all treaty body based complaint mechanisms have entered into force.**

Currently, seven of the human rights treaty bodies (CCPR, CERD, CAT, CEDAW, CRPD, CED, and CESCR) may, under certain conditions, receive and consider individual complaints or communications from individuals:

The **Human Rights Committee (CCPR)** may consider individual communications alleging violations of the rights set forth in the International Covenant on Civil and Political Rights by States parties to the First Optional Protocol to the International Covenant on Civil and Political Rights;

The **Committee on Elimination of Discrimination Against Women (CEDAW)** may consider individual communications alleging violations of the Convention on the Elimination of All Forms of Discrimination against Women by States parties to the Optional Protocol to the Convention on the Elimination of Discrimination against Women;

The **Committee Against Torture (CAT)** may consider individual complaints alleging violations of the rights set out in the Convention against Torture and Other Cruel, Inhuman or Degrading Treatment or Punishment by States parties who have made the necessary declaration under article 22 of the Convention;

The **Committee on the Elimination of Racial Discrimination (CERD)** may consider individual petitions alleging violations of the International Convention on the Elimination of All Forms of Racial Discrimination by States parties who have made the necessary declaration under article 14 of the Convention;

The **Committee on the Rights of Persons with Disabilities (CRPD)** may consider individual communications alleging violations of the Convention on the Rights of Persons with Disabilities by States parties to the Optional Protocol to the Convention;

The **Committee on Enforced Disappearances (CED)** may consider individual communications alleging violations of the International Convention for the Protection of All Persons from Enforced Disappearance by States parties who have made the necessary declaration under article 31 of the Convention.

The **Committee on Economic, Social and Cultural Rights (CESCR)** may consider individual communications alleging violations of the International Covenant on Economic, Social and Cultural Rights by States parties to the Optional Protocol to the International Covenant on Economic, Social and Cultural Rights.

**For two other treaty bodies** (the **Committee on Migrant Workers (CMW)**, and the **Committee on the Rights of the Child (CRC)**) the individual complaint mechanisms **have not yet entered into force**.

Article 77 of the International Convention on the Protection of the Rights of All Migrant Workers and Members of Their Families gives the Committee on Migrant Workers (CMW) competence to receive and consider individual communications alleging violations of the Convention by States parties who made the necessary declaration under article 77. This individual complaint mechanism will become operative when ten states parties have made the necessary declaration under article 77. For status of ratifications, click here.

[Author's Note: As of June, 2014, only two states have made an article 77 declaration.]

The Optional Protocol (on a communications procedure) to the Convention on the Rights of the Child gives competence to the Committee on the Rights of the Child (CRC) to receive and consider individual communications alleging violations of the Convention on the Rights of the Child and its Protocols (OPSC, OPAC) by States parties to the Optional Protocol (on a communications procedure). This individual complaint procedure will become operative when 10 states parties have ratified the Optional Protocol (on a communications procedure). For status of ratifications, click here.

[Author's Note: CRC Individual Communication Procedures came into effect April 14, 2014.]

*Who can complain?*

Anyone can lodge a complaint with a Committee against a State:

- That is party to the treaty in question (through ratification or accession) providing for the rights which have allegedly been violated;
- That accepted the Committee's competence to examine individual complaints, either through ratification or accession to an Optional Protocol (in the case of CCPR, CEDAW, CRPD, CESCR, and CRC) or by making a declaration to that effect under a specific article of the Convention (in the case of CERD, CAT, CED, and CMW).

Complaints may also be brought by third parties on behalf of individuals, provided they have given their written consent (without requirement as to its specific form). In certain cases, a third party may bring a case without such consent, for example, where a person is in prison without access to the outside world or is a victim of an enforced disappearance. In such cases, the author of the complaint should state clearly why such consent cannot be provided.

For more information on how to complain under the treaty bodies' complaint procedures, click here.

### Inter-State Complaints

Several of the human rights treaties contain provisions to allow for State parties to complain to the relevant treaty body (Committee) about alleged violations of the treaty by another State party.

**Note**: These procedures have never been used.

***

### Inquiries

Upon receipt of reliable information on serious, grave, or systematic violations by a State party of the conventions they monitor, the Committee Against Torture (article 20 CAT), the Committee on the Elimination of Discrimination Against Women (article 8 of the Optional Protocol to CEDAW), the Committee on the Rights of Persons with Disabilities (article 6 Optional Protocol to CRPD), the Committee on Enforced Disappearances (article 33 of CED), the Committee on Economic, Social and Cultural Rights (article 11 of the Optional Protocol to CESCR) and the Committee on the Rights of the Child (article 13 of the Optional Protocol (on a communications procedure) to CRC; Protocol not yet in force) may, on their own initiative, initiate inquiries if they have received reliable information containing well-founded indications of serious or systematic violations of the conventions in a State party.

*Which States may be subject to inquiries?*

Inquiries may only be undertaken with respect to States parties who have recognized the competence of the relevant Committee in this regard. States parties may opt out, at the time of signature, ratification, or accession (article 28 CAT; article 10 of the Optional Protocol to CEDAW; article 8 of the Optional Protocol to CRPD; article 13(7) of the Optional Protocol (on a communications procedure) to CRC), or anytime (article 11(8) of the Optional Protocol to CESCR) by making a declaration that they do not recognize the competence of the Committee in question to undertake inquiries.

*Inquiry Procedure*

1. The procedure may be initiated if the Committee receives reliable information indicating that the rights contained in the Convention it monitors are being systematically violated by the State party.

2. The Committee invites the State party to co-operate in the examination of the information by submitting observations.

3. The Committee may, on the basis of the State party's observations and other relevant information available to it, decide to designate one or more of its members to conduct an inquiry and report urgently to the Committee. Where warranted and with the consent of the State party concerned, an inquiry may include a visit to its territory.

4. The findings of the member(s) are then examined by the Committee and transmitted to the State party together with any comments and recommendations.

5. The State party is requested to submit its own observations on the Committee's findings, comments, and recommendations within a specific time frame (usually six months) and, where invited by the Committee, to inform it of the measures taken in response to the inquiry.

6. The inquiry procedure is confidential and the cooperation of the State party shall be sought at all stages of the proceedings.

b. Treaty Based Complaint Procedures: The Process

Each Committee determines its own processes for considering individual complaints. The U.N. OHCHR provides linked descriptions these various processes on its website under "Human Rights Bodies — Individual Communications." This webpage also includes "How to direct complains to the treaty bodies — Contact details." More detail, including model complaint forms, can typically be found on each Committee's webpage within the U.N. system: CCPR | CESCR | CEDAW | CERD | CRC | CRPD | CAT | SPT | CMW | CED . A good illustration of this is the webpage of the HRC, which provides a linked publication called "Fact Sheet 15." Fact Sheet 15 provides a fairly detailed description of the most important aspects of the Committee and its work, including the individual communications process. The webpage also provides a link to the current version of the Committee's "Rules of Procedure," which detail both the reporting process and individual communications brought under the Optional Protocol (Section XVII).

While there are some variations, most of the treaty based Committees utilize very similar processes that might be very loosely described as "quasi-judicial." Some important commonalities include exclusive reliance on written submissions of the alleged victim and accused state (no independent fact finding or oral hearings), interim measures in cases involving immediate irreparable harm, the ultimate expression of the Committee's "views" on the dispute including recommended remedies, and a "follow up" process encouraging state compliance. The HRC process is generally typical. Consider the following U.N. OHCHR description of how the HRC generally handles communications:

**Procedure Under the Optional Protocol to the International Covenant on Civil and Political Rights**

\*\*\*

### *Details of the procedure*

\*\*\*

If the case is registered, the Committee's usual course of action, given the large number of complaints received under this procedure, is to consider the admissibility and merits of the case simultaneously. To this end, the State party against whom the complaint is directed has six months to present its submissions on the admissibility and merits of the case. When it does so, you have two months to comment, following which the case is ready for a decision by the Committee. As noted above, if the State party fails to respond to your complaint, you are not disadvantaged. In such a case, the State party receives two reminders after the six-month deadline has passed. If there is still no reply, the Committee considers the complaint on the basis of the information you initially supplied. On the other hand, if the State party presents submissions after a reminder, they are transmitted to you and you have the opportunity to comment.

\*\*\*

You should be aware that, given the large number of cases brought under the Optional Protocol, there may be a delay of several years between the initial submission and the Committee's final decision.

### *Special circumstances of urgency*

For the Human Rights Committee, situations of urgency requiring immediate action fall under Rule 86 of its rules of procedure. In such cases, the Committee's Special Rapporteur on New Communications may issue a request to the State party for interim measures with a view to averting irreparable harm before your complaint is considered. The Committee views compliance with such a request as inherent in a State party's obligations under the Optional Protocol and any failure to comply as a breach thereof.

### *Additional pointers on the admissibility of your case*

\*\*\*

Two points may be made regarding the question of simultaneous examination of the same claim under another mechanism of international settlement. The Committee has decided that, for its purposes, the "1503 procedure" (described later in this Fact Sheet) and complaints to a special rapporteur of the Commission on Human Rights do not constitute such a mechanism. Accordingly, your claim to the Human Rights Committee will not be declared inadmissible if you are concurrently pursuing options such as these. Second, the Committee has taken the view that, inasmuch as the Covenant provides greater protection in some respects than is available under other international instruments, facts that have already been submitted to another international mechanism can be brought before the Committee if broader protections in the Covenant are invoked. It should be added that, in the Committee's view, complaints dismissed by other international mechanisms on procedural grounds have not been substantively examined; the same facts may, therefore, be brought before the Committee.

### *After the Committee's decision — some further remarks*

When the Committee decides that you have been the victim of a violation by the State party of your rights under the Covenant, the State is invited to provide information, within three months, on the steps it has taken to give effect to the Committee's views. The basis for this requirement is that the State party, in article 2, paragraph 3, of the Covenant, has guaranteed you an effective remedy for any violation of your rights. Its response will be transmitted to you for comment. The Committee often indicates what an appropriate remedy would be, for instance payment of compensation or release from detention. In the event of failure by the State party to take appropriate steps, the case is referred to a member of the Committee, the Special Rapporteur on Follow-up of Views, for consideration of further measures to be taken. The Special Rapporteur may, for example, issue specific requests to the State party or meet with its representatives to discuss the action taken. Unless, exceptionally, the information is suppressed, it is published together with the action taken by the Special Rapporteur in an annual report on follow-up.

When the Committee considers your case admissible, either in general or with reference to specific claims or articles, the State party is requested to present its submissions on the merits within six months. You then have a two-month period to comment on the submissions, following which the case is usually ready for consideration by the Committee.

The U.N. website also describes and provides practical advice and informational links about the process by which complaints may be filed under the various treaties:

The complaint mechanisms are designed to be accessible to the layperson. It is not necessary to be a lawyer or even familiar with legal and technical terms to bring a complaint under the treaties concerned.

Overview of individual complaints procedures

Against whom can a complaint under a treaty be brought?

Who can bring a complaint?

What information do you need to provide to bring a complaint?

When can you make a complaint under the human rights treaties?

The procedure

Special circumstances of urgency and sensitivity

The admissibility of your case

The merits of your case

<u>Consideration of your case</u>

<u>What happens once the Committee decides your case?</u>

[Authors' Note: All of these links are to different parts of the same webpage.]

If you are interested in learning more about the "how to" aspects of the individual petitioning processes, visit either the above U.N. webpage, or this <u>alternative web site</u> (Professor Bayefsky). UNESCO has also posted a <u>useful 200 page guide</u> to the various complaint processes.

c. Illustrative Committee Decisions

i. Overview

As of 2014, the treaty based committees have evaluated more than 3000 thousand individual complaints. The busiest committee, by far, is the HRC. As of August 2014, the HRC had considered 2271 petitions, declared its "views" in 1008 cases (850 finding a treaty violation), found 620 petitions "inadmissible," and is in the process of reviewing 388 "live" complaints. (See "<u>statistical survey</u>" at the HCR website. The NGO "Center for Civil and Political Rights" also provides a very <u>useful database</u> that organizes the HRC's decisions by country, article and subject matter.) Under its optional Article 22 procedures, <u>CAT has received</u> 570 petitions regarding 38 countries, expressing views in 221 cases. Curiously, these include a significant number of petitions filed against such notorious human rights violators as Switzerland (150 complaints), Sweden (116 complaints), and Canada (93 complaints) — perhaps alleging primarily inhuman and degrading treatment rather than torture. CAT reports that it is currently considering 124 pending petitions. Other treaty bodies with complaint procedures have been far less active. For example, <u>CEDAW has only decided</u> 16 cases and has 26 petitions pending. <u>CERD has decided</u> 30 cases and has only 6 pending. As Committees decide cases they also develop a form of legal <u>jurisprudence</u> regarding the Committees' interpretation of the treaty. Most, including the HRC, have begun to consolidate and organize this jurisprudence and make it available on their websites.

The following excerpt is from the HRC's concluding views regarding a petition against Venezuela brought by <u>Eligio Cedeño</u>. Cedeño was a prominent banker in Caracas who, he alleges, was the victim of retaliation by the government for his support of opposition candidates and other leaders. He is the same banker that Judge María Lourdes Afiuni released on bail after several years in detention without trial, thereby prompted her own prolonged detention without trial (recall facts provided at the beginning of this chapter). Omitted from the excerpt is the Committee's lengthy and detailed description of the factual allegations made by both the petitioner and Venezuela. In typical fashion, the Committee recites facts alleged by the petitioner, the government's responses and the petitioner's counter-responses but does not engage in independent fact finding, oral testimony, or argumentation.

The short version of the story goes like this. The petitioner was indicted in 2005 by the Attorney General's Office on charges of smuggling and tax evasion relating to transactions involving a subsidiary of the Banco Canarias that allegedly violated foreign exchange controls. On February 7, 2007, the Attorney General's Office applied to a "provisional" judge (a judge who is subject to dismissal without cause by the government) for Cedeño's pretrial detention, on new charges alleging embezzlement for having improperly used currency. Although he had voluntarily appeared in court, the judge ordered detention pending trial reasoning that there was a risk that Cedeño would abscond since he was wealthy and owned an aircraft.

The subsequent events giving rise to Cedeño's claims before the HRC involve the lengthy pre-trial detention caused by government delay and interference with the various courts and judges involved in the process. For example, at the preliminary stage of the trial, two judges recused themselves due to governmental pressures including a letter from the President of the Supreme Court threatening their dismissal. Trial proceedings began in March 2008, but after the evidence had been presented and closing arguments scheduled, the prosecution failed to appear in court without explanation. The Attorney General's Office then requested a two-year extension of the period of pre-trial detention without providing explanation or supporting reasons.

In 2009, the petitioner sought the help of the United Nations Working Group on Arbitrary Detention and the Special Rapporteur on the Independence of Judges and Lawyers (please recall these "specialized" procedures associated with the Charter-based Human Rights Council). Later in 2009, the Supreme Court agreed that the indictment was flawed and that the proceeding had violated the petitioner's right to a legal defense but did not order his release. A new indictment followed and another provisional judge added two additional years of allowable pre-trial detention. On September 1, 2009, the Working Group on Arbitrary Detention (with other U.N. mandate holders) found that the government had caused undue delay in the proceedings, and that Cedeño's pre-trial detention without bail, which exceeded the maximum term established under Venezuelan law, violated articles 9, 10, and 11 of the Universal Declaration of Human Rights and articles 9, 10, and 14 of the International Covenant on Civil and Political Rights, and was therefore arbitrary. Opinion No. 10/2009. (The Working Group also later found that Judge Afiuni's detention was arbitrary and involved improper interference with the judiciary.) At this point, after almost 3 years in detention without trial, Cedeño was brought before Judge Afiuni, who had been randomly assigned to resume the prosecution. She released Cedeño on bail and he promptly fled to the United States where he was granted political asylum. The excerpt below takes up the events from there and the international human rights claims those events engendered.

ii. Cedeño v. Venezuela

CCPR/C/106/D/1940/2010

**Human Rights Committee, Communication No. 1940/2010**

**Views adopted by the Committee at its 106th session (15 October–2 November 2012)**

**Submitted by: Eligio Cedeño**

**State party: Bolivarian Republic of Venezuela**

**Views under article 5, paragraph 4, of the Optional Protocol**

The facts as submitted by the author

\*\*\*

2.16 Subsequently, the thirty-first "control court" of first instance (the court responsible for the investigative and preliminary phases) of the criminal judicial circuit of the Caracas Metropolitan Area (Court No. 31) was selected at random to hear the case against the author [Cedeño]. On 10 December 2009, in view of the opinion of the Working Group on Arbitrary Detention, the absence of any risk of flight and the failure of the prosecution to appear on two consecutive occasions, the judge modified the precautionary measure of pretrial detention, ordering the author's release on condition that he report to the court every two weeks and did not leave the country, and ordering him to relinquish his passport.

2.17 Having learned of this measure and of the author's release, officers of the Intelligence and Prevention Services Directorate raided Court No. 31 and arrested all those present without a warrant, including the judge, Ms. M.L.A. [Afiuni], and two bailiffs. The judge was taken to the Directorate's headquarters. On 11 December 2009, it was reported that an order for the judge's detention had been issued by the first control court of the criminal judicial circuit of the Caracas Metropolitan Area. At the same time, the police attempted to find and detain the author even though they had no court order. The author's defence lawyers were subjected to intimidation. One of them was arrested and taken to the headquarters of the Military Intelligence Directorate where he was questioned for two days. On 11 December 2009, the President of the Republic referred to the author's case in a radio and television programme on a national channel, calling him a "bandit" and accusing him of having "fled". He also referred to the judge as a "bandit", insinuated that she was corrupt and called for her to be sentenced to 30 years' imprisonment. He stated that the lawyers defending the author had committed an offence in allegedly preparing in advance the decision issued by the judge. Lastly, he called for the President of the Supreme Court and the National Assembly to make the legislative amendments necessary to allow for the maximum sentence to be imposed upon the judge.

2.18 On 12 December 2009, the Attorney-General's Office indicted Judge M.L.A. before Control Court No. 50 on charges of corruption, assisting an escape, conspiracy and abuse of power.

\*\*\*

Issues and proceedings before the Committee

Consideration of admissibility

6.1 Before considering any claim contained in a communication, the Human Rights Committee must decide, in accordance with rule 93 of its rules of procedure, whether the communication is admissible under the Optional Protocol to the Covenant.

6.2 Under article 5, paragraph 2 (a), of the Optional Protocol, the Committee must ascertain that the same matter is not being examined under another procedure of international investigation or settlement. *** As the Working Group on Arbitrary Detention had already concluded its consideration of the case before the present communication was submitted to the Committee, the Committee will not address the issue of whether consideration of a case by the Working Group is "another procedure of international investigation or settlement" under article 5, paragraph 2 (a), of the Optional Protocol. Consequently, the Committee considers that there are no obstacles to the admissibility of the communication under article 5, paragraph 2 (b), of the Optional Protocol.

6.3 As for the exhaustion of domestic remedies, the Committee notes that the complaints submitted by the author under articles 9 and 14 of the Covenant relate to the proceedings against him, which have been in the investigation phase since the author was indicted by the Attorney-General's Office in 2005. Since the issue of the exhaustion of domestic remedies is intimately linked to the substantive issues, the Committee considers that article 5, paragraph 2 (b), of the Optional Protocol is not an obstacle to the admissibility of the communication.

6.4 The Committee takes note of the author's allegations concerning article 14, paragraph 3 (a) of the Covenant that he was not promptly informed of the charges of which he had been accused *** The Committee notes that the author challenged the legality of these acts before the courts and that as a result, on 7 May 2009 the Supreme Court ruled that the author had not been properly charged for embezzlement and annulled the proceedings related to this offence. In view of this decision, the Committee considers that the author's complaint was properly dealt with by the authorities of the State party and that, consequently, his submission to the Committee is unfounded. The Committee therefore considers that this complaint is inadmissible under article 2 of the Optional Protocol.

6.5 With regard to the right to have adequate time and facilities for the preparation of his defence (art. 14, para. 3 (b)), *** the Committee considers that the author, who had legal assistance throughout, has not provided detailed information on how the preparation of his defence was obstructed or hindered and how access was denied to decisive evidence. Consequently, the Committee considers that this complaint has not been sufficiently substantiated for the purposes of admissibility either, and declares that it too is inadmissible under article 2 of the Optional Protocol.

6.6 The Committee considers, therefore, that the author has sufficiently substantiated his claims under articles 9 and 14 paragraphs 1, 2, and 3 (c) of the Covenant, for the purposes of admissibility. The other admissibility requirements having been met, the Committee considers the communication admissible and proceeds to its examination on the merits.

Consideration of the merits

7.1 The Human Rights Committee has considered the present communication in the light of all the information made available to it by the parties, as required under article 5, paragraph 1, of the Optional Protocol.

7.2 With regard to the allegations in respect of article 14, paragraph 1, of the Covenant, the Committee notes that, according to the author, the judicial authorities who heard the case were not independent because the State party has imposed a system of provisional judges who are not secure in their positions and who can be removed at will without any predefined procedure; and that those who do not follow instructions from the executive branch are subject to reprisals. The Committee also takes note of the author's claims that the judges and prosecutors in his case were provisional, and that the judge presiding over Court No. 31, Ms. M.L.A., who ordered his release, acted in accordance with the law and, in retaliation, was arrested without a warrant immediately after doing so. ***

7.3 The Committee notes that the State party does not contest the provisional status of the judicial authorities involved in the proceedings against the author. The Committee also notes that the judge presiding over Court No. 31 was arrested on the same day as she ordered the release of the author and that on the following day the President of the Republic referred to her in the media as a "bandit" and suggested that she should be severely punished. The Committee recalls that States should take specific measures to guarantee the independence of the judiciary, protect judges from any form of political influence, and establish clear procedures and objective criteria for the appointment, remuneration, tenure, promotion, suspension, and dismissal of the members of the judiciary and for disciplinary sanctions against them. *** In view of this, together with the provisional nature of the judicial authorities involved in the proceedings against the author, the Committee concludes that in the case at hand the State party violated the independence of the judicial bodies involved and article 14, paragraph 1, of the Covenant.

7.4 With regard to the possible violation of article 14, paragraph 2, the Committee notes the author's claim that his right to be presumed innocent was not respected, since he was deprived of his liberty as a preventive measure even though none of the legal requirements for this action were satisfied, and that the proceedings against him were politically motivated. The Committee also notes that, after the author's release had been ordered, the President of the Republic called him a "bandit" on national radio and television and insinuated that his release had been illegally coordinated by his lawyers and the judge presiding over Court No. 31. The Committee has received no refutation or explanation of the President's statements from the State party. In this connection, the Committee recalls that the denial of bail does not affect the presumption of innocence. In general, all public authorities have a duty to refrain from prejudging the outcome of a trial, e.g. by abstaining from making public statements affirming the guilt of the accused. Consequently, as no judgement had been made as to the criminal liability of the author, the Committee considers that the direct reference to the author's case by the President of the Republic, and the form it took, violated the principle of the presumption of innocence, as set out in article 14, paragraph 2, of the Covenant, which applies to every accused person in the absence of a judgement to the contrary.

7.5  With regard to the author's claim in respect of article 14, paragraph 3 (c), that he was not tried within a reasonable time and without undue delay, the Committee takes note of the State party's arguments that it cannot be held responsible for the delay in the trial; ***

7.6  The Committee notes that the author was charged for the first time in 2005, formally indicted in March 2007 and held in pretrial detention from 8 February 2007 to 10 December 2009. When the communication was submitted, on 9 March 2010, no judgement had been made regarding his possible criminal liability, as the proceedings were at the stage of the preliminary hearing. The Committee also notes that the hearings were repeatedly suspended because no representative of the prosecution was in attendance, and because the author's request for cognizance by a higher court, submitted on 19 November 2008, was admitted by the Supreme Court seven months later, on 17 June 2008, and ruled upon 18 months later, on 7 May 2009.

7.7  The Committee recalls that the reasonableness of the delay in a trial has to be assessed in the circumstances of each case, taking into account the complexity of the case, the conduct of the accused and the manner in which the matter was dealt with by the administrative and judicial authorities. In the circumstances of this case, the Committee is of the view that the State party's observations do not adequately explain how the delays in the proceedings can be attributed to the conduct of the author or the complexity of the case. Consequently, the Committee considers that the proceedings against the author suffered from undue delay, contrary to the provisions of article 14, paragraph 3 (c), of the Covenant.

7.8  With regard to the alleged violations of article 9 of the Covenant, the Committee takes note of the author's claim that the pretrial detention order issued by Court No. 3 was arbitrary because it did not meet the requirements established by law; that he was not informed immediately of the charges against him which motivated his arrest; and that he did not have access to a rapid judicial review of the legality of his arrest within a reasonable period. Moreover, on completion of the maximum 2-year period of pretrial detention, on 8 February 2009, he was not released even though there were no serious grounds for refusing to do so and no formal decision in that respect. ***

7.9  The Committee notes that on 8 February 2007, when he learned that the Attorney-General's Office had ordered his pretrial detention, the author presented himself voluntarily to the authorities, who placed him in pretrial detention *** The Committee also notes that the maximum legal period of pretrial detention expired on 8 February 2009. However, the author was not released ***.

7.10  The Committee recalls that pretrial detention should be the exception and as short as possible. Also, pretrial detention must not only be lawful but also reasonable and necessary in all circumstances, for example to prevent flight, interference with the evidence or repetition of the crime. In the light of the information provided, the Committee considers that the State party has not given sufficient reasons, other than the mere assumption that he would try to abscond, to justify the initial pretrial detention of the author or its subsequent extension; nor has it explained why it could not take other measures to prevent his possible flight or why the detention order was not extended until months after the 2-year period had expired. Although it is true that in the end the author fled the country in spite of the arrest warrant issued by Court No. 31 on 18 December 2009, the Committee notes that it was the irregularities in the proceedings that prompted his flight, as recounted above. The Committee therefore concludes that the pretrial detention of the author violated article 9 of the Covenant.

8.  The Human Rights Committee, acting under article 5, paragraph 4, of the Optional Protocol to the International Covenant on Civil and Political Rights, is of the view that the information before it discloses a violation by the State party of articles 9 and 14, paragraphs 1, 2 and 3 (c), of the Covenant.

9.  In accordance with article 2, paragraph 3 (a), of the Covenant, the State party is under an obligation to provide the author with an effective remedy, including by: (a) if the author faces trial, ensuring the trial affords all the judicial guarantees provided for in article 14 of the Covenant; (b) assuring him that he will not be held in arbitrary detention for the duration of the proceedings; and (c) providing the author with redress, particularly in the form of appropriate compensation. The State party is also under an obligation to prevent similar violations in the future.

10.  Bearing in mind that, by becoming a party to the Optional Protocol, the State party has recognized the competence of the Committee to determine whether or not there has been a violation of the Covenant and that, pursuant to article 2 of the Covenant, the State party has undertaken to ensure to

all individuals within its territory or subject to its jurisdiction the rights recognized in the Covenant and to provide an effective and enforceable remedy when a violation has been established, the Committee wishes to receive from the State party, within 180 days, information about the measures taken to give effect to the Committee's Views. The State party is also requested to publish the present Views and to have them widely disseminated.

### d. Evaluating the Petition Process

How effective are the treaty based individual complaint processes? Do they serve useful functions? Are they credible and legitimate in terms of process, expertise, independence, accountability and authority? The answers to such questions depend, in part, on the criteria one uses. It also depends upon how one views the proper role and function of the committees. Even a voluminous caseload, followed by well-reasoned decisions would say little about the actual effectiveness of the petitioning processes absent evidence of state compliance. The record of the HRC is, in this regard, decidedly mixed. First, there is significant doubt about whether the final views of the committees are legally binding. The treaty itself does not say so and it appears that many states do not consider themselves bound to implement the HRC's views, or find it convenient to simply ignore them. Other states, and the HRC itself, reasonably dispute this conclusion on the premise that consent to the process implies mandatory compliance with the committee's views.[111] Either way, ambiguous legal authority hinders the effectiveness of the committee's work if measured by outcomes in which states modify their conduct.

Second, whether technically binding or not, there are currently no means of enforcing the committees' decisions. The only consequence of non-compliance is the limited moral suasion inherent in being called out in the Committee's annual report to the General Assembly. Remedies demanded by the Committee are strictly dependent upon the willingness of the state party to comply.

Third, the record of actual effective state compliance with committee views is, at best, spotty. Although questions of compliance are inherently subtle, it appears that most state parties have chosen to simply ignore the HRC without meaningful consequences.[112] Perhaps not surprisingly, this was precisely Venezuela's response to the Cedeño decision excerpted above. The HRC, to its credit, has become increasingly

---

111. The HRC typically includes in its views this statement which appears in the Cedeno case excerpt above:

> "Bearing in mind that, by becoming a party to the Optional Protocol, the State party has recognized the competence of the Committee to determine whether there has been a violation of the Covenant or not and that, pursuant to article 2 of the Covenant, the State party has undertaken to ensure to all individuals within its territory and subject to its jurisdiction the rights recognized in the Covenant and to provide an effective and enforceable remedy in case a violation has been established, the Committee wishes to receive from the State party, within 90 days, information about the measures taken to give effect to the Committee's Views."

112. The Civil and Political Rights Centre in Switzerland provides a database that purports to track state compliance on a case by case basis.

transparent about the problem of compliance and has instituted a follow process similar to that which it uses for state reports. Its last several annual reports to the General Assembly confirm the scope of the problem — despite more than 600 decisions demanding remedies by more than 60 state parties pending in 2013, only a small handful of cases (less than 10) had received what the Committee could describe as a "satisfactory" response.[113]

One explanation for weakness in state compliance, apart from the dearth of enforcement mechanisms, is that the committees arguably have not yet developed the institutional legitimacy nor earned respect needed for voluntary state compliance. All of the committees are drastically underfunded and, by rule, only meet part-time (for example, the HRC meets for 3–4 weeks, 3 times per year to conclude all of its work including state reports, general comments, and petitions). Committee members are not paid. They have very limited capacity for fact finding and generally do not engage in it other than considering documentary submissions. Although many members have excellent reputations, doubts may also reasonably be raised regarding the actual expertise, impartiality and independence of some committee members who are selected by the state parties, not infrequently drawn from the ranks of former public officials.[114]

Doubts about Committee legitimacy and authority may also, on some level, derive from the often controversial nature of the issues they confront. Not infrequently the Committees are asked to make decisions about domestically controversial issues — issues that may be highly contested within domestic systems, have significant political and cultural implications and are not clearly resolved by explicit treaty language. Capital punishment, religious based gender discrimination, freedom of speech, and issues of sexual orientation are examples. Committee decisions involving such issues inevitably create resentment in some quarters and raise questions about the Committees' legitimacy and cultural sensitivity, perhaps inevitably so given the array of cultural, religious and political viewpoints found among Committee

---

113. Annual Report of the Human Rights Committee, Vol. 1, Ch.VI (and Annex V), G.A. Doc. A/69/40 (2014); Annual Report of the Human Rights Committee, Vol. 2, Annex XI, G.A. Doc. A/68/40 (2013) available here.

114. Some Committees like the HRC have taken steps to improve the selection of its experts and ensure their independence. See, e.g., 1999, HRC, Annex III of A/53/40, vol. I. The 2012 U.N. Report on Strengthening the System also recommended changes in state practices regarding selection. These included:

"1. The nomination of candidates through an open and transparent selection process from among persons who have a proven record of expertise in the relevant area (through relevant work experience, publications, and other achievements) and the willingness to take on the full range of responsibilities related to the mandate of a treaty body member;

2. The avoidance of nominations or election of experts while they are holding positions in the government or any other positions that might expose them to pressures, conflict of interest or generate a real or perceived negative profile in terms of independence that would impact negatively on the credibility of the candidates personally as well as on the treaty body system as a whole; or their resignation from the Committee once elected." U.N. Doc. A/66/860 at 75–76.

members. Do the various Committees and their processes possess sufficient institutional competencies, authority, accountability, and democratic legitimacy such that member states ought to treat their views as authoritative? Does this depend on the specific right under consideration — fact-based, egregious violations of physical integrity versus contestable moral or social issues?

Arguably the HRC has not helped its own cause in this regard by sometimes asserting authority that many states are unlikely to willingly concede. The reactions of three Caribbean states to decisions of the HRC relating to the death penalty seem, at least in part, to reflect the reluctance of states to accept the Committee's authority over controversial domestic issues. In 1997–98, Jamaica, Guyana and Trinidad & Tobago each withdrew from the optional protocol of the CPRC after a series of decisions involving the death penalty. In 1994, the British "Privy Council" (the court of last resort for these former colonies) ruled in *Pratt & Morgan v. Attorney Gen. for Jamaica,* [1994] 2 A.C.1, 4 All E.R. 769 (P.C. 1993) that delays of more than five years from sentencing generally constituted cruel and inhumane treatment in violation of the Jamaican constitution. Since delays caused by petitions to the HRC (and the Inter-American Court of Human Rights) often exceeded three years, the decision created significant obstacles to the imposition of capital punishment in several Caribbean states.

Jamaica consequently withdrew from the Optional Protocol which authorized individual petitions to the HRC. Guyana, and Trinidad and Tobago, similarly denounced their adoption of the Optional Protocol (similarly withdrawing from the Inter-American Court process). These two states then immediately re-acceded to the Optional Protocol with a reservation forbidding review of capital cases.[115] As explored further below, the HRC refused to recognize these reservations in the case of Kennedy v. Trinidad and Tobago, finding them incompatible with the object and purposes of the Optional Protocol. Not surprisingly, the decision was applauded by some states but caused great consternation among others who viewed the Committee's actions as ultra vires interference in state sovereignty. A general comment from the Committee providing a rationale for this assertion of authority over state membership and reservations is described further below.

On the other hand, other states such as Finland, Canada, Norway, Sweden and Australia have accepted and complied with at least some prior HRC decisions. For example, Australia enacted federal laws overturning a Tasmanian law criminalizing homosexual conduct after the HRC expressed its views that such laws violated the CPRC's provisions on privacy and equal protection.[116] A cynic might observe that a committee's views are far more likely to enjoy compliance in those countries where it is needed least. Others complain that the HRC simply overreaches its authority. Consider the following brief comment on Toonen.

---

115. See generally Helfer, Overlegalizing Human Rights: International Relations Theory and the Commonwealth Caribbean Backlash Against Human Rights Regimes, 102 Col. L. Rev. 1832 (2002).
116. Toonen v. Australia, Communication No. 488/1992, U.N. Doc CCPR/C/50/D/488/1992 (1994).

ii. From Guzman, Meyer, International Common Law: The Soft Law of International Tribunals, 9 CHIJIL 515 (2009)

Consider, for example, one of the Committee's most famous decisions, Toonen v Australia. There, the Committee expressed the "view" that Tasmania's anti-sodomy laws violated the privacy and antidiscrimination provisions of the CCPR. This view, of course, was nonbinding on Australia, but nevertheless has been seen as a contributing factor in the Australian government's decision to effectively preempt the Tasmanian law. But the Toonen decision's consequences did not stop with Australia. In 1995, a year after the Toonen decision, the Committee expressed concern in its consideration of the American report made under Article 40 of the CCPR "at the serious infringement of private life in some states which classify as a criminal offence sexual relations between adult consenting partners of the same sex carried out in private, and the consequences thereof for their enjoyment of other human rights without discrimination."

This statement was a direct effort by the Committee to extend the reach of its Toonen decision to other contexts — in this case, contexts in which it lacked jurisdiction to hear individual disputes. The US, after all, has not signed the Optional Protocol to the CCPR, and thus cannot have its practices challenged by individuals. Nevertheless, as evidenced by its comments on American practices, the Committee, and likely other states as well, understood the Toonen decision to provide clarification of the CCPR's binding obligations. The Toonen decision, in other words, is itself a soft-law obligation piggybacking on the hard-law obligations of the CCPR.

Do the treaty based committees suffer from a deficit in authority and legitimacy? Consider the following commentary suggesting that they do.

ii. Donoho, Democratic Legitimacy in Human Rights: The Future of International Decision Making, 21 Wisconsin International Law Journal 1 (2003)

Essentially the offspring of states, it is not surprising that most international human rights organizations are currently limited to supervisory or monitoring roles rather than judicial or quasi-judicial functions. ***

On the one hand, it is clear that international human rights institutions with supervisory or monitoring functions lack certain democratic attributes. One might reasonably complain, for example, that the treaty-based committees are generally composed of unaccountable elite, chosen by national executive branches with no electoral or other meaningful connection to the populations whose rights are being addressed. More critically perhaps, the norms that they supervise are, by their nature, indeterminate and underdeveloped, allowing these experts significant interpretive flexibility. As explained below, it is often argued that unaccountable decision-makers are most problematic for democracy when they lack objective criteria for interpreting and applying indeterminate standards. Complaints may be raised, therefore, that any particular standard articulated by such supervisory bodies is not authentically democratic since it is not derived from a process responsive to the polity concerned.

\*\*\*

## B. Judicial and Quasi-Judicial Functions

The developing judicial and quasi-judicial functions of international human rights institutions present more critical potential implications for democracy. There are three such institutions of some prominence: the Inter-American Court of Human Rights (IACHR); the European Court of Human Rights (ECHR); and the HRC. While there are differences among these institutions in their basic processes, mandates and authority, each provides a means for redressing individual complaints that a government has violated its obligations under an international human rights treaty.

The judges or experts who serve on these bodies are not elected by popular vote or otherwise directly accountable to the general population. Nor are they selected through any confirmation or approval process that provides opportunities for meaningful public and political review of their qualifications. Other than the promotion and protection of human rights within their jurisdictional mandate, they have no political constituency and are not representative of any particular society. . . . While the practical authority of these institutions may vary, each has a theoretically authoritative role to play and, at minimum, the international system presumes eventual compliance with their decisions. Ultimately, the international system hopes to gain sufficient respect for the decisions of such institutions so that states will eventually choose to comply with their decision-making (as has been the case for the ECHR).

While many of these characteristics, particularly independence, may reasonably be seen as strengths with regard to the protection and promotion of human rights, their international context potentially creates some arguably troubling implications for domestic democracy. As explained below, the point of tension here is similar to that which confronts domestic constitutional systems utilizing the judiciary as a check on majoritarian rule. A group of generally unaccountable decision-makers is entrusted with the resolution of important social debates that have the potential to displace majoritarian choices regarding highly contested moral and social issues.

There are, of course, many sound reasons why any particular democratic society might favor this institutional arrangement. Such choices, however, typically reflect an on-going domestic political debate about the appropriate role for government institutions and the desired balance between individual rights and majoritarian rule. The persistent debate over judicial review in U.S. constitutional law clearly manifests this on-going process. Many of the considerations involved in that debate are relevant to the context of international human rights decision-making. The international context, however, presents important special considerations concerning the appropriate locus of, and constraints on, decision-making that may create problematic implications for domestic democracy.

# 3. General Comments

UN treaty based Committees also publish their interpretations regarding the meaning of their respective treaty provisions, known as <u>general comments</u>. These general comments or "recommendations" are typically abstract and, as their name suggests, general in nature, focusing on thematic issues or methods of work. These general comments have covered a wide range of topics from the nature of a state's obligation to implement human rights to the meaning of particular phrases in the treaty.

Some committees' General Comments have expansively interpreted the substance of state obligations and the committee's own authority. Such comments raise questions regarding the authority of the committees and the legal implications of General Comments — subjects which are not addressed in the treaty text itself. HRC General Comment 24 issued in 1994 (U.N. Doc. CCPR/C/21/Rev.1/Add.6) illustrates this point. In General Comment 24, the Committee complained that reservations were impeding the potential effectiveness of the CCPR.

a. HRC General Comment 24

**Human Rights Committee, General Comment 24 (52), U.N. Doc. CCPR/C/21/Rev.1/Add.6 (1994).**

1. As of 1 November 1994, 46 of the 127 States parties to the International Covenant on Civil and Political Rights had, between them, entered 150 reservations of varying significance to their acceptance of the obligations of the Covenant. Some of these reservations exclude the duty to provide and guarantee particular rights in the Covenant. Others are couched in more general terms, often directed to ensuring the continued paramountcy of certain domestic legal provisions. Still others are directed at the competence of the Committee. The number of reservations, their content and their scope may undermine the effective implementation of the Covenant and tend to weaken respect for the obligations of States Parties.

The HRC went on to criticize, without naming, countries like the United States which have imposed broad reservations to avoid changing aspects of domestic law:

11. The intention of the Covenant is that the rights contained therein should be ensured to all those under a State's party's jurisdiction. To this end certain attendant requirements are likely to be necessary. Domestic laws may need to be altered properly to reflect the requirements of the Covenant; and mechanisms at the domestic level will be needed to allow the Covenant rights to be enforceable at the local level. Reservations often reveal a tendency of States not to want to change a particular law. And sometimes that tendency is elevated to a general policy. Of particular concern are widely formulated reservations which essentially render ineffective all Covenant rights which would

require any change in national law to ensure compliance with Covenant obligations. No real international rights or obligations have thus been accepted. And when there is an absence of provisions to ensure that Covenant rights may be sued on in domestic courts, and, further, a failure to allow individual complaints to be brought to the Committee under the first Optional Protocol, all the essential elements of the Covenant guarantees have been removed.

Most controversially, the Committee also concluded that it was the final authority over the legitimacy of a reservation. It also asserted that any reservations it found incompatible with the treaty would simply be severed and void, leaving the state party obligated as if the reservation had not been declared:

> 18. It necessarily falls to the Committee to determine whether a specific reservation is compatible with the object and purpose of the Covenant. This is in part because, as indicated above, it is an inappropriate task for States parties in relation to human rights treaties, and in part because it is a task that the Committee cannot avoid in the performance of its functions. In order to know the scope of its duty to examine a State's compliance under article 40 or a communication under the first Optional Protocol, the Committee has necessarily to take a view on the compatibility of a reservation with the object and purpose of the Covenant and with general international law. Because of the special character of a human rights treaty, the compatibility of a reservation with the object and purpose of the Covenant must be established objectively, by reference to legal principles, and the Committee is particularly well placed to perform this task. The normal consequence of an unacceptable reservation is not that the Covenant will not be in effect at all for a reserving party. Rather, such a reservation will generally be severable, in the sense that the Covenant will be operative for the reserving party without benefit of the reservation.

The United States, joined by the United Kingdom and France, filed a written objection to the comment asserting that: "The Committee's position, while interesting, runs contrary to the Covenant scheme and international law." The HRC subsequently followed General Comment 24 with a decision in a case from Trinidad & Tobago that overtly rejected that state's reservation regarding capital punishment as incompatible with the treaty. The Committee further found the reservation "severable" and decided the case on the merits even though the state had previously declared that the Committee could not review its death penalty practices. As a consequence of this decision, Trinidad & Tobago denounced the entire Optional Protocol and is no longer subject to the individual complaint procedures. A short excerpt from its reasoning appears below.

b. Rawle Kennedy (represented by the London law firm Simons Muirhead & Burton) v. Trinidad and Tobago, Communication No. 845, U.N. Doc. CCPR/C/67/D/845/1999 (31 December 1999)

\*\*\*

6.2 On 26 May 1998, the Government of Trinidad and Tobago denounced the first Optional Protocol to the International Covenant on Civil and Political Rights. On the same day, it reacceded, including in its instrument of reaccession the reservation set out in paragraph 4.1 above.

6.3 To explain why such measures were taken, the State party makes reference to the decision of the Judicial Committee of the Privy Council in Pratt and Morgan v. the Attorney General for Jamaica2 A.C. 1, 1994, in which it was held that "in any case in which execution is to take place more than five years after sentence there will be strong grounds for believing that the delay is such as to constitute "inhuman or degrading punishment or other treatment"" in violation of section 17 of the Jamaican Constitution. The effect of the decision for Trinidad and Tobago is that inordinate delays in carrying out the death penalty would contravene section 5, paragraph 2(b), of the Constitution of Trinidad and Tobago, which contains a provision similar to that in section 17 of the Jamaican Constitution. . . . Thus, the State party chose to denounce the Optional Protocol:

***

6.4 As opined in the Committee's General Comment No. 24, it is for the Committee, as the treaty body to the International Covenant on Civil and Political Rights and its Optional Protocols, to interpret and determine the validity of reservations made to these treaties. ***. The Committee must, however, determine whether or not such a reservation can validly be made.

6.5 *** The issue at hand is therefore whether or not the reservation by the State party can be considered to be compatible with the object and purpose of the Optional Protocol.

6.6 In its General Comment No. 24, the Committee expressed the view that a reservation aimed at excluding the competence of the Committee under the Optional Protocol with regard to certain provisions of the Covenant could not be considered to meet this test . . .

***

6.7 The present reservation, which was entered after the publication of General Comment No. 24, does not purport to exclude the competence of the Committee under the Optional Protocol with regard to any specific provision of the Covenant, but rather to the entire Covenant for one particular group of complainants, namely prisoners under sentence of death. This does not, however, make it compatible with the object and purpose of the Optional Protocol. On the contrary, the Committee cannot accept a reservation which singles out a certain group of individuals for lesser procedural protection than that which is enjoyed by the rest of the population. In the view of the Committee, this constitutes a discrimination which runs counter to some of the basic principles embodied in the Covenant and its Protocols, and for this reason the reservation cannot be deemed compatible with the object and purpose of the Optional

Protocol. The consequence is that the Committee is not precluded from considering the present communication under the Optional Protocol.

General Comments have also been used to elaborate the Committee's view of what various rights require of the state parties. At times, these views provide significant detail which goes considerably beyond the express treaty language. Consider the following examples from the <u>Committee on Economic, Social and Cultural Rights</u> regarding rights to food and water.

c. GENERAL COMMENT 12

**The Right to Adequate Food (Art. 11:05/12/1999, E/C.12/199/5**

**Committee on ESCR**

<u>Obligations and violations</u>

14. The nature of the legal obligations of States parties are set out in article 2 of the Covenant and has been dealt with in the Committee's General Comment No. 3 (1990). The principal obligation is to take steps to achieve *progressively* the full realization of the right to adequate food. This imposes an obligation to move as expeditiously as possible towards that goal. Every State is obliged to ensure for everyone under its jurisdiction access to the minimum essential food which is sufficient, nutritionally adequate and safe, to ensure their freedom from hunger.

15. The right to adequate food, like any other human right, imposes three types or levels of obligations on States parties: the obligations to *respect*, to *protect* and to *fulfil*. In turn, the obligation to *fulfil* incorporates both an obligation to *facilitate* and an obligation to *provide*. [11] *** The obligation to *fulfil (facilitate)* means the State must pro-actively engage in activities intended to strengthen people's access to and utilization of resources and means to ensure their livelihood, including food security. Finally, whenever an individual or group is unable, for reasons beyond their control, to enjoy the right to adequate food by the means at their disposal, States have the obligation to *fulfil (provide)* that right directly. This obligation also applies for persons who are victims of natural or other disasters.

***

17. Violations of the Covenant occur when a State fails to ensure the satisfaction of, at the very least, the minimum essential level required to be free from hunger. In determining which actions or omissions amount to a violation of the right to food, it is important to distinguish the inability from the unwillingness of a State party to comply. Should a State party argue that resource constraints make it impossible to provide access to food for those who are unable by themselves to secure such access, the State has to demonstrate that every effort has been made to use all the resources at its disposal in an effort to satisfy, as a matter of priority, those minimum obligations. ***

20. While only States are parties to the Covenant and are thus ultimately accountable for compliance with it, all members of society — individuals, families, local communities, non-governmental organizations, civil society organizations, as well as the private business sector — have responsibilities in the realization of the right to adequate food. \*\*\*

### d. ESCRC General Comment 15 and the Right to Water

In similar fashion, the ESCRC adopted <u>General Comment 15</u> in 2002, declaring that the Covenant creates a "right to water." Such a right is not expressly mentioned in the treaty but rather, according to the Committee, is implicitly guaranteed as part of rights to an "adequate standard of living" (Art. 11) and to "health" (Art. 12). In addition to relying upon the fundamental human need for adequate water to sustain life, the Committee reasoned that water was an essential prerequisite for attainment of other rights explicitly recognized in the Convention, which utilizes a "catalogue of rights . . . not intended to be exhaustive."

General Comment 15 directly suggests that the right to water, as interpreted by the Committee, is legally binding for the 160 state parties to the Convention. It also describes the Committee's view of what such a right requires — in what critics might describe as flabbergasting detail. More charitably, the Committee's detailed pronouncements would, at minimum, undoubtedly cause deep consternation among national governments who might take the General Comment seriously, and among those who prefer democratically driven policy making. The General Comment includes, for example, the following assertions of state obligations under the implicit right to water:

> ". . . disadvantaged and marginalized farmers, including women farmers, [should] have equitable access to water and water management systems, including sustainable rain harvesting and irrigation technology;" "Water should be treated as a social and cultural good, and not primarily as an economic good;" "Water should be of an acceptable colour, odour and taste for each personal or domestic use;" "All water facilities and services must be of sufficient quality, culturally appropriate and sensitive to gender, life-cycle and privacy requirements;" "Even in times of severe resource constraints, the vulnerable members of society must be protected by the adoption of relatively low-cost targeted programmes;" "Investments should not disproportionately favour expensive water supply services and facilities that are often accessible only to a small, privileged fraction of the population, rather than investing in services and facilities that benefit a far larger part of the population;" "States parties should give special attention to those individuals and groups who have traditionally faced difficulties in exercising this right, including women, children, minority groups, indigenous peoples, refugees, asylum seekers, internally displaced persons, migrant workers, prisoners and detainees . . ."

One explanation for the Committee's venture into basic economic and social policy questions involving water is that it views its pronouncements as non-binding aspirational guidance. It is clear, however, that the CESCR does not view its positions on the implied right to water as merely aspirational goals. General Comment 15 provides in paragraphs 55 & 56 that specific justiciable remedies must be provided in the form of "adequate reparations, including restitution, compensation, satisfaction or guarantees of non-repetition . . ." as well as "legal assistance for obtaining remedies." Finally, the Committee portrays itself as the ultimate safeguard for its own policy directives regarding the right to water, demanding that states set "benchmarks" for the adequacy of water quantities, qualities and access, based on international standards which the Committee will then supervise. GC 15, Par. 53

While many may agree that General Comment 15 articulates excellent policy ideas, it is equally true that each of its detailed pronouncements reflect basic judgments about priorities that are typically assigned to domestic, democratic processes. Water is not only an essential need it is also both a commodity and a scarce resource. A legally recognized right to water, if taken seriously, would necessarily suggest a transfer and redistribution of resources both domestically and internationally. Currently, most people don't pay anything near the actual cost of water if one includes externalities, pollution control and infrastructure.[117] This reality is reflected in General Comment 15's stress on distributive goals:

> "To ensure that water is affordable, States parties must adopt the necessary measures that may include, inter alia: (a) use of a range of appropriate low-cost techniques and technologies; (b) appropriate pricing policies such as free or low-cost water; and (c) income supplements. Any payment for water services has to be based on the principle of equity, ensuring that these services, whether privately or publicly provided, are affordable for all, including socially disadvantaged groups. Equity demands that poorer households should not be disproportionately burdened with water expenses as compared to richer households."

Undoubtedly some may argue that General Comment 15 reflects an astonishing display of hubris for an unelected, unaccountable advisory body with no binding power and questionable degree of authoritativeness. In some ways, however, this depends on how one views the role of the Committee. Is its function to progressively

---

117. The Economist special report on water describes actual cost of water this way: "Dr Perry, the irrigation economist, says water is typically priced at 10-50% of the costs of operating and maintaining the system, and that in turn is only 10-50% of what water is worth in terms of agricultural productivity. So to bring supply and demand into equilibrium the price would have to rise by 4-100 times." See *Special Report on Water*, *"Trade and Conserve,"* available at: http://www.economist.com/node/16136292. In another article in the series titled, *"Clean Water is a Right,"* the author also cites the U.N. Development Fund for his observation that: "If the poor cannot pay, someone else must. Taxpayers already bear some of the costs of water, shovelling money into loss-making public utilities. Ms Foster and Mr Yepes reckon that almost 90% of water utilities in low-income countries do not charge their retail customers enough to cover the costs of operating and maintaining their pipes, let alone investing in them." The Economist, *Clean Water is a Right*, Nov. 9, 2006 available at: http://www.economist.com/node/8142904

promote full realization of basic rights, representing first the interests of people, pushing states for change? Or is it a legal institution with expertise in the interpretation of the treaty's text, beholden to the undoubtedly more limited meaning ascribed to it by member governments? Does the Committee's aggressive stance enhance or hinder its legitimacy and effectiveness?

General comments issued by the various committees can be accessed and researched on their respective <u>webpages</u>.

# D. Critiquing the U.N. Treaty Based System

## 1. Is It Really Working to Alter State Behavior?

**Emilie M. Hafner-Burton, Kiyoteru Tsutsui, Human Rights in a Globalizing World: The Paradox of Empty Promises,** *American Journal Sociology,* Volume 110 Number 5 (March 2005): 1373–1411

\*\*\*

The vast majority of states today bind themselves to an international regime designed to protect the fundamental rights of virtually every child, woman, and man through law. As a growing number of nations voluntarily join this regime, the regime itself is expanding to incorporate new core human rights (see table 1). These treaties supply various monitoring bodies that work to improve governments' practice in the specified areas of human rights by collecting and disseminating information, often with nongovernmental activists' cooperation. Yet, government violation of human rights is epidemic. Figure 1 compares the percentage of available international human rights treaties that the average state has ratified and the percentage of states reported to be repressive, over time. It is clear that (1) the average state has ratified a steadily increasing percentage of available human rights treaties, creating a world space characterized by the rapid and nearly universal acceptance of international human rights law, while (2) the percentage of states reported to repress human rights has grown over time, although the increase has tapered off in recent years. This rising gap between states' propensity to join the international human rights regime and to bring their human rights practice into compliance with that regime challenges the efficacy of international law and questions the authenticity of states' legal commitments to protect the lives of their citizens. There are many examples. \*\*\*

The problem in the current research is clear: theoretical expectations point in both directions, and systematic empirical evidence to support either side is rare. Furthermore, the tendency to isolate the two core aspects of the compliance process has led scholars to overlook the larger picture. Concern about the direct effects of formal treaty ratification has led to a pessimistic preoccupation with the apparent gap between ratification and domestic practices.

Belief that international civil society advocates can encourage better practices has led to a more optimistic preoccupation with the nature of activism.

Our core argument is that global institutionalization of human rights has been a double-edged sword. On the one hand, global human rights treaties supply weak institutional mechanisms to monitor and enforce regime norms, offering governments strong incentives to ratify human rights treaties as a matter of window dressing rather than a serious commitment to implement respect for human rights in practice. Moreover, these international agreements may at times provide governments with a shield for increasingly repressive behaviors after ratification, as treaty ratification confers on them human rights legitimacy and makes it difficult for others to pressure them for further action. As external pressures decrease, governments often spiral into worse repression after ratification, and the human rights legal regime remains powerless to stop this process.

On the other hand, human rights advocates regularly mobilize around these treaties, leveraging the emergent legitimacy of human rights as a global norm of appropriate state behavior to pressure states to improve actual human rights practices. In effect, we explain the impact of human rights treaties as a "paradox of empty promises." As nation-states make formal legal commitments to symbolize human rights compliance even while they are in violation, this process of "empty" institutional commitment to a weak regime paradoxically empowers nonstate advocates with the tools to pressure governments toward compliance.

***

EMPIRICAL ANALYSIS

Our basic aim in this section is to test our hypotheses:

Hypothesis 1. — *Ratification of human rights treaties has had no direct positive effect on states' compliance in practice and may even have a significantly negative effect, corresponding to increasing repression.* Hypothesis 2. — *Linkage to international civil society has had a positive effect on states' human rights behavior, decreasing repression.* ***

Results

Table 3 below displays our major findings. Two outcomes are striking.

First, *state commitment to the international human rights legal regime does not automatically translate into government respect for human rights.* States that ratify a greater number of human rights treaties are not more likely to protect human rights than states that ratify a small number of treaties. To the contrary, model 1 suggests that ratification is frequently coupled with noncompliance behavior and that state commitment to the international human rights legal regime at times leads to radical decoupling, exacerbating human rights abuse.

This finding is remarkably consistent when we disaggregate overall commitment to the human rights regime and examine ratification of specific U.N. treaties (models 2–7). In no instance does state ratification of any of the six core U.N. human rights treaties predict the likelihood of government respect for human rights. Rather, state ratification of all six treaties has a negative effect on signatories' behavior: treaty members are more likely to repress their citizens than nonratifiers.

Together, these findings draw a troubling picture: international human rights treaties do little to encourage better practices and cannot stop many governments from a spiral of increasing repressive behavior, and may even exacerbate poor practices. ***

Second, state linkage to international civil society poses a strong counterforce to this radical decoupling: states whose citizens belong to a greater number of INGOs are more likely to protect the rights of their citizens. The consistency of this effect across models indicates that the general institutional effect of global civil society is quite stable. Although we find that institutionalization of global human rights has no systematically positive impact through the treaty system, we also find that global human rights norms, embedded in the treaties and proffered by international civil society, do contribute to real improvements in human rights practices.

Table 3 also confirms that our estimates are consistent with the general findings of the human rights literature on key variables. Democracies are better protectors of human rights — in keeping with a vast majority of human rights scholars (Henderson 1991; Mitchell and McCormick 1988; Poe and Tate 1994; Poe et al. 1999) — as are states with a higher level of openness to the international economy (Meyer 1996; Richards, Gelleny, and Sacko 2001) and with higher levels of economic development. Consistent with current research in the field, one of the most important predictors of repression is state history of repression (Apodaca 2001; Poe et al. 1999).

***

Considered together, these findings offer strong support for our argument. There is no evidence to suggest a systematically positive correlation between official governmental acceptance of an international law to protect human rights and the actual behavior of government elites to protect those rights. More disturbing is evidence to suggest that the ratification of human rights treaties may actually hide worsening state compliance with human rights norms enshrined in those treaties, at least in the short term. On the other hand, evidence also suggests that linkage to global civil society improves human rights practices. Even though treaties often do not directly contribute to improvement in practice, the norms codified in these treaties are spread through INGOs that strategically leverage the human rights legal regime to pressure governments to change their human rights behavior.

# 2. Are There Problems with the Premises?

**Donoho, 35 Georgia J. Int'l L.1 (2006)**

\*\*\*

5 B. Designed For Failure

The apparent inability of the human rights system to deliver effectively on its lofty and noble promises is not, in many ways, surprising. It is, after all, a system designed with significantly limited enforcement capacity. Both Pollyannaish and cynical, the international system heavily relies upon the dubious premise that governments will faithfully implement international human rights standards within their own domestic systems and provide adequate domestic remedies to redress violations. This reliance on voluntary compliance is theoretically bolstered by a network of international mechanisms and institutions that are, in reality, anemic at best. Although not without exceptions, most international human rights institutions are generally limited to monitoring state compliance and promoting adherence to underdeveloped international standards through dialogue, condemnation, and moral suasion. Most of these institutions suffer from limited or ambiguous decision-making authority and lack effective, independent enforcement mechanisms.

Thus constrained, the international system has generally failed to check the abuse of repressive governments and meaningfully deliver the promise of human rights to those most in need of protection. In essence, the international system's approach to enforcement and implementation of human rights has proven unrealistic in a world characterized by oppression, autocratic governments, poverty, and armed conflict. Although there is no clear consensus regarding what enforcement of international human rights should look like, few would disagree that existing enforcement mechanisms remain the weakest link in the international human rights system.

\*\*\*

Theoretically, the international side of rights enforcement could take place under a vertical or "top-down" model in which authoritative international human rights institutions would directly compel compliance with human rights standards, utilizing means ranging from an "international marshal's office" to binding economic sanctions. As currently situated, however, international human rights institutions do not enjoy the capacity to directly enforce their own decisions. Lacking their own enforcement powers and mechanisms, these institutions must instead rely on the domestic enforcement capacities and goodwill of domestic governments.

Because of this forced reliance, the theoretical apex of enforceability for international institutions would occur if and when states recognized international decisions as authoritative and binding, and allowed the direct enforcement of such decisions by domestic institutions. In essence, states could choose to give the decisional output of human rights institutions "direct effect" without requiring prior legislative or executive action or approval. The reality is, however, that international law does not require that states adopt this approach to international decision-making and few, if any, states appear to have done so. For the vast majority of the international community, the decisions of international human rights institutions are simply not treated as binding or authoritative within the domestic legal order, even if technically "binding" under the relevant treaty regime.

Ultimately, most governments choose to enforce international decisions, if at all, solely through discretionary domestic legislative or executive action. Governments have generally reserved to themselves final discretion regarding the actual manner and method for enforcement of international institution decisions, if they enforce them at all. The key element to effective enforcement once again lies with each government's discretionary voluntary compliance, in this instance whether to treat the output of international human rights bodies as authoritative and translate those decisions into action.

It is fair to say that the traditional model for human rights enforcement involves a rather murky convergence between the two enforcement paths described above. International human rights treaties generally place primary responsibility for implementation and enforcement in the hands of national authorities subject to typically ambiguous international supervisory powers. International institutions monitor state compliance and may offer alternative forms of redress when the national system fails. These international processes are not generally authoritative, however, and even when technically binding lack clear enforcement mechanisms. The effectiveness of international remedies is, in turn, almost always dependent on the subject government's willingness to voluntarily comply. Since international institutions lack both authority and independent enforcement capacities, actual enforcement of international remedies ultimately depends upon the willingness of the perpetrators to meaningfully implement rights and comply with international supervisory authority.

## C. Institutional Failures and Ambiguous Authority

It is important to recognize initially that much of the work product of the current international human rights system is not designed for enforcement, at least in the sense described above. Rather, existing institutions are designed primarily to promote human rights through disclosure, dialogue, and technical assistance. For example, the United Nations charter-based system, which primarily involves the politically dominated work of the Commission on Human Rights [now Human Rights Council] and its various subsidiary organizations, does not seek to enforce human rights in any direct manner. Institutions created under the U.N.-sponsored network of multilateral human rights treaties are also primarily involved in work better described as promotion than enforcement. Each of the [nine] major multilateral human rights treaties sponsored by the U.N. creates a "committee" of experts who primarily serve fact-finding and promotional roles, reviewing state periodic reports on implementation and issuing "general comments."

Although there has been some effort to assert authority to bind states pursuant to the General Comments, it would be a misnomer to refer to such work as "enforcement," at least in the sense described above. The promotional activity of human rights institutions focuses almost exclusively on encouraging states to voluntarily change their behavior through dialogue, confrontation, and exposure regarding alleged violations of international standards. This activity has important benefits but cannot, at least in the short term, be relied upon as a meaningful way to compel compliance with rights where needed most.

Enforcement is probably more relevant to the various individual petitioning processes created by the regional systems and four of the major multilateral treaties. Each of the three regional human rights systems-the Inter-American, European, and African-administer individual petitioning processes under which human rights victims may bring their complaints, after exhaustion of domestic remedies, before a judicial or quasi-judicial body for resolution. CCPR, CAT, CERD, and CEDAW create similar processes that apply to any state that has voluntarily agreed to the relevant committee's petitioning jurisdiction.

***

The ECHR's [European Court of Human Rights] relative success in securing compliance, while not unblemished, stands in sharp contrast to the record of other international petitioning systems. The Inter-American system, for example, has had limited success in enforcing the decisions of its Commission and Court, even though those decisions are also technically "binding" under the American Convention on Human Rights. The enforcement record regarding decisions of the treaty-based bodies, such as the Human Rights Committee, is even more disappointing. Given the ambiguous legal status of its decisions and the absence of enforcement mechanisms, it is perhaps more accurate to describe this disappointing record as a lack of voluntary compliance rather than a failure of enforcement.

There are undoubtedly many reasons why it has proven difficult to enforce the adjudicatory decisions of international human rights institutions outside the context of Europe. Most significantly, however, states have found it easy to ignore such decisions as the result of three related factors: (1) ambiguous mandates and limited legal authority; (2) lack of meaningful legal or practical incentives to induce state compliance; and (3) insufficient institutional legitimacy to induce voluntary compliance.

Governments have not found it particularly painful to ignore the views and recommendations of most international human rights institutions because there are few, if any, serious consequences associated with doing so. Most governments comply with such decisions only when it is politically expedient to do so. Lacking mechanisms that compel compliance through sanction or other meaningful practical incentives, enforcement of international decisions depends entirely on the political goodwill of the government concerned. Given that the government is, by definition, the perpetrator of the alleged violation, it is hardly surprising that compliance is the exception, especially in states ruled by oppressive regimes. There is, in this sense, an inherent contradiction built into the system's approach to enforcement, which leaves compliance largely within the discretion of the perpetrators.

Reliance on voluntary compliance does not, of course, doom the human rights system to failure. Indeed, voluntary compliance with the decisions of respected international institutions should, ideally, have a central role in a rationally designed international enforcement regime. ***. In this regard, the European system appears to thrive by virtue of a happy coincidence of mutually reinforcing incentives and the respect that the ECHR has earned over time. Similarly, a critical reason for the dearth of voluntary compliance outside Europe undoubtedly lies in the fundamental lack of respect that states exhibit toward the authority of most other existing human rights institutions and the paucity of incentives to induce such respect and compliance.

This apparent lack of respect for the authority of international human rights institutions is undoubtedly related to ambiguity regarding their legal mandate and doubts over the legitimacy of "external" international decision-making regarding domestic practices. The problem in this sense is two-fold. On the one hand, most international institutions have ambiguous or ill-defined legal authority that potentially could be interpreted as including authoritative jurisdiction over an extremely wide range of human rights issues, including those with highly debatable or controversial substantive content. At the same time, these institutions lack the attributes of institutional legitimacy that might engender widespread state trust and respect. Outside of Europe, virtually all of these international institutions suffer from politicized appointment processes, lack of financial resources, poorly defined legal authority, failure to utilize full-time professional judges, and flawed fact-finding processes. These international decision-makers are generally unaccountable in the most literal sense, and render decisions that are, by definition, external to the body politic where the alleged violations occurred.

More significantly, these institutions have also failed to carefully and incrementally develop their own legitimacy and credibility over time in light of practical limitations on their powers and capacities. They have, in essence, failed to evolve an appropriate and realistic relationship vis-a-vis domestic authority and democratic institutions.

# E.  UN Humanitarian Work and Human Rights

The U.N. High Commissioner for Human Rights correctly points out that "there are other <u>United Nations bodies and entities</u> involved in the promotion and protection of human rights." Perhaps the U.N.'s greatest current contribution to human rights is in the form of the extensive humanitarian and development assistance it provides around the world. Here is a good sampling:

- <u>United Nations High Commissioner for Refugees</u> (UNHCR)
- <u>Office for the Coordination of Humanitarian Affairs</u> (OCHA)
- <u>Inter-Agency Internal Displacement Division</u>
- <u>International Labour Organization</u>
- <u>World Health Organization</u>
- <u>United Nations Educational, Scientific and Cultural Organization</u> (UNESCO)
- <u>Joint United Nations Programme on HIV/AIDS</u> (UNAIDS)
- <u>Inter-Agency Standing Committee</u> (IASC)
- <u>DESA (Department of Economic and Social Affairs)</u>
- <u>Commission on the Status of Women</u> (CSW)
- <u>Office of the Special Adviser on Gender Issues and the Advancement of Women</u> (OSAGI)
- <u>Division for the Advancement of Women</u> (DAW)
- <u>United Nations Population Fund</u> (UNFPA)
- <u>United Nations Children's Fund</u> (UNICEF)
- <u>United Nations Development Fund for Women</u> (UNIFEM)
- <u>United Nations Development Programme</u> (UNDP)
- <u>Food and Agriculture Organization of the United Nations</u> (FAO)
- <u>United Nations Human Settlements Programme</u> (HABITAT)
- <u>United Nations Mine Action</u>

# Chapter 9

# Regional Systems for the Protection of Human Rights: Introduction and Examination of the European System

## A. Introduction to Regional Systems of Human Rights Protection

### 1. Overview

The next two chapters focus on the work of "regional" human rights institutions. Currently, there are three major regional human rights institutions, each associated with a more comprehensive, regional political organization. Similar to the United Nations but geographically limited, these political organizations are involved in a wide variety of issues, but also have specific human rights agendas. The human rights mandates of the organizations are carried out by institutions specifically devoted to implementing human rights set out in regional treaties. Those three regional entities, and the human rights institutions they oversee include:

(1) The <u>Organization American States</u> ("OAS"), which is based in Washington, DC, oversees the **Inter-American Human Rights System**. The Inter-American System implements the OAS Charter human rights mandates as manifested in the <u>American Convention on Human Rights</u> and the <u>American Declaration of Human Rights</u>. The system primarily operates through two related human rights bodies, the <u>Inter-American Commission on Human Rights</u>, based in Washington, D.C., and the <u>Inter-American Court of Human Rights</u>, based in San Jose, Costa Rica.

(2) The <u>Council of Europe</u> is a political organization which consists of 47 European nations. The Council of Europe oversees the **European System of Human Rights**. The European System implements the <u>European Convention on Human Rights</u> through the <u>European Court of Human Rights</u> ("ECHR"), based in Strasbourg, France. In addition, we will see that a very distinct institution, the European Union,

has emerged as a significant force in the protection of the human rights of the 500 million citizens of its 28 member countries.

(3) The <u>African Union</u> is an economic and political organization whose members comprise most African countries. The AU also oversees the African System of Human Rights Protection, which implements the <u>African Charter of Human and Peoples' Rights</u>. The African System consists, for the time being, of the <u>African Court on Human and Peoples' Rights</u>, based in Arusha, Tanzania, and the <u>African Commission on Human and Peoples' Rights</u>, based in Banjul, The Gambia.

Like the U.N., each of these regional entities is created by treaty (commonly called a "charter") and has been given certain defined tasks and powers by its member states concerning issues of international peace, economics, social welfare, and human rights. Each regional organization is required to coordinate its activities with the United Nations under Articles 52–54 of the U.N. Charter. The basic idea is that these organizations and the subsidiary institutions they create should help to coordinate relations among states that share common interests in defined geographical regions.

As you read the materials, focus on understanding how each of these regional systems function. First and foremost, this means understanding the workings of the primary bodies charged with implementing the regional human treaties. **As with the U.N. institutions reviewed in prior chapters, you should critically consider how these institutions are structured, who sits on them, their mandate, their powers, and jurisdiction.** This chapter first focuses on the European System. Subsequently, we will turn our attention to the Inter-American and African Systems in Chapter 10. You will find strong parallels between each system. You should compare and contrast the regional systems with each other and with the U.N. system. A critical question to consider is why certain regional systems have proven more successful than the U.N. or other regional systems.

The article below provides an orientation by discussing how the regional systems of human rights protection complement the United Nations' system. The basic thesis of the paper is that the UN and regional systems serve different purposes, for very specific reasons, and thus have a kind of symbiotic relationship with each other. The UN, as a body incorporating almost all the world's countries, necessarily has a weaker human rights enforcement mechanism because of the diversity of its makeup. The regional bodies, however, have the ability to create stronger human rights norms and enforce them more effectively through shared values and culture, and economic incentives, since regional groupings frequently are also bound by economic ties as well.

## 2. James Wilets, Lessons from Kosovo: Towards a Multiple Track System of Human Rights Protection, 6 Int'l L. Students Ass'n J. Int'l & Comp. L. 645 (2000)

[I]t is the purpose of this article to suggest that the world is increasingly moving towards a system of human rights protection in which global bodies of human rights enforcement exist and function concurrently with regional human rights enforcement bodies. These regional human rights bodies have the capacity to enforce human rights in a manner consonant with the level of human rights development in those countries belonging to such a regional grouping. This developing system of enforcement can be referred to as a "Multiple Track System of Human Rights Protection."

The first track of global governance is universal and it incorporates the United Nations and its associated institutions. The United Nations system is the only truly global body with a mandate to develop and implement international law, including international human rights law. As such, it has adopted a comprehensive normative framework for human rights protection, even if the mechanisms for enforcement of those norms are frequently lacking. Nevertheless, cognizant of its global role as a representative body of liberal and illiberal states, it has adopted a procedurally statist approach with considerable deference towards state sovereignty and a strong bias against coercive intervention. Accordingly, consistent with its normative embrace of human rights, the United Nations has frequently condemned human rights abuses in member nations, but has only infrequently authorized coercive intervention in response to those violations with economic sanctions or military force. It is this gap between the normative human rights framework of the United Nations and its inability or unwillingness to enforce those rights in a more assertive manner, which provides the justification and need for regional human rights and security bodies to fill that gap. The implications of this still largely aspirational development are manifold.

First, the development of a Multiple Track System of Human Rights Protection avoids the problem of human rights protection being subject to the lowest common denominator. In other words, the level of enforcement in a Multiple Track System would be predicated upon the ability of smaller groups of countries agreeing on a common set of norms, permitting the greatest possible promulgation and enforcement of human rights norms within any regional grouping of countries. Thus, for example, the European Union has created political, civil, social, cultural, and economic rights that surpass the globally articulated norms in those United Nations human rights conventions.

Moreover, the actions of these associations of liberal, democratic states are not simply limited to addressing human rights violations within the borders of their member states. NATO's intervention in Kosovo are examples of the "democratic alliance's" refusal to recognize absolute state sovereignty in the face of systematic human rights violations occurring near the association's borders.

Second, a strong argument can be made that the relatively weaker systems of human rights protections contained in the United Nations system of human rights protection serve different functions than do the human rights systems of the regional groupings and may, in fact, be more appropriate for a system that contemplates protecting human rights for the entire world community. This argument takes some of the sting out of the widespread criticism of the ineffectiveness of the United Nations human rights system [and suggests] that it is necessarily limited in the extent to which it can do so given the extraordinarily diverse constituency it serves.

Third, the development of a Multiple Track System serves as a valid alternative to the approach of those international law commentators who have advocated the articulation of a universal set of human rights standards applicable to all countries and denying participation in the international community to those countries that fail to fulfill those global standards. This could be considered the "all-or-nothing" approach.

The normative justification for such an approach is quite obvious: human rights are good.

The problem with this approach, which admittedly enjoys an attractive philosophical clarity, is that it does not resolve what system of human rights protection, or even world order, would exist to regulate the conduct of those countries that do not comply with those global standards, but are short of constituting true international "outlaws." This all-or-nothing approach runs the risk of expelling these human rights violators out of the only international body that incorporates the vast majority of the world's nations: the United Nations. It certainly may be appropriate to expel certain countries from the United Nations that engage in systematic and severe human rights violations. But the "all-or-nothing" approach [would mean that] a substantially greater number of countries would have to be expelled from the United Nations. A truly useful institution for world dialogue among vastly different countries would then lose much of its original purpose.

The all-or-nothing approach does little to further human rights in those countries that opt out of the rigid universal human rights system that these legal commentators advocate. These all-or-nothing legal commentators arguably underestimate the importance of maintaining a system of global relations which permits liberal and illiberal countries to coexist peacefully and to maintain communication and dialogue. The all-or-nothing approach still leaves unanswered the question of what the international community's strategy should be with respect to those countries that are not eligible to "join the international community." Those countries that are ineligible will continue to exist and unless a system of international relations provides rules that allow all of the countries of the world to coexist, the potential for conflict can only increase.

Fourth, to the extent that the Multiple Track System recognizes a deeper integration and harmonization of the human rights norms existing in the member countries [of regional human rights protection regimes], it helps to protect, in a symbiotic fashion, the domestic system of human rights protection already existing in those countries. International law and domestic justice are fundamentally connected. However, a just system of international law will only be correlated with domestic justice, and vice versa, as long as countries are willing to recognize the authority of international law in their domestic legal systems. This recognition of the authority of international law is much more likely to occur in a regional context than in a global one. In part, this is because the economic integration that frequently accompanies the creation of these regional groupings of countries provides a clear economic incentive for members of regional groupings not to stray from their human rights commitments.

### Conclusion

While international law is far from attaining a world order based on respect for human rights norms, the world's institutions are, haltingly and unevenly, establishing the precedents on a regional and global level to realize that vision. In creating a Multiple Track System of Human Rights Protection, the world legal order is increasingly providing mechanisms for dealing with those nations who refuse to recognize the fundamental human rights of their citizens.

## 3. Chart of International and Regional Institutions with Significant Human Rights Mandates

| GLOBAL | AMERICAN | EUROPEAN | AFRICAN |
|---|---|---|---|
| United Nations (UN) | Organization of American States (OAS) | European Union (EU)<br><br>Council of Europe (CoE)<br><br>Also: OSCE (Organ. Sec. & Cooperation in Europe) | African Union (AU) |
| UN:<br>• ECOSOC<br>• HR Council<br>• Advisory Council<br>• High Commissioner for HR<br>• Treaty-based Committees<br>• Commission on Women | OAS:<br>• Inter-American Court of Human Rights (San Jose)<br>• Inter-American Commission (D.C.) | Council of Europe:<br>• European Court of Human Rights<br>• Others: e.g. Committees on Prevention of Torture, Racism, Human Trafficking, Corruption & Minorities<br><br>EU:<br>• ECJ<br>• Fund. Rts. Agency<br><br>OSCE:<br>• Office for Dem. Instit. & HR | AU:<br>• African Comm. of Human Rights<br>• African Ct of Human Rights |

*(Continued)*

| GLOBAL | AMERICAN | EUROPEAN | AFRICAN |
|---|---|---|---|
| Primary Treaties: U.N. Charter Art. 55–56 CPRC ESCRC CERD CEDAW CAT Children's Convention Refugee Convention CDP CMW | Primary Treaties: OAS Charter American Convention on Human Rights American Declaration of Human Rights | Primary Treaty (CoE): • European Convention on Human Rights and Fundamental Freedoms Primary Treaty (EU): • Charter of Fund. Rts OSCE — no treaty, set of voluntary commitments | Primary Treaty: AU Charter Banjul Charter |
| Judicial • International Ct of Justice (ICJ) • Intl Criminal Ct • Ad Hoc Tribunals | Judicial • IA Ct HR • IA Commission HR (quasi-judicial) | Judicial EU: • European Ct of Justice (ECJ) Council of Europe: • European Ct of HR (ECtHR) | Judicial • African Ct of Justice • African Commission & Court of HR |

# B. European System for the Protection of Human Rights

## 1. Overview

There are at least four significant regional institutions in Europe whose functions and purposes include protection of human rights. The first two of these institutions, the Council of Europe and European Court of Human Rights, are associated with the implementation and enforcement of the 1950 European Convention on Human Rights (ECHR). The third institution is the European Union, which has increasingly incorporated human rights into its wide ranging of authority. The fourth institution is the Organization for Security and Cooperation in Europe (OSCE), a group of 57 nations whose human rights mandate involves the entire European continent, Central Asia, and North America, with a primary focus on elections and democratic governance. Our primary focus in this chapter is on the work of the Council and Court under the ECHR and the emerging role of the European Union in the protection of human rights.

Historically, the term "European System of Human Rights" has referred to the ECHR as implemented and enforced through the Council of Europe (CoE) and European Court of Human Rights (ECtHR). The Council of Europe is a political organization of 47 European nations with populations of approximately 870 million people.

The Council of Europe should not be confused with the European Union, a quasi-federal international entity whose authority extends broadly over a wide range of economic, trade, political, and social issues. It is also necessary to distinguish the Council of Europe from a principle institution of the EU called, regrettably for students and teachers, the European Council. All 28 member states of the EU are also members of the Council of Europe. The European Union itself works in close cooperation with the Council of Europe and has traditionally committed itself to follow the decisions of the ECtHR, interpreting and applying the European Convention on Human Rights. More recently, EU member states adopted a treaty based commitment to join the European Convention. However, its accession to the Convention has been thwarted, at least temporarily, by a 2014 decision of the EU's judicial branch, the European Court of Justice. Significantly for the advancement of human rights, the EU also adopted, effective in 2009, the Charter of Fundamental Rights of the European Union. The Charter of Fundamental Rights goes further in its elaboration of human rights than the European Convention and will undoubtedly serve as a powerful instrument to protect and advance human rights for the over 500 million citizens of the European Union. (For a detailed breakdown of member states, see this map by Centre d'Information sur les Institutions Européennes (CIIE).)

As you examine and compare the work of the European CoE System and the EU in the materials presented below, consider important differences between their institutions, mandates, history, and geographic reach. The Council of Europe is, thus far, much broader in geographical scope than the European Union and includes countries with troubling human rights records like Russia, Ukraine, Romania, and Turkey. EU institutions, entrusted with binding authority over a wide range of economic related subjects, have the power to create and enforce law but human rights is not its primary agenda. In contrast, human rights and democracy are essentially the singular focus of the CoE, but it lacks the EU's muscular capacity for authoritative enforcement. On the other hand, members of the CoE and ECHR must, under Protocol 11 of that convention, consent to the jurisdiction of the European Court of Human Rights to hear complaints by individuals claiming violations of the Convention. Most of the Council's 47 members have also given the Convention direct domestic effect. You should recall that this generally means that individuals may seek to enforce the Convention's provisions within their own domestic legal system.

Which institutional arrangements are most effective in promoting human rights? Has the European CoE System become, since its expansion in recent years, less effective than the European Union in implementing its human rights norms? The comparison of these two entities seems to illustrate a fundamental characteristic of regional regimes: geographically broadening a human rights regime usually affects the ability of the regime to enforce its human rights norms effectively as the region encompasses more countries with more political diversity. In other words, as a general rule, the broader a regional regime, the less deep will be its elaboration and enforcement of human rights norms. An extreme example of this is the United Nations, where the global nature of the institution appears to generate a much less strict enforcement regime because of the need to include members with very low human rights standards. If the United Nations were to expel all members that did not comply with even the most basic human rights norms, it would cease to be a global body, defeating one of its initial purposes. Keep these distinctions and differences in mind as you examine the material which follows.

There are four specific learning objectives for this chapter. You should examine the materials that follow in order to understand and gain a working knowledge of:

1. The institutional characteristics of the European CoE System and the EU as it relates to human rights — how are the human rights bodies of the CoE and EU organized, what are their functions, mandates, and mechanisms of implementation and enforcement;

2. The legal relationship between the ECtHR (and its work) and the member states subject to its jurisdiction, as well as the EU — in particular the legal status of the European Convention and ECtHR decisions, the legal status of ECJ human rights decisions, and the function of the doctrines of Subsidiarity, European Supervision, European Consensus, and Margin of Appreciation;

3. The circumstances, institutional features, or other factors that might explain the ECtHR's general effectiveness and how these characteristics compare to those of the EU;

4. The distinctions and contrasts between the European Regional System and those institutions and conventions associated with the United Nations — how is the UN system different from the European system and how do such differences matter.

## 2. Historical Evolution of the CoE "European System"

The following excerpt from an article by Buergenthal provides an overview of the historical development of the European Human Rights System and how it operates. The excerpt provides useful context and background information but is somewhat lacking in two critical respects: (1) The article fails to account for how the significant expansion of the Council of Europe from 1996 through 2006 has recently effected its work and effectiveness; and (2) the article fails to recognize the growing role of the

Piece of the Berlin Wall in front of the European Court of Human Rights Building, Photo by <u>Francois, Wikimedia Commons</u>.

European Union's Court of Justice in adjudicating cases with human rights issues as European Union law has adopted its own human rights instruments, frequently surpassing in scope the rights contained in the European Convention.

Buergenthal, The Evolving International Human Rights System, 100 A.J.I.L. 683 (2006)

### The European Human Rights System

The European Convention for the Protection of Human Rights and Fundamental Freedoms established what has become most effective international system for the protection of individual human rights to date. It has also served as a model for the two other regional human rights systems. The Convention traces its origin to the late 1940s, when the states constituting the Council of Europe, then a grouping of Western European states only, concluded that UN efforts to produce a treaty transforming the lofty principles proclaimed in the Universal Declaration of Human Rights into a binding international bill of rights would take many years to come to fruition. Rather than wait, they decided that the Council of Europe should proceed on its own. The justification for not waiting was expressed in the preamble to the European Convention, which stated that the members of the Council of Europe were "resolved, as the Governments of European countries, which are like-minded and have a common heritage of political traditions, ideals, freedoms, and the rule of law, to take the first steps for the collective enforcement of certain of the rights stated in the Universal Declaration."

By 1953, the ten ratifications necessary to bring the Convention into force had been deposited and a total of forty-six states are now parties to it. This dramatic increase in its membership is due in large measure to the geopolitical transformation of Europe that resulted from the demise of the Soviet Union and the end of the Cold War. Today most European states are members of the Council of Europe, including Russia and some former Soviet Republics.

When the European Convention entered into force, it guaranteed only a dozen basic civil and political rights. The list of these rights has grown significantly over the years with the adoption of additional protocols that have expanded the Convention's catalog of rights. In the meantime, these rights have been extensively interpreted by the Convention institutions and the national courts of the member states. In the process, the meaning and scope of these rights also have increasingly come to reflect the contemporary needs of European society. The result is a modern body of human rights law to which other international, regional, and national institutions frequently look when interpreting and applying their own human rights instruments.

In addition, the institutions of the European Convention have undergone extensive changes. The original Convention machinery consisted of a European Commission and Court of Human Rights. The institutional structure of the European system was substantially changed with the adoption of Protocol No. 11 to the Convention, which entered into force in 1998. It abolished the Commission and gave individuals direct access to the Court. The Convention thus became the first human rights treaty to give individuals standing to file cases directly with the appropriate tribunal.

Today the European Court numbers forty-six judges, that is, a judge for each member state of the Council of Europe. The Plenary Court, which consists of all judges, exercises mainly administrative functions. The judicial work of the Court is performed by three bodies of judges: Committees (three judges), Chambers (seven judges), and the Grand Chamber (seventeen judges). The Committees are authorized to reject, by unanimous vote, individual applications as inadmissible. Chambers deal with the remaining admissibility issues and the merits of most interstate and individual applications. The Grand Chamber has a dual function. Under certain circumstances, particularly when a Chamber is called upon to decide serious questions of interpretation of the Convention or its protocols, it may opt to relinquish its jurisdiction in favor of the Grand Chamber. In certain "exceptional cases," the Grand Chamber may also act as an appellate tribunal and hear cases already decided by a Chamber.

Over time, the European Court of Human Rights for all practical purposes has become Europe's constitutional court in matters of civil and political rights. [Ed.: Until recently], its judgments are routinely followed by the national courts of the states parties to the Convention, their legislatures, and their national governments. The Convention itself has acquired the status of domestic law in most of the state parties and can be invoked as such in their courts. While at times some of the newer states parties find it difficult to live up to their obligations under the Convention, a substantial majority of states applies the Convention faithfully and routinely.

The success of the European Convention system has brought with it a caseload for the Court that it has found more and more difficult to cope with. To address this problem, the Council of Europe adopted Protocol No. 14 to the Convention. [T]he Protocol should enable the Court to reduce its caseload substantially by a variety of methods. It cannot be doubted, however, that the current caseload has become unmanageable, seriously impeding the effective implementation of the Convention.

## 3. Nuts & Bolts: How the ECtHR Works

Please visit the <u>website of the European Court of Human Rights</u>. You will find many informative links there that describe the Court's current operations. First, watch the 15 minute video about the Court, "<u>The Conscience of Europe</u>."

It is a bit boring, but it does provide a good overview of the Court and how it functions. You should then peruse the links provided under "<u>Home</u>," and "<u>How the Court Works</u>," at minimum reviewing the "case processing flow-chart," "life of an application," "<u>fact sheets</u>" and "<u>Case Law</u>."

Review these links and others to learn basic information on the Court's current operations — how cases are submitted, how many cases are pending, what kinds of claims are brought, who the defendants are and what the Court can do. More detailed information about the Court's decided cases, arranged by various subject matters (e.g., "sexual identity" or "forced labor and trafficking") in "case law guides," are linked to the main webpage.

Although not necessary, it is also instructive to visit the Court's webcasts of hearings and listen to an oral argument. (For example, the 2010 argument before the Grand Chamber in ***Al-Skeini*** *and others v. the United Kingdom* (no. 55721/07) and *Al Jedda v. the United Kingdom* (no. 27021/08) concerning the issue of whether the Convention applies to British activity during the war in Iraq in which six civilians were shot and killed.)

An important consideration for any system of human rights protection is the process of enforcement. As noted by Professor Buergenthal above, the ECtHR is generally well respected and has been relatively effective as measured by state compliance with its decisions. The judgments of the Court are legally binding under the treaty. States found out of compliance are expected to both remedy the particular violation (including payment of damages) and take action to prevent similar violations. Neither the Court nor the CoE itself, however, is given explicit powers to force compliance via sanction. Rather, the CoE puts substantial political pressure on state parties by creating an enforcement process, which relies upon reporting and follow up. Most member states comply with the Court's decisions interpreting and applying the Convention even when controversial. It is generally the task of the CoE (via its Council of government ministers) to pursue enforcement of the Court's decisions. The Council of Europe's Secretariat maintains a "Department for the Execution of Judgments of the European Court of Human Rights," which tracks compliance and reports to the Council. Its website provides detailed information about enforcement.

As noted above, the great majority of countries accept and implement the decisions of the ECtHR. There have, however, been some notable examples in which countries have resisted implementations of ECtHR decisions or norms explicitly provided by the European Convention. Consider these two recent illustrations of the problem.

a. Problems with Expansion: The Russian Connection

Even well before the Russian invasion of Ukraine and the government's massive crackdown on independent media, the CoE encountered significant on-going difficulties in effectively enforcing human rights in this recalcitrant, repressive state. As noted by the web news site, Russia Direct:

> According to the 2014 annual report of the ECHR, as of December 31, 2014, there were 69,900 cases pending before the ECHR. Of those, 9,990 were brought against Russia, which is more than were brought against any other member of the Council of Europe except for Italy (10,087) and Ukraine (13,635). Four nations — Italy, Russia, Turkey, and Ukraine — together account for 43,200 of the 69,900 pending cases before the ECHR (61.8 percent).

> In 2014, the ECHR issued a total of 129 judgments against Russia in which the Court found at least one violation of the provisions of the European

Convention on Human Rights. The leading bases for these judgments were violations of the right to liberty and security (56), inhuman or degrading treatment (50), and violations of the right to an effective remedy (30).

In 2014, the ECHR rendered more judgments against Russia than any other country. After the 129 judgments issued against Russia, the next highest totals were for Turkey (101) and Romania (87).

Things then got worse in 2014, when the President of Ukraine fled and sought refuge in Russia. Russian troops, at first disguised with non-descript uniforms, invaded Crimea, a region of Ukraine, and shortly thereafter annexed it to Russia. Shortly after that invasion of Crimea, Russia actively assisted Russian speaking separatists in eastern Ukraine, who began fighting to secede from Ukraine and join Russia. Russian involvement became more explicit, with Russian troops and arms actively invading several regions in Eastern Ukraine. In late 2014, a ceasefire was entered into between the Ukrainian government, the rebels, and Russia that essentially froze a Russian dominated autonomous region in parts of Eastern Ukraine. The Council of Europe ultimately suspended Russia over its actions in Crimea and Ukraine. What was notable, however, was the lack of strong action by the Council of Europe earlier in the conflict and the relatively more assertive action by the European Union in attempting to resolve Russia's violation of international law and international human rights norms, although those actions by the European Union have not proven strongly effective. In 2015, the Russian lower house of Parliament, the Duma, adopted a law which, in effect, enables Russian courts to ignore decisions of the ECtHR.

The suspension of Russia from the Council of Europe, at least temporarily, suggests that tolerance for Russian intransigence is not inexhaustible. The experience with Russia, however, appears to reinforce the suggestion made in the Wilets article on a Multiple Track of Human Rights Protection: "The geographically broader the entity, the less effective the entity will be in its ability to effectively enforce human rights norms." This has become abundantly clear after Russia's actions after its admission into the Council of Europe despite the reservations of many of the Council's members.

b. The European Roma

The Roma are an ethnic group that is widely dispersed throughout Europe. The Roma have been widely targeted for persecution, and some of those sentiments are summarized in these linked articles about the miserable conditions and expulsion of the Roma. As the articles note, what is notable about the Roma situation is the prevalence of resistance to complying with European human rights norms and ECtHR decisions by countries with otherwise good human rights records. The plight of the Roma provides a vivid illustration of countries' resistance to complying with the norms and decisions of even highly regarded international institutions, when public sentiment is unfavorable. The Council of Europe website also addresses Roma issues.

## 4. Critical Jurisprudence: ECtHR Case Law

a. Overview

After reviewing the basic information on the system available at the web pages provided above, you should read the case excerpts provided below. Pay particular attention to how the Court views its role vis-à-vis democratically elected national governments when faced with controversial moral issues under the Convention. What do the terms "margin of appreciation," "subsidiarity," "European supervision," and "European consensus," mean in the European system? How does the Court evaluate state imposed limitations on rights invoked as "necessary" in a democratic society?

b. Dudgeon v. UK (Northern Ireland)

PROCEDURE

1. The Dudgeon case was referred to the Court by the European Commission of Human Rights ("the Commission"). The case originated in an application against the United Kingdom of Great Britain and Northern Ireland lodged with the Commission on 22 May 1976 under Article 25 (art. 25) of the Convention for the Protection of Human Rights and Fundamental Freedoms ("the Convention") by a United Kingdom citizen, Mr. Jeffrey Dudgeon.

AS TO THE FACTS

13. Mr. Jeffrey Dudgeon, who is 35 years of age, is a shipping clerk resident in Belfast, Northern Ireland.

Mr. Dudgeon is a homosexual and his complaints are directed primarily against the existence in Northern Ireland of laws which have the effect of making certain homosexual acts between consenting adult males criminal offences.

**A. The relevant law in Northern Ireland**

14. The relevant provisions currently in force in Northern Ireland are contained in the Offences against the Person Act 1861, the Criminal Law Amendment Act 1885 and the common law.

Under sections 61 and 62 of the 1861 Act, committing and attempting to commit buggery are made offences punishable with maximum sentences of life imprisonment and ten years' imprisonment, respectively. Buggery consists of sexual intercourse per anum by a man with a man or a woman, or per anum or per vaginam by a man or a woman with an animal.

\*\*\*

15. Acts of homosexuality between females are not, and have never been, criminal offences, although the offence of indecent assault may be committed by one woman on another under the age of 17.

\*\*\*

## F. The personal circumstances of the applicant

33. On 21 January 1976, the police went to Mr. Dudgeon's address to execute a warrant under the Misuse of Drugs Act 1971. During the search of the house, a quantity of cannabis was found, which subsequently led to another person being charged with drug offences. Personal papers, including correspondence and diaries, belonging to the applicant in which were described homosexual activities were also found and seized. As a result, he was asked to go to a police station where for about four and a half hours he was questioned, on the basis of these papers, about his sexual life. The Director, in consultation with the Attorney General, decided that it would not be in the public interest for proceedings to be brought. Mr. Dudgeon was so informed in February 1977 and his papers, with annotations marked over them, were returned to him.

## PROCEEDINGS BEFORE THE COMMISSION

34. In his application, lodged with the Commission on 22 May 1976, Mr. Dudgeon claimed that:

— the existence, in the criminal law in force in Northern Ireland, of various offences capable of relating to male homosexual conduct and the police investigation in January 1976 constituted an unjustified interference with his right to respect for his private life, in breach of Article 8 (art. 8) of the Convention;

— he had suffered discrimination, within the meaning of Article 14 (art. 14) of the Convention, on grounds of sex, sexuality, and residence.

The applicant also claimed compensation.

35. By decision of 3 March 1978, the Commission declared admissible the applicant's complaints concerning the laws in force in Northern Ireland prohibiting homosexual acts between males (or attempts at such acts), but inadmissible as being manifestly ill-founded his complaints concerning the existence in Northern Ireland of certain common law offences.

In its report adopted on 13 March 1980 (Article 31 of the Convention) (art. 31), the Commission expressed the opinion that:

— the legal prohibition of private consensual homosexual acts involving male persons under 21 years of age was not in breach of the applicant's rights either under Article 8 (art. 8) (eight votes to two) or under Article 14 read in conjunction with Article 8 (art. 14+8) (eight votes to one, with one abstention);

— the legal prohibition of such acts between male persons over 21 years of age breached the applicant's right to respect for his private life under Article 8 (art. 8) (nine votes to one);

— it was not necessary to examine the question whether the last-mentioned prohibition also violated Article 14 read in conjunction with Article 8 (art. 14+8) (nine votes to one).

The report contains one separate opinion.

## AS TO THE LAW

## I. THE ALLEGED BREACH OF ARTICLE 8 (art. 8)

A. Introduction

37. The applicant complained that under the law in force in Northern Ireland he is liable to criminal prosecution on account of his homosexual conduct and that he has experienced fear, suffering, and psychological distress directly caused by the very existence of the laws in question — including fear of harassment and blackmail. He further complained that, following the search of his house in January 1976, he was questioned by the police about certain homosexual activities and that personal papers belonging to him were seized during the search and not returned until more than a year later.

He alleged that, in breach of Article 8 (art. 8) of the Convention, he has thereby suffered, and continues to suffer, an unjustified interference with his right to respect for his private life.

38. Article 8 (art. 8) provides as follows:

"1. Everyone has the right to respect for his private and family life, his home, and his correspondence.

2. There shall be no interference by a public authority with the exercise of this right except such as is in accordance with the law and is necessary in a democratic society in the interests of national security, public safety, or the economic well-being of the country, for the prevention of disorder or crime, for the protection of health or morals, or for the protection of the rights and freedoms of others."

## B. The existence of an interference with an Article 8 (art. 8) right

40. The Commission unanimously concluded that "the legislation complained of interferes with the applicant's right to respect for his private life guaranteed by Article 8 par. 1 (art. 8-1), in so far as it prohibits homosexual acts committed in private between consenting males" (see paragraphs 94 and 97 of the Commission's report).

The Government, without conceding the point, did not dispute that Mr. Dudgeon is directly affected by the laws and entitled to claim to be a "victim" thereof under Article 25 (art. 25) of the Convention. Nor did the Government contest the Commission's above-quoted conclusion.

41. The Court sees no reason to differ from the views of the Commission: the maintenance in force of the impugned legislation constitutes a continuing interference with the applicant's right to respect for his private life (which includes his sexual life) within the meaning of Article 8 par. 1 (art. 8-1). In the personal circumstances of the applicant, the very existence of this legislation continuously and directly affects his private life: either he

respects the law and refrains from engaging — even in private with consenting male partners — in prohibited sexual acts to which he is disposed by reason of his homosexual tendencies, or he commits such acts and thereby becomes liable to criminal prosecution.

## C. The existence of a justification for the interference found by the Court

45. It next falls to be determined whether the interference is aimed at "the protection of morals" or "the protection of the rights and freedoms of others", the two purposes relied on by the Government.

48. As the Commission rightly observed in its report (at paragraph 101), the cardinal issue arising under Article 8 (art. 8) in this case is to what extent, if at all, the maintenance in force of the legislation is "necessary in a democratic society" for these aims.

49. There can be no denial that some degree of regulation of male homosexual conduct, as indeed of other forms of sexual conduct, by means of the criminal law can be justified as "necessary in a democratic society" . . . [B]ut what distinguishes the law in Northern Ireland from that existing in the great majority of the member States is that it prohibits generally gross indecency between males and buggery whatever the circumstances. The question in the present case is whether the contested provisions of the law of Northern Ireland and their enforcement remain within the bounds of what, in a democratic society, may be regarded as necessary in order to accomplish those aims.

50. A number of principles relevant to the assessment of the "necessity," "in a democratic society," of a measure taken in furtherance of an aim that is legitimate under the Convention have been stated by the Court in previous judgments.

51. Firstly, "necessary" in this context does not have the flexibility of such expressions as "useful," "reasonable," or "desirable," but implies the existence of a "pressing social need" for the interference in question.

52. [Second], it is for the national authorities to make the initial assessment of the pressing social need in each case; accordingly, a margin of appreciation is left to them (ibid). However, their decision remains subject to review by the Court.

As was illustrated by the Sunday Times judgment, the scope of the margin of appreciation is not identical in respect of each of the aims justifying restrictions on a right. [T]he margin of appreciation will be more extensive where the protection of morals is in issue. It is an indisputable fact that "the view taken . . . of the requirements of morals varies from time to time and from place to place, especially in our era," and that "by reason of their direct and continuous contact with the vital forces of their countries, State authorities are in principle in a better position than the international judge to give an opinion on the exact content of those requirements."

However, not only the nature of the aim of the restriction but also the nature of the activities involved will affect the scope of the margin of appreciation. The present case concerns a most intimate aspect of private life. Accordingly, there must exist particularly serious reasons before interferences on the part of the public authorities can be legitimate for the purposes of paragraph 2 of Article 8.

53. Finally, in Article 8 (art. 8) as in several other Articles of the Convention, the notion of "necessity" is linked to that of a "democratic society". According to the Court's case-law, a restriction on a Convention right cannot be regarded as "necessary in a democratic society"—two hallmarks of which are tolerance and broadmindedness—unless, amongst other things, it is proportionate to the legitimate aim pursued.

54. The Court's task is to determine on the basis of the aforesaid principles whether the reasons purporting to justify the "interference" in question are relevant and sufficient under Article 8 par. 2. The Court is not concerned with making any value-judgment as to the morality of homosexual relations between adult males.

56. The Government drew attention to what they described as profound differences of attitude and public opinion between Northern Ireland and Great Britain in relation to questions of morality. Northern Irish society was said to be more conservative and to place greater emphasis on religious factors, as was illustrated by more restrictive laws even in the field of heterosexual conduct.

The Court acknowledges that such differences do exist to a certain extent and are a relevant factor. As the Government and the Commission both emphasized, in assessing the requirements of the protection of morals in Northern Ireland, the contested measures must be seen in the context of Northern Irish society.

The fact that similar measures are not considered necessary in other parts of the United Kingdom or in other member States of the Council of Europe does not mean that they cannot be necessary in Northern Ireland. Where there are disparate cultural communities residing within the same State, it may well be that different requirement, both moral and social, will face the governing authorities.

57. As the Government correctly submitted, it follows that the moral climate in Northern Ireland in sexual matters, in particular as evidenced by the opposition to the proposed legislative change, is one of the matters which the national authorities may legitimately take into account in exercising their discretion.

Although it may be out of line with current attitudes in other communities, its existence among an important sector of Northern Irish society is certainly relevant for the purposes of Article 8 par. 2 (art. 8-2).

60. The Government right affected by the impugned legislation protects an essentially private manifestation of the human personality.

As compared with the era when that legislation was enacted, there is now a better understanding, and in consequence an increased tolerance, of homosexual behaviour to the extent that in the great majority of the member States of the Council of Europe it is no longer considered to be necessary or appropriate to treat homosexual practices of the kind now in question as in themselves a matter to which the sanctions of the criminal law should be applied; the Court cannot overlook the marked changes which have occurred in this regard in the domestic law of the member States. In Northern Ireland itself, the authorities have refrained in recent years from enforcing the law in respect of private homosexual acts between consenting males over the age of 21 years capable of valid consent (see paragraph 30 above). No evidence has been adduced to show that this has been injurious to moral standards in Northern Ireland or that there has been any public demand for stricter enforcement of the law.

It cannot be maintained in these circumstances that there is a "pressing social need" to make such acts criminal offences, there being no sufficient justification provided by the risk of harm to vulnerable sections of society requiring protection or by the effects on the public. On the issue of proportionality, the Court considers that such justifications as there are for retaining the law in force unamended are outweighed by the detrimental effects which the very existence of the legislative provisions in question can have on the life of a person of homosexual orientation like the applicant. Although members of the public who regard homosexuality as immoral may be shocked, offended, or disturbed by the commission by others of private homosexual acts, this cannot on its own warrant the application of penal sanctions when it is consenting adults alone who are involved.

61. Accordingly, the reasons given by the Government, although relevant, are not sufficient to justify the maintenance in force of the impugned legislation in so far as it has the general effect of criminalising private homosexual relations between adult males capable of valid consent.

To sum up, the restriction imposed on Mr. Dudgeon under Northern Ireland law, by reason of its breadth and absolute character, is, quite apart from the severity of the possible penalties provided for, disproportionate to the aims sought to be achieved.

### D. Conclusion

63. Mr. Dudgeon has suffered and continues to suffer an unjustified interference with his right to respect for his private life. There is accordingly a breach of Article 8 (art. 8).

**FOR THE REASONS, THE COURT**

1. Holds by fifteen votes to four that there is a breach of Article 8 (art. 8) of the Convention;

2. Holds by fourteen votes to five that it is not necessary also to examine the case under Article 14 taken in conjunction with Article 8 (art. 14+8);c. The Doctrines of Necessity & Margin of Appreciation

i. The Term "Necessary"

In a number of articles, the European Convention explicitly addresses government restrictions on rights allegedly justified by competing public interests. The Court in Dudgeon, examines this language in reference to the right of privacy which may only be restricted as:

> "is necessary in a democratic society in the interest of national security, public safety or the economic well-being of the country, for the prevention of disorder or crime, for the protection of health or morals, or for the protection of the rights and freedoms of others."

Interpreting this language, the Court establishes several critical points that reflect both the degree of protection required for such rights and the relative roles of the Court and national authorities. First, the Court narrowly interprets the term "necessary" as lacking the "flexibility" of terms such as "useful," "reasonable," or "desirable," implying instead the existence of a "pressing social need" for the restrictions imposed. Second, the Court tells us that a restriction "cannot be regarded as "necessary in a democratic society" — two hallmarks of which are tolerance and broadmindedness — unless, amongst other things, it is proportionate to the legitimate aim pursued." Third, the Court indicates that such judgments must be made first by national authorities who, more familiar with national social and cultural circumstances, are to be given a "margin of appreciation" or deference, ultimately subject to European standards enforced by the Court.

How does the rigorous interpretation that the ECtHR places on the term "necessary" compare to the manner in which the U.S. Supreme Court has evaluated government restrictions on personal liberties under the U.S. Constitution? Under strict scrutiny, the government has the burden of demonstrating that its interference with a fundamental right was necessary to achieve a compelling public interest. For other non-fundamental rights, the challenger must show that the government interference lacked a rational basis (either no legitimate purposes or fails to achieve such objectives). How does this approach generally compare to that taken by the ECtHR? Does the Supreme Court make use of proportionality? Does it consider whether there is an "American" consensus? Should it do so, or are the issues concerning individual rights distinct in the context of a single, unified nation?

ii. "Margin of Appreciation"

As discussed in greater depth below, the ECtHR uses the "margin of appreciation" doctrine to establish a degree of deference to the judgments of a national legislature in determining how a particular right should be interpreted, protected, or restricted for the public interest. Arguably this is similar to the manner in which a U.S. court will sometimes accord certain deference to legislators who are presumed to be accountable to the people and reflect the values and norms of a democratic society. Similarly, the U.S. system of federalism might also reflect these concepts of deference when the Supreme Court interprets the Constitution as either not protecting a certain individual liberty interest or only providing a minimum floor of protection. In either case, states are given the deference to protect (or not) such liberties under their own law.

In considering Professor Donoho's article below, think about the possible similarities between the "margin of appreciation" employed by the European Court of Human Rights and aspects of rights jurisprudence from the US Supreme Court. The "margin" given by the ECtHR depends on several factors including the nature of the right involved and the degree to which the Court perceives a "European consensus" on the specific issue. To what degree do (or should) popular opinion, social consensus, or general moral standards affect the courts' interpretation of rights? Does the U.S. Supreme Court take into consideration national, international, or state law interpretations? Does consensus among U.S. states matter in interpreting a Constitutional right? Does the "margin of appreciation" occurring in the European human rights system have its analogy in U.S. Constitutional law?

Also consider to what extent doctrines like the margin of appreciation, necessity, subsidiarity, and European supervision discussed below, contribute (or not) to the effectiveness of the European system. How are these doctrines important to the success of ECtHR "mechanisms" or processes? Are these processes superior to others we have studied? Could they be successfully applied to the larger global setting or other regional systems? What role do shared economic interests, cultural similarities, and political will have to do with the successes of the European system?

iii. Interpreting the Case Law: Commentary on the Margin of Appreciation

Donoho, Autonomy, Self-Governance, and the Margin of Appreciation: Developing a Jurisprudence of Diversity within Universal Human Rights, 15 Emory Int'l L. Rev. 391 (2001).

***The Margin of Appreciation, Human Rights, and Diversity in Europe

Since the process of European unification began, nearly all of the issues described above have been played out before the supranational institutions of Europe. Distinct from domestic judicial processes, European institutions have been forced to confront diversity issues in light of critical concerns over domestic sovereignty, democratic self-governance, and institutional authority. In particular, the work of the European Court of Human Rights has involved dilemmas highly analogous to those raised by the international debate over the universal versus relative nature of human rights.

Perhaps the most relevant jurisprudence for present purposes is the ECHR's "margin of appreciation doctrine." The ECHR originally articulated the doctrine in its earliest cases to address state derogations of rights under alleged exigent circumstances. This doctrine has since evolved as one of the ECHR's primary tools for accommodating diversity, national sovereignty, and the will of domestic majorities, while enforcing effective implementation of rights under the European Convention. Under this doctrine, national governments are given a certain degree of discretion regarding the specific manner in which they implement European Convention rights. The rationale for the "margin of appreciation" rests upon the primacy of national implementation of rights and the notion that state authorities are often better situated to judge local conditions and the various public interests that inevitably compete with the claims of individuals. When a state's choices fall within a predictably amorphous range of acceptable alternatives, the ECHR will uphold the state's actions as being within its so-called "margin of appreciation."

The margin of appreciation that the ECHR will provide depends upon a number of factors, most prominently whether a European consensus on the issues exists. The importance of the right and the consequences of the state's conduct for the individual are also important factors in determining how wide the margin of appreciation should be in any particular case.

While recognizing the importance of national discretion, the ECHR has repeatedly emphasized that the margin is limited by, and must correspond to, the concept of "European supervision." Under this principle, the ECHR must assert its role as the final arbiter of European Convention rights and ultimately determine the consistency of state conduct with the European Convention and evolving European standards of human rights. The ECHR's teleological orientation to interpretation, demanding scrutiny of state justifications and emphasis on the "effectiveness" of rights, also tends to restrict state discretion.

Although not strictly limited to such rights, the doctrine is frequently invoked when the ECHR is evaluating the scope of personal liberties under Articles 8 through 11, which inevitably implicate the exception clauses of those provisions, requiring a balance of individual versus public interests. These articles, dealing with personal liberties, including freedom of speech, religion, family life, and privacy, expressly allow for limitations on those rights in order to protect certain categories of public interests where "necessary in a democratic society." The ECHR has relied on this language to fashion tests for evaluating and limiting the exercise of discretion allowed national authorities in their implementation of rights. Thus, limitations on such rights must be designed to accomplish a "pressing social need" and the means chosen must be "proportionate" to those ends. In this regard, the ECHR has recognized a hierarchy of rights, deeming some so fundamental to democratic society that little discretion is allowed to national governments. Similarly, some rights, such as criminal due process, are set out in detail in the European Convention and have not generally involved margin analysis, perhaps because they are less susceptible to legitimate variations among state parties.

Review of the ECHR's application of the doctrine reveals its central function: the ECHR utilizes the "margin of appreciation" doctrine to accommodate variations among state parties in their implementation of rights, while at the same time preserving the core "European" values they reflect. In this regard, the ECHR's application of the doctrine has involved resolution of precisely the same kind of conflicts presented in the compromise language of the Vienna Declaration. European governments have frequently defended against alleged violations of the European Convention by asserting cultural, religious, and moral interests, presumably representative of majoritarian will. When a government defends its action or omission on such grounds, the ECHR is called upon to strike a balance between a European (international) human rights standard and the cultural, social, or religious preferences of the state and its democratic majority. In a case challenging Irish legislation prohibiting divorce, for example, the ECHR was essentially asked to decide whether Ireland could follow a path different from the rest of Europe based on the Irish majority's deeply rooted religious and moral aversion to divorce.

Similar considerations have been raised in a variety of other cases brought before the ECHR, such as challenges to state policies involving the education of school children, transsexualism, criminalization of sodomy, abortion and free speech. The underlying question is whether the specific meaning and application of rights, such as free speech, privacy, and family life, may vary from state to state within the European system based upon context, history, religion, or moral preferences. In this context, the ECHR must not only weigh competing interests that may be couched in terms of culture or tradition, but also balance the tension between national prerogatives and self-governance, and the development of uniform European standards.

The ECHR's application of the margin of appreciation doctrine clearly recognizes that variations in the implementation of rights may be acceptable, particularly regarding questions of public morality or other issues for which no strong European consensus exists. In Handyside v. United Kingdom, for example, the ECHR found the lack of European consensus on issues of public morality required that the United Kingdom be given a wide margin of appreciation concerning its decision to ban a sexually explicit book designed for the education of children. In Muller v. Switzerland, the ECHR employed similar reasoning to uphold the decision of local Austrian authorities to close a sexually provocative art showing that was open to the public without restriction. By allowing such discretion, the ECHR has, in effect, endorsed variations in the implementation of rights reflective of European diversity.

As a result, the ECHR has tempered national discretion, and thus the degree of variation among states, where a European consensus on the issue exists, or the importance of the right demands it. Thus, when presented with a challenge to Ireland's anti-sodomy laws, the ECHR was forced to evaluate the competing claims of the Irish majority, which had exerted its moral and cultural preferences in criminal statutes, and individual claimants who were adversely affected by that legislation. The Irish Government defended the legislation by, among other things, relying on the prevailing moral sensibilities of its population. The ECHR explicitly acknowledged the significance of this dominant cultural position in Irish society but found that the existence of a contrary consensus among other parties to the European Convention should prevail.

In essence, that consensus helped the ECHR determine what the core value of the right of privacy included and how to use that consensus as a baseline upon which to evaluate the Irish legislation. In contrast, the ECHR has in other cases used the lack of European consensus to extend a wide margin of appreciation to national authorities. Significantly, the ECHR has recognized that consensus over rights, and acceptable state restrictions on them, is evolutionary as opposed to static. Presumably, the interpretation of a right's specific content will evolve along with European society, ensuring the progressive development of "European" standards.

The ECHR's view of the appropriate margin is also influenced by the nature of the right involved and the consequences to the individual claimant caused by its restriction. Private sexual conduct in Dudgeon v. United Kingdom, for example, involved the "most intimate aspects of private life" requiring significant justifications for state interference. In essence, the ECHR has recognized a hierarchy among rights protected by the European Convention. Thus, alleged infringements or restrictions on rights such as free press and speech and political participation have been subjected to a narrower margin of state discretion than less favored rights such as the use of property. One manifestation of this approach is the ECHR's frequent reference to — and reliance on — its perception of modern, liberal, and democratic society and its foundation based in "pluralism, tolerance, and broad-mindedness without which there is no democratic society". State interference with those rights that are deeply associated with these ideals requires a high level of justification.

For present purposes, the significance of the ECHR's use of the margin of appreciation doctrine does not rest on the complex nuances of that jurisprudence. Indeed, as discussed below, there are a number of obvious and significant differences in circumstances that counsel against wholesale adoption of the margin of appreciation doctrine in the global context. Rather, its potential significance lies in its most salient features. First, the ECHR uses the margin of appreciation doctrine to recognize a variable degree of state discretion in the implementation of rights based on, among other things, cultural, religious and social preferences. The acknowledgment of such preferences in the interpretation of human rights, as seemingly demanded by the language of the Vienna Declaration, probably requires the allowance of some such discretion. Second, the ECHR attempts to constrain that discretion by reliance on a number of relevant factors, among the most important of which is the existence of consensus over meaning, the importance of the right, and the consequences for the individual. Such factors, particularly reliance on evolving international consensus, reflect the benefits of international supervision and allow the progressive development of rights standards. The selection of appropriate criteria by which to limit state discretion is, of course, critical for avoiding abuse and preserving core human rights values.

Third, the ECHR recognizes a hierarchy among rights in measuring state discretion. While controversial for other reasons, hierarchies among rights in this context would allow human rights institutions to distinguish those rights susceptible to culturally based variation from those that are not. Such hierarchies similarly allow these institutions to demand greater justifications for state limitations on certain rights. Fourth, the ECHR couples the margin of appreciation doctrine with a dynamic and teleological view of interpretation such that the meaning of rights and its view of permissible restrictions generally favor an expansive view of rights and protection of the individual. In this way, human rights institutions may work toward the progressive development of rights, enhance the protection given to individuals, and avoid stagnation in the status quo of oppressive cultural traditions. The ECHR has adopted an approach to interpretation that ultimately emphasizes protection of the right holder by placing the burden of justification for restrictions on the state.

Finally, the ECHR remains the final arbiter of the meaning of rights, tempering state discretion with international supervision. Although, perhaps inevitably problematic in a state-centric system, the exercise of meaningful supervisory authority seems critical to the ultimate success of the international human rights system and to the progressive development of rights.

## 5. Protocol 14 (entered into force June 1, 2010)

From: protocol 14

### Need to increase the effectiveness of the control system established by the Convention

*Protocol No. 11*

3. Protocol No. 11 substituted a full-time single Court for the old system established by the 1950 Convention, namely, a Commission, a Court and the Committee of Ministers which played a certain "judicial" role.

4. Protocol No. 11, which was opened for signature on 11 May 1994 and came into force on 1 November 1998, was intended, firstly, to simplify the system

so as to reduce the length of proceedings, and, secondly, to reinforce their judicial character. This protocol made the system entirely judicial (abolition of the Committee of Ministers' quasi-judicial role, deletion of the optional clauses concerning the right of individual application and the compulsory jurisdiction of the Court) and created a single full-time Court.

5. ***Whereas the Commission and Court had given a total of 38,389 decisions and judgments in the forty-four years up to 1998 (the year in which Protocol No. 11 took effect), the single Court has given 61,633 in five years.[2] None the less, the reformed system, which originated in proposals first made in the 1980s, proved inadequate to cope with the new situation. Indeed, since 1990, there has been a considerable and continuous rise in the number of individual applications as a result, amongst other things, of the enlargement of the Council of Europe. Thus the number of applications increased from 5,279 in 1990 to 10,335 in 1994 (+96%), 18,164 in 1998 (+76%) and 34,546 in 2002 (+90%). ***

6. This increase is due not only to the accession of new States Parties (between the opening of Protocol No. 11 for signature in May 1994 and the adoption of Protocol No. 14, thirteen new States Parties ratified the Convention, extending the protection of its provisions to over 240 million additional individuals) and to the rapidity of the enlargement process, but also to a general increase in the number of applications brought against states which were party to the Convention in 1993. In 2004, the Convention system was open to no fewer than 800 million people. As a result of the massive influx of individual applications, the effectiveness of the system, and thus the credibility and authority of the Court, were seriously endangered.

*The problem of the Court's excessive caseload*

7. It is generally recognised that the Court's excessive caseload (during 2003, some 39,000 new applications were lodged and at the end of that year, approximately 65,000 applications were pending before it) manifests itself in two areas in particular: i. processing the very numerous individual applications which are terminated without a ruling on the merits, usually because they are declared inadmissible (more than 90% of all applications), and ii. processing individual applications which derive from the same structural cause as an earlier application which has led to a judgment finding a breach of the Convention (repetitive cases following a so-called "pilot judgment"). ***

12. The principle of subsidiarity underlies all the measures taken to increase the effectiveness of the Convention's control system. . . . In other words, securing rights and freedoms is primarily the responsibility of the Parties; the Court's role is subsidiary. ***

*Effectiveness of filtering and of subsequent processing of applications by the Court*

18. Filtering and subsequent processing of applications by the Court are the main areas in which Protocol No. 14 makes concrete improvements. . . .

38. The filtering capacity is increased by making a single judge competent to declare inadmissible or strike out an individual application. . . .

39. A new admissibility requirement is inserted in Article 35 of the Convention. . . . by empowering it to declare inadmissible applications where the applicant has not suffered a significant disadvantage and which, in terms of respect for human rights, do not otherwise require an examination on the merits by the Court. ***

40. The competence of the committees of three judges is extended to cover repetitive cases. They are empowered to rule, in a simplified procedure, not only on the admissibility but also on the merits of an application, if the underlying question in the case is already the subject of well-established case-law of the Court.

46. Finally, an amendment has been introduced with a view to possible accession of the European Union to the Convention.

# C.  The Increasing Role of the European Union ("EU") as an Enforcer of Human Rights Norms

## 1. Overview: Understanding the EU and its Historical Development Culminating in Charter of Fundamental Rights

Since its origins in 1951,[118] the European Union has evolved from a relatively small common market designed to eliminate certain trade barriers into what is sometimes called the federal government of Europe. Through a series of treaties (now commonly referred to as the EU's Constitution) the EU now consists of a single market of twenty-eight countries, which ensures free movement of not only twenty percent of the world's gross domestic product but also over 500 million people. EU institutions have the power to create binding law, which is superior to the law of its member states and is subject to direct application in their national courts. Nineteen of its twenty-eight member states share a common currency which is also used by the EU itself. Although during its evolution the EU has greatly expanded the scope of its jurisdiction from purely economic to more social issues, it only recently fully adopted a legally authorized human rights agenda.

The process of incorporating human rights into EU law began with decisions of the European Court of Justice (the judicial institution of the European Union) that declared that respect for human rights formed an important part of the general legal principles to be enforced by the Court. The Court further held that it would safeguard

---

118.  A good summary of the European Union's historical development from the European Coal and Steel Community to its present form can be found at Wikipedia.

human rights in accordance with not only the constitutional traditions of member states but also the European Convention of Human Rights, as interpreted by the European Court of Human Rights in Strasburg. In 2000, the Union created the Charter of Fundamental Rights which became legally binding on the Union and the member states in 2009 with the Treaty of Lisbon.

The European Union describes the Charter in the following terms.

Charter of Fundamental Rights

The Charter of Fundamental Rights recognises a range of personal, civil, political, economic and social rights of EU citizens and residents, enshrining them into EU law.

In December 2009, with the entry into force of the Lisbon Treaty, the charter was given binding legal effect equal to the Treaties. To this end, the charter was amended and proclaimed a second time in December 2007.

**Content**

The charter brings together in a single document rights previously found in a variety of legislative instruments, such as in national and EU laws, as well as in international conventions from the Council of Europe, the United Nations (UN) and the International Labour Organisation (ILO). By making fundamental rights clearer and more visible, it creates legal certainty within the EU.

The Charter of Fundamental Rights contains a preamble and 54 Articles, grouped in seven chapters:

**Chapter I: dignity** (human dignity, the right to life, the right to the integrity of the person, prohibition of torture and inhuman or degrading treatment or punishment, prohibition of slavery and forced labour);

**Chapter II: freedoms** (the right to liberty and security, respect for private and family life, protection of personal data, the right to marry and found a family, freedom of thought, conscience and religion, freedom of expression and information, freedom of assembly and association, freedom of the arts and sciences, the right to education, freedom to choose an occupation and the right to engage in work, freedom to conduct a business, the right to property, the right to asylum, protection in the event of removal, expulsion, or extradition);

**Chapter III**

**equality** (equality before the law, non-discrimination, cultural, religious and linguistic diversity, equality between men and women, the rights of the child, the rights of the elderly, integration of persons with disabilities);

**Chapter IV solidarity** (workers' right to information and consultation within the undertaking, the right of collective bargaining and action, the right of access to placement services, protection in the event of unjustified dismissal, fair and just working conditions, prohibition of child labour and protection of young people at work, family and professional life, social security and social assistance, health care, access to services of general economic interest, environmental protection, consumer protection);

**Chapter V: citizens' rights** (the right to vote and stand as a candidate at elections to the European Parliament and at municipal elections, the right to good administration, the right of access to documents, European Ombudsman, the right to petition, freedom of movement and residence, diplomatic and consular protection);

**Chapter VI: justice** (the right to an effective remedy and a fair trial, presumption of innocence and the right of defence, principles of legality and proportionality of criminal offences and penalties, the right not to be tried or punished twice in criminal proceedings for the same criminal offence);

**Chapter VII: general provisions.**

**Scope**

The charter applies to the European institutions, subject to the principle of subsidiarity, and may under no circumstances extend the powers and tasks conferred on them by the Treaties. The charter also applies to EU countries when they implement EU law.

If any of the rights correspond to rights guaranteed by the European Convention on Human Rights, the meaning and scope of those rights is to be the same as defined by the convention, though EU law may provide for more extensive protection. Any of the rights derived from the common constitutional traditions of EU countries must be interpreted in accordance to those traditions.

Protocol (No) 30 to the Treaties on the application of the charter to Poland and the United Kingdom restricts the interpretation of the charter by the Court of Justice and the national courts of these two countries, in particular regarding rights relating to solidarity (chapter IV).

An additional description and resource regarding the Charter can be found here.

# 2. Fundamental Rights Agency (FRA)

**From: Europa**

Fundamental Rights Agency (FRA)

This Regulation establishes the European Fundamental Rights Agency (FRA), in order to extend the mandate of the European Monitoring Centre on Racism and Xenophobia (EUMC). The objective of the Agency, which became operational on 1 March 2007, is to provide the Community institutions and the Member States of the European Union (EU) assistance and expertise on fundamental rights.

**Council Regulation (EC) No 168/2007 of 15 February 2007 establishing a European Union Agency for Fundamental Rights.**

## SUMMARY

The objective of the Agency is to provide Community institutions and bodies and Member States of the European Union (EU) with assistance and expertise on fundamental rights when implementing Community law. The Agency aims to help the institutions, bodies and Member States fully respect these rights.

The Agency must also establish close institutional relations at international, European and national levels, particularly with the Council of Europe, the Organisation for Security and Cooperation in Europe (OSCE), the competent Community agencies, and governmental agencies and public bodies, including national institutions for the protection of human rights. The aim is to cooperate and avoid duplication of work.

Agreement between the European Community and the Council of Europe on **cooperation between the European Union Agency for Fundamental Rights and the Council of Europe** [Official Journal L 186 of 15.7.2008].

This Agreement sets up a framework for the cooperation between the FRA and the Council of Europe. The purpose is first of all to avoid duplication, and secondly, to complement and provide added value to their work. The cooperation is based on regular contacts. To this end, a contact person is appointed in both organisations.

# D. Somewhere Between International Human Rights Law and Domestic Incorporation: The "Federalization of Human Rights Law"

The article below summarizes the similarities in the development of the federalization of human rights norms in the United States and the European Union and discusses how some of the greatest advances in human rights protection have occurred at the federal or quasi-federal level, rather than at the strictly international level.

## 1. J. Wilets, The Thin Line between International Law and Federalism: A Comparative Legal and Historical Perspective on US Federalism and European Union Law. 1 STUDI SULL'INTEGRAZIONE EUROPEA 35 (2010)

(Heavily abridged, footnotes omitted)

This article parallels the relationship between the US system of federalism and European law, and the similar operation of the two systems in the *domestic* legal arena *particularly with respect to human right enforcement.* This article will illustrate that the United States system of federalism, particularly in its early years, bore much more resemblance to contemporary international law than commonly supposed. The significant of that statement is, as we've already learned, international law is generally less effective at implementing human rights norms that domestic law. Conversely, this article will also argue the correlative: that European law is much more characteristic of US federal law in its application in the *domestic sphere* than international law.

The US Constitution

The process of political integration of the states of the United States following the ratification of the United States Constitution has been much misunderstood. The process of integration in the United States characteristic of what we would call contemporary "federalism" took centuries to develop, and it can be argued that the United States, in many respects, did not even achieve the level of political and economic integration achieved by the present-day European Union until the very recent past.

The discussion below more fully illustrates the ambiguous distinction between early American federalism and contemporary international law.

Prior to the passage of the 14th Amendment following the Civil War, the federal government had little Constitutional power to regulate US states' treatment of their own residents, even actions, such as slavery that are now characterized as crimes against humanity. States were largely free to treat their own citizens however cruelly or arbitrarily they wished, as long as such policies did not affect the common market, foreign policy, or other limited area of federal jurisdiction. At the risk of stating the obvious, states could even enslave their own inhabitants and no state was under any requirement to provide any of the rights contained in the federal bill of rights to their own citizens. There is no other historical example in the last three centuries of one legally unified country where a class of people were full citizens in some jurisdictions and slaves in other jurisdictions in the same country.

Prior to the passage of the post Civil War Amendments to the US Constitution, which imposed the requirements of equal protection on the states, the United States practiced one of the most racialized systems of slavery ever promulgated. The United States experience with slavery was not just unique to the Western World, but arguably to World History as well. As noted by the report of the Brown University Steering Committee on Slavery and Justice (the "Brown Report"):

If American slavery has any claims to being historically "peculiar," its peculiarity lay in its rigorous racialism, the systematic way in which racial ideas were used to demean and deny the humanity of people of even partial African descent. This historical legacy would make the process of incorporating the formerly enslaved as citizens far more problematic in the United States than in other New World slave societies.[119]

This would help explain the historical distinction in racial attitudes between the United States and other countries such as Brazil, with an even longer history of slavery than the United States. The United States was perhaps unique in the history of the world in its racialization of slavery. As noted by the Brown Report:

Few if any societies in history carried this logic further than the United States, where people of African descent came to be regarded as a distinct "race" of persons, fashioned by nature for hard labor.

In other words, prior to the post-Civil War 14th Amendment to the U.S. Constitution, the U.S. federal government had less legal power to regulate human rights abuses by U.S. states against their citizens than international law presently has to regulate human rights abuses by nations against their own citizens. In this respect, U.S. states enjoyed more sovereignty and autonomy from federal interference than individual nations currently enjoy in the international legal system.

The sovereign US states in pre-Civil War United States thus retained many of the attributes of what we would today normally consider independent states where sovereignty is regularly curtailed by certain supranational institutional rules affecting economics, taxation, labor, human and animal health, product safety, anti-trust and securities regulation, to name just a few.

At a minimum, therefore, the US states, prior to the Civil War, maintained much greater sovereignty over their *domestic law* than the member states of the contemporary European Union.

However, even after the Civil War and the passage of the 14th Amendment, U.S. states still enjoyed certain kinds of sovereignty that even independent countries do not currently enjoy under international law. The concept of sovereignty normally implies the power to regulate the activity of individuals residing within the territory of the sovereign. The U.S. Constitution originally envisioned the several states as the primary regulators of individual activity, not the federal government, and this regulatory division continued even after the Civil War.

The inability of federal law to protect, or regulate the conduct of, *individuals*, as opposed to the respective *states*, is much more characteristic of traditional international law, not domestic law. This division of power left the federal government unable to prevent creation by the states of a pervasive

---

119. Report of the Brown University Steering Committee on Slavery and Justice, "*Slavery and Justice*," at 8 ("Brown Report").

system of private segregation that would now be characterized as a violation of *jus cogens* international law.

The system of racial apartheid in southern US states was unique to the industrialized world and, as of the early 1960's, was officially practiced only in the outlaw nations of Rhodesia and South Africa. Even two individuals married in one state could be arrested in another state for the simple act of being married until 1967, hardly a legal characteristic of a country with one unified domestic legal system of human rights protection. Indeed, the parents of President Barack Obama would have been arrested simply for being married had they chosen to visit one of sixteen U.S. states that criminalized their marriage.

The enormous advances in human rights protection in the United States resulting from the elimination of American slavery did not result from a consensual political process within the United States, but because the values and mores of the North were imposed on the South through a violent, non-consensual strengthening of the federalist process. Similarly, the end of apartheid in the United States also came about only through a strengthening of the implied powers of federalism, piggybacking on the Commerce Clause of the Constitution. The Commerce Clause itself was originally intended only to create a common market, not create a national civil rights law. The U.S. Supreme Court was forced to resort to the Commerce Clause of the U.S. Constitution, and in some cases the "Spending Clause," because no other Constitutional authority existed for federal regulation of individual discrimination. As discussed below, the European Union's central lawmaking authorities have had much less difficulty in finding explicit or implicit authority in the EU treaties for more far-reaching "federal legislation" regarding human rights protection.

As in the EU, it was the creation of a unitary economic market, as provided by the Commerce Clause, which gave the federal government the implied power to regulate issues with only very attenuated relationships with interstate commerce, including the human rights of its citizens.

The European Union: From a common market to "Federalism"?

The domestic law of the European Union shares the four core legal characterizations of United States domestic federal law.

First, EU law enjoys supremacy over individual EU member state law, equivalent to US federal supremacy over state law in those areas where the federal government has authority to legislate.

Second, as in US federal law, much of European law, with the exception of directives, is directly effective in the domestic legal system of EU member states without further action by EU member states. [E]ven EU member states that do not recognize the direct incorporation of international law into their domestic law nevertheless accept this principle in the context of the European legal system. Thus, this characteristic of EU law is also much more typical of a federal system than international law.

Third, judicial review by the European Court of Justice ("ECJ") of member state judicial decisions for compliance with EU law is actually even more stringent and comprehensive than federal judicial review of US state law or judicial decisions. In the United States, federal judicial review of legislation or cases allegedly in conflict with the Constitution happens only when a specific case is brought to challenge the constitutionality of the statute and then review by the Supreme Court is infrequent and limited by judicial rules that require courts to avoid adjudicating constitutional issues if at possible. In Europe, on the other hand, review of lower court cases or legislation allegedly in conflict with EU law can happen in the lower courts at the discretion of the lower court when the EU issue will be sent up to the ECJ for determination of that particular issue. Moreover, the decisions of a country's highest court involving EU law is subject to mandatory review by the ECJ.

Fourth, the extensive implied powers of the EU lawmaking bodies to legislate on matters not explicitly delegated to it by the EU treaties are, as discussed above, the aspect of US federalism that ultimately enable the United States to forge what can now be considered a unified state.

Not only does EU law share the core fundamental legal characteristics of US federalism, EU treaty law codifies the four freedoms of movement of people, goods, services and capital that are the legal equivalent of the US Constitution's "Commerce Clause," Privileges and Immunities Clause of Article IV, and the Privileges or Immunities Clause of the XIV Amendment.

The European Union has thus witnessed a similar "federalization" of broad substantive areas of law as has the United States. Aside from defense and foreign policy, admittedly substantial exceptions, it is difficult to see how European Union law differs from US federal law in terms of its effect as *domestic law*. Moreover, increasing areas of law and policy related to foreign policy and external relations are being "federalized" to the extent that: (1) many foreign policy issues are trade issues, which by definition must be dealt with at the EU, not national, level; (2) the freedom of movement of people, goods, capital and services within the European Union has meant that the relevant borders for issues related to business regulation, immigration, criminal control, product safety, public safety are usually the borders of the EU, not the borders of each EU state

In many respects the evolution of European "federalism" has been even more dramatic than that of US federalism. Unlike the United States, the members of the European Union began the process of unification as independent countries with different languages and vast cultural differences, and as historical adversaries with violent histories of nationalist conflict. It was almost inconceivable in 1945 that the countries of Western and Central Europe would, in a span of approximately 50 years, emerge as a unified common market with almost all physical borders eliminated.

The European Union now enjoys a completely unified common market with legal rules regulating that market that are largely similar to those regulating the national economy of the United States. However, in certain ways the federalization and unification of the European Union has gone further than the United States, *at least domestically*. It is easier for lawyers to practice law in a different EU state than it is for lawyers in the United States. Unlike in the United States, students wishing to study in another EU state not only cannot be charged higher tuition than citizens of the other EU state, they are entitled to receive the same living stipends as students from the host country. In summary, the European Union frequently applies its principles of non-discrimination against individuals from other states, and the EU equivalent of the US Constitution's "privileges and immunities" clause and Commerce Clause, more rigorously than does the United States.

It is in the area of civil, political, economic and social human rights that the European Union has most clearly tracked the evolution of US federalism by linking the creation of a common market with the unification of other kinds of law.

The jurisdiction of the EU's European Court of Justice is technically limited to the law encompassed by the EU's treaties. Until relatively recently, the EU treaties have largely focused on issues relating to the creation of the common market and largely avoided addressing human rights issues *per se*, much like the original US Constitution before the creation of the Bill of Rights. Human rights in the European Union, and Europe in general, have been traditionally enforced by the European Court of Human Rights, which has jurisdiction over all the member countries of the Council of Europe, encompassing almost all of the countries of the continent of Europe.

The governing treaty of the European Court of Human Rights is the European Convention on Human Rights and Fundamental Freedoms. The European Court of Human Rights is an enormously respected institution, and, until recently, its decisions have been almost universally recognized and enforced by the member states of the Council of Europe. However, as the EU treaties have begun incorporating increasingly greater human rights protections above and beyond those guaranteed by the European Convention, the role of the EU's European Court of Justice as a guarantor of human rights has vastly increased. Moreover, the recent incorporation of the European Union Charter of Fundamental Rights into EU law has effectively given the European Union the equivalent a US Constitutional Bill of Rights, but even more far-reaching. This has resulted in the European Union's "federalization" of what were previously European international human rights norms. Because the benefits of EU membership are so much more valuable than membership in the Council of Europe because of the attendant economic and other benefits, the European Union is able to force all of its member states to comply with its more rigorous human rights norms. Moreover, with the admission of Russia into the Council of Europe, it has become more difficult for the Council of Europe to effectively enforce the norms in the European Convention, and more difficult to reach a consensus among the more numerous and politically diverse members of the Council of Europe regarding what precisely those norms are.

In this sense, the European Court of Human Rights has begun looking less like a European human rights Supreme Court, and is coming to resemble a more traditional international law court. This is occurring even as the European Court of Justice, by increasingly ruling on human rights protections explicitly provided or implied within the Treaty of Rome and the subsequent treaties, has come increasingly to resemble the United States Supreme Court to the extent that its jurisdiction has come to increasingly cover the full ambit of what one would normally characterize as domestic law.

The European Union has thus evolved from a common market into an entity that is perhaps the most potent protector of individual human, economic and social rights the world has ever seen, arguably surpassing the Council of Europe as the most effective and comprehensive protector of basic human rights in the world.

The failure of many human rights theorists to acknowledge, or even consider, this reality reflects this classical and increasingly outdated dichotomy between international and domestic law. When international norms are incorporated into "federal law" such as European Union law, with much more direct, expansive and binding authority than traditional international bodies such as the European Court of Human Rights, that federal body has now effectively become a much more effective enforcer of human rights norms. Similarly, the elimination of some of the most horrific human rights abuses, slavery and American apartheid, occurred not through application of international law through traditional international legal institutions, but through the forceful application of those norms through federal law.

CONCLUSION

It is clear that contemporary United States federalism is not international law. It is also clear that the European Union does not yet have all the attributes of a single political system like the United States, at least with respect to foreign and military affairs. Nevertheless, the European Union and the United States reached a very similar form of *domestic* federal structure coming from very different assumptions. The United States began the process of confederation and then federation from a desire to maintain a united front in international relations, creating a common market only under the later Constitutional process. The European Union, however, has begun from an assumption that the

EU countries would maintain full independence in foreign relations and security matters, and that the European Union project was more limited to the domestic goal of creating a common market, thereby avoiding conflict *inter se*.

Nevertheless, as illustrated in this article, the *domestic* legal realities of United States federalism and European Union law are highly similar. Moreover, with the passage of the Lisbon Treaty, the European Union has expanded the reach of European Union law into foreign policy areas that were previously strictly the jurisdiction of inter-governmental European legal institutions. [T]he European Union is illustrating that the line between international law and domestic federal law truly is thin and ambiguous, and that it is indeed possible for a political entity to enjoy a unitary territory and economy, but permit subdivisions of that entity to exercise independent sovereignty with respect to other countries.

Understanding the parallels in the development of both European law and United States federalism has the ability to create new opportunities for re-conceptualizing the role of federalism, international law, and hybrids of the two in the governance of the world's peoples, particularly with respect to their basic human rights.

# E. OSCE: Organization for Security and Cooperation in Europe & the "Human Dimension"

The underlying description of the OSCE is found on the organization's website.

The three OSCE dimensions

In the early 1970s, as tensions lessened between the two sides in the Cold War, contacts slowly increased and a number of understandings were reached, prominent among which was the signing by Richard Nixon and Leonid Brezhnev of the Anti-Ballistic Missile Treaty at the SALT-1 talks in May 1972.

The time was ripe for a Conference on Security and Co-operation in Europe, or CSCE. Finland offered to host the informal preparatory talks, which began in Dipoli on the outskirts of Helsinki in November 1972 and concluded in June the following year with a set of final recommendations, also known as the 'Blue Book'.

It is this 'Blue Book' which contains the seeds of the three OSCE 'dimensions'. It proposed that the conference agenda would be divided into three 'baskets':

1. Questions relating to security in Europe.

2. Co-operation in the fields of economics, of science and technology and of the environment.

3. Co-operation in humanitarian and other fields.

These three 'baskets' formed the core of the Helsinki Final Act, which was signed by the 35 CSCE Heads of State or Government on 1 August 1975. Today, these 'baskets' are usually referred to as the OSCE's three 'dimensions', which are as follows:

- The politico-military dimension
- The economic and environmental dimension
- The human dimension

The OSCE takes a comprehensive approach to the **politico-military dimension** of security, which includes a number of commitments by participating States and mechanisms for conflict prevention and resolution. The Organization also seeks to enhance military security by promoting greater openness, transparency and co-operation.

Activities in the **economic and environmental dimension** include the monitoring of developments in this area among participating States with the aim of alerting them to any threat of conflict; and assisting in the creation of economic and environmental policies and related initiatives to promote security in the OSCE region.

The commitments made by OSCE participating States in the **human dimension** aim to ensure full respect for human rights and fundamental freedoms; to abide by the rule of law; to promote the principles of democracy by building, strengthening, and protecting democratic institutions; and to promote tolerance throughout the OSCE area.

# Chapter 10

# Regional Human Rights Systems: The Inter-American and African Systems

## A. Introduction & Overview

The materials that follow examine the regional human rights systems currently functioning in the Americas and Africa. Each system operates as a component part of a larger regional political organization. The Organization of American States (OAS) maintains the Inter-American system of human rights consisting of the Inter-American Commission and Inter-American Court of Human Rights. The African Union conducts its human rights mandate through the African Commission and Court of Human Rights. As with other institutions we have studied, you should examine critical institutional characteristics of these regional bodies such as their composition, jurisdiction, procedures, and enforcement capacity. You should ultimately be able to compare and contrast these regional systems with the European system and the UN.

Before examining the institutional characteristics and mechanisms of the Inter-American and African Systems, you should read the material and links below to become familiar with the plight of children world-wide, but in particular in the United States, Latin America, and Africa. Consider what remedies might be available under either the Inter-American or African systems for the situations described, taking into account that the perpetrators of abuse are often private parties. How does the protection of children's rights under these systems compare with protections created under the UN system? Is a "rights" approach effective in addressing such abuses?

# B. Abuse and Exploitation of Children: Street Children, Child Labor & Child Soldiers

## 1. Overview

Children are abandoned, exploited, abused, and neglected world-wide on a shockingly grand scale. Human Rights Watch's Children's Rights Division puts it this way: "Millions of children have no access to education, work long hours under hazardous conditions and are forced to serve as soldiers in armed conflict. They suffer targeted attacks on their schools and teachers or languish in institutions or detention centers, where they endure inhumane conditions and assaults on their dignity. Young and immature, they are often easily exploited. In many cases, they are abused by the very individuals responsible for their care." Amnesty International similarly reports, "They miss out on their right to education. They are abandoned and left to fend for themselves on the street. They are recruited into armed forces. They are subjected to the death penalty, are disappeared, are punished by cruel and inhumane methods and suffer many other forms of violence."

Although children in poor and less developed countries perhaps are more likely to suffer such abuses, the situation for children in rich nations such as the United States is often also dismal. Covenant House describes how the problem of homelessness effects US children:

Every Year, More Than 2 Million Kids in America Will Face a Period of Homelessness

Behind the face of every homeless young person is another heartbreaking story — a teenage boy abused by his alcoholic parent, a pregnant girl rejected by her guardian, or a teenager trying to escape gang membership or a life of forced prostitution.

In case after case, the main cause of youth homelessness is physical, sexual, and/or emotional abuse from parents or guardians.

The facts about homelessness are staggering ... but acknowledging the depth of the problem is the first step in fixing it.

- 57% of homeless kids spend at least one day every month without food.
- In the United States, as many as 20,000 kids are forced into prostitution by human trafficking networks every year.
- According to a study of youth in shelters, nearly 50% reported intense conflict or physical harm by a family member as a major contributing factor to their homelessness.
- More than 25% of former foster children become homeless within two to four years of leaving the system.
- 50% of adolescents aging out of foster care and juvenile justice systems will be homeless within six months because they are unprepared

to live independently and have limited education and no social support.

- Almost 40% of the homeless in the United States are under 18.

[Authors' Note: Only the United States and Somalia are not parties to the <u>UN Convention on the Rights of the Child</u>.]

# 2. Street Children

a. Casa Alianza U.K. Network

6th June 2006

### GUATEMALAN SOLDIERS ATTACK STREET CHILDREN

Day after day children and teenagers continue to be murdered in Guatemala, their young bodies showing clear evidence of torture. Equally, street children are constantly threatened and intimidated by police forces. Many of them live in permanent fear of being murdered by police or by hired killers. And yet day after day the Guatemalan government continues to allow such acts to occur with impunity, making the state responsible by omission. Now the National Police is hiring ex-soldiers to impose security, violating peace agreements and bringing fear to several vulnerable groups of Guatemalan society.

Last week, a group of children on the streets of the central zone of Guatemala City told Casa Alianza's educators that a group of soldiers had attacked and humiliated them. They had arrived in two cars, bearing the licence plate numbers 007GDH and 010GDH.

According to the children this has been a regular occurrence in recent weeks; children are also reported to have been put into a pickup and assaulted. These events have been officially reported at the Public Prosecutor's Office, and put forward for investigation (Report No. MP001-2006-38029).

\*\*\*

On May 4th and 5th, the United Nations Committee Against Torture (CAT) held its 36th session in Geneva, examining Guatemala's compliance with the UN Convention Against Torture. The Committee recommended that every law authorising the Guatemalan Army to participate in routine police activities be repealed. The Committee also asked the State of Guatemala to provide information about the measures it has taken to apply recommendations relating to the "social cleansing" of children and adolescents, in particular, the murder of street children and children from marginalised areas, where there is often clear evidence of torture and ill-treatment.

During the past few years, the State of Guatemala has ***failed to respond to most of the UN and NGOs' concerns with regards to the impunity of***

***aggressors and the lack of reparation provided to victims of torture and ill treatment.*** Casa Alianza demands that the state of Guatemala implement a plan to combat this violence, in order to respect children's human rights.

<u>Casa Alianza U.K.</u> reports that only eight convictions involving abuse of street children occurred in Guatemala between 1994 and 1998, with eighty-six percent of the complaints remaining unresolved. In thirty-two percent of the cases authorities claim to have "lost the files." When known perpetrators of violence were members of the national police, ninety-three percent of abuse cases were unresolved.

b. Video Clip — Street Kids in Guatemala

Please watch the short video linked above concerning children living on the streets of Guatemala City.

c. From Human Rights Watch: "Easy Targets: Violence Against Children World-Wide"

Police Violence Against Street Children

*The police treat us badly. They hit us. Not for any particular reason . . . just because they feel like it. They've hit me lots of times. They hit with their rifles, or with sticks, on our backs and stomachs. And sometimes they just punch us in the stomach with their hands. They also take our paint thinner and pour it over our heads. They've done that to me five times. It's awful, it hurts really bad. It gets in your eyes and burns; for half an hour you can't see anything.*

— Beto R., fifteen, Guatemala

Street children risk violence at the hands of the authorities much more frequently than other children. Children on the street are beaten, tortured, sexually assaulted, and sometimes killed. Several factors contribute to this phenomenon: police perceptions of street children as vagrants and criminals, widespread corruption and a culture of police violence, the inadequacy and non-implementation of legal safeguards, and the level of impunity that officials enjoy.

Street children are easy targets because they are young, often small, poor, ignorant of their rights, and frequently do not have responsible adults to look out for them. Police also have financial incentives to resort to violence against children. They beat children for their money or demand payment for protection, to avoid false charges, or for release from (often illegal) custody. . . .

Girls on the street are additionally vulnerable to sexual attacks. Susana F., a sixteen-year-old, reported that she was raped by two police officers while a third kept watch. The officers threatened to put her in prison for having marijuana if she made any noise. "I'm sure this has happened to many other girls. But usually they won't say anything about it. . . . Ugly things happen on the street." . . .

In India, where more than 18 million children live and work on the streets, street children have been routinely detained illegally, beaten, and tortured and sometimes killed by police. In 1995 and 1996, Human Rights Watch interviewed one hundred street children; all reported a fear of the police, and sixty reported police abuse in the form of detentions, beatings, extortion, or verbal abuse. . . .

The scale of violence against street children in India sometimes included custodial deaths of children. Between 1986 and 1995, fourteen children are known to have died in custody in the Andhra Pradesh province, but no police officers were prosecuted in that period.

Street children in Kenya experience similar abuse at the hands of police. Children told Human Rights Watch in 1996 that they were frequently kicked, slapped, or hit with a rifle butt for no reason other than the fact that they were street children. Street children were often subject to extortion, and street girls were asked for sex in addition to money to avoid arrest or to be released from police custody. . . .

In 1996, eighteen months after the acquittal of one Kenyan police reservist for killing a street boy, another street boy was killed by a police reservist. Children present at the shooting could identify the police officers who came toward them with a whip and guns. Two boys had hidden in a ditch. One of them escaped through a tunnel, but the policeman pointed into the ditch and shot the other. The boy who escaped told Human Rights Watch that his friend was shot at point blank range, that he had his arms raised in surrender when he was shot, and that the reservist spat on his body before he walked away.

### d. Sexual Exploitation of Children

Casa Alianza conducted a study in 2004 concerning commercial sexual exploitation of minors in Guatemala. According to the Report:

Casa Alianza's field investigators visited 284 different establishments operating in the sex industry throughout the country. A total of 179 confirmed minors were found in these establishments, which consisted of bars, saunas, private clubs and massage parlours. Another 423 youths were presumed to be minors by Casa Alianza investigators who interviewed each of these children privately. A total of 668 minors were found in these 197 premises that sexually exploited children. Only 85 of establishments visited employed adults only.

## 3. Child Soldiers

Photo by Professor Peter Mantello

By <u>some estimates</u> there are 250–300,000 children under the age of 16 actively engaged in armed conflicts around the world. The proliferation of child soldiers, often forcibly recruited and always abused, has prompted the UN to sponsor the <u>Optional Protocol to the Convention on the Rights of the Child on the Involvement of Children in Armed Conflict</u>, which now has over 160 state parties. The problem is particularly pronounced in Africa. Simply search under images of "<u>child soldiers</u>" on the internet to better understand how shocking this really is. Time magazine also offers a <u>photo gallery</u> on the sad reality of child soldiers.

a. The Truth About Child Soldiers, Professor Mark Drumbl, March 19, 2015 (with numerous pictures online), CNN, Opinion

*(CNN)* Images last week from an ISIS video appearing to show a child executing a hostage were horrific. The very idea of the "cubs of the caliphate," as the Islamic State of Iraq and Syria dubs them, is stomach-churning.

But ISIS is far from the first or only group to treat children in such a wretched way. There are tens of thousands of child soldiers under age 18 around the world, from South America to Africa to Southeast Asia to recent conflicts in the Balkans. The Kony2012 video that went viral, for example, featured children in the Lord's Resistance Army in northern Uganda. Boko

Haram, in Nigeria, also dreadfully abuses children. Children associated with armed forces and armed groups typically serve as porters, sentries, spies, cooks or cleaners. Many are sex slaves. Some, however, carry weapons on their own, exercise authority over others and commit atrocities against adults and children alike.

There is, though, an oft-overlooked point that also highlights one of the difficulties we face if we are going to tackle the problem of child soldiers. Despite the dominant image of these soldiers as boys, it is estimated that globally as many as 40% of child soldiers are girls. . . .

Children who end up in armed groups arrive there from along a number of paths and for divergent reasons. And children are, of course, individuals. Hence, they act in different ways once they are in these armed groups. Some children are abducted, drugged, brainwashed and brutalized. Many refuse to kill, some kill to survive, others murder to thrive. Some are brought to armed groups by their own families. Others join willingly, often traveling long distances of their own volition. . . .

[C]hild soldiers have just as much right as adults to be reintegrated into communities. Society owes them a chance to contribute to peaceful transition and build their lives. But how is it best to do that? For certain child soldiers, a healthy path to transition may involve them fulfilling some kind of obligation to society. Dismissively (and patronizingly) telling them their violent actions weren't their fault isn't helpful. Neither, of course, is locking them away in prison — this is especially the case for children who have suffered horrid brainwashing as is the case for ISIS and Boko Haram.

b. Quotes from Child Soldiers (various sources reported at Child Soldiers.org and Trip Line, Origin Uncertain)

### Voices of Young Soldiers

### Central Africa

"I feel so bad about the things that I did. It disturbs me so much that I inflicted death on other people. When I go home I must do some traditional rites because I have killed. I must perform these rites and cleanse myself. I still dream about the boy from my village that I killed. I see him in my dreams, and he is talking to me, saying I killed him for nothing, and I am crying." A 16-year-old girl after demobilization from an armed group (Source: U.S. State Dept. TIP Report 2005)

### Democratic Republic of the Congo

"When they came to my village, they asked my older brother whether he was ready to join the militia. He was just 17 and he said no; they shot him in the head. Then they asked me if I was ready to sign, so what could I do — I didn't want to die." A former child soldier taken when he was 13. (BBC report.)

### Sudan

"I joined the SPLA when I was 13. I am from Bahr Al Ghazal. They demobilized me in 2001 and took me to Rumbek, but I was given no demobilization documents. Now, I am stuck here because my family was killed in a government attack and because the SPLA would re-recruit me. At times I wonder why I am not going back to SPLA, half of my friends have and they seem to be better off than me." Boy interviewed by Coalition staff, southern Sudan, February 2004.

### Uganda

"Early on when my brothers and I were captured, the LRA [Lord's Resistance Army] explained to us that all five brothers couldn't serve in the LRA because we would not perform well. So they tied up my two younger brothers and invited us to watch. Then they beat them with sticks until two of them died. They told us it would give us strength to fight. My youngest brother was nine years old." Former child soldier, aged 13.

### Zimbabwe

"There was no one in charge of the dormitories and on a nightly basis we were raped. The men and youths would come into our dormitory in the dark, and they would just rape us — you would just have a man on top of you, and you could not even see who it was. If we cried afterwards, we were beaten with hosepipes. We were so scared that we did not report the rapes. The youngest girl in our group was aged 11 and she was raped repeatedly in the base." Nineteen-year-old girl describing her experience in the National Youth Service Training Program.

c. Video Clips

   a.  https://www.youtube.com/watch?v=XIoJrrKixBM

   b.  http://www.youtube.com/watch?v=iZm1Vn3LPcg&feature=related

# 4.  Exploitation of Child Labor

According to the U.S. Department of Labor: "Child labor is work that interferes with the physical and mental development of children. This work also often interferes with children's opportunities to attend school fully or requires them to drop out of school entirely. There are still 168 million children working worldwide, 85 million in hazardous work. ILO Convention 182 on the Worst Forms of Child Labor calls on the global community, as a matter of urgency, to eradicate the use of children under 18 years of age in all forms of slavery, commercial sexual exploitation, illicit activities, and hazardous work that is likely to harm their health, safety or morals." UNICEF reports that in poor countries, particularly in Sub-Saharan Africa, as many as one in four children are engaged in work hazardous to their health. To better understand the reality of child labor please search for images of "child labor" on the internet.

Nepalese girls working in a brick factory. Photo by Krish Dulal, Wikimedia Commons.

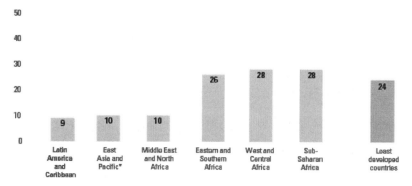

Percentage of children aged five to fourteen years engaged in child labour at the time of the survey, by region — see more at: http://data.unicef.org/child-protection/child-labour.html#sthash.n245fWpg.dpuf

# C. The Inter-American Human Rights System

## 1. The OAS

### a. Overview

The Inter-American system for human rights is a fundamental component part of the Organization of American States (OAS). The OAS is a regional political organization consisting of <u>thirty-five North American, South American, and Caribbean states</u> bound by the 1951 <u>OAS Charter and amending protocols</u>. It has granted permanent observer status to sixty-three states, as well as to the European Union. The OAS was established to achieve "an order of peace and justice, to promote their solidarity, to strengthen their collaboration, and to defend their sovereignty, their territorial integrity, and their independence." Similar to a "regional United Nations," the OAS provides a forum for collective negotiation, dialogue, and action regarding political, security and social issues for the Hemisphere based upon the four "pillars: democracy, human rights, security, and development." As described below, the OAS human rights functions are primarily carried out by two institutions—the Inter-American Commission and Inter-American Court of Human Rights. It is also important to consider, however, how the recent evolution of the OAS into an organization of states committed to democracy has contributed to respect for essential human rights in the Hemisphere.

### b. Evolution of the OAS & Its Promotion of Democracy

During much of the OAS' early history, particularly during the decades prior to the 1980s, Latin America was characterized by brutal authoritarian rule and military dictatorships. Earlier chapters in this book briefly described the egregious human rights violations associated with these authoritarian regimes, such those perpetrated by <u>General Auguto Pinochet</u> in Chile, <u>Rios Montt</u> in Guatemala and military leaders in Argentina's "<u>dirty war.</u>" Similarly tragic histories were repeated in <u>Uruguay,</u> <u>Paraguay,</u> and other states.[120]

However, during the last thirty years, starting in the 1980s, a dramatic movement towards democratic rule has swept through the Americas with a corresponding reduction in the most egregious types of human rights violations. The OAS has, in response, increasingly supported transitions to democracy as a vital component of its human rights and political agenda. These efforts have included sponsoring over 100 observer missions to ensure free and fair elections. In recent years, it ele-

---

120. Brian E. Lovemen's study "<u>Military Government in Latin America, 1959–1990</u>" provides this summary:

Long-term military governments, with changing leadership in most cases, controlled eleven Latin American nations for significant periods from 1964 to 1990: Ecuador, 1963–1966 and 1972–1978; Guatemala, 1963–1985 (with an interlude from 1966–1969); Brazil, 1964–1985; Bolivia, 1964–1970 and 1971–1982; Argentina, 1966–1973 and 1976–1983; Peru, 1968–1980; Panama, 1968–1989; Honduras, 1963–1966 and 1972–1982; Chile, 1973–1990; and Uruguay, 1973–1984. In El Salvador, the military dominated government from 1948 until 1984, but the last "episode" was from 1979 to 1984.

vated a commitment to democracy as a prerequisite to membership, adopting legal commitments to democratic rule such as the <u>Inter-American Democratic Charter</u>. The Democratic Charter provides for suspension from OAS membership for states experiencing a "disruption" of democratic rule. True to principle, the OAS <u>suspended Honduras</u> from membership after the June 28, 2009, military coup that deposed elected President Manuel Zelaya.

What role does democracy play in promoting respect for human rights? Is the OAS commitment to democracy an effective tool in achieving human rights? The UN has devoted significant resources to the promotion of democracy, which it explicitly describes as essential to human rights. As <u>described on the UN website</u>: "In 2011, UNDP [United Nations Development Program] helped more than 130 countries and devoted US $1.5 billion in resources to democratic governance, making UNDP the world's largest provider of democratic governance assistance. UNDP supports one in three parliaments in the developing world and an election every two weeks." The UN Security Council has even authorized the use of sanctions and force in response to a coup in Haiti, declaring that the disruption of democracy constituted a threat to international peace.[121] The UN Human Rights Council has also repeatedly affirmed that "democracy, development, and respect for all human rights and fundamental freedoms were interdependent and mutually reinforcing."

Is this emphasis on democracy a feasible approach for global realization of human rights? Is representative democracy an indispensable condition for human rights?

## 2. Overview of the Inter-American System for Human Rights

The following excerpts from OAS websites explain the evolution and operation of the OAS system. These sources focus on the historical development, composition, and the role of the two principle human rights institutions of the Inter-American System for Human Rights — the <u>Inter-American Commission</u> for Human Rights and the <u>Inter-American Court for Human Rights</u>.

It is important to highlight several key features of this system. First, note how the Commission has dual functions, which in turn reflects the bifurcated dual track system that has developed under the OAS. The Commission's first human rights mandate is based on its role as an OAS Charter institution (created by <u>OAS Charter Ch. XV, Art. 106</u>).[122] As a Charter institution, it has jurisdiction over all OAS members but only with regard to the Charter and the non-binding <u>American Declaration of the Rights and Duties of Man</u>. Arguably, the Declaration, although non-binding,

---

121. Donoho, <u>Evolution or Expediency: The United Nations Response to the Disruption of Democracy,</u> 29 Cornell Int'l L. J. at 329. (SC RES. 940, 1994).

122. Chapter XV, The Inter-American Commission on Human Rights, Article 106:

There shall be an Inter-American Commission on Human Rights, whose principal function shall be to promote the observance and protection of human rights and to serve as a consultative organ of the Organization in these matters.

is an expression of a binding OAS Charter commitment to respect human rights. (The Commission has extended this logic to also incorporate enforcement of rights declared in other international treaties as part of its mandate.)

The Commission's second role in the system derives from its status as an institution of the 1978 <u>American Convention on Human Rights</u>, a distinct OAS sponsored treaty. As an American Convention institution, the Commission has jurisdiction over all members of the Convention and the authority to hear individual petitions under that Convention against those states that accept its contentious (as opposed to advisory) jurisdiction.

Second, in contrast to the Commission, the Inter-American Court is strictly a Convention institution with authority only over those states that have consented to its jurisdiction to hear the individual petitions first reviewed and referred to it by the Commission. Eleven members of the OAS, Antigua and Barbuda, the Bahamas, Belize, Canada, Cuba, Guyana, Saint Lucia, Saint Kitts and Nevis, Saint Vincent and the Grenadines, Trinidad and Tobago and the United States, are not parties to the American Convention, and thus are not subject to the jurisdiction of the Court. Three countries, Grenada, Jamaica, and Dominica are parties to the Convention but have not accepted the Court's contentious jurisdiction.

As you review the materials that follow regarding the institutions of the Inter-American System, focus on how this system might be used to address the plight of abused and exploited children, as described above.

a. Brief History of the Inter-American Human Rights System

From the <u>Inter-American Commission Website</u>

The Inter-American Human Rights System was born with the adoption of the American Declaration of the Rights and Duties of Man in Bogotá, Colombia in April of 1948. The American Declaration was the first international human rights instrument of a general nature. The IACHR was created in 1959 and held its first session in 1960. Since that time, and until 2009, the Commission has held 134 sessions, some of them at its headquarters, others in different countries of the Americas.

By 1961, the IACHR had begun to carry out on-site visits to observe the general human rights situation in a country or to investigate specific situations. Since that time, the IACHR has carried out sixty-nine visits to twenty-three member States. In relation to its visits for the observation of the general human rights situation of a country, the IACHR has published forty-four special country reports to date.

In 1965, the IACHR was expressly authorized to examine complaints or petitions regarding specific cases of human rights violations. Up until 1997,

---

An Inter-American convention on human rights shall determine the structure, competence, and procedure of this Commission, as well as those of other organs responsible for these matters.

the IACHR has received thousands of petitions, which have resulted in 12,000 cases which have been processed or are currently being processed. (The procedure for the processing of individual cases is described below). The final published reports of the IACHR regarding these individual cases may be found in the Annual Reports of the Commission or independently by country.

In 1969, the American Convention on Human Rights was adopted. The Convention entered into force in 1978. As of August of 1997, it has been ratified by 25 countries: Argentina, Barbados, Brazil, Bolivia, Chile, Colombia, Costa Rica, Dominica, Dominican Republic, Ecuador, El Salvador, Grenada, Guatemala, Haiti, Honduras, Jamaica, Mexico, Nicaragua, Panama, Paraguay, Peru, Suriname, Trinidad and Tobago, Uruguay and Venezuela. The Convention defines the human rights that the ratifying States have agreed to respect and ensure. The Convention also creates the Inter-American Court of Human Rights and defines the functions and procedures of both the Commission and the Court. The IACHR also possesses additional faculties which pre-date and are not derived directly from the Convention, such as the processing of cases involving countries which are still not parties to the Convention.

\*\*\*

The Basic Documents include the American Declaration of the Rights and Duties of Man (hereinafter "the American Declaration") and the American Convention on Human Rights (hereinafter "the American Convention"). These are followed by the Inter-American Convention Against Torture, the additional protocols to the American Convention on Economic, Social and Cultural Rights and on the Death Penalty, the Inter-American Conventions on Violence Against Women, Forced Disappearance of Persons and Discrimination Against Persons with Disabilities; as well as a list of the OAS States that are signatories to those treaties and the current status of such ratifications. Also included are the OAS Charter and the Inter-American Democratic Charter; as well as the Declaration of Principles on Freedom of Expression, and Principles and Best Practices on the Protection of Persons Deprived of Liberty in the Americas. The Statutes and Rules of Procedure of the Inter-American Commission and Court are also included. Finally, the form for filing petitions alleging human rights violations before the Commission is attached. This edition of Basic Documents has been updated as of June 30, 2010.

# 3. Inter-American Commission

## a. Overview of the Commission & Its Functions

As an OAS Charter institution, the Commission carries on promotional and investigation activities similar to those engaged in by UN Charter-based human rights institutions. These include "rapporteurs" (on the rights of indigenous peoples, women, migrants, children, human rights defenders, persons deprived of liberty, afro-descendants, and LGTB persons), "thematic," and "country" reports. Country reports and visits are prompted by particular criteria including "[a] serious breach of the core requirement of representative democracy," and "massive, serious, and widespread violations of human rights." In 2013, the Commission chose to investigate and report on conditions in Cuba, Venezuela, and Honduras. By perusing this and other reports available on the Commission website, you can develop an understanding of these aspects of the Commission's mandate.

A distinct function of the Commission is resolving individual petitions alleging violations of either the American Declaration (for OAS members who are not parties to the American Convention) or American Convention on Human Rights. Cases decided under the American Convention may be referred to the Inter-American Court for final resolution if that state has accepted the Court's jurisdiction.

From the IA Commission website: Commission Website

Commission Processing of Individual Cases

The Commission is currently processing more than 1,450 individual cases. Any person, group of persons, or non-governmental organization may present a petition to the Commission alleging violations of the rights protected in the American Convention and/or the American Declaration. The petition may be presented in any of the four official languages of the OAS and may be presented on behalf of the person filing the petition or on behalf of a third person.

The Commission may only process individual cases where it is alleged that one of the member States of the OAS is responsible for the human rights violation at issue. The Commission applies the Convention to process cases brought against those States which are parties to that instrument. For those States that are not parties, the Commission applies the American Declaration.

The Commission may, of course, study those petitions alleging that human rights violations were committed by State agents. However, the Commission may also process cases where it is asserted that a State failed to act to prevent a violation of human rights or failed to carry out proper follow-up after a violation, including the investigation and sanction of those responsible as well as the payment of compensation to the victim.

The petitions presented to the Commission must show that the victim has exhausted all means of remedying the situation domestically. If domestic remedies have not been exhausted, it must be shown that the victim tried to exhaust domestic remedies but failed because: 1) those remedies do not provide for adequate due process; 2) effective access to those remedies was denied, or; 3) there has been undue delay in the decision on those remedies.

If domestic remedies were exhausted, the petition must be presented within six months after the final decision in the domestic proceedings. If domestic remedies have not been exhausted, the petition must be presented within a reasonable time after the occurrence of the events complained of. The petition must also fulfill other minimal formal requirements which are found in the Convention and the **Rules of Procedure of the Commission.**

***

When a case is opened and a number is assigned, the pertinent parts of the petition are sent to the Government with a request for relevant information. During the processing of the case, each party is asked to comment on the responses of the other party. The Commission also may carry out its own investigations, conducting on-site visits, requesting specific information from the parties, etc . . . The Commission may also hold a hearing during the processing of the case, in which both parties are present and are asked to set forth their legal and factual arguments. In almost every case, the Commission will also offer to assist the parties in negotiating a friendly settlement if they so desire.

When the parties have completed the basic back-and-forth of briefs and when the Commission decides that it has sufficient information, the processing of a case is completed. The Commission then prepares a report which includes its conclusions and also generally provides recommendations to the State concerned. This report is not public. The Commission gives the State a period of time to resolve the situation and to comply with the recommendations of the Commission.

Upon the expiration of this period of time granted to the State, the Commission has two options. The Commission may prepare a second report, which is generally similar to the initial report and which also generally contains conclusions and recommendations. In this case, the State is again given a period of time to resolve the situation and to comply with the recommendations of the Commission, if such recommendations are made. At the end of this second period granted to the State, the Commission will usually publish its report, although the Convention allows the Commission to decide otherwise.

Rather than preparing a second report for publication, the Commission may decide to take the case to the Inter-American Court. If it wishes to take the case to the Court, it must do so within three months from the date in which it transmits its initial report to the State concerned. The initial report of the Commission will be attached to the application to the Court. The Commission will appear in all proceedings before the Court.

The decision as to whether a case should be submitted to the Court or published should be made on the basis of the best interests of human rights in the Commission's judgment.

b. Petitioning the Commission

i. Overview of Petitioning Process

Briefly review the <u>Commission's guidelines for presenting a petition</u>, including an "online" format.

ii. Illustrative Petitions & Decisions

Review and evaluate the following petitions filed with the Commission against the United States. They are far too lengthy to study in full — simply review the allegations, and the rationales and conclusions reached. If you don't like these, others may be accessed from the Commission's website, "<u>cases in the court</u>," and "<u>merits</u>."

**Petitions**

Petition Alleging Violations of the <u>Human Rights of Juveniles</u> Sentenced to Life without Parole in the United States of America

[See especially pages 20–25]

Petition to Inter-American Commission on Human Rights on Behalf of the <u>Guantanamo Detainees</u> [note reliance on alleged violations of the Geneva Convention and CCPR]

Petition of the Boarder Action Network in Relation to Victims of <u>Anti-Immigrant Activities and Vigilante Violence</u> in Southern Arizona vs. United States of America

Petition to the Inter-American Commission on Human Rights Seeking Relief from Violations Resulting from <u>Global Warming Caused by Acts and Omissions of the United States</u>

**Commission Decisions**

Report 78/15, Case 12.831, <u>Kevin Cooper v. United States</u> (2105) (one of many cases finding violation of right to fair trial in capital conviction based on "heightened scrutiny" of US proceedings from trial and appeals through habeas corpus review)

Report 63/08, Case 12.534, <u>Mortlock v. United States</u> (2008) (finding violation of the right against cruel, inhumane treatment resulting from deportation of alien convicted of a felony to Jamaica given prospect of inadequate medical treatment for condition of HIV/AIDS and lack of other support)

Report 80/11, Case 12.626, <u>Jessica Lenahan v. United States</u> (2011) (finding various violations of rights including "adequate remedy" for state government's failure to "act with due diligence" to protect petitioner's three children from being murdered by their father — same case as previously decided by U.S. Supreme Court in <u>Castle Rock v. Gonzalez</u>, 545 U.S. 748 (2005) which rejected § 1983 civil rights claim based on failure to enforce restraining order)

iii. The Problem of State Compliance

As seems endemic to international human rights institutions outside of Europe, the Inter-American Commission has a mixed record in securing state compliance with its "recommendations." Other than reporting back to the OAS on noncompliance, the Commission lacks traditional enforcement power or mechanisms. In an effort to encourage greater compliance, the Commission's Annual Reports to the OAS now track state responses. By way of illustration, review the Commission's 2014 Annual Report to the OAS, particularly tab "D. Status of Compliance."

The failure of states to comply with the Commission's recommendations and findings could, of course, be the function of pure recalcitrance. In the case of Trinidad, Jamaica and Guyana, each of whom have withdrawn in some fashion from the Inter-American system, controversial decisions by the Commission and Court involving capital punishment resulted in a backlash of sorts against international processes.[123] A lack of compliance could also result from a lack of respect, or from recognition that the Commission has no power to enforce and can essentially be ignored without serious consequences. Others may believe that overreaching by the Commission, in particular application of the American Declaration as binding law, contributes to non-compliance. The United States has taken this position in the vast majority of petitions brought against it. The following response to a Commission decision relating to Cubans detained after the Mariel exodus summarizes the U.S. position:

> With regard to each implication or direct assertion in the Commission's report that the American Declaration of the Rights and Duties of Man itself accords rights or imposes duties, some of which the United States has supposedly violated, the United States reminds the Commission that the Declaration is no more than a recommendation to the American States. Accordingly, the Declaration does not create legally binding obligations and therefore cannot be "violated."

Based on the decisions linked above involving the United States, do you believe that the Commission's decisions ought to be respected and followed by our government? Does the Commission "overreach" beyond clear state obligations or its competency? How does the Commission go about deciding factual issues? Would you think differently if the decision involved factually clear violations of fundamental rights such as the torture of a prisoner?

## 4. Inter-American Court of Human Rights

The IACtHR website provides helpful overviews of its history, composition, cases and procedures. It also provides a database of decisions and judgments, and material relating to state compliance with judgments. (Unfortunately for English speakers, most of these reports are available only in Spanish, Portuguese or French.) Visit the site to review information regarding the Court's essential institutional characteristics and processes. Loyola Law School in Los Angeles maintains a case data base (IACHR Project) that provides summaries of certain decisions. The OAS also pro-

---

123. *See generally* Laurence R. Helfer, *Overlegalizing Human Rights: International Relations Theory and the Commonwealth Caribbean Backlash Against Human Rights Regimes*, 102 Columbia L. Rev. 1832 (2002).

vides <u>brief English summaries of cases</u> decided by the Court. Review these summaries to gain an understanding of the types of cases and decisions that the Court has rendered.

Please review the case of Street Children, <u>Villagrán Morales et al. v. Guatemala</u> (also available from the IACtHR <u>here</u>). Ismene Zarifis, in <u>Human Rights Briefs</u>, describes events leading up to the case this way:

> Before their deaths, the victims in the Bosques case — Anstraum Aman Villagrán Morales (age 17), Henry Giovanni Contreras (age 18), Julio Roberto Caal Sandoval (age 15), Federico Clemente Figueroa Tunchez (age 20), and Jovito Josué Juárez Cifuentes (age 17) — took part in rehabilitative programs run by Casa Alianza, a non-governmental children's rights organization. On June 17, 1990, the severely burned bodies of four of the victims were found mutilated in the woods, with their eyes and ears burned and their tongues severed. On June 25, 1990, the fifth victim was abducted and suffered the same fate as his friends. As a result of these crimes, and in reaction to unprecedented numbers of human rights violations committed against street children, Casa Alianza opened its legal aid office in 1990 with the initiation of the Bosques case.

Review of the Court's decisions reveals an active docket which has produced hundreds of decisions addressing a wide range of egregious human rights violations with a detailed and sophisticated jurisprudence. Alas, the glass is perhaps still only half full. State compliance with the Court's judgments, which often demand both payment of compensation to victims and equitable or institutional remedies, is far from impressive, particularly when compared to those of European human rights institutions (whose own record of state compliance has significantly weakened since expansion). Are there institutional reasons for this lack of compliance or might the reasons be contextual, including the presence of oppressive or recalcitrant state parties, entrenched political elites, weak national institutional structures and poverty? It what ways are the circumstances of the Inter-American Court distinct from those under which the European Courts operate? Consider the following commentary.

## D. Critiquing the Inter-American System

James Cavallaro & Stephanie Erin Brewer, <u>Re-evaluating Regional Human Rights Litigation in the Twenty-First Century</u>: The Case of the Inter-American Court, The American Journal of International Law, Vol. 102, p. 768, 2008

> Observing from the international level, scholars and practitioners interested in promoting human rights may at first instinctively assume that this growth of tribunals on the global stage necessarily signals an equivalent increase in the power of international human rights law to protect individuals throughout the world. Yet a disproportionate focus on these institutions' existence

in isolation may lead us to overlook the actual degree of success that such tribunals have had in the countries subject to their jurisdiction. While ideally the growth of human rights bodies with binding legal authority (and the expansion of these bodies' jurisprudence) should indeed translate into proportionately better human rights practices on the ground, evaluating the domestic impact of recent supranational decisions often reveals a vast gap between what regional courts order and what actually happens in a country. The mounting evidence that greater institutionalization of human rights protection at the supranational level does not necessarily increase respect for human rights on the ground points to the need for a new model of how and when supranational litigation can positively affect domestic human rights practices.

***

For nearly three decades, the European Court thus provided the only model for observing whether and how a regional human rights court could influence state practices. The model was widely hailed as a triumph by scholars and practitioners alike. Helfer and Slaughter, writing in 1997, called the ECHR a "remarkable and surprising success" and noted that the degree of compliance with its judgments in individual cases had been "extremely high." ***

Over the past fifteen years, however, supranational tribunals have sought to influence human rights situations far different from those seen in Western Europe in the first decades of the ECHR. Even the political landscape of the Council of Europe has changed considerably during this time with the entry of a significant number of new members (largely former Soviet bloc states). As we contend in the paragraphs that follow, given the complex and often severe human rights problems that regional tribunals must address today, the model of governmental compliance exemplified by the early ECHR cases is no longer the primary reference point for how regional courts influence state practice. In fact, it may now be the exception rather than the rule.

The reason for this discrepancy becomes clear when one considers the specific set of factors that characterized the European system through the early 1990s. Most salient, at this time the European Court exercised jurisdiction over a relatively homogeneous group of Western European states in which democratic governance and the rule of law were already well established. Many states in the Council of Europe prior to the collapse of the Berlin Wall shared a specific commitment to implement the decisions of the European Court in their domestic systems, a commitment that existed not only in law, but also in practice.

****

By contrast, the entry of roughly twenty new members into the Council of Europe beginning in the early 1990s — many of which are former Soviet bloc states typified by grave violations and more limited experience of the rule of law than Western Europe — has presented the ECHR with a significantly different political climate. Today, the notion of hierarchical implementation of jurisprudence is less and less relevant even in Europe, as the ECHR faces both challenges to its authority and an increased number of cases involving systematic, violent human rights violations. Its 2007 annual report notes that five member states — Russia, Turkey, Romania, Ukraine, and Poland — accounted for 59 percent of the Court's docket as of the end of that year. In the prior year's report, virtually all of the example cases involving deprivations of life, excessive use of force by state authorities, torture, and unlawful arrest arose from facts in new member states (notably Russia), and in Turkey. Further, the statistics of the Council of Europe's Committee of Ministers reveal that the majority of ECHR judgments awaiting compliance supervision by the committee (excluding the large family of similar cases involving delays in civil and criminal proceedings in Italy) now involve Eastern European member states and Turkey. ****

As this analogy suggests, the experience of the Inter-American system has been far different from that of the early ECHR. When the Inter-American Court came into being in 1979, it entered a region characterized largely by authoritarian regimes, mass atrocities, and violent human rights violations, such as massacres in indigenous communities and prisons, as well as widespread forced disappearances of political dissidents. By the time the Court received its first contentious cases in 1986, the landscape in the Americas was changing, but still included several conflict-ridden states and recent transitional democracies. Today, the Court continues to adjudicate cases of severe, endemic violations such as paramilitary violence, summary executions, use of torture by police, and brutal violations against detained individuals.

***

The experience of the Inter-American Court and the challenges now facing the European system confirm our belief that the early European Court is not a representative model of how regional courts influence states' human rights practices outside the entrenched democracies of Western Europe. This understanding is even more relevant when one considers that the African Court, too, will soon face significant challenges as it begins to operate in a climate of severe violations and lack of deep-rooted respect for the rule of law. In this regard, we note that the African Commission on Human and Peoples' Rights has operated in the context of limited compliance with its determinations. The question presented, as we see it, is, how can tribunals positively influence human rights practices when dealing with states that may not automatically implement supranational judgments?

Primarily on the basis of a survey of case studies in the inter-American system, we contend below that supranational tribunals will generally have the greatest impact when their procedures and judgments are relevant to the actors working to advance specific human rights in these countries, including not only state agents but also human rights organizations, social movements, and the media. \*\*\*

We suggest, however, that rather than viewing local actors as forces to be deployed to increase the power of a tribunal, human rights tribunals should understand that international rights courts are most effective when their work contributes to efforts deployed *by* domestic activists as part of their broader human rights campaigns. \*\*\*

In an analysis of compliance with recommendations of the African Commission from 1994–2003, Frans Viljoen and Lirette Louw likewise report that compliance is enhanced when a petition to the African Commission forms one part of a broader social movement. They consider several cases illustrating the role of international pressure and domestic mobilization in persuading states to comply with Commission recommendations.

\*\*\*

## II. OVERVIEW OF THE INTER-AMERICAN SYSTEM

\*\*\*

Thus, as currently structured, the Commission's fact-finding process in individual cases cannot be termed judicial. While one might imagine enhancing the procedures of the Commission to enable it to become the authoritative judicial fact-finder of the system, doing so would require significant changes that we do not foresee in the near future.

For cases in which it reaches a merits determination in favor of the petitioners, the Commission transmits its recommendations for remedying the violation in question to the state concerned. However, member states may ignore or otherwise fail to implement these recommendations, in which case the Commission may submit the matter to the Court.

\*\*\*

*The Inter-American Court*

\*\*\*

When the Court determines that a state is responsible for human rights violations, it publishes a judgment setting forth the violations found and orders the state to carry out reparations measures (discussed in parts III and IV below). On the basis of its own interpretation of its mandate, the Court retains jurisdiction to monitor compliance with its judgments and issues periodic compliance orders. As will be seen later, the Court faces considerable difficulties with respect to compliance with certain elements of its judgments. While states generally pay monetary damages, there are very few cases of full compliance, which is notably lacking as regards the obligation to bring perpetrators of violations to justice.

***

Although the Court now resolves a significantly increased number of cases each year, we emphasize that it remains an organ of extremely limited access for the vast majority of victims of human rights violations. From the Court's inception through the end of 2007, it had issued 174 determinations in ninety-five contentious cases. From 2004 to 2007 (following the systemic reforms discussed above), the Court resolved approximately fourteen cases annually, including a total of seventeen in 2006. Yet these numbers still represent an average of less than one case per year for each country that has recognized its contentious jurisdiction. Recalling that the Inter-American Commission receives more than thirteen hundred complaints each year — which already represent only a fraction of total victims of rights abuses — it is clear that the fourteen or so cases resolved by the Court each year make up a tiny percentage of the potential cases that would progress through the system if every victim of human rights violations had his or her proverbial day in court.

***

### State Compliance with Orders of the Inter-American Court

A review of the Inter-American Court's past cases demonstrates that the Court does face frequent non-implementation of its judgments. Governments may openly reject certain orders, but even more commonly they assert that they will comply or are in the process of complying, yet fail to take the steps necessary to bring their practices into line with the requirements of the Court's judgment.

***

Our review of the compliance orders of the Court reveals a clear (though not universal) pattern in states' reactions to its judgments. The pattern that emerges demonstrates that states generally pay some or all of the monetary damages awarded by the Court. In addition, states may comply with symbolic reparations, including those concerning public ceremonies. However, when it comes to more far-reaching measures to reduce impunity and advance human rights (such as prosecuting past violations or changing laws and practices), compliance is considerably less likely. Most salient, virtually no compliance decision records that a state has effectively investigated and punished the perpetrators of a human rights violation forming the basis of a Court decision. Even when states report taking some steps toward a full investigation of the case or having prosecuted some of the alleged perpetrators, they often do not progress to investigating fully or prosecuting all the parties involved, weakening the impact of those legal processes in combating impunity. States also frequently fail even to provide the Court with the data necessary to determine whether the state is complying with a judgment or not. In 2003 Panama challenged the principle that the Court even has the authority to monitor compliance with its orders. As of 2007, the Court reported full compliance in only 11.57 percent of resolved cases.

The picture that emerges from interviews with human rights groups regarding the Court's substantive impact on human rights issues is also troubling. To provide just a few examples, with respect to the cases of *Blanco Romero v. Venezuela* and *Montero Aranguren v. Venezuela*, involving, respectively, forced disappearances and a prison massacre, the state has yet to comply fully with any part of the judgments. Meanwhile, in the first half of 2007, the level of violence occurring in Venezuelan detention facilities — the problem at issue in *Montero Aranguren* — increased. In Paraguay, two cases in the past few years, *Yakye Axa Indigenous Community v. Paraguay* and *Sawhoyamaxa Indigenous Community v. Paraguay*, have brought before the Court the issue of indigenous communities' right to their traditional lands. In these cases, the displacement of indigenous communities from their lands caused their members to live in deplorable conditions and sometimes to die as a result of the state's subsequent failure to provide necessary medical services. Yet the state has not complied with the most important element of the Court's determinations on reparations: giving possession of the lands to the communities. The Court noted in February 2007 that since the publication of the judgment in *Sawhoyamaxa*, the state's failure to implement its orders on providing basic services to the community had led to the deaths of four additional individuals and the hospitalization of five more.

The examples listed above should not detract from the Court's achievements in other cases, which induced states to change laws and policies in response to Court judgments.

***

In more cases than not, however, the Court continues to confront problems in achieving meaningful and lasting implementation of its reparations orders. Lack of political will and the powerful position of the armed forces and police in various Latin American countries mean that the Court often faces particular difficulties in prompting states to punish the authors of past violations, a crucial challenge given the role of impunity in perpetuating tolerance for human rights violations. Governments may also be reluctant to deploy the resources necessary to carry out the systematic reforms needed to correct endemic human rights problems. This situation is complicated by the fact that states are not monolithic; even if a country's supreme court or national government is receptive to inter-American jurisprudence, resistance by the local authorities actually responsible for day-to-day implementation of ordered reforms may stymie efforts to advance human rights in practice.

# E.  African System for Human Rights Protection

## 1. Introduction and Overview

The African system for the protection of human rights had genesis in the 1981 adoption of the African Charter on Human and Peoples' Rights (commonly referred to as the "Banjul Charter") by the Organization of African States (OAS). The Charter came into force in 1986 after ratification of a majority of OAS members and has now been ratified by all African states within the union. In 1987, a Charter based institution for the promotion of human rights, the African Commission on Human Rights, was formed. In 2004 a protocol to the Charter creating the African Court for Human Rights came into force creating a second Charter based institution which is described below. The OAS was disbanded and replaced by the African Union in 2001.

Consider the following brief description of the AU and its functions. **Then, after reviewing the material describing the African system for human rights, evaluate how that system might be used to respond to the plight of children soldiers described at the beginning of this chapter.**

## 2. Evolution of the African Union

[From AU official website; Hyperlinks from website.]

The African Union (AU) is a supranational union consisting of fifty-three African states. Established in 2001, the AU was formed as a successor to the amalgamated African Economic Community (AEC) and the Organization of African Unity (OAU). Eventually, the AU aims to have a single currency (the Afro) and a single integrated defense force, as well as other institutions of state, including a cabinet for the AU Head of State. The purpose of the union is to help secure Africa's democracy, human rights, and a sustainable economy, especially by bringing an end to intra-African conflict and creating an effective common market.

***

The AU covers the entire continent except for Morocco, which opposes the membership of Western Sahara as the Sahrawi Arab Democratic Republic. However, Morocco has a special status within the AU and benefits from the services available to all AU states from the institutions of the AU, such as the African Development Bank. ***

The AU's first military intervention in a member state was the May 2003 deployment of a peacekeeping force of soldiers from South Africa, Ethiopia, and Mozambique to Burundi to oversee the implementation of the various agreements. AU troops are also deployed in Sudan for peacekeeping in the Darfur conflict. The AU also has pledged to send peacekeepers to Somalia, of which the peacekeepers from Uganda have already reached Somalia.

***

## 3. African Human Rights System

a. Overview

Buergenthal, *The Evolving International Human Rights System*, 100 A.J.I.L. 683 (2006)

*The African Human Rights System*

The African human rights system evolved in two distinct stages in a manner somewhat similar to that of its Inter-American counterpart. The first stage consisted of the adoption in 1981 by the Organization of African Unity, now the African Union, of the African Charter on Human and Peoples' Rights. It entered into force in 1986 and in the meantime has been ratified by all fifty-three member states of the African Union. The Charter created an African Commission on Human and Peoples' Rights, but not a court. The African Court of Human and Peoples' Rights was established later by means of a separate protocol that came into force in 2004. The Court was formally inaugurated only in 2006.

The catalog of rights that the African Charter guarantees differs from its European and Inter-American counterparts in several important respects. The Charter proclaims not only rights but also duties, and it guarantees both individual and peoples' rights. In addition to civil and political rights, the African Charter sets out a series of economic and social rights. The Charter permits the states parties to impose more extensive restrictions and limitations on the exercise of the rights it proclaims than the European and inter-American human rights instruments. It also does not contain a derogation clause, which leaves the question open whether all rights in the African Charter are derogable. . . .

The Commission's mandate is "to promote human and peoples' rights and ensure their protection in Africa." It is composed of eleven elected members who serve in their individual capacities. . . .

The Commission is also empowered to render interpretive opinions and to deal with interstate and individual complaints. The states parties, the African Union, and intergovernmental African organizations recognized by the latter may request advisory opinions from the Commission regarding interpretation of the African Charter on Human and Peoples' Rights.

\*\*\*

The powers of the African Commission to deal with interstate and individual communications are much more limited than those conferred by the European and Inter-American human rights treaties. The Commission is so constrained in part because its findings with regard to the communications it receives cannot be made public without the permission of the African Union's Assembly of Heads of State and Government, a political body that has traditionally not been inclined to take strong action against serious violators of human rights. The Commission's power to deal with individual petitions is limited, furthermore, to "cases which reveal the existence of a series of serious or massive violations of human and peoples' rights." Thus, what we have here is not really a mechanism for individual petitions as it exists in the two other regional human rights systems.

\*\*\*

The new African Court of Human and Peoples' Rights, whose function it is to "complement the protective mandate" of the African Commission, has contentious and advisory jurisdiction. Its contentious jurisdiction is broader than that of the European and Inter-American Courts; it extends to disputes arising not only under the Charter and the Protocol establishing the Court, but also "under any other relevant Human Rights instrument ratified by the States concerned."

\*\*\*

The future of the Court has been further complicated by the African Union's conclusion of yet another Protocol that calls for the establishment of an African Court of Justice. When this Protocol enters into force, the new court is supposed to be merged with the African Court of Human and Peoples' Rights. What impact such a merger will have on the latter Court's role is still too early to say. Moreover, the political, economic, and social problems Africa faces are much more severe than the comparable problems that plague the Americas or Europe. In addition to severe poverty and corruption, the African continent continues to be the victim of wars and internal armed conflicts that have killed millions of human beings, while AIDS is ravaging the entire populations of some countries. Africa has also not been able to rid itself of authoritarian regimes, some of which still hold power. It will therefore not be easy in the short term for the African Court and Commission to create an effective regional human rights system.

### b. African Commission on Human and Peoples' Rights

As described by Judge Buergenthal above, the <u>African Commission</u> is a quasi-judicial institution tasked with promoting human rights among the fifty-four members of the African Union, primarily under the <u>African Charter on Human and Peoples' Rights</u>. The Commission (ACHPR) consists of eleven independent experts elected by OAS member states, who serve in their personal capacities. The ACHPR's mandate includes consideration of individual complaints of violations of the Charter. As noted by Judge Buergenthal, Article 58 of the Charter would appear to significantly limit these cases to "serious and massive" violations of human rights. However, in its "Guidelines for Submission of Communication," the Commission has essential rejected this limitation:

From the wordings of Article 58(1), of the Charter, it would seem that the Commission can only consider a communication when the latter reveals a series of serious and massive violation of human and peoples' rights, and only after the Assembly of Heads of state and Government has requested it to do so. However, the practice of the Commission has been to consider every communication even if it refers to only a single violation of the Charter. The rationale behind this practice is that a single violation still violates the dignity of the victim and is an affront to international human rights norms.

The <u>communications procedures, guidelines, and past decisions</u>, organized by violation and country, can be found on the ACHPR's website. The Commission also prepares cases for submission to the African Court on Human and Peoples' Rights. The Commission has no binding authority nor enforcement mechanisms. According to the Project on International Courts and Tribunals: "The scantiness of the enforcement and compliance control mechanism contained in the African Charter, however, is hardly surprising. At the time the OAU adopted the African Charter, very few African States (i.e., Gambia, Senegal, and Botswana), could vaunt of a democratic regime respectful of at least the fundamental human rights."

Much like the Inter-American Commission, the ACHPR also investigates and promotes human rights in more general ways including review of state "<u>periodic reports</u>" on human rights conditions and the creation of "special mechanisms." The Commission, limited in resources, currently only meets twice per year in "<u>ordinary sessions</u>" of about two weeks. The <u>ACHPR website</u> lists the following special mechanisms:

### Special Mechanisms

The Commission may create subsidiary mechanisms such as special rapporteurs, committees, and working groups. The creation and membership of such subsidiary mechanisms may be determined by consensus, failing which, the decision shall be taken by voting.

The Commission shall determine the mandate and the terms of reference of each subsidiary mechanism. Each subsidiary mechanism shall present a report on its work to the Commission at each ordinary session of the Commission.

| Special Mechanism | Establishment | Missions | Resolutions |
| --- | --- | --- | --- |
| Special Rapporteur on Freedom of Expression and Access to Information | 2004 | 1 | 14 |
| The Special Rapporteur on Prisons, Conditions of Detention and Policing in Africa | 1996 | 16 | 9 |
| Special Rapporteur on Human Rights Defenders | 2004 | 1 | 14 |

*(Continued)*

| Special Mechanism | Establishment | Missions | Resolutions |
|---|---|---|---|
| Special Rapporteur on Refugees, Asylum Seekers, Migrants, and Internally Displaced Persons | 2004 | | 11 |
| Special Rapporteur on Rights of Women | 1999 | 5 | 10 |
| Committee for the Prevention of Torture in Africa | 2004 | 2 | 6 |
| Working Group on Economic, Social and Cultural Rights | 2004 | 1 | 6 |
| Working Group on Death Penalty and Extra-Judicial, Summary or Arbitrary Killings in Africa | 2005 | | 11 |
| Working Group on Indigenous Populations/Communities in Africa | 2000 | 14 | 15 |
| Working Group on Specific Issues Related to the work of the African Commission | 2004 | | 8 |
| Working Group on Rights of Older Persons and People with Disabilities | 2007 | | 10 |
| Working Group on Extractive Industries, Environment and Human Rights Violations | 2009 | | 8 |
| Committee on the Protection of the Rights of People Living With HIV (PLHIV) and Those at Risk, Vulnerable to and Affected by HIV | 2010 | | 8 |
| Advisory Committee on Budgetary and Staff Matters | 2009 | | 4 |
| Working Group on Communications | 2011 | | 5 |

## c. African Court on Human and Peoples' Rights

The African Court on Human and Peoples' Rights came into existence under a Protocol to the African Charter on Human and Peoples' Rights in 2004. The Court's website provides the following efficient summary of some basic facts and technical details about the Court. Note that, under the <u>Protocol on the Statute of the African Court of Justice and Human Rights</u>, the Court has been merged with the AU's proposed African Court of Justice into a single institution. (For further information on the merger, its history and implications see the <u>Project on International Courts and Tribunals</u>.) As of 2016, the Court has accomplished very little to report. Its credibility was not furthered when the <u>African Union voted in 2014</u>, contrary to prevailing international law,[124] to specifically exempt "senior government officials" from prosecution for crimes against humanity and other serious international crimes.

> The African Court on Human and Peoples' Rights (the Court) is a continental court established by African countries to ensure protection of human and peoples' rights in Africa. It complements and reinforces the functions of the African Commission on Human and Peoples' Rights.

***

> To date, only the following twenty nine (29) States have ratified the Protocol: Algeria, Benin, Burkina Faso, Burundi, Cote d'Ivoire, Comoros, Congo, Gabon, Gambia, Ghana, Kenya, Libya, Lesotho, Mali, Malawi, Mozambique, Mauritania, Mauritius, Nigeria, Niger, Rwanda, Sahrawi Arab Democratic Republic, South Africa, Senegal, Tanzania, Togo, Tunisia, Uganda, and Cameroon. . . .

> The Court has jurisdiction over all cases and disputes submitted to it concerning the interpretation and application of the African Charter on Human and Peoples' Rights, the (the Charter), the Protocol and any other relevant human rights instrument ratified by the States concerned. Specifically, the Court has two types of jurisdiction: contentious and advisory.

> The Court is composed of eleven Judges, nationals of Member States of the African Union. . . . The Judges of the Court are elected, after nomination by their respective States, in their individual capacities from among African jurists of proven integrity and of recognized practical, judicial or academic

---

124. As stated by the International Justice Resource Center:

This immunity provision differs from the mandates of other supranational criminal courts, including the International Criminal Court (ICC), the International Criminal Tribunal for the Former Yugoslavia (ICTY), and the International Criminal Tribunal for Rwanda. Article 27(1) of the <u>Rome Statute of the ICC</u>, for example, states that the Statute applies "equally to *all persons without any distinction based on official capacity*. In particular, official capacity as a Head of State or Government, a member of a Government or parliament, an elected representative or a government official shall in no case exempt a person from criminal responsibility under this Statute." The wording of Article 7(2) of the <u>Statute of the ICTY</u> and Article 6(2) of the <u>Statute of the ICTR</u> are identical; both state that the "official position of any accused person, whether as Head of state or government or as a responsible government official, *shall not relieve such person of criminal responsibility* nor mitigate punishment." In this way, all three courts—the ICC, the ICTY, and the ICTR—have the authority to prosecute sitting heads of state and senior officials. This is consistent with international law, which allows international courts to lift immunity from current heads of state and senior officials.

competence and experience in the field of human rights. . . . The President of the Court resides and works on a full time basis at the seat of the Court, while the other ten (10) judges work on a part-time basis. In the accomplishment of his duties, the President is assisted by a Registrar who performs registry, managerial, and administrative functions of the Court.

The Court officially started its operations in Addis Ababa, Ethiopia, in November 2006, but in August 2007, it moved to its seat in Arusha, the United Republic of Tanzania . . . and in June 2010, the Court adopted its final Rules of Court.

According to the Protocol (Article 5) and the Rules (Rule 33), the Court may receive complaints and/or applications submitted to it either by the African Commission of Human and Peoples' Rights or State parties to the Protocol or African Intergovernmental Organizations. Non-Governmental Organizations with observer status before the African Commission on Human and Peoples' Rights and individuals from States which have made a Declaration accepting the jurisdiction of the Court can also institute cases directly before the Court. As of March 2014, only seven countries had made such a Declaration.

The Court delivered its first judgment in 2009 following an application dated 11 August 2008 by Mr Michelot Yogogombaye against the Republic of Senegal. As of September 2013, the Court has received twenty-eight applications. It has already finalized twenty-three cases. Currently the Court has five pending cases on its table to examine including Requests for advisory opinion.

# Chapter 11

# International Criminal Law, Humanitarian Law & Human Rights

## A. Introduction & Overview

This chapter examines the emerging role of international criminal law as a vital tool in the enforcement of international human rights. International criminal law is a broad subject that traditionally has been understood to include international law enforcement and punishment of transnational crimes such as international drug trafficking, piracy, and terrorism. Since World War II and the Nuremberg Tribunals, however, criminal law has increasingly played an important role in enforcing fundamental human rights. Our primary focus will be on how international criminal processes can be used to bring certain human rights violators to justice.

International criminal human rights law involves a narrower set of rights and protections than those protected by international human rights law generally. There are two major types of international human rights crimes. The first type includes human rights violations involving egregious physical wrongs such as genocide, torture, summary execution and disappearances. The second type involves certain crimes and human rights abuses committed during armed conflicts — a subject that is often called humanitarian law based on its origins in the laws of war. Although it has separate (and much earlier) origins than current international human rights law, humanitarian law significantly overlaps with the interests and values protected by international human right law.

One major difference between general human rights law and humanitarian law is that humanitarian law concerns the treatment of people during times of armed conflict, while human rights apply generally during both war and peace. It is possible, therefore, for both human rights law and humanitarian law to apply to the very same situation. [125] A second major difference involves the types of accountability and remedies involved. In contrast to human rights law, international criminal law is generally

---

125. Note that many human rights treaties allow "derogation" for certain rights in times of national emergencies such as war. Typically these derogations do not apply for such fundamental

focused on the criminal accountability of individual perpetrators. Traditional human rights law, on the other hand, tends to focus on holding the offending government responsible, obtaining civil compensation for the victims, or bringing about changes in government law and policy. International criminal law is premised on the potential for individual and not governmental accountability.

In this regard, you should recall that international human rights law primarily focuses on creating international rules that concern the behavior of *governments and governmental actors* toward their own citizens. In general, non-state actors (private, non-governmental individuals and juridical entities) are not subject to and cannot technically violate international human rights standards except to the extent they act in an official government capacity or agent of the government. For some international human rights crimes, such as torture or summary execution, this limitation may still apply since such crimes are defined in terms of official conduct. There are, however, some major exceptions to this general rule. For example, genocide, crimes against humanity and war crimes cover a broad range of private individual conduct, primarily during armed conflict, which may violate international criminal law. (For a detailed discussion of this point see the <u>Kadic v. Karadzic</u> case.) Whether private or official, international criminal law is premised, just like criminal law generally, upon *individual responsibility* for violations of human rights resulting in punishment of the perpetrator.[126]

Recall that part of domestic enforcement of human rights includes using criminal law to punish perpetrators of certain universal crimes — perpetrators of such crimes being the "enemies of all human kind." The prospect of utilizing domestic institutions to prosecute international crimes as a part of domestic law is a significant alternative to international processes. The primary, although not only, distinction has to do with the institutions responsible for the prosecution. Many of the underlying concepts are the

---

rights as torture, genocide, slavery and life. The CPRC is a good example. Article 4 of this treaty provides:

Article 4

1. In time of public emergency, which threatens the life of the nation and the existence of which is officially proclaimed, the States Parties to the present Covenant may take measures derogating from their obligations under the present Covenant to the extent strictly required by the exigencies of the situation, provided that such measures are not inconsistent with their other obligations under international law and do not involve discrimination solely on the ground of race, colour, sex, language, religion or social origin.

2. No derogation from articles 6, 7, 8 (paragraphs I and 2), 11, 15, 16, and 18 may be made under this provision.

3. Any State Party to the present Covenant availing itself of the right of derogation shall immediately inform the other States Parties to the present Covenant, through the intermediary of the Secretary-General of the United Nations, of the provisions from which it has derogated and of the reasons by which it was actuated. A further communication shall be made, through the same intermediary, on the date on which it terminates such derogation.

126. Some human rights treaties, like the genocide and torture conventions, also require that State Parties criminalize violations and prosecute or extradite perpetrators. See Chapter 5.

same. For example, "universal jurisdiction" is an important concept that frequently justifies international prosecutions just as it often does in domestic prosecutions.

As you study the materials, focus on how the international tribunals are organized, how they function, the bases for their jurisdiction, the nature of the cases decided and effectiveness. Although we will start with a historical perspective by examining the World War II Nuremberg and Far East Criminal Tribunals, most of the chapter focuses on ad hoc criminal tribunals created by the U.N. Security Council and the Permanent International Criminal Court created through the 2002 "Rome Statute" (a treaty).

As you study the materials think about the following questions that you should be able to answer at the end of the lesson.

1) What were the legal justifications for creating the ad hoc tribunals in Yugoslavia and Rwanda? Do the same justifications apply to the Permanent International Criminal Court?

2) How are these tribunals — both ad hoc and the permanent ICC — organized and structured to accomplish their missions?

   a. What is the role of a "prosecutor" in the tribunals' work?

   b. To whom do these tribunals answer?

   c. Who decides which cases to pursue and how does this take place?

   d. Are there any political checks?

3) What specific crimes may these tribunals prosecute and what are their key elements?

4) Have U.S. officials committed international crimes in Iraq, Afghanistan or elsewhere in the war on terror? Has the group ISIL also committed international crimes in Iraq and Syria? What crimes would these be?

5) If the answer to question 4 is yes, is there a tribunal that would have jurisdiction to prosecute?

6) What would be your priorities if were you a tribunal prosecutor? Which individuals would first receive your attention?

7) How do these tribunals gain custody over potential defendants?

   a. May defendants be tried in absentia?

   b. If not, what obligation does the world community have to capture and present potential defendants to the tribunals?

   c. How will the tribunals effectively gather the evidence necessary to prosecute such individuals?

8) How will the guilty be punished and where?

9) Why has the United States opposed the Permanent International Criminal Court and is this opposition justified?

CHART OF IMPORTANT DIFFERENCES BETWEEN INTERNATIONAL CRIMINAL LAW
AND INTERNATIONAL HUMAN RIGHTS LAW

| | International Human Rights Law | International Criminal Law |
| --- | --- | --- |
| Generally | Focus is on the acts and responsibility of governments | Focus is on actions and accountability of individuals |
| Substance | Same or similar human rights norms although typically defined differently and from distinct sources | |
| | IHL: broader in scope and context covering many rights not subject to criminal liability<br>Rights typically vaguely defined in terms of general principles, values or ends; requires "state action" | ICL: narrower set of protections generally applicable in armed conflicts, and other egregious physical violations such as genocide or torture; crimes defined with detail & precision (actus reus, mens rea, defenses) |
| Process | Limited quasi-judicial international processes; civil in nature; government or government officials defendants. | Judicial processes with procedural requirements and protections similar to U.S. criminal courts |
| Jurisdiction | Universal jurisdiction applicable as a matter of subject matter and personal jurisdiction | |
| | Subject matter found in treaties & CIL; jurisdiction involves the state, not the individual<br>State consent to processes typically required | Subject matter strictly confined to treaty terms often including temporal & other limits (sometimes treaties binding as CIL); Subject of personal jurisdiction is the individual; referrals by state parties or UN Sec. Council |
| Enforcement | Decisions of human rights adjudicatory bodies generally do not have binding authority (except ECtHR, IACtHR); no capacity to enforce judgments | Enforcement actions very concrete including prison<br>Countries turn over individuals for adjudication; cooperation req'd under UN Charter. Possible S.C. enforcement |

# B. Historical Antecedents: Nuremberg & Tokyo Trials

## 1. Nuremberg Trials

Just like the modern concept of international human rights, recognition of individual criminal responsibility for certain human rights abuses began in earnest after

World War II. After the war, the victorious powers (United Kingdom, U.S.A., U.S.S.R., and France) created the first international process empowered to prosecute and punish individuals for international crimes.[127] Known as "Nuremberg" because of its location, the initial trial of twenty-one German leaders considered "major war criminals" was held before an "International Military Tribunal" (one additional defendant committed suicide before trial and another was tried *in absentia*; Adolf Hitler, Heinrich Himmler, and Joseph Goebbels all committed suicide before indictments were issued). Legal justifications for the novel tribunal and its prosecutions rested on murky grounds. Some scholars and historians assert that it was solely an exercise of "victors' justice." Indeed, jurisdiction was created in the German Instrument of Surrender and effectuated by allied control over German territory after the war. The judges and prosecutors were all from the four victorious powers, which also wrote the rules and defined the crimes, previously unrecognized under international law. As you review the following sources, consider some basic questions about the legal basis for such prosecutions — upon what authority was the tribunal created, what laws established the defendants' criminal liability and what legal precedents did the process establish?

**Opening Statement of Robert Jackson, Chief United States Prosecutor at Nuremberg.**

---

127. The agreement to try Nazi leaders was apparently first tentatively reached at a 1945 meeting of Churchill, Roosevelt, and Stalin in Yalta (Crimea Russia), and later confirmed after the war in the Potsdam conference. Recently released classified documents confirm the widespread belief that the British favored summary execution of Nazi leaders but the Russians favored the American proposal for a tribunal because of its propaganda value. It has also been widely reported that Stalin, perhaps in jest, urged in 1943 meeting in Tehran that 50–100 thousand German officers should also be summarily executed. When Churchill vehemently objected, Roosevelt supposedly replied (one hopes in jest) that 49,000 would be adequate.

MR. JUSTICE JACKSON: May it please Your Honors:

The privilege of opening the first trial in history for crimes against the peace of the world imposes a grave responsibility. The wrongs which we seek to condemn and punish have been so calculated, so malignant, and so devastating, that civilization cannot tolerate their being ignored, because it cannot survive their being repeated. That four great nations, flushed with victory and stung with injury stay the hand of vengeance and voluntarily submit their captive enemies to the judgment of the law is one of the most significant tributes that Power has ever paid to Reason.

This Tribunal, while it is novel and experimental, is not the product of abstract speculations nor is it created to vindicate legalistic theories. This inquest represents the practical effort of four of the most mighty of nations, with the support of 17 more, to utilize international law to meet the greatest menace of our times — aggressive war. The common sense of mankind demands that law shall not stop with the punishment of petty crimes by little people. It must also reach men who possess themselves of great power and make deliberate and concerted use of it to set in motion evils which leave no home in the world untouched. It is a cause of that magnitude that the United Nations will lay before Your Honors.

***

What makes this inquest significant is that these prisoners represent sinister influences that will lurk in the world long after their bodies have returned to dust. We will show them to be living symbols of racial hatreds, of terrorism and violence, and of the arrogance and cruelty of power. They are symbols of fierce nationalisms and of militarism, of intrigue and war-making, which have embroiled Europe generation after generation, crushing its manhood, destroying its homes, and impoverishing its life.

***

Unfortunately, the nature of these crimes is such that both prosecution and judgment must be by victor nations over vanquished foes. . . . The former high station of these defendants, the notoriety of their acts, and the adaptability of their conduct to provoke retaliation make it hard to distinguish between the demand for a just and measured retribution, and the unthinking cry for vengeance which arises from the anguish of war. It is our task, so far as humanly possible, to, draw the line between the two. We must never forget that the record on which we judge these defendants today is the record on which history will judge us tomorrow. To pass these defendants a poisoned chalice is to put it to our own lips as well. We must summon such detachment and intellectual integrity to our task that this [t]rial will commend itself to posterity as fulfilling humanity's aspirations to do justice.

Please watch and listen to at least some portion of Justice Jackson's opening statement on this <u>video</u> clip (or others also available online).

The defendants at Nuremberg. Front row, from left to right: Hermann Göring, Rudolf Hess, Joachim von Ribbentrop, Wilhelm Keitel, Ernst Kaltenbrunner, Alfred Rosenberg, Hans Frank, Wilhelm Frick, Julius Streicher, Walther Funk, Hjalmar Schacht. Back row from left to right: Karl Dönitz, Erich Raeder, Baldur von Schirach, Fritz Sauckel, Alfred Jodl, Franz von Papen, Arthur Seyss-Inquart, Albert Speer, Konstantin van Neurath, Hans Fritzsche.

*Courtesy of the National Archives.*

Contemporaneous video footage of the trial can be found on the website of the U.S. Holocaust Museum, if you are interested in further detail. You might also find interesting an excellent and fascinating BBC documentary *Nuremberg: Nazis on Trial* (2006) (sorry, no longer available on YouTube but it is on Netflix, BBC article summarizing content here) that examines, with dramatization, the particular defendants Albert Speer, Hermann Goering, and Rudolf Hess. Important documents relating to the proceedings are also available from multiple web sources, including Yale's Avalon Project and the Library of Congress.

The international crimes recognized by the Nuremberg Tribunal fell within three categories: "crimes of war," "crimes against peace" and "crimes against humanity." These are generally now known as the Nuremberg Principles.

# 2. The Nuremberg Charter

## JURISDICTION AND GENERAL PRINCIPLES

### Article 6

***

The following acts, or any of them, are crimes coming within the jurisdiction of the Tribunal for which there shall be individual responsibility:

**(a) CRIMES AGAINST PEACE**: namely, planning, preparation, initiation, or waging of a war of aggression, or a war in violation of international treaties, agreements, or assurances, or participation in a common plan or conspiracy for the accomplishment of any of the foregoing;

**(b) WAR CRIMES**: namely, violations of the laws or customs of war. Such violations shall include, but not be limited to, murder, ill-treatment or deportation to slave labor or for any other purpose of civilian population of or in occupied territory, murder or ill-treatment of prisoners of war or persons on the seas, killing of hostages, plunder of public or private property, wanton destruction of cities, towns or villages, or devastation not justified by military necessity;

**(c) CRIMES AGAINST HUMANITY**: namely, murder, extermination, enslavement, deportation, and other inhumane acts committed against any civilian population, before or during the war; or persecutions on political, racial, or religious grounds in execution of or in connection with any crime within the jurisdiction of the Tribunal, whether or not in violation of the domestic law of the country where perpetrated.

Leaders, organizers, instigators, and accomplices participating in the formulation or execution of a common plan or conspiracy to commit any of the foregoing crimes are responsible for all acts performed by any persons in execution of such plan.

### Article 7

The official position of defendants, whether as Heads of State or responsible officials in Government Departments, shall not be considered as freeing them from responsibility or mitigating punishment.

### Article 8

The fact that the Defendant acted pursuant to order of his Government or of a superior shall not free him from responsibility, but may be considered in mitigation of punishment if the Tribunal determines that justice so requires.

The indictments, tracking these general categories of crime, included specific allegations relating to the murder of over six million Jews, the pursuit of an unjustified war of aggression, brutality against civilian populations, maintenance of concentration camps, and use of slave labor. For additional background and historical context, review eye witness accounts posted on the website "Eye Witness to History," such as

Map from Wikipedia commons.

"Beginning of World War II" (territorial aggression), "The Nazi Occupation of Po-land," and "Inside a Nazi Death Camp" (atrocities against Jews), "The London Blitz 1940" and "The Siege of Leningrad 1941–1944"(attacks on civilian populations).

Led by Hitler's heir apparent Goering, most of the defendants denied the tribunal's authority, proclaimed innocence, denied knowledge of atrocities, or plead that they were simply following orders. Others, notably the armaments minister Speer, admitted collective guilt and condemned Nazism. Perhaps because of this, Speer was sentenced to only twenty years imprisonment despite his deep involvement in the extensive and brutal use of slave labor. After a ten month trial, eleven defendants were sentenced to death by hanging, seven were sentenced to life or lesser term of imprisonment and three were acquitted.

After the trial of these major Nazi leaders was concluded, each of the four victorious allies conducted numerous subsequent trials of other alleged war criminals in areas under their respective control. The defendants included military officers, concentration camp commandants, prison guards, industrialists, members of killing squads, and even doctors who participated in medical experiments on prisoners. Under occupation <u>Council Control Law No. 10</u>, the United States conducted twelve "subsequent Nuremberg trials" of 183 defendants of which twelve were sentenced to death, eight were sentenced to life, seventy-seven were sentenced to a lesser term and the remainder acquitted. A good summary of these twelve subsequent Nuremberg trials, with linked detailed descriptions, can be found at the websites maintained at the University of Missouri, Kansas City (<u>here</u>) or the U.S. Holocaust Memorial Museum (<u>here</u>), (original documents can be accessed at the Library of Congress <u>here</u>). Thousands of other individuals were also tried in other locations <u>outside of the Nuremberg process</u>. (<u>See map here</u>.)

## 3. Tokyo Trials

It wasn't just the Nazis who committed egregious atrocities during World War II. A similar tribunal, the International Military Tribunal for the Far East, was created to try twenty-eight major Japanese war criminals in Tokyo. As in Europe, thousands of so-called "lesser" war criminals were subsequently tried throughout the region.[128]

The Chinese News Daily provided this overview:

MAY 3, 1946 to NOVEMBER 12, 1948

All Japanese Class A war criminals were tried by the International Military Tribunal for the Far East (IMTFE) in Tokyo. The prosecution team was made up of justices from eleven Allied nations: Australia, Canada, China, France, Great Britain, India, the Netherlands, New Zealand, the Philippines, the Soviet Union, and the United States of America. The Tokyo trial lasted two and a half years, from May 1946 to November 1948. Other war criminals were tried in the respective victim countries. War crime trials were held at ten different locations in China.

I. THE INDICTMENT

Of the eighty (80) Class A war criminal suspects detained in the Sugamo prison after 1945, twenty-eight (28) men were brought to trial before the IMTFE. The accused included nine civilians and nineteen professional military men:

---

128. In an article reviewing the Far East prosecutions, <u>History.net states</u>:

Japanese soldiers had been killing, raping, looting, and torturing all across the East since the 1930s. In 1945, at long long last, the bill was coming due. Before the courts-martial and military commissions recessed for the last time, some 5,600 Japanese had been prosecuted in more than 2,200 trials. Of these men — and a few women — more than 4,400 were convicted, and about 1,000 were executed. Testifying to the Allies' determination to deal fairly with the enemy, there had also been about the same number of acquittals.

Four former premiers: Hiranuma, Hirota, Koiso, Tojo

Three former foreign ministers: Matsuoka, Shigemitsu, Togo

Four former war ministers: Araki, Hata, Itagaki, Minami

Two former navy ministers: Nagano, Shimada

Six former generals: Doihara, Kimura, Matsui, Muto, Sato, Umezu

Two former ambassadors: Oshima, Shiratori

Three former economic and financial leaders: Hoshino, Kaya, Suzuki

One imperial adviser: Kido

One radical theorist: Okawa

One admiral: Oka

One colonel: Hashimoto

The indictment accused the defendants of promoting a scheme of conquest that "contemplated and carried out . . . murdering, maiming and ill-treating prisoners of war (and) civilian internees . . . forcing them to labor under inhumane conditions . . . plundering public and private property, wantonly destroying cities, towns, and villages beyond any justification of military necessity; (perpetrating) mass murder, rape, pillage, brigandage, torture, and other barbaric cruelties upon the helpless civilian population of the over-run countries."

Joseph Keenan, the chief prosecutor representing the United States at the trial, issued a press statement along with the indictment: "[w]ar and treaty-breakers should be stripped of the glamour of national heroes and exposed as what they really are — plain, ordinary murderers."

The following excerpts from Wikipedia present this shocking portrayal of the crimes for which the Japanese war leadership was tried.

***Crimes

The Japanese military during the 1930s and 1940s is often compared to the military of Nazi Germany during 1933–45 because of the sheer scale of suffering. Much of the controversy regarding Japan's role in World War II revolves around the death rates of prisoners of war and civilians under Japanese occupation. The historian Chalmers Johnson has written that:

*It may be pointless to try to establish which World War Two Axis aggressor, Germany or Japan, was the more brutal to the peoples it victimised. The Germans killed six million Jews and [twenty] million Russians [i.e. Soviet citizens]; the Japanese slaughtered as many as [thirty] million Filipinos, Malays, Vietnamese, Cambodians, Indonesians and Burmese, at least [twenty-three] million of them ethnic Chinese. Both nations looted the countries they conquered on a monumental scale, though Japan plundered more, over a longer period, than the Nazis. Both conquerors enslaved millions and exploited them as* *forced labourers — and, in the case of the Japanese, as [forced] prostitutes for front-line troops. If you were a Nazi prisoner of war from <u>Britain</u>, <u>America</u>, <u>Australia</u>, <u>New Zealand</u> or <u>Canada</u> (but not Russia) you faced a [four percent] chance of not surviving the war; [by comparison] the death rate for Allied POWs held by the Japanese was nearly [thirty percent].*

***

Mass Killings

*** The most infamous incident during this period was the <u>Nanking Massacre</u> of 1937–38, when, according to the findings of the <u>International Military Tribunal for the Far East</u>, the Japanese army massacred as many as 300,000 civilians and prisoners of war, although the accepted figure is somewhere in the hundreds of thousands. A similar crime was the <u>Changjiao massacre</u>. In Southeast Asia, the <u>Manila massacre</u>, resulted in the deaths of 100,000 civilians in the Philippines. It is estimated that at least one out of every twenty Filipinos died at the hand of the Japanese during the occupation. In the <u>Sook Ching massacre</u>, between 50,000 and 90,000 ethnic Chinese in Singapore were taken to beaches and massacred. There were numerous other massacres of civilians e.g. the <u>Kalagong massacre</u>. ***

Human Experimentation and Biological Warfare

Special Japanese military units conducted experiments on civilians and POWs in <u>China</u>. One of the most infamous was <u>Unit 731</u> under <u>Shirō Ishii</u>. Victims were subjected to <u>vivisection</u> without anesthesia, amputations, and were used to test <u>biological weapons</u>, among other experiments. Anesthesia was not used because it was believed to affect results.

According to GlobalSecurity.org, the experiments carried out by Unit 731 alone caused 3,000 deaths.

***

Torture of Prisoners of War

Japanese imperial forces employed widespread use of <u>torture</u> on prisoners, usually in an effort to gather military intelligence quickly. Tortured prisoners were often later executed. A former Japanese Army officer who served in China, Uno Shintaro, stated:

*The major means of getting intelligence was to extract information by interrogating prisoners. Torture was an unavoidable necessity. Murdering and burying them follows naturally. You do it so you won't be found out. I believed and acted this way because I was convinced of what I was doing. We carried out our duty as instructed by our masters. We did it for the sake of our country. From our filial obligation to our ancestors. On the battlefield, we never really considered the Chinese humans. When you're winning, the losers look really miserable. We concluded that the <u>Yamato [i.e., Japanese] race</u> was superior.*

***

Shirō Ishii, commander of Unit 731.

Forced Labor

*Main article: Slavery in Japan*

The Japanese military's use of <u>forced labor</u>, by Asian civilians and POWs also caused many deaths. According to a joint study by historians including Zhifen Ju, Mitsuyoshi Himeta, Toru Kubo, and <u>Mark Peattie</u>, more than ten million Chinese civilians were mobilized by the <u>*Kōa-in*</u> (Japanese Asia Development Board) for forced labour. More than 100,000 civilians and POWs died in the construction of the <u>Burma-Siam Railway</u>.

\*\*\*

Comfort Women

*Main article: Comfort women*

The terms "comfort women" . . . or "military comfort women" . . . are <u>euphemisms</u> for women in Japanese military <u>brothels</u> in occupied countries, many of whom were recruited by force or deception, and regard themselves as having been <u>sexually assaulted</u> or <u>sex slaves</u>.

\*\*\*

The controversy was re-ignited on March 1, 2007, when Japanese Prime Minister <u>Shinzo Abe</u> mentioned suggestions that a <u>U.S. House of Representatives</u> committee would call on the Japanese Government to "apologize for and acknowledge" the role of the Japanese Imperial military in wartime sex slavery. However, Abe denied that it applied to comfort stations. "There is no evidence to prove there was coercion, nothing to support it." Abe's comments provoked negative reactions overseas. For example, a *New York Times* editorial on March 6 said:

*These were not commercial brothels. Force, explicit and implicit, was used in recruiting these women. What went on in them was serial rape, not prostitution. The Japanese Army's involvement is documented in the government's own defense files. A senior Tokyo official more or less apologized for this horrific crime in 1993. . . .*

\*\*\*

The atrocities described above are obviously criminal in nature. The question is what kind of crimes are they? Are such crimes committed by governments, committed systematically on a wide scale during armed conflict, different from ordinary crime? As you will see, the substance of the crimes defined and developed by Nuremberg and Tokyo form the foundation of modern international criminal law as it relates to human rights and humanitarian law. You can understand the factual foundation for defining such crimes, particularly crimes against humanity, in the descriptions of atrocities above.

The Nuremberg principles and its modern offspring, particularly crimes against humanity and war crimes, also substantively parallel certain international human rights we have already studied but typically have distinct characteristics and requirements. You should recall, for example, that harsh physical abuse or murder committed by a private citizen generally would not constitute human rights violations. These same acts, however, might become violations of human rights — perhaps torture and summary execution — if perpetrated by a government official under color of law. Those same violations of human rights committed by the public official might not constitute a war crime or crime against humanity unless other conditions were also present such as being part of a widespread and systematic set of violations committed against innocent civilians during armed conflict. To complicate matters just a bit further, private individuals may also commit crimes against humanity and war crimes even though the same conduct outside of armed conflict would not necessarily constitute a human rights violation since not committed by a government official. These distinctions and others are examined further below.

# C. Evolution of International Humanitarian Law: The Geneva Conventions

International criminal law has evolved significantly since Nuremberg and Tokyo. It is generally accepted that the Nuremberg principles, which have been endorsed by the U.N. General Assembly and Security Council, are binding customary international law. The Nuremberg principles now form part of international "humanitarian law" — a larger body of international law designed to prescribe rules on war, in particular the treatment of soldiers and civilians during armed conflicts. Such rules pre-date Nuremberg and have existed since at least the 1899 and 1907 Hague Conventions, in forms that have evolved along with the destructiveness of armed conflict. The modern manifestation of international humanitarian law is found in the four 1949 "Geneva Conventions" and subsequent protocols.[129]

- First Geneva Convention for the Amelioration of the Condition of the Wounded and Sick in Armed Forces in the Field, 1864

- Second Geneva Convention for the Amelioration of the Condition of Wounded, Sick and Shipwrecked Members of Armed Forces at Sea, 1906

- Third Geneva Convention relative to the Treatment of Prisoners of War, 1929

- Fourth Geneva Convention relative to the Protection of Civilian Persons in Time of War, 1949

---

129. The 1949 Conventions included the revision of three earlier international treaties on the law of war (regarding wounded or sick armed forces in the "field," or at "sea" and prisoners of war) and the addition of a new convention relating to civilian populations. There are three subsequently added protocols: Protocol I (1977) (Protection of Victims of International Armed Conflicts — clarifying & expanding original Geneva provisions); Protocol II (1977) (relating to the Protection of Victims of Non-International Armed Conflicts); Protocol III (2005) (Additional Distinctive Emblem for medical personnel).

With the explicit endorsement of the U.N. Security Council, the 1949 Geneva Conventions (which nearly all countries in the world are party to) have undoubtedly also become customary international law. The Harvard Research Initiative on Humanitarian Law provided this helpful summary describing the substantive pillars of the Geneva Convention:

> **Principles.** Though a number of complex questions and concerns may arise in applying IHL to contemporary conflicts, certain fundamental principles provide basic guidance. For instance, the principles of distinction, proportionality, and necessity, all of which are part of customary international law, always apply to the use of armed force.
>
> **Distinction:** Parties to an armed conflict must distinguish between the civilian population and combatants and between civilian objects and military objectives. Any intended target must be a military target.
>
> **Proportionality:** Attacks are prohibited if they cause incidental loss of civilian life, injury to civilians, or damage to civilian objects that is excessive in relation to the anticipated concrete and direct military advantage of the attack.
>
> **Necessity:** The use of military force is justified only to the extent it is necessary to achieve a military goal. This force used must not exceed the level required to stop the threatening activity.
>
> Other fundamental IHL principles include the duty to take precautions to spare the civilian population before and during an attack; the prohibition against infliction of unnecessary suffering or destruction, or of superfluous injury; and the prohibition against engaging in indiscriminate attacks.

"Human Rights Education Associates" provides a somewhat different but useful characterization of the fundamental principles of international humanitarian law:

> *Fundamental principles of humanitarian law*
>
> International humanitarian law aims to limit the suffering caused by war by forcing parties engaged in a conflict to:
>
> * engage in limited methods and means of warfare;
> * differentiate between civilian population and combatants, and work to spare civilian population and property;
> * abstain from harming or killing an adversary who surrenders or who can no longer take part in the fighting;
> * abstain from physically or mentally torturing or performing cruel punishments on adversaries.

The Geneva Conventions classify certain violations of the treaties as "grave breaches," which are essentially war crimes. Each Convention defines grave breaches in a similar way with variations relevant to that particular convention. The 4th Convention on protection of civilians, for example, provides:

Art. 147.

Grave breaches to which the preceding Article relates shall be those involving any of the following acts, if committed against persons or property protected by the present Convention: wilful killing, torture, or inhuman treatment, including biological experiments, wilfully causing great suffering or serious injury to body or health, unlawful deportation or transfer or unlawful confinement of a protected person, compelling a protected person to serve in the forces of a hostile Power, or wilfully depriving a protected person of the rights of fair and regular trial prescribed in the present Convention, taking of hostages and extensive destruction, and appropriation of property, not justified by military necessity and carried out unlawfully and wantonly.

Thus, a grave breach and war crime under the Geneva Conventions would include:

- willful killing, torture, or inhuman treatment, including biological experiments
- willfully causing great suffering or serious injury to body or health
- unlawful deportation, transfer, or confinement of protected persons
- compelling one to serve in the forces of a hostile power
- willfully depriving one of the right to a fair and regular trial
- taking of hostages
- extensive destruction and appropriation of property not justified by military necessity and carried out unlawfully and wantonly

The International Committee of the Red Cross website also provides links to texts and the text of the various conventions.

State parties to the Conventions must enact and enforce legislation criminalizing grave breaches. The International Committee for the Red Cross maintains a national implementation database by subject and country. Nations are also obligated to search for persons alleged to have committed such crimes, or ordered them to be committed, and to bring them to trial regardless of their nationality and regardless of the place where the crimes took place. The U.S. War Crimes Act of 1996 criminalizes grave breaches of the Geneva Conventions (including torture, cruel or inhumane treatment, biological experimentation on persons, murder, mutilation or maiming, intentionally causing serious bodily injury in violation of the laws of war, rape, sexual assault or abuse, and hostage taking, by or against U.S. nationals or a member of the armed forces).[130]

---

130. The 2006 Military Commission Act required that alleged war crimes perpetrated by those defined as "unlawful enemy combatants" in the war on terror be tried by military tribunal. In Boumediene v. Bush, the Supreme Court struck down as unconstitutional under the "Suspension Clause" the Act's prohibition against writs of habeas corpus challenging such prosecutions.

# D.  Contemporary International Criminal Processes Involving Humanitarian Law and Human Rights

Significant developments in international criminal law relating to human rights and humanitarian law have taken place recently. The first important development since Nuremberg has been the UN Security Council's creation of "ad hoc" international criminal tribunals to address particular situations, such as the atrocities in Rwanda and the former Yugoslavia. The second major development is the creation of the permanent International Criminal Court. These institutional developments have been accompanied by a quantum evolution of the underlying substantive law defining jurisdiction, the elements of crimes, command responsibility, complicity, and defenses. Customary international law and universal jurisdiction have played prominent roles in justifying the various tribunals' powers.

## 1. Ad Hoc International Criminal Tribunals

The most prominent "ad hoc" international tribunals are those created by the U.N. Security Council to prosecute violations of humanitarian law and genocide in the former Yugoslavia (1993) and Rwanda (1994). Other international tribunals, including "special" courts or tribunals compromised of both national and international judges, have been created under U.N. auspices for conflicts in <u>Sierra Leone</u> (2002), <u>Cambodia</u> (2003), <u>East Timor</u> (2006) and <u>Lebanon</u> (2007).

a. International Criminal Tribunal for the Former Yugoslavia (ICTY)

Beginning in 1991, the former Yugoslavia essentially disintegrated into what are now five independent sovereign states — Slovenia, Croatia, Bosnia-Herzegovina, Macedonia, and the Federal Republic of Yugoslavia (which consists of the former provinces of Serbia and Montenegro — and is often referred to as "Serbia"). The legal status of a sixth de-facto new sovereign state, <u>Kosovo, remains uncertain</u> even today. As the former Yugoslavia disintegrated along ethnic and religious lines, fighting almost immediately erupted.[131]

The conflict in Bosnia essentially revolved around the quest for power and property asserted by three competing ethnic groups — the Serbs, Croats and Muslims.[132] Approximately 43% of Bosnia is Muslim, 31% is Serbian, and 18% is Croatian. Ethnic Serbs living in Bosnia, covertly supported by Serbia, forcibly took over large portions

---

131. The United Nations Security Council first responded by imposing a mandatory embargo prohibiting arms sales in the region. Subsequently, this embargo included air and naval blockades and severe economic sanctions against "Serbia," which has supplied money, weaponry, and manpower to ethnic Serbs fighting in Bosnia and Croatia. Ultimately, NATO intervened militarily forcing an end to the various conflicts, including the 1999 war in Kosovo.

132. Technically of course, "Muslims" are not an ethnic group but a religious one. For historical reasons, however, Muslims in Bosnia have been considered as ethnically different from their Serbian and Croatian neighbors.

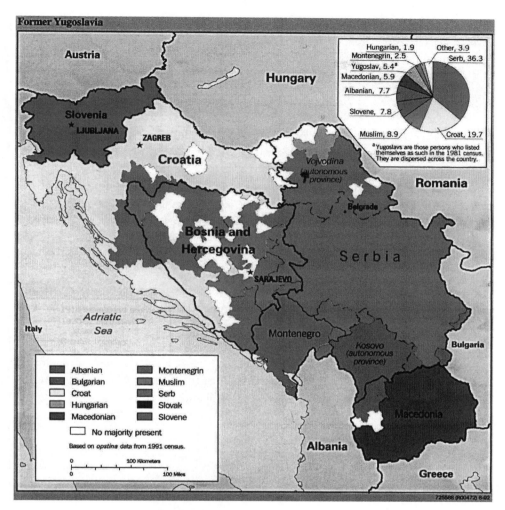

Map from <u>Wikimedia Commons</u>

of Bosnia formerly occupied by Bosnian Muslims (Serbs living in Croatia also forcibly captured portions of Croatia; and Croats in Bosnia also forcibly captured parts of Bosnia). The primary aim of these Serbian "nationalists," such as <u>Radovan Karadzic</u>, was to carve out an "ethnically pure" Serbian homeland in Bosnia that eventually could be joined with "Serbia proper." Ultimately, the parties in Bosnia (including Serbia) agreed to a peace settlement called the <u>Dayton Accords</u> that was promulgated and policed by NATO.

In Kosovo, over ninety percent of the population is ethnic Albanian. In 1989, Serbian nationalist leaders, such as Slobodan Milosevic, began reasserting the Serbs' historical claims over Kosovo, then a restive autonomous region, by oppressing of the ethnic Albanian population. This oppression culminated in the 1999 campaign of terror that forced over one million people into exile and resulted in the NATO bombing war on Serbia and eventual occupation of Kosovo. UN Security Council

Resolution 1244 placed Kosovo under transitional UN administration with self-governance. In 2008, Kosovo unilaterally declared its independence (again) which has been recognized by almost 100 other countries.

Additional general descriptions of the facts and the history of conflicts in this region (often called the "Balkans") can be found on Wikipedia. There are many other depictions, both fact and fiction, on the web including here.

Both of the above conflicts resulted in widespread atrocities against civilians. Among these atrocities was so-called "ethnic cleansing." Ethnic cleansing occurred when the Serbs (and, to a lesser extent, the Croats in Bosnia) forcibly removed a rival ethnic group (mostly Muslims and ethnic Albanians) from their homes, stole their property, killed them or forced them into concentration camps or exile. The Serbs, and to a lesser extent other warring factions including the Bosnian Muslims and ethnic Albanians, also committed a wide variety of other atrocities including systematic rape of women and girls, wide-scale torture, the massacre of civilians, and the creation of concentration camps — all reminiscent of the horrors that occurred during World War II. After a special Commission of Experts report confirmed widespread atrocities, the U.N. Security Council took the unprecedented step in 1993 (Resolution 827) of creating the International Criminal Tribunal for the Former Yugoslavia (ICTY) to prosecute its perpetrators.

Declaring that the atrocities in the former Yugoslavia constituted a breach and threat to international peace under Chapter VII of the Charter, the Council authorized the tribunal to prosecute and punish persons guilty of "serious violations of international humanitarian law committed in the territory of the former Yugoslavia since 1991 . . . ."

The "Statute" of the tribunal (adopted by the Council) provides that these violations include:

### Article 2
### Grave breaches of the Geneva Conventions of 1949

The International Tribunal shall have the power to prosecute persons committing or ordering to be committed grave breaches of the Geneva Conventions of 12 August 1949, namely the following acts against persons or property protected under the provisions of the relevant Geneva Convention:

(a) wilful killing;

(b) torture or inhuman treatment, including biological experiments;

(c) wilfully causing great suffering or serious injury to body or health;

(d) extensive destruction and appropriation of property, not justified by military necessity and carried out unlawfully and wantonly;

(e) compelling a prisoner of war or a civilian to serve in the forces of a hostile power;

(f) wilfully depriving a prisoner of war or a civilian of the rights of fair and regular trial;

(g)  unlawful deportation or transfer or unlawful confinement of a civilian;

(h)  taking civilians as hostages.

## Article 3
### Violations of the laws or customs of war

The International Tribunal shall have the power to prosecute persons violating the laws or customs of war. Such violations shall include, but not be limited to:

(a)  employment of poisonous weapons or other weapons calculated to cause unnecessary suffering;

(b)  wanton destruction of cities, towns or villages, or devastation not justified by military necessity;

(c)  attack or bombardment, by whatever means, of undefended towns, villages, dwellings, or buildings;

(d)  seizure of, destruction or wilful damage done to institutions dedicated to religion, charity and education, the arts and sciences, historic monuments, and works of art and science;

(e)  plunder of public or private property.

## Article 4
### Genocide

1. The International Tribunal shall have the power to prosecute persons committing genocide as defined in paragraph 2 of this article or of committing any of the other acts enumerated in paragraph 3 of this article.

2. Genocide means any of the following acts committed with intent to destroy, in whole or in part, a national, ethnical, racial, or religious group, as such:

(a)  killing members of the group;

(b)  causing serious bodily or mental harm to members of the group;

(c)  deliberately inflicting on the group conditions of life calculated to bring about its physical destruction in whole or in part;

(d)  imposing measures intended to prevent births within the group;

(e)  forcibly transferring children of the group to another group.

3.  The following acts shall be punishable:

(a)  genocide;

(b)  conspiracy to commit genocide;

(c)  direct and public incitement to commit genocide;

(d)  attempt to commit genocide;

(e)  complicity in genocide.

### Article 5
### Crimes against humanity

The International Tribunal shall have the power to prosecute persons responsible for the following crimes when committed in armed conflict, whether international or internal in character, and directed against any civilian population:

(a)  murder;

(b)  extermination;

(c)  enslavement;

(d)  deportation;

(e)  imprisonment;

(f)  torture;

(g)  rape;

(h)  persecutions on political, racial and religious grounds;

(i)  other inhumane acts.

Regarding individual responsibility, the Statute provides:

### Article 7
### Individual criminal responsibility

1. A person who planned, instigated, ordered, committed, or otherwise aided and abetted in the planning, preparation, or execution of a crime referred to in articles 2 to 5 of the present Statute, shall be individually responsible for the crime.

2. The official position of any accused person, whether as Head of State or Government or as a responsible Government official, shall not relieve such person of criminal responsibility nor mitigate punishment.

3. The fact that any of the acts referred to in articles 2 to 5 of the present Statute was committed by a subordinate does not relieve his superior of criminal responsibility if he knew or had reason to know that the subordinate was about to commit such acts or had done so and the superior failed to take the necessary and reasonable measures to prevent such acts or to punish the perpetrators thereof.

4. The fact that an accused person acted pursuant to an order of a Government or of a superior shall not relieve him of criminal responsibility, but may be considered in mitigation of punishment if the International Tribunal determines that justice so requires.

The Statute also provided for an "independent prosecutor," judicial review of "indictments," "rules of procedure and evidence," due process "rights of the accused," and an organizational chart and chart of the "key stages" in the process appear on the ICTY website. Although the Tribunal has concurrent jurisdiction over cases with national institutions, it also enjoys "primacy" allowing it to exclusively prosecute cases within its mandate if it chooses. The Tribunal offers this <u>video summary</u> of its work which is boring but informative.

By most measures, the Tribunal has enjoyed considerable success.[133] The Tribunal's "<u>Key Figures</u>" database indicates that it indicted 161 individual suspects, concluded proceeding in 141 cases and convicted and sentenced 74 defendants to prison terms up to 40 years. Importantly, these cases included prosecution of major political and military leaders responsible for atrocities committed during the war, such as Serbian President <u>Slobodan Milosevic</u> (who died during his trial). The Karadzic and Mladic cases are briefly described below. The <u>ICTY website</u> provides a wealth of useful information both about the tribunal and its cases, including live feeds and video recordings of major events during various trials. You should browse the Tribunal's website in order to find out more about how it is composed, its jurisdiction and information about the cases that it has decided.

The ICTY has recently concluded the prosecution of <u>Radovan Karadzic</u>, after 497 trial days and 580 witnesses. His prosecution is particularly significant given his role a political and military leader in the conflict.

Photo by Mikhail Evstafiev. Wikimedia Commons.

---

133. For a contrary view, casting the Tribunal as a "rogue" court and "crude political arm" of NATO, see Edward S. Herman, *Stacy Sullivan on Milosevic and Genocide*, <u>Global Policy Forum</u>.

The Tribunal's "Case Information Sheet" describes the charges against him this way:

Founding member of the Serbian Democratic Party (SDS); President of the SDS until his resignation on 19 July 1996; Chairman of the National Security Council of the so-called Serbian Republic of Bosnia and Herzegovina (later Republika Srpska — "RS"); President of the three-member Presidency of RS from its creation on 12 May 1992 until 17 December 1992, and thereafter sole President of Republika Srpska and Supreme Commander of its armed forces.

Crimes alleged in the indictment:

Genocide:

- He committed in concert with others, planned, instigated, ordered and/or aided and abetted genocide against a part of the Bosnian Muslim and/or Bosnian Croat national, ethnical, and/or religious groups as such. He participated in a joint criminal enterprise (JCE) to permanently remove Bosnian Muslims and Bosnian Croats from the territories of Bosnia and Herzegovina (BiH) claimed as Bosnian Serb territory;

- He participated in a JCE to eliminate the Bosnian Muslims in Srebrenica by killing the men and boys of Srebrenica and forcibly removing the women, young children and some elderly men from Srebrenica.

Persecutions, Extermination, Murder, Deportation, Inhumane acts

(Crimes against humanity):

- He committed in concert with others, planned, instigated, ordered and/or aided and abetted persecutions on political and/or religious grounds against Bosnian Muslims and/or Bosnian Croats in the following municipalities: Banja Luka, Bijeljina, Bosanski Novi, Bratunac, Brčko, Foča, Hadžići, Ilidža, Ključ, Novi Grad, Novo Sarajevo, Pale, Prijedor, Rogatica, Sanski Most, Sokolac, Višegrad, Vlasenica, Vogošća, and Zvornik as well as persecutions of the Bosnian Muslims of Srebrenica ("Municipalities");

- He is responsible for the acts of extermination and murder that formed part of the objective to permanently remove Bosnian Muslims and Bosnian Croats from Bosnian-Serb claimed territory, and which were carried out between March 1992 and 30 November 1995 by members of the Serb forces and Bosnian Serb political and governmental organs, including killings during and after takeovers in the Municipalities and killings related to detention facilities in the Municipalities;

Murder, acts of violence the primary purpose of which is to spread terror among the civilian population, unlawful attack on civilians, taking of hostages (violations of the laws or customs of war):

- Between April 1992 and November 1995, Karadžić, in concert with other members of a JCE, established and implemented a military strategy that used sniping and shelling to kill, maim, wound and terrorize the civilian inhabitants of Sarajevo. The sniping and shelling killed and wounded thousands of civilians of both sexes and all ages, including children and the elderly.

- Between approximately 26 May 1995 and 19 June 1995, Bosnian Serb forces detained over 200 UN peacekeepers and military observers in various locations, including Pale, Sarajevo, Banja Luka, and Goraţde, and held them at various locations in Republika Srpska. Threats were issued to third parties, including NATO and UN Commanders, that further NATO attacks on Bosnian Serb military targets would result in the injury, death or continued detention of the detainees. Some of the detainees were assaulted or otherwise maltreated during their captivity.

Video clips of the Karadzic proceedings, including the initial appearance and charges are available here and on the ICTY website video library. On March 24, 2016, the Tribunal announced its judgement that Karadzic was guilty of genocide, war crimes and crimes against humanity for leading a "campaign of terror against civilians." As reported by the NY Times: "Mr. Karadzic, 70, was sentenced to forty years in prison for his role in lethal ethnic cleansing operations, the siege of Sarajevo and the slaughter of 8,000 Muslim men and boys in Srebrenica in 1995, in proceedings that were likened to the Nuremberg trials of former Nazi leaders."

In 2011, Serbia extradited one of the last remaining high ranking figures accused of atrocities within the Tribunal's jurisdiction — the notorious "butcher of Bosnia," General Ratko Mladić. Like Karadzic before him, Mladić was protected by sympathizers inside and out of government for approximately fifteen years.

Serbian witnesses against such defendants were forced to assume new identities, sometimes at great personal costs, including exile. (See N.Y. Times, Witness in War Crimes Court Tallies Cost of a Decade in Hiding, Testifying Against Slobodan Milosevic at Tribunal for Former Yugoslavia.) Eventually the economic and political interests of Serbia, coveting E.U. membership, made it expedient to dispatch him to The Hague.

The fact that many people in Serbia consider loathsome villains such as Mladić, Karadzic and Milosevic to be national heroes, despite overwhelming evidence of their participation in crimes against humanity, may provide sobering insights into the origins of such crimes. Author Daniel Goldhagen's highly controversial book, *Hitler's Willing Executioners: Ordinary Germans and the Holocaust* (1996), coined an invocative but easily misunderstood and abused phrase about the role, participation and acquiescence of ordinary people in mass human rights crimes.[134] New Republic author Stacy Sullivan (later echoed by Goldhagen) has similarly suggested a form of

---

134. Goldhagen's thesis about the depth and culture of German "eliminationist" anti-Semitism leading up to the Holocaust has been strongly challenged on historical and other grounds. The Wikipedia page on his book provides a reasonable summary of Goldhagen's views and his critics.

Supporters of Ratko Mladic wave flags with his picture — "Serbian hero" rally. Photograph by Rade Nagraisalović, <u>Wikimedia Commons</u>.

<u>collective guilt regarding Serbs</u>, seeped in nationalism and ethnic exclusion rather than anti-Semitism. How is genocide possible?

b. International Criminal Tribunal for Rwanda (<u>ICTR</u>)

Events involving ethnic violence also took place in Rwanda in 1994 — but on a much greater scale than the atrocities in Bosnia. It is estimated that as many as 800,000 innocent people were massacred — many being hacked to death by mobs wielding machetes.

For more information, please visit **One hundred days** (BBC News), which explores the 1994 genocide in depth (includes audio and images). The UN Security Council also created a war crimes tribunal for prosecuting perpetrators of this genocide.

By Lydia Polgreen

International Herald Tribune

Friday, December 19, 2008

**ACCRA, Ghana:** A senior Rwandan military officer charged with being one of the masterminds of the 1994 genocide in Rwanda was convicted on Thursday by a United Nations court in Tanzania of genocide and sentenced to life in prison.

Colonel Theoneste Bagosora, 67, is the most senior military official to have been convicted in connection with the genocide, in which bands of Hutu massacred 800,000 Tutsi and moderate Hutu. He was a leading Hutu extremist and the cabinet director for Rwanda's Defense Ministry at the start of the slaughter. He and three other senior army officers had been on trial since 2002 at the International Criminal Tribunal for Rwanda, which is based in Arusha, Tanzania.

In a statement, the United Nations tribunal said it had sentenced Bagosora and two other Rwandan military officers who were also on trial, Major Aloys Ntabakuze and Colonel Anatole Nsengiyumva, to life imprisonment for "genocide, crimes against humanity and war crimes." A fourth co-defendant, General Gratien Kabiligi, was acquitted of all charges and released by the court.*** The trial lasted six years, during which 242 witnesses were heard.

The ICTR completed 75 prosecutions, sentencing over 50 defendants to prison terms, before transferring its remaining work to the Mechanism For International Tribunals in 2012. The Mechanism's top priority is the capture and trial of 9 remaining fugitives indicted by the ICTR [Fulgence Kayishema (referred 22 February 2012); Charles Sikubwabo (referred 26 March 2012); Ladislas Ntaganzwa (referred 8 May 2012); Aloys Ndimbati (referred 25 June 2012); Charles Ryandikayo (referred 20 June 2012); Pheneas Munyarugarama (referred 28 June 2012); Augustin Bizimana; Félicien Kabuga; Protais Mpiranya — *have you seen them?*]. If captured, six of these suspects will be turned over to Rwandan authorities for trial in the national system. After 21 years as a fugitive, Ladislas Ntaganzwa was arrested and brought into custody in 2015. Another highly sought after defendant, for whom the U.S. State Department had offered a 5 million dollar reward, Bernard Munyagishari, was captured after 17 years by the "tracking unit" of the ICTR in 2011.

### c. Case Law From the Ad Hoc Tribunals

The ICTY and ICTY have produced a significant body of jurisprudence regarding the definition and application of criminal responsibility for violations of humanitarian law. Consider the following excerpts from tribunal judgments.

### i. Akayesu Case

**Decision of: 2 September 1998**

**THE PROSECUTOR**
**VERSUS**
**JEAN-PAUL AKAYESU**

*Case No. ICTR-96-4-T*

1. This judgment is rendered by Trial Chamber I of the International Tribunal for the prosecution of persons responsible for genocide and other serious violations of international humanitarian law committed in the territory of Rwanda and Rwandan citizens responsible for genocide and other such violations committed in the territory of neighbouring States, between 1 January and 31 December 1994 (the "Tribunal"). The judgment follows the

indictment and trial of Jean Paul Akayesu, a Rwandan citizen who was bourgmestre of Taba commune, Prefecture of Gitarama, in Rwanda, at the time the crimes alleged in the indictment were perpetrated.

***

## Indictment

4. As bourgmestre, Jean Paul Akayesu was charged with the performance of executive functions and the maintenance of public order within his commune, subject to the authority of the prefect. He had exclusive control over the communal police, as well as any gendarmes put at the disposition of the commune. ***

12. *** At least 2000 Tutsis were killed in Taba between April 7

and the end of June, 1994, while he was still in power. The killings in Taba were openly committed and so widespread that, as bourgmestre, Jean Paul AKAYESU must have known about them. Although he had the authority and responsibility to do so, Jean Paul AKAYESU never attempted to prevent the killing of Tutsis in the commune in any way or called for assistance from regional or national authorities to quell the violence.

12A. Between April 7 and the end of June, 1994, hundreds of civilians (hereinafter "displaced civilians") sought refuge at the bureau communal. The majority of these displaced civilians were Tutsi. While seeking refuge at the bureau communal, female displaced civilians were regularly taken by armed local militia and/or communal police and subjected to sexual violence, and/or beaten on or near the bureau communal premises. Displaced civilians were also murdered frequently on or near the bureau communal premises. Many women were forced to endure multiple acts of sexual violence which were at times committed by more than one assailant. These acts of sexual violence were generally accompanied by explicit threats of death or bodily harm. ***

12B. Jean Paul AKAYESU knew that the acts of sexual violence, beatings and murders were being committed and was at times present during their commission. Jean Paul AKAYESU facilitated the commission of the sexual violence, beatings and murders by allowing the sexual violence and beatings and murders to occur on or near the bureau communal premises. By virtue of his presence during the commission of the sexual violence, beatings and murders and by failing to prevent the sexual violence, beatings and murders, Jean Paul AKAYESU encouraged these activities.

***

14. The morning of April 19, 1994, following the murder of Sylvere Karera, Jean Paul AKAYESU led a meeting in Gishyeshye sector at which he sanctioned the death of Sylvere Karera and urged the population to eliminate accomplices of the RPF, which was understood by those present to mean

Tutsis. Over 100 people were present at the meeting. The killing of Tutsis in Taba began shortly after the meeting.

***

20. On or about April 19, 1994, Jean Paul AKAYESU ordered the local people and militia to kill intellectual and influential people. Five teachers from the secondary school of Taba were killed on his instructions. The victims were Theogene, Phoebe Uwineze and her fiance (whose name is unknown), Tharcisse Twizeyumuremye and Samuel. The local people and militia killed them with machetes and agricultural tools in front of the Taba bureau communal.

***

### 1.4.2. The Accused's line of defence

31. The Defence claims that the Chamber should not require the Accused to be a hero, to have laid down his life — as, for example, did the bourgmestre of Mugina — in a futile attempt to prevent killings and beatings. *** Moreover, the Defence argue, no bourgmestre in the whole of Rwanda was able to prevent the massacres in his Commune, no matter how willing he was to do so.

***

### GENOCIDE IN RWANDA IN 1994

118. In the opinion of the Chamber, there is no doubt that considering their undeniable scale, their systematic nature and their atrociousness, the massacres were aimed at exterminating the group that was targeted. Many facts show that the intention of the perpetrators of these killings was to cause the complete disappearance of the Tutsi.

***

119. Furthermore, as mentioned above, Dr. Zachariah also testified that the Achilles' tendons of many wounded persons were cut to prevent them from fleeing. In the opinion of the Chamber, this demonstrates the resolve of the perpetrators of these massacres not to spare any Tutsi. Their plan called for doing whatever was possible to prevent any Tutsi from escaping and, thus, to destroy the whole group.

***

### Factual Findings

***

182. The Indictment alleges that the killings in Taba were openly committed and so widespread that the Accused must have known about them. *** The issue is not contested, and it has been established that the Accused knew that killings were taking place and were widespread in Taba during the period in question.

183. The final allegation of paragraph 12 is that although he had the authority and responsibility to do so, Jean Paul Akayesu never attempted to prevent the killing of Tutsi in the commune in any way or called for assistance from regional or national authorities to quell the violence . . .

***

313. The Chamber finds that it has been proved beyond reasonable doubt that on or about 19 April 1994, Akayesu ordered the local people and Interahamwe to kill intellectual people'. *** The Chamber finds that it has been proved beyond reasonable doubt that teachers from the commune of Taba were killed pursuant to the instructions of Akayesu. *** The Chamber finds that it has not been proved beyond reasonable doubt that Akayesu ordered the killing of influential people, nor that the victims were teachers from the secondary school of Taba.

314. The Chamber finds that it has been proved beyond reasonable doubt that the teachers were killed because they were Tutsi.

### 5.5 Sexual Violence (Paragraphs 12A & 12B of the Indictment)

### Events Alleged

416. Allegations of sexual violence first came to the attention of the Chamber through the testimony of Witness J, a Tutsi woman, who stated that her six year-old daughter had been raped by three Interahamwe when they came to kill her father. On examination by the Chamber, Witness J also testified that she had heard that young girls were raped at the bureau communal. . . . . .

421. Witness JJ testified that often the Interahamwe came to beat the refugees during the day, and that the policemen came to beat them at night. She also testified that the Interahamwe took young girls and women from their site of refuge near the bureau communal into a forest in the area and raped them. Witness JJ testified that this happened to her — that she was stripped of her clothing and raped in front of other people. At the request of the Prosecutor and with great embarrassment, she explicitly specified that the rapist, a young man armed with an axe and a long knife, penetrated her vagina with his penis. She stated that on this occasion she was raped twice. . . . . . . Witness JJ testified that she could not count the total number of times she was raped. She said, "each time you encountered attackers they would rape you," — in the forest, in the sorghum fields. Witness JJ related to the Chamber the experience of finding her sister before she died, having been raped and cut with a machete.

422. Witness JJ testified that when they arrived at the bureau communal the women were hoping the authorities would defend them but she was surprised to the contrary. In her testimony she recalled lying in the cultural center, having been raped repeatedly by Interahamwe, and hearing the cries

of young girls around her, girls as young as twelve or thirteen years old. . . . Witness JJ recalled seeing the Accused standing at the entrance of the cultural center and hearing him say loudly to the Interahamwe, "Never ask me again what a Tutsi woman tastes like," and "[t]omorrow they will be killed" (Ntihazagire umbaza uko umututsikazi yari ameze, ngo kandi mumenye ko ejo ngo nibabica nta kintu muzambaza. Ngo ejo bazabica). According to Witness JJ, most of the girls and women were subsequently killed, either brought to the river and killed there, after having returned to their houses, or killed at the bureau communal.

***

452. On the basis of the evidence set forth herein, the Chamber finds beyond a reasonable doubt that the Accused had reason to know and, in fact, knew that sexual violence was taking place on or near the premises of the bureau communal, and that women were being taken away from the bureau communal and sexually violated. There is no evidence that the Accused took any measures to prevent acts of sexual violence or to punish the perpetrators of sexual violence. In fact, there is evidence that the Accused ordered, instigated and otherwise aided and abetted sexual violence.

***

## 6. THE LAW

### 6.1 Cumulative Charges***

465. The Chamber takes due note of the practice of the ICTY. This practice was also followed in the *Barbie* case, where the French *Cour de Cassation* held that a single event could be qualified both as a crime against humanity and as a war crime.

469. Having regard to its Statute, the Chamber believes that the offences under the Statute — genocide, crimes against humanity, and violations of article 3 common to the Geneva Conventions and of Additional Protocol II — have different elements and, moreover, are intended to protect different interests. The crime of genocide exists to protect certain groups from extermination or attempted extermination. The concept of crimes against humanity exists to protect civilian populations from persecution. The idea of violations of article 3 common to the Geneva Conventions and of Additional Protocol II is to protect non-combatants from war crimes in civil war. These crimes have different purposes and are, therefore, never co-extensive. Thus, it is legitimate to charge these crimes in relation to the same set of facts. It may, additionally, depending on the case, be necessary to record a conviction for more than one of these offences in order to reflect what crimes an accused committed. If, for example, a general ordered that all prisoners of war belonging to a particular ethnic group should be killed, with the intent thereby to eliminate the group, this would be both genocide and a violation of common

article 3, although not necessarily a crime against humanity. Convictions for genocide and violations of common article 3 would accurately reflect the accused general's course of conduct.

470. Conversely, the Chamber does not consider that any of genocide, crimes against humanity, and violations of article 3 common to the Geneva Conventions and of Additional Protocol II are lesser included forms of each other.*** 477. In this respect, the International Criminal Tribunal for the former Yugoslavia found in the Tadic case that: "a person may only be criminally responsible for conduct where it is determined that he knowingly participated in the commission of an offence" and that "his participation directly and substantially affected the commission of that offence through supporting the actual commission before, during, or after the incident."

479. Therefore, as can be seen, the forms of participation referred to in Article 6 (1), cannot render their perpetrator criminally liable where he did not act knowingly, and even where he should have had such knowledge. This greatly differs from Article 6 (3) analyzed here below, which does not necessarily require that the superior acted knowingly to render him criminally liable; it suffices that he had reason to know that his subordinates were about to commit or had committed a crime and failed to take the necessary or reasonable measures to prevent such acts or punish the perpetrators thereof. In a way, this is liability by omission or abstention.***

489. The Chamber holds that it is necessary to recall that criminal intent is the moral element required for any crime and that, where the objective is to ascertain the individual criminal responsibility of a person Accused of crimes falling within the jurisdiction of the Chamber, such as genocide, crimes against humanity and violations of Article 3 Common to the Geneva Conventions and of Additional Protocol II thereto, it is certainly proper to ensure that there has been malicious intent, or, at least, ensure that negligence was so serious as to be tantamount to acquiescence or even malicious intent.

497. Contrary to popular belief, the crime of genocide does not imply the actual extermination of group in its entirety, but is understood as such once any one of the acts mentioned in Article 2(2)(a) through 2(2)(e) is committed with the specific intent . . .

498. Genocide is distinct from other crimes inasmuch as it embodies a special intent or *dolus specialis*. Special intent of a crime is the specific intention, required as a constitutive element of the crime, which demands that the perpetrator clearly seeks to produce the act charged. Thus, the special intent in the crime of genocide lies in "the intent to destroy, in whole or in part, a national, ethnical, racial or religious group, as such".***

505. The Chamber holds that the expression deliberately inflicting on the group conditions of life calculated to bring about its physical destruction in whole or in part, should be construed as the methods of destruction by

which the perpetrator does not immediately kill the members of the group, but which, ultimately, seek their physical destruction.

506. For purposes of interpreting Article 2(2)(c) of the Statute, the Chamber is of the opinion that the means of deliberate inflicting on the group conditions of life calculated to bring about its physical destruction, in whole or part, include, *inter alia*, subjecting a group of people to a subsistence diet, systematic expulsion from homes and the reduction of essential medical services below minimum requirement.

### Imposing measures intended to prevent births within the group (paragraph d):

533. As regards the physical elements of complicity in genocide *(Actus Reus)*, three forms of accomplice participation are recognized in most criminal Civil Law systems: complicity by instigation, complicity by aiding and abetting, and complicity by procuring means.

538. The intent or mental element of complicity implies in general that, at the moment he acted, the accomplice knew of the assistance he was providing in the commission of the principal offence. In other words, the accomplice must have acted knowingly.

544. The findings of the Israeli courts in this case support the principle that the *mens rea*, or special intent, required for complicity in genocide is *knowledge* of the genocidal plan, coupled with the *actus reus* of participation in the execution of such plan. Crucially, then, it does not appear that the specific intent to commit the crime of genocide, as reflected in the phrase "with intent to destroy, in whole or in part, a national, ethnical, racial or religious group, as such," is required for complicity or accomplice liability.

545. In conclusion, the Chamber is of the opinion that an accused is liable as an accomplice to genocide if he knowingly aided or abetted or instigated one or more persons in the commission of genocide, while knowing that such a person or persons were committing genocide, even though the accused himself did not have the specific intent to destroy, in whole or in part, a national, ethnical, racial or religious group, as such.

### Crimes against Humanity in Article 3 of the Statute of the Tribunal

578. The Chamber considers that Article 3 of the Statute confers on the Chamber the jurisdiction to prosecute persons for various inhumane acts which constitute crimes against humanity. This category of crimes may be broadly broken down into four essential elements, namely :

(i)  the act must be inhumane in nature and character, causing great suffering, or serious injury to body or to mental or physical health;

(ii)  the act must be committed as part of a wide spread or systematic attack;

(iii)  the act must be committed against members of the civilian population;

(iv) the act must be committed on one or more discriminatory grounds, namely, national, political, ethnic, racial or religious grounds. ***

**LEGAL FINDINGS**

### ... Count 15 — Violations of Common Article 3 and Additional Protocol II (outrages upon personal dignity, in particular rape ... )

685. In the light of its factual findings with regard to the allegations of sexual violence set forth in paragraphs 12A and 12B of the Indictment, the Tribunal considers the criminal responsibility of the Accused on Count 13, crimes against humanity (rape), punishable by Article 3(g) of the Statute of the Tribunal and Count 14, crimes against humanity (other inhumane acts), punishable by Article 3(i) of the Statute.

687. The Tribunal considers that rape is a form of aggression and that the central elements of the crime of rape cannot be captured in a mechanical description of objects and body parts. The Tribunal also notes the cultural sensitivities involved in public discussion of intimate matters ... Like torture, rape is used for such purposes as intimidation, degradation, humiliation, discrimination, punishment, control or destruction of a person. Like torture, rape is a violation of personal dignity, and rape in fact constitutes torture when it is inflicted by or at the instigation of or with the consent or acquiescence of a public official or other person acting in an official capacity.

693. The Tribunal finds, under Article 6(1) of its Statute, that the Accused aided and abetted the following acts of sexual violence, by allowing them to take place on or near the premises of the bureau communal, while he was present on the premises in respect of (i) and in his presence in respect of (ii) and (iii), and by facilitating the commission of these acts through his words of encouragement in other acts of sexual violence, which, by virtue of his authority, sent a clear signal of official tolerance for sexual violence, without which these acts would not have taken place: ...

731. With regard, particularly, to the acts described in paragraphs 12(A) and 12(B) of the Indictment, that is, rape and sexual violence, the Chamber wishes to underscore the fact that in its opinion, they constitute genocide in the same way as any other act as long as they were committed with the specific intent to destroy, in whole or in part, a particular group, targeted as such. Indeed, rape and sexual violence certainly constitute infliction of serious bodily and mental harm on the victims and are even, according to the Chamber, one of the worst ways of inflict harm on the victim as he or she suffers both bodily and mental harm. In light of all the evidence before it, the Chamber is satisfied that ... These rapes resulted in physical and psychological destruction of Tutsi women, their families and their communities. Sexual violence was an integral part of the process of destruction,

specifically targeting Tutsi women and specifically contributing to their destruction and to the destruction of the Tutsi group as a whole.

732. The rape of Tutsi women was systematic and was perpetrated against all Tutsi women and solely against them.... Sexual violence was a step in the process of destruction of the Tutsi group — destruction of the spirit, of the will to live, and of life itself.

733. On the basis of the substantial testimonies brought before it, the Chamber finds that in most cases, the rapes of Tutsi women in Taba, were accompanied with the intent to kill those women.... In this respect, it appears clearly to the Chamber that the acts of rape and sexual violence, as other acts of serious bodily and mental harm committed against the Tutsi, reflected the determination to make Tutsi women suffer and to mutilate them even before killing them, the intent being to destroy the Tutsi group while inflicting acute suffering on its members in the process.

734. In light of the foregoing, the Chamber finds firstly that the acts described *supra* are indeed acts as enumerated in Article 2 (2) of the Statute, which constitute the factual elements of the crime of genocide, namely the killings of Tutsi or the serious bodily and mental harm inflicted on the Tutsi. The Chamber is further satisfied beyond reasonable doubt that these various acts were committed by Akayesu with the specific intent to destroy the Tutsi group, as such. Consequently, the Chamber is of the opinion that the acts alleged in paragraphs 12, 12A, 12B, 16, 18, 19, 20, 22, and 23 of the Indictment and proven above, constitute the crime of genocide, but not the crime of complicity; hence, the Chamber finds Akayesu individually criminally responsible for genocide.

Akayesu is currently serving a life sentence in Mali.

ii. ICTY Judgment in "Foca" (Press Release, Summary of Decision)

The Hague, 22 February 2001 JL/P.I.S./566-e

JUDGEMENT OF TRIAL CHAMBER II,
IN THE KUNARAC, KOVA^ AND VUKOVI] CASE

DRAGOLJUB KUNARAC SENTENCED TO 28 YEARS RADOMIR KOVA^ SENTENCED TO 20 YEARS ZORAN VUKOVI] SENTENCED TO 12 YEARS

Today, the Trial Chamber delivers its Judgement in the proceedings against the accused. The full text will be distributed to the parties. I shall read out only a summary and the disposition.

The three accused, who are ethnic Serbs, have been charged by the Prosecution with violations of the laws or customs of war and with crimes against humanity — rape, torture, enslavement and outrages upon personal dignity.

They participated in a Serb campaign in the wider area of the municipality of Foca from early 1992 up to about mid-1993. The campaign was part of an armed conflict between the Serb and Muslim forces in the wider region of Foca, which existed at all times material to the indictments against the accused.

One *purpose* of the campaign was, among others, to cleanse the Foca area of Muslims; to that end the campaign was successful. Even the town's name was cleansed.

Foca was renamed Srbinje and now lies in the territory of the Republika Srpska. There are hardly any Muslims left in Srbinje today.

One *target* of that campaign, apart from the Muslim armed forces, were Muslim civilians. In the present case, especially Muslim women.

The *method employed* was mostly expulsion through terror.

On a *general* level, the terror expressed itself in the violent destruction of the religious symbols of the Muslims. All mosques in Foca were blown up and the ruins razed to the ground.

Civilian Muslim men and women were rounded up in the villages surrounding Foca, and even as far as the neighbouring municipalities of Kalinovik and Gacko. The men were separated from the women and children.

The *men* often had to suffer long periods of detention in the Foca KP Dom prison. Detention without justification. Some were severely mistreated when they were captured. Some were killed on the spot, often in the presence or within earshot of their families. The *women and children* from the Foca region were taken to collection points, such as Buk Bijela, a settlement south of Foca. From there, they were transferred by bus to Foca High School, where they were detained. Some of them were later taken to other places in and around Foca, such as Partizan Sports Hall, which was about a stone's throw away from the police station, and to private houses in Miljevina and Trnovace. There they would meet women and girls from the other two municipalities.

In the above-mentioned places, the terror took on another, very *personal* dimension.

---

The trial against the three accused has sometimes been called the "rape camp case", an example of the systematic rape of women of another ethnicity being used as a "weapon of war".

It is to some extent misleading to say that systematic rape was employed as a "weapon of war". This could be understood to mean a kind of concerted approach or an order given to the Bosnian Serb armed forces to rape Muslim women as part of their combat activities in the wider meaning. There is no sufficient evidence for such a finding before the Trial Chamber.

*What the evidence shows*, is that the rapes were used by members of the Bosnian Serb armed forces as an instrument of terror. An instrument they were given free rein to apply whenever and against whomsoever they wished.

*What the evidence shows*, is that it was possible for the Serb forces to set up and maintain a detention centre for scores of Muslim women such as Partizan Sports Hall, next to the municipal police building in Foca, from which women and young girls were taken away on a regular basis to other locations to be raped.

*What the evidence shows*, is that the authorities who were meant to protect the victims, such as the local police which had been taken over by the Serbs, turned a blind eye to their suffering. Instead, they helped guard the women, and even joined in their maltreatment when approached by them for help against their oppressors.

*What the evidence shows*, are Muslim women and girls, mothers and daughters together, robbed of the last vestiges of human dignity, women and girls treated like chattels, pieces of property at the arbitrary disposal of the Serb occupation forces, and more specifically, at the beck and call of the three accused.

*What the sum of the evidence* **manifestly demonstrates**, is the effect a criminal personality will have in times of war on helpless members of the civilian population:

The actions of the three accused were part of a systematic attack against Muslim civilians. Some of their acts, in peacetime, could doubtlessly be characterised as organised crime.

They knew of the military conflict in the Foca region, because they participated in it as soldiers in different units.

They knew that one of the main purposes of that campaign was to drive the Muslims out of the region.

They knew that one way to achieve this was to terrorise the Muslim civilian population in a manner that would make it impossible for them ever to return.

They also knew of the general pattern of crimes, especially of detaining women and girls in different locations where they would be raped. The actions of all three accused, as will be described below, show beyond any doubt their knowledge of the detention centres, and of the practice of systematically transferring the women and girls to locations where they would be abused by Serb men.

The three accused were not just following orders, if there *were* such orders, to rape Muslim women. The evidence shows free will on their part. Of the women and girls so detained, one was a child of only 12 years at the time. She has not been heard of since she was sold by one of the accused. The women and girls were either lent or "rented out" to other soldiers for the sole purpose of being ravaged and abused. Some of the women and girls were kept in servitude for months on end.

The three accused are not ordinary soldiers, whose morals were merely loosened by the hardships of war. These are men with no known criminal past. However, they thrived in the dark atmosphere of the dehumanisation of those believed to be enemies, when one would not even ask, in the words of Eleanor Roosevelt,

*"Where, after all, do universal human rights begin? In small places, close to home . . ."*

The three accused are certainly not in the category of the political or military masterminds behind the conflicts and atrocities. However, the Trial Chamber wishes to make it perfectly clear that, although in these cases before this Tribunal it is generally desirable to prosecute and try those in the higher echelons of power, the Trial Chamber will not accept low rank or a subordinate function as an escape from criminal prosecution.

Political leaders and war generals are powerless if the ordinary people refuse to carry out criminal activities in the course of war. Lawless opportunists should expect no mercy, no matter how low their position in the chain of command may be.

Indeed, it is opportune to state that, in time of peace as much as in time of war, men of substance do not abuse women.

The Trial Chamber will now set out its verdict with regard to each accused.

### WOULD THE ACCUSED DRAGOLJUB KUNARAC PLEASE STAND:

Dragoljub Kunarac, under Counts 1 to 4 you were charged with rape and torture, both as a violation of the laws or customs of war and as a crime against humanity.

***

According to the test set out by the Trial Chamber in its Judgement with respect to cumulative convictions for the same conduct, namely that such convictions are permissible when each offence charged contains at least one distinct element not contained in the other, your conduct can be punished as both rape and torture, both under Article 3 of the Statute as a violation of the laws or customs of war and under Article 5 of the Statute as a crime against humanity. This legal principle applies equally in the indictments against the three accused.

The Trial Chamber therefore finds you GUILTY

under Count 1 of torture as a crime against humanity,
under Count 2 of rape as a crime against humanity,
under Count 3 of torture as a violation of the laws or customs of war and
under Count 4 of rape as a violation of the laws or customs of war.

The Trial Chamber therefore finds you NOT GUILTY under Counts 5, 6, 7 and 8.

Under Counts 9 and 10 you were charged with rape as a violation of the laws or customs of war and as a crime against humanity.

The Trial Chamber therefore finds you GUILTY
under Count 9 of rape as a crime against humanity and
under Count 10 as a violation of the laws or customs of war

Under **Counts 18 to 21** you are charged with enslavement and outrages upon personal dignity as crimes against humanity, and with rape both as a violation of the laws or customs of war and as a crime against humanity.

By the totality of these acts you have shown the most glaring disrespect for the women's dignity and their fundamental human right to sexual self-determination, on a scale that far surpasses even what one might call, for want of a better expression, the "average seriousness of rapes during wartime". You abused and ravaged Muslim women because of their ethnicity, and from among their number, you picked whomsoever you fancied on a given occasion.

***

You not only mistreated women and girls yourself, but you also organised their transfer to other places, where, as you were fully aware, they would be raped and abused by other soldiers.

This behaviour calls for a severe penalty commensurate with the gravity of your crimes.

The Trial Chamber therefore sentences you, Dragoljub Kunarac, to a single sentence of **28 years imprisonment.**

The sentence shall run from today. The time you have spent in custody shall be credited towards the sentence. You may sit down.

*****

### d. Completion Strategy & Mechanism for International Criminal Tribunals

When created, the ICTY an ICTR were envisioned as temporary, relatively short lived institutions. The number of eventual cases and their complexity, however, overwhelmed such expectations. In 2003, the U.N. Security Council adopted a "Completion Strategy" developed by the Tribunals. Security Council Resolution <u>1503</u> (2003) provides:

> *Recalling* and *reaffirming* in the strongest terms the statement of 23 July 2002 made by the President of the Security Council (S/PRST/2002/21), which endorsed the ICTY's strategy for completing investigations by the end of 2004, all trial activities at first instance by the end of 2008, and all of its work in 2010 (ICTY Completion Strategy) (S/2002/678), by concentrating on the prosecution and trial of the most senior leaders suspected of being most responsible for crimes within the ICTY's jurisdiction and transferring cases involving those who may not bear this level of responsibility to competent

national jurisdictions, as appropriate, as well as the strengthening of the capacity of such jurisdictions;***

"*Calls on* the ICTY and the ICTR to take all possible measures to complete investigations by the end of 2004, to complete all trial activities at first instance by the end of 2008, and to complete all work in 2010."

There have been, of course, further delays caused by late arrests and the complexity of the pending cases.

In 2010, nearly 20 years after their creation, the U.N. created an institutional process to consolidate, wrap up and preserve the work of the Tribunals. The oddly labelled "<u>Mechanism For International Tribunals</u>" is described by the U.N. as "a new small, temporary and efficient body, tasked with continuing the 'jurisdiction, rights and obligations and essential functions' (UNSC Resolution 1966) of the ICTR and the ICTY; and maintaining the legacy of both institutions." With a renewable 4 year term (beginning in 2013–14) the Mechanism continues but consolidates the work of the Tribunals retaining some (25) judges, prosecutors and staff assigned responsibility for pending appeals, prosecuting still at-large Rwandan fugitives, enforcement of sentences and preserving Tribunal records.

# E. International Criminal Court (ICC)

## 1. Overview

Without doubt the most important development toward establishing criminal responsibility for human rights atrocities is the creation of a permanent international criminal court in 2002. Perhaps prompted by the surprising successes of the ad hoc tribunals, the U.N. sponsored a revitalized effort to form a permanent international criminal court in the late 1990s. Despite strong and active, <u>continuing opposition by the United States</u>,[135] the International Criminal Court (ICC) (<u>website</u>) is now fully operational with by <u>123 countries</u> subject to its jurisdiction under the "<u>Rome Statute</u>."

The Court's jurisdiction is, under Article 1, only over the "most serious" international crimes (genocide, crimes against humanity, war crimes and crimes of aggression) and "complementary" to national criminal prosecutions. The Court's jurisdiction extends only to crimes taking place within the territory of a state party, or committed by a national of a state party. Non-party states may also specially consent to jurisdiction over a specific situation. Since the Court's jurisdiction can established by the location of alleged crimes, the actions of non-state party nationals could clearly be adjudicated by the Court. Under Article 17, however, a case is "inadmissi-

---

135. A significant component of U.S. opposition has been a campaign pressuring states to enter into so-called "Bilateral Immunity Agreements" under which the state promises not to surrender U.S. persons to the ICC. Under the threat of suspended aid, <u>102 countries have concluded</u> such agreements with the U.S. as on 2009.

ble" if a state with jurisdiction over it is genuinely investigating or has decided not to prosecute for legitimate reasons.

Some important provisions of the Rome Statute appear below. Examine the statute to answer, at minimum, the following basic questions:

- What crimes are subject to the ICC's jurisdiction?
- What kinds of elements must be shown from the crimes of Genocide, Crimes against Humanity and War Crimes?
- What are the "preconditions" and "admissibility" requirements to the Court's exercise of jurisdiction?
- Under what circumstances is an individual actor, including commanders or public officials, responsible for criminal conduct?
- How does the statute define the requisite mens rea for criminal guilt?

## 2. Statute of ICC

### Article 6

### Genocide

For the purpose of this Statute, 'genocide' means any of the following acts committed with intent to destroy, in whole or in part, a national, ethnical, racial or religious group, as such:

(a) Killing members of the group;

(b) Causing serious bodily or mental harm to members of the group;

(c) Deliberately inflicting on the group conditions of life calculated to bring about its physical destruction in whole or in part;

(d) Imposing measures intended to prevent births within the group;

(e) Forcibly transferring children of the group to another group.

### Article 7
### Crimes against humanity

1. For the purpose of this Statute, 'crime against humanity' means any of the following acts when committed as part of a widespread or systematic attack directed against any civilian population, with knowledge of the attack:

(a) Murder;

(b) Extermination;

(c) Enslavement;

(d) Deportation or forcible transfer of population;

(e) Imprisonment or other severe deprivation of physical liberty in violation of fundamental rules of international law;

(f)  Torture;

(g)  Rape, sexual slavery, enforced prostitution, forced pregnancy, enforced sterilization, or any other form of sexual violence of comparable gravity;

(h)  Persecution against any identifiable group or collectivity on political, racial, national, ethnic, cultural, religious, gender as defined in paragraph 3, or other grounds that are universally recognized as impermissible under international law, in connection with any act referred to in this paragraph or any crime within the jurisdiction of the Court;

(i)  Enforced disappearance of persons;

(j)  The crime of apartheid;

(k)  Other inhumane acts of a similar character intentionally causing great suffering, or serious injury to body or to mental or physical health.

## Article 8
### War crimes

1.  The Court shall have jurisdiction in respect of war crimes in particular when committed as part of a plan or policy or as part of a large-scale commission of such crimes.

2.  For the purpose of this Statute, 'war crimes' means:

(a)  Grave breaches of the Geneva Conventions of 12 August 1949, namely, any of the following acts against persons or property protected under the provisions of the relevant Geneva Convention:

(i)  Wilful killing;

(ii)  Torture or inhuman treatment, including biological experiments;

(iii)  Wilfully causing great suffering, or serious injury to body or health;

(iv)  Extensive destruction and appropriation of property, not justified by military necessity and carried out unlawfully and wantonly;

(v)  Compelling a prisoner of war or other protected person to serve in the forces of a hostile Power;

(vi)  Wilfully depriving a prisoner of war or other protected person of the rights of fair and regular trial;

(vii)  Unlawful deportation or transfer or unlawful confinement;

(viii)  Taking of hostages.

(b)  Other serious violations of the laws and customs applicable in international armed conflict, within the established framework of international law, namely, any of the following acts:

(i)  Intentionally directing attacks against the civilian population as such or against individual civilians not taking direct part in hostilities;

(ii) Intentionally directing attacks against civilian objects, that is, objects which are not military objectives;

(iii) Intentionally directing attacks against personnel, installations, material, units or vehicles involved in a humanitarian assistance or peacekeeping mission in accordance with the Charter of the United Nations, as long as they are entitled to the protection given to civilians or civilian objects under the international law of armed conflict;

(iv) Intentionally launching an attack in the knowledge that such attack will cause incidental loss of life or injury to civilians or damage to civilian objects or widespread, long-term and severe damage to the natural environment which would be clearly excessive in relation to the concrete and direct overall military advantage anticipated;

(v) Attacking or bombarding, by whatever means, towns, villages, dwellings or buildings which are undefended and which are not military objectives;

(vi) Killing or wounding a combatant who, having laid down his arms or having no longer means of defence, has surrendered at discretion;

(vii) Making improper use of a flag of truce, of the flag or of the military insignia and uniform of the enemy or of the United Nations, as well as of the distinctive emblems of the Geneva Conventions, resulting in death or serious personal injury;

(viii) The transfer, directly or indirectly, by the Occupying Power of parts of its own civilian population into the territory it occupies, or the deportation or transfer of all or parts of the population of the occupied territory within or outside this territory;

(ix) Intentionally directing attacks against buildings dedicated to religion, education, art, science or charitable purposes, historic monuments, hospitals and places where the sick and wounded are collected, provided they are not military objectives;

(x) Subjecting persons who are in the power of an adverse party to physical mutilation or to medical or scientific experiments of any kind which are neither justified by the medical, dental or hospital treatment of the person concerned nor carried out in his or her interest, and which cause death to or seriously endanger the health of such person or persons;

(xi) Killing or wounding treacherously individuals belonging to the hostile nation or army;

(xii) Declaring that no quarter will be given;

(xiii) Destroying or seizing the enemy's property unless such destruction or seizure be imperatively demanded by the necessities of war;

(xiv) Declaring abolished, suspended or inadmissible in a court of law the rights and actions of the nationals of the hostile party;

(xv) Compelling the nationals of the hostile party to take part in the operations of war directed against their own country, even if they were in the belligerent's service before the commencement of the war;

(xvi) Pillaging a town or place, even when taken by assault;

(xvii) Employing poison or poisoned weapons;

(xviii) Employing asphyxiating, poisonous or other gases, and all analogous liquids, materials or devices;

(xix) Employing bullets which expand or flatten easily in the human body, such as bullets with a hard envelope which does not entirely cover the core or is pierced with incisions;

(xx) Employing weapons, projectiles and material and methods of warfare which are of a nature to cause superfluous injury or unnecessary suffering or which are inherently indiscriminate in violation of the international law of armed conflict, provided that such weapons, projectiles and material and methods of warfare are the subject of a comprehensive prohibition and are included in an annex to this Statute, by an amendment in accordance with the relevant provisions set forth in articles 121 and 123;

(xxi) Committing outrages upon personal dignity, in particular humiliating and degrading treatment;

(xxii) Committing rape, sexual slavery, enforced prostitution, forced pregnancy, as defined in article 7, paragraph 2 (f), enforced sterilization, or any other form of sexual violence also constituting a grave breach of the Geneva Conventions;

(xxiii) Utilizing the presence of a civilian or other protected person to render certain points, areas or military forces immune from military operations;

(xxiv) Intentionally directing attacks against buildings, material, medical units and transport, and personnel using the distinctive emblems of the Geneva Conventions in conformity with international law;

(xxv) Intentionally using starvation of civilians as a method of warfare by depriving them of objects indispensable to their survival, including wilfully impeding relief supplies as provided for under the Geneva Conventions;

(xxvi) Conscripting or enlisting children under the age of fifteen years into the national armed forces or using them to participate actively in hostilities.

(c) In the case of an armed conflict not of an international character, serious violations of article 3 common to the four Geneva Conventions of 12 August 1949, namely, any of the following acts committed against persons taking no active part in the hostilities, including members of armed forces who have laid down their arms and those placed *hors de combat* by sickness, wounds, detention or any other cause:

(i)  Violence to life and person, in particular murder of all kinds, mutilation, cruel treatment and torture;

(ii)  Committing outrages upon personal dignity, in particular humiliating and degrading treatment;

(iii)  Taking of hostages;

(iv)  The passing of sentences and the carrying out of executions without previous judgement pronounced by a regularly constituted court, affording all judicial guarantees which are generally recognized as indispensable.

(d)  Paragraph 2 (c) applies to armed conflicts not of an international character and thus does not apply to situations of internal disturbances and tensions, such as riots, isolated and sporadic acts of violence or other acts of a similar nature.

(e)  Other serious violations of the laws and customs applicable in armed conflicts not of an international character, within the established framework of international law, namely, any of the following acts:

(i)  Intentionally directing attacks against the civilian population as such or against individual civilians not taking direct part in hostilities;

(ii)  Intentionally directing attacks against buildings, material, medical units and transport, and personnel using the distinctive emblems of the Geneva Conventions in conformity with international law;

(iii)  Intentionally directing attacks against personnel, installations, material, units or vehicles involved in a humanitarian assistance or peacekeeping mission in accordance with the Charter of the United Nations, as long as they are entitled to the protection given to civilians or civilian objects under the international law of armed conflict;

(iv)  Intentionally directing attacks against buildings dedicated to religion, education, art, science or charitable purposes, historic monuments, hospitals and places where the sick and wounded are collected, provided they are not military objectives;

(v)  Pillaging a town or place, even when taken by assault;

(vi)  Committing rape, sexual slavery, enforced prostitution, forced pregnancy, as defined in article 7, paragraph 2 (f), enforced sterilization, and any other form of sexual violence also constituting a serious violation of article 3 common to the four Geneva Conventions;

(vii)  Conscripting or enlisting children under the age of fifteen years into armed forces or groups or using them to participate actively in hostilities;

(viii)  Ordering the displacement of the civilian population for reasons related to the conflict, unless the security of the civilians involved or imperative military reasons so demand;

(ix) Killing or wounding treacherously a combatant adversary;

(x) Declaring that no quarter will be given;

(xi) Subjecting persons who are in the power of another party to the conflict to physical mutilation or to medical or scientific experiments of any kind which are neither justified by the medical, dental or hospital treatment of the person concerned nor carried out in his or her interest, and which cause death to or seriously endanger the health of such person or persons;

(xii) Destroying or seizing the property of an adversary unless such destruction or seizure be imperatively demanded by the necessities of the conflict;

(f) Paragraph 2 (e) applies to armed conflicts not of an international character and thus does not apply to situations of internal disturbances and tensions, such as riots, isolated and sporadic acts of violence or other acts of a similar nature. It applies to armed conflicts that take place in the territory of a State when there is protracted armed conflict between governmental authorities and organized armed groups or between such groups.

3. Nothing in paragraph 2 (c) and (e) shall affect the responsibility of a Government to maintain or re-establish law and order in the State or to defend the unity and territorial integrity of the State, by all legitimate means.

## Article 12
### Preconditions to the exercise of jurisdiction

1. A State which becomes a Party to this Statute thereby accepts the jurisdiction of the Court with respect to the crimes referred to in article 5.

2. In the case of article 13, paragraph (a) or (c), the Court may exercise its jurisdiction if one or more of the following States are Parties to this Statute or have accepted the jurisdiction of the Court in accordance with paragraph 3:

(a) The State on the territory of which the conduct in question occurred or, if the crime was committed on board a vessel or aircraft, the State of registration of that vessel or aircraft;

(b) The State of which the person accused of the crime is a national.

3. If the acceptance of a State which is not a Party to this Statute is required under paragraph 2, that State may, by declaration lodged with the Registrar, accept the exercise of jurisdiction by the Court with respect to the crime in question. The accepting State shall cooperate with the Court without any delay or exception in accordance with Part 9.

## Article 17
### Issues of admissibility

1. Having regard to paragraph 10 of the Preamble and article 1, the Court shall determine that a case is inadmissible where:

(a) The case is being investigated or prosecuted by a State which has jurisdiction over it, unless the State is unwilling or unable genuinely to carry out the investigation or prosecution;

(b) The case has been investigated by a State which has jurisdiction over it and the State has decided not to prosecute the person concerned, unless the decision resulted from the unwillingness or inability of the State genuinely to prosecute;

(c) The person concerned has already been tried for conduct which is the subject of the complaint, and a trial by the Court is not permitted under article 20, paragraph 3;

(d) The case is not of sufficient gravity to justify further action by the Court.

2. In order to determine unwillingness in a particular case, the Court shall consider, having regard to the principles of due process recognized by international law, whether one or more of the following exist, as applicable:

(a) The proceedings were or are being undertaken or the national decision was made for the purpose of shielding the person concerned from criminal responsibility for crimes within the jurisdiction of the Court referred to in article 5;

(b) There has been an unjustified delay in the proceedings which in the circumstances is inconsistent with an intent to bring the person concerned to justice;

(c) The proceedings were not or are not being conducted independently or impartially, and they were or are being conducted in a manner which, in the circumstances, is inconsistent with an intent to bring the person concerned to justice.

3. In order to determine inability in a particular case, the Court shall consider whether, due to a total or substantial collapse or unavailability of its national judicial system, the State is unable to obtain the accused or the necessary evidence and testimony or otherwise unable to carry out its proceedings.

**Article 25**

**Individual criminal responsibility**

1. The Court shall have jurisdiction over natural persons pursuant to this Statute.

2. A person who commits a crime within the jurisdiction of the Court shall be individually responsible and liable for punishment in accordance with this Statute.

3. In accordance with this Statute, a person shall be criminally responsible and liable for punishment for a crime within the jurisdiction of the Court if that person:

(a) Commits such a crime, whether as an individual, jointly with another or through another person, regardless of whether that other person is criminally responsible;

(b) Orders, solicits or induces the commission of such a crime which in fact occurs or is attempted;

(c) For the purpose of facilitating the commission of such a crime, aids, abets or otherwise assists in its commission or its attempted commission, including providing the means for its commission;

(d) In any other way contributes to the commission or attempted commission of such a crime by a group of persons acting with a common purpose. Such contribution shall be intentional and shall either:

(i) Be made with the aim of furthering the criminal activity or criminal purpose of the group, where such activity or purpose involves the commission of a crime within the jurisdiction of the Court; or

(ii) Be made in the knowledge of the intention of the group to commit the crime;

(e) In respect of the crime of genocide, directly and publicly incites others to commit genocide;

(f) Attempts to commit such a crime by taking action that commences its execution by means of a substantial step, but the crime does not occur because of circumstances independent of the person's intentions. However, a person who abandons the effort to commit the crime or otherwise prevents the completion of the crime shall not be liable for punishment under this Statute for the attempt to commit that crime if that person completely and voluntarily gave up the criminal purpose.

4. No provision in this Statute relating to individual criminal responsibility shall affect the responsibility of States under international law.

## Article 27

### Irrelevance of official capacity

1. This Statute shall apply equally to all persons without any distinction based on official capacity. In particular, official capacity as a Head of State or Government, a member of a Government or parliament, an elected representative or a government official shall in no case exempt a person from criminal responsibility under this Statute, nor shall it, in and of itself, constitute a ground for reduction of sentence.

2. Immunities or special procedural rules which may attach to the official capacity of a person, whether under national or international law, shall not bar the Court from exercising its jurisdiction over such a person.

## Article 28
### Responsibility of commanders and other superiors

In addition to other grounds of criminal responsibility under this Statute for crimes within the jurisdiction of the Court:

(a)  A military commander or person effectively acting as a military commander shall be criminally responsible for crimes within the jurisdiction of the Court committed by forces under his or her effective command and control, or effective authority and control as the case may be, as a result of his or her failure to exercise control properly over such forces, where:

(i)  That military commander or person either knew or, owing to the circumstances at the time, should have known that the forces were committing or about to commit such crimes; and

(ii)  That military commander or person failed to take all necessary and reasonable measures within his or her power to prevent or repress their commission or to submit the matter to the competent authorities for investigation and prosecution.

(b)  With respect to superior and subordinate relationships not described in paragraph (a), a superior shall be criminally responsible for crimes within the jurisdiction of the Court committed by subordinates under his or her effective authority and control, as a result of his or her failure to exercise control properly over such subordinates, where:

(i)  The superior either knew, or consciously disregarded information which clearly indicated, that the subordinates were committing or about to commit such crimes;

(ii)  The crimes concerned activities that were within the effective responsibility and control of the superior; and

(iii)  The superior failed to take all necessary and reasonable measures within his or her power to prevent or repress their commission or to submit the matter to the competent authorities for investigation and prosecution.

## Article 30
### Mental element

1.  Unless otherwise provided, a person shall be criminally responsible and liable for punishment for a crime within the jurisdiction of the Court only if the material elements are committed with intent and knowledge.

2.  For the purposes of this article, a person has intent where:

(a)  In relation to conduct, that person means to engage in the conduct;

(b)  In relation to a consequence, that person means to cause that consequence or is aware that it will occur in the ordinary course of events.

3. For the purposes of this article, 'knowledge' means awareness that a circumstance exists or a consequence will occur in the ordinary course of events. 'Know' and 'knowingly' shall be construed accordingly.

## 3. Institutional Structure and Process

The ICC Website provides an effective overview of the Court's <u>composition, organization and structure</u>. It also describes "<u>How the Court Works</u>" (at the page bottom) the process of bringing charges, securing a defendant and other procedures leading to trial. Please review that information to gain a general understanding of how the Court is designed to operate. How can a case come to the Court and how will it be handled?

## 4. Situations and Cases under ICC Review

In addition to providing useful information about the Court's structure and processes, the ICC website also summarizes "<u>situations and cases</u>" pending before the Court (examine the tabs listing investigations, pretrial proceedings, and trial). These summaries are also useful in understanding the Court's current processes. Here is an excerpt:

**Situations and cases**

21 cases in 10 situations have been brought before the International Criminal Court.

Pursuant to the Rome Statute, the Prosecutor can initiate an investigation on the basis of a referral from any State Party or from the United Nations Security Council. In addition, the Prosecutor can initiate investigations proprio motu on the basis of information on crimes within the jurisdiction of the Court received from individuals or organisations ("communications").

To date, four States Parties to the Rome Statute—Uganda, the Democratic Republic of the Congo, the Central African Republic and Mali—have referred situations occurring on their territories to the Court. In addition, the Security Council has referred the situation in Darfur, Sudan, and the situation in Libya—both non-States Parties. After a thorough analysis of available information, the Prosecutor has opened and is conducting investigations in all of the above-mentioned situations.

On 31 March 2010, Pre-Trial Chamber II granted the Prosecution authorisation to open an investigation proprio motu in the situation of Kenya. In addition, on 3 October 2011, Pre-Trial Chamber III granted the Prosecutor's request for authorisation to open investigations proprio motu into the situation in Côte d'Ivoire.

## Situation in Uganda

The case, The Prosecutor v. Joseph Kony, Vincent Otti, Okot Odhiambo and Dominic Ongwen is currently being heard before Pre-Trial Chamber II. In this case, five warrants of arrest have been issued against [the] five top members of the Lords Resistance Army (LRA).

Following the confirmation of the death of Mr Lukwiya, the proceedings against him have been terminated. The four remaining suspects are still at large.

## Situation in the Democratic Republic of the Congo

In this situation, five cases have been brought before the relevant Chambers: The Prosecutor v. Thomas Lubanga Dyilo; The Prosecutor v. Bosco Ntaganda; The Prosecutor v. Germain Katanga; The Prosecutor v. Mathieu Ngudjolo Chui; The Prosecutor v. Callixte Mbarushimana; and The Prosecutor v. Sylvestre Mudacumura. Thomas Lubanga Dyilo, Germain Katanga and Bosco Ntaganda are currently in the custody of the ICC. Sylvestre Mudacumura remains at large.

Trial Chamber I convicted Mr Lubanga Dyilo on 14 March 2012. The trial in this case, The Prosecutor v. Thomas Lubanga Dyilo, had started on 26 January 2009. On 10 July 2012, he was sentenced to a total period of 14 years of imprisonment. The time he spent in the ICC's custody will be deducted from this total sentence. On 7 August 2012, Trial Chamber I issued a decision on the principles and the process to be implemented for reparations to victims in the case. All three decisions are currently subject to appeal.

\*\*\*

## Situation in Darfur, Sudan

There are five cases in the situation in Darfur, Sudan: The Prosecutor v. Ahmad Muhammad Harun ("Ahmad Harun") and Ali Muhammad Ali Abd-Al-Rahman ("Ali Kushayb"); The Prosecutor v. Omar Hassan Ahmad Al Bashir; The Prosecutor v. Bahar Idriss Abu Garda; The Prosecutor v. Abdallah Banda Abakaer Nourain; and The Prosecutor v. Abdel Raheem Muhammad Hussein.

Warrants of arrest have been issued by Pre-Trial Chamber I for Messrs Harun, Kushayb, Al Bashir and Hussein. The four suspects remain at large.

\*\*\*

## Situation in the Republic of Kenya

\*\*\*

## Situation in Libya

***

Situation in Côte d'Ivoire

***

Situation in Mali

***

Situation in the Central African Republic II

***

The OTP is currently conducting preliminary examinations in a number of situations including Afghanistan, Georgia, Guinea, Colombia, Honduras, Korea and Nigeria.

## 5. Evaluating the ICC

Has the ICC been a success? Can it be? A critical consideration in evaluating the potential success of the ICC is the manner in which cases reach it. Even a causal survey of the mainstream world news reveals many on-going situations in which crimes falling within those defined by the ICC Statute have occurred. The conduct of Boko Haram in Nigeria and the Islamic State in Iraq and the Levant (or ISIL or ISIS) in Syria and Iraq, come immediately to mind. In four reports beginning in 2011, the U.N. Independent Commission of Inquiry on Syria has found "massive evidence" of atrocities by all participants in the Syrian civil war. In 2013, fifty eight countries submitted a petition to the U.N. Security Council asking it to refer the situation in Syria to the ICC for investigation. The New York Times has reported that the United States and United Kingdom have financed investigative teams in Syria who are working to collect evidence for future war crimes prosecutions. The U.N. has similarly documented "a staggering array" of widespread atrocities by ISIS. U.N. Reports (Commission of Inquiry on Human Rights in the Republic of Korea) similarly urge the Security Council to refer the situation in the North Korea to the ICC. Would other candidates include U.S. use of targeted drone strike assassinations and conduct of the Iraq war, Israeli bombardments in the Gaza Strip, and the indiscriminate shelling and killing of innocents by their enemy Hamas? What are the criteria and mechanisms by which any of the above situations could find its way before the ICC? How does the ICC decide which cases should be investigated and then prosecuted? You should think through these questions by reviewing the provisions of the Court's Statute provided above.

Is the ICC only designed to address friendless states, rogues and terrorist organizations? Is it another example of the West trying to dominate the rest through political manipulation? Does it have a racial bias and obsession with Africa? Consider the opinion pieces provided below regarding the Court and its legitimacy.

———————

\*\*\*

Meanwhile, the Bush administration condemned the International Criminal Court in a rush to pre-emptive judgment. . . . .

Although the U.S. dominated the drafting of the 1998 Rome Treaty leading to the court's establishment, the Bush administration has "unsigned" that document, characterizing the ICC as a "rogue court" and "political menace" to U.S. military personnel and politicians . . . ..

But the administration argues that the International Criminal Court threatens the security of U.S. service members and politicians with its more comprehensive enforcement mandate. In July 2002, it threatened to veto an extension for peacekeeping forces in Bosnia-Herzegovina unless U.S. peacekeepers were granted immunity from ICC prosecution. The U.S. ultimately accepted a compromise that extended immunity for one year to nations that do not accept the court.

And late last summer John Bolton, undersecretary of state for arms control and international security, led the Bush administration initiative to enlist nations in bilateral pledges not to extradite Americans to the international court. Israel and Romania signed first; about a dozen, mostly small and beholden, countries have signed since.

. . . . The real concern, found in Bolton's earlier writing, is that high-level officials, such as Henry Kissinger, rather than ordinary soldiers, are "the potential targets of the politically unaccountable prosecutor created by Rome."

. . . . If our generals and politicians can face down foreign tyrants bent on mass destruction to defend such ideals, surely they also can confront the non-violent and unlikely provocations of a civilian prosecutor in an international court.

\*\*\*

Even without endorsing or participating in its efforts, the U.S. can perform a service by letting the International Criminal Court begin its work unimpeded by pre-emptive attacks on its presumed politics.

---

b. The ICC Is No Kangaroo Court, Tracy Gurd for the Open Society Blog, part of the <u>Guardian Legal Network</u>, guardian.co.uk, Monday 26 July 2010 17.30 BST

By releasing Congo militia leader Thomas Lubanga, the ICC shows it is operating as a court should: according to the law

Thomas Lubanga Dyilo, <u>Picture from Witness.org</u>

The first man to be tried by the <u>International Criminal Court</u> (ICC) has been handed a "get out of jail free" card again. Following repeated clashes with prosecutors over security measures for an anonymous source, <u>judges halted the trial</u> and decided to release <u>Thomas Lubanga Dyilo</u>, a Congolese politician charged with recruiting child soldiers.

. . .

Indeed, the potential collapse of the case will no doubt be viewed as deeply disappointing by many Congolese victims who have waited years to see individuals held accountable for their alleged role in brutal crimes unleashed in eastern DRC. . . .

But the trial chamber's decision does send a deeply important message about the ICC: this is no kangaroo court. If the process is not fundamentally fair, then the accused must be released.

Sceptics have portrayed the ICC as a tool used by politicians in power to eliminate rival leaders and have noted that any ICC prosecutor could be riskily unpredictable if not kept in check.

Instead, this episode demonstrates that the ICC is serious about its mission to provide a fair hearing to those who come before it. . . .

To make sure Lubanga gets a fair trial, the court said "it is necessary that its orders, decisions, and rulings are respected."

The judges then said that continuing to hold Lubanga would be "unfair," given the "wholesale uncertainty" of whether the trial would restart, along with the length of jail time (five years) Lubanga has already served.

But whatever the outcome of the appeal, the ICC has demonstrated that the court is serious. . . .

c. Can the International Criminal Court Play Fair in Africa? By Mwangi S. Kimenyi, October 17, 2013

<u>Africa in Focus, Brookings Institute</u>

Currently, there is a great deal of criticism directed at the International Criminal Court (ICC) by Africans. The criticisms have intensified following the indictment of Kenya's president and his deputy by the court. . . .

The other criticism directed at the ICC by Africans is that the court has tended to focus almost exclusively on Africans and — more specifically — black Africans. Worse atrocities in other countries have not featured prominently in the court's agenda. African critics of the ICC cite many examples that suggest that there are biases in the selection of countries and cases followed up by the court.

. . . Africans cite the examples of Burma, Venezuela, Colombia, Iraq, Syria, Afghanistan and even Egypt where crimes against humanity have not been a focus of ICC.

Last week, the African Union demanded that the cases against Kenya's leadership be deferred and threatened to withdraw its membership should this request not be honored by the U.N. Security Council. The AU also advised President Uhuru Kenyatta not to honor the summons to appear before the ICC. . . .

A common criticism of the ICC by Africans is that the court is subject to political manipulation. This fear of political manipulation appears to be a concern to many other countries, including the United States. . . .

U.S. criticism of the court has also focused on the fairness and even the quality of Judges . . . the U.S. does not consider the court appropriately staffed with qualified judges.

. . . There is also concern about the wide-ranging powers endowed on the prosecutor who is "not accountable to any government or institution."

Another good example of a country that is concerned about the politicization of ICC is Israel. . . . Like the United States, Israel considers the "powers given to the prosecutor as excessive and the geographical appointment of judges as disadvantaging Israel."

Similarly, China and India have categorically refused to cede to the Rome Statute and have expressed concern over various issues, including powers of the prosecutor and the court's jurisdiction, among others. . . .

How far should the concept of international crimes go?

Corporate Extraction Commerce an International Crime:
http://www.nytimes.com/2013/01/30/opinion/treat-greed-in-africa-as-a-war-crime.html?ref=warcrimesgenocideandcrimesagainsthumanity

# Chapter 12

# Universal Human Rights, Relativism & the Challenge of Diversity

## A. Introduction & Overview

One of the aspects of International Human Rights Law that distinguishes it from other types of law is its global or universal characteristic. If you recall from the earliest chapters, human rights are accorded to an individual simply by virtue of being born, and those rights belong to the *individual*, not the community or country in which they reside. Therefore, if human rights are derived simply from being born a human, and human beings are equal regardless of where they are born, then it would follow that those rights should not vary simply by nature of where, when, or into which culture a person is born. This sentiment is real and important but may obscure more subtle and complex legal realities.

This concept of universal human rights, not surprisingly, is sometimes challenged by practices, attitudes and rules based on tradition, religion, or other communal concepts. At least from some points of view, such religious or cultural practices coerce or strongly encourage a person to abdicate internationally defined human rights to which they are otherwise entitled. As described below, for example, a particular cultural or religious practice may often deny the rights of women their basic human rights to equality in work, political participation, freedom of expression or education.

Some have argued that the concept of universal human rights — that is, that human rights must mean the same thing in all places for all people regardless of context — ignores the reality of a diverse world and, more controversially, is frequently inappropriate when those rights clash with genuine tradition, religion or culture. Those who make this argument, sometimes referred to as "cultural relativism," would argue that no culture is inherently superior to another culture when considering systems of law, morality, and rights. Usually, those who take this position would argue that the concept of universal human rights is itself based in a particular cultural view of the world rooted in a particular time in the development of

Western European and North American culture, morality and politics. This position, based upon a view of international human rights as inherently hegemonic, suggests that the "West" is attempting to force its particular notions of an appropriate society on the rest of the world. A less strident version of this argument would suggest that the particular specifics of rights ought to be interpreted to accommodate various religious, political or cultural traditions in order to accommodate diversity and toleration for difference. Whatever its form, this approach endorses the view that human rights may vary by context and, thus, is seemingly inconsistent with the premise of universality.

There are several possible responses to this relativist critique of the universality of international human rights. First, the concept of universal human rights is also, and has traditionally been, in tension with the traditional power structures of the "West" itself. The concept of human rights developed not in response to non-Western social practices but rather in opposition to Western political and cultural institutions that violated individual human dignity and freedom. One has only to think of the oppressive governments, and religious and racial intolerance, that led to the death of millions at the hands of "Western" institutions. Indeed, as discussed earlier in the book, modern human rights were institutionalized as a legal construct precisely because of the atrocities committed during the Second World War by both Western and Japanese regimes — atrocities that are not restricted to a particular cultural or social viewpoint. Moreover, current human rights similarly challenge a broad range of traditional Western culture which has its own deep history of suppressing human dignity, particularly for women, minorities, and the socially disfavored.

Second, while it may be true that the legal notion of universal individual human rights owes much to Western culture, it is Western centric to think that the concepts of individual liberty and empowerment are somehow foreign to, inappropriate or inconsistent with other, non-Western, societies. It is perhaps no accident that many of the world's authoritarian political and religious leaders endorse cultural relativism as a moral justification for their abuses of human rights.

Third, it must be recognized that relativists may be correct that the concept of universal human rights is inherently in conflict with certain traditions, wherever those traditions may exist in the world. Human rights necessarily challenge those traditions, however entrenched or grounded in culture or religion, which deny any individual essential human dignity as defined by the international community. That is, in fact, the basic idea.

The challenge of relativism, however, cannot be so easily dismissed as simply the rhetoric of oppressive forces. The article below, by Professor Donoho, discusses the challenges posed by the issue of relativism and, more specifically, diversity within the global legal system, including its system of human rights protection. He recognizes that the more extreme relativist positions, often advocated by dictators or those who personally benefit from those positions, are largely discredited. Nevertheless, relativism is an idea that reflects a deeper challenge to the concept of universal rights which, he argues, must somehow develop legal doctrines that can accommodate genuine and persistent global diversity, while protecting essential and universal human rights. Must human rights mean precisely the same thing, particularly in their specific applications, in all contexts?

# B. Global Diversity: Can the Meaning of Rights Be Relative to Cultural, Social or Religious Circumstances?

## 1. Donoho, Autonomy, Self-Governance, and the Margin of Appreciation: Developing a Jurisprudence of Diversity within Universal Human Rights, 15 Emory Int'l L. J 391

Profound diversity is a persistent characteristic of the international community. The implications of this diversity, however, have increasingly generated controversy within the international human rights system, challenging its tendency toward universalism. Many human rights advocates, particularly Westerners, have uncritically assumed that the widespread adoption of international treaties has established human rights that are universal in scope and content. Yet the manifestations of many human rights are still nascent and their specific meanings unclear. In practical terms, rights are contextual in many important respects. For example, the degree to which free speech protects sexually explicit expression from government censorship varies significantly among different societies and cultures. Rights appear to have different implications among different peoples depending upon their particular political, religious, social, and cultural orientations.

The power of this empirical observation, coupled with a deep sensitivity to the ideals of self-determination, democratic self-governance, autonomy, and cultural diversity, has posed significant and lingering dilemmas for the international human rights system. How can human rights be sufficiently universal to make them appropriate subjects for meaningful international regulation and yet consistent with, and appropriate to, the world's diversity? Can international organizations effectively promote and protect universal rights and yet respect and accommodate local preferences reflecting genuine cultural, political, religious, and moral diversity? Should they?

These questions are not abstract. The potential for divergent interpretations of rights is enormous and will ultimately affect the lives of millions. Practices such as veiling, female genital surgeries, and gender segregation are attacked as barbaric anachronisms and violations of human rights while simultaneously defended as cultural or religious imperatives. Similarly, governments and social majorities frequently invoke the "cultural card" to justify such things as unequal inheritance, denial of same sex marriage, and expulsion of homosexuals from the military. Laws preventing divorce, abortion, consensual sodomy, or assisted suicide may reflect genuine and deeply ingrained local values and yet be manifestly inconsistent with international human rights standards. The crux of such controversies concerns the complex and subtle interplay between the desire for universal international standards and the need to accommodate the diverse views found throughout the world.

These fundamental conflicts are complicated by repressive governments, bent on deflecting the heat of international scrutiny, that have feigned concern over cultural diversity and autonomy to serve their political purposes. Such disingenuous claims of diversity, often under the guise of cultural relativism, have left most international human rights bodies largely preferring to ignore the issues posed by diversity rather than develop a coherent jurisprudence to account for them.

To a significant degree, the political rhetoric surrounding the tired debate over cultural relativism has obscured the deeper issues that global diversity presents for the international human rights system. Relativism is neither synonymous with, nor necessary to, a pluralistic approach to human rights that acknowledges diversity, autonomy, and the value of self-governance. Indeed, the vast majority of states have long discredited the extreme relativist position of some repressive states, who claim that diversity delegitimizes international scrutiny or renders some human rights inapplicable. There remains, however, a genuine and persistent desire among some non-Western societies to manifest their cultural and social preferences — and avoid Western domination — in the development of human rights norms. Ultimately, acknowledgment of diversity and accommodation of self-governance and autonomy within the international human rights system seems inevitable, necessary, and appropriate. Whether for right or wrong, the political organizations of the United Nations have apparently endorsed this view, reflecting the international community's seemingly contradictory impulses toward universalism and diversity. Perhaps more importantly, by relying upon the primacy of state implementation and weak mechanisms for international supervision, the international system is already structured to allow for diverse interpretations of the system's generally abstract rights.

The critical question addressed in this Article is how international institutions can develop a jurisprudence that strikes an appropriate balance between universal rights and the competing values of self-governance, autonomy, and diversity, while simultaneously providing effective international supervision of human rights standards . . . .

[P]arallels exist between these competing forces and the accommodations that judicial institutions have traditionally made between individual rights, democratic majorities, and the public interest. Accordingly, I consider whether useful analogies may be drawn from European and North American jurisprudence that has, to some degree, developed judicial doctrines that balance similar competing concerns. I evaluate doctrines involving hierarchies of rights, levels of scrutiny, and the European Human Rights System's "margin of appreciation" doctrine, among others. I conclude that much of this jurisprudence, particularly to the extent that it addresses critical questions about appropriate standards of review and institutional competency, provides important insights regarding how international human rights institutions might successfully navigate the international communities' seemingly contradictory impulses toward universal rights and diversity . . . .

Many academics have recognized, sometimes implicitly, that the debate over relativism and universal human rights need not be cast in "either/or" terms. These writers believe that "universal" international human rights may vary at some level of understanding without undermining their basic purpose. For example, the core values underlying the right to free speech may be universally shared and preserved even though specific applications of the right vary among societies. Internationally, unencumbered political expression might be preserved even if some societies chose to severely restrict pornography while others do not.

Upon close examination, most of this "middle ground" literature reveals endorsement of a relativist perspective, if at all, solely as a means to an end: the promotion of diversity, pluralism, self-governance, and autonomy. Some undoubtedly would promote diversity as a value in its own right, or simply to preserve cultural or religious traditions. For many others, the priority is to stave off the relentless and seemingly inevitable domination by Western liberal values. Most writers stress the importance of local cultural expression and decision-making and argue that human rights must evolve contextually in order to be meaningful.

What is clear, however, is that one need not endorse "relativism" per se or its implications in order to argue that some degree of diversity in our understanding, application, and appreciation of certain international human rights is necessary or good. This is particularly true when the issues are viewed from a legal rather than purely philosophical perspective. Ultimately, the real issue is not legitimacy of relativism but rather the degree to which diversity, pluralism, self-governance, and autonomy values will be accounted for within the international human rights system.

It is in the context of gender, the principal focus of the next chapter, where issues over relativism are often most intensely contested. As discussed in the next chapter, and in the case immediately below, some governments and cultures argue that certain rights, including the rights of women, should be interpreted in accordance with their cultural, social, religious and political traditions. This could mean, for example, that differences in how women are treated in Islamic states rather than in Europe might be justified by cultural and religious traditions, at least in some particular applications. Again, this position is described here as "relativism" because these states are arguing that the meaning of international human rights should be "relative" to their particular national circumstances. Consider how these arguments play out in the following case.

## 2. When Culture Collides with International Human Rights Norms: The Case of Sandra Lovelace v. Canada

The case of Sandra Lovelace v. Canada involved a direct conflict between a Canadian statute that, in deference to tribal law and custom, required an indigenous female to lose her full status as an indigenous person if she married a non-tribal male. The rule was different for indigenous men who married non-indigenous females. While the rule would seem on its face to violate rights against gender discrimination contained in the Canadian Bill of Rights and the International Covenant on Civil and Political Rights, it also supported traditional tribal practices for which Canadian law provided deference. Sandra Lovelace, who lost her status as a member of her tribe after marrying a non-Indian man, brought a petition against Canada before the CCPR's Human Rights Committee alleging violation of her international human rights.

**Sandra Lovelace v. Canada, Communication No. 24/1977 (30 July 1981), U.N. Doc. CCPR/C/OP/1 at 83 (1984)**

\*\*\*

1. The author of the communication . . . .is a 32 year old woman, living in Canada. She was born and registered as "Maliseet Indian" but has lost her rights and status as an Indian in accordance with section 12 (1)(b) of the Indian Act, after having married a non-Indian on 23 May 1970. Pointing out that an Indian man who marries a non-Indian woman does not lose his Indian status, she claims that the Act is discriminatory on the grounds of sex and contrary to articles 2(1), 3, 23(1) and 4, 26 and 27 of the Covenant. As to the admissibility of the communication, she contends that she was not required to exhaust local remedies since the Supreme Court of Canada . . . held that [law] was fully operative, irrespective of its inconsistency with the Canadian Bill of Rights on account of discrimination based on sex . . .

5. In its submission under article 4 (2) of the Optional Protocol concerning the merits of the case, dated, April 1980, the State party recognized that "many of the provisions of the . . . Indian Act, including section 12 (1) (b), require serious reconsideration and reform". The Government further referred to an earlier public declaration to the effect that it intended to put a reform bill before the Canadian Parliament. It none the less stressed the necessity of the Indian Act as an instrument designed to protect the Indian minority in accordance with article 27 of the Covenant. A definition of the Indian was inevitable in view of the special priv-

ileges granted to the Indian communities, in particular their right to occupy reserve lands. Traditionally, patrilineal family relationships were taken into account for determining legal claims. Since, additionally, in the farming societies of the nineteenth century, reserve land was felt to be more threatened by non-Indian men than by non-Indian women, legal enactments as from 1869 provided that an Indian woman who married a non-Indian man would lose her status as an Indian. These reasons were still valid. A change in the law could only be sought in consultation with the Indians themselves who, however, were divided on the issue of equal rights. The Indian community should not be endangered by legislative changes. Therefore, although the Government was in principle committed to amending section 12 (1) (b) of the Indian Act, no quick and immediate legislative action could be expected.

6. The author of the communication, in her submission of 20 June 1980, disputes the contention that legal relationships within Indian families were traditionally patrilineal in nature. Her view is that the reasons put forward by the Canadian Government do not justify the discrimination against Indian women in section 12 (1) (b) of the Indian Act. She concludes that the Human Rights Committee should recommend the State party to amend the provisions in question.

7.1 In an interim decision, adopted on 31 July 1980, the Human Rights Committee set out the issues of the case in the following considerations:

7.2 The Human Rights Committee recognized that the relevant provision of the Indian Act, although not legally restricting the right to marry as laid down in article 23 (2) of the Covenant, entails serious disadvantages on the part of the Indian woman who wants to marry a non-Indian man and may in fact cause her to live with her fiancé in an unmarried relationship. There is thus a question as to whether the obligation of the State party under article 23 of the Covenant with regard to the protection of the family is complied with. Moreover, since only Indian women and not Indian men are subject to these disadvantages under the Act, the question arises whether Canada complies with its commitment under articles 2 and 3 to secure the rights under the Covenant without discrimination as to sex. On the other hand, article 27 of the Covenant requires States parties to accord protection to ethnic and linguistic minorities and the Committee must give due weight to this obligation. To enable it to form an opinion on these issues, it would assist the Committee to have certain additional observations and information.

\*\*\*

7.4 Since the author of the communication is ethnically an Indian, some persisting effects of her loss of legal status as an Indian may, as from the entry into force of the Covenant for Canada, amount to a violation of rights protected by the Covenant. The Human Rights Committee has been informed that persons in her situation are denied the right to live on an Indian reserve with resultant separation from the Indian community and members of their families. Such prohibition may affect rights which the Covenant guarantees in articles 12 (1), 17, 23 (1), 24 and 27. There may be other such effects of her loss of status,

***

9.3 As to the legal basis of a prohibition to live on a reserve, the State party offers the following explanations:

Section 14 of the Indian Act provides that "(an Indian) woman who is a member of a band ceases to be a member of that band if she marries a person who is not a member of that band". As such, she loses the right to the use and benefits, in common with other members of the band, of the land allotted to the band. It should, however, be noted that "when (an Indian woman) marries a member of another band, she thereupon becomes a member of the band of which her husband is a member". As such, she is entitled to the use and benefit of lands allotted to her husband's band.

An Indian (including a woman) who ceases to be a member of a band ceases to be entitled to reside by right on a reserve. None the less it is possible for an individual to reside on a reserve if his or her presence thereon is tolerated by a band or its members. It should be noted that under section 30 of the Indian Act, any person who trespasses on a reserve is guilty of an offence. In addition, section 31 of the Act provides that an Indian or a band (and of course its agent, the Band Council) may seek relief or remedy against any person, other than an Indian, who is or has been

(a) unlawfully in occupation or possession of,

(b) claiming adversely the right to occupation or possession of, or (c) trespassing upon a reserve or part thereof.

9.4 As to the reasons adduced to justify the denial of the right of abode on a reserve, the State party states that the provisions of the Indian Act which govern the right to reside on a reserve have been enacted to give effect to various treaty obligations reserving to the Indians exclusive use of certain lands.

***

9.6 As to Mrs. Lovelace's place of abode prior to her marriage both parties confirm that she was at that time living on the Tobique Reserve with her parents. Sandra Lovelace adds that as a result of her marriage, she was denied the right to live on an Indian reserve. As to her abode since then the State party observes:

Since her marriage and following her divorce, Mrs. Lovelace has, from time to time, lived on the reserve in the home of her parents, and the

Band Council has made no move to prevent her from doing so. However, Mrs. Lovelace wishes to live permanently on the reserve and to obtain a new house. To do so, she has to apply to the Band Council. Housing on reserves is provided with money set aside by Parliament for the benefit of registered Indians. The Council has not agreed to provide Mrs. Lovelace with a new house. It considers that in the provision of such housing priority is to be given to registered Indians.

9.7 In this connection the following additional information has been submitted on behalf of Mrs. Lovelace:

At the present time, Sandra Lovelace is living on the Tobique Indian Reserve, although she has no right to remain there. She has returned to the Reserve, with her children because her marriage has broken up and she has no other place to reside. She is able to remain on the reserve in violation of the law of the local Band Council because dissident members of the tribe who support her cause have threatened to resort to physical violence in her defence should the authorities attempt to remove her.

9.8 As to the other persisting effects of Mrs. Lovelace's loss of Indian status the State party submits the following:

When Mrs. Lovelace lost her Indian status through marriage to a non-Indian, she also lost access to federal government programs for Indian people in areas such as education, housing, social assistance, etc. At the same time, however, she and her children became eligible to receive similar benefits from programs the provincial government provides for all residents of the province.

Mrs. Lovelace is no longer a member of the Tobique band and no longer an Indian under the terms of the Indian Act. She however is enjoying all the rights recognized in the Covenant, in the same way as any other individual within the territory of Canada and subject to its jurisdiction.

9.9 On behalf of Sandra Lovelace the following is submitted in this connection:

All the consequences of loss of status persist in that they are permanent and continue to deny the complainant rights she was born with.

A person who ceases to be an Indian under the Indian Act suffers the following consequences:

(1) Loss of the right to possess or reside on lands on a reserve (ss. 25 and 28 (1)). This includes loss of the right to return to the reserve after leaving, the right to inherit possessory interest in land from parents or others, and the right to be buried on a reserve;

(2) An Indian without status cannot receive loans from the Consolidated Revenue Fund for the purposes set out in section 70;

(3) An Indian without status cannot benefit from instruction in farming and cannot receive seed without charge from the Minister (see section 71);

{4} An Indian without status cannot benefit from medical treatment and health services provided under section 73 (1) (g);

(5) An Indian without status cannot reside on tax exempt lands (section 87);

(6) A person ceasing to be an Indian loses the right to borrow money for housing from the Band Council (Consolidated Regulations of Canada, 1978, c. 949);

(7) A person ceasing to be an Indian loses the right to cut timber free of dues on an Indian reserve (section 4 — Indian Timber Regulations, c. 961, 1978 Consolidated Regulations of Canada);

(8) A person ceasing to be an Indian loses traditional hunting and fishing rights that may exist;

(9) The major loss to a person ceasing to be an Indian is the loss of the cultural benefits of living in an Indian community, the emotional ties to home, family, friends and neighbours, and the loss of identity.

***

13.1 The Committee considers that the essence of the present complaint concerns the continuing effect of the Indian Act, in denying Sandra Lovelace legal status as an Indian, in particular because she cannot for this reason claim a legal right to reside where she wishes to, on the Tobique Reserve. This fact persists after the entry into force of the Covenant, and its effects have to be examined, without regard to their original cause. Among the effects referred to on behalf of the author (see para. 9.9, above), the greater number, ((1) to (8)), relate to the Indian Act and other Canadian rules in fields which do not necessarily adversely affect the enjoyment of rights protected by the Covenant. In this respect the significant matter is her last claim, that "the major loss to a person ceasing to be an Indian is the loss of the cultural benefits of living in an Indian community, the emotional ties to home, family, friends and neighhours, and the loss of identity".

13.2 Although a number of provisions of the Covenant have been invoked by Sandra Lovelace, the Committee considers that the one which is most directly applicable to this complaint is article 27, which reads as follows:

> In those States in which ethnic, religious or linguistic minorities exist, persons belonging to such minorities shall not be denied the right, in community with the other members of their group, to enjoy their own culture, to profess and practise their own religion, or to use their own language.

It has to be considered whether Sandra Lovelace, because she is denied the legal right to reside on the Tobique Reserve, has by that fact been denied the right guaranteed by article 27 to persons belonging to minorities, to enjoy their own culture and to use their own language in community with other members of their group.

14. The rights under article 27 of the Covenant have to be secured to "persons belonging" to the minority. At present Sandra Lovelace does not qualify as an Indian under Canadian legislation. However, the Indian Act deals primarily with a number of privileges which, as stated above, do not as such come within the scope of the Covenant. Protection under the Indian Act and protection under article 27 of the Covenant therefore have to be distinguished. Persons who are born and brought up on a reserve, who have kept ties with their community and wish to maintain these ties must normally be considered as belonging to that minority within the meaning of the Covenant. Since Sandra Lovelace is ethnically a Maliseet Indian and has only been absent from her home reserve for a few years during the existence of her marriage, she is, in the opinion of the Committee, entitled to be regarded as "belonging" to this minority and to claim the benefits of article 27 of the Covenant. The question whether these benefits have been denied to her, depends on how far they extend.

15. The right to live on a reserve is not as such guaranteed by article 27 of the Covenant. Moreover, the Indian Act does not interfere directly with the functions which are expressly mentioned in that article. However, in the opinion of the Committee the right of Sandra Lovelace to access to her native culture and language "in community with the other members" of her group, has in fact been, and continues to be interfered with, because there is no place outside the Tobique Reserve where such a community exists . . .

16. In this respect, the Committee is of the view that statutory restrictions affecting the right to residence on a reserve of a person belonging to the minority concerned, must have both a reasonable and objective justification and be consistent with the other provisions of the Covenant, read as a whole. Article 27 must be construed and applied in the light of the other provisions mentioned above, such as articles 12, 17 and 23 in so far as they may be relevant to the particular case, and also the provisions against discrimination, such as articles 2, 3 and 26, as the case may be. . . .

17. The case of Sandra Lovelace should be considered in the light of the fact that her marriage to a non-Indian has broken up. It is natural that in such a situation she wishes to return to the environment in which she was born, particularly as after the dissolution of her marriage her main cultural attachment again was to the Maliseet band. Whatever may be the merits of the Indian Act in other respects, it does not seem to the Committee that to deny Sandra Lovelace the right to reside on the reserve is reasonable, or necessary to preserve the identity of the tribe. The Committee therefore concludes that to prevent her recognition as belonging to the band is an

unjustifiable denial of her rights under article 27 of the Covenant, read in the context of the other provisions referred to.

18. In view of this finding, the Committee does not consider it necessary to examine whether the same facts also show separate breaches of the other rights invoked. The specific rights most directly applicable to her situation are those under article 27 of the Covenant. The rights to choose one's residence (article 12), and the rights aimed at protecting family life and children (articles 17, 23 and 24) are only indirectly at stake in the present case. The facts of the case do not seem to require further examination under those articles. The Committee's finding of a lack of a reasonable justification for the interference with Sandra Lovelace's rights under article 27 of the Covenant also makes it unnecessary, as suggested above (para. 12), to examine the general provisions against discrimination (arts. 2, 3 and 26) in the context of the present case, and in particular to determine their bearing upon inequalities predating the coming into force of the Covenant for Canada.

19. Accordingly, the Human Rights Committee, acting under article 5 (4) of the Optional Protocol to the International Covenant on Civil and Political Rights, is of the view that the facts of the present case, which establish that Sandra Lovelace has been denied the legal right to reside on the Tobique Reserve, disclose a breach by Canada of article 27 of the Covenant.

How did the Human Rights Committee resolve the apparent tension between the indigenous peoples' rights to their own customs and Ms. Lovelace's right to non-discrimination? What if the indigenous legal provisions providing for separate treatment of women and men are considered integral to indigenous tradition? Couldn't the decision of the Human Rights Committee be viewed as violating those cultural traditions of the tribe?

This "heads-on" conflict between cultural customs and human rights is even more starkly illustrated in the conflict over whether genital mutilation should be tolerated under international human rights law, particularly when the participants are fully consenting.

## 3. When Culture and International Rights Collide: Female Genital Mutilation

a. Background

More than two million girls undergo genital mutilation each year pursuant to traditional religious and cultural customs. The World Health Organization provides the following overview of the practice and its health consequences.

Female genital mutilation,

Key facts

Female genital mutilation (FGM) includes procedures that intentionally alter or cause injury to the female genital organs for non-medical reasons.

The procedure has no health benefits for girls and women.

Procedures can cause severe bleeding and problems urinating, and later cysts, infections, as well as complications in childbirth and increased risk of newborn deaths.

More than 200 million girls and women alive today have been cut in 30 countries in Africa, the Middle East and Asia where FGM is concentrated.

FGM is mostly carried out on young girls between infancy and age 15.

FGM is a violation of the human rights of girls and women.

Female genital mutilation (FGM) comprises all procedures that involve partial or total removal of the external female genitalia, or other injury to the female genital organs for non-medical reasons.

The practice is mostly carried out by traditional circumcisers, who often play other central roles in communities, such as attending childbirths. In many settings, health care providers perform FGM due to the erroneous belief that the procedure is safer when medicalized. WHO strongly urges health professionals not to perform such procedures.

FGM is recognized internationally as a violation of the human rights of girls and women. It reflects deep-rooted inequality between the sexes, and constitutes an extreme form of discrimination against women. It is nearly always carried out on minors and is a violation of the rights of children. The practice also violates a person's rights to health, security and physical integrity, the right to be free from torture and cruel, inhuman or degrading treatment, and the right to life when the procedure results in death.

Procedures

Female genital mutilation is classified into 4 major types.

Type 1: Often referred to as clitoridectomy, this is the partial or total removal of the clitoris (a small, sensitive and erectile part of the female genitals), and in very rare cases, only the prepuce (the fold of skin surrounding the clitoris).

Type 2: Often referred to as excision, this is the partial or total removal of the clitoris and the labia minora (the inner folds of the vulva), with or without excision of the labia majora (the outer folds of skin of the vulva).

Type 3: Often referred to as infibulation, this is the narrowing of the vaginal opening through the creation of a covering seal. The seal is formed by cutting and repositioning the labia minora, or labia majora, sometimes through stitching, with or without removal of the clitoris (clitoridectomy).

Type 4: This includes all other harmful procedures to the female genitalia for non-medical purposes, e.g. pricking, piercing, incising, scraping and cauterizing the genital area.

Deinfibulation refers to the practice of cutting open the sealed vaginal opening in a woman who has been infibulated, which is often necessary for improving health and well-being as well as to allow intercourse or to facilitate childbirth.

No health benefits, only harm

FGM has no health benefits, and it harms girls and women in many ways. It involves removing and damaging healthy and normal female genital tissue, and interferes with the natural functions of girls' and women's bodies. Generally speaking, risks increase with increasing severity of the procedure.

\*\*\*

Health complications of female genital mutilation

Who is at risk?

Procedures are mostly carried out on young girls sometime between infancy and adolescence, and occasionally on adult women. More than 3 million girls are estimated to be at risk for FGM annually.

More than 200 million girls and women alive today have been cut in 30 countries in Africa, the Middle East and Asia where FGM is concentrated.

The practice is most common in the western, eastern, and north-eastern regions of Africa, in some countries the Middle East and Asia, as well as among migrants from these areas. FGM is therefore a global concern.

Cultural and social factors for performing FGM

The reasons why female genital mutilations are performed vary from one region to another as well as over time, and include a mix of sociocultural factors within families and communities. The most commonly cited reasons are:

Where FGM is a social convention (social norm), the social pressure to conform to what others do and have been doing, as well as the need to be accepted socially and the fear of being rejected by the community, are strong motivations to perpetuate the practice. In some communities, FGM is almost universally performed and unquestioned.

FGM is often considered a necessary part of raising a girl, and a way to prepare her for adulthood and marriage.

FGM is often motivated by beliefs about what is considered acceptable sexual behaviour. It aims to ensure premarital virginity and marital fidelity. FGM is in many communities believed to reduce a woman's libido and therefore believed to help her resist extramarital sexual acts. When a vaginal opening is covered or narrowed (type 3), the fear of the pain of opening it, and the fear that this will be found out, is expected to further discourage extramarital sexual intercourse among women with this type of FGM.

Where it is believed that being cut increases marriageability, FGM is more likely to be carried out.

FGM is associated with cultural ideals of femininity and modesty, which include the notion that girls are clean and beautiful after removal of body parts that are considered unclean, unfeminine or male.

Though no religious scripts prescribe the practice, practitioners often believe the practice has religious support.

Religious leaders take varying positions with regard to FGM: some promote it, some consider it irrelevant to religion, and others contribute to its elimination.

Local structures of power and authority, such as community leaders, religious leaders, circumcisers, and even some medical personnel can contribute to upholding the practice.

In most societies, where FGM is practised, it is considered a cultural tradition, which is often used as an argument for its continuation.

In some societies, recent adoption of the practice is linked to copying the traditions of neighbouring groups. Sometimes it has started as part of a wider religious or traditional revival movement.

In December 2012, the UN General Assembly adopted a resolution on the elimination of female genital mutilation.

### b. Does FGM Violate International Human Rights: Perspective of <u>Amnesty International</u>

- *I was genitally mutilated at the age of ten. When the operation began, I put up a big fight. The pain was terrible and unbearable . . . I was badly cut and lost blood . . . I was genitally mutilated with a blunt penknife. After the operation, no one was allowed to aid me to walk . . . Sometimes I had to force myself not to urinate for fear of the terrible pain. I was not given any anesthetic in the operation to reduce my pain, nor any antibiotics to fight against infection. Afterwards, I hemorrhaged and became anemic. This was attributed to witchcraft. I suffered for a long time from acute vaginal infections."* — Hannah Koroma, Sierra Leone

Why FGM is practiced

- FGM is traditionally practiced as a ritual signifying the acceptance of a woman into society and establishes her eligibility for marriage. It is believed to inspire submissiveness in young women. Reasons given for FGM range from beliefs that touching the clitoris will kill a baby during childbirth, to hygienic reasons, to enhancing fertility and ensuring chastity.

- In many societies, an important reason given for FGM is the belief that it reduces a woman's desire for sex, therefore reducing the chance of sex outside marriage. In FGM-practicing societies it is extremely difficult, if not impossible, for a woman to marry if she has not undergone mutilation. . . . Restricting women's sexuality is vital because the honour of the whole family is seen to be dependent on it.

How FGM reinforces gender stratification

- FGM is rooted in a culture of discrimination against women. It is a human rights abuse that functions as an instrument for socializing girls into prescribed gender roles within the family and community. It is therefore intimately linked to the unequal position of women in the political, social, and economic structures of societies where it is practiced.

- Alternatively, women who do not undergo FGM in societies where it is the norm are often ostracized by their communities and are considered ineligible for marriage. . . . . Because marriage is seen as the only significant and acceptable role for women in FGM-practicing societies — and only women who are mutilated are eligible to marry — FGM reasserts women's relegation to the domestic sphere, conferring upon women an inferior status and are reduced to mere child-bearers and objects of the male sexual fulfillment.

FGM as a human rights violation

- . . . . Violence against women and girls in the home or in the community is regarded as a "private" issue; the fact that perpetrators are private actors rather than state officials has often precluded FGM from being seen as a human rights concern.

- FGM is a manifestation of gender-based human rights violations that exist in all cultures that aim to control women's sexuality and autonomy. . . . . .

- A human rights perspective sets FGM in the context of women's social and economic powerlessness. Recognizing that civil, political, social, economic, and cultural rights are indivisible and interdependent is a crucial starting point for addressing the range of factors that perpetuate FGM. . . . .

**QUESTIONS TO ANSWER:**

1. In a recent case before the U.S. Immigration & Naturalization service, a Nigerian woman claimed a right to asylum in this country because she feared that her two daughters, both U.S. citizens, would be compelled by family members to submit to the traditional Nigerian practice of female genital circumcision.

A. Would this treatment of her daughters constitute a violation of international human rights law?

B. What if the mother and daughters, out of respect for tradition, agree to the procedures?

C. Assuming that it is a socially important and deeply honored cultural tradition in Nigeria, does the international community have a right to demand its elimination?

D. Should countries be able to ban the practice in countries where immigrants live who come from countries where the practice is common?

E.  Are such demands simply an example of insensitive, ethnocentric, Western cultural imperialism?

Although it may seem far-fetched by many, there have been some efforts to criminalize circumcision of males as a kind of genital mutilation without their consent.

c. Male Circumcision: Is a Gender Distinction Valid?

From Circumcision Information Australia:

Considering the similarities between the male and female genitals, the nature of the surgery, the justifications offered, and the support (in Western societies) for the principle that the genders should be treated equally, it may at first seem surprising that male and female circumcision enjoy such strikingly different reputations, at least in Anglophone countries. The first is regarded as a mild and harmless adjustment that should be tolerated, if not actively promoted, the second as a cruel abomination that must be stopped by law, no matter how culturally significant to its practitioners. . . . to call circumcision of boys male genital mutilation is likely to elicit accusations of emotionalism, even by those who agree that routine circumcision of males is unnecessary and should generally not be performed.

WHO double standards

While the World Health Organization (WHO), the United Nations and other international agencies devote substantial resources on programs to eradicate female genital cutting (FGC), they have been conspicuously silent about the circumcision of boys. . . . .. For all the rhetoric about the science behind such programs, it is really no more than an expression of the nineteenth century assumption that circumcision of boys is health-giving while circumcision of girls or women is a mutilation. . . . . Double standards reign.

**Time to ban male circumcision?**, Neil Howard and Rebecca Steinfeld, The Guardian, June 14, 2011

Voters in San Francisco, California, have been asked to ban the custom, much to the anger of Jews and Muslims.

San Francisco voters will decide later this year whether, like its female counterpart, male infant circumcision should be outlawed. If passed, article 50 — the "Genital Cutting of Male Minors" — would make it unlawful to circumcise, cut, or mutilate the foreskin, testicles, or penis of another person aged under 18. The bill includes an exemption for cases of medical necessity, but not for custom or ritual, which has profound implications for the many Jews and Muslims who consider it an essential part of their religious or cultural practice.

. . . . are the differences between male and female circumcision really so straightforward?

According to research, the sexual damage caused by female and male genital cutting can be extensive. . . . .

With female genital cutting, the desire to control female sexuality remains key: believed to reduce a woman's libido, the practice is said to help her resist "illicit" sexual acts, thus aiding the maintenance of premarital virginity and marital fidelity.

Male circumcision has similarly been associated with managing sexuality. . . . .

Clearly, significant similarities exist between male and female genital cutting, and the question asked by those behind article 50 is: why the legal difference between boys and girls?

. . . . What about religious freedom? Certainly, the ability to freely practise one's religion remains a vital component of any liberal democracy. But should this trump an individual's right to their <u>bodily integrity</u>? And shouldn't such a principle be extended to all those who, by virtue of their age, are too young to decide on which body parts they would or would not like to keep?

Some may point to state overreach here, suggesting that a ban on child ear-piercing will be next. But it is the irreversibility of circumcision that invalidates such comparisons. . . . .

. . . . If we oppose female genital mutilation, has the time not come for us also to oppose male genital mutilation?

In your opinion, should the meaning of rights be relative or universal? Is this an either/or issue? What are the disadvantages or advantages to the relativist view point — assuming that your goal is the effective implementation of international human rights standards? Can or should respect for cultural or religious differences and local diversity be accommodated by the international human rights system? Can there ever be universal rights given the vast cultural diversity that characterizes the modern world? All of these issues are pertinent to the issues facing women and sexual minorities as described in the next chapter.

# Chapter 13

# Gender Rights as Human Rights

## A. Introduction & Overview

This chapter is designed to achieve three goals:

The first goal is to explore what international human rights law currently provides substantively with regard to gender based rights, in particular, regarding the treatment of women. Much of this chapter focuses on the plight of women worldwide and how the international human rights system has responded. The second goal is to explore the boundaries of what gender means and the implications of different understandings on the development of human rights. For example, the Supreme Courts of India, Nepal and Bangladesh have each recognized a "third gender," similar to how Western societies increasingly have recognized the existence and interests of transgendered people. The third goal is directly related to the above and the preceding chapter on "relativism" and global diversity. Because gender based rights, and the meaning of gender itself, sit at the crossroads of religion, culture and international human rights standards, they are an excellent illustration of this debate and the forces that lie behind it.

The readings and referenced links first provide some basic information concerning the conditions and circumstances of women around the world and at home. Why are gender based rights necessary? As you read this material you should think carefully about why certain rights for women are resisted in some cultures. Also consider the so-called "public-private" distinction that suggests family life is "private" and therefore beyond the reach of international human rights standards. In the eyes of some, this is a false distinction merely used to deflect the application of human rights standards relating to gender discrimination. Others argue that such distinctions are necessary for protection of family, individual choice and deeply held cultural, religious and social values.

After you review this material about the conditions that women face world-wide (and do some exploring on your own) you should consult the <u>Convention on the Elimination of Discrimination Against Women</u> (CEDAW or "Women's Convention").

Review the first 16 articles of the Convention, paying particular attention to articles 1, 2, 5 & 16 and the response of CEDAW to reservations that would condition women's rights on consistency with religious law.

**Please be ready to answer the following questions for class.**

1. Why was it necessary for the international community to create rights specifically designed for the protection of women? What practices, abuses or conditions prompted the recognition of such rights?

2. What are the most basic rights that international human rights law provides for women? Are these rights different from other rights you have studied?

3. Should the international human rights system broaden its view of gender to address the needs and interests of those who do not fall neatly within traditional definitions and roles?

**"Under guarantees of international rights, as well as in everyday life, a woman is not yet a name for a way of being human." Catharine A. MacKinnon, Are Women Human? (2007 Harvard University Press)**

In this context, consider Justice Scalia's comments that women should not be included as "persons" within the meaning of the 14th Amendment Equal Protection Clause.

Time Magazine, Case Study

Adam Cohen, Justice Scalia Mouths Off on Sex Discrimination, Sept. 22, 2010

Leave it to Supreme Court Justice Antonin Scalia to argue that the Constitution does not, in fact, bar sex discrimination.

Even though the court has said for decades that the equal-protection clause protects women (and, for that matter, men) from sex discrimination, the outspoken, controversial Scalia claimed late last week that women's equality is entirely up to the political branches. "If the current society wants to outlaw discrimination by sex," he told an audience at the University of California's Hastings College of the Law, "you have legislatures."

*** 

But Justice Scalia's attack on the constitutional rights of women — and of gays, whom he also brushed off — is not just his usual mouthing off.

. . . . He focuses on the fact that the 14th Amendment was drafted after the Civil War to help lift up freed slaves to equality. "Nobody thought it was directed against sex discrimination," he told his audience.

. . . . It is no small thing to talk about writing women out of equal protection — or Jews, or Latinos or other groups who would lose their protection by the same logic. . . . .

Justice Scalia doesn't even have consistency on his side. After all, he has been happy to interpret the equal-protection clause broadly when it fits his purposes. . . .

It is a strange view of the Constitution to say that when it says every "person" must have "equal protection," it does not protect women, but that freedom of "speech" — something only humans were capable of in 1787 and today — guarantees corporations the right to spend unlimited amounts of money to influence elections.

# B. The Circumstances of Women That Necessitate Gender Based Rights

## 1. The Condition of Women World-Wide

From Speak Out Now

The Condition of Women Today

March 8th is celebrated around the world as International Women's Day. It began in the United States but is now a day celebrated throughout the world to recognize the role women have played in history and to draw awareness to the situation of women. Despite the gains women have achieved in society, they still remain underpaid in the workplace, are overburdened with childcare and housework, and face discrimination and abuse on a daily basis. Here's a look at the reality women face in our world today:

Sexual Violence

Over 12 percent of women in the Congo have been raped — that is 48 women every hour

In the US: one out of every three women will be sexually assaulted in their lifetime, one out of five women have been raped in their lives, and one in four women have been the victims of severe physical violence by an intimate partner

A woman born in South Africa has a greater chance of being raped than learning how to read. On average a woman is raped every 17 seconds in South Africa. While in the US, a woman is raped every two minutes

Between 2001 and 2009, 95,000 women have been raped in the ongoing conflict in Colombia.

Domestic Violence

Domestic violence has killed 34 women in Minnesota in 2011, one woman every five days in Spain, and 10,000 women in Mexico over the past ten years

In 2010, 8,391 dowry death cases were reported in India, meaning a bride was burned every 90 minutes

Thousands of acid attacks occur every year in Bangladesh, Cambodia, Pakistan, Afghanistan and India among others. 70 percent of the victims are women and girls

Trafficking and Slavery

There are over 32 million people enslaved around the world in fields, factories, brothels and homes, where they are exploited for sex or labor. 74 percent of them are women and girls

More than two million women and children are sold into the sex trade every year

Eighty-three percent of all sex trafficking in the US is of girls, a majority of whom are 17 or under

Exploitation at Home, Exploitation in the Workplace

Today, women worldwide are paid 10 to 30 percent less than men for the same work

In the US, women are paid 20 percent less on average than men

In a review of 126 countries, in more than a third, women are prohibited from working in the same industries as men

In rural Malawi women spend over eight times more than men on the same domestic chores

Women in Sub-Saharan Africa spend about 40 billion hours a year collecting water

In the US, married women without children do 17 hours of housework a week while men do 7 hours

Highlights from UNWomen.org Report on the Status of Women Facts & Figures: Economic Empowerment

- Women continue to participate in labour markets on an unequal basis with men. In 2013, the male employment-to-population ratio stood at 72.2 per cent, while the ratio for females was 47.1 per cent [8].

- Globally, women are paid less than men. Women in most countries earn on average only 60 to 75 per cent of men's wages [9]. . . .

- Women bear disproportionate responsibility for unpaid care work. Women devote 1 to 3 hours more a day to housework than men; 2 to 10 times the amount of time a day to care (for children, elderly, and the sick), and 1 to 4 hours less a day to market activities [13]. . . .

- Gender inequalities in time use are still large and persistent in all countries. When paid and unpaid work are combined, women in developing countries work more than men, with less time for education, leisure, political participation

and self-care [15]. Despite some improvements over the last 50 years, in virtually every country, men spend more time on leisure each day while women
spend more time doing unpaid housework [16].

- Women are more likely than men to work in informal employment [17]. In
  South Asia, over 80 per cent of women in non-agricultural jobs are in informal
  employment, in sub-Saharan Africa, 74 per cent, and in Latin America and the
  Caribbean, 54 per cent [18]. . . .

- Gender differences in laws affect both developing and developed economies,
  and women in all regions. Almost 90 per cent of 143 economies studied have at
  least one legal difference restricting women's economic opportunities [22]. Of
  those, 79 economies have laws that restrict the types of jobs that women can
  do [23]. And husbands can object to their wives working and prevent them from
  accepting jobs in 15 economies [24]. . . .

- Ethnicity and gender interact to create especially large pay gaps for minority
  women. In 2013 in the US for instance, "women of all major racial and ethnic
  groups earn less than men of the same group, and also earn less than white
  men . . . Hispanic women's median earnings were USD 541 per week of full-
  time work, only 61.2 per cent of white men's median weekly earnings, but 91.1
  per cent of the median weekly earnings of Hispanic men (because Hispanic
  men also have low earnings). The median weekly earnings of black women were
  USD 606, only 68.6 per cent of white men's earnings, but 91.3 per cent of black
  men's median weekly earnings, which are also fairly low. . . .

### Essential to agriculture

- Women comprise an average of 43 per cent of the agricultural labour force
  in developing countries, varying considerably across regions from 20 per
  cent or less in Latin America to 50 per cent or more in parts of Asia and
  Africa [27]. . . .

- Women farmers control less land than do men, and also have limited access to
  inputs, seeds, credits, and extension services [28]. Less than 20 per cent of land-
  holders are women [29]. . . . ..

- Women and children bear the main negative impacts of fuel and water collection and transport, with women in many developing countries spending from
  1 to 4 hours a day collecting biomass for fuel [34]. A study of time and water
  poverty in 25 sub-Saharan African countries estimated that women spend at
  least 16 million hours a day collecting drinking water; men spend 6 million
  hours; and children, 4 million hours [35].

  Also see UNWomen.org Report on the Progress of Women

## 2. Education, Marriage, Family Practices: A Question of Culture?

This cartoon is so true that we have to see it again.

By Edna Evans.

### i. Arranged Child Marriage

**Top Saudi cleric: OK for young girls to wed , CNN, January 17, 2009**

(CNN) — The debate over the controversial practice of child marriage in Saudi Arabia was pushed back into the spotlight this week,

with the kingdom's top cleric saying that it's OK for girls as young as 10 to wed.

"It is incorrect to say that it's not permitted to marry off girls who are 15 and younger," Sheikh Abdul Aziz Al-Sheikh, the kingdom's grand mufti, said in remarks quoted Wednesday in the regional Al-Hayat newspaper. "A girl aged 10 or 12 can be married. Those who think she's too young are wrong and they are being unfair to her."

The issue of child marriage has been a hot-button topic in the deeply conservative kingdom in recent weeks.

Late last month, a Saudi judge refused to annul the marriage of an 8-year-old girl to a 47-year-old man.

. . . . The judge required the girl's husband to sign a pledge that he would not have sex with her until she reaches puberty.

ii. Tiny Voices Defy Child Marriage in Yemen, Robert Worth, NY Times, June 29, 2008

JIBLA, Yemen — One morning last month, Arwa Abdu Muhammad Ali walked out of her husband's house here and ran to a local hospital, where she complained that he had been beating and sexually abusing her for eight months. . . .

That alone would be surprising in Yemen, a deeply conservative Arab society where family disputes tend to be solved privately. What made it even more unusual was that Arwa was 9 years old.

Within days, Arwa — a tiny, delicate-featured girl — had become a celebrity in Yemen, where child marriage is common but has rarely been exposed in public. She was the second child bride to come forward in less than a month; in April, a 10-year-old named Nujood Ali had gone by herself to a courthouse to demand a divorce, generating a landmark legal case. . . . .

The average age of marriage in Yemen's rural areas is 12 to 13, a recent study by Sana University researchers found. The country, at the southern corner of the Arabian Peninsula, has one of the highest maternal mortality rates in the world.

. . . . Child marriage is deeply rooted in local custom here, and even enshrined in an old tribal expression: "Give me a girl of 8, and I can give you a guarantee" for a good marriage.

. . . .The trouble started on the first night, when her 30-year-old husband, Faez Ali Thamer, took off her clothes as soon as the light was out. She ran crying from the room, but he caught her, brought her back and forced himself on her. Later, he beat her as well.

. . . To break a marriage would expose the family to shame. Finally, her uncle told her to go to court. On April 2, she said, she walked out of the house by herself and hailed a taxi. . . . After Nujood's case became public, Ms. Nasser said she received angry letters from conservative women denouncing her for her role. . . . .

Photographs of this 10 year old divorcee bring home the brutal reality of child marriage.

### iii. U.N. Population Fund on Child Marriage

The UN Population Fund has long campaigned for an end to child marriages. Its website provides multi-media resources including interviews, facts and data, and describes work being done to eradicate the practice. The organization notes that "Child marriage is a human rights violation. Despite laws against it, the practice remains widespread, in part because of persistent poverty and gender inequality. In developing countries, one in every three girls is married before reaching age 18. One in nine is married under age 15 . . . .Child marriage threatens girls' lives and health, and it limits their future prospects."

In its 2012 report "Marrying Too Young" the Fund found "For the period 2000–2011, just over one third (an estimated 34 per cent) of women aged 20 to 24 years in developing regions were married or in union before their eighteenth birthday. In 2010 this was equivalent to almost 67 million women. About 12 per cent of them were married or in union before age 15. The prevalence of child marriage varies substantially among countries, ranging from only 2 per cent in Algeria to 75 per cent in Niger. In 41 countries, 30 per cent or more of women aged 20 to 24 were married or in union when they were still children."

## C.  Religious Law & Women's Rights

It is an uncomfortable fact that many practices that have traditionally oppressed women find their origins in religious traditions. The following material presents commentary about the role religion sometimes plays in the lives of women — equally critical of each of the world's major religions, starting with Christianity.

Consider the following, provocative and clearly strident view of how religious practices derived from the Bible have affected women, presented by the "Freedom from Religion Foundation."

## 1. Nontract #10, Freedom From Religion Foundation, Inc.,

### by Annie Laurie Gaylor

Organized religion always has been and remains the greatest enemy of women's rights. In the Christian-dominated Western world, two bible verses in particular sum up the position of women:

"I will greatly multiply thy sorrow and thy conception; in sorrow thou shalt bring forth children; and thy desire shall be to thy husband, and he shall rule over thee." — Genesis 3:16

By this third chapter of Genesis, woman lost her rights, her standing — even her identity, and motherhood became a God-inflicted curse degrading her status in the world.

In the New Testament, the bible decrees:

"Let the woman learn in silence with all subjection. But I suffer not a woman to teach, nor to usurp authority over the man, but to be in silence. For Adam was first formed, then Eve. And Adam was not deceived, but the woman being deceived was in the transgression." — 1 Tim. 2:11-14

One bible verse alone, "Thou shalt not suffer a witch to live" (Exodus 22:18) is responsible for the death of tens of thousands, if not millions, of women. Do women and those who care about them need further evidence of the great harm of Christianity, predicated as it has been on these and similar teachings about women?

Church writer Tertullian said "each of you women is an Eve . . . You are the gate of Hell, you are the temptress of the forbidden tree; you are the first deserter of the divine law."

Martin Luther decreed: "If a woman grows weary and at last dies from childbearing, it matters not. Let her die from bearing, she is there to do it."

***

Why do women remain second-class citizens? Why is there a religion-fostered war against women's rights? Because the bible is a handbook for the subjugation of women. The bible establishes woman's inferior status, her "uncleanliness," her transgressions, and God-ordained master/servant relationship to man. Biblical women are possessions: fathers own them, sell them into bondage, even sacrifice them. The bible sanctions rape during wartime and in other contexts. Wives are subject to Mosaic-law sanctioned "bedchecks" as brides, and male jealousy fits and no-notice divorce as wives. The most typical biblical labels of women are "harlot" and "whore." . . .

There are more than 200 bible verses that specifically belittle and demean women. . . .

(See Woe To The Women: The Bible Tells Me So for a more comprehensive list)

# 2. Nicholas D. Kristof, Religion and Women, Opinion NY Times, January 9, 2010

Religions derive their power and popularity in part from the ethical compass they offer. So why do so many faiths help perpetuate something that most of us regard as profoundly unethical: the oppression of women?

On the Ground

It is not that warlords in Congo cite Scripture to justify their mass rapes (although the last warlord I met there called himself a pastor and wore a button reading "rebels for Christ"). It's not that brides are burned in India as part of a Hindu ritual. And there's no verse in the Koran that instructs Afghan thugs to throw acid in the faces of girls who dare to go to school.

Yet these kinds of abuses — along with more banal injustices, like slapping a girlfriend or paying women less for their work — arise out of a social context in which women are, often, second-class citizens. That's a context that religions have helped shape, and not pushed hard to change.

"Women are prevented from playing a full and equal role in many faiths, creating an environment in which violations against women are justified," former President Jimmy Carter noted in a speech last month to the Parliament of the World's Religions in Australia.

"The belief that women are inferior human beings in the eyes of God," Mr. Carter continued, "gives excuses to the brutal husband who beats his wife, the soldier who rapes a woman, the employer who has a lower pay scale for women employees, or parents who decide to abort a female embryo."

Mr. Carter, who sees religion as one of the "basic causes of the violation of women's rights," is a member of The Elders, a small council of retired leaders brought together by Nelson Mandela. The Elders are focusing on the role of religion in oppressing women, and they have issued a joint statement calling on religious leaders to "change all discriminatory practices within their own religions and traditions."

***

There is of course plenty of fodder, in both the Koran and the Bible, for those who seek a theology of discrimination.***

## 3. Sharia Law

a. What isn't wrong with Sharia law? Maryam Namazie, The Guardian, July 2010
"To safeguard our rights there must be one law for all and no religious courts"

The recent global day against the imminent stoning of Sakine Mohammadi-Ashtiani in Iran for adultery is an example of the outrage sparked by the brutality associated with sharia law's penal code.

What of its civil code though — which the Muslim Council of Britain's Shaykh Ibrahim Mogra describes as "small aspects" that concern "marriage, divorce, inheritance, custody of children"? According to human rights campaigner Gita Sahgal, "there is active support for sharia laws precisely because it is limited to denying women rights in the family. No hands are being cut off, so there can't be a problem . . . "

<u>Now a report</u>, Sharia Law in Britain: A Threat to One Law for All and Equal Rights, reveals the adverse effect of sharia courts on family law. Under sharia's civil code, a woman's testimony is worth half of a man's. A man can divorce his wife by repudiation, whereas a woman must give justifications, some of which are difficult to prove. Child custody reverts to the father at a preset age; women who remarry lose custody of their children even before then; and sons inherit twice the share of daughters. . . .

b. Pakistan Hudood Laws

From: <u>Wikipedia</u>

[the neutrality of this entry has been challenged]

> The **Hudood Ordinance** (<u>Urdu</u>: حدود مسوده) (also spelled **Hudud**) was a law in <u>Pakistan</u> that was enacted in 1979 as part of then military ruler <u>Zia-ul-Haq's Islamization</u> process, and replaced/revised in 2006 by the <u>Women's Protection Bill</u>.
>
> The Hudood Law was intended to implement Islamic <u>Shari'a</u> law, by enforcing punishments mentioned in the <u>Quran</u> and <u>Sunnah</u> for *Zina* (extramarital sex), *Qazf* (false accusation of zina), Offence Against Property (theft), and Prohibition (the drinking of alcohol).
>
> The ordinance has been criticized as leading to "*hundreds of incidents where a woman subjected to rape, or even gang rape, was eventually accused of <u>Zina</u>*" and incarcerated, and defended as punishment ordained by God and victim of "extremely unjust propaganda".
>
> *** The ordinance is mostly criticized for making it exceptionally difficult and dangerous to prove an allegation of <u>rape</u>. A woman alleging rape is required to provide four adult male witnesses of good standing of "*the act of penetration*". In practice this is virtually impossible, as no man of good standing would stand there and watch the violent act. Failure to find such proof of the rape places the woman at risk of prosecution for adultery, which does not require such strong evidence. Moreover, to prove rape the female victim has to admit that sexual intercourse had taken place. If the alleged offender, however, is acquitted for want of further evidence the woman now faces charges for either adultery, if she is married, or for fornication, if she is not married. According to a report by Pakistan National Commission on the Status of Women (NCSW) "an estimated 80% of women" in jail in 2003 were there as because "they had failed to prove rape charges and were consequently convicted of adultery." . . . .

The evidence of guilt was there for all to see: a newborn baby in the arms of its mother, a village woman named Zafran Bibi. Her crime: she had been raped. Her sentence: death by stoning. Now Ms. Zafran Bibi, who is about 26, is in solitary confinement in a death-row cell.

Thumping a fat red statute book, the white-bearded judge who convicted her, Anwar Ali Khan, said he had simply followed the letter of the Koran-based law, known as hudood, that mandates punishments.

"The illegitimate child is not disowned by her and therefore is proof of zina," he said, referring to laws that forbid any sexual contact outside marriage. Furthermore, he said, in accusing her brother-in-law of raping her, Ms. Zaf-ran had confessed to her crime.

## 4. Jewish Rabbinical Law

Every morning, orthodox Jewish males still recite the following benediction:

Blessed art thou, O Lord our God, King of the Universe, who hast not made me a woman.

a. <u>Women, Religious Law and Religious Courts in Israel</u> — The Jewish Case, by Margit Cohn

***

### IV. Jewish Rabbinate-Halakhic Law and the Status of Women

Traditional cultures, such as monotheistic religions, tend to be patriarchic in nature. As Frances Raday forcefully argues, the fundamental tenets of monotheistic religions are at odds with the basis of human rights doctrine. This is evidenced in the divergent bases of the two concepts: religious duty, central to Jewish religion, and human rights, which stem from individualistic and atomistic premises.

Gender differentiation is indeed integral to Halakhic Judaism. I present below some of the expressions of discrimination against women and, worse, of negative and demeaning attitudes towards women.

Some limited caveats are nevertheless in place. Alternative Jewish streams (i.e., Conservative, Reform and Liberal Judaism), express different levels of departure from scripturalism towards concepts of a living, evolving tradition. Even within Orthodox Judaism, the scriptures include lesser denigrating rules, but the following obligations and perceptions are deeply woven into the Halakhic fabric and cannot be ignored. Finally, the majority of the opinions and Halakhic rulings cited below are centuries old; one could expect a scripture dating from the 2nd, 12th and even 19th Century to express a world-view that demeans women and their role in society. Yet it must be stressed that the perceptions below still constitute, and frame, the Halakhic-Orthodox decision making process I will discuss below in the context of the state of Israel. Small shifts in emphasis do not signify a conceptual change away from the sanctity and completeness of the rabbinical Jewish scriptures.

***

A woman's role in the home was clearly defined long ago as fully subservi-ent to her husband in all respects. On the basis of God's decree in the Book of Genesis, the following excerpt from the Talmud is but one example: Rabbi Johanan said: a man may do whatever he pleases with his wife [at intercourse].

\*\*\*

Maimonides, a great Jewish philosopher in the 12th Century, ruled, perhaps more benignly: [The Sages]. ordained that the wife should honor her hus-band exceedingly and hold him in awe that she should arrange all her af-fairs according to his instructions, and that he should be in her as if he were a prince or a king, while she behaves according to his heart's desire, and keeps away from anything that is hateful to him.

\*\*\*

The last, but not final, example pertains to the exclusion of women from legal life. Women, together with minors and idiots, are disqualified as witnesses in court. Only men can sit as judges under Jewish law, a rule strictly followed in the rabbinical court system, discussed below. Some of the newer writings within the Halakhic tradition attempt to rationalize these rulings. Under such rationalization, women have been granted the supposed benefit of a bet-ter psyche, which could justify their diminished status or lesser obligations.

\*\*\*

How does Halakhic law discriminate against women in divorce proceed-ings? Jewish Law's starting point seems quite advanced, since it decrees that mutual consent of the spouses is sufficient ground for divorce. In the absence of consent, however, disparities take over. Grounds for divorce are limited, and a wife's gross misbehavior is an important one; misbehavior is assessed by Halakhic terms rather than modern ones. Extramarital affairs on the side of the husband do not carry serious effects, while the effects of an extra-marital affair of a woman can be devastating. A wife against whom such an affair is found is considered a rebellious wife and can be divorced without pecuniary effect; moreover, she is then prohibited from later marrying her lover (or remarrying her ex-husband). Any children with her lover, con-ceived while married to another, would be considered, *mamzerim*, a pariah status that entails exclusion from the proper Jewish community, and leaves such second-rate people the right to only marry between themselves and re-main pariahs for ten generations.

This law serves as a powerful threat to women, and has no equal with regard to men who conceive outside marriage. A man whose wife refuses to grant a divorce may ultimately receive a permit to remarry, and will thus be le-gally married to two women. Although this is not a common remedy, it is not available to women. Refusing husbands may be threatened with civil sanctions and ultimately jailed an even rarer occurrence.

But the more mundane differences between sexes are in fact more significant and painful than the striking examples above, since they are regular elements of rabbinical divorce proceedings. From child maintenance and custody to the division of assets, Halakhic law is not based on a concept of spouse equality; considering the above examples from its scriptures, this is not surprising. Under Halakha, a divorced wife is granted the sum fixed in the religious marriage contract, made by the husband on the day of the wedding (*ketubah*), with additional compensation. Joint ownership of assets and shared effort in acquiring assets during marriage are not at all part of Jewish law as found in the scriptures. Under Jewish law, custody of boys after the age of six is normally granted to the father. In general, spouses who show allegiance to Orthodox Judaism receive preferential treatment with regard to child custody.

Rabbinical courts have flexed some of the rules, but a large portion remains fully faithful to their medieval and earlier roots. Considering the status of women under Jewish law, as applied by the rabbinical courts (an issue discussed in the next section), it is not surprising that the state of Israel, on signing the Convention on Elimination of all Forms of Discrimination against Women (CEDAW), attached two reservations. The first reservation derogates from Article 16, which addresses equality in Marriage and Family; the second pertains to Article 7, which protects equality in political and public life, and was required to uphold the exclusion of women from the rabbinical court bench. A similar reservation was added to the Covenant on Civil and Political Rights, ratified in 1992. The reservation to Article 23 (protection of the family) expressly refers to the religious basis of Israel's family law, and could be interpreted as applying also to Article 18 (Freedom of Religion and Conscience) and Article 26 (Equality before the Law), in the context of family law.

\*\*\*

### Concluding remarks

What is the future of religious law in the state of Israel, and what are the implications for women? The *Bavli* case represents some of the problems ingrained in the interface between the protection of basic universal values and religious-political forces. The picture is not encouraging. Institutional monopoly of religious-based institutions tends to embed religious-based preconceptions about the lesser status of women. State-backed restraining mechanisms are difficult to maintain, especially when the arrangements and the constraints are politically volatile. International human rights arrangements do not necessarily apply as corrective forces, as the case of Israel shows. Political and social concern about women's rights can be marginalized in social climates under which public opinion is either concerned with issues that are viewed as more pressing, or maintains a deference towards religious values.

b. <u>Mary F. Radford, The Inheritance Rights of Women Under Jewish and Islamic Law</u>

***

## II. Women's Place in the Two Religions

The status of women under both Judaism and Islam is the subject of continuing debate. In both arenas, there are those who praise the religion for the dignified status to which it elevates women and those who criticize the religion for its sexist and discriminatory treatment of women. As will be noted, a modern resurgence of fundamentalism in both religions reinforces and emphasizes to women's detriment religious rules and historical traditions that relegate women to an inferior status.

### A. *Women in Judaism*

***

Several women appear throughout the Bible who are powerful in their own right. Yet Biblical references to women in general indicate that a woman's highest honor is to be found in her role as wife and mother. The *Mishnah* order that deals with women concentrates on marriage and divorce. The Talmud emphasizes further "the husbands' and fathers' duties with regard to the maintenance and care for his wife and daughters." The Talmud also adds to the role of the woman/wife/mother the important task of freeing her husband from mundane household tasks so that he will be free to study the Torah. Generally, women did not study the Torah, although history records the story of one woman scholar, Beruriah, who was purportedly able to "absorb over three hundred laws each day, . . . some of her legal decisions were accepted as *Halachah,* despite the opposing views of some Rabbis."

The status of Jewish women in modern times varies in Reform, Conservative, and Orthodox Judaism. For example, Orthodox Jews continue to restrict women from participating in religious rituals even though Reform Jews now admit women to the rabbinate. Jewish feminists continue to fight for the equalization of women's status in the religion against the traditionalist view that this equalization is contrary to talmudic legislation.

Jewish women, particularly in Israel, remain threatened by the political influence that may be wielded by Jewish "Ultra-Orthodox fundamentalists." Like Islamic fundamentalism, Jewish fundamentalism dictates an inferior and submissive status for women. Jewish fundamentalism "does not explicitly declare that a wife must be submissive and obedient to her husband [but] the overall structure of marriage and divorce laws delegates such a degree of authority and power to the husband as to allow him effectively to coerce his wife's obedience." Additionally, Jewish fundamentalists, in the name of "guard[ing] women's chastity [and] prevent[ing] women from tempting men into adultery," segregate the sexes, relegate women to the home, and restrict women's public dress.

B. *Women in Islam*

One scholar has noted that "[t]o attempt to talk about women in Islam is of course to venture into an area fraught with the perils of overgeneralization, oversimplification, and the almost unavoidable limitations of a Western bias." Islam is criticized by some as having created a "male-dominated society" and praised by others as having "elevated the status of women, providing them with an independent legal and spiritual identity." The Prophet's legislation is praised by some as having declared "a new equal status for women in society," yet criticized by others as setting forth a set of rules on family life with "almost all of them favoring men." ***

The Prophet replaced the tribe with the family as the primary social unit. He adopted the patrilineal system as the framework for his scheme of inheritance, but he established explicit inheritance rights for women. The Prophet restricted to four the number of wives that a man could have and forbade a woman from having more than one husband. He abolished the practice of female infanticide.

Strong women played an important role in the life of the Prophet and the foundation of the religion. . . . Despite these forceful feminine influences, some believe that women as a class do not fare particularly well in those segments of the Qur'an and the *Shari'a* that deal with topics other than inheritance and property rights. This belief is summarized as follows:

The purpose of women, according to the Koran, is to compliment men. Women's rights to employment and participation in public life, freedom of movement and freedom of organization, are severely restricted through a combination of the Shari'a principles of qawam (men's guardianship over women), hijab (the veil) and segregation between men and women. Examples of women's inequality can be found in the administration of justice and in certain aspects of family law. A woman's judicial testimony is deemed to be of half the value of that of a man, in civil cases, and is not accepted at all in serious criminal cases. In certain types of wrongful homicide, monetary compensation paid to the heirs of a female victim is less than that paid to the heirs of a male victim and a woman's share in inheritance is half that of a man's. Additionally, no woman may hold any public office which involves exercising authority over men.

*** 

Women played no part in interpretation of the Qur'an, and their absence "has been mistakenly equated with voicelessness in the text itself." Furthermore, social norms in many male-dominated countries may have obscured many of the original purposes of the Qur'anic legislation. Former Prime Minister of Pakistan, Benazir Bhutto, claims that the subjugation of women in Islam "has got nothing to do with the religion, but it has got very much to do with material or man-made considerations." She concludes, "It is not Islam which is averse to women rulers, I think — it is men."

An example of the effect of male interpretation and social norms appears in the development of the concept of "the veil." The required covering of a woman's face and body when she ventures out in public is seen by many as a symbol of the Islamic subordination of women. \*\*\*

c. Women in Islam Versus Women in the Judaeo-Christian Tradition: The Myth & the Reality, by Dr. Sherif Abdel Azeem

## 1. INTRODUCTION

Five years ago, I read in the Toronto Star issue of Juoy 3, 1990 an article titled "Islam is not alone in patriarchal doctrines", by Gwynne Dyer. The article described the furious reactions of the participants of a conference on women and power held in Montreal to the comments of the famous Egyptian feminist Dr. Nawal Saadawi. Her "politically incorrect" statements included : "the most restrictive elements towards women can be found first in Judaism in the Old Testament then in Christianity and then in the Quran"; "all religions are patriarchal because they stem from patriarchal societies"; and "veiling of women is not a specifically Islamic practice but an ancient cultural heritage with analogies in sister religions".

\*\*\*

## 2. EVE'S FAULT

The three religions agree on one basic fact: Both women and men are created by God, The Creator of the whole universe. However, disagreement starts soon after the creation of the first man, Adam, and the first woman, Eve. \*\*\*

A careful look into the two accounts of the story of the Creation reveals some essential differences. The Quran, contrary to the Bible, places equal blame on both Adam and Eve for their mistake. Nowhere in the Quran can one find even the slightest hint that Eve tempted Adam to eat from the tree or even that she had eaten before him. Eve in the Quran is no temptress, no seducer, and no deceiver. Moreover, Eve is not to be blamed for the pains of childbearing. God, according to the Quran, punishes no one for another's faults. Both Adam and Eve committed a sin and then asked God for forgiveness and He forgave them both.

\*\*\*

## 3. EVE'S LEGACY

The image of Eve as temptress in the Bible has resulted in an extremely negative impact on women throughout the Judaeo-Christian tradition. All women were believed to have inherited from their mother, the Biblical Eve, both her guilt and her guile. Consequently, they were all untrustworthy, morally inferior, and wicked. ***

If we now turn our attention to what the Quran has to say about women, we will soon realize that the Islamic conception of women is radically different from the Judaeo-Christian one. ***

It is clear that the Quranic view of women is no different than that of men. They, both, are God's creatures whose sublime goal on earth is to worship their Lord, do righteous deeds, and avoid evil and they, both, will be assessed accordingly. The Quran never mentions that the woman is the devil's gateway or that she is a deceiver by nature. The Quran, also, never mentions that man is God's image; all men and all women are his creatures, that is all. . . .

***

# D.  Cultural Practices

## 1. "Honor" Killing

From Wikipedia:

An honor killing or shame killing is the homicide of a member of a family by other members, due to the perpetrators' belief that the victim has brought shame or dishonor upon the family, or has violated the principles of a community or a religion, usually for reasons such as refusing to enter an arranged marriage, being in a relationship that is disapproved by their family, having sex outside marriage, becoming the victim of rape, dressing in ways which are deemed inappropriate, engaging in non-heterosexual relations or renouncing a faith.

From National Geographic News, February 12, 2002,
Hillary Mayell, Thousands of Women Killed for Family "Honor"

Hundreds, if not thousands, of women are murdered by their families each year in the name of family "honor." It's difficult to get precise numbers on the phenomenon of honor killing; the murders frequently go unreported, the perpetrators unpunished, and the concept of family honor justifies the act in the eyes of some societies.

Most honor killings occur in countries where the concept of women as a vessel of the family reputation predominates, said Marsha Freemen, director of International Women's Rights Action Watch at the Hubert Humphrey Institute of Public Affairs at the University of Minnesota.

. . . .

In India, for example, more than 5,000 brides die annually because their dowries are considered insufficient, according to the United Nations

Children's Fund (UNICEF). Crimes of passion, which are treated extremely leniently in Latin America, are the same thing with a different name, some rights advocates say.

"In countries where Islam is practiced, they're called honor killings, but dowry deaths and so-called crimes of passion have a similar dynamic in that the women are killed by male family members and the crimes are perceived as excusable or understandable," said Widney Brown, advocacy director for Human Rights Watch.

The practice, she said, "goes across cultures and across religions."

Amnesty International, among others, provides informative "fact sheets" regarding the most common violations of human rights facing women. Just take note of the array of problematic issues facing women, revealed in their list.

### *Fact Sheets*

- CEDAW: Treaty for the Rights of Women
- Domestic Violence as Torture
- Economic, Social & Cultural Rights
- Female Genital Mutilation
- HIV/AIDS, Women and Human Rights
- "Honor" Killings
- Human Trafficking
- Reproductive Rights
- Violence Against Women
- Violence Against Women in Armed Conflict
- Women in Post-Conflict Situations
- Women's Human Rights

See also: The Advocates for Human Rights, Violence Against Women Project.

## E.  Human Rights Law: Convention on Elimination of Discrimination Against Women (CEDAW)

Please read the description of CEDAW presented at the UN High Commissioner's website, including the treaty text. Review articles 1 through 16 or the Convention (especially 1, 2 & 5) and consider their relevance to the various circumstances facing women described in the materials above. Also consider the response of CEDAW to reservations that would condition women's rights on consistency with religious law.

**Does CEDAW create rights that address the circumstances and practices that oppress women as described above?** Does the CEDAW Committee have the power or processes necessary to make effective those rights? Consider the following commentary on CEDAW.

## 1. The Women's Convention And Its Optional Protocol, Empowering Women To Claim Their Internationally Protected Rights, Laboni Amena Hoq, 32 Colum. Hum. Rts. L. Rev. 677

\*\*\* The goal of the Convention is to go beyond existing human rights conventions, many of which nominally entitle the equal application of their respective human rights laws to men and women, so as to provide more focused protection of human rights for women. As the drafters of the Convention understood, systematic obstacles originating in the historic discrimination faced by women in all societies have inhibited the equal application of international human rights laws. Thus the essence of the Convention, as articulated in Article 1, is to focus on the elimination of such discrimination, in all its forms, that has either the "purpose" or "effect" of limiting women's full participation and development in their respective societies.

\*\*\*

The Convention further transcends the scope of other human rights treaties in its commitment to addressing discrimination by non-State actors, including any person, organization, or enterprise. In addition, the preamble of the Convention makes a commitment to supporting women's rights in the private spheres of women's lives. It states, "a change in the traditional role of men as well as the role of women in society and in the family is needed to achieve full equality."

\*\*\*In this regard, the Convention recognizes the influence of culture and tradition in restricting women's enjoyment of rights. Article 2 refers to "customs and practices which constitute discrimination"; Article 5 calls on State Parties to modify social and cultural patterns to eliminate prejudices and stereotyping; and Article 9 requires State Parties to recognize a woman's nationality, regardless of the nationality of her husband, when protecting her rights. Article 11 prohibits dismissal from employment on grounds of marriage or maternity and calls for the provision of maternity leave and social services to enable parents to combine family obligations with employment and participation in public life. Article 16 covers equal rights and responsibilities in marital and familial relationships.

 Not surprisingly, these are the provisions of the Convention (particularly Articles 2 and 16) that are the most contentious in terms of their interpretation and implementation by State Parties. These provisions reflect some of the essential dilemmas facing women's equality, including whether women can or should be viewed as equal to men, or whether their unique reproductive functions, marriage, and religious/cultural group membership support differential treatment. While the Women's Convention symbolizes an international consensus that women's equality need not be limited by these conditions, the numerous reservations and uneven adherence to the Convention has shown that symbolic measures cannot ensure equality for women.

## B. Challenges to the Women's Convention

### 1. Weak Enforcement Mechanisms

\*\*\*

### 2. Debilitating Effects of Reservations

Another hindrance to the Women's Convention is the expansive number of reservations that State Parties have made to their obligations. The Convention is among the most reserved of U.N. human rights instruments. \*\*\*

The debates surrounding reservations to the Convention are closely related to the fundamental normative controversies that challenge the universal commitment to international women's rights. \*\*\* Differing cultural and religious practices are often at the heart of this lack of consensus. For example, many reservations deal with the conflict between full equality rights and some interpretations of Islam that qualify the definition of sexual equality to something significantly less than the expansive notion of sexual equality embodied in the Convention. "Other prominent reservations deal with national religious or customary laws that restrict women's inheritance and property rights; nationality laws that do not accord women the same rights as men to acquire, change or retain their nationality upon marriage and laws limiting women's economic opportunities, freedom of movement and choice of residence." \*\*\*

### 3. Weak Adherence to the Normative Principles of the Convention

Both the weak enforcement mechanisms and the general acceptance of the numerous reservations to the fundamental obligations of the Convention indicate the larger lack of commitment to the basic norms and values that inform the international women's rights regime. Some have criticized the Convention as acting only as a symbolic commitment to these norms and values, demonstrating that "[t]he international community is prepared to formally acknowledge the considerable problems of inequality faced by women, but only, it seems, if individual States are not required as a result to alter patriarchal practices that subordinate women." The purported ideological resistance to advancing women's rights, coupled with the multiple problems of enforcement, has greatly hampered the Convention in its ability to work towards the goal of further equality for women. \*\*\*

## B. Avenues of Reinforcement

### 1. Combating the Marginalization of Women's Rights

The Women's Convention was itself born out of the reality that effective focus was not being placed on the rights of women in the existing human rights instruments, mainly the CCPR and the International Covenant on

Economic, Social and Cultural Rights (CESCR). At the heart of the short-comings of these existing conventions was their focus on human rights protections in the public sphere and their concomitant failure to apply similar protections in the private sphere. This focus had the normative effect of privileging rights protections for men over women as "women are relegated to the private sphere of home, hearth and family. The public sphere of workplace, law, economics, politics, intellectual and cultural life is regarded as the province of men." This failure to apply human rights in a gender-neutral fashion prompted the feminist community to urge the creation of both women-specific human rights and a Women's Convention to lay out the comprehensive context of these rights. The new instrument was meant to fill the existing gaps in international human rights law that failed to apply human rights equally to both men and women. ***

 *** For example, the very failure of the CCPR to contextualize the relative right to privacy alongside the more absolute right of a woman to be protected from oppressive conditions in characteristically private spheres such as "family and home" demonstrates this problem. Likewise, the CESCR's right to just and favorable conditions of work is defined in terms of work in the public sphere, which ignores working conditions faced by the majority of the world's women. ***

**2. An Expanded Role for CEDAW**

Until now, CEDAW has not had the authority to hear individual complaints or investigate claims of serious and systematic violations of the Convention. This is in stark contrast with other treaty bodies, most relevantly the Race Convention Committee, which had such authority from the inception of the Race Convention. The Optional Protocol now provides CEDAW with both the authority and procedures with which to carry out both of these tasks, placing it on par with other human rights treaty bodies. ***

***

**2. Prospects to Advance Women's Rights Through Rights Discourse**

   **a. Piercing the Private Sphere**

*** As noted earlier, an important attribute of the Women's Convention is its attempt to introduce elements of State obligation to bring domestic laws and policies in conformity with international rights and to place obligations on States to effectuate women's rights in the private sphere. This progressive development in international human rights law acknowledges the need to move beyond the 'public' sphere as the only realm of possible State action or international intervention.

*** At the heart of the private sphere is domestic and family life, a realm in which women continue to be the central occupants. The challenge women face in this sphere is that "the privacy of domestic life makes women's concerns invisible and ensures preservation of the status quo." [FN166] The limited public regulation in the private sphere, in such areas as domestic violence and rape in marriage, "supports and legitimates" the lack of protection of women by the law. From a normative perspective, the lack of regulation on issues particularly relevant to women demonstrates women's devalued position in society. Thus the lack of direct State intervention, often justified by the protection of privacy, can disguise the inequality and domination exercised in the private sphere.

The Women's Convention takes the important position that the private sphere is not off-limits when it comes to State obligations to protect women's rights. Yet the provisions of the Convention that de-emphasize the public/private distinction are the most reserved and least respected by State Parties. ***

****

# F. Relativism & the Public-Private Distinction: Are Women's Issues Different from Other Human Rights Issues?

Think about the distinction between state action and private action discussed just above and in the materials below. Reflect on how human rights violations by private parties can be endorsed, explicitly or implicitly, by the state. Think also about gender as a much larger concept than simply men and women, and how the roles of men and women are enforced by society, culture, religion and tradition. Should such variations among societies in cultural or religious orientation be taken into account in interpreting international human rights?

## 1. Wilets, Conceptualizing Private Violence Against Sexual Minorities as Gendered Violence: An International and Comparative Law Perspective, 60 Alb. L. Rev. 989 (1997)

... Thomas and Beasley made the important observation that "[a]lthough international law is gender neutral in theory, in practice it interacts with gender-biased domestic laws and social structures that relegate women and men to separate spheres of existence: private and public." ... This Article will continue this discussion of the limits and potential of international law in addressing gendered violence by focusing on the similarities and differences between violence based on gender and violence based on sexual minority status, with a particular focus on gendered violence in the private sphere. ...

## II.

## Defining the Problem: Private Violence Against Women and
## Sexual Minorities

When examining human rights abuses against women and sexual minorities from a global perspective, it is important to recognize that violations against the bodily integrity of both groups frequently occur outside the reach of the legal system. To the extent legal systems only address violations of bodily integrity occurring outside the home — in the "public sphere" — they fail to provide protection against the numerous abuses which occur within the home — in the "private sphere."

For example, in many countries, domestic violence has only recently been recognized as a crime. In other countries, it is considered to be outside the state's jurisdiction. As human rights lawyer Julie Mertus notes, "in most regions of the world, including many states in the United States, husbands are free to rape their wives without fear of legal reprisal." Mertus further documents that "[i]n Brazil, until 1991 wife killings were considered to be noncriminal 'honor killings'; in just one year, nearly eight hundred husbands killed their wives. Similarly, in Colombia, until 1980, a husband legally could kill his wife for committing adultery." In Egypt, a husband who kills his wife to defend his "honor" may receive a maximum sentence of three years in prison. The penalty for a wife who kills her husband under similar circumstances is prison and hard labor for three years to life.

\*\*\*

The public/private distinction in both domestic and international law has important implications for analyzing human rights abuses against lesbians and women generally. In many cultures, the principal instrument of societal control over women is the family. To the extent women lack legal status outside of their role within the family, they do not enjoy the legal protections accorded to men. Thus, a lesbian may be beaten or killed by a family member for her orientation/identity, yet this domestic violence may not be the concern of law enforcement officials. This contrasts with the status of male sexual minorities in many societies where they enjoy an independent legal status vis-a-vis the state. Therefore, achieving basic civil and political rights relating to an individual's relationship to the state, such as the right to privacy, is more likely to have an immediate, practical effect on the civil rights of gay men. The right to privacy involves a zone of sovereignty that the state may not reach. The right to privacy may offer less protection for women, for whom the state is not as frequently the primary instrument of control.

\*\*\* Nevertheless, states have traditionally been very willing to discard the private/public distinction in order to punish sexual minorities for violating gender norms. Thus, while a man's beating of his wife has been traditionally considered a private, "domestic" concern, same-gender private sexual activity between two consenting adults has been considered within the legitimate scope of the state's concern. In both cases, an actor representing the interests of male supremacy enforces gender norm expectations. The private/public distinction enables men to enforce these norms against members of their household. Conversely, when violations of gender norms are committed by individuals outside of the male dominated heterosexual household paradigm, such as sexual minorities, piercing the public/private distinction enables the state to intervene and perform the role of the husband or father. ***

In other countries, states are complicitous in the extra-judicial murder of sexual minorities or are passive in their approach to stopping the killings or apprehending the perpetrators. In other countries, sexual minorities suffer systematic torture, police abuse and arbitrary arrest. For example, in Australia, the government-funded Australian Institute of Criminology found that "11 percent of lesbians and 20 percent of gay men had been assaulted. Of those, 12 percent of [the] gay women and 18 percent of [the] gay men had been assaulted by the police." *** To the extent the state does not punish individuals who murder or otherwise injure sexual minorities, the state may be viewed as an accomplice in the act. ***

## IV.
### Piercing the Public/Private Distinction: Overcoming International Law's Deference to National Law and Local Custom

It is important to recognize that international law has traditionally maintained a certain deference to domestic law and custom. This deference has resulted because international law is based on values, traditions, standards, and norms accepted globally, although not necessarily by every culture or country. As Louis Henkin has observed, international human rights law is the law of the "lowest common denominator." International human rights law thus consists, in large part, of those rights which are deemed fundamental to human beings in all parts of the world and which inure to individuals because of their status as human beings and not because they are citizens of a specific country. . . . Yet, for far too long, countries have used this traditional deference to avoid addressing human rights abuses against women and sexual minorities. Thus, a threshold task for those seeking remedies under international law for violence against women and sexual minorities is obtaining a global consensus that such violence is, as a normative matter, unacceptable.

With respect to women, some progress has been made under international law toward establishing an international norm against gendered violence in cases of domestic violence and rape. ***

Nevertheless, women have only made limited progress in developing remedies to enforce those norms against states for their failure to enforce those norms against private actors.

Sexual minorities, however, have only sporadically obtained even this nominal normative recognition of their most fundamental human rights to bodily integrity and equal protection of the laws. In obtaining even this limited recognition, sexual minorities face several obstacles. The first obstacle is that, unlike the case with women, the very existence of sexual minorities in many cultures is questioned, or is seen as an import from the West. The second obstacle is that sexual minorities, unlike women, are frequently considered a criminal class per se in many countries . . . it is incumbent upon sexual minorities to demonstrate, through cross-cultural documentation, that sexual minorities are a global phenomenon, of relevance to all cultures and societies, and thus an appropriate object of regulation by international law. The accomplishment of this task is necessary to rebut cultural relativist arguments against providing protection for sexual minorities under international law. ***

# Chapter 14

# Gender Identity and Sexual Orientation as Subsets of Gender Rights

## A. Overview

This, the final chapter in the book, attempts to push at the current boundaries of international human rights law by examining the situation of sexual minorities. The chapter begins with links to several sources that provide information both about abuses of sexual minorities internationally and potential responses under current international human rights law. When you read through these materials it should become clear how extensive the abuse of sexual minorities is world-wide. It is also clear that sexual minorities are not well protected under current international law, and that attempts to interpret existing standards to protect them will face stiff resistance in many parts of the world. The 2011 Report of the UN High Commissioner for Human Rights to the Human Rights Counsel, a link to which appears below, is particularly good for establishing this background.

After examining the relatively bleak situation of sexual minorities internationally, the chapter explores this reality through two sources. The first is an excerpt from an article by Professor Wilets which examines gender identity and societal responses to it. The second is a remarkable opinion by the Indian Supreme Court regarding the rights of transsexual people. The chapter does not purport to present a particular theme but rather is designed to allow you to think critically, based on what they have learned in the course, about a new frontier in the promotion of essential human dignity.

## B. Treatment of Sexual Minorities World-Wide

Review the following sources, or those you may find on your own, concerning the treatment of sexual minorities around the world. Read as much of the reports as you need to inform yourself. Here are four basic resources:

UNHCHR Publication, Born Free and Equal: Sexual Orientation and Gender Identity in International Human Rights Law;

UNHCHR Report on Discriminatory Laws and Practices and Acts of Violence Against Individuals Based on Their Sexual Orientation and Gender Identity;

UNESCO Report on Sexual Minorities in Insular Southeast Asia;

Human Rights Watch Report, Iran.

# C. Potential International Human Rights Law Protections for Sexual Minorities

While significant legal protections exist under the European System of Human Rights[136] and within the domestic law of many nations, there are currently no global international agreements that explicitly provide protection for the rights and interests of sexual minorities. The UN itself has only recently, and with clear resistance among some states, taken up the cause of protecting sexual minorities from discrimination and violence.

In the UN documents linked above, various arguments are presented for interpretations of existing human rights norms to include sexual minorities, primarily based on principles of non-discrimination in the exercise of human rights based on "other status." Please review these legal arguments, which are summarized in paragraphs 5-19 in the UN Report on Discriminatory Law and Practices, linked above. Consider the decision of the Human Rights Committee in the Toonen case, below.

## 1. Toonen v. Australia, Communication No. 488/1992, U.N. Doc CCPR/C/50/D/488/1992 (1994)

Views of the Human Rights Committee under article 5, paragraph 4,
of the Optional Protocol to the International Covenant
on Civil and Political Rights

— Fiftieth session —
concerning
Communication No. 488/1992

Submitted by:                              Nicholas Toonen

---

136. Sexual minorities are not explicitly protected under the European Convention on Human Rights but the European Court for Human Rights has rendered a number decisions interpreting the treaty to protect LGBT persons. These include Dudgeon v. UK, 1981; Norris v. Ireland, 1988; and Modinos v. Cyprus, 1993 (prohibiting the criminalization of private, consensual sex between adults under Article 8, Respect for Private Life); Lustig-Prean and Beckett v. UK, 2000 (Convention prohibits ban on homosexuals in the military); Salgueiro da Silva Mouta v. Portugal (Convention prohibits denial of child custody based on sexual orientation).

| | |
|---|---|
| **Victim**: | The author |
| **State party**: | Australia |
| **Date of communication**: | 25 December 1991 |
| **Date of decision on admissibility**: | 5 November 1992 |

**The Human Rights Committee**, established under article 28 of the International Covenant on Civil and Political Rights,

**Meeting** on 31 March 1994,

**Having concluded** its consideration of communication No. 488/1992, submitted to the Human Rights Committee by Mr. Nicholas Toonen under the Optional Protocol to the International Covenant on Civil and Political Rights,

**Having taken into account** all written information made available to it by the author of the communication and the State party,

**Adopts** its Views under article 5, paragraph 4, of the Optional Protocol.

1. The author of the communication is Nicholas Toonen, an Australian citizen born in 1964, currently residing in Hobart in the state of Tasmania, Australia. He is a leading member of the Tasmanian Gay Law Reform Group (TGLRG) and claims to be a victim of violations by Australia of articles 2, paragraphs 1, 17 and 26 of the International Covenant on Civil and Political Rights.

### The facts as submitted by the author:

2.1 The author is an activist for the promotion of the rights of homosexuals in Tasmania, one of Australia's six constitutive states. He challenges two provisions of the Tasmanian Criminal Code, namely Sections 122(a) and (c) and 123, which criminalize various forms of sexual contacts between men, including all forms of sexual contacts between consenting adult homosexual men in private.

### The complaint:

3.1 The author affirms that Sections 122 and 123 of the Tasmanian Criminal Code violate articles 2, paragraphs 1, 17 and 26 of the Covenant because:

(a) they do not distinguish between sexual activity in private and sexual activity in public and bring private activity into the public domain. In their enforcement, these provisions result in a violation of the right to privacy, since they enable the police to enter a household on the mere suspicion that two consenting adult homosexual men may be committing a criminal offence. Given the stigma attached to homosexuality in Australian society (and especially in Tasmania), the violation of the right to privacy may lead to unlawful attacks on the honour and the reputation of the individuals concerned.

(b) they distinguish between individuals in the exercise of their right to privacy on the basis of sexual activity, sexual orientation and sexual identity, and

(c) the Tasmanian Criminal Code does not outlaw any form of homosexual activity between consenting homosexual women in private and only some forms of consenting heterosexual activity between adult men and women in private. That the laws in question are not currently enforced by the judicial authorities of Tasmania should not be taken to mean that homosexual men in Tasmania enjoy effective equality under the law.

**The State party's observations on the merits and author's comments thereon:**

6.1 In its submission under article 4, paragraph 2, of the Optional Protocol, dated 15 September 1993, the State party concedes that the author has been a victim of arbitrary interference with his privacy, and that the legislative provisions challenged by him cannot be justified on public health or moral grounds. It incorporates into its submission the observations of the government of Tasmania, which denies that the author has been the victim of a violation of the Covenant.

6.2 With regard to article 17, the Federal Government notes that the Tasmanian government submits that article 17 does not create a "right to privacy" but only a right to freedom from arbitrary or unlawful interference with privacy, and that as the challenged laws were enacted by democratic process, they cannot be an unlawful interference with privacy. The Federal Government, after reviewing the travaux préparatoires of article 17, subscribes to the following definition of "private": matters which are individual, personal, or confidential, or which are kept or removed from public observation". The State party acknowledges that based on this definition, consensual sexual activity in private is encompassed by the concept of "privacy" in article 17.

6.6 None the less, the State party cautions that the formulation of article 17 allows for some infringement of the right to privacy if there are reasonable grounds, and that domestic social mores may be relevant to the reasonableness of an interference with privacy. The State party observes that while laws penalizing homosexual activity existed in the past in other Australian states, they have since been repealed with the exception of Tasmania. Furthermore, discrimination on the basis of homosexuality or sexuality is unlawful in three of six Australian states and the two self-governing internal Australian territories. The Federal Government has declared sexual preference to be a ground of discrimination that may be invoked under ILO Convention No. 111 (Discrimination in Employment or Occupation Convention), and created a mechanism through which complaints about discrimination in employment on the basis of sexual preference may be considered by the Australian Human Rights and Equal Opportunity Commission.

6.7 On the basis of the above, the State party contends that there is now a general Australian acceptance that no individual should be disadvantaged on the basis of his or her sexual orientation. Given the legal and social situation in all of Australia except Tasmania, the State party acknowledges that a complete prohibition on sexual activity between men is unnecessary to sustain the moral fabric of Australian society. On balance, the State party "does not seek to claim that the challenged laws are based on reasonable and objective criteria".

6.9 In respect of the alleged violation of article 26, the State party seeks the Committee's guidance as to whether sexual orientation may be subsumed under the term " . . . or other status" in article 26. In this context, the Tasmanian authorities concede that sexual orientation is an "other status" for the purposes of the Covenant. . . .

6.10 The State party continues that <u>if</u> the Committee considers sexual orientation as "other status" for purposes of the Covenant, the following issues must be examined:

— whether Tasmanian laws draw a distinction on the basis of sex or sexual orientation;

— whether Mr. Toonen is a victim of discrimination;

— whether there are reasonable and objective criteria for the distinction; and

— whether Tasmanian laws are a proportional means to achieve a legitimate aim under the Covenant.

7.2 In response to the Tasmanian authorities' argument that moral considerations must be taken into account when dealing with the right to privacy, the author notes that Australia is a pluralistic and multi-cultural society whose citizens have different and at times conflicting moral codes. In these circumstances it must be the proper role of criminal laws to entrench these different codes as little as possible; in so far as some values must be entrenched in criminal codes, these values should relate to human dignity and diversity.

7.5 In the light of the above, the author urges the Committee to take account of the fact that the State party has consistently found that sexual orientation is a protected status in international human rights law and, in particular, constitutes an "other status" for purposes of articles 2, paragraphs 1 and 26. The author notes that a precedent for such a finding can be found in several judgements of the European Court of Human Rights.[1]

**Examination of the merits**:

8.1 The Committee is called upon to determine whether Mr. Toonen has been the victim of an unlawful or arbitrary interference with his privacy, contrary to article 17, paragraph 1, and whether he has been discriminated against in his right to equal protection of the law, contrary to article 26.

8.2 Inasmuch as article 17 is concerned, it is undisputed that adult consensual sexual activity in private is covered by the concept of "privacy", and that Mr. Toonen is actually and currently affected by the continued existence of the Tasmanian laws. The Committee considers that Sections 122(a), (c) and 123 of the Tasmanian Criminal Code "interfere" with the author's privacy, even if these provisions have not been enforced for a decade. In this context, it notes that the policy of the Department of Public Prosecutions not to initiate criminal proceedings in respect of private homosexual conduct does not amount to a guarantee that no actions will be brought against homosexuals in the future, particularly in the light of undisputed statements of the Director of Public Prosecutions of Tasmania in 1988 and those of members of the Tasmanian Parliament. The continued existence of the challenged provisions therefore continuously and directly "interferes" with the author's privacy.

8.3 The prohibition against private homosexual behaviour is provided for by law, namely, Sections 122 and 123 of the Tasmanian Criminal Code. As to whether it may be deemed arbitrary, the Committee recalls that pursuant to its General Comment 16[32] on article 17, the "introduction of the concept of arbitrariness is intended to guarantee that even interference provided for by the law should be in accordance with the provisions, aims and objectives of the Covenant and should be, in any event, reasonable in the circumstances".[4] The Committee interprets the requirement of reasonableness to imply that any interference with privacy must be proportional to the end sought and be necessary in the circumstances of any given case.

8.4 While the State party acknowledges that the impugned provisions constitute an arbitrary interference with Mr. Toonen's privacy, the Tasmanian authorities submit that the challenged laws are justified on public health and moral grounds, as they are intended in part to prevent the spread of HIV/AIDS in Tasmania, and because, in the absence of specific limitation clauses in article 17, moral issues must be deemed a matter for domestic decision.

8.5 As far as the public health argument of the Tasmanian authorities is concerned, the Committee notes that the criminalization of homosexual practices cannot be considered a reasonable means or proportionate measure to achieve the aim of preventing the spread of AIDS/HIV. . . .

8.6 The Committee cannot accept either that for the purposes of article 17 of the Covenant, moral issues are exclusively a matter of domestic concern, as this would open the door to withdrawing from the Committee's scrutiny a potentially large number of statutes interfering with privacy. It further notes that with the exception of Tasmania, all laws criminalizing homosexuality have been repealed throughout Australia and that, even in Tasmania, it is apparent that there is no consensus as to whether Sections 122 and 123 should not also be repealed. Considering further that these provisions are not currently enforced, which implies that they are not deemed essential to the protection of morals in Tasmania, the Committee concludes that the provisions do not meet the "reasonableness" test in the circumstances of the case, and that they arbitrarily interfere with Mr. Toonen's right under article 17, paragraph 1.

8.7 The State party has sought the Committee's guidance as to whether sexual orientation may be considered an "other status" for the purposes of article 26. The same issue could arise under article 2, paragraph 1, of the Covenant. The Committee confines itself to noting, however, that in its view the reference to "sex" in articles 2, paragraph 1, and 26 is to be taken as including sexual orientation.

9. The Human Rights Committee, acting under article 5, paragraph 4, of the Optional Protocol to the International Covenant on Civil and Political Rights, is of the view that the facts before it reveal a violation of articles 17, paragraph 1, juncto 2, paragraph 1, of the Covenant.

10. Under article 2(3)(a) of the Covenant, the author, victim of a violation of articles 17, paragraph 1, juncto 2, paragraph 1, of the Covenant, is entitled to a remedy. In the opinion of the Committee, an effective remedy would be the repeal of Sections 122(a), (c) and 123 of the Tasmanian Criminal Code.

11. Since the Committee has found a violation of Mr. Toonen's rights under articles 17(1) and 2(1) of the Covenant requiring the repeal of the offending law, the Committee does not consider it necessary to consider whether there has also been a violation of article 26 of the Covenant.

# D.  Sexual Minorities

## 1.  Note to Students from Professor Wilets

The article below posits 3 essential points:

1. Usually, people dislike LGBT people not because of any acts they engage in *per se*, but the gender of the person with whom they are engaging in these acts. The underlying reason for this hostility is that same-gender sexual relations are perceived as violating gender norms in the most fundamental way.

2. Moreover, the manner in which society views these gender transgressions speaks more to how society views women than anything about homosexual acts themselves. For example, a man having sex with another man, particularly if he performs the "traditional female" role, is perceived as degrading himself. In prison and other contexts, for example, a man penetrating another man is not perceived as violating gender roles as opposed to the man being penetrated. The "dominant" male will almost never consider himself "gay" nor will others consider him "gay," even though he is having sex with another man. In other words,

for the male to adopt a traditional female sexual role is perceived as "lowering" himself. Indeed, if one examines the slang used in English for the acts of sexual intercourse, one can see that the sexual act performed on the female is perceived as degrading her, unless performed in defined social contexts. Examples include such vulgar expression as "that person got "f——d" or "that person got "screwed." Women who have frequent sex with men are considered "sluts, whores, etc." Men who have sex with women are rarely branded with such degrading epithets.

Similarly, a "sissy boy" is usually perceived as a much greater gender norm transgression than a "tomboy." Society has traditionally laughed at men dressed as women, but few people laugh at women dressed like men. People ridicule men who exhibit female characteristics, but although people may dislike "masculine" women, the reaction is rarely one of laughter.

3. Thus, the roots of opposition to homosexuality are to the violation of gender norms, rather than the act itself.

4. Finally, most people in society, even those who oppose homosexuality, would recognize that violence against LGBT people motivated by hatred is a "hate crime." However, violence against women is rarely viewed as a "hate crime" even though the roots of much of the violence against women and LGBT people are rooted in the same or similar sources. This article argues that because women are everyone's mother, sister, daughter, it is difficult to recognize that violence on women could be part of a more systemic, society wide view of women. Thus, by understanding the common roots of violence against LGBT people and women suggests that violence against women are not simply isolated incidents of deranged males, but a kind of hate, not entirely different from that expressed against LGBT individuals.

\*\*\*

## 2. Wilets, Conceptualizing Private Violence Against Sexual Minorities as Gendered Violence: An International and Comparative Law Perspective, 60 ALB. L. REV. 989 (1997)

### III.

#### Sexual Minorities as "Gender Outlaws"

Oppression based on sexual orientation or identity involves a great deal more than social intolerance of homosexual relations. The oppression discussed in this Article is fueled by any group which challenges traditionally defined gender roles. For example, focusing solely on groups defined by their sexual orientation, such as gays, lesbians or bisexuals would not address human rights violations against a wide range of other individuals who violate norms of gender conformity through their dress and other social, non-sexual forms of expression, such as transgendered individuals. \*\*\*

Comparing the oppression of sexual minorities as such with the oppression of women is useful in understanding this continuum of resistance to gender conformity. The rigid bi-polar construction of gender existing in many societies oppresses women and sexual minorities in similar ways. Thus, sexual minorities and women who attempt to transcend societal gender role expectations frequently find themselves struggling against similar adversaries for similar underlying reasons.

Thus, how a society views gender roles often determines how it treats sexual minorities. As a general rule, to the extent a society does not assume a connection between same-gender sexual behavior and violation of gender roles (and the power relationships reinforced by gender roles), that same-gendered sexual behavior will be accepted.

The corollary to this proposition is that as a society broadens its definition of acceptable gender norms for all persons, that society will tend to accept not just same sex sexual activity, but also same-gender relationships where one of the partners is not obligated to assume an opposite gender role. This corollary thus suggests that efforts by social movements such as feminism to broaden the definition of acceptable gender behavior, particularly with respect to societal power relationships, are closely connected to the efforts by sexual minorities to obtain societal recognition of the many forms their identities and relationships may assume. ***

***

Homosexuality, particularly in a contemporary context, cannot be separated from the larger context of gender norm expectations and male-female gender role stereotypes. Sexual minority rights groups and feminists have not always acknowledged the connection between the struggle for gay and lesbian rights and the effort to eliminate discriminatory and arbitrary gender roles and stereotypes. Lesbians have been frequently marginalized and isolated within the feminist movement in numerous countries, and gay men have frequently failed to see the connection between their struggle and the struggle to abolish gender role norms and stereotypes with respect to all people.

***

In some societies, male homosexual activity was sanctioned only so long as it occurred between individuals of different classes or generations. Greenberg notes that in ancient Greece, "[p]reoccupation with status pervaded sexual culture to the point where the Greeks could not easily conceive of a relationship based on equality. Sex always involved superiority." There is thus considerable documentation of what one would call bisexuality in societies where it was considered appropriate to engage in either sexual relations with women or members of a subaltern class or younger generation, as long as the individual in the socially superior position did the "penetrating." ***

***

## IV.

### A. Hate Crime

Some jurisdictions are making progress in combating gendered "private" violence with legislation imposing harsher penalties for crimes motivated by hatred towards women and sexual minorities. For example, in June of 1995, Canada passed Bill C-41, a hate crimes bill, which requires that hate motivation be treated by judges as an aggravating factor in sentencing a person convicted of a crime. As noted by various commentators, "[t]he bill allows harsher sentences for crimes motivated by hate towards a victim's race, religion, language, color, gender, age, mental or physical disability or sexual orientation."] To some extent, this was already the case in Canada since the Ontario Court of Appeal ruled that harsher sentences are appropriate if the crime was motivated by hatred of the personal characteristics of the victim, such as, inter alia, gender or sexual orientation.

# E. Comparative Law in the Interpretation of the Indian Constitution in the Context of Transgendered Persons

## 1. Notes to Students from Professor Wilets

1. Note the confluence of history, domestic law, comparative law, and international law in this case and in *Bowers, Lawrence* and *Roper.*

2. The Court notes the traditional Indian Subcontinent's accept of hijras in the both the religion and the culture. The criminalization of hijra status occurred with British colonial rule. What does this tell us about some of the "cultural relativist" critiques treating tolerance of gender nonconformity as a "western" human rights concept?

3. Note the recognition of the Yogyakarta principles. What kind of international law are those principles?

4. Note Yogyakarta discussion of not requiring sex reassignment surgery to be recognized as another sex. Why is this important?

5. Note use of the word "aim" in paragraph 48 of the opinion. Is this an accurate description of the "aim" of the international instruments to which the Court cites?

6. Note in paragraph 49 that the Court states: "especially when [transgender] rights have gained universal recognition and acceptance." Is this accurate?

7. Note in paragraph 50 the Indian Court's interpretation of the Supremacy Clause and US treatment of international law generally. Is the Court giving the U.S. too much credit with respect to international law?

8. In paragraph 51, isn't the Indian court essentially articulating a "Charming Betsy" rule?

9. In Par. 54, isn't the Court discussing the same issue as the use of the word "person" in the 14th Amendment of the US Constitution?

10. The Court's discussion in paragraph 58 is directly analogous to the US Supreme Court's opinion in *Price Waterhouse v. Hopkins*, interpreting Title VII's

prohibition of sex discrimination as prohibiting sex stereotyping as well as more traditional forms of discrimination.

11. It should be noted that other countries have taken directly opposite approaches towards the relationship between transgenderism and sexual orientation. In Iran, for example, homosexual acts are not only illegal, they can result in the imposition of the death penalty. On the other hand, sex reassignment surgery is not only legal, it is partially subsidized by the Iranian government. What explains this apparent contradiction? Or is it a contradiction at all?

12. In Paragraph 53, how consistent is the Court's language with that in *Charming Betsy*?

## 2. In the Supreme Court of India, National Legal Services Authority v. Union of India

### JUDGMENT

### K.S. Radhakrishnan, J.

1. Seldom, our society realizes or cares to realize the trauma, agony and pain which the members of Transgender community undergo, nor appreciates the innate feelings of the members of the Transgender community, especially of those whose mind and body disown their biological sex. Our society often ridicules and abuses the Transgender community and in public places like railway stations, bus stands, schools, workplaces, malls, theatres, hospitals, they are sidelined and treated as untouchables, forgetting the fact that the moral failure lies in the society's unwillingness to contain or embrace different gender identities and expressions, a mindset which we have to change. ***

6. Shri Anand Grover, learned senior counsel appearing for the Intervener, traced the historical background of the third gender identity in India and the position accorded to them in the Hindu Mythology, Vedic and Puranic literatures, and the prominent role played by them in the royal courts of the Islamic world etc. Learned senior counsel also submitted that various International Forums and U.N. Bodies have recognized their gender identity and referred to the Yogyakarta Principles and pointed out that those principles have been recognized by various countries around the world. Reference was also made to few legislations giving recognition to the trans-sexual persons in other countries. Learned senior counsel also submitted that non-recognition of gender identity of the transgender community violates the fundamental rights guaranteed to them, who are citizens of this country.

***

11. Transgender is generally described as an umbrella term for persons whose gender identity, gender expression or behavior does not conform to their biological sex. TG may also takes in persons who do not identify with their sex assigned at birth, which include Hijras/Eunuchs who, in this writ petition,

describe themselves as "third gender" and they do not identify as either male or female. Hijras are not men by virtue of anatomy appearance and psychologically, they are also not women, though they are like women with no female reproduction organ and no menstruation. Since Hijras do not have reproduction capacities as either men or women, they are neither men nor women and claim to be an institutional "third gender". Among Hijras, there are emasculated (castrated, nirvana) men, non-emasculated men (not castrated/akva/akka) and inter-sexed persons (hermaphrodites). TG also includes persons who intend to undergo Sex Re-Assignment Surgery (**SRS**) or have undergone **SRS** to align their biological sex with their gender identity in order to become male or female. They are generally called transsexual persons. Further, there are persons who like to cross-dress in clothing of opposite gender, i.e. transvestites. Resultantly, the term "transgender", in contemporary usage, has become an umbrella term that is used to describe a wide range of identities and experiences, including but not limited to pre-operative, post-operative and non-operative transsexual people, who strongly identify with the gender opposite to their biological sex; male and female.

## HISTORICAL BACKGROUND OF TRANSGENDERS IN INDIA:

12. TG Community comprises of *Hijras,* eunuchs, *Kothis, Aravanis, Jogappas, Shiv-Shakthis* etc. and they, as a group, have got a strong historical presence in our country in the Hindu mythology and other religious texts. The Concept of *tritiya prakrti* or *napunsaka* has also been an integral part of vedic and puranic literatures. The word *'napunsaka'* has been used to denote absence of procreative capability.

***

16. We notice that even though historically, Hijras/transgender persons had played a prominent role, with the onset of colonial rule from the 18th century onwards, the situation had changed drastically. During he British rule, a legislation was enacted to supervise the deeds of *Hijras*/TG community, called the Criminal Tribes Act, 1871, which deemed the entire community of *Hijras* persons as innately 'criminal'.

17. Section 377 of the IPC found a place in the Indian Penal Code, 1860, prior to the enactment of Criminal Tribles Act that criminalized all penile-nonvaginal sexual acts between persons, including anal sex and oral sex, at a time when transgender persons were also typically associated with the prescribed sexual activity.

## GENDER IDENTITY AND SEXUAL ORIENTATION

19. Gender identity is one of the most-fundamental aspects of life which refers to a person's intrinsic sense of being male, female or transgender or transsexual person. A person's sex is usually assigned at birth, but a relatively small group of persons may born with bodies which incorporate both

or certain aspects of both male and female physiology. At times, genital anatomy problems may arise in certain persons, their innate perception of themselves, is not in conformity with the sex assigned to them at birth and may include pre and post-operative transsexual persons and also persons who do not choose to undergo or do not have access to operation and also include persons who cannot undergo successful operation. Countries, all over the world, including India, are grappled with the question of attribution of gender to persons who believe that they belong to the opposite sex. Few persons undertake surgical and other procedures to alter their bodies and physical appearance to acquire gender characteristics of the sex which conform to their perception of gender, leading to legal and social complications since official record of their gender at birth is found to be at variance with the assumed gender identity. Gender identity refers to each person's deeply felt internal and individual experience of gender, which may or may not correspond with the sex assigned at birth, including the personal sense of the body which may involve a freely chosen, modification of bodily appearance or functions by medical, surgical or other means and other expressions of gender, including dress, speech and mannerisms. Gender identity, therefore, refers to an individual's self-identification as a man, woman, transgender or other identified category.

20. Sexual orientation refers to an individual's enduring physical, romantic and/or emotional attraction to another person. Sexual orientation includes transgender and gender-variant people and their sexual orientation may or may not change during or after gender transmission, which also includes homo-sexuals, bysexuals, heterosexuals, asexual etc. Gender identity and sexual orientation, as already indicated, are different concepts. Each person's self-defined sexual orientation and gender identity is integral to their personality and is one of the most basic aspects of self-determination, dignity and freedom and no one shall be forced to undergo medical procedures, including *SRS*, sterilization or hormonal therapy, as a requirement for legal recognition of their gender identity.

## UNITED NATIONS AND OTHER HUMAN RIGHTS BODIES — ON GENDER IDENTITY AND SEXUAL ORIENTATION

21. United Nations has been instrumental in advocating the protection and promotion of rights of sexual minorities, including transgender persons. Article 6 of the Universal Declaration of Human Rights, 1948 and Article 16 of the International Covenant on Civil and Political Rights, 1966 (CCPR) recognize that every human being has the inherent right to live and this right shall be protected by law and that no one shall be arbitrarily denied of that right. Everyone shall have a right to recognition, everywhere as a person before the law. Article 17 of the CCPR states that no one shall be subjected to arbitrary or unlawful interference with his privacy, family, home or correspondence, nor to unlawful attacks on his honour and reputation and that

everyone has the right to protection of law against such interference or attacks. . . . .A distinguished group of human rights experts has drafted, developed, discussed and reformed the principles in a meeting held at Gadjah Mada, University in Yogyakarta, Indonesia from 6 to 9 November, 2006, which unanimously adopted the Yogyakarta Principles on the application of International Human Rights Law in relation to Sexual Orientation and Gender Identity. Yogyakarta Principles address a broad range of human rights standards and their application to issues of sexual orientation gender identity. [see Yogyakarta Principles at

 http://www.yogyakartaprinciples.org/principles_en.htm]

23. UN bodies, Regional Human Rights Bodies, National Courts, Government Commissions and the Commissions for Human Rights, Council of Europe, etc. have endorsed the Yogyakarta Principles and have considered them as an important tool for identifying the obligations of States to respect, protect and fulfill the human rights of all persons, regardless of their gender identity.

The United Nations Committee on Economic, Social and Cultural Rights in its Report of 2009 speaks of gender orientation and gender identity as follows:-

**"Sexual orientation and gender identity**

'Other status' as recognized in article 2, paragraph 2, includes sexual orientation. States parties should ensure that a person's sexual orientation is not a barrier to realizing Covenant rights, for example, in accessing survivor's pension rights. In addition, gender identity is recognized as among the prohibited grounds of discrimination, for example, persons who are transgender, transsexual or intersex, often face serious human rights violations, such as harassment in schools or in the workplace."

24. In this respect, reference may also be made to the General Comment No.2 of the Committee on Torture and Article 2 of the Convention against Torture and Other Cruel, Inhuman or Degrading Treatment or Punishment in 2008 and also the General Comment No.20 of the Committee on Elimination of Discrimination against Woman, responsible for the implementation of the Convention on the Elimination of All Forms of Discrimination against Woman, 1979 and 2010 report.

. . . ..

25. Various countries have given recognition to the gender identity of such persons, mostly, in cases where transsexual persons started asserting their rights after undergoing *SRS* of their re-assigned sex. \*\*\*

In New Zealand in *Attorney-General v. Otahuhu Family Court* (1995) 1 NZLR 603, Justice Ellis noted that once a transsexual person has undergone surgery, he or she is no longer able to operate in his or her original sex. It was held that there is no social advantage in the law for not recognizing the validity of the marriage of a transsexual in the sex of reassignment. The Court held that an adequate test is whether the person in question has undergone surgical and medical procedures that have effectively given the person the physical conformation of a person of a specified sex. In *Re Kevin (Validity of Marriage of Transsexual)* (2001) Fam CA 1074, in an Australian case, Chisholm J., held that there is no 'formulaic solution' to determine the sex of an individual for the purpose of the law of marriage. It was held that all relevant matters need to be considered, including the person's life experiences and self perception.

27. Lockhart, J. in *Secretary, Department of Social Security v. "SRA"*, (1993) 43 FCR 299 and Mathews, J. in *R v. Harris & McGuiness* (1988) 17 NSWLR 158, made an exhaustive review of the various decisions with regard to the question of recognition to be accorded by Courts to the gender of a transsexual person who had undertaken a surgical procedure. Lockhart. J. in *SRA* observed that the development in surgical and medical techniques in the field of sexual reassignment, together with indications of changing social attitudes towards transsexuals, would indicate that generally they should not be regarded merely as a matter of chromosomes, which is purely a psychological question, one of self-perception, and partly a social question, how society perceives the individual.

28. *A.B. v. Western Australia* (2011) HCA 42 was a case concerned with the Gender Reassignment Act, 2000. In that Act, a person who had undergone a reassignment procedure could apply to Gender Reassignment Board for the issue of a recognition certificate. Under Section 15 of that Act, before issuing the certificate, the Board had to be satisfied, inter alia, that the applicant believed his or her true gender was the person's reassigned gender and had adopted the lifestyle and gender characteristics of that gender. Majority of Judges agreed with Lockhart, J. in *SRA* that gender should not be regarded merely as a matter of chromosomes, but partly a psychological question, one of self-perception, and partly a social question, how society perceives the individual.

32. [**Here we have a judgment of the European Court of Human Rights**]. In *Christine Goodwin v. United Kingdom* (Application No.28957/95 — Judgment dated 11th July, 2002), the **European Court of Human Rights** examined an application alleging violation of Articles 8, 12, 13 and 14 of the Convention for Protection of Human Rights and Fundamental Freedoms, 1997 in respect of the legal status of transsexuals in UK and particularly their treatment in the sphere of employment, social security, pensions and marriage. Applicant in that case had a tendency to dress as a woman from early childhood and underwent aversion therapy in 1963-64. In the mid-1960s she was diagnosed as a transsexual. Though she married a woman and they had four children, her inclination was that her "brain sex" did not fit her

body. From that time until 1984 she dressed as a man for work but as a woman in her free time. In January, 1985, the applicant began treatment at the Gender Identity Clinic. In October, 1986, she underwent surgery to shorten her vocal chords. In August, 1987, she was accepted on the waiting list for gender re-assignment surgery and later underwent that surgery at a National Health Service hospital. The applicant later divorced her former wife. She claimed between 1990 and 1992 she was sexually harassed by colleagues at work, followed by other human rights violations. The Court after referring to various provisions and Conventions held as follows:-

> "Nonetheless, the very essence of the Convention is respect for human dignity and human freedom. Under Article 8 of the Convention in particular, where the notion of personal autonomy is an important principle underlying the interpretation of its guarantees, protection is given to the personal sphere of each individuals, including the right to establish details of their identity as individual human beings (see, *inter alia, Pretty v. the United Kingdom* no.2346/02, judgment of 29 April 2002, 62, and *Mikulic v. Croatia*, no.53176/99, judgment of 7 February 2002, 53, both to be published in ECHR 2002 . . .). In the twenty first century the right of transsexuals to personal development and to physical and moral security in the full sense enjoyed by others in society cannot be regarded as a matter of controversy requiring the lapse of time to cast clearer light on the issues involved. In short, the unsatisfactory situation in which postoperative transsexuals live in an intermediate zone as not quite one gender or the other is no longer sustainable."

33. The **European Court of Human Rights** in the case of ***Van Kuck v. Germany*** (Application No.35968/97 — Judgment dated 12.9.2003) dealt with the application alleging that German Court's decisions refusing the applicant's claim for reimbursement of gender reassignment measures and the related proceedings were in breach of her rights to a fair trial and of her right to respect for her private life and that they amounted to discrimination on the ground of her particular "psychological situation". Reliance was placed on Articles 6, 8, 13 and 14 of the Convention for Protection of Human Rights and Fundamental Freedoms, 1997. The Court held that the concept of "private life" covers the physical and psychological integrity of a person, which can sometimes embrace aspects of an individual's physical and social identity. For example, gender identifications, name and sexual orientation and sexual life fall within the personal sphere protected by Article 8.

The Court also held that the notion of personal identity is an important principle underlying the interpretation of various guaranteed rights and the very essence of the Convention being respect for human dignity and human freedom, protection is given to the right of transsexuals to personal development and to physical and moral security.

34. Judgments referred to above are mainly related to transsexuals, who, whilst belonging physically to one sex, feel convinced that they belong to the other, seek to achieve a more integrated unambiguous identity by undergoing medical and surgical operations to adapt their physical characteristic to their psychological nature. When we examine the rights of transsexual persons, who have undergone **SRS**, the test to be applied is not the "Biological test", but the "Psychological test", because psychological factor and thinking of transsexual has to be given primacy than binary notion of gender of that person. Seldom people realize the discomfort, distress and psychological trauma, they undergo and many of them undergo "Gender Dysphoria" which may lead to mental disorder. Discrimination faced by this group in our society, is rather unimaginable and their rights have to be protected, irrespective of chromosomal sex, genitals, assigned birth sex, or implied gender role. Rights of transgenders, pure and simple, like Hijras, eunuchs, etc. have also to be examined, so also their right to remain as a third gender as well as their physical and psychological integrity. Before addressing those aspects further, we may also refer to few legislations enacted in other countries recognizing their rights.

## LEGISLATIONS IN OTHER COUNTRIES ON TGs

35. We notice, following the trend, in the international human rights law, many countries have enacted laws for recognizing rights of transsexual persons, who have undergone either partial/complete SRS, including United Kingdom, Netherlands, Germany, Australia, Canada, Argentina, etc. United Kingdom has passed the General Recommendation Act, 2004, following the judgment in **Christine Goodwin** (supra) passed by the European Courts of Human Rights. The Act is all encompassing as not only does it provide legal recognition to the acquired gender of a person, but it also lays down provisions highlighting the consequences of the newly acquired gender status on their legal rights and entitlements in various aspects such as marriage, parentage, succession, social security and pensions etc. One of the notable features of the Act is that it is not necessary that a person needs to have undergone or in the process of undergoing a **SRS** to apply under the Act. Reference in this connection may be made to the Equality Act, 2010 (UK) which has consolidated, repealed and replaced around nine different anti-discrimination legislations including the Sex Discrimination Act, 1986. The Act defines certain characteristics to be "protected characteristics" and no one shall be discriminated or treated less favourably on grounds that the person possesses one or more of the "protected characteristics". The Act also imposes duties on Public Bodies to eliminate all kinds of discrimination, harassment and victimization. Gender reassignment has been declared as one of the protected characteristics under the Act, of course, only the transsexuals i.e. those who are proposing to undergo, is undergoing or has undergone the process of the gender reassignment are protected under the Act.

36. In Australia, there are two Acts dealing with the gender identity, (1) Sex Discrimination Act, 1984; and (ii) Sex Discrimination Amendment (Sexual Orientation, Gender Identity and Intersex Status) Act, 2013 (Act 2013). Act 2013 amends the Sex Discrimination Act, 1984. Act 2013 defines gender identity as the appearance or mannerisms or other gender-related characteristics of a person (whether by way of medical intervention or not) with or without regard to the person's designated sex at birth.

37. We may in this respect also refer to the European Union Legislations on transsexuals. Recital 3 of the Preamble to the Directive 2006/54/EC of European Parliament and the Council of 5 July 2006 makes an explicit reference to discrimination based on gender reassignment for the first time in European Union Law.

Recital 3 reads:- "The Court of Justice has held that the scope of the principle of equal treatment for men and women cannot be confined to the prohibition of discrimination based on the fact that a person is of one or other sex. In view of this purpose and the nature of the rights which it seeks to safeguard, it also applies to discrimination arising from the gender reassignment of a person."

38. European Parliament also adopted a resolution on discrimination against transsexuals on 12th September, 1989 and called upon the Member States to take steps for the protection of transsexual persons and to pass legislation to further that end.

Following that Hungary has enacted Equal Treatment and the Promotion of Equal Opportunities Act, 2003, which includes sexual identity as one of the grounds of discrimination. 2010 paper on 'Transgender Persons' Rights in the EU Member States prepared by the Policy Department of the European Parliament presents the specific situation of transgender people in 27 Member States of the European Union.

In the **United States of America** some of the laws enacted by the States are inconsistent with each other. The Federal Law which provides protection to transgenders is The Matthew Shepard and James Byrd. Jr. Hate Crimes Prevention Act, 2009, which expands the scope of the 1969 United States Federal Hate-crime Law by including offences motivated by actual or perceived gender identity. Around 15 States and District of Colombia in the United States have legislations which prohibit discrimination on grounds of gender identity and expression. Few States have issued executive orders prohibiting discrimination.

39. The Parliament of South Africa in the year 2003, enacted Alteration of Sex Description and Sex Status Act, 2003, which permits transgender persons who have undergone gender reassignment or people whose sexual characteristics have evolved naturally or an intersexed person to apply to the Director General of the National Department of Home Affairs for alteration

of his/her sex description in the birth register, though the legislation does not contemplate a more inclusive definition of transgenders.

40. The **Senate of Argentina** in the year 2012 passed a law on Gender Identity that recognizes right by all persons to the recognition of their gender identity as well as free development of their person according to their gender identity and can also request that their recorded sex be amended along with the changes in first name and image, whenever they do not agree with the self-perceived gender identity. Not necessary that they seemed to prove that a surgical procedure for total or partial genital reassignment, hormonal therapies or any other psychological or medical treatment had taken place. Article 12 deals with dignified treatment, respecting the gender identity adopted by the individual, even though the first name is different from the one recorded in their national identity documents.

Further laws also provide that whenever requested by the individual, the adopted first name must be used for summoning, recording, filing, calling and any other procedure or service in public and private spaces.

41. In Germany, a new law has come into force on 5th November, 2013, which allows the parents to register the sex of the children as 'not specified' in the case of children with intersex variation. According to Article 22, Section 3 of the German Civil Statutes Act reads as follows:

> "If a child can be assigned to neither the female nor the male sex then the child has to be named without a specification"

42. The law has also added a category of X, apart from "M" and "F" under the classification of gender in the passports.

**Indian Scenario**

43. We have referred exhaustively to the various judicial pronouncements and legislations on the international arena to highlight the fact that the recognition of "sex identity gender" of persons, and "guarantee to equality and non-discrimination" on the ground of gender identity or expression is increasing and gaining acceptance in international law and, therefore, be applied in India as well.

44. Historical background of Transgenders in India has already been dealt with in the earlier part of this Judgment indicating that they were once treated with great respect, at least in the past, though not in the present.

**INDIA TO FOLLOW INTERNATIONAL CONVENTIONS**

47. **International Conventions and norms are significant for the purpose of interpretation of gender equality**. Article 1 of the Universal declaration on Human Rights, 1948, states that all human-beings are born free and equal in dignity and rights. Article 3 of the Universal Declaration of Human Rights states that everyone has a right to life, liberty and security of person.

Article 6 of the International Covenant on Civil and Political Rights, 1966 affirms that every human-being has the inherent right to life, which right shall be protected by law and no one shall be arbitrarily deprived of his life. Article 5 of the Universal Declaration of Human Rights and Article 7 of the International Covenant on Civil and Political Rights provide that no one shall be subjected to torture or to cruel inhuman or degrading treatment or punishment.

[The] United Nations Convention against Torture and Other Cruel Inhuman and Degrading Treatment or Punishment (dated 24th January, 2008) specifically deals with protection of individuals and groups made vulnerable by discrimination or marginalization.

Para 21 of the Convention states that States are obliged to protect from torture or ill-treatment all persons regardless of sexual orientation or transgender identity and to prohibit, prevent and provide redress for torture and ill-treatment in all contests of State custody or control. Article 12 of the Universal Declaration of Human Rights and Article 17 of the International Covenant on Civil and Political Rights state that no one shall be subjected to "arbitrary or unlawful interference with his privacy, family, home or correspondence".

48. [The] Above-mentioned International Human Rights instruments which are being followed by various countries in the world are **aimed** to protect the human rights of transgender people since it has been noticed that transgenders/transsexuals often face serious human rights violations, such as harassment in work place, hospitals, places of public conveniences, market places, theaters, railway stations, bus stands, and so on.

49. *** We have exhaustively referred to various articles contained in the Universal Declaration of Human Rights, 1948, the International Covenant on Economic, Social and Cultural Rights, 1966, the International Covenant on Civil and Political Rights, 1966 as well as the Yogyakarta principles. Reference was also made to legislations enacted in other countries dealing with rights of persons of transgender community. Unfortunately we have no legislation in this country dealing with the rights of transgender community. Due to the absence of suitable legislation protecting the rights of the members of the transgender community, they are facing discrimination in various areas and hence the necessity to follow the International Conventions to which India is a party and to give due respect to other non-binding International Conventions and principles.

Constitution makers could not have envisaged that each and every human activity be guided, controlled, recognized or safeguarded by laws made by the legislature. Article 21 has been incorporated to safeguard those rights and a constitutional Court cannot be a mute spectator when those rights are violated, but is expected to safeguard those rights knowing the pulse and feeling of that community, though a minority, especially when their rights have gained universal recognition and acceptance.

50. Article 253 of the Constitution of India states that the Parliament has the power to make any law for the whole or any part of the territory of India for implementing any treaty, agreement or convention. Generally, therefore, a legislation is required for implementing the international conventions, unlike the position in the United States of America where the rules of international law are applied by the municipal courts on the theory of their implied adoption by the State, as a part of its own municipal law. Article VI, Cl. (2) of the U.S. Constitution reads as follows:

". . . . . . ..all treaties made, or which shall be made, under the authority of the united States, shall be the *supreme law of the land*, and the judges in every State shall be bound thereby, *anything in the Constitution or laws of any State to the contrary not-withstanding.*"

51. In the United States, however, it is open to the courts to supersede or modify international law in its application or it may be controlled by the treaties entered into by the United States. But, till an Act of Congress is passed, the Court is bound by the law of nations, which is part of the law of the land. Such a 'supremacy clause' is absent in our Constitution. Courts in India would apply the rules of International law according to the principles of comity of Nations, unless they are overridden by clear rules of domestic law. *** But, certainly, if the Indian law is not in conflict with the International covenants, particularly pertaining to human rights, to which India is a party, the domestic court can apply those principles in the Indian conditions. The Interpretation of International Conventions is governed by Articles 31 and 32 of the Vienna Convention on the Law of Treaties of 1969.

52. Article 51 of the Directive Principles of State Policy, which falls under Part IV of the Indian Constitution, reads as under:

"**Art. 51.** The State shall endeavour to

(a)  promote international peace and security;

(b)  maintain just and honourable relations between nations;

(c)  Foster respect for international law and treaty obligation in the dealings of organised peoples with one another; and

(d)  Encourage settlement of international disputes by arbitration."

53. Article 51, as already indicated, has to be read along with Article 253 of the Constitution. If the parliament has made any legislation which is in conflict with the international law, then Indian Courts are bound to give effect to the Indian Law, rather than the international law. However, in the absence of a contrary legislation, municipal courts in India would respect the rules of international law. In *His Holiness Kesavananda Bharati Sripadavalvaru v. State of Kerala* (1973) 4 SCC 225, it was stated that in view of Article 51 of the

Constitution, the Court must interpret language of the Constitution, if not intractable, in the light of United Nations Charter and the solemn declaration subscribed to it by India. In *Apparel Export Promotion Council v. A. K. Chopra* (1999) 1 SCC 759, it was pointed out that domestic courts are under an obligation to give due regard to the international conventions and norms for construing the domestic laws, more so, when there is no inconsistency between them and there is a void in domestic law. [T]his Court under Article 141 laid down various guidelines to prevent sexual harassment of women in working places, and to enable gender equality relying on Articles 11, 24 and general recommendations 22, 23 and 24 of the Convention on the Elimination of All Forms of Discrimination against Women. Any international convention not inconsistent with the fundamental rights and in harmony with its spirit must be read into those provisions, e.g., Articles 14, 15, 19 and 21 of the Constitution to enlarge the meaning and content thereof and to promote the object of constitutional guarantee. Principles discussed hereinbefore on TGs and the International Conventions, including *Yogyakarta principles*, which we have found not inconsistent with the various fundamental rights guaranteed under the Indian Constitution, must be recognized and followed, which has sufficient legal and historical justification in our country.

## ARTICLE 14 AND TRANSGENDERS

54. Article 14 of the Constitution of India states that the State shall not deny to "any person" equality before the law or the equal protection of the laws within the territory of India. Equality includes the full and equal enjoyment of all rights and freedom. Right to equality has been declared as the basic feature of the Constitution and treatment of equals as unequals or unequals as equals will be violative of the basic structure of the Constitution. Article 14 of the Constitution also ensures equal protection and hence a positive obligation on the State to ensure equal protection of laws by bringing in necessary social and economic changes, so that everyone including TGs may enjoy equal protection of laws and nobody is denied such protection. Article 14 does not restrict the word 'person' and its application only to male or female. Hijras/ transgender persons who are neither male/female fall within the expression 'person' and, hence, entitled to legal protection of laws in all spheres of State activity, including employment, healthcare, education as well as equal civil and citizenship rights, as enjoyed by any other citizen of this country.

## ARTICLES 15 & 16 AND TRANSGENDERS

56. Articles 15 and 16 prohibit discrimination against any citizen on certain enumerated grounds, including the ground of 'sex'. In fact, both the Articles prohibit all forms of gender bias and gender based discrimination.

57. Article 15 states that the State shall not discriminate against any citizen, inter alia, on the ground of sex[.]

58. Article 16 states that there shall be equality of opportunities for all the citizens in matters relating to employment or appointment to any office under the State. Article 16 (2) of the Constitution of India reads as follows :

> "16(2). No citizen shall, on grounds only of religion, race, caste, sex, descent, place of birth, residence or any of them, be ineligible for, or discriminated against in respect or, any employment or office under the State."

Article 16 not only prohibits discrimination on the ground of sex in public employment, but also imposes a duty on the State to ensure that all citizens are treated equally in matters relating to employment and appointment by the State.

59. Articles 15 and 16 sought to prohibit discrimination on the basis of sex, recognizing that sex discrimination is a historical fact and needs to be addressed. Constitution makers, it can be gathered, gave emphasis to the fundamental right against sex discrimination so as to prevent the direct or indirect attitude to treat people differently, for the reason of not being in conformity with stereotypical generalizations of binary genders. Both gender and biological attributes constitute distinct components of sex.

Biological characteristics, of course, include genitals, chromosomes and secondary sexual features, but gender attributes include one's self image, the deep psychological or emotional sense of sexual identity and character. The discrimination on the ground of 'sex' under Articles 15 and 16, therefore, includes discrimination on the ground of gender identity. The expression 'sex' used in Articles 15 and 16 is not just limited to biological sex of male or female, but intended to include people who consider themselves to be neither male or female.

63. We may, in this connection, refer to few judgments of the US Supreme Courts on the rights of TG's freedom of expression. The Supreme Court of the State of Illinois in the *City of Chicago v. Wilson et al.,* 75 III.2d 525(1978) struck down the municipal law prohibiting cross-dressing, and held as follows "- "the notion that the State can regulate one's personal appearance, unconfined by any constitutional strictures whatsoever, is fundamentally inconsistent with "values of privacy, self-identity, autonomy and personal integrity that . . . .. the Constitution was designed to protect."

64. In *Doe v. Yunits et al.,* 2000 WL33162199 (Mass. Super.), the Superior Court of Massachusetts, upheld the right of a person to wear school dress that matches her gender identity as part of protected speech and expression and observed as follows :- "by dressing in clothing and accessories traditionally associated with the female gender, she is expressing her identification with the gender. In addition, plaintiff's ability to express herself and her gender identity through dress is important for her health and wellbeing.

Therefore, plaintiff's expression is not merely a personal preference but a necessary symbol of her identity."

65. Principles referred to above clearly indicate that the freedom of expression guaranteed under Article 19(1)(a) includes the freedom to express one's chosen gender identity through varied ways and means by way of expression, speech, mannerism, clothing etc.

***

71. The Supreme Court of Nepal in *Sunil Babu Pant & Ors. v. Nepal Government* (Writ Petition No.917 of 2007 decided on 21st December, 2007), spoke on the rights of Transgenders as follows:-

> "the fundamental rights comprised under Part II of the Constitution are enforceable fundamental human rights guaranteed to the citizens against the State. For this reason, the fundamental rights stipulated in Part III are the rights similarly vested in the third gender people as human beings. The homosexuals and third gender people are also human beings as other men and women are, and they are the citizens of this country as well . . . . Thus, the people other than 'men' and 'women', including the people of 'third gender' cannot be discriminated. The State should recognize the existence of all natural persons including the people of third gender other than the men and women. And it cannot deprive the people of third gender from enjoying the fundamental rights provided by Part III of the Constitution."

72. The Supreme Court of Pakistan in *Dr. Mohammad Aslam Khaki & Anr. V. Senior Superintendent of Police (Operation) Rawalpindi & Ors.* (Constitution Petition No.43 of 2009) decided on 22nd March, 2011, had occasion to consider the rights of eunuchs and held as follows:-

> "Needless to observe that eunuchs in their rights are citizens of this country and subject to the Constitution of the Islamic Republic of Pakistan, 1973, their rights, obligations including right to life and dignity are equally protected. Thus no discrimination, for any reason, is possible against them as far as their rights and obligations are concerned. The Government functionaries both at federal and provincial levels are bound to provide them protection of life and property and secure their dignity as well, as is done in case of other citizens."

73. We may remind ourselves of the historical presence of the third gender in this country as well as in the neighbouring countries.

. . . .

129. We, therefore, declare:

(1) Hijras, Eunuchs, apart from binary gender, be treated as **"third gender"** for the purpose of safeguarding their rights under Part III of our Constitution and the laws made by the Parliament and the State Legislature.

(2)  Transgender persons' right to decide their self-identified gender is also upheld and the Centre and State Governments are directed to grant legal recognition of their gender identity such as male, female or as third gender.

(3)  We direct the Centre and the State Governments to take steps to treat them as socially and educationally backward classes of citizens and extend all kinds of reservation in cases of admission in educational institutions and for public appointments.

(5)  Centre and State Governments should seriously address the problems being faced by Hijras/Transgenders such as fear, shame, gender dysphoria, social pressure, depression, suicidal tendencies, social stigma, etc. and any insistence for SRS for declaring one's gender is immoral and illegal.

(6)  Centre and State Governments should take proper measures to provide medical care to TGs in the hospitals and also provide them separate public toilets and other facilities.

(7)  Centre and State Governments should also take steps for framing various social welfare schemes for their betterment.

(8)  Centre and State Governments should take steps to create public awareness so that TGs will feel that they are also part and parcel of the social life and be not treated as untouchables.

(9)  Centre and the State Governments should also take measures to regain their respect and place in the society which once they enjoyed.

# Index